Scooters
Service and Repair Manual

by Phil Mather and Alan Ahlstrand

Automatic Transmission, 50 to 250cc Two-wheel, Carbureted Models

Models covered:

Daelim A-Four (2006 and later), Cordi (2006 and later), Delfino (2006 and later), E-Five (2006 and later), History (2006 and later), S-Five (2006 and later), S2-250 (2006 and later)

Honda CHF50 Metropolitan (2002 through 2009), NB50 Aero (1985 through 1987), NPS50 Ruckus (2003 through 2009), NQ50 Spree (1984 through 1987), SA50 Elite (1988 through 2001), SB50 Elite (1988 through 2001), SE50 Elite (1987), NH80 Aero (1985), CH80 Elite (1985 through 2007), CH150 Elite (1985 through 1987), CH250 Elite (1985 through 1990), CN250 Helix (1985 through 2007), NS250 Reflex (2001 through 2007), PS250 Big Ruckus (2005 and 2006)

Kymco Agility 50 (2006 and later), People S-50 (2006 and later), Agility 125 (2006 and later), People S-125 (2006 and later), People S-200 (2006 and later)

Piaggio Typhoon 50 (2005 and later), Fly 150 (2005 and later), BV200 (2002 and later), BV250 (2005 and later)

Vespa LX50 (2005 and later), ET-4 150 (2005 and later), LX150 (2005 and later), GT200 (2004 and later)

Yamaha CA50 Riva (1985 and 1986), CE50 and CG50 Jog (1986 and 1987), CW50 Zuma/Zuma II (1997 through 2000), CY50 Riva/Riva Jog (1992 and later), XC50 Vino (2006 through 2008), JY50 Vino (2001 through 2004), YW50 Zuma (2002 through 2004), CV80 Zuma (1984 through 1987), XC125 Riva (1985 through 2001), YJ125 Vino (2004 through 2008), XC200 Riva (1987 through 1991)

ABCDE
FGHIJ
KLMNO
PQRST

ISBN-13: **978-1-56392-760-7**
ISBN-10: **1-56392-760-8**

Library of Congress Control Number 2009920149
Printed in the USA

Haynes Publishing
Sparkford, Nr Yeovil, Somerset BA22 7JJ, England

Haynes North America, Inc
861 Lawrence Drive, Newbury Park, California 91320, USA

© Haynes North America, Inc. 2009
With permission from J.H. Haynes & Co. Ltd.

A book in the **Haynes Service and Repair Manual Series**

09-368

Contents

LIVING WITH YOUR SCOOTER

Introduction

Daily (pre-ride) checks

MAINTENANCE

Contents

Scooters
from Novelty to Mass Transit

by Julian Ryder and Alan Ahlstrand

Scooters - for decades a tiny segment of the US motorcycle market - have steadily increased in popularity in the last several years. The belt-drive automatic transmission - known as "twist and go" because it eliminates the need to shift gears manually - has made scooters easier to ride. High fuel prices have led to a dramatic jump in scooter sales. Once the exclusive preserve of Italian company Piaggio, the scooter market has seen the entry of major manufacturers such as Honda and Yamaha, with more recent entries from companies such as Kymco (Taiwanese) and Daelim (Korean).

Outside of its native Italy, Piaggio is in a strange position. Everyone has heard of one of its products while comparatively few people know the name of the parent company itself. That product is, of course, the Vespa, the first mass-produced scooter and the vehicle that got Italy mobile after World War II before becoming a style icon for generations all over the world.

The first Vespa was completed in April 1946, after just three months design work by the gifted aeronautical engineer Corradinio d'Ascanio. Given the assignment of development by Enrico Piaggio - one of the heirs of company founder Rinaldo Piaggio - d'Ascanio laid out a totally new and original vehicle that it still recognizable today. He attached the motor to a load-bearing single-sided swingarm with direct gearing to the rear wheel, put the gearshift on the handlebar, and used an aircraft-undercarriage for the strut design front suspension, thus allowing instant wheel changing both front and rear. He clothed the whole thing in lightweight bodywork that protected the rider from the elements.

It was christened when Piaggio himself saw the first prototype, the MP6, and he remarked that with its wide engine housing and narrow central "waist," it looked like a wasp. The Italian word for wasp is Vespa.

The first 98cc Vespa was an instant success. In the first year, 2484 were sold, 10,535 in the following year, and in 1948 just under 20,000 were built. Piaggio did his first deal for licensed production in 1950 with Germany. Already, the Vespa was becoming a cult object. The ten-millionth Vespa was produced in 1980, and production is now past 15 million. Worldwide, the Vespa is still Piaggio's top-selling two-wheeler.

Of course, the original 98cc Vespa has developed over the years. It grew to 125cc as early as 1948 and the 150cc model of 1955 was the first of the really modern scooters.

Honda entered the US market in 1984 with the NQ50 Spree, followed a year later by Yamaha with the CA50 Riva. Kymco entered in 2000 with several 50cc scooters, and Daelim entered in 2006 with a range of bikes from 50 to 250cc. Piaggio also sells some scooters, such as the Beverly (BV) 200, under its own name. All of these manufacturers sell nationwide except Daelim, which at the time of printing had dealers in 28 states.

All the scooters covered in this manual, from all manufacturers, have the same basic powertrain. Power is supplied by a single-cylinder engine, either two-stroke or overhead cam four-stroke. The engine crankcase casting is combined into a single unit with the transmission casting. A reduction gear unit is mounted in the rear of the casting, and the engine crankshaft is connected to the reduction gears through a constantly-variable belt drive transmission and centrifugal clutch. Fuel is supplied to the engine by a slide-type carburetor (for two-strokes) or a constant vacuum (CV) carburetor (four-strokes). The rear wheel is mounted on a spindle that protrudes from the reduction gear unit. The

Classic styling is still available in some Vespa models, as well as in Japanese scooters such as the Yamaha Vino

entire assembly acts as a swingarm. The rear suspension consists of one or two coil-over shock absorbers. The front suspension is either the early aircraft-type strut design, or a pair of damper-rod forks of the type used in motorcycles. A drum brake is used at the front on some earlier and smaller models, while most use a front disc brake. Smaller models generally use a drum brake at the rear, while more powerful scooters use a rear disc brake.

Technical development, in addition to the change from manual shift to twist and go, has included a trend toward bigger engines. This manual covers scooters displacing up to 250cc, but there are a number of larger models available, up to and including the twin-cylinder Suzuki Burgman 650. Honda is now using a constantly variable transmission in a new sport-bike styled motorcycle, the 2009 DN-01. The transmission can be used in the usual stepless manner, or set to five pre-set ratios to give the feel of a conventional transmission.

The engines themselves are evolving, in large part due to emission regulations. Two-strokes, formerly universal, now are used in fewer and fewer models. Direct fuel injection may bring two-strokes back into more common use, but for now, four-strokes dominate the industry. Electronic fuel injection is being used in some scooters, and will doubtless become more common as emission rules tighten and the technology becomes less expensive.

As of this writing, gasoline prices have fallen dramatically, in some cases by more than half, from their recent peaks. Does this mean a drop-off in scooter sales? Probably not - the same economic slump that caused a drop in gasoline demand makes the

Some newer scooters feature sporty "street fighter" styling

economical transportation offered by scooters a choice very well suited to the times.

Acknowledgements

Thanks to Grand Prix, Santa Clara, California, and to San Jose BMW/Vespa, San Jose, California, for supplying some of the scooters used in these photographs. Special thanks to Lisa Malachowsky, Director of Parts and Service at San Jose BMW/Vespa, for supplying valuable technical information. Thanks also to Piaggio VE SpA, Italy, for permission to reproduce artwork from their publications.

About this manual

The aim of this manual is to help you get the best value from your scooter. It can do so in several ways. It can help you decide what work must be done, even if you choose to have it done by a dealer; it provides information and procedures for routine maintenance and servicing; and it offers diagnostic and repair procedures to follow when trouble occurs.

We hope you use the manual to tackle the work yourself. For many simpler jobs, doing it yourself may be quicker than arranging an appointment to get the scooter into a dealer and making the trips to leave it and pick it up. More importantly, a lot of money can be saved by avoiding the expense the shop must pass on to you to cover its labor and overhead costs. An added benefit is the sense of satisfaction and accomplishment that you feel after doing the job yourself.

References to the left or right side of the scooter assume you are sitting on the seat, facing forward.

We take great pride in the accuracy of information given in this manual, but scooter manufacturers make alterations and design changes during the production run of a particular scooter of which they do not inform us. No liability can be accepted by the authors or publishers for loss, damage or injury caused by any errors in, or omissions from, the information given.

Scooters manufacturers have added bigger, faster and more luxurious models, such as this Honda NS250 Reflex

Identification numbers

The frame serial number, or VIN (Vehicle Identification Number) as it is often known, is stamped into the frame, and also appears on the identification plate. The engine number is stamped into the rear of the transmission case. Both of these numbers should be recorded and kept in a safe place so they can be furnished to law enforcement officials in the event of a theft.

The frame and engine numbers should also be kept in a handy place (such as with your driver's license) so they are always available when purchasing or ordering parts for your scooter.

Each model type can be identified by its engine and frame number prefix.

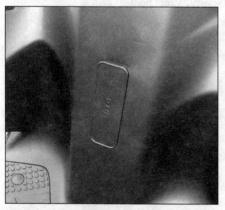

The Vehicle Identification number (VIN) is stamped on the frame - on some models, it's on a lower frame member and on others, it's on the steering head and can be found under a cover like this one

The VIN is also printed on a placard attached to the bodywork

The engine number is at the rear of the transmission/crankcase casting - on some models it's on the underside

Buying spare parts

When ordering new parts, it is essential to identify exactly the machine for which the parts are required. While in some cases it is sufficient to identify the machine by its title, eg, 'Piaggio BV200' or 'Yamaha Vino 50', any modifications made to components mean that it is usually essential to identify the scooter by its year of production, or better still by its frame or engine number prefix.

To be absolutely certain of receiving the correct part, not only is it essential to have the scooter engine or frame number prefix on hand, but it is also useful to take the old part for comparison (where possible). Note that where a modified component has replaced the original, a careful check must be made that there are no related parts which have also been modified and must be used to enable the new part to be correctly installed; where such a situation is found, purchase all the necessary parts and install them, even if this means replacing apparently unworn items.

Purchase parts from an authorized dealer or someone who specializes in scooter parts; they are more likely to have the parts in stock or can order them quickly from the importer. Pattern parts are available for certain components; if used, ensure these are of recognized quality brands which will perform as well as the original.

Expendable items such as lubricants, spark plugs, some electrical components, bearings, bulbs and tires can usually be obtained at lower prices from accessory shops or from specialists advertising in the national motorcycle press.

Professional mechanics are trained in safe working procedures. However enthusiastic you may be about getting on with the job at hand, take the time to ensure that your safety is not put at risk. A moment's lack of attention can result in an accident, as can failure to observe simple precautions.

There will always be new ways of having accidents, and the following is not a comprehensive list of all dangers; it is intended rather to make you aware of the risks and to encourage a safe approach to all work you carry out on your bike.

Asbestos

● Certain friction, insulating, sealing and other products - such as brake pads, clutch linings, gaskets, etc. - may contain asbestos. Extreme care must be taken to avoid inhalation of dust from such products since it is hazardous to health. If in doubt, assume that they do contain asbestos.

Fire

● Remember at all times that gasoline is highly flammable. Never smoke or have any kind of naked flame around, when working on the vehicle. But the risk does not end there - a spark caused by an electrical short-circuit, by two metal surfaces contacting each other, by careless use of tools, or even by static electricity built up in your body under certain conditions, can ignite gasoline vapor, which in a confined space is highly explosive. Never use gasoline as a cleaning solvent. Use an approved safety solvent.

● Always disconnect the battery ground terminal before working on any part of the fuel or electrical system, and never risk spilling fuel onto a hot engine or exhaust.

● It is recommended that a fire extinguisher of a type suitable for fuel and electrical fires is kept handy in the garage or workplace at all times. Never try to extinguish a fuel or electrical fire with water.

Fumes

● Certain fumes are highly toxic and can quickly cause unconsciousness and even death if inhaled to any extent. Gasoline vapor comes into this category, as do the vapors from certain solvents such as trichloro-ethylene. Any draining or pouring of such volatile fluids should be done in a well ventilated area.

● When using cleaning fluids and solvents, read the instructions carefully. Never use materials from unmarked containers - they may give off poisonous vapors.

● Never run the engine of a motor vehicle in an enclosed space such as a garage. Exhaust fumes contain carbon monoxide which is extremely poisonous; if you need to run the engine, always do so in the open air or at least have the rear of the vehicle outside the workplace.

The battery

● Never cause a spark, or allow a naked light near the vehicle's battery. It will normally be giving off a certain amount of hydrogen gas, which is highly explosive.

● Always disconnect the battery ground terminal before working on the fuel or electrical systems (except where noted).

● If possible, loosen the filler plugs or cover when charging the battery from an external source. Do not charge at an excessive rate or the battery may burst.

● Take care when topping up, cleaning or carrying the battery. The acid electrolyte, even when diluted, is very corrosive and should not be allowed to contact the eyes or skin. Always wear rubber gloves and goggles or a face shield. If you ever need to prepare electrolyte yourself, always add the acid slowly to the water; never add the water to the acid.

Electricity

● When using an electric power tool, inspection light etc., always ensure that the appliance is correctly connected to its plug and that, where necessary, it is properly grounded. Do not use such appliances in damp conditions and, again, beware of creating a spark or applying excessive heat in the vicinity of fuel or fuel vapor. Also ensure that the appliances meet national safety standards.

● A severe electric shock can result from touching certain parts of the electrical system, such as the spark plug wires (HT leads), when the engine is running or being cranked, particularly if components are damp or the insulation is defective. Where an electronic ignition system is used, the secondary (HT) voltage is much higher and could prove fatal.

Remember...

✗ **Don't** start the engine without first ascertaining that the transmission is in neutral.

✗ **Don't** suddenly remove the pressure cap from a hot cooling system - cover it with a cloth and release the pressure gradually first, or you may get scalded by escaping coolant.

✗ **Don't** attempt to drain oil until you are sure it has cooled sufficiently to avoid scalding you.

✗ **Don't** grasp any part of the engine or exhaust system without first ascertaining that it is cool enough not to burn you.

✗ **Don't** allow brake fluid or antifreeze to contact the machine's paintwork or plastic components.

✗ **Don't** siphon toxic liquids such as fuel, hydraulic fluid or antifreeze by mouth, or allow them to remain on your skin.

✗ **Don't** inhale dust - it may be injurious to health (see Asbestos heading).

✗ **Don't** allow any spilled oil or grease to remain on the floor - wipe it up right away, before someone slips on it.

✗ **Don't** use ill-fitting wrenches or other tools which may slip and cause injury.

✗ **Don't** lift a heavy component which may be beyond your capability - get assistance.

✗ **Don't** rush to finish a job or take unverified short cuts.

✗ **Don't** allow children or animals in or around an unattended vehicle.

✗ **Don't** inflate a tire above the recommended pressure. Apart from overstressing the carcass, in extreme cases the tire may blow off forcibly.

✔ **Do** ensure that the machine is supported securely at all times. This is especially important when the machine is blocked up to aid wheel or fork removal.

✔ **Do** take care when attempting to loosen a stubborn nut or bolt. It is generally better to pull on a wrench, rather than push, so that if you slip, you fall away from the machine rather than onto it.

✔ **Do** wear eye protection when using power tools such as drill, sander, bench grinder etc.

✔ **Do** use a barrier cream on your hands prior to undertaking dirty jobs - it will protect your skin from infection as well as making the dirt easier to remove afterwards; but make sure your hands aren't left slippery. Note that long-term contact with used engine oil can be a health hazard.

✔ **Do** keep loose clothing (cuffs, ties etc.)

and long hair) well out of the way of moving mechanical parts.

✔ **Do** remove rings, wristwatch etc., before working on the vehicle - especially the electrical system.

✔ **Do** keep your work area tidy - it is only too easy to fall over articles left lying around.

✔ **Do** exercise caution when compressing springs for removal or installation. Ensure that the tension is applied and released in a controlled manner, using suitable tools which preclude the possibility of the spring escaping violently.

✔ **Do** ensure that any lifting tackle used has a safe working load rating adequate for the job.

✔ **Do** get someone to check periodically that all is well, when working alone on the vehicle.

✔ **Do** carry out work in a logical sequence and check that everything is correctly assembled and tightened afterwards.

✔ **Do** remember that your vehicle's safety affects that of yourself and others. If in doubt on any point, get professional advice.

● If in spite of following these precautions, you are unfortunate enough to injure yourself, seek medical attention as soon as possible.

1a Two-stroke engine oil level check

The correct oil

● Keep the oil tank topped up with a good quality two-stroke oil suitable for injector systems. Certain scooters require a specific grade of two-stroke oil – see the *Data* section at the end of this manual.

● Don't rely on the oil level warning light to tell you that the oil needs topping-up. Get into the habit of checking the oil level at the same time as you fill up with fuel.

● If the engine is run without oil, even for a short time, serious engine damage and engine seizure will occur. It is advised that a bottle of engine oil is carried in the storage compartment at all times.

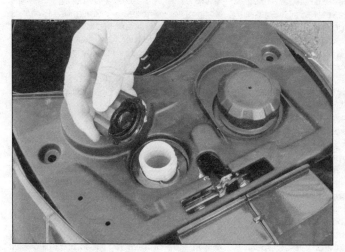

1 Remove the filler cap to check the oil level.

2 If the level is low, top-up with the recommended grade and type of oil, then install the filler cap securely.

1b Four-stroke engine oil level check

Before you start:
✔ Park the scooter outside or in some other well-ventilated area.
✔ Start the engine and let it idle for five minutes. If the air temperature is less than 50-degrees F (10-degrees C), allow it to run for five more minutes.

✔ After the bike has idled for the specified amount of time, turn it off. Support the bike in an upright position. The easiest way to do this when by yourself is to simply sit on the seat while checking the oil level. Immediately proceed to check the oil level.

Scooter care:
● If you have to add oil frequently, you should check whether you have any oil leaks.

The correct oil
● Modern engines place great demands on their oil. It is very important to use the correct oil for your engine.

● Always top-up with a good quality oil of the specified type and viscosity – see the *Data* section at the end of this manual.

● Check the oil level carefully. Make sure you know the correct level for your scooter.

1 On models without a sight glass for the engine oil level, the engine oil filler cap and dipstick are threaded into the crankcase casting, either on the left side (shown) . . .

2 . . . or on the right side - the oil level should be between the marks on the dipstick

2 Coolant level check (liquid-cooled engines)

 Warning: Never remove the radiator cap while the engine is warm or scalding coolant will spray out. Let the engine cool down before removing the cap.

 Warning: Antifreeze is poisonous. Do not leave open containers of coolant lying around.

Warning: Do not run the engine in an enclosed space such as a garage or workshop.

Before you start:
✔ Make sure you have a supply of coolant available. A mixture of 50% distilled water and 50% corrosion inhibited ethylene glycol antifreeze is needed. Keep in mind that many brands of coolant are pre-mixed, so be sure to check the container. Do not add water to pre-mixed coolant, as this would dilute the mixture.
✔ Always check the coolant level when the engine is cold.
✔ Ensure the scooter is held vertical while checking the coolant level. Make sure the scooter is on level ground.

Scooter care:
● Use only the specified coolant mixture. It is important that antifreeze is used in the system all year round, and not just in the winter. Do not top the system up using only water, as the system will become too diluted.
● Make sure you know the correct level for your scooter - refer to your scooter handbook for details. If there are no minimum and maximum marks, top-up the coolant level to just below the bottom of the filler neck
● Do not overfill the reservoir tank. If the coolant is significantly above the F (full) level line at any time, the surplus should be siphoned or drained off to prevent the possibility of it being expelled out of the overflow hose.
● If the coolant level falls steadily, check the system for leaks (see Chapter 1). If no leaks are found and the level continues to fall, it is recommended that the machine is taken to a dealer or other repair shop for a pressure test.

On many scooters, you will need to detach a body panel to view the coolant reservoir. To top up, unscrew the filler cap and top up to the bottom of the filler neck or level marks. On other scooters, the coolant reservoir has level marks on the side, which are visible through the body panel, and topping up is done through a filler cap at the top of the panel.

3 Suspension and steering checks

● Check that the front and rear suspension operates smoothly without binding.

● Check that the steering moves smoothly from lock-to-lock.

4 Fuel check

● This may seem obvious, but check that you have enough fuel to complete your journey. Do not rely on the fuel gauge or warning light to tell you that the level in the tank is low before filling up.

● If you notice any fuel leaks, you must rectify the cause immediately.

● Ensure you use the correct grade of unleaded gasoline. Note that the use of unleaded gasoline will increase spark plug life and have obvious benefits to the environment.

5 Brake fluid level check

> **Warning: Brake fluid can harm your eyes and damage painted or some plastic surfaces, so use extreme caution when handling and pouring it and cover surrounding surfaces with rag. Do not use fluid that has been standing open for some time, as it absorbs moisture from the air which can cause a dangerous loss of braking effectiveness.**

Before you start:

✔ Support the machine in an upright position on level ground and turn the handlebars until the hydraulic reservoir is as level as possible – remember to check both reservoirs if your scooter is equipped with front and rear disc brakes.

✔ Make sure you have a supply of the correct hydraulic fluid. Refer to the reservoir cover or the *Data* section of this manual.

✔ Access to the reservoir is restricted on most models by the upper handlebar cover. Remove the cover if the reservoir requires topping-up.

✔ Wrap a rag around the reservoir to prevent any hydraulic fluid coming into contact with painted or plastic surfaces.

Scooter care:

● The fluid in the hydraulic reservoir will drop slightly as the brake pads wear down.

● If the reservoir requires repeated topping-up, this is an indication of a fluid leak somewhere in the system, which should be investigated immediately.

● Check for signs of fluid leaks from the brake hoses and components – if found, rectify immediately.

● Check the operation of the brake before riding the machine; if there is evidence of air in the system (a spongy feel to the lever), it must be bled as described in Chapter 8.

1 The brake fluid level is visible through the sight glass in the reservoir body - it must be above the LOWER mark when the reservoir is level.

2 The fluid type is usually cast into the reservoir cover. Remove the reservoir cap screws and remove the cover, diaphragm plate and diaphragm. Top up with the specified brake fluid until the level is between the marks on the sight glass. Do not overfill and take care to avoid spills (see **Warning** above). Be sure the diaphragm is correctly seated before installing the plate and cover. Tighten the cover screws securely.

6 Legal and safety checks

Lighting and signalling

● Take a minute to check that the headlight, tail light, brake light, instrument lights and turn signals all work correctly.

● Check that the horn sounds when the switch is operated.

● A working speedometer graduated in mph may be a requirement in your state.

Safety

● Check that the throttle twistgrip rotates smoothly and snaps shut when released, in all steering positions.

● Check that the stand return spring holds the stand securely up when retracted.

● Check that both brakes work correctly when applied and free off when released.

7 Tire checks

The correct pressures:

● The tires must be checked when **cold**, not immediately after riding. Note that low tire pressures may cause the tire to slip on the rim or come off. High tire pressures will cause abnormal tread wear and unsafe handling.
● Use an accurate pressure gauge.
● Proper air pressure will increase tire life and provide maximum stability and ride comfort.
● Refer to the *Data* section at the end of this manual for the correct tire pressures for your model.

Tire care:

● Check the tires carefully for cuts, tears, embedded nails or other sharp objects and excessive wear. Operation of the scooter with excessively worn tires is extremely hazardous, as traction and handling are directly affected.
● Check the condition of the tire valve and ensure the dust cap is in place.

● Pick out any stones or nails which may have become embedded in the tire tread. If left, they will eventually penetrate through the casing and cause a puncture.
● If tire damage is apparent, or unexplained loss of pressure is experienced, seek the advice of a tire fitting specialist without delay.

Tire tread depth:

● Tire tread depth must be at least 1/16 of an inch all the way around the tire, with no bald patches.

● Many tires now incorporate wear indicators in the tread. Identify the triangular pointer on the tire sidewall to locate the indicator bar and replace the tire if the tread has worn down to the bar.

1 Check the tire pressures when the tires are **cold** and keep them properly inflated.

2 Measure tread depth at the center of the tire using a tread depth gauge.

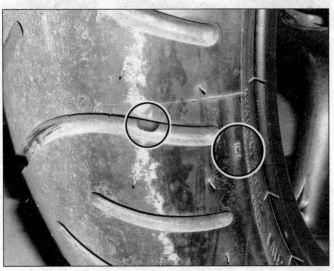

3 Tire tread wear indicator bar and its location marking (usually either an arrow, a triangle or the letters TWI) on the sidewall.

Chapter 1
Routine maintenance and servicing

Contents

Degrees of difficulty

Easy, suitable for novice with little experience	**Fairly easy,** suitable for beginner with some experience	**Fairly difficult,** suitable for competent DIY mechanic	**Difficult,** suitable for experienced DIY mechanic	**Very difficult,** suitable for expert DIY or professional

Specifications

Refer to the *Data* section at the end of this manual for servicing specifications.

1 Introduction

1 This Chapter is designed to help the home mechanic maintain his/her scooter for safety, economy, long life and peak performance.
2 Whenever you ride your scooter, and in some cases even when it is not in use, components wear and deteriorate. To counteract this process, every scooter has a service schedule – relating to either a period of time or mileage – which stipulates when checks and adjustments should be made.
3 The majority of service items are common to all scooters, but some, like the radiator on a liquid-cooled model or the valves on a four-stroke engine, are specific to certain models. The *Data* section at the end of this manual will help you identify the various systems on your scooter and their components, and provide you with the specifications necessary to ensure their continued reliable performance.
4 Deciding where to start or adopt a service schedule depends on several factors. If the warranty period on your scooter has just expired, and if it has been maintained

according to the warranty standards, you will want to pick up routine maintenance as it coincides with the next mileage or calendar interval. If you have owned the machine for some time but have never performed any maintenance on it, then you may want to start at the nearest interval and include some additional procedures to ensure that nothing important is overlooked. If you have just had a major engine overhaul, then you will want to start the maintenance routine from the beginning as with a new scooter. If you have a used scooter and have no knowledge of its history or maintenance record, it would be best to combine all the checks into one large initial service, then settle into a regular routine schedule.

5 Don't worry if you haven't got a service schedule for your particular scooter; use the information in this Chapter to identify the service items on your scooter – air filter, battery, brakes, etc – then create your own service schedule based on the examples we give.
Note: *Certain maintenance information is sometimes printed on decals attached to the scooter. If the information on the decals differs from that included here, use the information on the decal.*
6 Before beginning any maintenance or repair, clean your scooter thoroughly, especially around the suspension, brakes, engine and transmission covers. Cleaning will help ensure that dirt does not contaminate the working parts, and will allow you to detect

wear and damage that could otherwise easily go unnoticed.
Note 1: *The daily (pre-ride) checks detailed at the beginning of this manual cover those items which should be inspected on a daily basis. Always perform the pre-ride inspection at every maintenance interval (in addition to the procedures listed).*
Note 2: *The intervals listed below are the intervals generally recommended by manufacturers but are not specific to any make or model. The owner's handbook for your model may have different intervals to those shown. If available, always refer to the maintenance booklet supplied with your scooter for the correct intervals.*

Routine maintenance and servicing procedures

2 Typical service items

Identifying service items
1 Use the accompanying list and the owner's handbook to identify the service items on your scooter and their locations **(see illustrations)**. The service items have been grouped under headings which identify the overall systems to which they belong. The headings also relate to the Chapters in this manual.
2 Not all the service items under each heading will require attention at the same time, but when you are working on a particular system, it is useful to note all the parts that require servicing and check them at the same time. For example, when the drivebelt cover has been removed to inspect the variator and the condition of the belt, the general condition of the clutch and the kickstart mechanism can be checked. Also, if the belt has worn prematurely and is close to its service limit, a new one can be installed earlier than scheduled to prevent any damage caused by a broken belt.

Two-stroke engines
- ☐ *Engine oil level*
- ☐ *Oil filter*
- ☐ *Oil pump adjustment*
- ☐ *Oil pump drivebelt*
- ☐ *Cylinder head decarbonizing*

Four-stroke engines
- ☐ *Engine oil level*
- ☐ *Engine oil change*
- ☐ *Oil filter*
- ☐ *Engine oil pressure*
- ☐ *Valve clearances*

Cooling system (air-cooled engines)
- ☐ *Cooling fan*
- ☐ *Engine cowling*

Cooling system (liquid-cooled engines)
- ☐ *Coolant*
- ☐ *Radiator*
- ☐ *Water pump*
- ☐ *Hoses*
- ☐ *Draining, flushing and refilling*

Fuel and exhaust system
- ☐ *Air filters*
- ☐ *Throttle cable*
- ☐ *Carburetor*
- ☐ *Fuel hose*
- ☐ *Idle speed*

Ignition system
- ☐ *Spark plug*

Transmission
- ☐ *Drivebelt*
- ☐ *Variator*
- ☐ *Kickstart mechanism*
- ☐ *Clutch pulley*
- ☐ *Gearbox oil change*
- ☐ *Gearbox oil level*

Frame and suspension
- ☐ *Front suspension*
- ☐ *Rear suspension*
- ☐ *Stand*
- ☐ *Steering head bearings*

Brakes, wheels and tires
- ☐ *Brake cable*
- ☐ *Brake fluid (disc brake)*
- ☐ *Brake hose (disc brake)*
- ☐ *Brake levers*
- ☐ *Brake pads (disc brake)*
- ☐ *Brake shoes and cam (drum brake)*
- ☐ *Wheel bearings*
- ☐ *Tire condition*

Bodywork
- ☐ *Fasteners*
- ☐ *Panel condition*

Electrical systems
- ☐ *Battery*
- ☐ *Headlight aim*
- ☐ *Brake light*
- ☐ *Horn*
- ☐ *Speedometer cable*

General
- ☐ *Nuts and bolts*

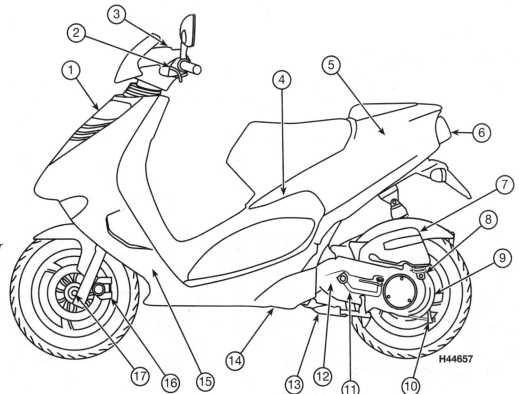

1   Headlight
2   Brake levers
3   Speedometer cable
4   Battery
5   Engine oil – two-stroke
    engine
6   Brake light
7   Air filter
8   Rear suspension
9   Gearbox oil
10 Rear drum brake adjuster
11 Kickstarter
12 Transmission – variator,
    drivebelt and clutch
13 Stand
14 Engine oil – four-stroke
    engine
15 Horn
16 Front brake
17 Wheel bearings

2.1a Component locations – left-hand side

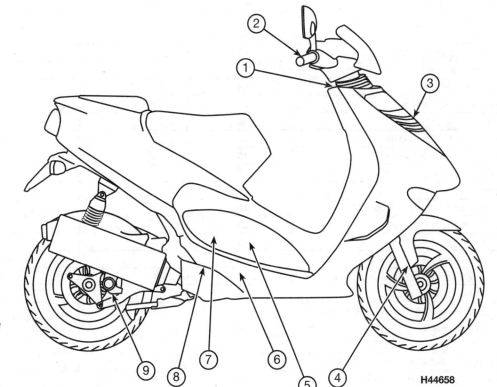

1   Steering head bearings
2   Throttle cable
3   Cooling system –
    liquid-cooled engine
4   Front suspension
5   Valves – four-stroke
    engine
6   Spark plug
7   Carburetor – idle speed
8a Water pump –
    liquid-cooled engine
8b Cooling fan – air-cooled
    engine
9   Rear brake – disc
    brake model

2.1b Component locations – right-hand side

Two-stroke engine

Note: *Always perform the daily (pre-ride) checks before every service interval – see the beginning of this Manual.*
Note: *Severe conditions are regarded as intensive urban use, short journeys with cold engine or use in dusty conditions.*
Note: *The 2500 mile tasks should be included with the 5000 mile service, etc.*

	Text section in this Chapter	Every 2500 miles (4000 km) or 12 months 1500 miles (2500 km) for severe conditions	Every 5000 miles (8000 km) or 2 years 3000 miles (5000 km) for severe conditions	Every 10,000 miles (16,000 km) or 3 years
Air filters – clean/replace	3	✓		
Battery – check	4	✓		
Brake cable – check and lubricate	7	✓		
Brake fluid – check	8	✓		✓*
Brake hose – check	9	✓		✓*
Brake lever pivots – lubricate	6	✓		
Brake pads – check	10	✓		
Brake shoes – check	11	✓		
Brake shoe cam – check and lubricate	12		✓	
Brake system – check	5	✓		
Carburetor – clean	15		✓	
Clutch pulley and bearing – check and lubricate	26		✓	
Cooling system – check	21	✓		✓**
Cylinder head – decarbonize	31		✓	
Drivebelt – check	22	✓		
Drivebelt – replace	23		✓	
Engine oil system – check	17	✓		
Engine oil filter – change	18		✓	
Fuel system – check	14	✓		
Gearbox oil level – check	27	✓		
Gearbox oil – change	28		✓	
Headlight, brake light and horn – check	33	✓		
Idle speed – check and adjust	16	✓		
Kickstart mechanism – check	25		✓	
Nuts and bolts – tightness check	39	✓		
Oil pump cable – check and adjust	19	✓		
Oil pump drivebelt – replace	20			✓
Spark plug – gap check and adjust	29	✓		
Spark plug – replace	30		✓	
Speedometer cable and drive gear – lubricate	36		✓	
Stand – check and lubricate	35	✓		
Steering head bearings – check and adjust	37		✓	
Suspension – check	38		✓	
Throttle cable – check and adjust	13	✓		
Variator pulley and rollers – check and lubricate	24	✓		
Wheels and tires – check	34	✓		

* The brake fluid must be changed every 2 years and the brake hose replaced every 3 years, regardless of mileage
** Drain and refill a liquid-cooled system with fresh coolant every 2 years, regardless of mileage

Four-stroke engine

Note: *Always perform the daily (pre-ride) checks before every service interval – see the beginning of this Manual.*
Note: *Severe conditions are regarded as intensive urban use, short journeys with cold engine or use in dusty conditions.*
Note: *The 2500 mile tasks should be included with the 5000 mile service, etc.*

	Text section in this Chapter	Every 2500 miles (4000 km) or 12 months *1500 miles (2500 km) for severe conditions*	Every 5000 miles (8000 km) or 2 years *3000 miles (5000 km) for severe conditions*	Every 10,000 miles (16,000 km) or 3 years
Air filters – clean/replace	3	✓		
Battery – check	4	✓		
Brake cable – check and lubricate	7	✓		
Brake fluid – check	8	✓		✓*
Brake hose – check	9	✓		✓*
Brake lever pivots – lubricate	6	✓		
Brake pads – check	10	✓		
Brake shoes – check	11	✓		
Brake shoe cam – check and lubricate	12		✓	
Brake system – check	5	✓		
Carburetor – clean	15		✓	
Clutch pulley and bearing – check and lubricate	26		✓	
Cooling system – check	21	✓		✓**
Drivebelt – check	22	✓		
Drivebelt – replace	23		✓	
Engine oil system – check	17	✓		
Engine oil and filter – change	18	✓		
Fuel system – check	14	✓		
Gearbox oil level – check	27	✓		
Gearbox oil – change	28		✓	
Headlight, brake light and horn – check	33	✓		
Idle speed – check and adjust	16	✓		
Kickstart mechanism – check	25		✓	
Nuts and bolts – tightness check	39	✓		
Spark plug – gap check and adjust	29	✓		
Spark plug – replace	30		✓	
Speedometer cable and drive gear – lubricate	36		✓	
Stand – check and lubricate	35	✓		
Steering head bearings – check and adjust	37		✓	
Suspension – check	38		✓	
Throttle cable – check and adjust	13	✓		
Valve clearances – check and adjust	32			✓
Variator pulley and rollers – check and lubricate	24	✓		
Wheels and tires – check	34	✓		

* The brake fluid must be changed every 2 years and the brake hose replaced every 3 years, regardless of mileage
** Drain and refill a liquid-cooled system with fresh coolant every 2 years, regardless of mileage

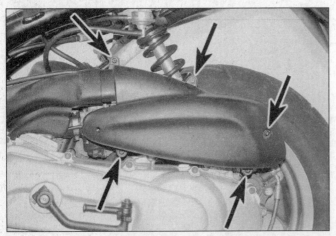

3.1a Undo the air filter cover screws (arrows) . . .

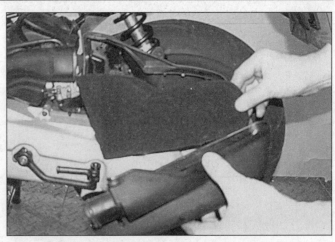

3.1b . . . and remove the cover and filter element

3.1c A typical filter element panel

3 Air filters – cleaning and replacement

Caution: If the scooter is continually ridden in wet or dusty conditions, the filters should be checked more frequently.

Engine air filter

1 Remove the screws securing the air filter cover and detach the cover (see illustration). Remove the filter element – note that some filter elements are installed in a removable panel (see illustrations).

2 Some manufacturers recommend that the filter element is replaced at every service interval – refer to your scooter handbook for details. However, foam filters can usually be cleaned and re-used if they are in good condition.

3 Wash the filter in hot soapy water, then blow dry using compressed air.

4 Soak the filter in dedicated air filter oil, or a mixture of gasoline and 10% two-stroke oil or four-stroke engine oil, as recommended. Lay it on an absorbent surface and squeeze out the excess liquid, making sure you do not damage the filter by twisting it.

5 Allow the filter to dry for a while, then install it back into the housing and install the cover and tighten the screws securely.

6 If the filter is excessively dirty and cannot be cleaned properly, or is torn or damaged in any way, replace it.

7 If the filter housing is equipped with a drain, undo the plug and release any trapped fluid (see illustration)

Transmission air filter

8 Some scooters have a filter installed on the belt drive housing. Remove the filter unit and lift out the filter element (see illustrations). Clean and, if required, re-oil the element as described in Steps 3 to 5.

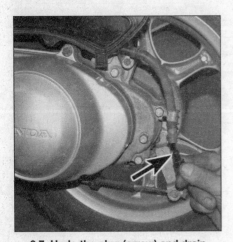

3.7 Undo the plug (arrow) and drain the hose

3.8a Remove the belt drive housing filter unit . . .

3.8b . . . and lift out the filter element

4.1 Check the electrolyte level through the battery case

4.2 Top-up the battery to the upper mark with distilled water

Secondary air system

9 A secondary air system is installed on two-stroke models with a catalytic converter exhaust system. The system sucks fresh air into the exhaust pipe to promote the burning of unburnt gases, reducing the emission of hydrocarbons into the atmosphere.
10 Remove any body panels as necessary to access the system components (see Chapter 9).
11 Undo the screws securing the housing cover and detach the cover, then lift out the reed valve and the filter element. Discard the cover O-ring or gasket if installed, as a new one must be used on reassembly.
12 Where installed, pry the breather cap out of the drivebelt cover with a small screwdriver and carefully pull the filter element out of the cap.
13 Wash the filters in hot soapy water, then blow them dry using compressed air. Never wring the filters dry, as they may tear. If the filters are excessively dirty and cannot be cleaned properly, or are torn or damaged in any way, install new ones.
14 To check the condition of the reed valve, hold it up to the light. The valve should be closed. If light can be seen around the edge of the reed, a new valve should be installed. Clean the reed carefully with a suitable solvent to remove any gum.
15 Install the components in the reverse order of disassembly, remembering to install a new O-ring or gasket to the filter housing cover if required.

4 Battery – check

Caution: Be extremely careful when handling or working around the battery. The electrolyte is very caustic and an explosive gas (hydrogen) is given off when the battery is charging.

Conventional battery

1 Remove the battery access panel and partially lift the battery out of its holder. Check the electrolyte level which is visible through the translucent battery case – it should be between the UPPER and LOWER level marks **(see illustration)**.
2 If the electrolyte is low, disconnect the battery terminals (see Chapter 10) and move the battery to the work bench. Remove the cell caps and fill each cell to the upper level mark with distilled water **(see illustration)**. Do not use tap water (except in an emergency), and do not overfill. The cell holes are quite small, so it may help to use a clean plastic squeeze bottle with a small spout to add the water. Install the battery cell caps, tightening them securely, then install the battery (see Chapter 10).

Maintenance-free battery

3 On machines equipped with a sealed battery, no maintenance is required. **Note:** *Do not attempt to remove the battery caps to check the electrolyte level or battery specific gravity. Removal will damage the caps, resulting in electrolyte leakage and battery failure.* All that should be done is to check that the battery terminals are clean and tight and that the casing is not damaged. See Chapter 10 for further details.

5 Brake system – check

1 A routine check of the brake system will ensure that any problems are discovered and remedied before the rider's safety is jeopardized.
2 Check that the brake levers are not loose or damaged, and that the lever action is smooth without excessive play. Replace any worn or damaged parts (see Chapter 8).
3 Make sure all brake fasteners are tight. Check the brake pads (disc brake) and brake shoes (drum brake) for wear (see Sections 10 and 11).
4 Where disc brakes are installed, make sure the fluid level in the hydraulic reservoir is correct (see *Daily (pre-ride) checks*). Look for leaks at the hose connections and check for cracks and abrasions in the hoses and replace them if necessary (see Chapter 8). If the lever action is spongy, bleed the brakes (see Chapter 8).
5 Where drum brakes are installed, check the cable for damage or stiff action (see Section 7).
6 Make sure the brake light operates when each brake lever is pulled in. The brake light switches are not adjustable. If they fail to operate properly, check them (see Chapter 10, Section 6).

6 Brake lever pivots – lubrication

1 The lever pivots should be lubricated periodically to reduce wear and ensure safe and trouble-free operation.
2 In order for the lubricant to be applied where it will do the most good, the lever should be removed (see Chapter 8). However, if chain or cable lubricant is being used, it can be applied to the pivot joint gaps and will work its way into the areas where friction occurs. If motor oil or light grease is being used, apply it sparingly as it may attract dirt (which could cause the controls to bind or wear at an accelerated rate). **Note:** *One of the best lubricants for the control lever pivots is a dry-film lubricant.*

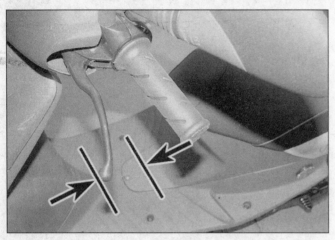

7.1 Measuring brake lever freeplay

7.2 Brake cable adjuster nut (arrow)

7 Brake cable – check, adjustment and lubrication

Check and adjustment

Drum brake

1 Check that there is no excessive freeplay in the handlebar lever before the brake takes effect **(see illustration)**. The wheel should spin freely when the brake is off, but the brake should come on before the lever is pulled back against the handlebar.

2 To reduce freeplay in the lever, turn the adjuster nut on the brake drum end of the cable clockwise; to increase freeplay, turn the adjuster nut counterclockwise **(see illustration)**. If there is a locknut on the adjuster, tighten it securely on completion.

3 If the brake is binding without the lever being pulled, first check that the lever is moving freely (see Section 6). Next, disconnect the cable from the handlebar lever (see Chapter 8) and check that the inner cable slides smoothly in the outer cable. If the action is stiff, inspect along the length of the outer cable for splits and kinks, and the ends

of the inner cable for frays, and replace either one if necessary (see Chapter 8).

4 If there are no signs of damage, lubricate the cable (see Step 9). If the cable is still stiff after lubrication, replace it (see Chapter 8).

5 If the handlebar lever and brake cable are in good condition, check the operation of the brake cam (see Section 12).

Disc brake

6 If the hydraulic master cylinder is activated by a cable from the handlebar lever, remove the front panel (see Chapter 9) and check that there is no freeplay in the cable. If there is, loosen the cable adjuster locknut and turn the adjuster counterclockwise until all the slack is taken up, but make sure the lever arm is not

activated and pressurizing the system **(see illustration)**.

7 If the brake is binding without the lever being pulled, turn the adjuster clockwise until the lever arm is at rest, but make sure that no freeplay is created in the cable. Tighten the locknut securely on completion. To check the cable operation, follow the procedure in Step 3.

Lubrication

8 The cable should be lubricated periodically to ensure safe and trouble-free operation.

9 To lubricate the cable, disconnect it at its upper end and lubricate it with a pressure adapter, or using the set-up shown **(see illustration)**.

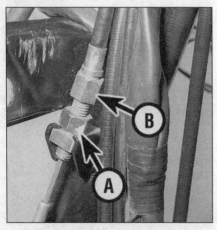

7.6 Loosen the locknut (A) and turn the adjuster (B) as required

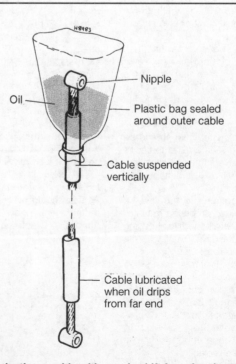

7.9 Lubricating a cable with a makeshift funnel and motor oil

Oil — Nipple

Plastic bag sealed around outer cable

Cable suspended vertically

Cable lubricated when oil drips from far end

9.1 Inspect the brake hose (A) and banjo fitting (B)

10.1 Check brake pad wear at the underside of the caliper

10 Reconnect the cable and adjust the handlebar lever freeplay.

8 Brake fluid – check

1 The fluid level in the hydraulic reservoir should be checked before riding the scooter (see *Daily (pre-ride) checks*).
2 Brake fluid will degrade over a period of time. It should be changed every two years or whenever a new master cylinder or caliper is installed. Refer to the brake bleeding and fluid change section in Chapter 8.

 HAYNES HINT *Old brake fluid is much darker in color than new fluid, making it easy to see when all old fluid has been expelled from the system.*

9 Brake hose – check

1 Twist and flex the hose while looking for cracks, bulges and seeping fluid. Check extra carefully where the hose connects to the banjo fittings as this is a common area for hose failure **(see illustration)**.
2 Inspect the banjo fittings; if they are rusted, cracked or damaged, install new hoses.
3 Inspect the banjo union connections for leaking fluid. If they leak when tightened securely, unscrew the banjo bolt and install new washers (see Chapter 8).
4 Flexible hydraulic hose will deteriorate with age and should be replaced every three years regardless of its apparent condition (see Chapter 8).

10 Brake pads – wear check

1 The extent of friction material wear can normally be checked by looking at the underside of the caliper **(see illustration)**. If the pads are dirty, or if you are in any doubt as to the amount of friction material remaining, remove the pads for inspection (see Chapter 8).
2 If the amount of friction material remaining on the pads is below the service limit, new pads must be installed.

 Warning: Brake pads often wear at different rates. If there is any doubt about the condition of either of the pads in a caliper, remove the caliper and check. Brake failure will result if the friction material wears away completely.

3 Refer to Chapter 8 for details of pad removal, inspection and replacement.

11 Brake shoes – wear check

1 Drum brakes are normally equipped with a wear indicator **(see illustration)**.
2 As the brake shoes wear and the cable is adjusted to compensate, the indicator moves closer to the index mark on the casing. To check the extent of brake wear, have an assistant apply the brake firmly; if the indicator aligns with the index mark, the brake shoes are worn to their limit and must be replaced (see Chapter 8, Section 9).
3 If there is no wear indicator, remove the wheel to check the amount of friction material remaining on the brake shoes (see Chapter 8, Section 9).
4 If the amount of friction material remaining on the shoes is below the service limit, new shoes must be installed.

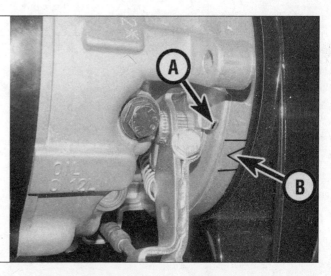

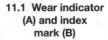 11.1 Wear indicator (A) and index mark (B)

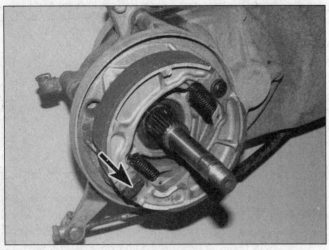

12.1 Typical brake shoe arrangement – note the brake cam (arrow)

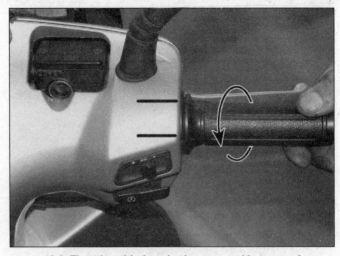

13.3 Throttle cable freeplay is measured in terms of twistgrip rotation

12 Brake shoe cam – check and lubrication

1 Remove the wheel; on front brakes, the brake shoes and brake cam are installed to the back plate, on rear brakes the shoes and cam are installed to the back of the gearbox casing **(see illustration)**.
2 Remove the brake shoes, then remove the brake arm and pull the brake cam out of the back plate or casing (see Chapter 8, Section 9).
3 Clean the shaft and cam and inspect the bearing surfaces for wear; replace the cam if necessary.
4 Apply some copper grease to the bearing surfaces of the cam and the shaft before reassembly.

Caution: Do not apply too much grease, otherwise there is a risk of it contaminating the brake drum and shoe linings.

13 Throttle cable – check and adjustment

Twistgrip cable

1 Ensure the throttle twistgrip rotates easily from fully closed to fully open with the handlebars turned at various angles. The twistgrip should return automatically from fully open to fully closed when released.
2 If the throttle sticks, this is probably due to a cable fault. Remove the cable (see Chapter 4) and lubricate it following the procedure in Section 7.
3 With the throttle operating smoothly, check for a small amount of freeplay in the cable, measured in terms of the amount of twistgrip rotation before the throttle opens **(see illus-**

tration). Compare the amount of freeplay to the specifications in the *Data* section at the end of this manual.
4 If there is insufficient or excessive freeplay, loosen the locknut on the cable adjuster, then turn the adjuster until the correct amount of freeplay is evident, then retighten the locknut **(see illustration)**. If the adjuster has reached its limit, replace the cable (see Chapter 4).
5 Start the engine and check the idle speed. If the idle speed is too high, this could be due to incorrect adjustment of the cable. Loosen the locknut and turn the adjuster in – if the idle speed falls as you do, there is insufficient freeplay in the cable. Reset the adjuster (see Step 4). **Note:** *The idle speed should not change as the handlebars are turned. If it does, the throttle cable is routed incorrectly. Rectify the problem before riding the scooter (see Chapter 4).*

Oil pump cable (two-stroke engines)

Note: *Two-stroke engines are installed with either a cable-controlled or centrifugal oil pump. A quick visual check will confirm which pump is installed to your engine (see Section 17).*

6 There should be no freeplay in the cable from the splitter to the carburetor **(see illustration)**.
7 Remove the air filter housing (see Chapter 4) and pull back the boot on the cable adjuster on the top of the carburetor.
8 Screw the adjuster into the top of the carburetor to create a small amount of freeplay in the cable, then screw the adjuster out until the carburetor slide just begins to lift. Now turn the adjuster in a quarter turn **(see illustration)**. Reinstall the boot and the filter housing.
9 Check the adjustment of the oil pump cable (see Section 19).

14 Fuel system – check

 Warning: Gasoline is extremely flammable, so take extra precautions when you work on any part of the fuel system.
Don't smoke or allow open flames or bare light bulbs near the work area, and

13.4 Adjusting the throttle cable freeplay
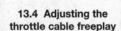

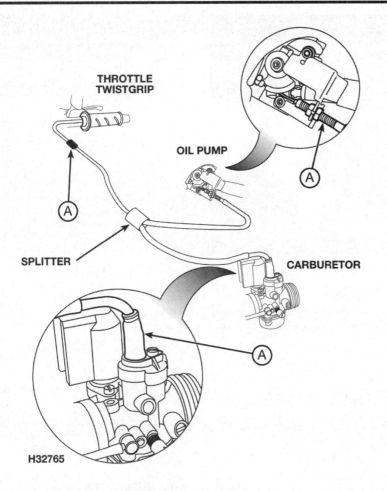

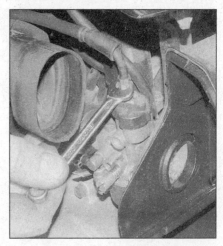

13.8 Adjusting the cable at the carburetor end

13.6 Cable arrangement for models equipped with a cable-operated oil pump
Location of cable adjusters (A)

pected (see Chapter 4).
5 Check that the fuel tank cap breather hole is clear. If the hole becomes blocked, fuel starvation will occur.
6 If your scooter is equipped with a fuel pump, ensure the fuel and vacuum hoses are securely attached to the pump and check the pump body for leaks. If you suspect that the pump is damaged or faulty, follow the procedure in Chapter 4 to test it.
7 If the carburetor gaskets are leaking, the carburetor should be disassembled and rebuilt using new gaskets and seals (see Chapter 4).
8 If the fuel gauge is believed to be faulty, check the operation of the sender (see Chapter 10).

15 Carburetor – cleaning

1 Remove the air filter housing (see Chapter 4) and the storage compartment (see Chapter 9) to access the carburetor.
2 The exterior of the carburetor and the

don't work in a garage where a gas-type appliance is present. If you spill any fuel on your skin, rinse it off immediately with soap and water. When you perform any kind of work on the fuel system, wear safety glasses and have a fire extinguisher suitable for a Class B type fire (flammable liquids) on hand.

Check

1 Remove the body panels as necessary to access the fuel tank, tap or pump (as applicable to your scooter) and carburetor (see Chapter 9). Check the fuel tank, the tap or pump, and the fuel hose for signs of leaks, deterioration or damage; in particular check that there are no leaks from the fuel hose. Replace the fuel hose if it is cracked or deteriorated.
2 If a fuel tap is installed to the tank, inspect the tap-to-tank fitting and ensure that the hose clip around the fitting is tight **(see illustration)**. If the fitting is leaking, remove the tap and check the condition of the fuel tap O-ring (see Chapter 4).
3 The fuel tap is vacuum-operated and should be closed when the engine is not

running. Disconnect the hose from the tap to check that the valve inside is not leaking **(see illustration 14.2)**. If the valve is leaking, install a new tap (see Chapter 4).
4 Cleaning or replacement of the fuel filter is advised after particularly high mileage has been reached, or if fuel starvation is sus-

14.2 Fuel tap hose clip (A), fuel hose (B) and vacuum hose (C)

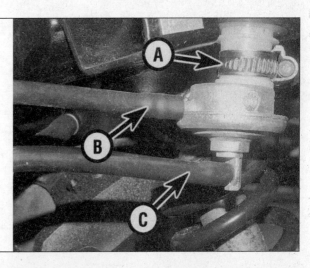

15.2 Keep the carburetor body and throttle mechanism free from dirt. Note the idle speed adjuster (arrow)

throttle mechanism should be kept clean and free of road dirt **(see illustration)**. Wash it carefully with hot soapy water, ensuring no water enters the carburetor body, and dry it with compressed air. Clean away any grit with a small paint brush. Oil deposits can be removed with a rag soaked in a suitable solvent. Take care to ensure the idle speed setting is not disturbed during cleaning.

3 Provided the air filter element is kept clean (see Section 3), the carburetor will give many thousands of miles of satisfactory service. However, dirt particles and varnish will gradually accumulate inside the body, and the carburetor should be removed and disassembled periodically to avoid the jets becoming blocked (see Chapter 4).

4 If the scooter has not been used for a long period, a sticky residue may form in the carburetor, jamming the throttle slide. Disassemble the carburetor and clean the components with a suitable solvent or carburetor cleaner (see Chapter 4). **Note:** *If the carburetor is being disassembled, read through the entire procedure and make sure that you have obtained a new gasket set first.*

16 Idle speed – check and adjustment

1 The idle speed (engine running with the throttle twistgrip closed) should be checked and adjusted when it is obviously too high or too low. Before adjusting the idle speed, make sure the throttle cable is correctly adjusted (see Section 13) and check the spark plug gap (see Section 29). On four-stroke engines, the valve clearances must be correct to achieve a satisfactory idle speed (see Section 32).

2 The engine should be at normal operating temperature, which is usually reached after 10 to 15 minutes of stop-and-go riding. Support the scooter on its center stand with the rear wheel clear of the ground.

 Warning: Do not allow exhaust gases to build-up in the work area; either perform the check outside or use an exhaust gas extraction system.

3 Although most manufacturers specify idle speed in engine revolutions per minute (rpm),

for scooters not equipped with a tachometer, it is sufficient to ensure that at idle the engine speed is steady and does not falter, and that it is not so high that the automatic transmission engages.

4 The idle speed adjuster screw is located on the carburetor or adjacent to the carburetor – refer to your scooter handbook for details. With the engine running, turn the screw clockwise to increase idle speed, and counterclockwise to decrease it **(see illustrations)**.

5 Snap the throttle open and shut a few times, then recheck the idle speed. If necessary, repeat the adjustment procedure.

6 If a smooth, steady idle can't be achieved, the fuel/air mixture may be incorrect (see Chapter 4) or the carburetor may need cleaning (see Section 15). If a satisfactory idle speed still cannot be achieved, have the ignition timing checked (see Chapter 5).

7 With the idle speed correctly adjusted, recheck the throttle cable freeplay (see Section 13).

17 Engine oil system – check

1 A routine check of the engine oil system will ensure that any problems are discovered and remedied before the engine is damaged.

2 Check the engine oil level (see *Daily (pre-ride) checks*).

Two-stroke engines

3 Check the operation of the oil level warning light in the instrument cluster. The light should come on temporarily when the ignition is first turned on as a check of the warning circuit, and then extinguish. If the light stays on, the oil level is low and should be topped-up. If the light stays on when the tank is full, check the oil level warning circuit (see Chapter 10). If the light doesn't come on at all, check the bulb and oil level warning circuit (see Chapter 10, Section 8). **Note:** *On most scooters,*

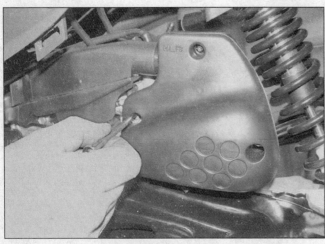

16.4a Adjusting the idle speed with a screwdriver . . .

16.4b . . . or directly on the carburetor

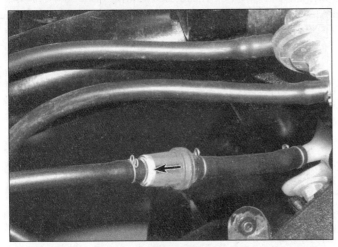

17.4 Two-stroke engine oil filter – arrow indicates direction of oil flow

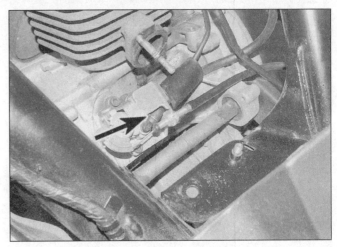

17.5a Inspect the oil hose connections (arrow) . . .

the oil level sensor is part of the safety circuit which prevents the engine starting if there is insufficient oil in the oil tank.

4 If a filter is installed in the hose from the oil tank to the pump, inspect the filter **(see illustration)**. Air bubbles should be bled from the filter by tilting it to allow the trapped air to rise through the hose into the oil tank. Check for sediment in the filter and replace the filter if necessary (see Section 18).

5 Check the condition of the oil inlet and outlet hoses. In particular check that there are no leaks from the hose connections to the oil tank, filter, oil pump and carburetor **(see illustration)**. Replace any hoses that are cracked or deteriorated and ensure they are properly secured by clips **(see illustration)**.

6 Two-stroke engines are equipped with either a cable-operated or centrifugal oil pump; the pump can be either mounted externally or inside part of the engine casing. On engines equipped with a cable-operated oil pump, check that the reference marks on the oil pump cam and pump body align with the throttle fully open. If the marks do not align, adjust the pump cable as necessary (see Section 19).

17.5b . . . and ensure they are secured by clips

Four-stroke engines

7 Check the operation of the oil pressure warning light in the instrument cluster. The light should come on when the ignition is turned on as a check of the warning circuit, and then extinguish when the engine is started.

8 If the light stays on, or comes on when the scooter is being ridden, stop the engine immediately. Check the oil level and top-up as necessary. If the level is correct, check for a fault in the oil pressure warning circuit. If the light doesn't come on at all, check the bulb and oil pressure warning circuit. **Note:** *If there is any doubt about the performance of the engine lubrication system, the oil pressure should be checked by a scooter dealer. Seri-*

ous damage to the engine will result if there is a failure in the engine lubrication system.

18 Engine oil and oil filter – change

Two-stroke engines

1 The oil filter should be changed at the specified service interval, or sooner if there is sediment in it.

2 Remove any body panels or the storage compartment as necessary to access the oil filter. Release the clips securing the inlet and outlet hoses to the filter and slide them along the hoses away from the filter **(see illustration 17.4)**. Detach the hoses and clamp them to prevent oil loss.

3 The oil filter body is marked with an arrow indicating the direction of oil flow. Connect the hoses to the filter fittings, ensuring the arrow points towards the oil pump, then install the hose clips.

4 Ensure any trapped air is bled from the filter (see Section 17) before reinstalling the body panels.

Four-stroke engines

⚠️ *Warning: Be careful when draining the oil, as the exhaust pipe, the engine, and the oil itself can cause severe burns.*

5 Oil and filter changes are the single most important maintenance procedure you can perform on a four-stroke engine. The oil not only lubricates the internal parts of the engine, but it also acts as a coolant, a cleaner, a sealant, and a protector. Because of these demands, the oil takes a terrific amount of abuse and should be replaced at the specified service interval with oil of the recommended grade and type.

6 Before changing the oil, warm-up the engine so the oil will drain easily. Stop the engine and turn the ignition OFF. Support the scooter on its center stand, and position a clean drain tray below the engine.

7 Unscrew the oil filler plug to vent the crank-

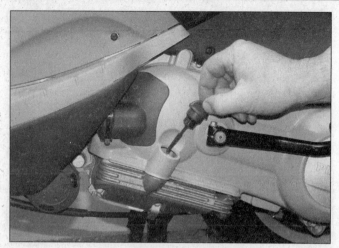

18.7 Unscrew the oil filler plug

18.8a The oil drain plug is situated on the underside . . .

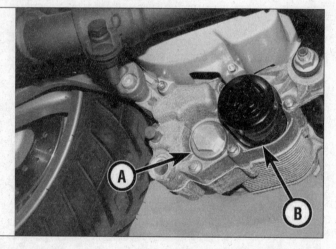

18.8b . . . or the side of the crankcase (A). Note the oil filter (B)

Step 8. Install the strainer, install a new sealing washer or O-ring to the plug as necessary, then install the plug and tighten it securely.

10 When the oil has completely drained, install the drain plug using a new sealing washer or O-ring. Tighten the plug to the specified torque, if available (see the *Data* section at the end of this manual). Avoid overtightening, as damage to the threads will result.

11 Place the drain tray below the oil filter. On some engines the filter element is installed inside a cover; unscrew the cover bolts, then remove the cover, the spring and the filter (see illustrations). Tip any residual oil into the drain tray. Discard any O-rings on the cover and in the filter housing as new ones should be used. As required, install the new housing O-ring, then install the new filter and install the spring and the cover, again using a new O-ring (see illustration 18.11b). Tighten the cover bolts securely.

12 Some engines have a spin-on type filter (see illustration 18.8b). Unscrew the filter and tip any residual oil into the drain tray. Smear clean engine oil onto the seal of the new filter, then install the filter and tighten it securely by hand.

case and to act as a reminder that there is no oil in the engine (see illustration).

8 Unscrew the oil drain plug and allow the oil to flow into the drain tray (see illustrations). Discard the sealing washer or O-ring on the drain plug, as a new one must be used on reassembly. On some engines, a gauze strainer is installed behind the drain plug; withdraw the strainer, clean it in solvent and remove any debris caught in the mesh (see illustration). Check the gauze for splits or holes and replace it if necessary.

9 A separate oil strainer is installed on some engines; unscrew the strainer plug and withdraw the strainer (see illustration). Clean and check the strainer as described in

18.8c If equipped, remove the strainer (arrow)

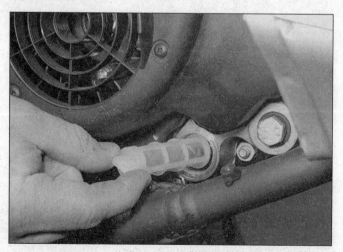

18.9 Some engines have a separate oil strainer

18.11a Unscrew the bolts (arrows) . . .

18.11b . . . and remove the cover, spring and filter

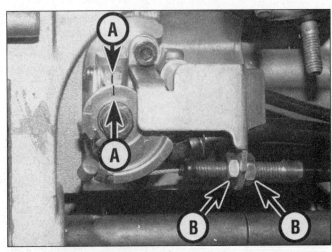

19.3a Externally-mounted oil pump. Note the index marks (A) and
adjuster locknuts (B)

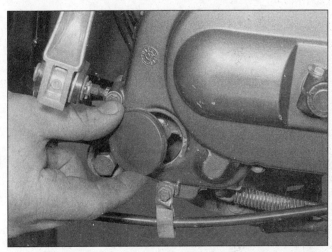

19.3b Remove the plug in the drivebelt cover . . .

13 Refill the engine to the correct level using the recommended type and amount of oil (see the *Data* section at the end of this manual). Install the filler plug and tightening it by hand.

14 Start the engine and let it run for two or three minutes. Shut it off, wait five minutes, then check the oil level. If necessary, top-up the oil to the correct level (see *Daily (pre-ride) checks*). Check around the drain plug and the oil filter/strainer for leaks.

15 The old oil drained from the engine cannot be re-used and should be disposed of properly. Check with your local parts store, disposal facility or environmental agency to see whether they will accept the used oil for recycling. Don't pour used oil into drains or onto the ground.

**HAYNES
HiNT** *Check the old oil carefully – if it is very metallic colored, then the engine is experiencing wear from break-in (new engine) or from insufficient lubrication. If there are flakes or chips of metal in the oil, then something is drastically wrong internally and the*

engine will have to be disassembled for inspection and repair.

19 Oil pump cable (two-stroke engines) – check and adjustment

1 Where the oil pump is cable-controlled, the cable is connected to the throttle twist-grip via a splitter **(see illustration 13.6)**.

2 Ensure the throttle twistgrip rotates easily from fully closed to fully open with the handlebars turned at various angles, and check that the throttle cable freeplay is correct (see Section 13).

3 Remove any body panels or the storage compartment as necessary to access the oil pump. Where the pump is located inside the drivebelt cover, remove the inspection plug **(see illustrations)**.

4 At the pump end, the cable is connected to the pump cam. With the cable correctly adjusted, an index mark on the cam should align with a mark on the pump body, either

with the throttle closed or with the throttle fully open – check with your scooter hand-book for details **(see illustrations 19.3a and 19.3c)**. Note: *The oil pump cable will*

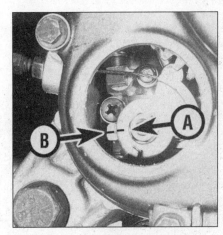

19.3c . . . to access the internally-mounted pump. Note index marks (A) and (B)

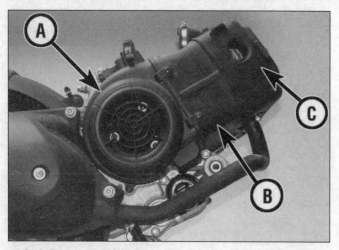

21.2 Fan cowling (A) and engine cowling sections (B and C)

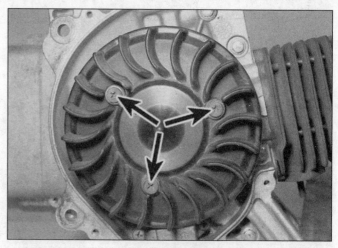

21.3a Check the fan for broken vanes and ensure the bolts (arrows) are tight

stretch slightly in use, so only a small amount of adjustment should be necessary to re-align the marks. As a guide, there should be no discernible freeplay in the pump cable with the throttle closed and the pump cam should turn as the throttle is opened. If the cable is over-adjusted (too tight), too much oil will be fed into the engine causing a fouled spark plug and a smoky exhaust. If there is any doubt about the adjustment of the pump cable, consult a scooter dealer.

5 If the marks are not aligned, loosen the cable adjuster locknut and turn the adjuster as required until the marks align, then retighten the locknut. If the adjuster has reached its limit of adjustment, replace the cable (see Chapter 4, Section 12).

20 Oil pump drivebelt (two-stroke engines) – replacement

1 On some engines, the oil pump is driven by a small belt from either the left or right-hand side of the crankshaft. To access the belt, it is necessary to remove either the variator or the alternator.

2 Refer to you scooter handbook or check with a scooter dealer to confirm that belt replacement is a service item, then follow the appropriate procedure in Chapter 2A to replace the drivebelt.

21 Cooling system – check

Air-cooled engines

1 On air-cooled models, a fan mounted on the alternator rotor forces air into the engine cowling to cool the cylinder and cylinder head.

2 Check that the air intake in the fan cowling is unobstructed and that the sections of the engine cowling are installed together correctly and secured with their mounting screws (see illustration). Note: If any sec-

tions of the engine cowling are missing, the engine will not be properly cooled.

3 Remove the fan cowling and inspect the fan (see illustration). If any of the vanes are broken, replace the fan. Check that the fan mounting bolts are tight; if the bolts are loose or if the bolt holes are worn oversize, the fan will run out of true and cause engine vibration. Note: On some engines, the holes for the mounting bolts in the cooling fan are oversize and it is important to centralize the fan on the bolts before tightening them, otherwise the fan will run out of true and cause engine vibration. Use two shouldered bolts, or wrap a short length of electrical tape tightly around two bolts, and install them in opposite holes to centralize the fan, then install two mounting bolts (see illustrations). Remove the centralizing bolts and install the remaining bolts.

Liquid-cooled engines

⚠ Warning: The engine must be cool before beginning this procedure.

21.3b Use shouldered bolts to centralize the fan . . .

21.3c . . . then install the mounting bolts

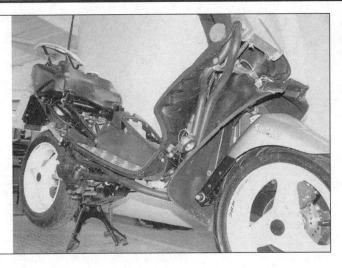

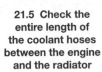
21.5 Check the entire length of the coolant hoses between the engine and the radiator

4 Check the coolant level (see *Daily (pre-ride) checks*).
5 The entire cooling system should be checked for evidence of leaks. Remove any body panels as necessary and examine each coolant hose along its entire length **(see illustration)**. Look for cracks, abrasions and other damage. Squeeze the hoses at various points. They should feel firm, yet pliable, and return to their original shape when released. If they are hard or deteriorated, replace them (see Chapter 3).
6 Check for evidence of leaks at each cooling system joint. Ensure that the hoses are pushed fully onto their fittings and that the hose clips are tight. **Note:** *Check the tension of any hose spring clips and replace them if they are loose.*
7 Check the underside of the water pump for evidence of leaks (see Chapter 3).
8 Check the radiator for leaks and other damage. Leaks in the radiator leave tell-tale scale deposits or coolant stains on the outside of the core below the leak. If leaks are noted, remove the radiator (see Chapter 3) and have it repaired or replace it.

Caution: Do not use a liquid leak stopping compound to try to repair leaks.

9 Inspect the radiator fins for mud, dirt and insects which will impede the flow of air through the radiator. If the fins are dirty, remove the radiator (see Chapter 3) and clean it using water or low pressure compressed air directed through the fins from the back. If the fins are bent or distorted, straighten them carefully with a screwdriver. If the air flow is restricted by bent or damaged fins over more than 30% of the radiator's surface area, install a new radiator.
10 Check the condition of the coolant in the reservoir. If it is rust-colored or if accumulations of scale are visible, drain, flush and refill the system with new coolant (see Chapter 3).
11 Check the antifreeze content of the coolant with an antifreeze hydrometer. Sometimes coolant looks like it's in good condition, but is too weak to offer adequate protection.

If the hydrometer indicates a weak mixture, drain, flush and refill the system (see Chapter 3). **Note:** *The cooling system should be drained and refilled with fresh coolant every 2 years.*
12 Start the engine and let it reach normal operating temperature, then check for leaks again.
13 If the coolant level is consistently low, and no evidence of leaks can be found, have the entire system pressure-checked by a scooter dealer.

22 Drivebelt – check

1 Referring to Chapter 6, remove the drivebelt cover and inspect the belt. Some manufacturers specify service limits for drivebelt wear (see the *Data* section at the end of this manual).
2 If there is any doubt about the condition of the belt, replace it. In the event of premature belt wear, the cause should be investigated (see Chapter 6).

23 Drivebelt – replacement

The drivebelt must be replaced at the specified service interval, or earlier dependant on belt condition (see Chapter 6).

24 Variator pulley and rollers – check and lubrication

Referring to Chapter 6, remove the drive pulley and the variator. Disassemble the variator and check all components for wear as described. If applicable, grease the rollers and the roller tracks in the variator housing before reassembly. **Note:** *The self-locking variator center nut and, where applicable, the variator housing O-ring, must be replaced on reassembly.*

25 Kickstart gear and spindle bushing – check

1 The kickstart lever should move smoothly and return to the rest position under the tension of the return spring **(see illustration)**. It is good practice to periodically check the operation of the kickstart to ensure it is in good working order.
2 Referring to Chapter 6, remove the drivebelt cover. Inspect the component parts of the kickstart mechanism for damage and wear and replace any parts as necessary. Lubricate the kickstart spindle with high-temperature grease before reassembly.

26 Clutch pulley and bearing – check and lubrication

1 Referring to Chapter 6, remove the drivebelt cover.

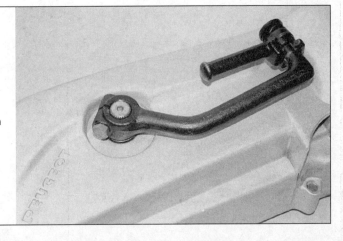

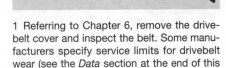
25.1 Kickstart lever rest position

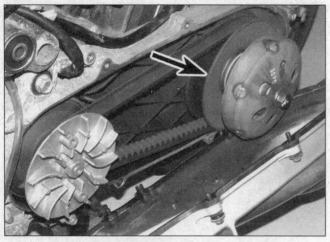

26.2 Check for play in the bearings of the clutch pulley hub (arrow)

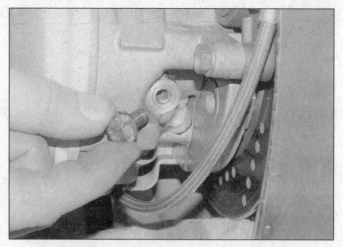

27.1a Gearbox oil level plug on the rear of the casing

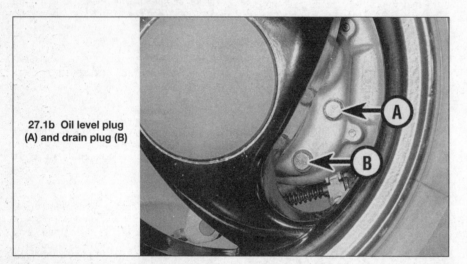

27.1b Oil level plug (A) and drain plug (B)

2 The outer half of the clutch pulley should slide outwards on the clutch hub, against the pressure of the clutch center spring. Next, grasp the pulley assembly and check for play in the pulley hub bearings **(see illustration)**.

3 To disassemble the clutch and pulley assembly in order to check the condition of the clutch and to lubricate the pulley bearing surfaces, follow the procedure in Chapter 6. **Note:** *The self-locking clutch center nut must be replaced on reassembly.*

27 Gearbox oil level – check

1 Some scooters are equipped with an integral gearbox filler cap and dipstick, while most have a filler plug which also acts as a level plug; the filler plug may be on the rear of the gearbox casing or on the side facing the rear wheel **(see illustrations)**. On some scooters, where the manufacturer does not require the oil level to be checked or the oil drained unless the gearbox is being over-

hauled, the filler plug is inside the belt drive casing.

2 The oil level should be checked either with the machine supported upright on level ground, or with it supported on its center stand. It is important to clarify the correct procedure for your scooter. On gearboxes

equipped with a dipstick, it is important to identify which mark on the dipstick is to be used, and whether or not the dipstick should be screwed back into the casing when the level reading is being taken. Either refer to your scooter handbook or a scooter dealer for details.

⚠ *Warning: It is important to have the right information for checking the gearbox oil level on your scooter. Do not risk under-filling or over-filling the gearbox, as a transmission seizure or dangerous oil leakage may result.*

3 Clean the area around the filler cap or plug, then unscrew the cap or plug from the gearbox casing. Discard the filler plug sealing washer, as a new one should be used on reassembly. If you are using a dipstick, use a clean rag or paper towel to wipe off the oil.

4 On gearboxes with a level plug, the oil level should come up to the lower threads so that it is just visible on the threads **(see illustration)**. On gearboxes with a dipstick, insert the dipstick, then read the level on the stick in accordance with the manufacturer's recommendations.

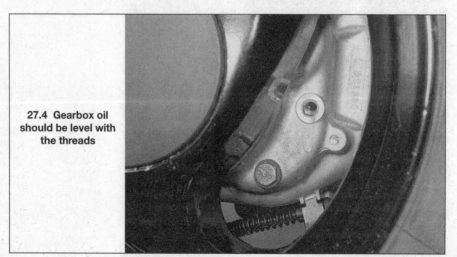

27.4 Gearbox oil should be level with the threads

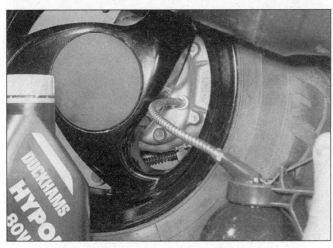
27.5a Use a pump-type can to top up the oil . . .

27.5b . . . or a bottle of specified gear oil

5 If required, top the gearbox up with the recommended grade and type of oil (see the *Data* section at the end of this manual). Use a pump-type oil can or oil bottle to top-up gearboxes with a level plug (see illustrations). Do not overfill.
6 Install the filler cap and tighten it securely by hand, or install a new sealing washer to the level plug and tighten it securely.
7 If the oil level is very low, or oil is leaking from the gearbox, refer to Chapter 6 and inspect the condition of the case seals and gaskets and replace them if necessary.

28 Gearbox oil – change

1 If required to gain access to the gearbox drain plug, remove the rear wheel (see Chapter 8).
2 Position a clean drain tray below the gearbox. Unscrew the filler cap or level plug (as applicable) to vent the case and to act as a reminder that there is no oil in it.

3 Unscrew the oil drain plug (see illustration 27.1b), and allow the oil to flow into the drain tray. Discard the sealing washers on the drain and level plugs, as new ones should be used.
4 When the oil has completely drained, install the drain plug using a new sealing washer, and tighten it securely. Avoid overtightening, as damage to the casing will result. If available, tighten the drain plug to the specified torque setting (see the *Data* section at the end of this manual)
5 Refill the gearbox to the proper level using the recommended type and amount of oil (see Section 27). Install the filler cap and tighten it securely by hand, or install a new sealing washer to the level plug and tighten it securely.
6 Check the oil level again after riding the scooter for a few minutes and, if necessary, add more oil. Check around the drain plug for leaks.
7 The old oil drained from the gearbox cannot be re-used and should be disposed of properly. Check with your local parts store, disposal facility or environmental agency to see whether they will accept the used oil for

recycling. Don't pour used oil into drains or onto the ground.

29 Spark plug gap – check and adjustment

Warning: Access to the spark plug is extremely restricted on some scooters. Ensure the engine and exhaust system are cool before attempting to remove the spark plug.

1 Make sure your spark plug socket is the correct size before attempting to remove the plug – a suitable plug wrench is usually supplied in the scooter's tool kit.
2 As required, remove the engine access panel or side cover. Remove any access panel in the engine cowling (see illustrations).
3 Pull off the spark plug cap, then ensure the spark plug socket is located correctly over the plug and unscrew the plug from the cylinder head.

29.2a Remove the engine access panel . . .

29.2b . . . or the spark plug panel in the engine cowling

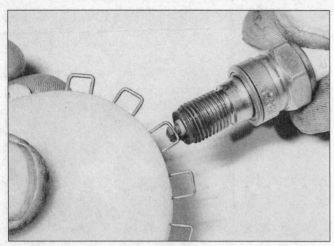

29.7a Using a wire type gauge to measure the spark plug electrode gap

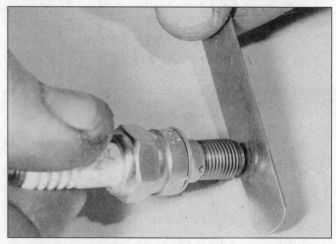

29.7b Using a feeler gauge to measure the spark plug electrode gap

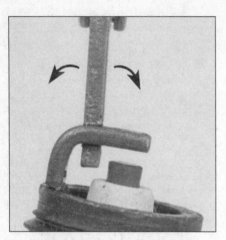

29.7c Adjust the electrode gap by bending the side electrode only

4 Inspect the electrodes for wear. Both the center and side electrode should have square edges and the side electrode should be of uniform thickness. Look for excessive deposits and evidence of a cracked or chipped insulator around the center electrode. Compare your spark plug to the color spark plug reading chart at the end of this manual. Check the condition of the threads and washer, and the ceramic insulator body for cracks and other damage.

5 If the electrodes are not excessively worn, and if the deposits can be easily removed with a wire brush, the plug can be regapped and re-used (if no cracks or chips are visible in the insulator). If in doubt concerning the condition of the plug, replace it, as the expense is minimal.

6 Cleaning a spark plug by sandblasting is permitted, provided you clean it with a high flash-point solvent afterwards.

7 Before installing the plug, make sure it is the correct type (see the *Data* section at the end of this manual). Check the gap between the electrodes **(see illustrations)**. Compare the gap to that specified and adjust as necessary. If the gap must be adjusted, bend the

side electrode only and be very careful not to chip or crack the insulator nose **(see illustration)**.

8 Make sure the washer is in place before installing the plug. Smear the plug threads with a little copper-based grease then thread it into the head by hand until it is finger-tight. Since the cylinder head is made of aluminium which is soft and easily damaged, ensure the plug threads are not crossed before tightening it securely with the spark plug socket. Reconnect the plug cap.

 HAYNES HINT *A stripped plug thread in the cylinder head can be repaired with a thread insert.*

30 Spark plug – replacement

Remove the old spark plug as described in Section 29 and install a new one. Ensure the new plug is the correct type (see the *Data* section at the end of this manual). Check the gap between the electrodes and adjust it if necessary.

31 Cylinder head (two-stroke engines) – decarbonization

Note: *The use of modern, low ash engine oils specifically designed for use in two-stroke engines has considerably reduced the need to decarbonize the engine. However, some manufacturers still recommend decarbonizing as part of the routine service schedule, and if the machine is continually ridden on short journeys which do not allow the engine to reach and maintain its normal operating temperature, the cylinder head should be decarbonized more frequently.*

1 Remove the cylinder head (see Chapter 2A).

2 Remove all accumulated carbon from inside the cylinder head using a blunt scraper. Small traces of carbon can be removed with very fine abrasive paper or a kitchen scourer.

Caution: The cylinder head and piston are made of aluminium which is relatively soft. Take great care not to gouge or score the surface when scraping.

3 Press the cylinder down against the crankcase to avoid breaking the cylinder base gasket seal, then turn the engine over until the piston is at the very top of its stroke. Smear grease all around the edge of the piston to trap any particles of carbon, then clean the piston crown, taking care not to score or gouge it or the cylinder bore. Finally, lower the piston and wipe away the grease and any remaining particles of carbon.

HAYNES HINT *Finish the piston crown and cylinder head off using a metal polish. A shiny surface is more resistant to the build-up of carbon deposits.*

4 With the piston at the bottom of its stroke, check the exhaust port in the cylinder and scrape away any carbon. If the exhaust port is heavily coked, remove the exhaust system and clean the port and the exhaust pipe thoroughly (see Chapter 4).

5 Install the cylinder head (see Chapter 2A).

32 Valve clearances (four-stroke engines) – check and adjustment

Note: *Many Honda models have external valve adjusters, which eliminate the need to remove the valve cover(s). To use these, place the engine at TDC compression (see Steps 4 and 5). Loosen the lockbolt on each adjuster, turn it outward until resistance is felt, then turn it back one mark on the adjuster scale. Tighten the lockbolt.*

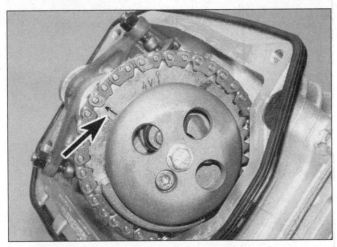

32.5a **Check for camshaft sprocket timing mark (arrow) . . .**

32.5b **. . . or a line on the camshaft sprocket (arrow)**

32.5c **Check for timing marks on the alternator rotor (A) and crankcase (B) . . .**

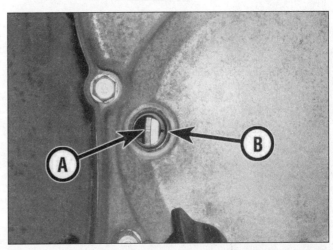

32.5d **. . . or alternator rotor (A) and inside the inspection hole (B) in the engine side cover**

1 The engine must be completely cold for this maintenance procedure, so let the machine sit overnight before beginning. Remove any body panels necessary to gain access to the alternator and cylinder head (see Chapter 9).

2 Remove the spark plug (see Section 29).

3 Remove the valve cover (see Chapter 2B). Discard the cover gasket or O-ring, as a new one must be installed on reassembly.

4 The valve clearances are checked with the piston at top dead center (TDC) on its compression stroke (the valves are closed and a small clearance can be felt at each rocker arm). Turn the engine in the normal direction of rotation until the piston is at TDC; you can do this by rotating the crankshaft via the alternator rotor or the variator center nut. **Note:** *On liquid-cooled engines with the water pump located on the alternator cover, it should not be necessary to remove the water pump or disconnect the coolant hoses in order to displace the cover.* If there is access, the position of the piston can be checked by inserting a screwdriver down the spark plug hole.

5 Look for timing marks on the camshaft sprocket and the camshaft holder or cylinder head **(see illustrations)**. Alternatively, look for timing marks on the alternator rotor and the crankcase **(see illustrations)**. With the piston at TDC on its compression stroke and the timing marks aligned, the valve clearances can be checked. **Note:** *On some engines with options for two or four valve heads there may be alternative timing marks.*

6 Insert a feeler gauge of the same thickness as the correct valve clearance between the rocker arm and stem of each valve (see the *Data* section at the end of this manual). The feeler gauge should be a firm sliding fit – you should feel a slight drag when the you pull the gauge out **(see illustration)**.

7 If the clearance is either too small or too large, loosen the locknut and turn the

32.6 **Checking the valve clearance with a feeler gauge**

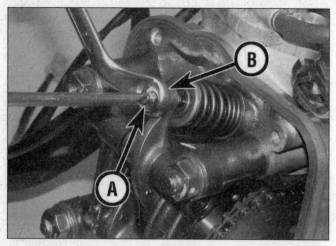

32.7 Hold the adjuster (A) while tightening the locknut (B)

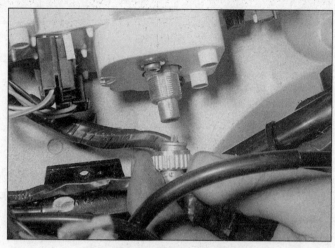

36.1a Unscrew the knurled ring . . .

adjuster until a firm sliding fit is obtained, then tighten the locknut securely, making sure the adjuster does not turn as you do so **(see illustration)**. Recheck the clearances.
8 Apply some engine oil to the valve assemblies, rockers and camshaft before installing the valve cover and install a new cover gasket or O-ring. Install the remaining components in the reverse order of removal.

33 Headlight, brake light and horn – check

Note: *An improperly adjusted headlight may cause problems for oncoming traffic or provide poor, unsafe illumination of the road ahead. Before adjusting the headlight aim, be sure to consult with local traffic laws and regulations.*
1 Before making any adjustment, check that the tire pressures are correct and the suspension is adjusted as required. Make any adjustments to the headlight aim with the scooter on level ground, with the fuel tank half full and with an assistant sitting on the seat. If the scooter is usually ridden with a passenger on the back, have a second assistant to do this.
2 All headlight units have provision for vertical (up and down) adjustment. The headlight adjuster screw will be located either at the front of the unit, adjacent to the light, accessible through a hole or grille, or behind a body panel. Alternatively, an adjuster at the rear of the unit will be accessible through a hole in the kick panel or inside the glovebox. Refer to your scooter handbook for details.
3 Position the scooter in a straight line facing a brick wall. The scooter must be off its stand, upright and with a rider seated. Measure the height from the ground to the center of the headlight and mark a horizontal line on the wall at this height. Position the scooter 12.5 feet from the wall and draw a vertical line up the wall central to the centerline of the scooter. Switch to low beam and check that

the beam pattern falls slightly lower than the horizontal line and to the right of the vertical line. Turn the adjuster screw to move the beam up or down as required.
4 The brake light should come on when either the front or rear brake levers are pulled in. If it does not, check the operation of the brake light switch and tail/brake light bulb (see Chapter 10). **Note:** *In most cases, check the operation of the brake light with the engine running.*
5 If the horn fails to work, check the operation of the handlebar switch and the horn itself (see Chapter 10). **Note:** *In most cases, check the operation of the horn with the engine running.*

34 Wheels and tires – general check

Wheels

1 Wheels are virtually maintenance free, but they should be kept clean and corrosion-free and checked periodically for damage to the rims. Check cast wheels for cracks. Also check the wheel runout and alignment (see Chapter 8). Never attempt to repair damaged cast wheels; they must be replaced.
2 Wheel bearings will wear over a period of time and result in handling problems. Support the machine on its center stand and check for any play in the bearings by pushing and pulling the wheel against the hub. Also rotate the wheel and check that it turns smoothly.
3 If any play is detected in the hub, or if the wheel does not rotate smoothly (and this is not due to brake or transmission drag), the wheel bearings must be inspected for wear or damage (see Chapter 8).

Tires

4 Check the tire condition and tread depth thoroughly – see *Daily (pre-ride) checks*. Check the valve rubber for signs of damage or deterioration and have it replaced if nec-

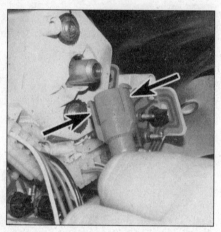

36.1b . . . or press the clips to release the speedometer cable

essary. Also, make sure the valve stem cap is in place and tight.

35 Stand – check and lubrication

1 Since the stand pivots are exposed to the elements, they should be lubricated periodically to ensure safe and trouble-free operation.
2 In order for the lubricant to be applied where it will do the most good, the component should be disassembled. However, if chain or cable lubricant is being used, it can be applied to the pivot joint gaps and will usually work its way into the areas where friction occurs. If motor oil or light grease is being used, apply it sparingly as it may attract dirt (which could cause the controls to bind or wear at an accelerated rate).
3 The return spring must be capable of retracting the stand fully and holding it retracted when the machine is in use. If the spring has sagged or broken, it must be replaced (see Chapter 7).

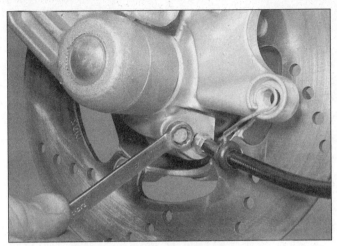

36.3a Loosen the retaining plate bolt . . .

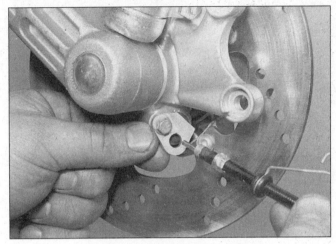

36.3b . . . and withdraw the cable

36 Speedometer cable and drive gear – lubrication

Note: *Some scooters are equipped with electronic speedometers. On these machines, only the drive gear needs lubricating. Do not attempt to disconnect the electrical wire from the drive housing.*

1 Remove the handlebar cover (see Chapter 9), then disconnect the speedometer cable from the underside of the instrument panel **(see illustrations)**.
2 Withdraw the inner cable from the outer cable and lubricate it with motor oil or cable lubricant. Do not lubricate the upper few inches of the cable as the lubricant may travel up into the instrument head.
3 On some scooters, the drive gear is contained within the hub (see Chapter 8). On some other scooters, the drive gear is sealed and requires no maintenance other than to check that the gear rotates smoothly when the hub is being overhauled. On others, the drive

36.3c Remove the drive gear and regrease it

gear is retained by a plate. Loosen the bolt and withdraw the speedometer cable, then undo the bolt and remove the plate **(see illustrations)**. Pull out the drive gear and regrease it **(see illustration)**. Install the drive gear and cable in the reverse order of removal.

4 Some scooters are equipped with a separate speedometer drive housing. Remove the cap from the housing and press some general purpose grease into it **(see illustrations)**. Reinstall the cap and tighten it securely.

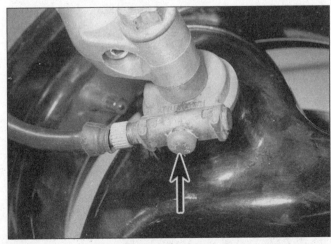

36.4a Remove the cap (arrow) . . .

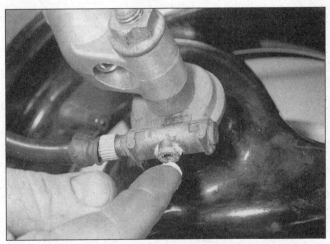

36.4b . . . and press some grease into the housing

37.4 Checking for play in the steering head bearings

37 Steering head bearings – check

1 Most scooters are equipped with ball steering head bearings which run in races at the top and bottom of the steering head. The races can become dented or rough during normal use and the balls will gradually wear. In extreme cases, worn or loose steering head bearings can cause steering wobble – a condition that is potentially dangerous.

2 Place the scooter on the centerstand. Raise the front wheel off the ground either by having an assistant push down on the rear or by placing a support under the frame. **Note:** *Do not rest the weight of the scooter on the bodywork; if necessary, remove the belly panel to expose the frame (see Chapter 9).*

3 Point the front wheel straight-ahead and slowly turn the handlebars from side-to-side. Any dents or roughness in the bearing races will be felt and the bars will not move smoothly and freely. If the bearings are damaged, they must be replaced (see Chapter 7).

4 Next, grasp the front suspension and try to move it forwards and backwards **(see illustration)**. Any freeplay in the steering head bearings will be felt as front-to-rear movement of the steering stem. **Note:** *On leading or trailing link front suspension, grasp the lower end of the suspension leg by the suspension arm pivot bolt for this test. If play is felt in the bearings, follow the procedure described in Chapter 7 to adjust them.*

5 Over a period of time the grease in the bearings will harden or may be washed out. Disassemble the steering head for regreasing of the bearings. Refer to Chapter 7 for details.

38 Suspension – check

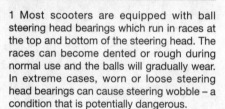

1 The suspension components must be maintained in top operating condition to ensure rider safety. Loose, worn or damaged suspension parts decrease the scooter's stability and control.

Front suspension

2 While standing alongside the scooter, apply the front brake and push on the handlebars to compress the suspension several times. See if it moves up-and-down smoothly without binding. If binding is felt, the suspension should be disassembled and inspected (see Chapter 7).

3 On models with leading or trailing link suspension, inspect the shock for fluid leaks and corrosion on the damper rod. If the shock is faulty it should be replaced (see Chapter 7). Check that the shock mounting bolts are tight.

4 On models with telescopic forks, inspect the area around the dust seal for signs of grease or oil leaks, then carefully pry off the dust seal using a flat-bladed screwdriver and inspect the area behind it **(see illustration)**. If corrosion is evident, the seals must be replaced (see Chapter 7). The chromed finish on the forks is prone to corrosion and pitting, so it is advisable to keep them as clean as possible and to spray them regularly with a rust inhibitor, otherwise the seals will not last long. If corrosion and pitting is evident, tackle it as early as possible to prevent it getting worse.

5 Check the tightness of all suspension nuts and bolts to ensure none have worked loose.

Rear suspension

Note: *For scooters equipped with twin rear shocks, both shocks must be in good condition. If either is found to be faulty, replace the shocks as a pair.*

6 Inspect the rear shock for fluid leaks and corrosion on the damper rod. If a shock is faulty, it should be replaced (see Chapter 7). Check that the shock mounting bolts are tight.

7 With the aid of an assistant to support the scooter, compress the rear suspension several times. It should move up-and-down freely without binding. If any binding is felt, the worn or faulty component must be identified and replaced. The problem could be due to either the shock absorber or the front pivot assembly.

8 Support the scooter so that the rear wheel is off the ground. Grab the engine/transmission unit at the rear and attempt to rock it from side-to-side – there should be no discernible freeplay felt between the engine and frame. If there is movement, inspect the tightness of the rear suspension mountings and the front engine mounting (referring to the torque settings specified in the *Data* section), then recheck for movement. If freeplay is felt, disconnect the rear shock absorber lower mounting and remove the shock and check again – any freeplay in the front engine mounting should be more evident. If there is freeplay, inspect the mounting bolts and brackets for wear (see Chapter 7).

9 Reconnect the rear shock, then grasp the top of the rear wheel and pull it upwards – there should be no discernible freeplay before the shock absorber begins to compress. Any freeplay indicates a worn or shock mountings. The worn components must be replaced (see Chapter 7).

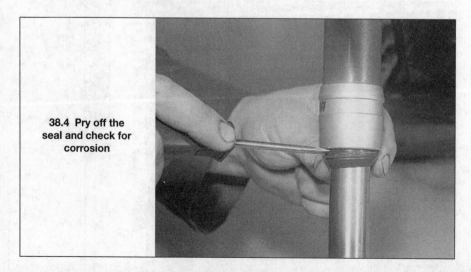

38.4 Pry off the seal and check for corrosion

39 Nuts and bolts – tightness check

1 Since vibration tends to loosen fasteners, all nuts, bolts, screws, etc, should be periodically checked for proper tightness.
2 Pay particular attention to the following:

Spark plug
Carburetor clamps
Gearbox oil filler and drain plugs (where installed)
Engine oil drain plug (four-stroke engines)
Stand bolts
Engine mounting bolts
Suspension bolts

Wheel bolts
Handlebar clamp bolts
Brake caliper and disc mounting bolts (disc brakes)
Brake hose banjo bolts (disc brakes)
Exhaust system bolts/nuts

3 If a torque wrench is available, use it along with the torque specifications given in the *Data* section at the end of this manual.

Notes

Chapter 2 Part A
Two-stroke engines

Contents

Degrees of difficulty

Easy, suitable for novice with little experience	**Fairly easy,** suitable for beginner with some experience	**Fairly difficult,** suitable for competent DIY mechanic	**Difficult,** suitable for experienced DIY mechanic	**Very difficult,** suitable for expert DIY or professional

Specifications

Refer to the *Data* section at the end of this manual for servicing specifications.

1 General information

The engine is a single cylinder two-stroke, with either fan-assisted air cooling (see Chapter 1) or pumped liquid cooling (see Chapter 3). The crankshaft assembly is pressed together, incorporating the connecting rod. The piston runs on a needle roller bearing installed in the small-end of the connecting rod. The crankshaft runs in caged ball main bearings.

The crankcase divides vertically – the left-hand crankcase is an integral part of the drivebelt casing and gearbox.

2 Operations possible with the engine in the frame

Most components and assemblies, with the obvious exception of the crankshaft assembly and its bearings, can be worked on without having to remove the engine/transmission unit from the frame. However, access to some components is severely restricted, and if a number of areas require attention at the same time, removal of the engine is recommended, as it is an easy task to undertake.

3 Major engine repair – general information

1 It is not always easy to determine if an engine should be completely overhauled, as a number of factors must be considered.

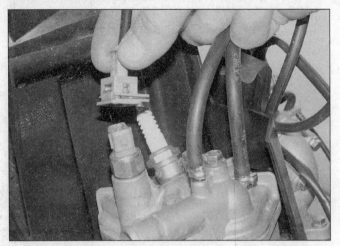

4.6a Disconnect the temperature sender wiring connector

4.6b Detach the carburetor heater fitting

2 High mileage is not necessarily an indication that an overhaul is needed, while low mileage, on the other hand, does not preclude the need for an overhaul. Frequency of servicing is probably the single most important consideration. An engine that has regular and frequent maintenance will most likely give many miles of reliable service. Conversely, a neglected engine, or one which has not been broken in properly, may require an overhaul very early in its life.

3 If the engine is making obvious knocking or rumbling noises, the connecting rod and/or main bearings are probably at fault.

4 Loss of power, rough running, excessive noise and high fuel consumption rates may also point to the need for an overhaul, especially if they are all present at the same time. If a complete service as detailed in Chapter 1 does not remedy the situation, major mechanical work is the only solution.

5 An engine overhaul generally involves restoring the internal parts to the specifications of a new engine. This may require installing new piston rings and crankcase seals, or, with high mileage, replacing the piston, cylinder and crankshaft assembly. The end result should be a like-new engine that will give as many trouble-free miles as the original.

6 Before beginning the engine overhaul, read through the related procedures to familiarize yourself with the scope and requirements of the job. Overhauling an engine is not all that difficult, but it is time-consuming. Check on the availability of parts and make sure that any necessary special tools and materials are obtained in advance.

7 Most work can be done with typical workshop hand tools, although manufacturers often produce a number of service tools for specific purposes such as disassembling the clutch and separating the crankcase halves. Precision measuring tools are required for inspecting parts to determine if they must be replaced. Alternatively, a dealer will handle the inspection of parts and offer advice concerning reconditioning and replacement. As a general rule, time is the primary cost of an

overhaul, so it does not pay to install worn or substandard parts.

8 As a final note, to ensure maximum life and minimum trouble from a rebuilt engine, everything must be assembled with care in a spotlessly clean environment.

4 Engine – removal and installation

Caution: The engine/transmission unit is not heavy, however removal and installation should be carried out with the aid of an assistant; personal injury or damage could occur if the engine falls or is dropped.

Removal

1 Support the scooter securely in an upright position. Work can be made easier by raising the machine to a suitable height on a hydraulic ramp or a suitable platform. Make sure it is secure and will not topple over.

2 Remove any body panels as necessary to access the engine (see Chapter 9).

3 Remove the exhaust system (see Chapter 4).

4 If the engine is dirty, particularly around its mountings, wash it thoroughly before starting any major disassembly work. This will make work much easier and rule out the possibility of dirt falling inside.

5 Disconnect the negative battery cable (see Chapter 10) and pull the spark plug cap off the plug.

6 On liquid-cooled engines, disconnect the wire to the temperature sender on the cylinder head **(see illustration)**. Drain the cooling system and disconnect the coolant hoses from the fittings on the water pump, cylinder and cylinder head (see Chapter 3). If installed, undo the screw securing the carburetor heater union to the carburetor **(see illustration)**.

7 Trace the wiring from the alternator/igni-

tion pulse generator coil and disconnect it at the connectors. Free the wiring from any clips or ties on the engine. Either remove the starter motor or disconnect the starter motor leads (see Chapter 10). If installed, disconnect the ground wire between the frame and the engine.

8 If required, remove the air filter housing and the air intake duct (see Chapter 4).

9 Either remove the carburetor, leaving the throttle cable attached if required, or just disconnect the fuel hose and fuel tap vacuum hose from their unions on the carburetor and inlet manifold respectively, and disconnect the throttle cable (see Chapter 4). Where installed, disconnect the automatic choke wiring connector.

10 Where installed, disconnect the fuel pump vacuum hose from the engine.

11 Where installed, detach the oil pump control cable from the pump pulley and detach the cable from its bracket (see Section 12).

12 Release the clip securing the hose from the oil tank to the union on the oil pump and detach the hose from the pump (see Section 12). Clamp the hose and secure it in an upright position to minimize oil loss. Wrap a clean plastic bag around the end to prevent dirt entering the system.

13 If required, remove the rear wheel (see Chapter 8). **Note:** *On machines where the center stand is bolted to the underside of the engine unit, the rear wheel and stand provide a convenient support for the unit once it is removed from the scooter. However, it is useful to loosen the rear wheel nut at this point before disconnecting the rear brake.*

14 On models installed with a rear drum brake, disconnect the brake cable from the brake arm (see Chapter 8). Undo any screws securing the cable to the underside of the drivebelt casing and detach the cable **(see illustration)**.

15 On models installed with a rear disc brake, displace the brake caliper (see Chapter 8). Unclip the brake hose from the underside of the drivebelt casing **(see illustration 4.14)**.

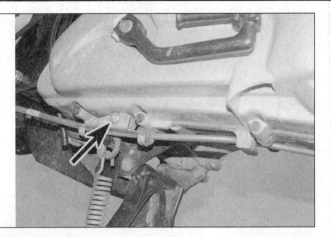

4.14 Undo the clip (arrow) to detach the brake cable

16 Check that all wiring, cables and hoses are clear of the engine/transmission unit.

17 With the aid of an assistant, support the weight of the machine on the rear of the frame, then remove the bolt securing the rear shock absorber to the gearbox casing. If the rear wheel has been removed, support the gearbox on a wood block to prevent damage to the casing. Undo the nut securing the upper end of the shock to the frame and remove the shock. **Note:** *On scooters installed with twin rear shocks, remove both shocks.*

18 Remove the front engine mounting bolt **(see illustrations)**. Note that on some scooters the engine is supported by a bracket on the top of the engine/transmission unit. If the stand is installed to the frame, maneuver the engine unit back and out of the frame. If the stand is bolted to the engine unit, lift the frame away **(see illustration)**.

19 If required, remove the stand (see Chapter 7) and the rear wheel (see Chapter 8).

Installation

20 Installation is the reverse of removal, noting the following:

Make sure no wires, cables or hoses become trapped between the engine and the frame when installing the engine.

Tighten the front engine mounting bolt and shock absorber bolt to the torque settings specified in the Data section at the end of this manual.

Make sure all wires, cables and hoses are correctly routed and connected, and secured by any clips or ties.

On liquid-cooled engines, fill the cooling system (see Chapter 3).

Bleed the oil pump (see Section 12) and check the adjustment of the oil pump cable, where installed (see Chapter 1).

Check the operation of the rear brake before riding the machine (see Chapter 8).

5 Disassembly and reassembly – general information

Disassembly

1 Before disassembling the engine, the external surfaces of the unit should be thoroughly cleaned and degreased. This will prevent contamination of the engine internals, and will also make working a lot easier and cleaner. A high flash-point solvent, such as

paraffin can be used, or better still, a proprietary engine degreaser such as Gunk. Use an old paintbrush to work the solvent into the various recesses of the engine casings. Take care to keep solvent or water away from the electrical components and inlet and exhaust ports.

⚠️ *Warning: The use of gasoline as a cleaning agent should be avoided because of the risk of fire.*

2 When clean and dry, arrange the unit on the workbench, leaving suitable clear area for working. Gather a selection of small containers and plastic bags so that parts can be grouped together in an easily identifiable manner. Some paper and a pen should be on hand to write notes and make labels where necessary. A supply of clean rag is also required.

3 Before commencing work, read through the appropriate Section so that some idea of the necessary procedure can be gained. When removing components, it should be noted that great force is seldom required, unless specified. In many cases, a component's reluctance to be removed is indicative of an incorrect approach or removal method – if in any doubt, recheck with the text.

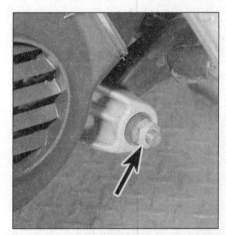

4.18a Undo the nut (arrow) . . .

4.18b . . . and withdraw the bolt

4.18c Separate the engine unit from the frame

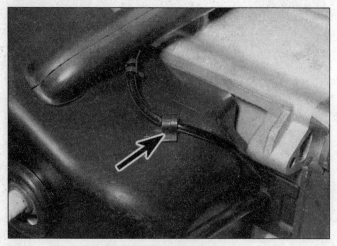

6.2a Unclip any wires or hoses . . .

6.2b . . . then undo the cowling fixing bolts (arrows)

4 When disassembling the engine, keep mated parts that have been in contact with each other during engine operation together. These mated parts must be re-used or replaced as an assembly.

5 Complete engine disassembly should be done in the following general order with reference to the appropriate Sections (refer to Chapter 6 for details of transmission components disassembly):

   Remove the cylinder head.
   Remove the cylinder.
   Remove the piston.
   Remove the alternator.
   Remove the variator (see Chapter 6).
   Remove the starter motor (see
     Chapter 10).
   Remove the oil pump.
   Remove the water pump if installed
     internally (see Chapter 3).
   Remove the reed valve (see Chapter 4).
   Separate the crankcase halves.
   Remove the crankshaft.

Reassembly

6 Reassembly is accomplished by reversing the order of disassembly.

6.3b . . . or the
cylinder head bolts

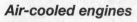

6.3a Undo the cylinder
head nuts . . .

6 Cylinder head – removal, inspection and installation

Note: *This procedure can be carried out with the engine in the frame. If the engine has been removed, ignore the steps that do not apply.*

Caution: The engine must be completely cool before beginning this procedure or the cylinder head may become warped.

Air-cooled engines

Removal

1 Remove the body panels as necessary to access the cylinder head (see Chapter 9).

2 Pull the spark plug cap off the spark plug. It will be necessary to remove the engine cowling, or part of the cowling, to access the cylinder head. On some engines, the cooling fan cowling forms part of the engine cowling. Check around the cowling and disconnect any wires or hoses clipped to it, then undo the bolts securing the cowling and remove it, noting how it fits **(see illustrations)**.
Note: *Some cowlings are clipped together – take care not to damage the fixing lugs when separating them.* Remove any spacers for the cowling bolts for safekeeping if they are loose.

3 Remove the spark plug, then unscrew the cylinder head bolts, or cylinder head nuts, evenly and a little at a time in a criss-cross sequence until they are all loose and remove them, together with any washers **(see illustra-**

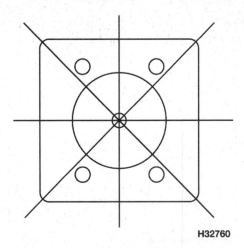

6.10 Check the cylinder head for warpage with a straight-edge

H32760

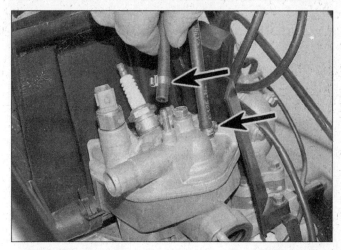

6.14 Disconnect the coolant hoses from the cylinder head

tions). **Note:** *Some cylinder heads are secured by long bolts which pass down through the cylinder and screw into the crankcase, others are secured by nuts on long studs. In both cases, once the cylinder head is loose, care must be taken not to break the cylinder base gasket seal - otherwise, a new base gasket will have to be installed before reinstalling the head (see Section 7).*

4 Lift the head off the cylinder. If the head is stuck, tap around the joint face between the head and cylinder with a soft-faced mallet to free it. Do not attempt to free the head by inserting a screwdriver between the head and cylinder – you'll damage the sealing surfaces.

5 If installed, remove the cylinder head gasket and discard it. A new one must be used on reassembly.

Inspection

6 Refer to Chapter 1 and decarbonize the cylinder head.

7 Inspect the head very carefully for cracks and other damage. If cracks are found, a new head will be required.

8 Inspect the threads in the spark plug hole.

Damaged or worn threads can be repaired using a thread insert (see *Tools and Workshop Tips* in the *Reference* section). Most scooter dealers and small engineering firms offer a service of this kind.

9 Check the mating surfaces on the cylinder head and cylinder for signs of leaks, which could indicate that the head is warped.

10 Using a precision straight-edge and a feeler gauge, check the head mating surface for warpage. **Note:** *Clean all traces of old gasket material from the cylinder head and cylinder with a suitable solvent. Take care not to scratch or gouge the soft aluminium.* Lay the straight-edge across the surface and try to slip the feeler gauge under it on either side of the combustion chamber. If the feeler gauge can be inserted between the straight-edge and the cylinder head, the head is warped and must be either machined or, if warpage is excessive, replaced. Check vertically, horizontally and diagonally across the head, making four checks in all **(see illustration)**. If there is any doubt about the condition of the head, consult a scooter dealer or repair shop.

Installation

11 Installation is the reverse of removal, noting the following:
Ensure both cylinder head and cylinder mating surfaces are clean.
Lubricate the cylinder bore with the specified type of two-stroke oil.
Install the new head gasket if required. **Note:** *The gasket may be marked to identify which side should face up when it is in place, or there may be a raised section around the inner edge of the gasket. If so, install the gasket with the raised section uppermost.*
Tighten the cylinder head fasteners evenly and a little at a time in a criss-cross pattern to the torque setting specified in the Data section.
Ensure the engine cowling is correctly secured.

Liquid-cooled engines
Removal

12 Remove the body panels as necessary to access the cylinder head (see Chapter 9). Remove any heat shield that may prevent access to the head.

13 Disconnect the negative battery cable (see Chapter 10). Pull the spark plug cap off the plug and disconnect the wire to the temperature sender on the cylinder head **(see illustration 4.6a)**.

14 Drain the cooling system and disconnect the coolant hoses from the fittings on the cylinder head **(see illustration)**. If installed, disconnect the carburetor heater hoses **(see illustration 4.6b)**.

15 On some engines, the thermostat housing is mounted on the top of the cylinder head; if required, undo the bolts and remove the housing, then lift out the thermostat **(see illustration)**.

16 Some engines are installed with a separate cylinder head cover which forms part of

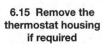

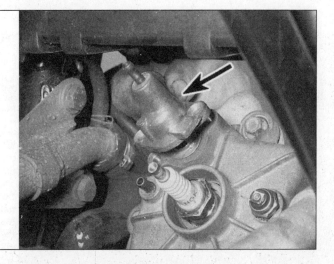

6.15 Remove the thermostat housing if required

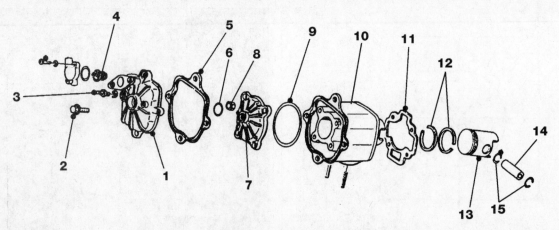

6.16 Liquid-cooled engine with separate cylinder head cover

1	Cylinder head cover	6	O-ring	11	Base gasket
2	Cover bolt – 4 off	7	Cylinder head	12	Piston rings
3	Temperature sender	8	Cylinder head nut – 4 off	13	Piston
4	Thermostat	9	O-ring	14	Piston pin
5	Cover seal	10	Cylinder	15	Snap-rings

6.17 Components of a conventional liquid-cooled engine

1 Cylinder head
2 Cylinder head nut – 4 off
3 Temperature sender
4 Thermostat
5 Cylinder head gasket
6 O-ring
7 Cylinder
8 Base gasket
9 Piston rings
10 Piston
11 Piston pin
12 Snap-rings

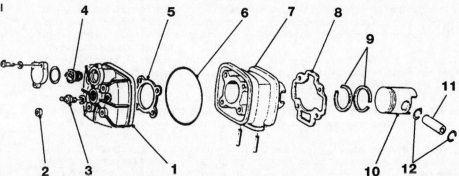

the engine cooling water jacket **(see illustration)**. Undo the bolts and remove the cover. Discard any gasket or O-ring, as a new one

must be used on reassembly.
17 Follow Steps 3 and 4 and remove the cylinder head. Discard any gasket or O-ring, as

new ones must be used **(see illustration)**.
18 If the thermostat is installed inside the cylinder head, lift out the thermostat **(see illustration)**.

Inspection

19 Follow Steps 6 to 10 to decarbonize and check the cylinder head. If the thermostat is installed inside the cylinder head, ensure that the thermostat bypass passage is clear **(see illustration)**. Check the condition of the thermostat (see Chapter 3).

Installation

20 Installation is the reverse of removal, noting the following:
    Ensure both cylinder head and cylinder
        mating surfaces are clean.
    Lubricate the cylinder bore with the
        specified type of two-stroke oil.
    Assemble the components with new
        gaskets and O-rings.

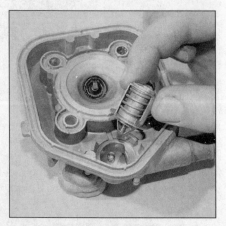

6.18 Where installed, lift out the thermostat

6.19 Thermostat bypass passage must be clear

7.1 Detach the coolant hose (arrow) from the cylinder

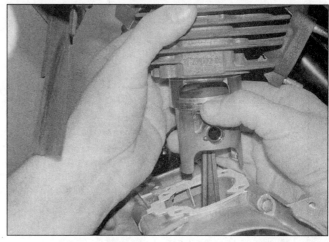

7.2 Support the piston as the cylinder is lifted off

Tighten the cylinder head, and head cover where installed, fixings evenly and a little at a time in a criss-cross pattern to the torque setting specified in the Data section.

Ensure the thermostat and coolant system hoses are installed correctly (see Chapter 3).

Refill the cooling system (see Chapter 1).

7 Cylinder – removal, inspection and installation

Note: *This procedure can be carried out with the engine in the frame.*

Removal

1 Remove the exhaust system (see Chapter 4) and the cylinder head (see Section 6). On liquid-cooled engines, where applicable, detach the coolant hose from the cylinder **(see illustration)**.

2 Lift the cylinder up off the crankcase, supporting the piston as it becomes accessible to prevent it hitting the crankcase opening **(see illustration)**. If the cylinder is stuck, tap around the joint face between the cylinder and the crankcase with a soft-faced mallet to free it. Don't attempt to free the cylinder by inserting a screwdriver between it and the crankcase – you'll damage the sealing surfaces. When the cylinder is removed, stuff a clean rag into the crankcase opening around the piston to prevent anything falling inside.

3 Remove the cylinder base gasket and discard it, as a new one must be installed on reassembly.

4 Scrape off any carbon deposits that may have formed in the exhaust port, then wash the cylinder with a suitable solvent and dry it thoroughly. Compressed air will speed the drying process and ensure that all holes and recesses are clean.

Inspection

5 Check the cylinder bore carefully for scratches and score marks.

6 If available, use a telescoping gauge and micrometer to measure the diameter of the cylinder bore to assess the amount of wear, taper and ovality (see *Tools and Workshop Tips* in the *Reference* section). Measure near the top (but below the level of the top piston ring at TDC), center and bottom (but above the level of the bottom ring at BDC) of the bore both parallel to and across the crankshaft axis **(see illustration)**. Calculate any differences between the measurements taken to determine any taper or ovality in the bore.

7 Now measure an unworn part of the cylinder bore (below the level of the bottom ring at BDC) and compare the result to the previous measurements to determine overall wear.

8 If the bore is tapered, oval, or worn excessively, or badly scratched, scuffed or scored, the cylinder and piston will have to be replaced. **Note:** *If no service limit specifications (see Data section) are available to*

assess cylinder wear, calculate the piston-to-bore clearance to determine whether the cylinder is useable (see Section 8).

9 If there is any doubt about the serviceability of the cylinder, consult a scooter dealer. **Note:** *On some engines, the surface of the cylinder has a wear-resistant coating which, when damaged or worn through, requires a new cylinder. On others, the cylinder can be rebored and an oversize piston installed (see Data section). Oversize pistons are not necessarily marked as such; in many cases the only way to determine if a cylinder has been rebored is to measure an unworn area of the bore and compare the result with the specifications in the Data section. Most manufacturers mark cylinders and pistons with a size code during production; the size code (usually a letter) is stamped into the cylinder gasket surface and the top of the piston* **(see illustration)**. *It is important that new parts have matching codes.*

10 If applicable, inspect the cylinder head bolt threads in the crankcase (see Section 13). If

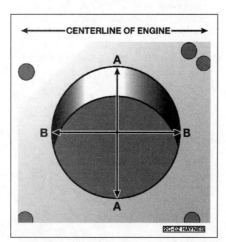

7.6 Measure the cylinder diameter in two directions, at the top, center and bottom of travel

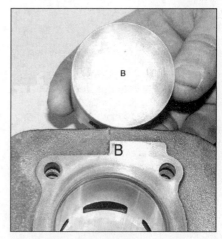

7.9 Cylinders and pistons are size-coded and should always match

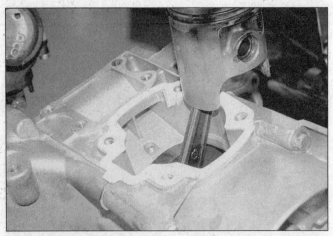

7.11 Ensure the new gasket is positioned correctly on the crankcase

7.12 Ring locating pins (arrows) must be between the ring ends

7.13 Position the cylinder over the top of the piston . . .

7.14 . . . then carefully feed the piston into the cylinder

the head is secured by studs, check that they are tight. If any are loose, remove them and clean their threads. Apply a suitable permanent thread locking compound and tighten them securely.

Installation

Note: *On some engines, cylinder base gaskets are available in a range of thicknesses; the appropriate thickness depends on the height of the piston crown at TDC in relation to the cylinder top gasket surface. Consult a scooter dealer for details. In these instances, the correct gasket thickness must be calculated before reassembly (see Steps 17 to 21).*

11 Check that the mating surfaces of the cylinder and crankcase are clean, then remove any rags from the crankcase opening. Lay the new base gasket in place on the crankcase, making sure it is correctly positioned **(see illustration)**.

12 Check that the piston rings are correctly positioned so that the ring locating pins in the piston grooves are between the ring ends **(see illustration)**.

13 Lubricate the cylinder bore, piston and piston rings, and the connecting rod big and

small ends, with the specified type of two-stroke oil, then position the cylinder over the top of the piston **(see illustration)**.

14 Ensure the piston enters the bore squarely and does not get cocked sideways. Carefully compress and feed each ring into the bore as the cylinder is lowered, taking care that the rings do not rotate out of position **(see illustration)**. Do not use force if the

cylinder appears to be stuck, as the piston and/or rings will be damaged.

15 When the piston is correctly installed in the cylinder, check that the base gasket has not been displaced, then press the cylinder down onto the gasket **(see illustration)**.

16 Install the remaining components in the reverse order of removal.

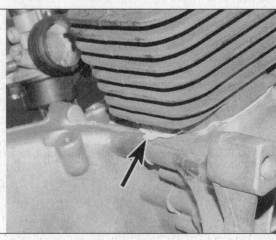

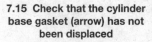

7.15 Check that the cylinder base gasket (arrow) has not been displaced

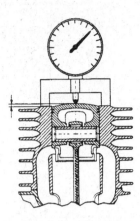

7.17 Set-up for calculating the thickness of the cylinder base gasket

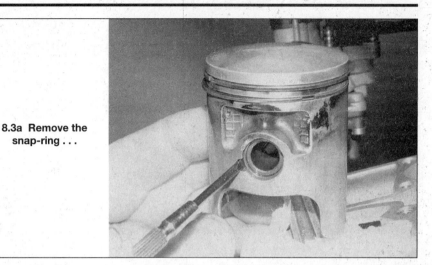

8.3a Remove the snap-ring . . .

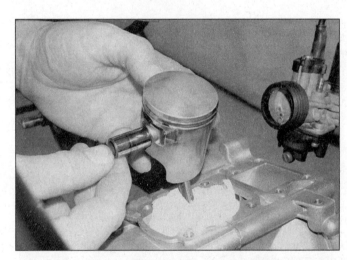

8.3b . . . then push out the piston pin

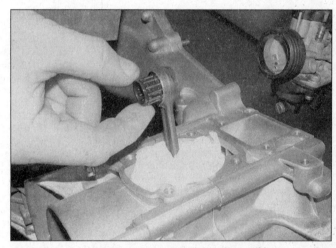

8.4 Remove the small-end bearing

Cylinder base gasket thickness

17 To measure the height of the piston crown at TDC in relation to the cylinder top gasket surface, you will require a dial gauge and a mounting plate (see illustration).

18 Assemble the cylinder on the piston as described in Steps 12 to 14, but without a base gasket, and press the cylinder down onto the crankcase.

19 Set the dial gauge in the mounting plate, and with the mounting plate feet and gauge tip resting against the cylinder top gasket surface, zero the gauge. Rotate the crankshaft so that the piston is part way down the bore.

20 Clamp the mounting plate diagonally across the cylinder using the cylinder fasteners and tighten them to ensure that the cylinder is held firmly against the crankcase.

21 Rotate the crankshaft via the alternator rotor nut so the piston rises to the top of its stroke (TDC). At this point read off the dial gauge (see illustration 7.17). The reading represents the distance between the cylinder top gasket surface and the top of the piston crown. Use this measurement, together with the manufacturer's information, to identify the appropriate gasket thickness.

8 Piston – removal, inspection and installation

Note: *This procedure can be carried out with the engine in the frame.*

Removal

1 Remove the cylinder and stuff a clean rag into the crankcase opening around the piston to prevent anything falling inside (see Section 7).

2 The piston top should be marked with an arrow which faces towards the exhaust. If this is not visible, mark the piston accordingly so that it can be installed in the correct position. Note that the arrow may not be visible until the carbon deposits have been scraped off and the piston cleaned.

3 Carefully pry the snap-ring out from one side of the piston using needle-nose pliers or a small flat-bladed screwdriver inserted into the notch (see illustration). Check for burring around the snap-ring groove and remove any with a very fine file or penknife blade, then push the piston pin out from the other side

and remove the piston from the connecting rod (see illustration). Use a socket extension to push the piston pin out if required. Remove the other snap-ring and discard them both, as new ones must be used on reassembly.

 To prevent the snap-ring from flying away or from dropping into the crankcase, pass a rod or screwdriver, with a greater diameter than the gap between the snap-ring ends, through the piston pin. This will trap the snap-ring if it springs out.

 If the piston pin is a tight fit in the piston bosses, heat the piston gently with a hot air gun – this will expand the alloy piston sufficiently to release its grip on the pin.

4 The connecting rod small-end bearing is a loose fit in the rod; remove it for safekeeping, noting how it is installed (see illustration).

5 Before the inspection process can be carried out, the piston rings must be removed and the piston must be cleaned. Note: *If the cylinder is being replaced or rebored, pis-*

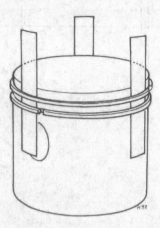

8.5 Remove the piston rings carefully

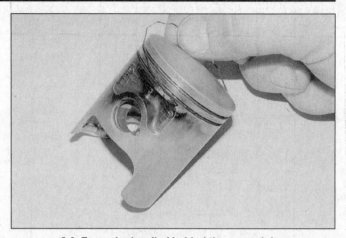

8.6 Expander insalled behind the second ring

ton inspection can be overlooked, as a new one will be installed. The piston rings can be removed by hand; using your thumbs, ease the ends of each ring apart and carefully lift it off the piston, taking care not to expand it any more than is necessary **(see illustration)**. Do not nick or gouge the piston in the process.

6 Note which way up each ring fits and in which groove, as they must be installed in their original positions if being re-used. The upper surface of each ring should be marked at one end (see Section 9). Some pistons have an expander installed behind the second ring **(see illustration)**. Note: *It is good practice to replace the piston rings when an engine is being overhauled. Ensure that the piston and bore are serviceable before purchasing new rings.*

7 Clean all traces of carbon from the top of the piston. A hand-held wire brush or a piece of fine emery cloth can be used once most of the deposits have been scraped away. Do not, under any circumstances, use a wire brush mounted in a drill motor; the piston material is soft and is easily damaged.

8 Use a piston ring groove cleaning tool to remove any carbon deposits from the ring grooves. If a tool is not available, a piece

broken off an old ring will do the job. Be very careful to remove only the carbon deposits. Do not remove any metal and do not nick or gouge the sides of the ring grooves.

9 Once the carbon has been removed, clean the piston with a suitable solvent and dry it thoroughly. If the identification previously marked on the piston is cleaned off, be sure to re-mark it correctly.

Inspection

10 Inspect the piston for cracks around the skirt, at the pin bosses and at the ring lands. Check that the snap-ring grooves are not damaged. Normal piston wear appears as even, vertical wear on the thrust surfaces of the piston and slight looseness of the top ring in its groove. If the skirt is scored or scuffed, the engine may have been suffering from overheating and/or abnormal combustion, resulting in excessively high operating temperatures.

11 A hole in the top of the piston, in one extreme, or burned areas around the edge of the piston crown, indicate that pre-ignition or knocking under load have occurred. If you find evidence of any problems, the cause must be corrected or the damage will occur again. Refer to Chapter 4 for carburetion checks and Chapter 5 for ignition checks.

12 Check the piston-to-bore clearance by measuring the cylinder bore (see Section 7)

and the piston diameter. Measure the piston approximately 25 mm down from the bottom of the lower piston ring groove and at 90° to the piston pin axis **(see illustration)**. Note: *The precise point of measurement differs between manufacturers and engines, but the aim is to measure the piston in an area where it is worn. Subtract the piston diameter from the bore diameter to obtain the clearance. If it is greater than the specified figure, check whether it is the bore or piston that is worn the most (see Data section at the end of this manual). If the bore is good, install a new piston and rings. Note: Oversize pistons installed in a rebored cylinder are not necessarily marked as such; in many cases the only way to determine if a cylinder has been rebored is to measure an unworn area of the bore and compare the result with the specifications in the Data section. Most manufacturers mark cylinders and pistons with a size code during production; the size code (usually a letter) is stamped into the cylinder gasket surface and the top of the piston (see illustration 7.9). It is important that new parts have matching codes. It is essential to supply the size code and any rebore specifications when purchasing a new piston.*

13 Use a micrometer to measure the piston pin in the middle, where it runs in the small-end bearing, and at each end where it runs in the piston **(see illustration)**. If there is any

8.12 Measure the piston at 90° to the piston pin axis

8.13 Measuring the piston pin where it runs in the small-end bearing

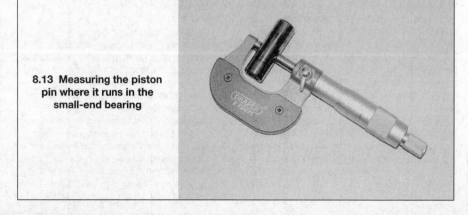

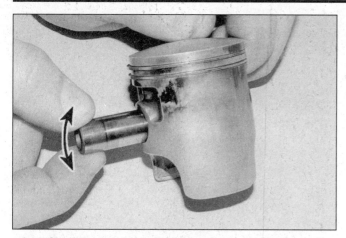

8.14 Check for freeplay between the piston and the piston pin

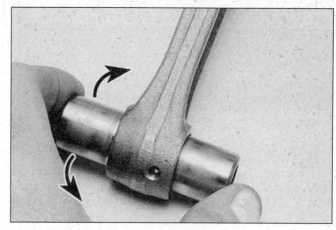

8.15 Rock the piston pin back-and-forth to check for freeplay

difference in the measurements, the pin is worn and must be replaced.

14 If the piston pin is good, lubricate it with clean two-stroke oil, then insert it into the piston and check for any freeplay between the two **(see illustration)**. There should be no freeplay.

15 Next, check the condition of the connecting rod small-end bearing. A worn small-end bearing will produce a metallic rattle, most audible when the engine is under load, and increasing as engine speed rises. This should not be confused with connecting rod bearing wear, which produces a pronounced knocking noise. Inspect the bearing rollers for flat spots and pitting. Install the bearing in the connecting rod, then slide the piston pin into the bearing and check for freeplay **(see illustration)**. There should only be slightly discernible freeplay between the piston pin, the bearing and the connecting rod.

16 If there is freeplay, measure the internal diameter of the connecting rod small-end **(see illustration)**. Take several measurements; if there is any difference between the measurements, the small end is worn and either a new connecting rod or crankshaft assembly will have to be installed (see Section 14). Con-

sult a scooter dealer about the availability of parts. **Note:** *If a new rod is available, installing it is a specialist task which should be left to a scooter dealer or machine shop. If a new rod is installed, the connecting rod bearing should be replaced at the same time.*

17 If the small-end is good, install a new small-end bearing. **Note:** *On some engines, a mark on the connecting rod indicates the matching size code of the small end bearing – the bearing will have the same mark or will be color-coded. Refer to these marks when purchasing a new bearing.*

Installation

18 Install the piston rings (see Section 9).
19 Lubricate the piston pin, the piston pin bore in the piston and the small-end bearing with the specified two-stroke oil and install the bearing in the connecting rod.
20 Install a new snap-ring in one side of the piston, line up the piston on the connecting rod, making sure the arrow on the piston top faces towards the exhaust, and insert the piston pin from the other side. Secure the pin with the other new snap-ring. When installing the snap-rings, compress them only just enough to fit them in the piston, and make

sure they are properly seated in their grooves with the open end away from the removal notch.
21 Install the cylinder (see Section 7).

9 Piston rings – inspection and installation

1 New piston rings should be installed whenever an engine is being overhauled. It is important that you get new rings of the correct size for your piston, so ensure that any information relating to piston size, including rebore size, and size-coding is available when purchasing new parts.

2 Before installing the new rings onto the piston, the ring end gaps must be checked. Insert the top ring into the bottom of the cylinder bore and square it up by pushing it in with the top of the piston. The ring should be about 15 to 20 mm from the bottom edge of the cylinder. To measure the end gap, slip a feeler gauge between the ends of the ring and compare the measurement to the specification in the *Data* section at the end of this manual **(see illustration)**.

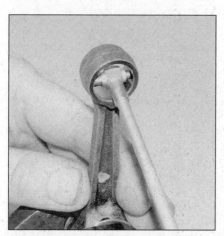

8.16 Measuring the internal diameter of the connecting rod small-end

9.2 Measuring installed ring end gap

9.7 Using a thin blade to install the piston ring

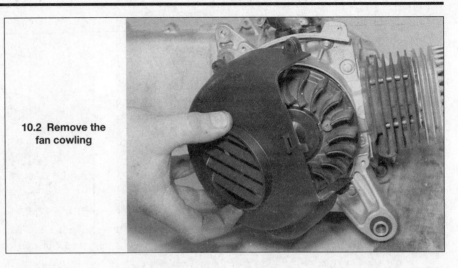

10.2 Remove the fan cowling

3 If the gap is larger or smaller than specified, check to make sure that you have the correct rings before proceeding. If the gap is larger than specified, it is likely the cylinder bore is worn. If the gap is too small, the ring ends may come into contact with each other during engine operation, causing serious damage.

4 Repeat the procedure for the other ring.

5 Once the ring end gaps have been checked, the rings can be installed on the piston. First identify the ring locating pin in each piston ring groove – the ring must be positioned so that the pin is in between the ends of the ring **(see illustration 7.12)**.

6 If the piston has an expander installed behind the lower ring, install that first, ensuring that the ends of the expander do not overlap the ring locating pin **(see illustration 8.6)**.

7 The upper surface of each ring should be marked at one end; make sure you install the rings the right way up. Install the lower ring first. Do not expand the ring any more than is necessary to slide it into place and check that the locating pin is between the ends of the ring **(see illustration)**.

8 Install the top ring. Always ensure that the

ring end gaps are positioned each side of the locating pins before installing the piston into the cylinder.

10 Alternator – removal and installation

Note: *This procedure can be carried out with the engine in the frame. If the engine has been removed, ignore the steps that do not apply.*

Removal

1 Remove the body panels as necessary to access the alternator (see Chapter 9). If required, remove the exhaust system (see Chapter 4).

2 On air-cooled engines, unclip any wiring or hoses from the fan cowling, then undo the bolts securing the fan cowling and remove it **(see illustration)**. Note that on some models the fan cowling is clipped to the engine cowling – take care not to damage the attachment lugs when separating them. Remove any spacers for the cowling bolts for safekeeping if they are loose. Undo the bolts securing the

cooling fan to the alternator rotor and remove the fan (see Chapter 1, Section 21).

3 On liquid-cooled engines where the water pump is mounted on the outside of the alternator cover, first drain the coolant and disconnect all the coolant hoses from the pump (see Chapter 3). Undo the cover mounting bolts and lift off the cover. Depending on the tools available for removing the alternator rotor, it may be necessary to unscrew the pump drive dampers **(see illustration)**.

4 On some engines, the alternator is located behind the right-hand engine side cover. **Note:** *If the water pump is mounted on the outside of the engine side cover, first drain the coolant and disconnect all the coolant hoses from the pump (see Chapter 3).* Trace the wiring from the cover and disconnect it at the connector, then undo the cover bolts and lift off the cover **(see illustration)**. Discard the gasket (as a new one must be installed) and remove the cover dowels for safekeeping if they are loose. If applicable, remove the starter pinion assembly (see Section 11).

5 To remove the rotor center nut, it is necessary to stop the rotor from turning; some manufacturers produce a service tool for this purpose. If the rotor face is accessible, you

10.3 The water pump is driven by dampers on the alternator rotor

10.4 Lift off the side cover and alternator stator

10.5 Hold the rotor and undo the center nut (arrow)

10.6 Using a strap wrench to hold the rotor

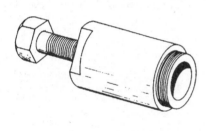

10.8a Typical service tool for removing the rotor

10.8b Using a screw-in type puller

10.8c Using a two-legged puller

can make up a tool which engages the slots or holes **(see illustration)**. **Note:** *Take great care not to damage the coils of the alternator when locating any tools through the rotor.*

> 🔧 **TOOL TIP** *A rotor holding tool can easily be made using two strips of steel bolted together in the middle, with a bolt through each end which locates into the slots or holes in the rotor. Do not allow the bolts to extend too far through the rotor, otherwise the coils could be damaged.*

6 If the alternator stator is located in the engine side cover, the rotor can be held with a strap wrench **(see illustration)**.

7 With the rotor securely held, unscrew the center nut.

8 To remove the rotor from the shaft, it is necessary to use a puller – either a manufacturer's service tool or a commercially available puller **(see illustrations)**. To use the service tool, first screw the body of the tool all the way into the threads provided in the rotor. Hold the tool steady with a wrench on its flats and tighten the center bolt, exerting steady pressure to draw the rotor off the crankshaft.

To use a puller, engage the puller legs either in the slots in the rotor or thread them into the threaded holes in the rotor, then tighten the center bolt, exerting steady pressure to draw the rotor off the crankshaft. Remove the Woodruff key from the shaft for safekeeping, noting how it fits **(see illustrations)**.

9 In most cases, the alternator stator coils and ignition pulse generator coil are wired together and have to be removed as an assembly. If not already done, trace the wiring back from the alternator and pulse generator, and disconnect it at the connectors. Free the wiring from any clips or guides and

10.8d Remove the Woodruff key for safekeeping

10.8e Note the alignment of the key (A) and the slot in the rotor (B)

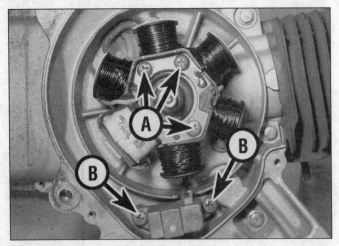

10.10a Undo the stator screws (A) and the pulse generator coil screws (B) . . .

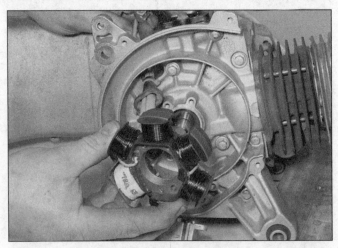

10.10b . . . and remove the assembly, noting how the wiring fits

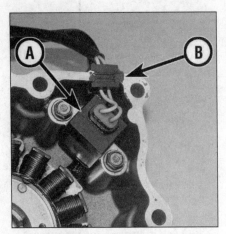

10.10c Note the position of the pulse generator (A) and the wiring grommet (B)

11.1 Starter pinion assembly is driven by the starter motor shaft (arrow)

Make sure that no metal objects have attached themselves to the magnets on the inside of the rotor.

Clean the tapered end of the crankshaft and the corresponding mating surface on the inside of the rotor with a suitable solvent.

Install the Woodruff key into its slot in the shaft, then install the rotor.

Tighten the rotor center nut to the torque setting specified in the Data section at the end of this manual.

Secure the wiring with any clips or ties.

If applicable, refill the cooling system and bleed it (see Chapter 3).

11 Starter pinion assembly and starter clutch – removal, inspection and installation

feed it through to the alternator.

10 Undo the screws securing the stator and the pulse generator and lift them off together (see illustration). Where installed, draw any rubber wiring boot out of the crankcase or engine side cover and carefully pull the wiring away, noting how it fits (see illustrations).

Installation

11 Installation is the reverse of removal, noting the following:

Ensure the wiring is correctly routed before installing the stator and pulse generator.

Note 1: *Two different set-ups are used to transfer the starter motor drive to the engine – a sliding pinion assembly or a starter (one-way) clutch. The sliding pinion assembly engages with the driven gear on the variator pulley, or a driven gear on the crankshaft behind the variator. The starter clutch is located either on the back of the alternator rotor or on the crankshaft behind the variator. Note the point at which the starter motor shaft enters the engine case to locate the appropriate assembly.*

Note 2: *This procedure can be carried out with the engine in the frame.*

Starter pinion assembly

Removal

1 Note the position of the starter motor, then remove the drivebelt cover (see Chapter 6) and locate the pinion assembly adjacent to the variator pulley (see illustration).

2 Where necessary, undo the bolts securing the starter pinion outer support and remove the support.

3 Withdraw the starter pinion assembly (see illustration).

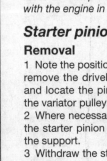

11.3 Remove the pinion assembly, noting how it fits

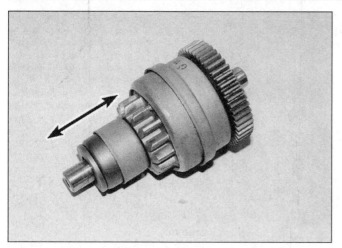

11.5 Check the pinion teeth. The outer pinion should move smoothly on the shaft

11.13 Starter idler gear (A) and driven gear (B)

Inspection

4 Some pinion assemblies are installed with a rubber boot. If the boot shows signs of damage or deterioration, remove it. If a new boot is available, install it on reassembly.

5 Check the starter pinion assembly for any signs of damage or wear, particularly for chipped or broken teeth on either of the pinions **(see illustration)**. Check the corresponding teeth on the starter motor pinion and the variator driven gear.

6 Rotate the outer pinion and check that it moves smoothly up-and-down the shaft, and that it returns easily to its rest position.

7 The starter pinion assembly is supplied as a complete unit; if any of the component parts is worn or damaged, the unit will have to be replaced.

8 Most manufacturers recommend that the starter pinion mechanism should not be lubricated, as any excess grease may contaminate the drivebelt and cause it to slip. However, a smear of grease should be applied to both ends of the pinion shaft before reassembly.

Installation

9 Installation is the reverse of removal. Ensure the inner pinion engages with the starter motor shaft **(see illustration 11.1)**.

Starter (one-way) clutch

Removal

10 Note the position of the starter motor, then remove either the alternator cover (see Section 10) or the drivebelt cover (see Chapter 6).

11 The operation of the starter clutch can be checked while it is in place. Check that the starter driven gear is able to rotate freely in the opposite direction of engine rotation, but locks when rotated in the other direction **(see illustration 11.13)**. If not, the starter clutch is faulty and should be removed for inspection.

Removal

12 Remove the variator (see Chapter 6) or the alternator rotor (see Section 10) as appropriate. If the starter clutch is mounted

on the crankshaft behind the variator, slide the clutch assembly off the shaft.

13 Remove the idler gear, noting how it fits **(see illustration)**.

Inspection

14 Inspect the teeth on the idler gear and replace it if any are chipped or worn **(see illustration)**. Check the idler shaft and bearing surfaces for signs of wear or damage, and replace it if necessary. Inspect the teeth of the driven gear.

15 Hold the starter clutch assembly or the alternator rotor, as appropriate, and check that the starter driven gear rotates freely in one direction and locks in the other direction **(see illustration)**. If it doesn't, the starter clutch is faulty and should be replaced. If individual components are available, follow Steps 16 and 17 and check the condition of the one-way mechanism. If there is any doubt about the condition of the starter clutch, have it tested by a scooter dealer.

16 Slowly rotate the driven gear and with-

11.14 Examine the idler gear teeth for wear and damage

11.15 The gear should rotate freely in one direction only

11.16a Withdraw the gear from the clutch

11.16b Undo the bolts to remove the starter clutch from the alternator rotor

draw it from the clutch (see illustration). If the starter clutch is on the back of the alternator rotor, use a strap wrench to hold the rotor and undo the clutch mounting bolts (see illustration).

17 Inspect the hub of the driven gear for wear and scoring. Inspect the clutch one-way mechanism; if a ring of sprags is used, the individual sprags should be smooth and free to rotate in their cage (see illustration); if individual sprags are spring-loaded, check that the spring plungers are free to move.

Installation

18 Installation is the reverse of removal, noting the following:

> Apply a drop of thread locking compound to the clutch mounting bolts.
> Lubricate the driven gear hub with clean engine oil.
> Rotate the driven gear to install it in the starter clutch.
> Ensure the idler gear engages with the pinion on the starter motor shaft.

12 Oil pump – removal, inspection, installation and bleeding

Note 1: Generally the oil pump is located on the outside of the crankcase, either in front of or behind the cylinder, or inside the engine unit either behind the variator or behind the alternator rotor. Externally-mounted pumps are generally driven via a shaft and worm gear on the crankshaft and the rate of oil delivery is either cable-controlled (from the throttle twistgrip via a cable splitter – see Chapter 1) or automatic (centrifugal pump). Internally-mounted pumps are generally either belt- or gear-driven and rate of oil delivery is either cable-controlled or automatic.

Note 2: This procedure can be carried out with the engine in the frame. If the engine has been removed, ignore the steps that do not apply.

Externally-mounted pump

Removal

1 Remove the body panels as necessary to access the oil pump (see Chapter 9). If required, remove the exhaust system (see Chapter 4). **Note:** On some engines, the externally-mounted pump is located behind a cover on the side of the crankcase; the pump is driven by an extension of the water pump driveshaft. Remove the cover to access the pump.

2 On engines installed with a cable-operated pump, detach the cable from the pump pulley, then unscrew the bolts securing the cable bracket and remove the bracket with the cable attached (see illustration).

3 On all models, release the clip securing the oil inlet hose from the oil tank to the union on the pump and detach the hose (see illustration). Clamp the hose and secure it in an upright position to minimize oil loss. Release the clip securing the oil outlet hose to the fitting on the pump and detach the hose. Wrap clean plastic bags around the hose ends to prevent dirt entering the system. **Note:** On some engines, the inlet and outlet hoses are protected from the exhaust pipe by a heat-proof sheath. Remove the sheath if necessary but don't forget to reinstall it on reassembly.

4 On models installed with a centrifugal pump (without cable operation), unscrew the pump mounting bolts and remove the bolts.

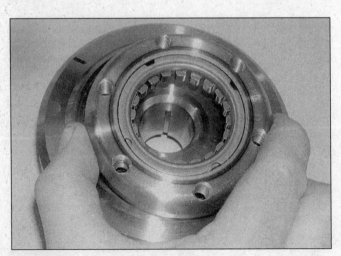

11.17 Check the condition of the clutch sprags – they should be flat on one side

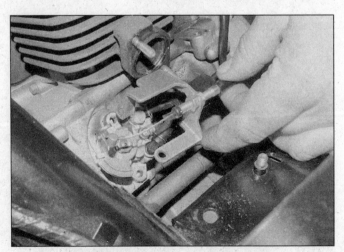

12.2 Remove the oil pump cable and bracket

12.3 Detach the oil hoses (arrows) from the pump unions

12.5 Remove the wave washer

5 Withdraw the pump from the crankcase and remove the wave washer (see illustration). Note how the tab on the back of the pump locates in the slot in the pump driveshaft.

6 Stuff a clean rag into the crankcase opening to prevent dirt falling inside.

7 Remove the O-ring from the pump body and discard it, as a new one must be installed on reassembly.

8 If installed, remove the two nuts from the underside of the pump mounting on the crankcase for safekeeping.

9 Ensure no dirt enters the pump body. Clean it using a suitable solvent, then dry the pump thoroughly.

Inspection

10 Check the pump body for obvious signs of damage, especially around the mounting bolt holes. Turn the pump drive by hand and check that the pump rotates smoothly. Where installed, check that the cable pulley turns freely and returns to rest under pressure of the return spring.

11 No individual internal components are available for the pump. If it is damaged or, if after bleeding the operation of the pump is suspect, replace it.

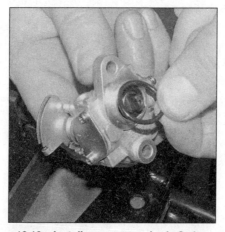

12.12a Install a new pump body O-ring

Installation

12 Installation is the reverse of removal, noting the following:

  Install a new O-ring on the pump body and lubricate it with a smear of grease (see illustration).

  Install the wave washer, then install the pump.

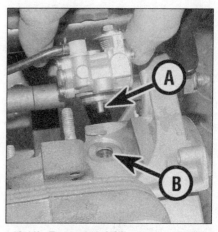

12.12b Ensure tab (A) locates in slot (B)

  Ensure the tab on the back of the pump engages with the slot in the driveshaft (see illustration).

  Ensure the hoses are secured to the pump fittings with clips.

  Bleed the pump (see Step 24).

  On models installed with a cable-operated pump, check the operation of the cable (see Chapter 1).

Caution: Accurate cable adjustment is important to ensure that the oil pump delivers the correct amount of oil to the engine and is correctly synchronized with the throttle.

Internally-mounted pump

Removal

13 Trace the oil inlet hose from the oil tank to the engine unit and remove either the drivebelt cover or the alternator cover. Remove either the variator (see Chapter 6) or the alternator rotor (see Section 10) as applicable.

14 Undo the screws securing the oil pump, then withdraw the pump (see illustration). Where installed, slide the rubber grommet

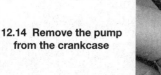

12.14 Remove the pump from the crankcase

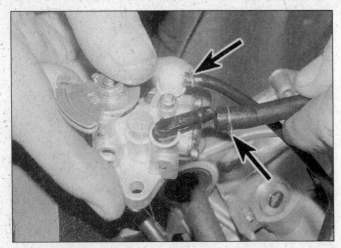

12.16 Detach the oil hoses from the pump

12.18a Remove the pump drivebelt cover

12.18b Remove the belt . . .

securing the hoses out of its cutout in the crankcase.

15 If the pump is belt-driven, note how the drive tab on the back of the pump locates in the slot in the driven pulley. If the pump is being removed rather than just being displaced for belt replacement, detach the cable from the pump pulley, noting how it fits.

16 Release the clip securing the oil inlet hose from the oil tank to the fitting on the pump and detach the hose **(see illustration)**. Clamp the hose to minimize oil loss. Release the clip securing the oil outlet hose to the fitting on the pump and detach the hose. Wrap clean plastic bags around the hose ends to prevent dirt entering the system.

17 Ensure no dirt enters the pump body and clean it using a suitable solvent, then dry the pump thoroughly.

18 To remove the pump drivebelt, first undo the screw securing the belt cover, where installed, then remove the cover and the plate behind it, noting how they fit **(see illustration)**. If a spacer is installed to the crankshaft, slide it off. Slip the belt off the pulleys, then slide off the drive pulley, noting how it fits **(see illustrations)**.

19 Remove the pump driven pulley and the thrustwasher behind it **(see illustration)**. On engines where the water pump is located inside the crankcase halves, note how the

oil pump drive locates on the water pump shaft.

20 To remove the pump drive gear, use snap-ring pliers to remove the snap-ring, then slide the gear off the shaft. If the drive gear, or drive pulley, is retained by a ring nut, hold the crankshaft to prevent it turning, then use a peg wrench or punch to undo the ring nut. Note the drive pin in the shaft and remove it for safekeeping if it is loose.

Inspection

21 Follow Steps 10 and 11 to check the condition of the pump. If the pump is gear driven, check the condition of the pump drive and driven gears and replace them if necessary.

22 If the pump is belt-driven, check along the length of the pump drivebelt for splits, cracks or broken teeth and replace the belt if necessary. The belt should be replaced regardless of its condition at the service interval specified in Chapter 1, or during the course of assembly.

Installation

23 Installation is the reverse of removal, noting the following:

12.18c . . . then slide off the drive pulley

12.19 Remove the pump driven pulley

12.25a Bleed screw on the cable-operated pump

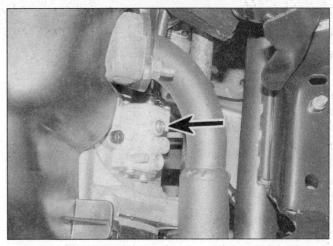

12.25b Bleed screw on the centrifugal pump

Slide the drive pulley onto the crank-shaft with the shoulder innermost.
Install the thrustwasher between the crankcase and the driven pulley.
Where installed, secure the pump drivegear with a new snap-ring.
Where installed, fit a new O-ring on the pump body and lubricate it with a smear of grease.
Ensure the hoses are secured to the pump fittings with clips.
Bleed the pump (see Step 24).
On models installed with a cable-oper-ated pump, check the operation of the cable (see Chapter 1).

Caution: Accurate cable adjustment is important to ensure that the oil pump delivers the correct amount of oil to the engine and is correctly synchronized with the throttle.

Bleeding

24 Bleeding the pump is the process of removing air from it and allowing it to be filled with oil. First ensure that the inlet hose from the oil tank and the oil filter are completely filled with oil. If necessary, detach the hose from the pump and wait until oil flows from the hose, then reconnect it.
25 Loosen the bleed screw on the pump and wait until oil, without any air mixed with it, flows out the hole, then tighten the screw **(see illustrations).**
26 Ensure the ignition switch is OFF. Disconnect the oil outlet hose from the carburetor and crank the engine with the kickstarter until oil, without any air mixed with it, flows out the hose, then reconnect the hose and secure it with the clip. Alternatively, fill an auxiliary fuel tank with a 2% (50:1) gasoline/two-stroke oil mix and connect it to the carburetor. Disconnect the oil outlet hose from the carburetor, start the engine and run it until oil, without any air mixed with it, flows out the hose, then reconnect the hose and secure it with the clip.

Warning: Never run the engine without an oil supply or crank the engine on the electric starter without an oil supply. Never crank the engine with the ignition ON and the spark plug cap disconnected from the spark plug, as the ignition system may be damaged.

13 Crankcase halves and main bearings

Note: *To separate the crankcase halves, the engine unit must be removed from the frame.*

Separation

1 Follow the procedure in Section 4 and remove the engine from the frame.
2 Before the crankcase halves can be separated the following components must be removed:

Alternator (see Section 10).
Variator (see Chapter 6).
Cylinder head (see Section 6).
Cylinder (see Section 7).
Piston (see Section 8).
Starter motor (see Chapter 10).
Oil pump (see Section 12).
Water pump (see Chapter 3).
Reed valve (see Chapter 4).

3 Tape some rag around the connecting rod to prevent it knocking against the cases, then loosen the crankcase bolts evenly, a little at a time and in a criss-cross sequence until they are all finger-tight, then remove them **(see illustration). Note:** *Ensure that all the crankcase bolts have been removed before attempting to separate the cases.*

HAYNES HiNT *Make a cardboard template of the crankcase and punch a hole for each bolt location. This will ensure all bolts are installed correctly on reassembly – this is important as some bolts may be of different lengths.*

4 Remove the right-hand crankcase half from the left-hand half by drawing it off the

13.3 Loosen the crankcase bolts evenly in a criss-cross sequence

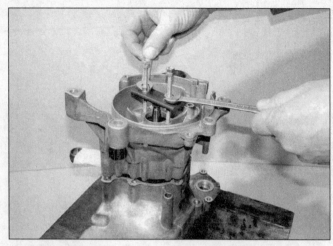

13.4 Drawing the right-hand crankcase half off the crankshaft

13.5 Pressing the crankshaft out of the left-hand crankcase half

right-hand end of the crankshaft. The cases will be a tight fit on the crankshaft and most manufacturers produce a service tool to facilitate this procedure. Alternatively, use the set-up shown, ensuring equal pressure is applied on both sides of the puller arrangement at all times **(see illustration)**. If the puller is placed across the end of the crankshaft, thread the old alternator center nut on first to protect the threads. **Note:** *If the crankcase halves do not separate easily, first ensure all fasteners have been removed. Apply steady pressure with the tools described and heat the bearing housings with a hot air gun. Do not try and separate the halves by levering against the mating surfaces as they are easily scored and will not seal correctly afterwards. Do not strike the ends of the crankshaft with a hammer as damage to the end threads or the shaft itself will result.*

5 Now press the crankshaft assembly out of the left-hand crankcase half – again, a service tool will be available. Alternatively, use the set-up shown **(see illustration)**. Thread the old variator nut onto the end of the crankshaft to protect the threads and make

sure the crankshaft assembly is supported to prevent it dropping if it suddenly comes free.
6 If installed, remove the crankcase gasket and discard it. A new one must be used on reassembly.
7 Remove the dowels from either crankcase half for safekeeping if they are loose.
8 On engines where the oil pump is driven off the crankshaft, remove the pump driveshaft and the shaft bushing. If necessary, heat crankcase around the bushing while applying pressure to the shaft.
9 On engines where the water pump is located inside the crankcase halves, remove the snap-ring from the outer end of the pump shaft, then press the shaft and its bearings out of the crankcase. Check the condition of the bearings and replace them if necessary (see *Tools and Workshop Tips* in the *Reference* section). The pump seal is located in the crankcase – have a new seal installed by a scooter dealer or automotive engineer.
10 Note the position of the crankshaft oil seals and measure any inset before removing them **(see illustration)**. Note how the seals are installed. Remove the seals by tapping

them gently on one side and pulling them out with pliers **(see illustration)**. Discard the seals, as new ones must be installed on reassembly.
11 The main bearings will either remain in place in the crankcase halves during disassembly or come out with the crankshaft assembly (see Section 14). If the main bearings have failed, excessive rumbling and vibration will be felt when the engine is running. Sometimes this may cause the oil seals to fail, resulting in a loss of compression and poor running. Check the condition of the bearings (see *Tools and Workshop Tips* in the *Reference* section) and only remove them if they are unserviceable. Always replace both main bearings at the same time, never individually.
12 To remove the bearings from the cases, heat the bearing housings with a hot air gun and tap them out using a bearing driver or suitable socket **(see illustration)**. Note how the bearings are installed. If the bearings are stuck on the crankshaft, they must be removed with an external bearing puller to avoid damaging the crankshaft assembly. **Note:** *On some engines, the main bear-*

13.10a Measuring crankshaft oil seal inset

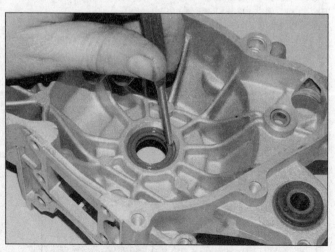

13.10b Tap the seals with a punch to displace them

13.12 Driving a main bearing out of the crankcase

13.18 Inspect the mount bushings (A) and the main bearing housings (B)

ings are installed in the crankcases prior to assembly, on others, they are installed to the crankshaft. Consult a scooter dealer for details before installing new bearings.

13 If required, remove the transmission assembly from the left-hand crankcase half (see Chapter 6).

Inspection

14 Remove all traces of old gasket from the crankcase mating surfaces, taking care not to nick or gouge the soft aluminium if a scraper is used. Wash all the components in a suitable solvent and dry them with compressed air.

Caution: Be very careful not to damage the crankcase mating surfaces, which may result in loss of crankcase pressure causing poor engine performance. Check both crankcase halves very carefully for cracks and damaged threads.

15 Small cracks or holes in aluminium castings can be repaired with an epoxy resin adhesive as a temporary measure. Permanent repairs can only be effected by welding, and only a spe-

cialist in this process is in a position to advise on the economy or practical aspect of such a repair. On some engines, the crankcase halves can be replaced individually, on others the two halves are only available together as a matching set – consult a scooter dealer for details.

16 Damaged threads can be economically reclaimed by using a thread insert (see *Tools and Workshop Tips* in the *Reference* section). Most scooter dealers and small engineering firms offer a service of this kind. Sheared screws can usually be removed with screw extractors (see *Tools and Workshop Tips* in the *Reference* section). If you are in any doubt about removing a sheared screw, consult a scooter dealer or automotive engineer.

17 Always wash the crankcases thoroughly after any repair work to ensure no dirt or metal shavings are trapped inside when the engine is rebuilt.

18 Inspect the engine mount bushings **(see illustration)**. If they show signs of deterioration, replace them all at the same time. To remove a bushing, first note its position in the casing. Heat the casing with a hot air gun, then support the casing and drive the bushing out with a hammer and a suitably-

sized socket. Alternatively, use two suitably-sized sockets to press the bushing out in the jaws of a vise. Clean the bushing housing with steel wool to remove any corrosion, then reheat the casing and install the new bushing. **Note:** *Always support the casing when removing or installing bushings to avoid breaking the casing.*

19 If the main bearings came out with the crankshaft assembly, or if they have been removed from the cases for replacement, inspect the bearing housings **(see illustration 13.18)**. If a bearing outer race has spun in its housing, the inside of the housing will be damaged. A bearing locking compound can be used to fix the outer race in place on reassembly if the damage is not too severe. **Note:** *If a bearing has spun in its housing, the bearing itself is likely to be damaged internally and should be replaced.*

20 Inspect the crankshaft assembly and bearings (see Section 14).

Reassembly

21 If the main bearings are to be installed into the crankcase halves, heat the bearing housings with a hot air gun, then install them using a bearing driver or suitable socket which bears onto the outer race only.

22 If the main bearings are to be installed onto the crankshaft, heat them first in an oil bath to around 212°F, then press them onto the shaft using a suitable length of tube that just fits over the shaft and bears onto the inner race only **(see illustration)**. If the bearings are difficult to install, they are not hot enough.

⚠ *Warning: This must be done very carefully to avoid the risk of personal injury.*

23 Install the new crankshaft oil seals into the crankcase halves and drive them to the previously measured inset using a seal driver or socket (see Step 10). Ensure the seals are installed properly and that they enter the

13.22 Tap the bearing onto the crankshaft – do not use excessive force

13.23 Ensure the new oil seals are installed correctly

13.25a Pulling the crankshaft into the case with a service tool . . .

cases squarely **(see illustration)**.

24 On engines where the water pump is located inside the crankcase halves, ensure the pump components are installed before joining the cases (see Step 9).

25 Install the crankshaft assembly into the left-hand crankcase half first, ensuring that the connecting rod is aligned with the crankcase mouth. Lubricate the shaft, seal and bearing with the specified two-stroke oil and tape some rag around the connecting rod to prevent it knocking against the cases. If the main bearing is in the crankcase half, pull the assembly into place either with a service tool or using the set-up shown **(see illustrations)**. If the main bearing is on the crankshaft, heat the bearing housing in the crankcase with a hot air gun before installing the crank assembly. **Note:** *Avoid applying direct heat onto the crankshaft oil seal.* If required, a freeze spray can be used on the bearing itself to aid installation. Ensure the bearing is installed fully into its housing.

26 If applicable, allow the case to cool, then wipe the mating surfaces of both crankcase halves with a rag soaked in a suitable solvent and install the dowels. Install the crankcase gasket or apply a small amount of suitable sealant to the mating surface of the left-hand case as required **(see illustration)**.

27 Now install the right-hand crankcase half. Lubricate the shaft, seal and bearing with the specified two-stroke oil. If the main bearing is in the crankcase half, press the crankcase half into place, either with a service tool or with the set-up used in Step 25 **(see illustration)**. If necessary, place a thick washer over the center of the right-hand crankcase to protect the aluminium. If the main bearing is on the crankshaft, heat the bearing housing with a hot air gun before installing the crankcase half and, if required, use a freeze spay on the bearing. **Note:** *Avoid applying direct heat onto the crankshaft oil seal.*

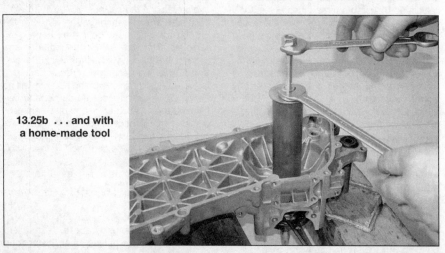

13.25b . . . and with a home-made tool

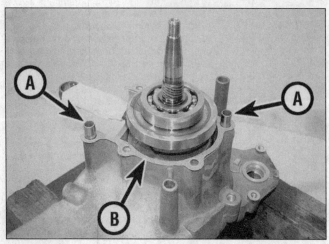

13.26 Install the crankcase dowels (A) and gasket (B)

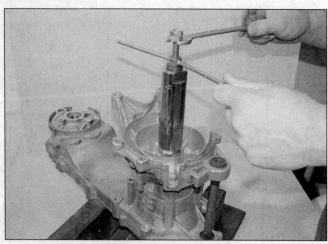

13.27 Installing the right-hand crankcase half

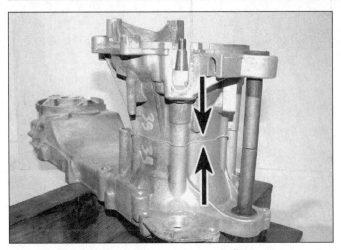

13.28a Ensure the crankcase halves are seated on the gasket

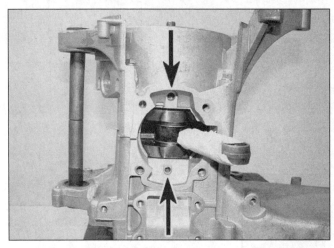

13.28b Position of main bearings can be checked through oilways (arrows)

28 Check that the crankcase halves are seated all the way around and that the main bearings are pressed fully into their housings **(see illustrations)**. If the casings are not correctly seated, heat the bearing housings while applying firm pressure with the assembly tools used previously. **Note:** *Do not attempt to pull the crankcase halves together using the crankcase bolts, as the casing will crack and be ruined.*

29 Clean the threads of the crankcase bolts and install them finger-tight, then tighten them evenly a little at a time in a criss-cross sequence to the torque setting specified in the *Data* section. Support the connecting rod and rotate the crankshaft by hand – if there are any signs of undue stiffness, tight or rough spots, or of any other problem, the fault must be rectified before proceeding further.

30 If necessary, trim the crankcase gasket flush with the mating surface for the cylinder **(see illustration)**.

31 Where installed, lubricate the oil pump

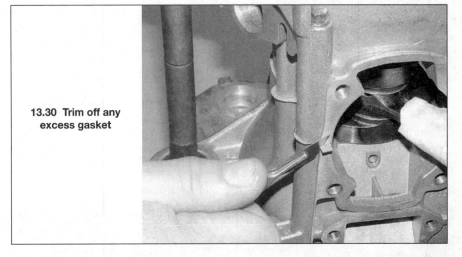

13.30 Trim off any excess gasket

driveshaft and install the shaft and the shaft bushing; tap the bushing into its seat with a hammer and suitable-sized socket **(see illustrations)**. Rotate the crankshaft to

ensure the oil pump drivegears are correctly engaged.

32 Install the remaining components in the reverse order of removal.

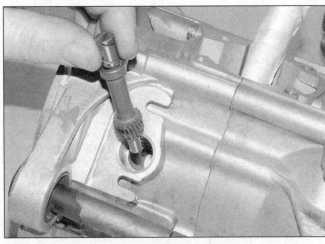

13.31a Install the oil pump shaft . . .

13.31b . . . and shaft bushing

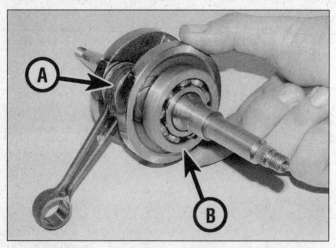

14.2 The connecting rod big-end (A) and main bearings (B)

14.3 Any freeplay indicates a worn connecting rod bearing

14 Crankshaft assembly and connecting rod bearing

1 To access the crankshaft and the connecting rod bearing, the crankcase must be split into two parts (see Section 13).

2 The crankshaft assembly should give many thousands of miles of service. The most likely problem to occur will be worn connecting rod bearings due to poor lubrication **(see illustration)**. A worn connecting rod big-end bearing will produce a pronounced knocking noise, most audible when the engine is under load, and increasing as engine speed rises. This should not be confused with connecting-rod small-end bearing wear, which produces a lighter, metallic rattle (see Section 8).

Inspection

3 To assess the condition of the connecting rod bearing, hold the crankshaft assembly firmly and push and pull on the connecting rod, checking for any up-and-down freeplay between the two **(see illustration)**. If any freeplay is noted, the bearing is worn and either the bearing or the crankshaft assembly will have to be replaced. **Note:** *A small amount of big-end side clearance (side-to-side movement) is acceptable on the connecting rod.* Consult a scooter dealer about the availability of parts. **Note:** *If a new bearing is available, installing it is a specialist task which should be left to a scooter dealer or repair shop.*

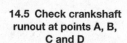
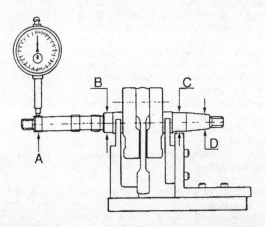

14.5 Check crankshaft runout at points A, B, C and D

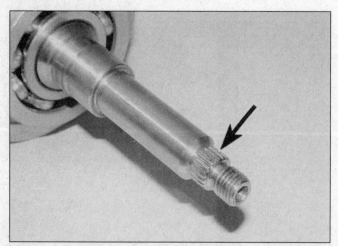

14.6a Inspect the shaft end threads and the variator pulley splines (arrow)

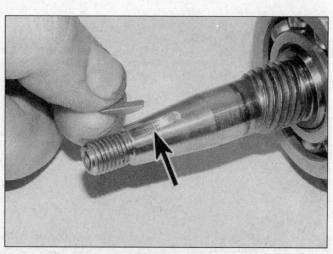

14.6b Inspect the shaft taper and slot (arrow) for the Woodruff key

14.7 Inspect the oil pump drivegear teeth

4 Inspect the crankshaft where it passes through the main bearings for wear and scoring. The shaft should be a press fit in the bearings; if it is worn or damaged a new assembly will have to be installed. Evidence of extreme heat, such as discoloration or blueing, indicates that lubrication failure has occurred. Be sure to check the oil pump and bearing oil ways before reassembling the engine.

5 If available, place the crankshaft assembly on V-blocks and check the runout at the main bearing journals (B and C) and at either end (A and D) using a dial gauge **(see illustration)**. If the crankshaft is out-of-true it will cause excessive engine vibration. If there is any doubt about the condition of the crankshaft, have it checked by a scooter dealer or machine shop. **Note:** *The crankshaft assembly is pressed together and is easily damaged if it is dropped.*

6 Inspect the threads on each end of the crankshaft and ensure that the retaining nuts for the alternator rotor and the variator are a good fit **(see illustration)**. Inspect the splines for the variator pulley on the left-hand end of the shaft. Inspect the taper and the slot in the right-hand end of the shaft for the alternator Woodruff key **(see illustration)**. Damage or wear that prevents the rotor from being installed securely will require a new crankshaft assembly.

7 Where applicable, inspect the oil pump drivegear teeth on the crankshaft and on the pump driveshaft for damage or wear **(see illustration)**. Inspect the ends of pump driveshaft where it runs in its bearings. Replace any components that are worn or damaged.

Reassembly

8 Follow the procedure in Section 13 to install the crankshaft assembly.

15 Initial start-up after overhaul

1 Make sure the oil tank is at least partly full and the pump is correctly adjusted (see Chapter 1) and bled of air (see Section 12).

2 On liquid-cooled models, make sure the coolant level is correct (see *Daily (pre-ride) checks*).

3 Make sure there is fuel in the tank.

4 With the ignition OFF, operate the kickstart to check that the engine turns over easily.

5 Turn the ignition ON, start the engine and allow it to run at a slow idle until it reaches operating temperature. Do not be alarmed if there is a little smoke from the exhaust –

this will be due to the oil used to lubricate the engine components during assembly and should subside after a while.

6 If the engine won't start, remove the spark plug and check that it has not become wet and oily. If it has, clean it and try again. If the engine refuses to start, go through the fault finding charts at the end of this manual to identify the problem.

7 Check carefully for fuel and oil leaks and make sure the transmission and controls, especially the brakes, function properly before road testing the machine. Refer to Section 16 for the recommended break-in procedure.

8 Upon completion of the road test, and after the engine has cooled-down completely, check for air bubbles in the engine oil inlet and outlet hoses (see Section 12). On liquid-cooled models, check the coolant level (see *Daily (pre-ride) checks*).

16 Recommended break-in procedure

1 Treat the engine gently for the first few miles to allow any new parts to bed-in.

2 If a new piston, cylinder or crankshaft assembly has been installed, the engine will have to be broken-in as when new. This means a restraining hand on the throttle until at least 300 miles (500 km) have been covered. There's no point in keeping to any set speed limit – the main idea is to keep from laboring the engine and to gradually increase performance up to the 600 mile (1000 km) mark. Make sure that the throttle position is varied to vary engine speed, and use full throttle only for short bursts. Experience is the best guide, since it's easy to tell when an engine is running freely.

3 Pay particular attention to the *Daily (pre-ride) checks* at the beginning of this manual and investigate the cause of any oil or, on liquid-cooled models, coolant loss immediately. Check the tightness of all relevant nuts and bolts.

Notes

Chapter 2 Part B
Four-stroke engines

Contents

Degrees of difficulty

Easy, suitable for novice with little experience	**Fairly easy,** suitable for beginner with some experience	**Fairly difficult,** suitable for competent DIY mechanic	**Difficult,** suitable for experienced DIY mechanic	**Very difficult,** suitable for expert DIY or professional

Specifications

Refer to the *Data* section at the end of this manual for servicing specifications.

1 General information

The engine is a single cylinder, overhead-camshaft four-stroke, with either fan-assisted air cooling (see Chapter 1) or pumped liquid cooling (see Chapter 3). The camshaft is chain-driven off the crankshaft and operates the valves via rocker arms.

The crankshaft assembly is pressed together, incorporating the connecting rod. The crankcase divides vertically – the left-hand crankcase is an integral part of the drivebelt casing and gearbox.

2 Operations possible with the engine in the frame

Most components and assemblies, with the obvious exception of the crankshaft assembly and its bearings, can be worked on without having to remove the engine/ transmission unit from the frame. However, access to some components is severely restricted, and if a number of areas require attention at the same time, removal of the engine is recommended, as it is an easy task to undertake.

3 Major engine repair – general information

1 It is not always easy to determine if an engine should be completely overhauled, as a number of factors must be considered.
2 High mileage is not necessarily an indication that an overhaul is needed, while low mileage, on the other hand, does not preclude the need for an overhaul. Frequency of servicing is probably the single most important consideration. An engine that has regular and frequent oil and filter changes, as well as other required maintenance, will most likely give many miles of reliable service. Conversely, a neglected engine, or one which has not been broken-in properly, may require an overhaul very early in its life.
3 Exhaust smoke and excessive oil consumption are both indications that the piston rings and/or valve guide oil seals are in need of attention.
4 If the engine is making obvious knocking or rumbling noises, the connecting rod and/ or main bearings are probably at fault.
5 Loss of power, rough running, excessive noise and high fuel consumption rates may also point to the need for an overhaul, especially if they are all present at the same time. If a complete service as detailed in Chapter 1 does not remedy the situation, major mechanical work is the only solution.
6 An engine overhaul generally involves restoring the internal parts to the specifications of a new engine. The piston and piston rings are replaced and the cylinder is rebored. The valve seats are reground and new valve springs are installed. If the connecting rod bearings are worn, a new crankshaft assembly is installed and, where possible, the main bearings in the crankcase are replaced. The end result should be a like-new engine that will give as many trouble-free miles as the original.
7 Before beginning the engine overhaul, read through the related procedures to familiarize yourself with the scope and requirements of the job. Overhauling an engine is not all that difficult, but it is time-consuming. Check on the availability of parts and make sure that any necessary special tools and materials are obtained in advance.
8 Most work can be done with typical workshop hand tools, although precision measuring tools are required for inspecting parts to determine if they must be replaced. Often a dealer will handle the inspection of parts and offer advice concerning reconditioning and

replacement. As a general rule, time is the primary cost of an overhaul so it does not pay to install worn or substandard parts.
9 As a final note, to ensure maximum life and minimum trouble from a rebuilt engine, everything must be assembled with care in a spotlessly clean environment.

4 Engine – removal and installation

Caution: *The engine/transmission unit is not heavy, however, removal and installation should be carried out with the aid of an assistant; personal injury or damage could occur if the engine falls or is dropped.*

Removal

1 The procedure for removing the four-stroke engine is the same as for two-stroke models. If required, drain the engine oil (see Chapter 1). **Note:** *There is no external oil feed or external oil pump on four-stroke engines.*
2 Refer to Chapter 2A, Section 4, for the rest of the procedure.

Installation

3 Installation is the reverse of the procedure in Chapter 2A. Note that if the engine oil was drained, or if any oil has been lost during overhaul, the engine must be filled with the specified quantity of oil (see *Data* section at the end of this manual) and the oil level checked as described in *Daily (pre-ride) checks.*

5 Disassembly and reassembly – general information

Disassembly

1 Before disassembling the engine, the external surfaces of the unit should be thoroughly cleaned and degreased. This will prevent contamination of the engine internals, and will also make working a lot easier and cleaner. A high flash-point solvent, such as paraffin, can be used, or better still, a proprietary engine degreaser such as Gunk. Use old paintbrushes and toothbrushes to work the solvent into the various recesses of the engine casings. Take care to keep solvent or water away from the electrical components and intake and exhaust ports.

 Warning: *The use of gasoline as a cleaning agent should be avoided because of the risk of fire.*

2 When clean and dry, arrange the unit on the workbench, leaving a suitable clear area

for working. Gather a selection of small containers and plastic bags so that parts can be grouped together in an easily identifiable manner. Some paper and a pen should be on hand to permit notes to be made and labels attached where necessary. A supply of clean rag is also required.
3 Before commencing work, read through the appropriate Section so that some idea of the necessary procedure can be gained. When removing components, it should be noted that great force is seldom required, unless specified. In many cases, a component's reluctance to be removed is indicative of an incorrect approach or removal method – if in any doubt, recheck with the text.
4 When disassembling the engine, keep mated parts that have been in contact with each other during engine operation together. These mated parts must be re-used or replaced as an assembly.
5 Complete engine disassembly should be done in the following general order with reference to the appropriate Sections (refer to Chapter 6 for details of transmission components disassembly):

> *Remove the valve cover.*
> *Remove the camshaft and rockers.*
> *Remove the cylinder head.*
> *Remove the cylinder.*
> *Remove the piston.*
> *Remove the alternator.*
> *Remove the starter motor (see Chapter 10).*
> *Remove the water pump if installed internally (see Chapter 3).*
> *Remove the oil pump.*
> *Separate the crankcase halves.*
> *Remove the crankshaft.*

Reassembly

6 Reassembly is accomplished by reversing the order of disassembly.

6 Valve cover – removal and installation

Note: *This procedure can be carried out with the engine in the frame. If the engine has been removed, ignore the Steps that do not apply.*

Removal

1 Remove the body panels as necessary to access the cylinder head (see Chapter 9).
2 On some air-cooled engines, the engine cowling covers the valve cover – pull the cap off the spark plug, then remove the screws securing the engine cowling and remove it. Note that it may also be necessary to remove the fan cowling to access the valve cover. **Note:** *Some cowlings are clipped together – take care not to damage the fixing lugs when separating them.*
3 Loosen the clips securing any breather

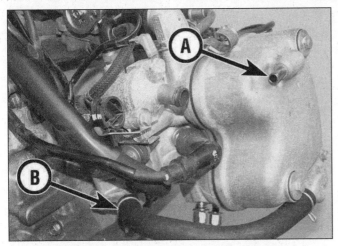

6.3 Location of breather hose (A) and PAIR valve hose (B)

6.4 Lift off the valve cover – note the gasket (arrow)

hose or PAIR valve hose to the valve cover and detach the hoses **(see illustration)**.

4 Unscrew the bolts securing the valve cover and remove them, together with any washers, then lift the cover off **(see illustration)**. If the cover is stuck, tap around the joint face between the cover and the cylinder head with a soft-faced mallet to free it. Do not try to lever the cover off as this may damage the sealing surfaces.

5 Remove the gasket and discard it, as a new one must be used. Note that on some engines, the gasket incorporates a camshaft end cap.

Installation

6 Clean the mating surfaces of the cylinder head and the valve cover with a suitable solvent to remove any traces of old gasket or sealant.

7 Lay the new gasket onto the valve cover, making sure it fits correctly into the groove **(see illustration)**. If a camshaft end cap is used, apply a suitable sealant around the edge of the cap before installing it.

8 Position the valve cover on the cylinder head, making sure the gasket stays in place.

Install the cover bolts with their washers, if equipped, then tighten the bolts evenly and in a criss-cross sequence to the torque setting specified in the *Data* section.

9 Install the remaining components in the reverse order of removal.

7 Oil cooler and pipes – removal and installation

Note: *This procedure can be carried out with the engine in the frame. If the engine has been removed, ignore the Steps that do not apply.*

Removal

1 Remove the body panels as necessary to access the oil cooler (see Chapter 9).

2 Drain the engine oil (see Chapter 1).

3 On air-cooled engines, remove the screws securing the engine cowling and remove the cowling.

4 Unscrew the banjo bolt securing each pipe fitting to the engine **(see illustration)**. Now

unscrew the cooler mounting bolts, noting the washers where installed, and remove the cooler and pipes.

5 If required, unscrew the banjo bolt securing each pipe to the cooler and detach the pipes. Discard the pipe sealing washers, as new ones must be used.

Installation

6 Installation is the reverse of removal, noting the following:

  Always use new sealing washers on the pipe unions.
  Tighten the banjo bolts securely.
  Fill the engine with oil (see Chapter 1) and check the oil level (see Daily (pre-ride) checks).

8 Cam chain tensioner – removal, inspection and installation

Note: *This procedure can be carried out with the engine in the frame. If the engine has been removed, ignore the Steps that do not apply.*

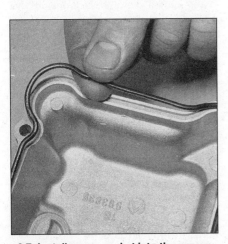

6.7 Install a new gasket into the groove

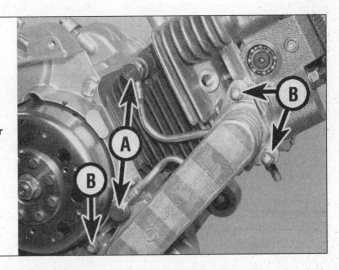

7.4 Oil pipe banjo bolts (A) and cooler mounting bolts (B)

8.4 Cam chain tensioner cap bolt (arrow)

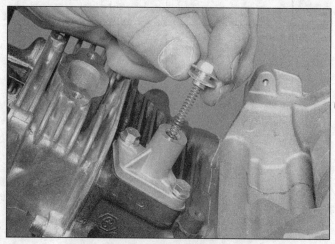

8.5a Remove the cap bolt and spring . . .

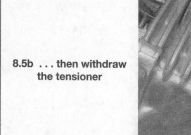

8.5b . . . then withdraw the tensioner

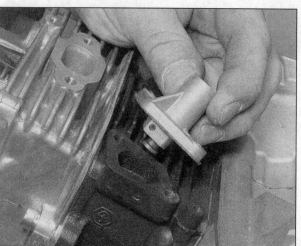

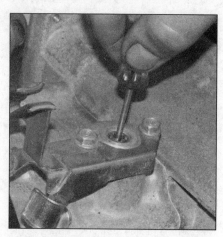

8.5c Use a small screwdriver to retract the plunger . . .

Removal

1 Remove the body panels as necessary to access the engine (see Chapter 9).

2 If necessary, displace the carburetor to access the cam chain tensioner (see Chapter 4).

3 On air-cooled engines, remove the screws securing the engine cowling and remove the cowling.

4 Undo the tensioner cap bolt (see illustration). Note any sealing washer or O-ring installed to the bolt and discard it, as a new one must be installed.

5 On some tensioners, the cap bolt retains a spring in the tensioner body; withdraw the spring, then unscrew the tensioner mounting bolts and withdraw the tensioner from the cylinder (see illustrations). On others, the tensioner is a sealed unit; to release the tensioner plunger before removing the tensioner, insert a small flat-bladed screwdriver into the end of the tensioner so that it engages the slotted plunger, then turn the screwdriver clockwise to retract the plunger. Hold the screwdriver in this position while undoing the tensioner mounting bolts and withdraw the tensioner from the cylinder (see illustrations). Release the screwdriver – the plunger will be released, but it can easily be reset for installation.

6 Remove the gasket from the base of the tensioner or from the cylinder and discard it, as a new one must be used.

Inspection

7 Examine the tensioner components for signs of wear or damage.

8 Release the ratchet mechanism from the tensioner plunger and check that the plunger moves freely in and out of the tensioner body (see illustration).

8.5d . . . while the tensioner is removed

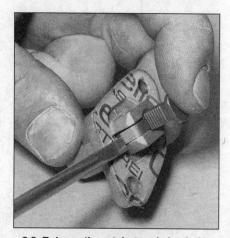

8.8 Release the ratchet and check the operation of the plunger

9.3a If equipped, remove the oil seal holder. . .

9.3b . . . and pry out the seal

9 Individual components are generally not available – if the tensioner or any of its components are worn or damaged, or if the plunger is seized in the body, a new tensioner must be installed.

Installation

10 Turn the engine in the normal direction of rotation using the kickstarter or a wrench on the alternator rotor nut. This removes all the slack between the crankshaft and the camshaft in the front run of the chain and transfers it to the back run where it will be taken up by the tensioner.

11 Install a new gasket on the tensioner body.

12 If the spring has been removed from the tensioner, release the ratchet mechanism and press the tensioner plunger all the way into the tensioner body (see illustration 8.8). Install the tensioner in the cylinder and tighten the bolts. Install a new sealing washer on the cap bolt, then install the spring and tighten the bolt securely.

13 If the tensioner is a sealed unit, retract the plunger as before with a small screwdriver, then hold it in this position while the tensioner is installed and the mounting bolts are tightened. The plunger should extend when the screwdriver is withdrawn. Install a new washer or O-ring to the cap bolt and tighten the bolt securely.

14 It is advisable to remove the valve cover (see Section 6) and check that the cam chain is tensioned. If it is slack, the tensioner plunger did not release. Remove the tensioner and check the operation of the plunger again.

15 Install the remaining components in the reverse order of removal.

9 Cam chain, blades and sprockets – removal, inspection and installation

Note 1: *This procedure can be carried out with the engine in the frame, although on* *some scooters, access to the top of the engine is extremely restricted.*

Note 2: *The general procedure for removing the cam chain, blades and sprockets is the same for all engines. However, since the positioning of the cam chain differs according to manufacturer, it will be necessary to remove components from the left- or right-hand side of the engine as applicable.*

Removal

1 Remove the valve cover (see Section 6).

2 On some engines, the camshaft is supported in a journal on the outside of the camshaft sprocket. On these engines, follow the procedure below to remove the sprocket and chain from the camshaft, but note that the camshaft itself must be removed in order to remove the sprocket and chain from the engine (see Section 10).

3 If the cam chain and, in some cases, the tensioner blade is being removed, access to the crankcase and crankshaft will be required. If the cam chain is on the left-hand side of the engine, refer to the procedure in Chapter 6 and remove the variator. If the left-hand crankcase oil seal is installed in a holder behind the variator, remove the holder and the seal (see illustrations). If the oil pump is driven by a chain from the left-hand side of the crankshaft, remove the oil pump driven sprocket, drive chain and drive sprocket (see Section 18). If the cam chain is on the right-hand side of the engine, remove the alternator (see Section 16). If the oil pump drive is on the right-hand side, remove the oil pump driven sprocket, drive chain and drive sprocket (see Section 18).

4 If not already done, remove the spark plug.

5 Turn the crankshaft in the normal direction of rotation, using a wrench on the alternator rotor nut, until the piston is at top dead center (TDC) on the compression stroke (all valves are closed and a small clearance can be felt at each rocker arm).

6 Look for timing marks on the camshaft sprocket and the camshaft holder or cylinder head, or alternatively, look for timing marks on the alternator rotor and the crankcase to confirm the position of the piston (see Chapter 1, Section 32). Note the alignment of the timing marks.

7 Remove the cam chain tensioner (see Section 8).

8 If an automatic decompressor mechanism is installed to the camshaft sprocket, follow the procedure in Steps 18 to 26 to remove, inspect and install the mechanism.

9 If the camshaft is supported in a journal on the outside of the camshaft sprocket, undo the bolts securing the journal and remove it. Remove any dowels for safekeeping if they are loose.

10 Unscrew the bolt(s) securing the camshaft sprocket to the camshaft. To prevent the sprocket from turning, hold the alternator or use a suitable holding tool installed into the hole(s) in the sprocket (see illustration).

Note: *Some manufacturers recommend that new bolts and washers are used on reassembly – check with a scooter dealer.*

11 Draw the sprocket off the end of the camshaft, noting how it locates on the shaft, and disengage it from the camchain (see

9.10 Hold the sprocket and undo the sprocket bolts

9.11 Draw the sprocket off the shaft and out of the chain

9.12a Remove the crankshaft thrustwasher if equipped

9.12b Lower the camchain down the tunnel . . .

9.12c . . . and draw it out of the engine

9.12d Note how the sprocket locates on the pin (arrow)

illustration). Where installed, remove the sprocket spacer for safekeeping.

12 Mark the chain with paint so that if it is to be re-used, it can be installed in the same position. Where installed, remove the thrust-

9.13 The tensioner blade is secured by a pivot bolt (arrow)

washer from the end of the crankshaft, then lower the cam chain down its tunnel, slip it off the sprocket on the crankshaft, and draw it out of the engine **(see illustrations)**. On some engines the sprocket is a sliding fit on the shaft; remove the sprocket, noting how it fits **(see illustration)**.

13 If required, undo the bolt securing the cam chain tensioner blade and withdraw the blade, noting how it fits **(see illustration)**. The guide blade can be removed when the cylinder head has been removed (see Section 11).

Inspection

14 Check the sprockets for wear and damaged teeth, replacing them if necessary. If the sprocket teeth are worn, the chain is also worn and should be replaced. If the sprocket is a press-fit on the crankshaft, pull it off with a bearing puller. If access is limited, it may be necessary to remove the crankshaft assembly from the crankcases (see Sections 19 and 20).

15 Check the chain tensioner blade and

guide blade for wear or damage and replace them if necessary. Check the operation of the cam chain tensioner (see Section 8).

16 Where installed, check the components of the automatic decompressor mechanism (see Step 22)

Installation

17 Installation is the reverse of removal, noting the following:

Ensure the tensioner blade and guide blade are installed correctly.

Ensure any spacers and thrustwashers are installed correctly.

Ensure the piston is at TDC on the compression stroke and that all the timing marks align as described in Step 6.

Ensure any slack in the chain is in the back run where it will be taken up by the tensioner.

Use new bolts and washers to secure the camshaft sprocket if recommended by the manufacturer.

9.18a Undo the center bolt . . .

9.18b . . . and remove the cover

Caution: After installing the cam chain tensioner, turn the crankshaft and check that all the timing marks still align correctly. If the timing marks are not aligned exactly as described, the valve timing will be incorrect and the valves may strike the piston, causing extensive damage to the engine.

Automatic decompressor mechanism

Removal

18 Undo the camshaft sprocket center bolt and lift off the decompressor mechanism cover **(see illustrations)**. Hold the alternator to prevent the sprocket from turning.

19 Undo the decompressor mechanism bolt, then hold the bob weight return spring and withdraw the bolt and static weight **(see illustrations)**.

20 Lift off the bob weight – note the nylon bushing on the back of the weight and how it locates in the slot in the cam chain sprocket **(see illustration)**. Remove the bushing for safekeeping.

21 Lift the sprocket and its backing plate off

9.19a Undo the automatic decompressor mechanism bolt . . .

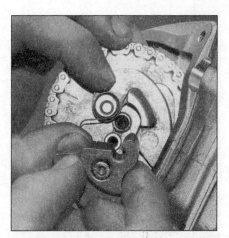

9.19b . . . and remove the static weight

the end of the camshaft, then disengage it from the camchain **(see illustration)**.

Inspection

22 Inspect the components of the decompressor mechanism. Check the nylon bush-

ing for wear and flat spots and replace it if necessary. Temporarily assemble the mechanism on the camshaft (start at Step 23) and check its operation – check the spring tension and ensure the bob weight does not bind on the cover.

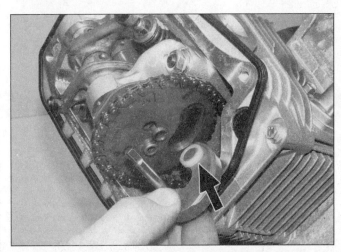

9.20 Note how the bushing (arrow) locates in the slot

9.21 Disengage the sprocket from the camchain

9.23a Install the camshaft sprocket backing plate . . .

9.23b . . . and the camshaft sprocket

10.1 Remove the rubber pad (if equipped)

10.4 Mark the end of the camshaft to aid reassembly

Installation

23 Check that the piston is at TDC on the compression stroke (see Step 6). Install the camshaft sprocket backing plate on the end of the camshaft (see illustration). Slip the camshaft sprocket into the top of the chain, then take up the slack in the lower run of the chain and install the sprocket onto the camshaft, aligning the timing mark on the sprocket with the index mark on the camshaft holder (see illustration). Note: To prevent the backing plate falling off the end of the camshaft while the sprocket is being installed, pass the blade of a small screwdriver through the center of the sprocket, the backing plate and the camshaft.

24 Apply some silicone grease to the nylon bushing and install it onto the back of the cam timing bob weight, then install the bob weight – ensure the bushing locates in the slot in the cam chain sprocket (see illustration 9.20).

25 Lift the bob weight return spring and install the static weight, ensuring that the spring is located over the top of the static weight. Tighten the decompressor mecha-

nism bolt to the specified torque setting. Check the operation of the mechanism – the bob weight should move freely on its spindle and return to the rest position under the tension of the spring.

26 Install the decompressor mechanism cover, aligning the small hole in the cover with the head of the mechanism bolt. Install the camshaft sprocket center bolt and tighten it securely. Hold the alternator to prevent the sprocket from turning.

10 Camshaft and rockers – removal, inspection and installation

Note: This procedure can be carried out with the engine in the frame, although on some scooters, access to the top of the engine is extremely restricted.

Removal

1 Remove the valve cover (see Section 6). Where installed, remove the rubber insulating

pad from the top of the camshaft holder for safekeeping, noting how it fits (see illustration).

2 Remove the cam chain tensioner (see Section 8).

3 Where possible, remove the camshaft sprocket (see Section 9), then secure the cam chain using a cable tie to prevent it dropping into the engine. If the camshaft is supported in a journal on the outside of the camshaft sprocket, remove the journal, then displace the sprocket and lift off the chain (see Section 9).

4 Stuff a clean rag into the cam chain tunnel to prevent anything falling into the engine. Mark the end of the camshaft so that it can be installed in the same position (TDC, all valves closed) (see illustration).

5 On some engines, the camshaft and rockers are located in a separate holder. If the holder is retained by long studs that also secure the cylinder head and cylinder to the crankcases, check to see if the head is also secured by any smaller bolts, and if so, undo them first (see illustration). Now unscrew the camshaft holder nuts or bolts, evenly

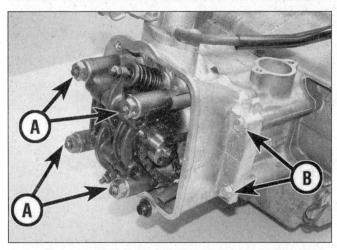

10.5a The camshaft holder is retained by four nuts (A), but the smaller bolts (B) must be loosened first

10.5b Lift off the camshaft holder

and a little at a time in a criss-cross pattern, until they are all loose, then remove them. Lift off the camshaft holder (see illustration). If the camshaft remains in the cylinder head, lift it out and remove the sprocket, then detach the chain; secure the chain to prevent it dropping into the engine. If the camshaft is in the camshaft holder, remove the retaining plate or snap-ring and withdraw the camshaft from the holder (see illustrations). Note that the bearings may come out with the camshaft.

6 If the camshaft housing is an integral part of the cylinder head, remove the retaining plate or snap-ring and withdraw the camshaft (see illustrations). Note that the bearings, where installed, may come out with the camshaft.

7 Mark the rocker arms so that they can be installed in their original positions. On some engines, the rocker shafts are retained in the camshaft housing by the camshaft housing bolts; once the housing has been removed, withdraw the shafts carefully and remove the rockers, noting the position of any thrustwashers on the shafts. On other engines, the

shafts are retained by a stopper bolt or snap-ring; remove the bolt or snap-ring, as applicable, and withdraw the shafts. Assemble the rockers and any thrustwashers on their shafts in the correct order so that they can be installed in their original positions. **Note:** *On*

some engines the rockers are located on one shaft, on others the intake and exhaust valve rockers have separate shafts. On engines with four-valve heads, the rockers are forked so that they bear on two valves simultaneously.

10.5c Remove the snap-ring . . .

10.5d . . . and withdraw the camshaft

10.6a Remove the retaining plate . . .

10.6b . . . and withdraw the camshaft

10.9 Measuring the camshaft lobe height with a micrometer

10.12 Inspect the contact surfaces (arrows) on the rocker arms for wear and pitting

Inspection

8 Clean all of the components with a suitable solvent and dry them.

9 Inspect the camshaft lobes for heat discoloration (blue appearance), score marks, chipped areas, flat spots and spalling. Measure each camshaft lobe height with a micrometer and compare the results with the specifications in the *Data* section at the end of this manual **(see illustration)**. If damage is noted or wear is excessive, the camshaft must be replaced.

10 Check the condition of the camshaft bearings and replace them if necessary (see *Tools and Workshop Tips* in the *Reference* Section). If the bearing is on the camshaft it must be removed using a suitable bearing puller to avoid damaging the shaft. If the bearing is in the housing or cylinder head, it may be possible to remove it with a bearing driver or suitable socket that bears on the outer race only. Alternatively, a puller will be required. **Note:** *Take great care when removing the bearings to avoid damaging other components. If necessary, consult a scooter*

dealer or repair shop.

11 If the camshaft runs directly in the cylinder head, inspect the bearing surfaces of the head and camshaft holder and the corresponding journals on the camshaft. Look for score marks, scratches and spalling. If damage is noted the relevant parts must be replaced.

12 Blow through the oil passages in the rocker arms with compressed air, if available. Inspect the face of the rocker arm and the contact area between the adjuster screw and the valve stem for pits and spalling **(see illustration)**. Where installed, check the articulated tip of the adjuster screw for wear; the tip should move freely, but not be loose. Check the rocker shaft for wear; if available, use a micrometer to measure the diameter of the shaft in several places - any difference in the measurements is an indication of wear. Assemble the rocker arm on its shaft – it should be a sliding fit with no discernible freeplay. Replace any components that are worn or damaged.

Installation

13 Installation is the reverse of removal, noting the following:

    Ensure the piston is at TDC on the compression stroke before you start.

    Lubricate the shafts, bearing surfaces and bearings with clean engine oil before installation.

    It is good practice to use new snaprings, where installed.

    Tighten the main cylinder head fasteners before any smaller bolts.

    Tighten the cylinder head fasteners a little at a time in a criss-cross sequence to the torque setting specified in the Data section.

    Check the valve clearances (see Chapter 1).

11 Cylinder head – removal and installation

Caution: *The engine must be completely cool before beginning this procedure or the cylinder head may become warped.*

Note: *On most scooters, this procedure can be carried out with the engine in the frame. However, in some cases there is insufficient clearance between the cylinder head and the frame to allow the head to be removed. If so, support the rear frame, then detach the lower end of the rear shock absorber(s) and displace the shock(s). Raise the rear wheel until there is enough clearance to remove the head.*

Removal

1 If equipped, remove the oil cooler (see Section 7).

2 Remove the carburetor and exhaust system (see Chapter 4).

3 On liquid-cooled engines, drain the cool-

11.5a Undo the smaller bolts (arrows) first . . .

11.5b . . . then undo the main nuts (arrows)

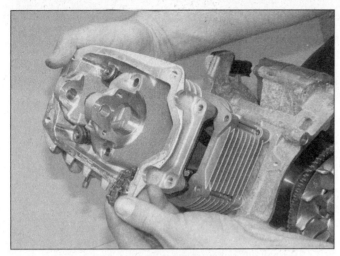

11.6 Lift off the cylinder head

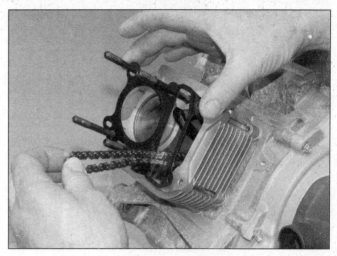

11.7a Discard the old cylinder head gasket

ing system (see Chapter 3). Detach the coolant hoses from the fittings on the cylinder head, noting where they fit. Disconnect the coolant temperature sensor wiring connector. If required, remove the thermostat housing (see Chapter 3).

4 Remove the camshaft and rockers (see Section 10). **Note:** *On some engines it is possible to remove the cylinder head with the camshaft and rockers in place, but in practice, the camshaft and rockers must be removed in order to service the valves. The fasteners for the camshaft holder may also secure the cylinder head.*

5 Check to see which bolts secure the cylinder head; on some engines, in addition to the main internal fasteners, the head is also secured by smaller, external bolts. Undo the smaller bolts first, then undo the main nuts or bolts, evenly and a little at a time in a crisscross pattern, until they are all loose, and remove them **(see illustrations).**

6 Lift the cylinder head off carefully, feeding the cam chain down through the tunnel in the head **(see illustration)**. If the head is stuck, tap around the joint face between the head and the cylinder with a soft-faced mallet to free it. Do not try to lever the head off, as this may damage the sealing surfaces. **Note:** *Avoid lifting the cylinder off the crankcase when the head is removed, otherwise a new cylinder base gasket will have to be installed (see Section 13).*

7 Remove the old cylinder head gasket and discard it, as a new one must be installed on reassembly; note any dowels in the head or cylinder and remove them for safekeeping if they are loose **(see illustrations).**

8 Secure the cam chain to prevent it dropping into the engine.

9 Inspect the cylinder head gasket and the mating surfaces on the cylinder head and cylinder for signs of leaks, which could indicate that the head is warped. Refer to Section 12 and check the head mating surface for warpage.

10 Clean all traces of old gasket material from the cylinder head and cylinder with a suitable solvent. Take care not to scratch or gouge the soft aluminium. Be careful not to let any of the gasket material fall into the crankcase, the cylinder bore or the oil or coolant passages.

Installation

11 Installation is the reverse of removal, noting the following:

Lubricate the cylinder bore with clean engine oil.

Install a new head gasket – never re-use the old gasket.

Ensure the oil and coolant holes in the gasket align with the cylinder.

Tighten the main cylinder head fasteners first before the smaller, external bolts.

Tighten the main cylinder head fasteners evenly and a little at a time in a crisscross pattern to the torque setting specified in the Data section.

On liquid-cooled engines, refill the cooling system.

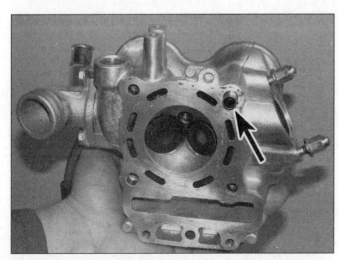

11.7b Note the position of dowels (arrow) in the head . . .

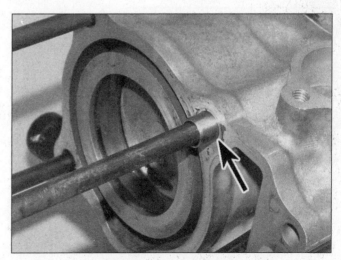

11.7c . . . or the cylinder

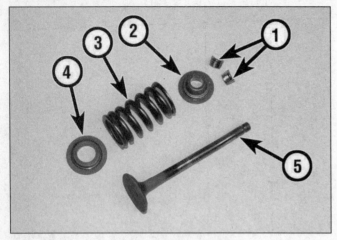

12.1 Valve components

1 Keepers
2 Spring retainer
3 Valve spring

4 Spring seat
5 Valve

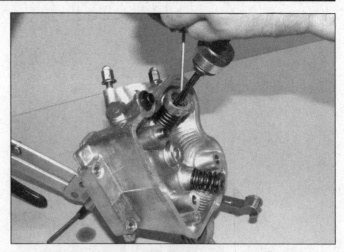

12.3 Compress the valve spring carefully and remove
the keepers

12 Cylinder head and valves – disassembly, inspection and reassembly

Note: If a valve spring compressor is available, the home mechanic can remove the valves from the cylinder head, grind in the valves and replace the valve stem seal. If the necessary measuring tools are available, you can assess the amount of wear on the valves and guides and measure the valve-to-seat contact areas.

Disassembly

1 Before you start, arrange to label and store the valves and their related components so that they can be returned to their original locations without getting mixed up (see illustration).
2 If not already done, clean all traces of old gasket material from the cylinder head with a

suitable solvent. Take care not to scratch or gouge the soft aluminium. On liquid-cooled engines, if the thermostat is installed in the cylinder head, remove the thermostat (see Chapter 3).
3 Compress the valve spring on the first valve with a spring compressor, making sure it is correctly located onto each end of the valve assembly (see illustration). On the underside of the head, make sure the plate on the compressor only contacts the valve and not the soft aluminium of the head – if the plate is too big for the valve, use a spacer between them. Do not compress the spring any more than is absolutely necessary to release the keepers.
4 Remove the keepers, using either needle-nose pliers, a magnet or a screwdriver with a dab of grease on it. Carefully release the valve spring/compressor and remove the spring retainer (noting which way up it fits), the spring, the spring seat, and the valve from the head. If the valve binds in the guide (won't pull through), push it back into the head and deburr the area around the keeper

groove with a very fine file (see illustration).
Note: On some engines, two springs are installed to each valve.
5 Once the valve has been removed, pull the valve stem oil seal off the top of the valve guide with pliers and discard it, as a new one must be used on reassembly (see illustration).
6 Repeat the procedure for the remaining valve(s). Remember to keep the parts for each valve together and in order so they can be reinstalled in the correct location.
7 Next, clean the cylinder head with solvent and dry it thoroughly. Compressed air will speed the drying process and ensure that all holes and recessed areas are clean.
8 Clean the valve springs, keepers, retainers and spring seats with solvent. Work on the parts from one valve at a time so as not to mix them up.
9 Scrape off any carbon deposits that may have formed on the valve, then use a motorized wire brush to remove deposits from the valve heads and stems. Again, make sure the valves do not get mixed up.

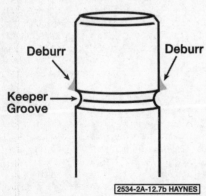

12.4 If the valve binds in the guide, deburr the area above the keeper groove

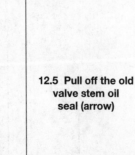

12.5 Pull off the old valve stem oil seal (arrow)

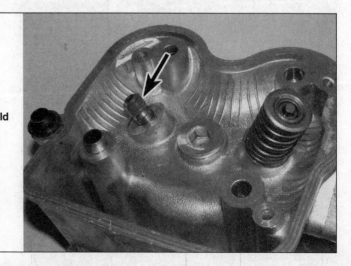

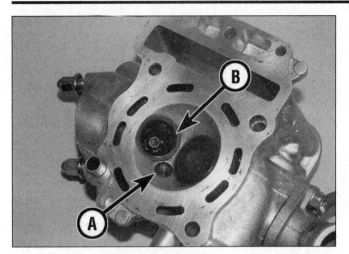

12.10 Check the head for cracks. Inspect the spark plug hole (A) and the valve seats (B)

12.12 Check the cylinder head for warpage in the directions shown

Inspection

10 Inspect the head very carefully for cracks and other damage **(see illustration)**. If cracks are found, a new head will be required.

11 Inspect the threads in the spark plug hole. Damaged or worn threads can be reclaimed using a thread insert (see *Tools and Workshop Tips* in the *Reference* section). Most scooter dealers and machine shops offer a service of this kind.

12 Using a precision straight-edge and a feeler gauge, check the head mating surface for warpage. Lay the straight-edge across the surface and try to slip the feeler gauge under it on either side of the combustion chamber. If the feeler gauge can be inserted between the straight-edge and the cylinder head, the head is warped and must be either machined or, if warpage is excessive, replaced. Check vertically, horizontally and diagonally across the head, making four checks in all **(see illustration)**. If there is any doubt about the condition of the head, consult a scooter dealer or machine shop.

13 Examine the valve seats in the combustion chamber. If they are deeply pitted,

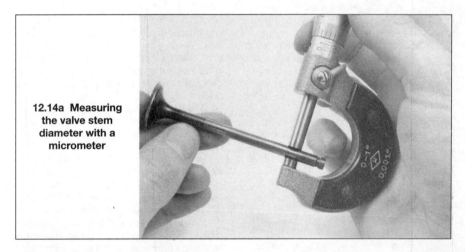

12.14a Measuring the valve stem diameter with a micrometer

cracked or burned, it may be possible to have them repaired and recut by a specialist engineer, otherwise a new head will be required. The valve seats should be a uniform width all the way around **(see illustration 12.10)**.

14 If available, use a micrometer to measure

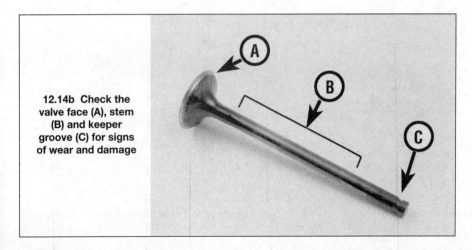

12.14b Check the valve face (A), stem (B) and keeper groove (C) for signs of wear and damage

the valve stem diameter in several places **(see illustration)**. Any difference in the measurements is an indication of wear. Inspect the valve face for cracks, pits and burned spots. Check the valve stem and the collet groove area for cracks **(see illustration)**. Rotate the valve and check for any obvious indication that it is bent. Check the end of the stem for pitting and excessive wear. If any of the above conditions are found, install a new valve. If the stem end is pitted or worn, also check the contact area of the adjuster screw in the rocker arm.

15 Insert a known good valve into its guide – it should be a sliding fit with no discernible freeplay. If there is freeplay, the guide is probably worn. Have the guides checked by a scooter dealer or machine shop. If new valve guides are available, have them installed by a specialist who will also recut the valve seats. If new guides are not available, a machine shop may be able to bore out the old ones and install sleeves in them. Otherwise a new cylinder head will have to be installed. **Note:** *Carbon build-up inside the guide is an indication of wear.*

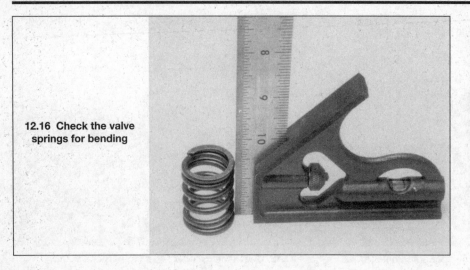

12.16 Check the valve springs for bending

12.19 Apply the grinding compound sparingly, in small dabs, to the valve face only

16 Check the end of each valve spring for wear and pitting. Stand the spring upright on a flat surface and check it for bend by placing a square against it **(see illustration)**. If the spring is worn, or the bend is excessive, it must be replaced. Some manufacturers specify a service limit for the spring free length (consult a scooter dealer), but it is good practice to install new springs when the head has been disassembled for valve servicing. Always install new valve springs as a set.

17 Check the spring retainers and keepers for obvious wear and cracks. Any questionable parts should not be re-used, as extensive damage will occur in the event of failure during engine operation.

Reassembly

18 Unless the valve seats have been recut, before installing the valves in the head, they should be ground-in (lapped) to ensure a positive seal between the valves and seats. This procedure requires coarse and fine valve grinding compound and a valve grinding tool. If a grinding tool is not available, a piece of rubber or plastic hose can be slipped over the valve stem (after the valve has been installed in the guide) and used to turn the valve.

19 Apply a small amount of coarse grinding compound to the valve face, then slip the valve into the guide **(see illustration)**. **Note:** *Make sure each valve is installed in its correct guide and be careful not to get any grinding compound on the valve stem.*

20 Attach the grinding tool (or hose) to the valve and rotate the tool between the palms of your hands. Use a back-and-forth motion (as though rubbing your hands together) rather than a circular motion, so that the valve rotates alternately clockwise and counterclockwise rather than in one direction only **(see illustration)**. Lift the valve off the seat and turn it at regular intervals to distribute the grinding compound properly. Continue the grinding procedure until the valve face and seat contact areas are of uniform width and unbroken around the circumference **(see illustration)**.

21 Carefully remove the valve from the guide and wipe off all traces of grinding compound. Use solvent to clean the valve and wipe the seat area thoroughly with a solvent-soaked cloth.

22 Repeat the procedure with fine valve grinding compound, then repeat the entire procedure for the other valve(s).

HAYNES HINT *Check for proper sealing of each valve by pouring a small amount of solvent into the valve port while holding the valve shut. If the solvent leaks past the valve into the combustion chamber, the valve grinding operation should be repeated.*

23 Working on one valve at a time, lay the spring seat in place in the cylinder head, then install a new valve stem seal onto the guide. Use an appropriate size deep socket to push the seal over the end of the valve guide until it is felt to clip into place. Don't twist or cock it, or it will not seal properly against the valve stem. Also, don't remove it again or it will be damaged.

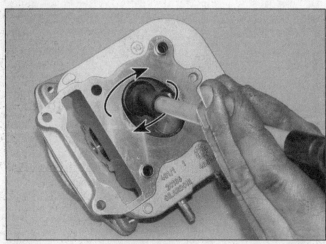

12.20a Rotate the grinding tool back and forth between the palms of your hands

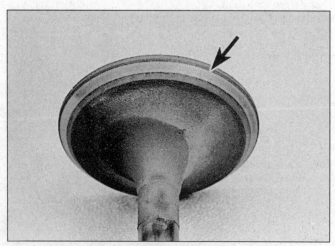

12.20b The valve face and seat should show a uniform unbroken ring

12.25 A small dab of grease helps to keep the keepers in place during installation

13.3 Lift out the cam chain guide blade

24 Lubricate the valve stem with molybdenum disulphide grease, then install it into its guide, rotating it slowly to avoid damaging the seal. Check that the valve moves up and down freely in the guide. Next, install the spring, with its closer-wound coils facing down into the cylinder head, followed by the spring retainer, with its shouldered side facing down so that it fits into the top of the spring. **Note:** *On some engines, two springs are installed to each valve.*

25 Apply a small amount of grease to the keepers to hold them in place as the pressure is released from the spring. Compress the spring with the valve spring compressor and install the keepers **(see illustration)**. When compressing the spring, depress it only as far as is absolutely necessary to slip the keepers into place. Make certain that the keepers are securely locked in their retaining grooves.

26 Repeat the procedure for the remaining valve(s).

27 Support the cylinder head on blocks so the valves can't contact the workbench top,

then very gently tap each of the valve stems with a soft-faced hammer. This will help seat the keepers in their grooves.

13 Cylinder – removal, inspection and installation

Note: *On most scooters, this procedure can be carried out with the engine in the frame. However, in some cases there is insufficient clearance between the cylinder and the frame to allow the cylinder to be removed. If so, support the rear frame, then detach the lower end of the rear shock absorber(s) and displace the shock(s). Raise the rear wheel until there is enough clearance to remove the cylinder.*

Removal

1 Remove the cylinder head (see Section 11).

2 On liquid-cooled engines, where applicable, detach the coolant hose from the cylinder (see Chapter 3).

3 Note the location of the cam chain guide blade, then lift out the blade **(see illustration)**.

4 Where installed, undo the bolt(s) securing the cylinder to the crankcase **(see illustration)**.

5 Lift the cylinder up off the crankcase, supporting the piston as it becomes accessible to prevent it hitting the crankcase opening **(see illustration)**. If the cylinder is stuck, tap around the joint face between the cylinder and the crankcase with a soft-faced mallet to free it. Don't attempt to free the cylinder by inserting a screwdriver between it and the crankcase – you'll damage the sealing surfaces. When the cylinder is removed, stuff a clean rag into the crankcase opening around the piston to prevent anything falling inside.

6 Remove the cylinder base gasket and discard it, as a new one must be installed on reassembly.

13.4 Bolt (arrow) secures the cylinder to the crankcase

13.5 Support the piston as the cylinder is removed

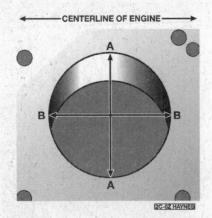

13.8 Measure the cylinder diamater in two directions, at the top, center and bottom of travel

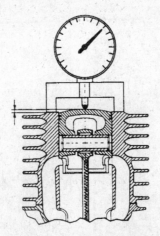

13.21 Set-up for checking the cylinder surface-to-piston crown relationship

Inspection

7 Check the cylinder bore carefully for scratches and score marks.

8 If available, use a telescoping gauge and micrometer to measure the diameter of the cylinder bore to assess the amount of wear, taper and ovality (see *Tools and Workshop Tips* in the *Reference* section). Measure near the top (but below the level of the top piston ring at TDC), center and bottom (but above the level of the bottom ring at BDC) of the bore both parallel to and across the crankshaft axis **(see illustration)**. Calculate any differences between the measurements to determine any taper or ovality in the bore.

9 Now measure an unworn part of the cylinder bore (below the level of the bottom ring at BDC) and compare the result to the previous measurements to determine overall wear.

10 If the bore is tapered, oval, worn excessively, or badly scratched, scuffed or scored, the cylinder and piston will have to be replaced. **Note:** *If no service limit specifications (see Data section) are available to assess cylinder wear, calculate the piston-to-bore clearance to determine whether the cylinder is useable (see Section 14). Alternatively, check for a lip around the (unworn) top edge of the cylinder bore as a rough indication of wear.*

11 If there is any doubt about the serviceability of the cylinder, consult a scooter dealer. **Note:** *On some engines, the surface of the cylinder has a wear-resistant coating which, when damaged or worn through, requires a new cylinder. On others, the cylinder can be rebored and an oversize piston installed (see Data section). Oversize pistons are not necessarily marked as such; in many cases the only way to determine if a cylinder has been rebored is to measure an unworn area of the bore and compare the result with the specifications in the Data section. Some manufacturers mark cylinders and pistons with a size code during production; the size code (usually a letter) is stamped into the cylinder gasket surface and the top of the*

piston. It is important that new parts have matching codes.

12 Where installed, check that all the cylinder head studs are tight in the crankcase halves. If any are loose, remove them and clean their threads. Apply a suitable permanent thread locking compound and tighten them securely.

Installation

Note: *On some engines, cylinder base gaskets are available in a range of thicknesses; the appropriate thickness depends on the height of the piston crown at TDC in relation to the cylinder top gasket surface. Consult a scooter dealer for details. In these instances, the correct gasket thickness must be calculated before reassembly (see Steps 21 to 25).*

13 Check that the mating surfaces of the cylinder and crankcase are clean, then remove any rag from the crankcase opening. Lay the new base gasket in place on the crankcase, making sure it is correctly installed.

14 If required, install a piston ring clamp onto the piston to ease its entry into the bore as the cylinder is lowered. This is not essential if the cylinder has a good lead-in enabling the piston rings to be hand-fed into the bore.

If possible, have an assistant to support the cylinder while this is done. Check that the piston ring end gaps are positioned as described in Section 15.

15 Lubricate the cylinder bore, piston and piston rings, and the connecting rod big- and small-ends, with the clean engine oil, then lower the cylinder down until the piston crown fits into the bore.

16 Gently push down on the cylinder, making sure the piston enters the bore squarely and does not get cocked sideways. If a piston ring clamp is not being used, carefully compress and feed each ring into the bore as the cylinder is lowered. If necessary, use a soft mallet to gently tap the cylinder down, but do not use force if it appears to be stuck, as the piston and/or rings will be damaged. If a clamp is used, remove it once the piston is in the bore.

17 When the piston is correctly installed in the cylinder, check that the base gasket has not been displaced, then press the cylinder down onto the base gasket.

18 Install the cylinder bolt(s) finger-tight only at this stage (see Step 4).

19 Install the cam chain guide blade, then install the cylinder head (see Section 11).

20 Tighten the cylinder bolt(s) and, on liquid-cooled engines, install the coolant hose on the cylinder and secure it with the clip.

Cylinder base gasket thickness

21 To measure the height of the piston crown at TDC in relation to the cylinder top gasket surface you will require a dial gauge and a mounting plate **(see illustration)**.

22 Assemble the cylinder on the piston as described in Steps 13 to 16, but without a base gasket, and press the cylinder down onto the crankcase.

23 Clamp the mounting plate across the top of the cylinder using the cylinder fixings and tighten them to ensure that the cylinder is held firmly against the crankcase. Rotate the crankshaft so that the piston is part way down the bore.

24 Set the dial gauge on the mounting plate, and with the gauge tip resting against the cylinder top gasket surface, zero the gauge **(see illustration)**.

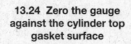

13.24 Zero the gauge against the cylinder top gasket surface

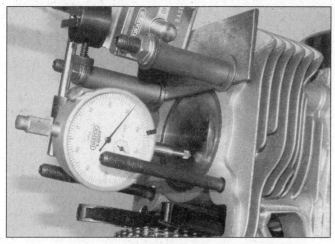

13.25 Measuring the piston height at TDC

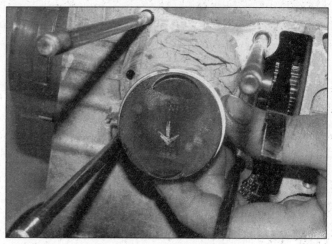

14.2 Mark the top of the piston

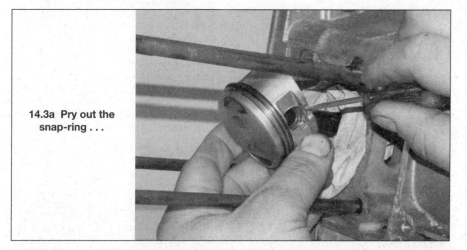

14.3a Pry out the snap-ring . . .

side of the piston using needle-nose pliers or a small flat-bladed screwdriver inserted into the notch **(see illustration)**. Check for burring around the snap-ring groove and remove any with a very fine file or penknife blade, then push the piston pin out from the other side and remove the piston from the connecting rod **(see illustration)**. Use a socket extension to push the piston pin out if required. Remove the other snap-ring and discard them both, as new ones must be used on reassembly.

 HAYNES HiNT *To prevent the snap-ring from flying away or from dropping into the crankcase, pass a rod or screwdriver, with a greater diameter than the gap between the snap-ring ends, through the piston pin. This will trap the snap-ring if it springs out.*

 HAYNES HiNT *If the piston pin is a tight fit in the piston bosses, heat the piston gently with a hot air gun – this will expand the alloy piston sufficiently to release its grip on the pin.*

25 Now rest the gauge tip against the top of the piston. Rotate the crankshaft via the alternator rotor nut so the piston rises to the top of its stroke (TDC). At this point read off the dial gauge **(see illustration)**. The reading represents the distance between the cylinder top gasket surface and the top of the piston crown. Use this measurement, together with the manufacturer's information, to identify the appropriate gasket thickness.

direction it should be installed. If no mark is visible, scratch one lightly on the top of the piston **(see illustration)**. Note that the manufacturer's mark may not be visible until the carbon deposits have been scraped off and the piston cleaned.

3 Carefully pry out the snap-ring on one

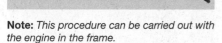

14 Piston – removal, inspection and installation

Note: *This procedure can be carried out with the engine in the frame.*

Removal

1 Remove the cylinder and stuff a clean rag into the crankcase opening around the piston to prevent anything falling inside (see Section 13).

2 The top of the piston should be marked with an arrow or lettering (IN on the intake side, nearest the carburetor) to show which

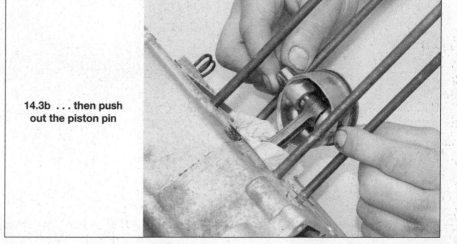

14.3b . . . then push out the piston pin

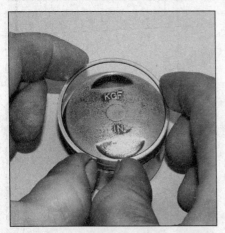

14.4 Remove the piston rings carefully

14.8 Manufacturer's mark on piston crown

4 Before the inspection process can be carried out, the piston rings must be removed and the piston must be cleaned. **Note:** *If the cylinder is being rebored, piston inspection can be overlooked as a new one will be installed.* The piston rings can be removed by hand; using your thumbs, ease the ends of each ring apart and carefully lift it off the piston, taking care not to expand it any more than is necessary **(see illustration)**. Do not nick or gouge the piston in the process.

5 Note which way up each ring fits and in which groove, as they must be installed in their original positions if being re-used. The upper surface of each ring should be marked at one end (see Section 15). Some pistons are installed with a three-piece third (oil control) ring; there will be an upper and lower side rail and a central rail spacer. **Note:** *It is good practice to replace the piston rings when an engine is being overhauled. Ensure that the piston and bore are serviceable before purchasing new rings.*

6 Clean all traces of carbon from the top of the piston. A hand-held wire brush or a piece of fine emery cloth can be used once most of the deposits have been scraped away. Do not, under any circumstances, use a wire brush mounted in a drill motor; the piston material is soft and is easily damaged.

7 Use a piston ring groove cleaning tool to remove any carbon deposits from the ring grooves. If a tool is not available, a piece broken off an old ring will do the job. Be very careful to remove only the carbon deposits. Do not remove any metal and do not nick or gouge the sides of the ring grooves.

8 Once the carbon has been removed, clean the piston with a suitable solvent and dry it thoroughly. If the identification previously marked on the piston is cleaned off, be sure to re-mark it correctly **(see illustration)**.

Inspection

9 Inspect the piston for cracks around the skirt, at the pin bosses and at the ring lands. Check that the snap-ring grooves are not damaged. Normal piston wear appears as even, vertical wear on the thrust surfaces of the piston and slight looseness of the top ring in its groove. If the skirt is scored or scuffed, the engine may have been suffering from overheating and/or abnormal combustion, which caused excessively high operating temperatures.

10 A hole in the top of the piston, in one extreme, or burned areas around the edge of the piston crown, indicate that pre-ignition or knocking under load have occurred. If you find evidence of any problems, the cause must be corrected or the damage will occur again. Refer to Chapter 4 for carburation checks and Chapter 5 for ignition checks.

11 Check the piston-to-bore clearance by measuring the cylinder bore (see Section 13) and the piston diameter. Measure the piston approximately 25 mm down from the bottom of the lower piston ring groove and at 90° to the piston pin axis **(see illustration)**. **Note:** *The precise point of measurement differs between manufacturers and engines, but the aim is to measure the piston in an area where it is worn.* Subtract the piston diameter from the bore diameter to obtain the clearance. If it is greater than the specified figure, check whether it is the bore or piston that is worn the most (see *Data* section at the end of this manual). If the bore is good, install a new piston and rings. **Note:** *Oversize pistons installed in a rebored cylinder are not necessarily marked as such; in many cases the only way to determine if a cylinder has been rebored is to measure an unworn area of the bore and compare the result with the specifications in the Data section. Some manufacturers mark cylinders and pistons with a size code during production; the size code (usually a letter) is stamped into the cylinder gasket surface and the top of the piston. It is important that new parts have matching codes. It is essential to supply the size code and any rebore specifications when purchasing a new piston.*

12 Use a micrometer to measure the piston pin in the middle, where it runs in the small-end bearing, and at each end where it runs in the piston **(see illustration)**. If there is any

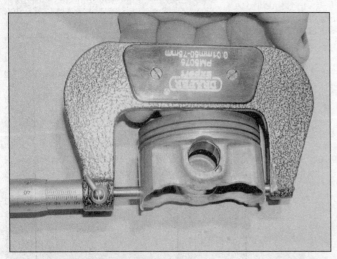

14.11 Measuring the piston diameter with a micrometer

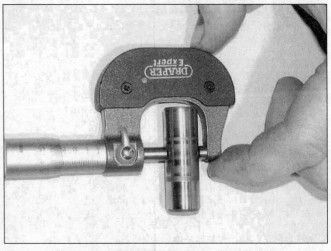

14.12 Measuring the diameter of the piston pin

14.13 Checking for freeplay between the piston and piston pin

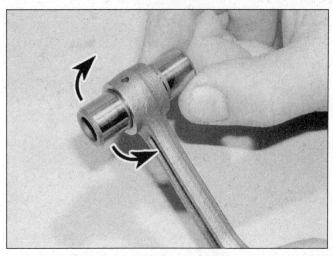

14.14 Rock the piston pin back-and-forth in the small-end to check for wear

difference in the measurements, the pin is worn and must be replaced.

13 If the piston pin is good, lubricate it with clean engine oil, then insert it into the piston and check for any freeplay between the two **(see illustration)**. There should be no freeplay.

14 Next, check the condition of the connecting rod small-end. A worn small-end will produce a metallic rattle, most audible when the engine is under load, and increasing as engine speed rises. This should not be confused with connecting rod bearing wear, which produces a pronounced knocking noise. Lubricate the piston pin with clean engine oil, then slide it into the small-end and check for freeplay **(see illustration)**. There should only be slightly discernible freeplay between the piston pin and the connecting rod.

15 If there is freeplay, measure the internal diameter of the connecting rod small-end **(see illustration)**. Take several measurements; if there is any difference between the measurements, the small end is worn and either a new connecting rod or crankshaft assembly will have to be installed (see Section 20). Consult a scooter dealer about the availability of parts. **Note:** *If a new rod is available, installing it is a specialized task which should be left to a scooter dealer or machine shop. If a new rod is installed, the connecting rod bearing should be replaced at the same time.*

16 If the small-end is good, install a new piston pin. **Note:** *On some engines, the piston pin and small-end are marked with a size code during production; look for identification marks or colors on the components and refer to them when ordering new parts.*

Installation

17 Install the piston rings (see Section 15).
18 Lubricate the piston pin, the piston pin bore in the piston and the connecting-rod small-end with clean engine oil.

19 Install a new snap-ring in one side of the piston, then line up the piston on the connecting rod, making sure it is correctly installed (see Step 2), and insert the piston pin from the other side. Secure the pin with the other new snap-ring. When installing the snap-rings, compress them only just enough to fit them in the piston, and make sure they are properly seated in their grooves with the open end away from the removal notch.
20 Install the cylinder (see Section 13).

15 Piston rings – inspection and installation

1 New piston rings should be installed whenever an engine is being overhauled. It is important that you get new rings of the correct size for your piston, so ensure that any information relating to piston size - including rebore size and size coding - is available when purchasing new parts.
2 Before installing the new rings onto the piston, the ring end gaps must be checked. Insert the top ring into the bottom of the cylinder bore and square it up by pushing it in

14.15 Measuring the internal diameter of the connecting rod small-end

with the top of the piston. The ring should be about 15 to 20 mm from the bottom edge of the cylinder. To measure the end gap, slip a feeler gauge between the ends of the ring and compare the measurement to the specification in the *Data* section at the end of this manual **(see illustration)**.

15.2 Measuring the installed piston ring end gap

15.6a Install the oil ring expander first . . .

15.6b . . . then the lower side rail

3 If the gap is larger or smaller than specified, check to make sure that you have the correct rings before proceeding. If the gap is larger than specified, it is likely the cylinder bore is worn. If the gap is too small, the ring ends may come into contact with each other during engine operation, causing serious damage.

4 Repeat the procedure for the other two rings. **Note:** *If the piston is installed with a three-piece third (oil control) ring, check the end gap on the upper and lower side rails only. The ends of the central rail spacer should contact each other when it is installed on the piston.*

5 Once the ring end gaps have been checked, the rings can be installed on the piston. Do not expand the rings any more than is necessary to slide them into place. **Note:** *A ring installation tool can be used on the two compression rings, and on a one-piece oil control ring, if desired, but not on the side rails of a three-piece oil control ring.*

6 The oil control ring (lowest on the piston) is installed first. If a three-piece ring is used, fit the rail spacer into the groove, then install the lower side rail **(see illustrations)**. Place one end of the side rail into the groove between the spacer and the lower ring land. Hold it firmly in place, then slide a finger around the piston while pushing the rail into the groove. Install the upper side rail the same way. Ensure the ends of the spacer touch but do not overlap, then check that both side rails turn smoothly in the ring groove.

7 Next install the 2nd compression ring, noting that there is usually a marking or letter near the gap to denote the upper surface of the ring. Finally install the top ring into its groove.

8 Once the rings are correctly installed, check they move freely without snagging, then stagger their end gaps before installing the piston into the cylinder **(see illustrations)**.

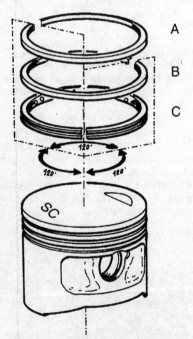

15.8a If a one-piece oil control ring is used, position the end gaps at 120°intervals

A   *First (top) compression ring*
B   *Second (middle) compression ring*
C   *Oil control ring*

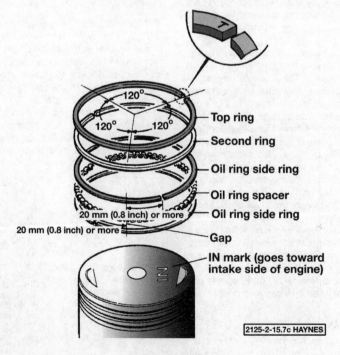

- Top ring
- Second ring
- Oil ring side ring
- Oil ring spacer
- Oil ring side ring
- Gap
- IN mark (goes toward intake side of engine)

20 mm (0.8 inch) or more
20 mm (0.8 inch) or more

2125-2-15.7c HAYNES

15.8b Ring details

16.2 Where necessary, remove the fan cowling

16.3 The water pump is driven by dampers on the alternator rotor

16 Alternator – removal and installation

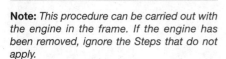

Note: *This procedure can be carried out with the engine in the frame. If the engine has been removed, ignore the Steps that do not apply.*

Removal

1 Remove the body panels as necessary to access the alternator (see Chapter 9). If required, remove the exhaust system (see Chapter 4).

2 On some air-cooled engines, the alternator is located behind the fan cowling. Unclip any wiring or hoses from the fan cowling, then undo the bolts securing the fan cowling and remove it **(see illustration)**. Note that on some models the fan cowling is clipped to the engine cowling – take care not to damage the fixing lugs when separating them. Remove any spacers for the cowling bolts for

safekeeping if they are loose. Undo the bolts securing the cooling fan to the alternator rotor and remove the fan (see Chapter 1, Section 21).

3 On liquid-cooled engines where the water pump is mounted on the outside of the alternator cover, first drain the coolant and disconnect all the coolant hoses from the pump (see Chapter 3). Undo the cover mounting bolts and lift off the cover. Depending on the tools available for removing the alternator rotor, it may be necessary to unscrew the pump drive dampers **(see illustration)**.

4 On some engines, the alternator is located behind the right-hand engine side cover. **Note:** *If the water pump is mounted on the outside of the engine side cover, first drain the coolant and disconnect all the coolant hoses from the pump (see Chapter 3). Drain the engine oil (see Chapter 1). Trace the wiring from the cover and disconnect it at the connector, then undo the cover bolts and lift off the cover* **(see illustration)**.

Discard the gasket, as a new one must be installed, and remove the cover dowels for safekeeping if they are loose. If applicable, remove the starter pinion assembly (see Section 17).

5 To remove the rotor center nut, it is necessary to stop the rotor from turning; some manufacturers produce a service tool for this purpose. If the rotor face is accessible, you can make up a tool which engages the slots or holes **(see illustration)**. **Note:** *Take great care not to damage the coils of the alternator when locating any tools through the rotor.*

HAYNES HINT *A rotor holding tool can easily be made using two strips of steel bolted together in the middle, with a bolt through each end which locates into the slots or holes in the rotor. Do not allow the bolts to extend too far through the rotor, otherwise the coils could be damaged.*

6 If the alternator stator is located in the engine side cover, the rotor can be held with

16.4 Lift off the side cover and alternator stator

16.5 Hold the rotor and undo the center nut (arrow)

16.6 Using a strap wrench to hold the rotor

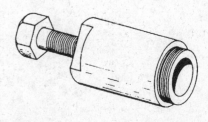

16.8a Typical service tool for removing the rotor

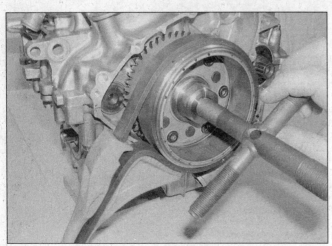

16.8b Using a screw-in type puller

16.8c Using a two-legged puller

a strap wrench **(see illustration)**.

7 With the rotor securely held, unscrew the center nut.

8 To remove the rotor from the shaft, it is necessary to use a puller – either a manufacturer's service tool or a commercially available puller **(see illustrations)**. To use the service tool, first screw the body of the tool all the way into the threads provided in the rotor. Hold the tool steady with a wrench on its flats and tighten the center bolt, exerting steady pressure to draw the rotor off the crankshaft. To use a puller, engage the puller legs either in the slots in the rotor or thread them into the threaded holes in the rotor, then tighten the center bolt, exerting steady pressure to draw the rotor off the crankshaft. Remove the Woodruff key from the shaft for safekeeping, noting how it fits **(see illustrations)**.

9 In most cases, the alternator stator coils

16.8d Remove the Woodruff key for safekeeping

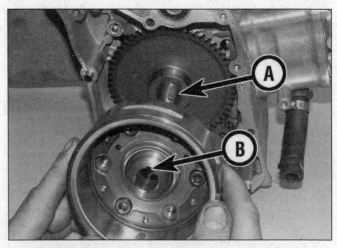

16.8e Note the alignment of the key (A) and the slot (B) in the rotor

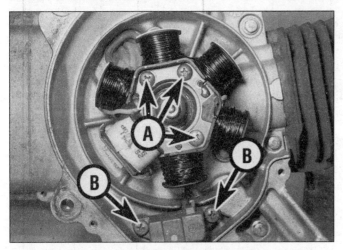

16.10a Undo the stator screws (A) and the pulse generator coil screws (B) . . .

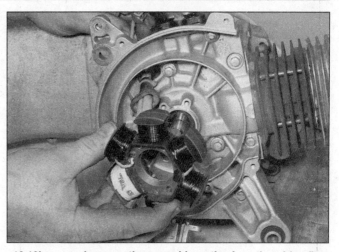

16.10b . . . and remove the assembly, noting how the wiring fits

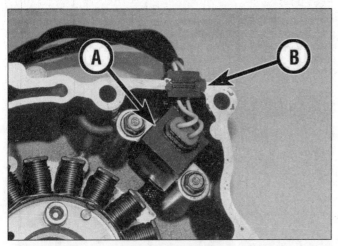

16.10c Note the position of the pulse generator (A) and the wiring grommet (B)

18.2 Undo the screws (arrows) and remove the cover

and ignition pulse generator coil are wired together and have to be removed as an assembly. If not already done, trace the wiring back from the alternator and pulse generator and disconnect it at the connectors. Free the wiring from any clips or guides and feed it through to the alternator.

10 Undo the screws securing the stator and the pulse generator and lift them off together. Where installed, draw any rubber wiring boot out of the crankcase or engine side cover and carefully pull the wiring away, noting how it fits **(see illustrations)**.

Installation

11 Installation is the reverse of removal, noting the following:

Ensure the wiring is correctly routed before installing the stator and pulse generator.

Make sure that no metal objects have attached themselves to the magnets on the inside of the rotor.

Clean the tapered end of the crankshaft and the corresponding mating sur-

face on the inside of the rotor with a suitable solvent.

Fit the Woodruff key into its slot in the shaft, then install the rotor.

Tighten the rotor center nut to the torque setting specified in the Data section at the end of this manual.

Secure the wiring with any clips or ties.

If applicable, fill the engine with the correct type and quantity of oil (see Chapter 1).

If applicable, refill the cooling system and bleed it (see Chapter 3).

17 Starter pinion assembly and starter clutch – removal, inspection and installation

Note: *This procedure can be carried out with the engine in the frame.*

The procedure for removal, inspection and installation of either the starter pinion assembly or the starter (one-way) clutch is the same as for two-stroke engines (see

Chapter 2A, Section 17). Note that details for removal of the alternator on four-stroke engines are given in Section 16.

18 Oil pump – removal, inspection and installation

Note 1: *Generally, the oil pump is located inside the engine unit and is chain-driven from either the left- or right-hand side of the crankshaft. On some engines, the pump drive sprocket is integral with the crankshaft.*

Note 2: *This procedure can be carried out with the engine in the frame.*

Removal

1 Remove either the variator (see Chapter 6) or the alternator rotor (see Section 16) as applicable.

2 The pump drive sprocket is located on the crankshaft behind the variator, remove the cover **(see illustration)**.

18.3 Undo the bolts (arrows) and remove the oil pan cover

assembly, then remove the dowel and thrust-washer from the pump shaft.

7 If the pump sprocket is retained by a snap-ring, use snap-ring pliers to remove the snap-ring, then withdraw the chain and sprocket(s) **(see illustrations)**.

8 If the sprocket is retained by a bolt, insert a pin punch or screwdriver through one of the holes in the sprocket and locate it against part of the casing to prevent the sprocket turning, then unscrew the bolt **(see illustration)**. Withdraw the chain and sprocket(s) **(see illustrations)**.

9 Where installed, undo the pump retaining bolts, then withdraw the pump from the engine. If a gasket is installed behind the pump, discard it, as a new one must be installed.

Inspection

10 Check the pump body for obvious signs of damage, especially around the mounting bolt holes. Turn the pump shaft by hand and check that the pump rotates smoothly. Some pumps cannot be disassembled for inspection – if the operation of the pump is suspect, replace it.

3 If the pump is located in a separate oil pan, remove the oil pan cover and discard the gasket, as a new one must be installed on reassembly **(see illustration)**. **Note:** *On some engines, the lubrication system incorporates an oil pressure relief valve. If the valve is located in the oil pan, remove it for safekeeping, noting how it fits. If the valve is equipped with an O-ring, discard it and install a new one on reassembly.*

4 Where installed, remove the screws securing the pump drive chain cover and remove the cover **(see illustrations)**.

5 Mark the chain so that it can be installed the same way.

6 On some pumps, the pump sprocket is retained by the chain cover. Withdraw the chain and sprockets from the engine as an

18.4a Undo the screws (arrows) . . .

18.4b . . . securing the pump drive chain cover

18.7a Remove the snap-ring . . .

18.7b . . . and lift off the sprocket and chain

18.8a Undo the sprocket bolt . . .

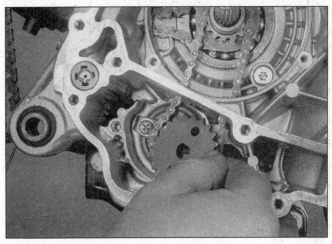

18.8b . . . then remove the sprocket . . .

18.8c . . . and lift off the chain

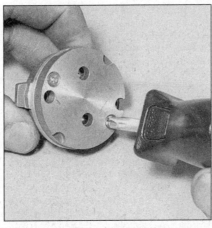

18.11a Remove the screws . . .

18.11b . . . and lift off the cover

11 Remove the screws securing the cover to the pump body, then remove the cover **(see illustrations)**. Note any reference marks on the pump rotors; even if the rotors are not marked, it is essential that they are reassembled correctly. Lift out the inner and outer rotor and the pump shaft **(see illustration)**. Note the location of any drive pin in the shaft. **Note:** *On some pumps, the rotors are secured by a snap-ring – use a new snap-ring on reassembly.*

12 Clean the pump components with a suitable solvent and dry them with compressed air, if available. Inspect the pump body, rotors and shaft for scoring and wear. If any damage, scoring, uneven or excessive wear is evident, replace the pump (individual components are not available).

13 If the pump is good, reassemble all the components in the correct order and lubricate them with clean engine oil.

14 Install the cover and tighten the screws securely, then rotate the pump shaft by hand to check that the rotors turn smoothly and freely.

15 Inspect the pump drive chain and sprockets for wear or damage, and replace them as a set if necessary. If the drive sprocket is not

a sliding fit on the crankshaft, check to see if it is a press-fit or an integral part of the shaft. If the sprocket is a press-fit and needs to be replaced, measure its position from the end of the shaft, then pull it off with a bearing puller (see *Tools and Workshop Tips* in the *Reference* section). Heat the new sprocket in an oil bath to around 212°F, then press it onto the shaft using a suitable length of tube that just fits over the shaft. Ensure that the

sprocket is installed at the correct distance from the end of the shaft.

Installation

16 Installation is the reverse of removal, noting the following:

If required, install a new gasket to the pump.

Where installed, secure the pump drive gear with a new snap-ring.

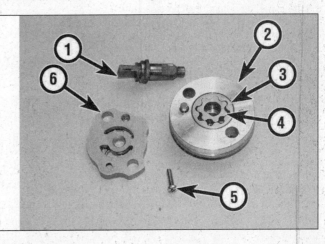

18.11c Oil pump components

1 Pump shaft
2 Pump body
3 Outer rotor
4 Inner rotor
5 Body screw
6 Cover

19.3 Undo the crankcase bolts evenly in a criss-cross sequence

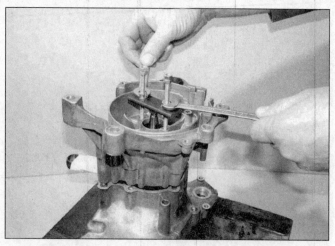

19.6 Drawing the right-hand crankcase half off the crankshaft

Ensure the chain is installed correctly. Where installed, ensure the oil pressure relief valve is correctly installed. Install a new gasket to the oil pan. If applicable, fill the engine with the correct type and quantity of oil (see Chapter 1).

19 Crankcase halves and main bearings

Note: *To separate the crankcase halves, the engine must be removed from the frame.*

Separation

1 Follow the procedure in Section 4 and remove the engine from the frame.
2 Before the crankcase halves can be separated, the following components must be removed:

> *Camchain, blades and sprockets (see Section 9).*
> *Cylinder head (Section 11).*
> *Cylinder (Section 13).*
> *Alternator rotor (Section 16).*
> *Variator (Chapter 6).*
> *Starter motor (Chapter 10).*
> *Oil pump (Section 18).*

3 Tape some rag around the connecting rod to prevent it knocking against the cases, then loosen the crankcase bolts evenly, a little at a time and in a criss-cross sequence until they are all finger-tight, then remove them **(see illustration)**. **Note:** *Ensure that all the crankcase bolts have been removed before attempting to separate the cases.*

HAYNES HiNT *Make a cardboard template of the crankcase and punch a hole for each bolt location. This will ensure all bolts are installed correctly on reassembly – this is important as some bolts may be of different lengths.*

4 On some engines, the crankshaft is secured against the right-hand main bearing

by a large nut. Lock the crankshaft by passing a bar through the connecting rod small-end and resting it on two pieces of wood to protect the cylinder gasket surface, then undo the nut.
5 If the crankshaft oil seals are installed to the outside of the crankcases, remove the oil seals. Note that on some engines, the seals are held in a fixing plate; undo the bolts and remove the plate, do not try to remove the seal from the plate.
6 Remove the right-hand crankcase half from the left-hand half by drawing it off the right-hand end of the crankshaft. On most engines, the cases will be a tight fit on the crankshaft and most manufacturers produce a service tool to facilitate this procedure. Alternatively, use the set-up shown, ensuring equal pressure is applied on both sides of the puller arrangement at all times **(see illustration)**. If the puller is placed across the end of the crankshaft, thread the old alternator center nut on first to protect the threads. **Note:** *If the crankcase halves do not separate easily, first ensure all fasteners have been removed. Apply steady pressure with the tools described and heat the bearing hous-*

ings with a hot air gun. Do not try and separate the halves by prying against the mating surfaces, as they are easily scored and will not seal correctly afterwards. Do not strike the ends of the crankshaft with a hammer as damage to the end threads or the shaft itself will result.
7 Now press the crankshaft assembly out of the left-hand crankcase half – again, a service tool will be available. Alternatively, use the set-up shown **(see illustration)**. Thread the old variator nut onto the end of the crankshaft to protect the threads and make sure the crankshaft assembly is supported to prevent it dropping if it suddenly comes free.
8 Note the position of the crankshaft oil seals (if not already removed) and measure any inset before removing them **(see illustration)**. Note how the seals are installed. Pry the seals out carefully with a large, flat-bladed screwdriver and a piece of wood, taking care not to damage the crankcase. Discard the seals, as new ones must be installed on reassembly.
9 Remove any dowels from either crankcase half for safekeeping if they are loose.
10 The main bearings will either remain in place in the crankcase halves during dis-

19.7 Pressing the crankshaft out of the left-hand crankcase half

19.8 Measuring crankshaft oil seal inset

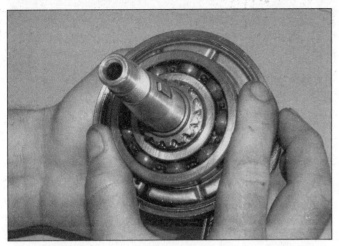

19.10 Checking the main bearing on the crankshaft

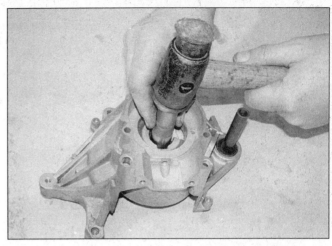

19.11 Driving a main bearing out of the crankcase

assembly or come out with the crankshaft assembly **(see illustration)**. If the main bearings have failed, excessive rumbling and vibration will be felt when the engine is running. Check the condition of the bearings (see *Tools and Workshop Tips* in the *Reference* section) and only remove them if they are unserviceable. Always replace both main bearings at the same time, never individually. Note that on some engines, plain (non-roller) main bearings are installed in the crankcases. These bearings are generally not replaceable, and if they are worn, new crankcases will have to be installed. Check the availability of new parts with a scooter dealer.

11 To remove the bearings from the cases, heat the bearing housings with a hot air gun and tap them out using a bearing driver or suitable socket **(see illustration)**. Note how the bearings are installed. If the bearings are stuck on the crankshaft, they must be removed with an external bearing puller to avoid damaging the crankshaft assembly. **Note:** *On some engines, the main bearings are installed in the crankcases prior to assembly, on others they are installed to the crankshaft. Consult a scooter dealer for*

details before installing new bearings.
12 If required, remove the transmission assembly from the left-hand crankcase half (see Chapter 6).

Inspection

13 Remove all traces of old sealant from the crankcase mating surfaces with a suitable solvent. Take care not to nick or gouge the soft aluminium. Wash the cases in a suitable solvent and dry them with compressed air.
14 The procedure for inspecting the crankcase halves and repairing minor damage is the same as for two-stroke engines (see Chapter 2A, Section 13).
15 Inspect the crankshaft assembly and bearings (see Section 20).

Reassembly

16 If the main bearings are to be installed into the crankcase halves, heat the bearing housings with a hot air gun, then install them using a bearing driver or suitable socket which bears onto the outer race only.
17 If the main bearings are to be installed onto the crankshaft, heat them first in an oil bath to around 212°F, then press them onto the shaft using a suitable length of tube that just fits over the shaft and bears onto the

inner race only. If the bearings are difficult to install, they are not hot enough.

⚠ *Warning: This must be done very carefully to avoid the risk of personal injury.*

18 Install the new crankshaft oil seals into the crankcase halves and drive them to the previously-measured inset using a seal driver or socket (see Step 8). Ensure the seals are correctly installed and that they enter the cases squarely.
19 Install the crankshaft assembly into the left-hand crankcase half first, ensuring that the connecting rod is aligned with the crankcase mouth. Lubricate the shaft, seal and bearing with clean engine oil and tape some rag around the connecting rod to prevent it knocking against the cases. If the main bearing is in the crankcase half, pull the assembly into place either with a service tool or using the set-up shown **(see illustration)**. If the main bearing is on the crankshaft, heat the bearing housing in the crankcase with a hot air gun before installing the crank assembly. **Note:** *Avoid applying direct heat onto the crankshaft oil seal.* If required, a freeze spray can be used on the bearing itself to aid installation. Ensure the bearing is installed fully into its housing **(see illustration)**.

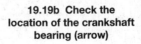

19.19a Installing the crankshaft assembly in the left-hand crankcase half

19.19b Check the location of the crankshaft bearing (arrow)

2B•28 Four-stroke engines

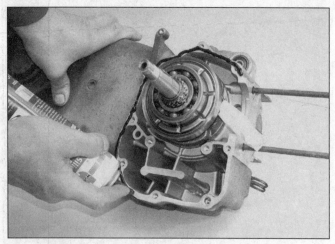

19.20 Apply sealant to the crankcase mating surface

19.21 Installing the right-hand crankcase half

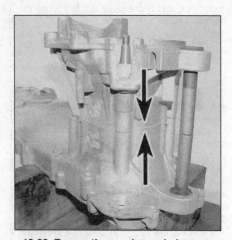

19.22 Ensure the crankcase halves are correctly seated

20 If applicable, allow the case to cool, then wipe the mating surfaces of both crankcase halves with a rag soaked in a suitable solvent and install the dowels. Apply a small amount of suitable sealant to the mating surface of the left-hand case (see illustration).

21 Install the right-hand crankcase half. Lubricate the shaft, seal and bearing with clean engine oil. If the main bearing is in the crankcase half, press the crankcase half into place, either with a service tool or with the set-up shown (see illustration). If the main bearing is on the crankshaft, heat the bearing housing with a hot air gun before installing the crankcase half and, if required, use a freeze spray on the bearing. Note: Avoid applying direct heat onto the crankshaft oil seal.

22 Check that the crankcase halves are seated all the way around (see illustration). If the casings are not correctly seated, heat the bearing housings while applying firm pressure with the assembly tools used previously. Note: Do not attempt to pull the crankcase halves together using the crankcase bolts, as the casing will crack and be ruined.

23 Clean the threads of the crankcase bolts and install them finger-tight, then tighten them evenly a little at a time in a criss-cross sequence to the torque setting specified in the *Data* section. Support the connecting rod and rotate the crankshaft by hand – if there are any signs of excess stiffness, tight or rough spots, or of any other problem, the fault must be rectified before proceeding further.

24 If equipped, install the crankshaft nut (see Step 4). The nut should be tightened to a specific torque setting – check with a scooter dealer for details.

25 On engines where the crankshaft oil seals are installed to the outside of the crankcases (see Step 5), lubricate the new seals with clean engine oil and install them in the cases.

26 Install the remaining components in the reverse order of removal.

20 Crankshaft assembly and connecting rod bearing

1 To access the crankshaft and the connecting rod bearing, the crankcase must be split into two parts (see Section 19).

2 The crankshaft assembly should give many thousands of miles of service. The most likely problems to occur will be a worn small or connecting rod bearing due to poor lubrication. A worn connecting rod bearing will produce a pronounced knocking noise, most audible when the engine is under load, and increasing as engine speed rises. This should not be confused with small-end bearing wear, which produces a lighter, metallic rattle (see Section 14).

Inspection

3 To assess the condition of the connecting rod bearing, hold the crankshaft assembly firmly and push-and-pull on the connecting rod, checking for any up-and-down freeplay between the two (see illustration). If any

freeplay is noted, the bearing is worn and either the bearing or the crankshaft assembly will have to be replaced. **Note:** *A small amount of big-end side clearance (side-to-side movement) is acceptable on the connecting rod. Consult a scooter dealer about the availability of parts.* **Note:** *If a new bearing is available, installing it is a specialized task which should be left to a scooter dealer or machine shop.*

4 Inspect the crankshaft where it passes through the main bearings for wear and scoring – if required, remove the bearings carefully with a bearing puller to avoid damaging the shaft (see illustration). The shaft should be a press-fit in the bearings; if it is worn or damaged, a new assembly will have to be installed. Evidence of extreme heat, such as discoloration or blueing, indicates that lubrication failure has occurred. Be sure to check the oil pump and bearing oilways in the crankcases before reassembling the engine.

5 If available, place the crankshaft assembly on V-blocks and check the runout at the main bearing journals (B and C) and at either end (A and D) using a dial gauge (see illustra-

20.3 Check for up-and-down play in the connecting rod bearing

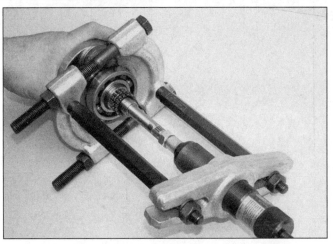

20.4 Removing a main bearing using a bearing puller

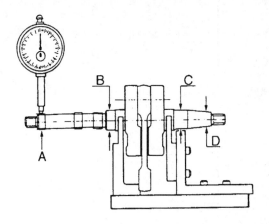

20.5 Support the crankshaft on V-blocks and check the runout at points A, B, C and D

tion). **Note:** *The main bearings will have to be removed for this check.* If the crankshaft is out-of-true, it will cause excessive engine vibration. If there is any doubt about the condition of the crankshaft, have it checked by a scooter dealer or automotive engineer. **Note:** *The crankshaft assembly is pressed together and is easily damaged if it is dropped.*

6 Inspect the threads on each end of the crankshaft and ensure that the retaining nuts for the alternator rotor and the variator are a good fit. Inspect the splines for the variator pulley on the left-hand end of the shaft. Inspect the taper and the slot in the right-hand end of the shaft for the alternator Woodruff key **(see illustration)**. Damage or wear that prevents the rotor from being installed securely will require a new crankshaft assembly.

7 Where applicable, inspect the oil pump and/or the camshaft drive sprocket teeth on the crankshaft for damage or wear **(see illustration 20.6)**. If the sprocket is integral with the shaft, a new crankshaft assembly will have to be installed. If the sprocket is a press-fit and needs to be replaced, measure its position from the end of the shaft, then pull it off with a bearing puller **(see illustration 20.4)**. Heat the new sprocket in an oil bath to around 212°F, then press it onto the

shaft using a suitable length of tube that just fits over the shaft. Ensure that the sprocket is installed at the correct distance from the end of the shaft.

Reassembly

8 Follow the procedure in Section 19 to install the crankshaft assembly.

21 Initial start-up after overhaul

1 Make sure the engine oil level is correct (see *Daily (pre-ride) checks*).
2 On liquid-cooled models, make sure the coolant level is correct (see *Daily (pre-ride) checks*).
3 Make sure there is fuel in the tank.
4 With the ignition OFF, operate the kickstart a couple of times to check that the engine turns over easily.
5 Turn the ignition ON, start the engine and allow it to run at a slow idle until it reaches operating temperature. Do not be alarmed if there is a little smoke from the exhaust – this will be due to the oil used to lubricate the piston and bore during assembly and should

subside after a while.
6 If the engine proves reluctant to start, remove the spark plug and check that it has not become wet and oily. If it has, clean it and try again. If the engine refuses to start, refer to *Troubleshooting* at the end of this manual to identify the problem.
7 Check carefully for fuel and oil leaks and make sure the transmission and controls, especially the brakes, function properly before road testing the machine. Refer to Section 22 for the recommended break-in procedure.
8 Upon completion of the road test, and after the engine has cooled down completely, recheck the valve clearances (see Chapter 1). Check the engine oil level and, on liquid-cooled models, check the coolant level (see *Daily (pre-ride) checks*).

22 Recommended break-in procedure

1 Treat the engine gently for the first few miles to allow any new parts to bed-in.
2 If a new piston, cylinder or crankshaft assembly has been installed, the engine will have to be broken-in as when new. This means a restraining hand on the throttle until at least 300 miles (500 km) have been covered. There's no point in keeping to any set speed limit – the main idea is to keep from laboring the engine and to gradually increase performance up to the 600 mile (1000 km) mark. Make sure that the throttle position is varied to vary engine speed, and use full throttle only for short bursts. Experience is the best guide, since it's easy to tell when an engine is running freely.
3 Pay particular attention to the *Daily (pre-ride) checks* at the beginning of this manual and investigate the cause of any oil or, on liquid-cooled models, coolant loss immediately. Check the tightness of all relevant nuts and bolts.

20.6 Inspect the crankshaft taper (A), location of the Woodruff key (B), thread (C) and sprocket teeth (D)

Notes

Chapter 3
Cooling system (liquid-cooled engines)

Contents

Degrees of difficulty

Easy, suitable for novice with little experience	**Fairly easy,** suitable for beginner with some experience	**Fairly difficult,** suitable for competent DIY mechanic	**Difficult,** suitable for experienced DIY mechanic	**Very difficult,** suitable for expert DIY or professional

Specifications

Refer to the *Data* section at the end of this manual for servicing specifications.

1 General information

The cooling system uses a water/antifreeze coolant to carry excess energy away from the engine in the form of heat. The coolant is contained within a water jacket inside the cylinder and cylinder head which is connected to the radiator and the water pump by the coolant hoses.

Coolant heated by the engine is circulated by thermo-syphonic action, and the action of the pump, to the radiator. It flows across the radiator core, where it is cooled by the passing air, then through the water pump and back to the engine, where the cycle is repeated.

A thermostat is installed in the cylinder head to prevent the coolant flowing to the radiator when the engine is cold, therefore accelerating the speed at which the engine reaches normal operating temperature. A coolant temperature sender mounted in the cylinder head is connected to the temperature gauge on the instrument panel.

 Warning 1: Do not remove the reservoir cap when the engine is hot. Scalding hot coolant and steam may be blown out under pressure, which could cause serious injury.

 Warning 2: Do not allow antifreeze to come in contact with your skin or painted or plastic surfaces of the scooter. Rinse off any spills immediately with plenty of water. Antifreeze is highly toxic if ingested. Never leave antifreeze lying around in an open container or in puddles on the floor; children and

pets are attracted by its sweet smell and may drink it. Check with the local authorities about disposing of used antifreeze. Many communities will have collection centers which will see that antifreeze is disposed of safely. Antifreeze is also combustible, so don't store it near open flames.

Caution: At all times, use the specified type of antifreeze, and always mix it with distilled water in the correct proportion. The antifreeze contains corrosion inhibitors which are essential to avoid damage to the cooling system. A lack of these inhibitors could lead to a build-up of corrosion which would block the coolant passages, resulting in overheating and severe engine damage. Distilled water must be used as opposed to tap water to avoid a build-up of scale which would also block the passages.

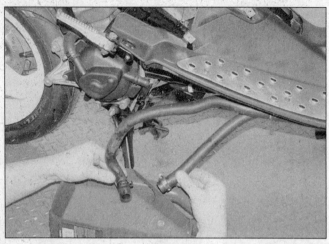

2.3a Drain the cooling system into a suitable container

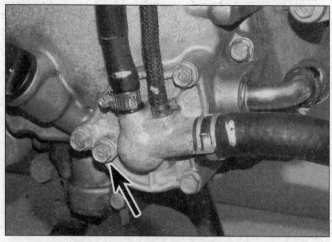

2.3b Water pump drain bolt (arrow)

2 Draining, flushing and refilling

⚠ **Warning: Allow the engine to cool completely before performing this maintenance operation. Also, don't allow antifreeze to come into contact with your skin or the painted or plastic surfaces of the scooter. Rinse off spills immediately with plenty of water.**

Draining

1 Remove any body panels as necessary to access the hose connection either to the water pump or, if more easily accessible, the bottom of the radiator, and the coolant system filler cap (see Chapter 9). **Note:** *On some systems, the filler cap is on the radiator, on others it is on the coolant reservoir; refer to your scooter handbook for details.*
2 Remove the filler cap. If you hear a hissing sound as you unscrew it (indicating there is still pressure in the system), wait until it stops.

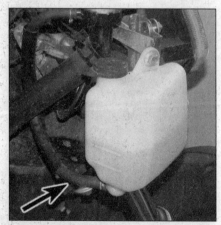

2.4 Detach the hose (arrow) to drain the reservoir

3 To drain the coolant, first loosen the clip securing the coolant hose either to the union on the water pump or the bottom of the radiator. Position a suitable container beneath the hose, then detach it and allow the coolant to drain from the system **(see illustration)**. Note that some water pumps are installed with a drain bolt **(see illustration)**; if applicable, undo the bolt to drain the system without disturbing the coolant hoses. Retain the old sealing washer for use while flushing the system.
4 Where installed, check that the coolant has drained from the coolant reservoir. If necessary, detach the hose from the bottom of the reservoir and drain the coolant **(see illustration)**.

Flushing

5 Flush the system with clean tap water by inserting a garden hose in the filler neck. Allow the water to run through the system until it is clear and flows cleanly out of either the detached hose or the drain hole. If there is a lot of rust in the water, remove the radiator and have it professionally cleaned (see Section 8). If the drain hole appears to be clogged with sediment, remove the pump cover and clean the inside of the pump (see Section 9). If necessary, remove the coolant reservoir and rinse the inside with clean water, then install it.
6 As applicable, attach the coolant hoses and secure them with the clips, and install the drain bolt using the old sealing washer.
7 Fill the system with clean water mixed with a flushing compound. **Note:** *Make sure the flushing compound is compatible with aluminium components and follow the manufacturer's instructions carefully.* If the system is installed with a bleed valve, loosen the valve to release any trapped air, then tighten it securely **(see illustration)**. Alternatively, rock the scooter from side-to-side and bleed any trapped air out through the filler neck. Install the filler cap.
8 If necessary, fill the coolant reservoir separately with clean water.

9 Start the engine and allow it to reach normal operating temperature. Let it run for about five minutes.
10 Stop the engine. Let it cool for a while, then remove the filler cap (see Step 2) and drain the system (see Step 3).
11 Reconnect the coolant hoses and the drain bolt as applicable, then fill the system with clean water only and repeat the procedure in Steps 7 to 10. Where installed, check that the water has drained from the coolant reservoir.

Refilling

12 Ensure all the hoses are correctly attached and secured with their clips. If applicable, install a new sealing washer onto the drain bolt and tighten the bolt securely.
13 Fill the system with the proper coolant mixture (see the *Data* section at the end of this manual). **Note:** *Pour the coolant in slowly to minimize the amount of air entering the system.* Release any trapped air as described in Step 7. If necessary, top-up the coolant reservoir. Install the filler cap.
14 Start the engine and allow it to idle for 2 to 3 minutes. Flick the throttle twistgrip part open 3 or 4 times, so that the engine speed rises, then stop the engine. Release any trapped air (see Step 7) and check the system for leaks.

⚠ **Warning: Make sure that the machine is on its center stand and that the rear wheel is off the ground before bleeding the cooling system. If necessary, place a support under the stand to prevent the rear wheel contacting the ground.**

15 Let the engine cool and check the coolant level (see *Daily (pre-ride) checks*), then install the body panels (see Chapter 9).
16 Do not dispose of the old coolant by pouring it down the drain. Pour it into a heavy plastic container, cap it tightly and take it into an authorized disposal site or garage – see **Warning 2** in Section 1.

2.7 Release any trapped air through the bleed valve (arrow)

3.1 Some systems are installed with a pressure cap

4.2 Temperature sender wiring connector

3 Pressure cap

1 Where installed, the pressure cap is designed to retain a specific working pressure within the cooling system and, in extreme cases, to release pressure before it becomes a danger **(see illustration)**.
2 If, after checking the cooling system (see Chapter 1), problems such as overheating or loss of coolant still occur, have the cap opening pressure checked by a scooter dealer with the special tester required for the job. If the cap is defective, replace it.

4 Temperature gauge and sender

Temperature gauge
Check

1 The circuit consists of the sender mounted in the cylinder head or thermostat housing and the gauge or warning light in the instrument panel. If the system malfunctions, first check the coolant level (see *Daily (pre-ride) checks*). If the level is correct, check that the battery is fully-charged and that the fuse is good (see Chapter 10). If a warning light is installed, check the condition of the bulb.
2 If the gauge or warning light is still not working, disconnect the wire from the sender and connect it to ground with a jumper wire **(see illustration)**. Turn the ignition switch ON; the temperature gauge needle should swing over to the H on the gauge or the bulb should illuminate. If the gauge or warning light work as described, check the operation of the sender (see Steps 4 to 6). **Note:** *It is possible for a faulty gauge or light to register a reading in this check, but not when connected to the sender. Only replace the sender if it fails the checks described below.*

Caution: If the needle moves, turn the ignition OFF immediately to avoid damaging the gauge.

3 If the gauge or warning light is still not working, the fault lies in the wiring or the gauge itself. Check all the relevant wiring and wiring connectors; if all appears to be well, the gauge is defective and must be replaced. **Note:** *On some scooters, the temperature gauge is an integral part of the instrument cluster and cannot be replaced as a separate item.*

Temperature gauge sender
Check

4 Disconnect the negative battery cable, then disconnect the sender wiring connector **(see illustration 4.2)**. Using a multimeter or continuity tester, check for continuity between the sender body and ground. There should be continuity. If there is no continuity, check that the sender mounting is secure, then recheck the operation of the gauge.
5 Remove the sender (see Steps 7 and 8 below). Fill a small heatproof container with coolant and place it on a stove. Using a multimeter set to the ohms scale, connect the positive probe to the terminal on the sender and the negative probe to the sender body. Using some wire or other support, suspend the sender in the coolant so that just the sensing portion and the threads are submerged **(see illustration)**. Also place a thermometer capable of reading temperatures up to approximately 250°F in the coolant so that its bulb is close to the sensor. **Note:** *None of the components should be allowed to directly touch the container.*
6 Check the resistance of the sender at approximately 68°F and keep the coolant temperature constant at 68°F for 3 minutes before continuing the test. Then increase the heat gradually, stirring the coolant gently. As the temperature of the coolant rises, the resistance of the sender should fall. Check that the correct resistance is obtained at the temperatures specified in the *Data* section at the end of this manual. If the meter readings obtained are different, or they are obtained

at different temperatures, then the sender is faulty and must be replaced.

> **⚠ Warning: This must be done very carefully to avoid the risk of personal injury.**

Replacement

> **⚠ Warning: The engine must be completely cool before carrying out this procedure.**

7 Disconnect the negative battery cable and drain the cooling system (see Section 2).
8 Disconnect the sender wiring connector **(see illustration 4.2)**. Unscrew the sender and remove it.
9 Apply a smear of a suitable non-permanent sealant to the threads of the new sender, then install it into the cylinder head or thermostat housing and tighten it securely. Connect the sender wiring.
10 Refill the cooling system (see Section 2) and reconnect the negative battery cable.

5 Cooling fan and switch

Cooling fan
Note: *Where installed, the cooling fan is located either on the front or the back of the radiator.*

Check

1 If the engine is overheating and the cooling fan isn't coming on, first check the cooling fan circuit fuse (see Chapter 10), then the fan switch as described in Steps 8 and 9 below.
2 If the fan does not come on (and the fan switch is good), the fault lies in either the fan motor or the relevant wiring. Test all the wiring and connections as described in Chapter 10.

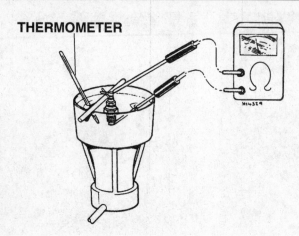

THERMOMETER

4.5 Set-up for testing the temperature gauge sender

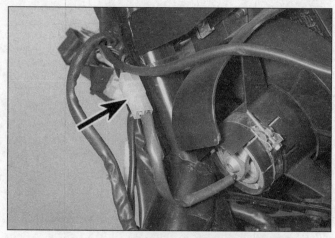

5.3 Disconnect the fan wiring connector (arrow)

3 To test the fan motor, disconnect the fan wiring connector **(see illustration)**. Using a 12 volt battery and two jumper wires, connect the positive battery cable to the positive wire terminal and the negative battery cable to the ground wire terminal on the fan motor side of the connector. Once connected, the fan should operate. If it does not, and the wiring is all good, then the fan motor is faulty and must be replaced

Replacement

 Warning: The engine must be completely cool before carrying out this procedure.

4 Disconnect the negative battery cable.
5 If required, remove the radiator (see Section 8). Ensure the wiring for the fan and the fan switch is free from any ties. Remove the screws securing the fan assembly to the radiator and lift it off, noting how it fits **(see illustration)**.
6 Installation is the reverse of removal.

Cooling fan switch

Check

7 If the engine is overheating and the cooling fan isn't coming on, first check the cooling fan circuit fuse (see Chapter 10). If the fuse is blown, check the fan circuit for a short to ground.
8 If the fuse is good, disconnect the wiring connectors from the fan switch on the radiator **(see illustration)**. Using a jumper wire, connect the wiring connector terminals together. The fan should come on when the ignition is turned ON. If it does, the fan switch is confirmed faulty and must be replaced. If it does not come on, the fan motor should be tested (see Step 3).
9 If the fan motor is on all the time, even when the engine is cold, disconnect the switch wiring connectors and keep them apart. The fan should stop. If it does, the fan switch is defective and must be replaced. If

it keeps running, check the wiring between the switch and the fan motor for a short to ground.

Replacement

 Warning: The engine must be completely cool before carrying out this procedure.

10 Disconnect the negative battery cable. Drain the cooling system (see Section 2).
11 Disconnect the wiring connectors from the fan switch on the radiator. Unscrew the switch and withdraw it from the radiator. Discard the seal or O-ring, as a new one must be used.
12 Apply a suitable sealant to the switch threads, then install the switch using a new seal and tighten it securely. Take care not to overtighten the switch, as the radiator could be damaged.
13 Reconnect the switch wiring and refill the cooling system (see Section 2). Reconnect the negative battery cable.

5.5 Fan assembly is mounted on the radiator

6 Thermostat

 Warning: The engine must be completely cool before carrying out this procedure.

Removal

1 The thermostat is automatic in operation and should give many years service without requiring attention. In the event of a failure, the thermostat valve will probably jam open, in which case the engine will take much longer to reach its normal operating temperature, resulting in increased fuel consumption. If the valve jams shut, the coolant will be unable to circulate and the engine will overheat with the risk of seizure. In either case, if the thermostat is found to be faulty, a new unit should be installed immediately.
2 Generally, the thermostat is located in a housing on the cylinder head or alongside

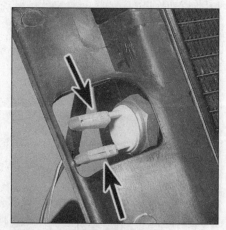

5.8 Disconnect the fan wiring connectors (arrows)

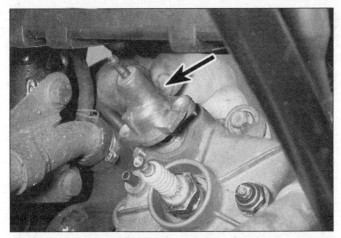

6.2a Thermostat housing on the cylinder head

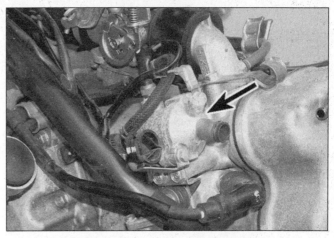

6.2b Separate thermostat housing assembly

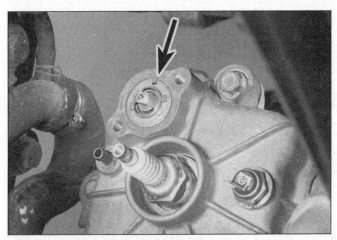

6.4a Note how the thermostat fits . . .

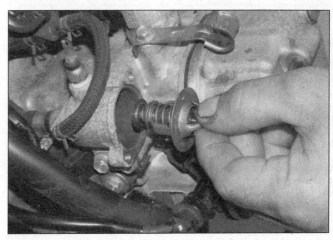

6.4b . . . before removing it

the cylinder head **(see illustrations)**. On some two-stroke engines, the thermostat is located inside the cylinder head **(see illustration 6.4c)**. A visual check should identify the location of the thermostat.

3 Drain the cooling system (see Section 2).

Loosen the clips securing any coolant hoses to the thermostat housing cover and detach the hoses. Where installed, disconnect the temperature sender wiring connector.

4 Undo the bolts securing the thermostat housing cover, then lift out the thermostat,

noting how it fits **(see illustrations)**. Note the position of any cover gasket or O-ring. If required, refer to Chapter 2A to remove the cylinder head, then lift out the thermostat **(see illustrations)**. Note the position of any spring or O-ring.

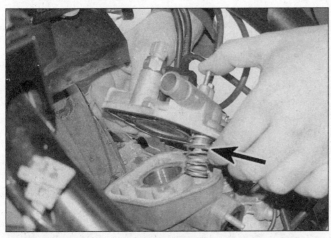

6.4c Remove the cylinder head with the thermostat assembly (arrow) . . .

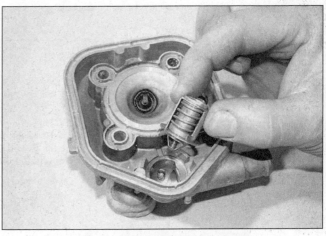

6.4d . . . then lift out the thermostat

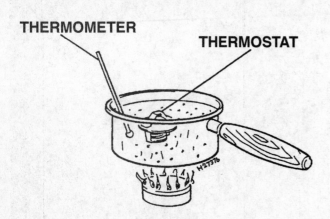

6.6 Set-up for testing the thermostat

7.4 Note how the reservoir fits on its mounting (arrow)

5 Examine the thermostat visually before carrying out the test. If it remains in the open position at room temperature (68°F approximately), it should be replaced.
6 Fill a small, heatproof container with cold water and place it on a stove. Using a piece of wire, suspend the thermostat in the water (see illustration). Heat the water and see whether the thermostat opens. Opening temperatures vary between 158 and 176°F and the thermostat valve should open between 3 to 5 mm approximately. If the valve has not opened by the time the water starts to boil, the thermostat is faulty and must be replaced.
7 Where installed, inspect the thermostat spring and replace it if it is corroded or damaged (see Step 4).

Installation

8 Installation is the reverse of removal, noting the following:
  Ensure any air bleed hole in the thermostat is at the top.
  Install new gaskets and O-rings.
  Ensure the coolant hoses are secured with the clips.
  Refill the cooling system and bleed it (see Section 2).

7 Coolant reservoir – removal and installation

⚠ **Warning: Ensure that the engine is cold before working on the coolant reservoir.**

Removal

1 Generally, the coolant reservoir is located next to the radiator; remove any body panels as necessary to access the reservoir (see Chapter 9).
2 Remove the reservoir cap, then detach the hose from the bottom of the reservoir and

drain the coolant into a suitable container (see Section 2).
3 Where installed, detach the upper hose from the reservoir.
4 Undo the reservoir mounting bolts and lift it off; note any rubber bushings on the reservoir mounting (see illustration).

Installation

5 Installation is the reverse of removal, noting the following:
  Replace the reservoir mounting bushings if they are worn or damaged.
  Ensure the hose(s) are correctly installed and secured with their clips.
  Refill the reservoir with the proper coolant mixture (see Daily (pre-ride) checks).

8 Radiator – removal and installation

⚠ **Warning: Ensure that the engine is cold before working on the radiator.**

Removal

1 Remove any body panels as necessary to access the radiator and the radiator hose connections (see Chapter 9).
2 Drain the cooling system (see Section 2).
3 Where installed, disconnect the wiring from the cooling fan and the fan switch and release the wiring from any ties (see Section 5).
4 Loosen the clips securing the coolant hoses to the radiator and detach the hoses (see illustration).

 HAYNES HiNT *If a radiator hose is corroded in place on its fitting, cut the hose with a sharp knife then slit it lengthwise and peel it off the fitting. While this means replacing the hose, it is preferable to buying a new radiator.*

Caution: The radiator fittings are fragile. Do not use excessive force when attempting to remove the hoses.

5 Where installed, loosen the clips securing the coolant reservoir hoses to the radiator and detach the hoses; if necessary, remove the reservoir (see Section 7).
6 Undo the radiator mounting bolts and

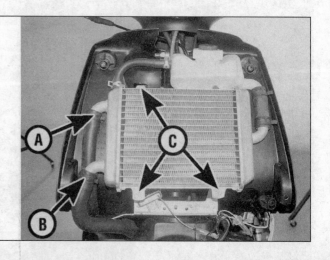

8.4 Radiator coolant hoses (A and B) and mounting bolts (C)

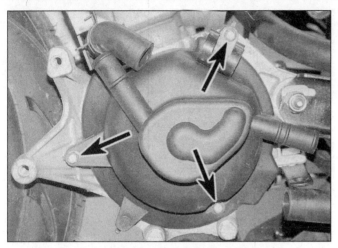

9.5a Undo the alternator cover mounting bolts

9.5b Water pump is driven by dampers on the alternator rotor . . .

remove the radiator **(see illustration 8.4)**. Note the position of any washers and rubber bushings.

7 Check the radiator for signs of damage and clear any dirt or debris that might obstruct air flow and inhibit cooling (see Chapter 1, Section 21).

Installation

8 Installation is the reverse of removal, noting the following:

Replace the radiator mounting bushings if they are worn or damaged.

Ensure the hoses are in good condition (see Chapter 1, Section 21).

Ensure the hoses are correctly installed and secured with their clips.

Refill the cooling system and bleed it (see Section 2).

9.5c . . . which engage in holes in the back of the pump

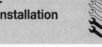

9 Water pump – removal and installation

Note: *A variety of pump designs are used; the pump may be mounted in the alternator cover, on the outside of the crankcase, inside the engine side cover, or in the crankcase. Trace the main coolant hoses to determine the location of the pump. On some two-stroke engines the pump can only be removed after the crankcase halves have been separated (see Chapter 2A).*

1 An internal seal prevents leakage of coolant from the pump; if the seal fails, coolant will either drain out of the bottom of the pump housing or the crankcase, depending on the location of the pump.

2 Leaks leave tell-tale scale deposits or coolant stains. Ensure the coolant is leaking from inside the pump and not from a hose connection or damaged hose. If the pump is leaking, a new seal must be installed or the pump must be replaced. **Note:** *If a new internal seal is available, installing it is a spe-*

cialized task which should be left to a scooter dealer or machine shop.

Mounted on alternator cover

Removal and installation

3 Drain the coolant and detach both the hoses from the pump (see Section 2).

4 Where installed, undo the pump cover mounting screws and remove them. Remove the cover and discard the O-ring, as a new one must be used. **Note:** *On some scooters, the pump is integral with the alternator cover; if the pump seal or bearing fails, a new cover must be installed.*

5 Undo the alternator cover mounting bolts, noting the position of any hose guides secured by the bolts **(see illustration)**. Lift the cover away from the engine, noting how the pump drive dampers are attached to the alternator rotor and how the dampers fit into the back of the pump **(see illustrations)**.

6 If required, hold the alternator rotor to prevent it turning and unscrew the dampers. Replace the damper seals as a set if they are worn.

7 The pump impeller is a press-fit in the pump bearings. To remove the impeller, support the alternator cover upside down on the work surface with sufficient clearance below it to allow the impeller to be driven out. **Note:** *Take great care not to damage the sealing surface of the alternator cover. Use a soft drift (preferably aluminium or brass) to carefully drive the impeller out.*

8 Check the condition of the bearings in the alternator cover and replace them if necessary (see *Tools and Workshop Tips* in the *Reference* section). **Note:** *It may be necessary to remove the pump seals before the bearings can be removed; if available, have new seals and bearings installed by a scooter dealer or machine shop.*

9 Installation is the reverse of removal, noting the following:

Make sure the drive dampers fit correctly into the back of the pump.

Ensure the coolant hoses are pushed fully onto the pump fittings and secured with the clips.

Refill the cooling system and bleed it (see Section 2).

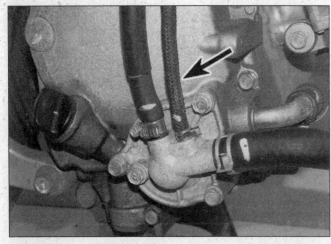

9.10 Side cover mounted pump – note the carburetor heater hose (arrow)

9.11 Lift off the pump cover

9.12a Hold the pump impeller with grips . . .

9.12b . . . then undo the impeller center nut (arrow)

Mounted on engine side cover
Removal and installation

10 Drain the coolant and, if required, detach the hoses, including the carburetor heater hose, from the pump (see illustration).

11 Undo the pump cover bolts and lift off the cover (see illustration). Discard the cover O-ring, as a new one must be installed. Clean any sediment out of the cover.

12 Hold the pump impeller with pipe grips to prevent it turning, then undo the impeller nut (see illustrations).

⚠️ *Warning: The impeller nut may have a left-hand thread (undoes clockwise). Check before you undo the nut to avoid damaging the thread.*

13 On four-stroke engines, drain the engine oil (see Chapter 1).

14 Trace any wiring from the engine side cover and disconnect it at the connector, then undo the cover bolts and lift it off. Note how the pump shaft locates in the drive from the oil pump (see illustration). Discard the engine cover gasket, as a new one must be installed, and remove the cover dowels for safekeeping if they are loose.

15 The pump shaft and bearing are secured in the engine cover by snap-rings (see illustration 9.14). Use snap-ring pliers to remove them, then pull out the shaft and bearing.

16 Check the condition of the bearing and replace it if necessary (see Tools and Workshop Tips in the Reference section).

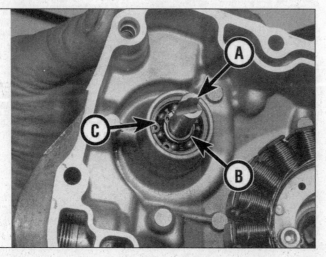

9.14 Oil pump shaft locates in slot (A). Note the water pump shaft snap-ring (B) and bearing snap-ring (C)

9.21 Discard the pump body O-ring (arrow)

9.22 Remove the pump cover and O-ring

17 The pump seal and an oil seal are located in the engine cover – have then both replaced by a scooter dealer or repair shop.

18 Installation is the reverse of removal, noting the following:

Where removed, install new snap-rings.
Install a new engine side cover gasket.
Ensure the pump shaft locates correctly in the drive from the oil pump.
Install a new pump cover O-ring.
Ensure the coolant hoses are pushed fully onto the pump fittings and secured with the clips.
Refill the cooling system and bleed it (see Section 2).
If applicable, fill the engine with the correct type and quantity of oil (see Chapter 1).

Mounted on external crankcase

Removal and installation

19 Drain the coolant and detach the hose(s) from the pump (see Section 2).

20 On four-stroke engines, drain the engine oil (see Chapter 1).

21 Undo the pump mounting bolts and withdraw the pump from the crankcase. Note how the pump shaft locates in the drive from the oil pump. Discard the pump body O-ring as a new one must be installed **(see illustration)**.

22 Undo the pump cover screws and remove the cover. Discard the cover O-ring, as a new one must be installed **(see illustration)**. Clean any sediment out of the cover.

23 The pump shaft is secured by a snap-ring; ease the snap-ring off with a small screwdriver, then pull the shaft and impeller out of the pump body, noting any sealing ring installed behind the impeller **(see illustration)**. The impeller is integral with the shaft.

24 The pump seal and an oil seal are located in the pump body – have both replaced by a scooter dealer or repair shop. Check the condition of the pump bearing and, if necessary, have it replaced at the same time.

25 Installation is the reverse of removal, noting the following:

Install a new sealing ring behind the pump impeller.
Install a new snap-ring to the pump shaft.
Install new O-rings to the pump body and pump cover.
Ensure the pump shaft locates correctly in the drive from the oil pump.
Ensure the coolant hoses are pushed fully onto the pump fittings and secured with the clips.
Refill the cooling system and bleed it (see Section 2).
If applicable, fill the engine with the correct type and quantity of oil (see Chapter 1).

Mounted on internal crankcase

Removal and installation

26 On this type of water pump the seal is installed directly into the crankcase, so unless the engine has been removed from the frame as part of an overhaul, it may be practical to have the entire procedure undertaken by a scooter dealer.

27 Before the seal can be replaced, the fol-lowing components have to be removed:

Alternator rotor (see Chapter 2A or 2B).
If applicable, the oil pump.
Water pump cover.

28 The pump shaft is driven by a belt from the crankshaft; the crankshaft pulley is located behind the alternator. To remove the pump shaft, first hold the pump shaft pulley to prevent it turning, then undo the pump rotor nut and pull off the rotor. Withdraw the pump shaft, together with the pulley and belt, from the crankcase.

29 The pump drive pulley is retained by a snap-ring or ring nut (see Chapter 2A, Section 12).

30 Check the condition of the pump bearing and replace it if necessary.

10 Coolant hoses –
**   removal and installation**

Removal

1 Before removing a hose, drain the coolant (see Section 2).

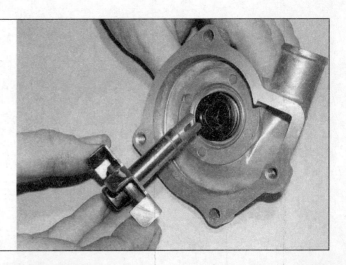

9.23 Pull the impeller out of the pump body

10.2a Loosen the hose clip (arrow) and slide it back along the hose . . .

10.2b . . . then pull the hose off the fitting (arrow)

2 Loosen the hose clip, then slide it back along the hose clear of the fitting. Pull the hose off its fitting (see illustrations).

3 If a hose proves stubborn, release it by rotating it on its fitting before working it off. If all else fails, slit the hose with a sharp knife at the fitting (see *Haynes Hint* in Section 8).

Caution: The radiator fittings are fragile. Do not use excessive force when attempting to remove the hoses.

4 Check the condition of the hose clips; if they are corroded or have lost their tension, replace them.

Installation

5 Slide the clips onto the hose first, then work the hose all the way onto its fitting up to the index mark (see illustration).

HAYNES HiNT *If the hose is difficult to push on its fitting, it can be softened by soaking it in very hot water, or alternatively a little soapy water can be used as a lubricant.*

6 Rotate the hose on its fittings to settle it in position before sliding the clips into place and tightening them securely.

7 Refill the cooling system and bleed it correctly (see Section 2).

10.5 Work the hose on all the way to the index mark

Chapter 4
Fuel and exhaust systems

Contents

Degrees of difficulty

Easy, suitable for novice with little experience	**Fairly easy,** suitable for beginner with some experience	**Fairly difficult,** suitable for competent DIY mechanic	**Difficult,** suitable for experienced DIY mechanic	**Very difficult,** suitable for expert DIY or professional

Specifications

Refer to the *Data* section at the end of this manual for servicing specifications.

1 General information and precautions

The fuel system consists of the fuel tank, fuel tap with filter, carburetor, fuel hoses and control cables. On some scooters, either due to the position of the fuel tank or the use of a fuel header tank in the system, a fuel pump is installed.

The fuel tap is automatic in operation and is opened by engine vacuum. Generally, the fuel filter is installed inside the fuel tank and is part of the tap. On some models, an additional fuel filter is installed in the fuel line.

For cold starting, an electrically-operated automatic choke is installed in the carburetor. Some models also have an electrically-operated carburetor heater.

Air is drawn into the carburetors via an air filter, which is housed above the transmission casing. **Note:** *On two-stroke engines, lubricating oil is mixed with the fuel in the intake manifold. See Chapter 2A for details of the oil pump.*

Several fuel system service procedures are considered routine maintenance items and for that reason are included in Chapter 1.

Precautions

 Warning: Gasoline is extremely flammable, so take extra precautions when you work on any part of the fuel system. Don't smoke or allow open flames or bare light bulbs near the work area, and don't work in a garage where a gas-type appliance is present. If you spill any fuel on your skin, rinse it off immediately with soap and water. When you perform any kind of work on the fuel system, wear safety glasses and have a fire extinguisher suitable for a class B type fire (flammable liquids) on hand.

2.2a Detach the fuel hose from the carburetor . . .

2.2b . . . and the vacuum hose from the manifold . . .

Always perform service procedures in a well-ventilated area to prevent a build-up of fumes.

Never work in a building containing a gas appliance with a pilot light, or any other form of naked flame. Ensure that there are no naked light bulbs or any sources of flame or sparks nearby.

Do not smoke (or allow anyone else to smoke) while in the vicinity of gasoline or of components containing it. Remember the possible presence of vapor from these sources and move well clear before smoking.

Check all electrical equipment belonging to the house, garage or workshop where work is being undertaken (see the Safety first! section of this manual). Remember that certain electrical appliances such as drills, cutters, etc, create sparks in the normal course of operation and must not be used near gasoline or any component containing it. Again, remember the possible presence of fumes before using electrical equipment.

Always mop up any spilled fuel and safely dispose of the rag used.

Any stored fuel that is drained off during servicing work must be kept in sealed containers that are suitable for holding gasoline, and clearly marked as such; the containers themselves should be kept in a safe place.

Read the Safety first! section of this manual carefully before starting work.

2 Fuel tap and filter – check, removal and installation

⚠️ **Warning: Refer to the precautions given in Section 1 before starting work.**

Fuel tap

Note: *Some scooters do not have a separate fuel tap – instead the tap function is controlled by the fuel pump, which will only allow fuel to flow when the engine is turning over.*

See Section 13 for fuel pump check and replacement. On these machines, the fuel filter is installed to the fuel supply hose (see Steps 10 to 14).

Check

1 Where installed, the fuel tap is located on the underside of the fuel tank. Remove any body panels as required for access (see Chapter 9). The tap is automatic, operated by a vacuum created when the engine is running, which opens a diaphragm inside the tap. If the tap is faulty, it must be replaced – it is a sealed unit for which no individual components are available. The most likely problem is a hole or split in the tap diaphragm.

2 To check the tap, detach the fuel hose from the carburetor and place the open end in a small container **(see illustration)**. Detach the vacuum hose from the inlet manifold or carburetor, according to model **(see illustrations)**, and apply a vacuum to it (suck on the hose end) – if you are not sure which hose is which on your model, trace the hoses from the tap. Fuel should flow from the tap and into the container **(see illustration)** – if it doesn't, the diaphragm is probably split.

3 Before replacing the tap, check that the

2.2c . . . or the carburetor

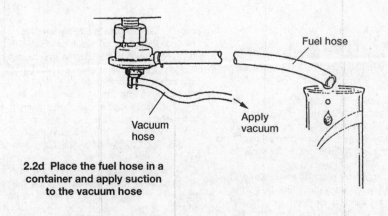

2.2d Place the fuel hose in a container and apply suction to the vacuum hose

Fuel hose

Vacuum hose

Apply vacuum

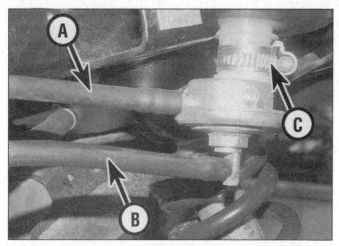

2.6 Fuel hose (A), vacuum hose (B) and retaining clip (C)

2.11 Check the condition of the in-line fuel filter

vacuum hose is securely attached, and that there are no splits or cracks in the hose. If in doubt, attach a spare hose to the vacuum union on the tap and again apply a vacuum. If fuel still does not flow, remove the tap and install a new one.

Removal

4 The tap should not be removed unnecessarily from the tank, otherwise the O-ring or filter may be damaged.

5 Before removing the tap, connect a drain hose to the fuel hose union and insert its end in a container suitable and large enough for storing the fuel. Detach the vacuum hose from the inlet manifold and apply a vacuum to it, to allow the tank to drain.

6 Loosen the clamp securing the tap and withdraw the tap assembly (see illustration). Check the condition of the O-ring. If it is in good condition, it can be re-used, though it is better to use a new one. If it is in any way deteriorated or damaged, it must be replaced.

7 Clean the gauze filter to remove all traces of dirt and fuel sediment. Check the gauze

for holes. If any are found, a new tap should be installed, as the filter is not available individually.

Installation

8 Install the fuel tap into the tank, preferably using a new O-ring, and tighten the clamp securely.

9 Install the fuel and vacuum hoses onto their respective fittings and secure them with their clips.

In-line filter

10 Remove any body panels as required for access (see Chapter 9).

11 Check the filter for signs of sediment or a clogged element (see illustration).

12 To remove the filter, first clamp the fuel hoses to prevent leaks, then loosen the clips securing the fuel hoses to each end of the filter and detach the hoses. If the filter is installed in a bracket, note which way up it fits.

13 The filter is a sealed unit. If it is dirty or clogged, install a new one.

14 Installation is the reverse of removal,

making sure the filter is the correct way up – there should be an arrow marked on the body indicating direction of fuel flow. Replace the clips on the fuel hoses if the old ones are loose or corroded. Remember to remove the clamps from the fuel hoses.

3 Air filter housing – removal and installation

Removal

1 Where applicable, remove the body panels to access the filter housing, which is located above the drivebelt cover on the left-hand side of the scooter. Release the clips or cut the plastic ties securing the air inlet and outlet ducts and, where installed, the breather hose, and detach them from the housing (see illustrations).

2 Where installed, release the idle speed adjuster from its clip on the front of the housing.

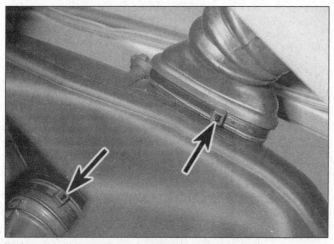

3.1a Release the ties securing the air ducts . . .

3.1b . . . and clips securing the hoses

3.3 Detach the hose for the air temperature sensor (arrow)

3.4a Undo the fixings . . .

3 Where installed, release the air temperature sensor hose from the housing **(see illustration)**

4 Remove the bolts securing the air filter housing to the engine unit and maneuver the housing away, noting how it fits **(see illustrations)**.

Installation

5 Installation is the reverse of removal. Use new plastic cable ties to secure the air inlet and outlet ducts where the originals were cut free.

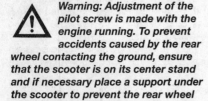

3.4b . . . for the air filter housing

4 Idle fuel/air mixture adjustment – general information

⚠️ *Warning: Adjustment of the pilot screw is made with the engine running. To prevent accidents caused by the rear wheel contacting the ground, ensure that the scooter is on its center stand and if necessary place a support under the scooter to prevent the rear wheel contacting the ground.*

1 Idle fuel/air mixture is set using the pilot screw **(see illustration 8.1 or 9.1)**. Adjustment of the pilot screw is not normally necessary and should only be performed if the engine is running roughly, stalls continually, or if a new pilot screw has been installed.

2 If the pilot screw is removed during a carburetor overhaul, record its current setting by turning the screw it in until it seats lightly, counting the number of turns necessary to achieve this, then unscrew it fully. On installation, turn the screw in until it seats lightly, then back it out the number of turns you've recorded. If installing a new pilot screw, turn the screw in until it seats, then back it out the number of turns specified in the *Data* section at the end of this manual.

3 Pilot screw adjustment must be made with the engine running and at normal working temperature. Stop the engine and screw the pilot screw in until it seats lightly, then back it out the number of turns specified in the *Data* section. Start the engine and set the idle speed to the specified amount (see Chapter 1).

4 Now try turning the pilot screw inwards by no more than a small amount, noting its effect on the idle speed, then repeat the process, this time turning the screw outwards.

5 The pilot screw should be set in the position which gives the most consistent, even idle speed without the automatic transmission engaging, and so that the engine does not stall when the twistgrip is opened. **Note:** *It will not be possible to achieve an even idle speed if the spark plug needs adjustment or if the air filter element is dirty. On four-stroke engines, ensure the valve clearances are correctly set.*

6 Once a satisfactory pilot screw setting has been achieved, further adjustments to the idle speed can be made with the idle speed adjuster screw (see Chapter 1).

7 If it is not possible to achieve a satisfactory idle speed after adjusting the pilot screw, take the machine to a scooter dealer and have the fuel/air mixture adjusted with the aid of an exhaust gas analyser.

5 Automatic choke unit – check

1 Poor starting or poor engine performance and an increase in fuel consumption are possible signs that the automatic choke is not working properly.

2 The resistance of the choke should be checked with a multimeter after the engine has been warmed to normal operating temperature, then allowed to cool for ten minutes. Remove the engine access panel (see Chapter 9) and trace the wiring from the automatic choke unit on the carburetor and disconnect it at the connectors **(see illustrations)**.

3 Measure the resistance between the terminals on the choke unit side of the connector with the multimeter set to the ohms scale. If the result is not as specified in the *Data* section at the end of this manual, replace the choke unit (see Section 8 or Section 9).

4 To check that the plunger is not seized in the choke body, first remove the choke unit from the carburetor (see Section 8 or Section 9). Measure the protrusion of the plunger from the body **(see illustration)**. Next, use

5.2a Automatic choke unit (arrow) on a slide type carburetor . . .

5.2b . . . and on a CV type carburetor

jumper wires to connect a good 12V battery to the choke unit terminals and measure the protrusion again after 5 minutes. If the measurement has not increased by approximately 3 to 6 mm (depending on the type of carburetor) the unit is faulty and should be replaced.

6 Carburetor overhaul – general information

1 Poor engine performance, difficult starting, stalling, flooding and backfiring are all signs that carburetor maintenance may be required.
2 Keep in mind that many so-called carburetor problems can often be traced to mechanical faults within the engine or ignition system malfunctions. Try to establish for certain that the carburetor is in need of maintenance before beginning a major overhaul.
3 Check the fuel tap and filter, the fuel and vacuum hoses, the fuel pump (where installed), the intake manifold joints, the air filter, the ignition system and the spark plug before assuming that a carburetor overhaul is required.
4 Most carburetor problems are caused by dirt particles, varnish and other deposits

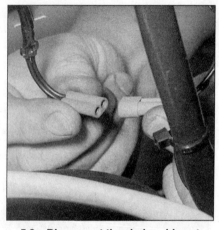

5.2c Disconnect the choke wiring at the connector

which build up in - and eventually block - the fuel jets and air passages inside the carburetor. Also, in time, gaskets and O-rings deteriorate and cause fuel and air leaks which lead to poor performance.
5 When overhauling the carburetor, disassemble it completely and clean the parts thoroughly with a carburetor cleaning solvent. If available, blow through the fuel jets and air passages with compressed air to

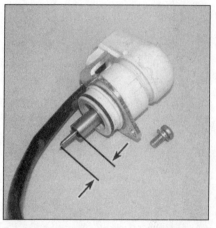

5.4 Measure the protrusion of the plunger from the body

ensure they are clear. Once the cleaning process is complete, reassemble the carburetor using new gaskets and O-rings.
6 Before disassembling the carburetor, make sure you have the correct carburetor gasket set, some carburetor cleaner, a supply of clean rags, some means of blowing out the carburetor passages and a clean place to work.

7 Carburetor – removal and installation

 Warning: Refer to the precautions given in Section 1 before starting work.

Removal

1 Remove the body panels as required on your scooter to access the carburetor (see Chapter 9). Where installed, remove the carburetor cover, noting how it fits **(see illustration)**.

7.1 Remove the cover (arrow), noting how it fits

7.2 Release the clip (arrow) and detach the air duct

7.3 Disconnect the carburetor heater hoses (arrows)

7.4a Remove the screw . . .

7.4b . . . or unscrew the top . . .

2 Remove the air filter housing (see Section 3). Where installed, release the clip or cut the tie securing the air intake duct and detach it from the carburetor (see illustration).

3 Trace the wiring from the automatic choke unit and disconnect it at the connector. Where installed, trace the wiring from the carburetor heater and disconnect it at the connector. Free the wiring from any clips or ties. Where

installed on liquid-cooled engines, undo the bolt securing the heater union to the carburetor or disconnect the heater hoses (see illustration).

4 If the throttle cable is attached to a slide inside the carburetor (see Section 8), undo the carburetor top cover, then lift off the cover and withdraw the throttle slide assembly (see illustrations). Secure the cable where the slide assembly will not be damaged. To detach the slide assembly from the cable, see Section 8.

5 If the throttle cable is attached to a pulley on the outside of the carburetor, first detach the outer cable from its bracket, then detach the cable end from the pulley (see illustration).

6 If the idle speed adjuster is mounted adjacent to the carburetor, release the adjuster from its clip and feed it through to the carburetor.

7 Release the clips securing the fuel hose and vacuum hose, and oil hose on two-stroke engines, noting which fits where (see Section 2). Be prepared to catch any residual fuel in a suitable container. The fuel and oil

7.4c . . . then withdraw the throttle slide assembly

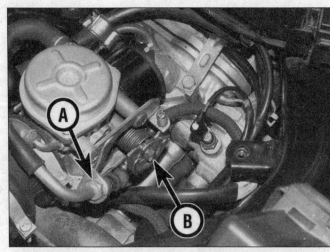

7.5 Detach the cable from the bracket (A), then the pulley (B)

7.8 Carburetor drain screw (arrow)

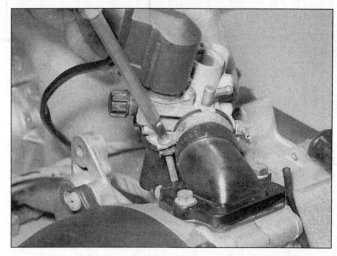

7.9a Loosen the carburetor clamp . . .

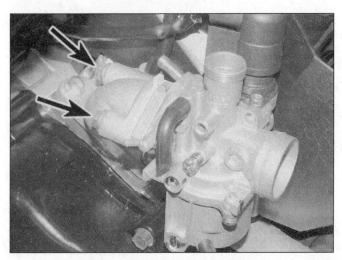

7.9b . . . undo the carburetor bolts . . .

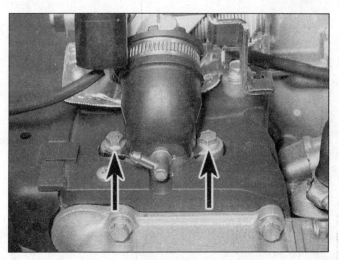

7.9c . . . or remove the manifold bolts

hoses should be clamped to prevent leaks using any of the methods shown (see *Tools and Workshop Tips* in the *Reference* section). Where installed, the breather and drain hoses can usually be left attached and withdrawn with the carburetor, as their lower ends are not secured. Note their routing as they are withdrawn. **Note:** *If the vacuum and oil hoses are connected to the intake manifold, they can be left attached if the carburetor is being removed without it.*

8 Loosen the drain screw and drain all the fuel from the carburetor into a suitable container **(see illustration)**. Discard the drain screw O-ring, as a new one must be used. On installation, install the new O-ring and tighten the drain screw securely. **Note:** *If a cleaning solvent is going to be used, install the new O-ring after the cleaning process.*

9 Either loosen the clamp or undo the bolts securing the carburetor to the inlet manifold on the engine and remove the carburetor. Or, undo the bolts securing the manifold to the engine and remove it and the carbure-

tor together **(see illustrations)**. Discard the manifold gasket or O-ring and install a new one on reassembly.

Caution: Stuff clean rag into the intake after removing the carburetor to prevent anything from falling inside.

Installation

10 Installation is the reverse of removal, noting the following:

Make sure the carburetor is fully engaged with the intake manifold and the clamp is securely tightened.

Make sure all hoses are correctly routed and secured and not trapped or kinked.

Check the throttle cable adjustment (see Chapter 1).

On liquid-cooled models, top-up the cooling system if necessary.

Check the idle speed and adjust as necessary (see Chapter 1).

8 Slide carburetor – overhaul

  Warning: Refer to the precautions given in Section 1 before starting work.

Note: *Carburetor design differs for two-stroke and four-stroke engines. Two-stroke engines use a slide type carburetor, whereas four-stroke engines generally use a constant-vacuum (CV) type – refer to the specifications in the Data section at the end of this manual to ensure that you follow the correct procedure either in this Section or Section 9.*

Disassembly

1 Remove the carburetor (see Section 7). Take care when removing components to note their exact locations and any springs or

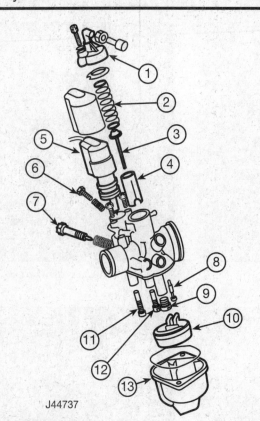

8.1 Slide-type carburetor components

1   Top cover
2   Slide spring
3   Needle
4   Slide
5   Automatic choke unit
6   Pilot screw
7   Idle speed adjuster screw
8   Float needle valve
9   Main jet
10 Float
11 Starter jet
12 Pilot jet
13 Float chamber

J44737

8.2a Remove the choke unit cover . . .

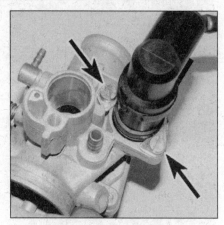

8.2b . . . then undo the clamp screws (arrows) . . .

O-rings that may be installed **(see illustration)**.

2 Where installed, remove the cover on the automatic choke unit, then remove the clamp securing the unit in the carburetor **(see illustrations)**. Withdraw the choke unit, noting how it fits **(see illustration)**.

3 To remove the throttle slide assembly from the cable if the top cover and slide assembly have already been removed from the

8.2c . . . and pull out the choke unit

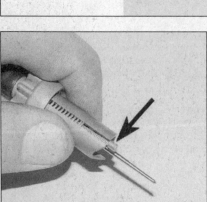

8.3a Compress the spring until the cable end (arrow) is free . . .

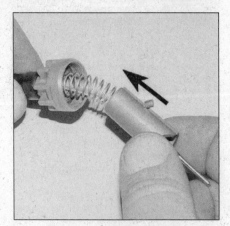

8.3b . . . then slot it up through the slide . . .

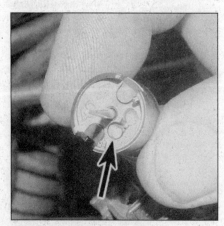

8.3c . . . or through the hole (arrow) in the bottom of the slide

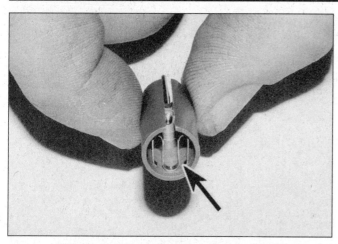

8.4 Remove the spring clip, where installed

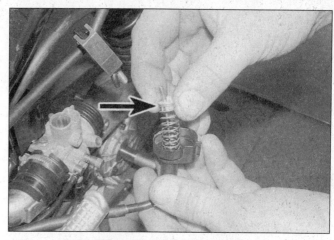

8.5a Remove the spring seat (arrow) . . .

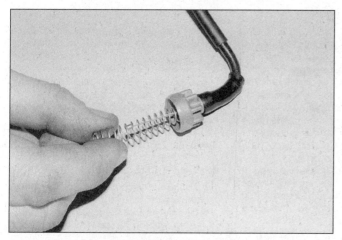

8.5b . . . then pull the spring . . .

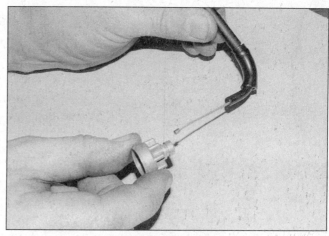

8.5c . . . and carburetor top cover off the cable

carburetor, first compress the slide spring. Either slot the cable end up through the side of the slide and detach the slide, or slot the cable end out of its recess and through the hole in the bottom of the slide **(see illustrations)**.

4 On some carburetors, the needle is retained by a spring clip – remove the clip,

noting how it fits **(see illustration)**. Lift the needle out of the slide.

5 Remove the spring and, where installed, the spring seat from the cable, then pull the carburetor top cover off the cable **(see illustrations)**.

6 If the carburetor top cover is still in place, unscrew the cover retaining screws, then lift

off the cover and withdraw the slide assembly (see Section 7). Unhook the spring retaining the slide assembly, then twist the needle holder and withdraw it from the slide.

7 Undo the screws securing the float chamber to the base of the carburetor and remove it – discard the gasket, as a new one must be used **(see illustrations)**.

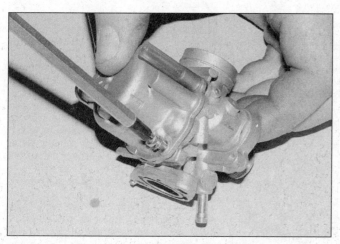

8.7a Undo the float chamber screws

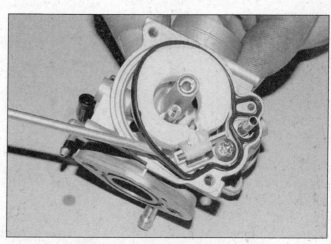

8.7b Lift out the float chamber gasket

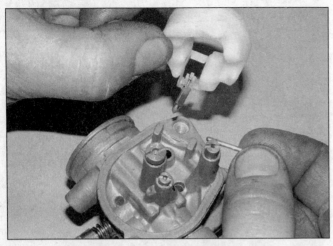

8.8a Remove the float pin and lift out the float

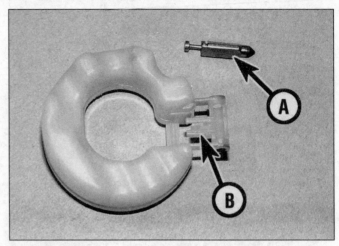

8.8b Note how the float needle valve (A) fits onto the tab (B)

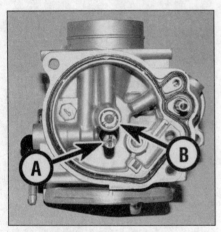

8.9a Carburetor with two removable jets – pilot jet (A) and main jet (B)

8 Using a pair of thin-nose pliers, carefully withdraw the float pin (see illustration). Note: *The float pin may be retained by a small screw.* If necessary, displace the pin using a small punch or a nail. Remove the float and unhook the float needle valve, noting how it fits onto the tab on the float (see illustration).

9 Some carburetors are installed with two removable jets (pilot jet and main jet), some have three removable jets (pilot jet, main jet and starter jet) (see illustrations). Note the location of the jets, then unscrew them. The main jet screws into the base of the atomizer; if the atomizer is slotted, unscrew it if required. Note: *The jets will be marked with an identification number or code; check the jets against the specifications in the* Data *section at the end of this manual.*

10 The pilot screw can be removed if required, but note that its setting will be disturbed (see *Haynes Hint*). Unscrew and remove the pilot screw along with its spring and O-ring, where installed.

HAYNES HINT *To record the pilot screw's current setting, turn the screw in until it seats lightly, counting the number of turns necessary to achieve this, then unscrew it fully. On installation, turn the screw in until it seats, then back it out the number of turns you've recorded.*

Cleaning

Caution: Use only a petroleum-based solvent for carburetor cleaning. Don't use caustic cleaners.

11 Use carburetor cleaning solvent to loosen and dissolve the varnish and other deposits on the carburetor body and float chamber; use a nylon-bristled brush to remove the stubborn deposits. Dry the components with compressed air. Note: *Avoid soaking the carburetor body in solvent if any O-ring seals remain inside.*

12 If available, use compressed air to blow out all the fuel jets and the air passages in the carburetor body, not forgetting the passages in the carburetor intake.

Caution: Never clean the jets or passages with a piece of wire or a drill bit, as they will be enlarged, causing the fuel and air metering rates to be upset.

Inspection

13 If removed, check the tapered portion of the pilot screw and the spring for wear or damage. Install a new O-ring and replace the screw or spring if necessary.

14 Check the carburetor body, float chamber and top cover for cracks, distorted sealing surfaces and other damage. If any defects are found, replace the faulty component, although a new carburetor will probably be necessary.

15 Insert the throttle slide in the carburetor body and check that it moves up-and-down smoothly. Check the surface of the slide for wear. If it's worn or scored excessively or doesn't move smoothly, replace the components as necessary.

16 Where installed, check that the clip is correctly positioned on the needle (see *Data* section). If necessary, remove the clip and check the needle for straightness by rolling it on a flat surface such as a piece of glass. Install a new needle if it's bent or if the tip is worn. Reinstall the clip for safekeeping.

17 Inspect the tip of the float needle valve. If it has grooves or scratches in it, or is in any way worn, it must be replaced. If the valve seat is damaged, check the availability of new parts, otherwise a new carburetor body will have to be installed. Note: *On scooters*

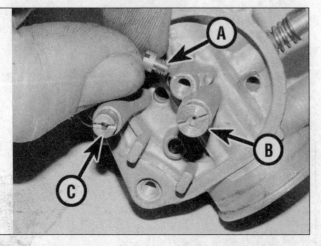

8.9b Carburetor with three removable jets – pilot jet (A), main jet (B) and starter jet (C)

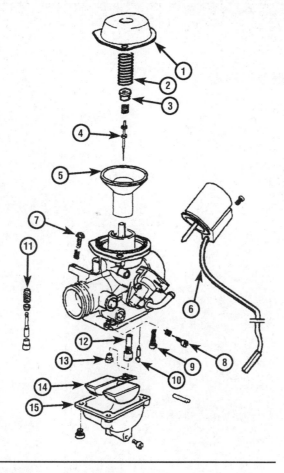

9.1 Constant vacuum (CV) type carburetor components

1   Top cover
2   Spring
3   Needle retainer
4   Needle
5   Diaphragm and piston assembly
6   Automatic choke unit
7   Idle speed adjuster screw
8   Pilot screw
9   Pilot jet
10 Float needle valve
11 Accelerator pump assembly
12 Needle jet
13 Main jet
14 Float
15 Float chamber

as described in Step 6, install the needle holder in the slide and twist the holder to lock it in place. Secure the slide assembly to the cover with the spring, then install the slide assembly and the cover and tighten the cover screws securely.

27 Install the carburetor (see Section 7).

28 If applicable, install the needle in the throttle slide (see Step 4). Reverse the procedure in Steps 3 and 5 to install the throttle slide assembly onto the cable, then install the carburetor top cover.

9   Constant-vacuum (CV) carburetor – overhaul

⚠️ **Warning: Refer to the precautions given in Section 1 before proceeding.**

Note: *Carburetor design differs for two-stroke and four-stroke engines. Two-stroke engines use a slide type carburetor, whereas four-stroke engines generally use a constant-vacuum (CV) type – refer to the specifications in the Data section at the end of this manual to ensure that you follow the correct procedure either in this Section or Section 8.*

Disassembly

1   Remove the carburetor (see Section 7). Take care when removing components to note their exact locations and any springs or O-rings that may be installed **(see illustration)**.

2   Where installed, remove the cover on the automatic choke unit, then remove the clamp securing the choke in the carburetor. Withdraw the choke, noting how it fits **(see illustration)**. On some carburetors, it is possible to undo the screws securing the choke unit mounting and remove it. Discard the gasket, as a new one must be installed. If required, undo the screw securing the accelerator pump lever and remove the lever and return spring.

with a pumped and pressurized fuel system, a worn or incorrectly-sized carburetor float needle valve seat will not be able to shut off the fuel supply sufficiently to prevent carburetor flooding and excessive use of fuel.

18 Check the float for damage. This will usually be apparent by the presence of fuel inside the float. If the float is damaged, it must be replaced.

19 Inspect the automatic choke unit plunger and needle for signs of wear and replace the unit if necessary **(see illustration 5.4)**. To check the operation of the choke unit, see Section 5.

Reassembly

Note: *When reassembling the carburetor, be sure to use new O-rings and gaskets. Do not overtighten the carburetor jets and screws, as they are easily damaged.*

20 If removed, install the pilot screw, spring and O-ring; adjust the screw to the setting as noted on removal (see Step 10).

21 If removed, install the atomizer. Screw the main jet into the end of the atomizer.

22 Install the pilot jet and, if applicable, the starter jet.

23 Hook the float needle valve onto the float tab, then position the float assembly in the carburetor, making sure the needle valve enters its seat. Install the float pin, making sure it is secure. If necessary, the carburetor

float height should be checked at this point (see Section 10).

24 Install a new gasket onto the float chamber, making sure it is seated properly in its groove, then install the chamber onto the carburetor and tighten the screws securely. If necessary, the carburetor fuel height should be checked at this point (see Section 10).

25 Install the choke unit and secure it with the clamp and screws. Install the choke unit cover, if equipped.

26 If the carburetor top cover was removed

9.2 Withdraw the choke unit

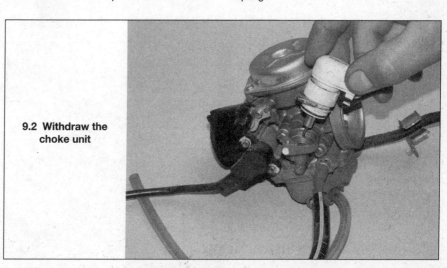

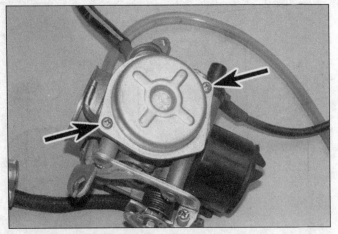

9.3a Undo the top cover retaining screws (arrows)

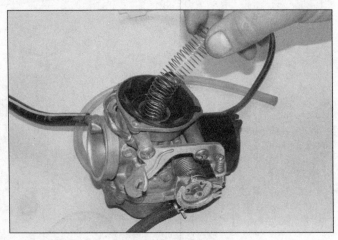

9.3b Lift out the spring

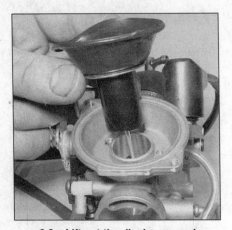

9.3c Lift out the diaphragm and piston assembly

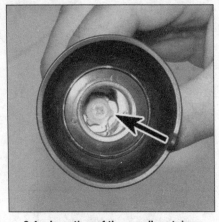

9.4a Location of the needle retainer (arrow)

9.4b Push the needle up from the bottom

3 Unscrew and remove the top cover retaining screws, then lift off the cover and remove the spring from inside the piston (see illustrations). Carefully peel the diaphragm away from its sealing groove in the carburetor and withdraw the diaphragm and piston assembly (see illustration). Note how the tab on the diaphragm fits in the recess in the carburetor body.

Caution: Do not use a sharp instrument to displace the diaphragm as it is easily damaged.

4 On some carburetors it is necessary to unscrew the needle retainer, otherwise lift out the needle retainer, noting any spring or washer installed underneath, then push the needle up from the bottom of the piston and withdraw it from the top (see illustrations).

5 Remove the screws securing the float chamber to the base of the carburetor and remove it (see illustration). Discard the gasket, as a new one must be used.

6 On carburetors with an accelerator pump, either withdraw the accelerator pump spring and plunger from the carburetor body, noting how it fits, or unscrew the accelerator pump assembly from the float chamber (see illus-

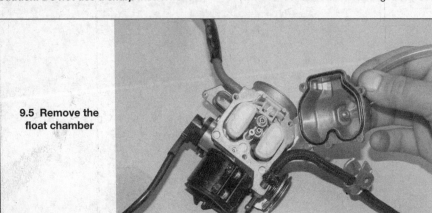

9.5 Remove the float chamber

9.6 Withdraw the accelerator pump assembly

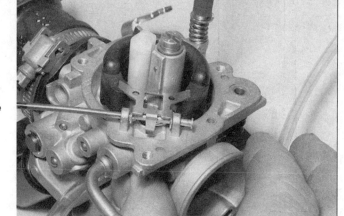

9.7a Displace the float pin

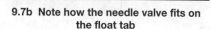

9.7b Note how the needle valve fits on the float tab

tration). Discard the O-ring, as a new one must be installed.

7 Using a pair of long-nose pliers, carefully withdraw the float pin; if necessary, displace the pin using a small punch or a nail (see illustration). Remove the float and unhook the float needle valve, noting how it fits onto the tab on the float (see illustration).

8 Where installed, undo the screw secur-

ing the float needle valve seat clamp, then withdraw the valve seat (see illustrations). Discard the O-ring, as a new one should be used.

9 Where installed, remove the plastic jet cover. Unscrew the pilot jet and the main jet (see illustrations). The main jet screws into the base of the needle jet; if the needle jet is slotted, unscrew it if required.

10 The pilot screw can be removed if required, but note that its setting will be disturbed (see *Haynes Hint* following this Step). Unscrew and remove the pilot screw along with its spring and O-ring, where installed. **Note:** *Do not remove the screws securing the throttle butterfly to the throttle shaft.*

9.8a Remove the clamp screw (arrow) . . .

9.8b . . . and withdraw the valve seat

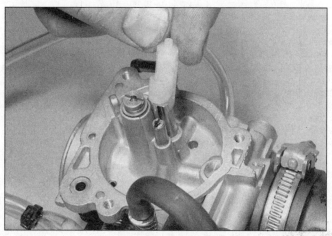

9.9a Remove the jet cover . . .

9.9b . . . then unscrew the main jet (A) and the pilot jet (B)

9.27 Insert the needle into the piston

9.28 Ensure the diaphragm and the tab (arrow) are correctly seated

HAYNES HiNT *To record the pilot screw's current setting, turn the screw in until it seats lightly, counting the number of turns necessary to achieve this, then unscrew it fully. On installation, turn the screw in until it seats, then back it out the number of turns you've recorded.*

Cleaning

Caution: Use only a petroleum-based solvent for carburetor cleaning. Don't use caustic cleaners.

11 Follow Steps 11 and 12 in Section 8 to clean the carburetor body and jets. If the carburetor has an accelerator pump, pay particular attention to the fuel passage in the float chamber. On some carburetors, the fuel passage is installed with a one-way valve; blow through the fuel passage with compressed air from the bottom of the pump piston housing. **Note:** *Avoid soaking the carburetor body in solvent if any O-ring seals remain inside.*

Caution: Never clean the jets or passages with a piece of wire or a drill bit, as they will be enlarged, causing the fuel and air metering rates to be upset.

Inspection

12 If removed, check the tapered portion of the pilot screw and the spring for wear or damage. Install a new O-ring and replace the screw or spring if necessary.
13 Check the carburetor body, float chamber and top cover for cracks, distorted sealing surfaces and other damage. If any defects are found, replace the faulty component, although replacement of the entire carburetor will probably be necessary.
14 Inspect the piston diaphragm for splits, holes and general deterioration. Holding it up to a light will help to reveal problems of this nature. Insert the piston in the carburetor body and check that the piston moves up-and-down smoothly. Check the surface of the

piston for wear. If it's worn or scored excessively or doesn't move smoothly, replace the components as necessary.
15 Where installed, check that the clip is correctly positioned on the needle (see *Data* section). If necessary, remove the clip and check the needle for straightness by rolling it on a flat surface such as a piece of glass. Install a new needle if it's bent or if the tip is worn. Reinstall the clip for safekeeping.
16 Inspect the tip of the float needle valve. If it has grooves or scratches in it, or is in any way worn, it must be replaced. If the valve seat is damaged, check the availability of new parts, otherwise a new carburetor body will have to be installed. **Note:** *On scooters with a pumped and pressurized fuel system, a worn or incorrectly-sized carburetor float needle valve seat will not be able to shut off the fuel supply sufficiently to prevent carburetor flooding and excessive use of fuel.*
17 Operate the throttle shaft to make sure the throttle butterfly valve opens and closes smoothly. If it doesn't, cleaning the throttle linkage may help. Otherwise, replace the carburetor.
18 Check the float for damage. This will usually be apparent by the presence of fuel inside the float. If the float is damaged, it must be replaced.
19 Inspect the automatic choke unit plunger and needle for signs of wear and replace the unit if necessary. To check the operation of the choke unit, see Section 5.
20 Inspect the accelerator pump piston and its seat in the float chamber for signs of wear. Ensure that the spring and the rubber boot are not damaged or deformed and replace them if necessary.

Reassembly

Note: *When reassembling the carburetor, be sure to use new O-rings and seals. Do not overtighten the carburetor jets and screws as they are easily damaged.*
21 If removed, install the pilot screw, spring and O-ring; adjust the screw to the setting as

noted on removal (see Step 10).
22 If removed, install the needle jet.
23 Install the main jet and the pilot jet; install the plastic jet cover where installed.
24 If removed, install the float needle valve seat using a new O-ring, then install the clamp and tighten the screw.
25 Hook the float needle valve onto the float tab, then position the float assembly in the carburetor, making sure the needle valve enters its seat. Install the pin, making sure it is secure. If necessary, the carburetor float height should be checked at this point (see Section 10).
26 On carburetors with an accelerator pump, either install the accelerator pump spring and plunger in the carburetor body, or install a new O-ring to the accelerator pump assembly, then screw the assembly into the float chamber (see Step 6). Install a new gasket onto the float chamber, making sure it is seated properly in its groove, then install the chamber onto the carburetor and tighten the screws securely. If necessary, the carburetor fuel height should be checked at this point (see Section 10).
27 Check that the clip is correctly positioned on the needle, then insert the needle into the piston **(see illustration)**. If applicable, install the spring and spring seat, then install the needle retainer.
28 Insert the piston assembly into the carburetor body and push it down lightly, ensuring the needle is correctly aligned with the needle jet. Align the tab on the diaphragm with the recess in the carburetor body, then press the diaphragm outer edge into its groove, making sure it is correctly seated **(see illustration)**. Check the diaphragm is not creased, and that the piston moves smoothly up-and-down in its bore.
29 Install the spring into the piston and install the top cover to the carburetor, making sure the spring locates over the raised section on the inside of the cover, then tighten the cover screws securely **(see illustration)**.
30 Where installed, install the choke unit mounting with a new gasket.

9.29 Ensure the spring locates correctly inside the cover

31 Install the automatic choke unit and secure it with its clamp. If equipped, install the choke unit cover.
32 If removed, install the accelerator pump lever and return spring and secure them with the screw.
33 Install the carburetor (see Section 7).

10 Fuel level and float height – check

1 If the carburetor floods when the scooter is in use, and the float needle valve and the valve seat are good, the fuel or float height should be checked and the result compared to the specification in the *Data* section at the end of this manual.

Fuel level check

2 If not already done, remove the carburetor (see Section 7).
3 Support the carburetor upright in a vise and connect a length of clear fuel hose to the drain union on the base of the float chamber. Secure the hose up against the side of

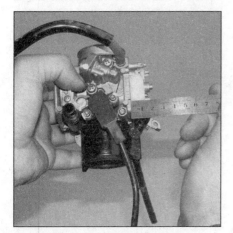

10.7 Measuring the carburetor float height

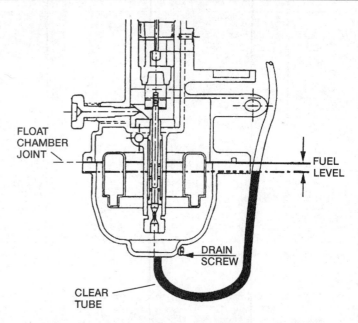

10.3 Set-up for measuring the fuel level in the carburetor

the carburetor and mark it level with the float chamber-to-carburetor body joint, or the level mark on the side of the carburetor body **(see illustration)**.
4 Carefully pour a small amount of fuel into the carburetor via the fuel hose fitting, then undo the drain screw in the bottom of the float chamber enough to allow fuel to flow into the clear hose. Continue pouring fuel into the carburetor until the float needle valve shuts off the supply, at which point the level in the clear hose should be at the specified height in relation to the mark (see *Data* section at the end of this manual).
5 If the fuel level is incorrect, remove the float chamber and check the float tab for wear or damage (see Section 8 or 9). If the float tab is metal, it can be adjusted carefully to correct the fuel height, otherwise a new float will have to be installed.

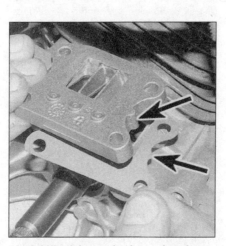

11.2 Lift off the reed valve and gasket – note the tabs (arrows) for positioning

Float height check

6 If not already done, remove the carburetor (see Section 7). Remove the float chamber (see Section 8 or 9).
7 Angle the carburetor so that the float needle valve is resting against the valve seat and measure the distance between the float chamber gasket face and the bottom of the float **(see illustration)**.
8 Compare the result with the measurement in the *Data* section. **Note:** *On some carburetors, it is sufficient that the bottom straight-edge of the float should be parallel with the gasket face.*
9 If the float height is incorrect, check the float tab for wear or damage (see Section 8 or 9). If the float tab is metal, it can be adjusted carefully to correct the fuel height, otherwise a new float will have to be installed.

11 Reed valve (two-stroke engines) – removal, inspection and installation

Removal

1 Remove the carburetor, along with the intake manifold (see Section 7).
2 Withdraw the reed valve from the crankcase, noting how it fits **(see illustration)**.
3 Discard any seals or gaskets, as new ones must be installed.

Inspection

4 Check the reed valve body closely for cracks, distortion and any other damage, particularly around the mating surfaces between the crankcase and the intake manifold – a

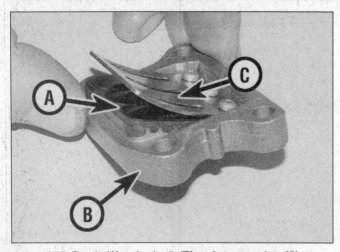

11.5 Reeds (A), valve body (B) and stopper plate (C)

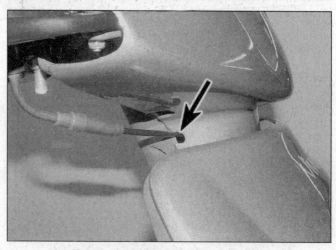

12.3 Release the cable from the grommet (arrow)

good seal must be maintained between the components, otherwise crankcase pressure - and therefore engine performance - will be affected.

5 Check the reeds for cracks, distortion and any other damage. Check also that there are no dirt particles trapped between the reeds and their seats. The reeds should sit flat against the valve body so that a good seal is obtained when the crankcase is under pressure **(see illustration)**. After prolonged use, the reeds tend to become bent and will not therefore seal properly, in which case the assembly should be replaced. A good way to check is to hold the valve up to the light – if light is visible between the reeds and the body, they are not sealing properly. If the engine is difficult to start or idles erratically, this could be the problem.

6 Check that the stopper plate retaining screws are tight; do not disassemble the reed valve unnecessarily as individual components are not available.

Installation

7 Installation is the reverse of removal, noting the following:

> Ensure all mating surfaces are clean and perfectly smooth.
> Use new gaskets.

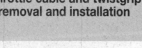

12 Throttle cable and twistgrip – removal and installation

Warning: Refer to the precautions given in Section 1 before proceeding.

Note: *All four-stroke engines and two-stroke engines equipped with centrifugal oil pumps (see Chapter 2A) are equipped with one-piece throttle cables. Two-stroke engines with cable-controlled oil pumps are equipped with three-piece cables.*

One-piece cable
Removal

1 Remove the upper or front handlebar cover, the engine access panel and any body panels as required on your scooter to access the cable (see Chapter 9). Where installed, remove the carburetor cover, noting how it fits **(see illustration 7.1)**.

2 Disconnect the cable from the twistgrip (see Steps 20 to 23).

3 If necessary, release the cable from the grommet where it passes through the handlebar cover **(see illustration)**.

4 Detach the cable from the throttle slide (see Section 8) or the carburetor pulley (see Section 9).

5 Ensure the cable is free from any clips or guides, then withdraw it from the machine, noting the correct routing.

 When installing a new cable, tape the lower end of the new cable to the upper end of the old cable before removing it from the machine. Slowly pull the lower end of the old cable out, guiding the new cable down into position. Using this method will ensure the cable is routed correctly.

Installation

6 Installation is the reverse of removal, noting the following:

> Lubricate the upper end of the cable with grease before installing it into the twistgrip.
> Ensure the cable is correctly routed and clipped into place.
> Adjust the cable freeplay (see Chapter 1).
> Check the cable operation before riding the scooter.

Three-piece cable
Removal

7 The throttle cable consists of three sections – the main cable from the twistgrip goes into a splitter, with separate cables from this going

to the carburetor and oil pump (see Chapter 1, Section 13).

8 If a cable problem is diagnosed, check the availability of new parts – on some scooters it is possible to replace individual cables rather than the whole assembly.

9 Remove the upper or front handlebar cover, the engine access panel and any body panels as required on your scooter to access the cables (see Chapter 9). Where installed, remove the carburetor cover, noting how it fits **(see illustration 7.1)**.

10 Disconnect the cable from the twistgrip (see Steps 20 to 23).

11 If necessary, release the cable from the grommet where it passes through the handlebar cover **(see illustration 12.3)**.

12 Either detach the cable from the throttle slide assembly and the carburetor top cover (see Section 8) or the carburetor pulley (see Section 9).

13 If required, to access the cable at the oil pump, remove the plug in the engine case or the pump cover on the engine side cover (see Chapter 1, Section 19). Loosen the cable adjuster locknut, then detach the cable end from the pump pulley and detach the outer cable from its bracket or the engine case **(see illustration)**.

12.13 Unscrew the locknut (arrow) and detach the cable

12.17a Pull off the cable covers . . .

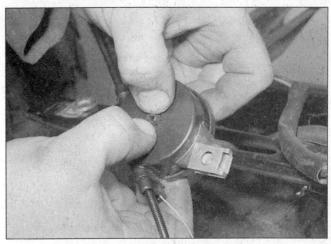

12.17b . . . then press in the tabs . . .

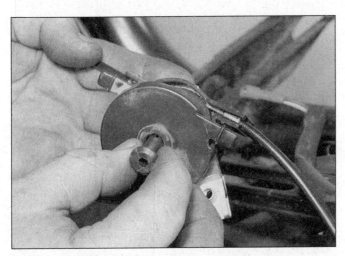

12.17c . . . and remove the peg and cover

12.17d Draw out the outer cables . . .

14 If the complete cable assembly is being removed, ensure the cables are free from any clips or guides, then withdraw the assembly from the machine, noting the correct routing.

HAYNES HiNT *When installing a new cable, tape the lower end of the new cable to the upper end of the old cable before removing it from the machine. Slowly pull the lower end of the old cable out, guiding the new cable down into position. Using this method will ensure the cable is routed correctly.*

15 If an individual cable is being removed, first detach the cable from the twistgrip, carburetor or oil pump as applicable, then detach the cable from the splitter as follows.
16 Two types of cable splitter are used. One operates with the throttle cable pulling on a pivoted cam, while the other operates with the throttle cable pulling on a slider.
17 On models with the cam type splitter, first remove the screw securing the splitter to its mounting and draw the cable covers off the splitter. Depress the tabs on the bottom

of the peg securing the splitter cover, then draw the peg out of the splitter and remove the cover **(see illustrations)**. Draw the outer cables out of their sockets, then lift the cam off its pivot and detach the cable ends from

the cam as required, noting their relative positions **(see illustrations)**.
18 On models with the slider type splitter, first detach the splitter holder from the frame and draw the covers off the splitter housing **(see**

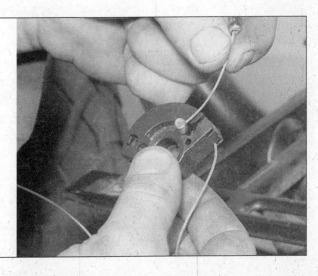

12.17e . . . then lift out the cam and detach the inner cable ends

12.18a Detach the splitter (arrow) from the frame . . .

12.18b . . . then pull off the covers

illustrations). Remove the cap from the splitter and pull the slider out of the housing with the throttle cable **(see illustrations)**. Detach the cable(s) from the splitter as required, noting their relative positions **(see illustration)**.

Caution: Before removing a cable, make a careful note of its routing to ensure correct installation.

Installation

19 Installation is the reverse of removal, noting the following:

Lubricate the cable ends with grease.
Ensure the cables are correctly routed and clipped into place – they must not interfere with any other component and should not be kinked or bent sharply.
Adjust the cable freeplay and check the oil pump setting (see Chapter 1).
Check the cable operation before riding the scooter.

Throttle twistgrip

20 Two types of twistgrip are used. Some scooters have a motorcycle type twistgrip,

12.18c Remove the cap . . .

where the end of the inner cable fits into a socket in the twistgrip. Others have a sliding type twistgrip, where the end of the inner cable is secured in a slider with a screw. The slider runs in a spiral track inside the twistgrip.

21 To access the cable at the twistgrip, first remove the upper or front handlebar cover (see Chapter 9).

22 On models with a motorcycle type twistgrip, loosen the cable adjuster locknut and thread the adjuster fully in to loosen the cable

12.18d . . . and pull out the slider

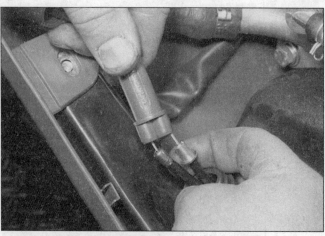

12.18e Detach the cables from the splitter

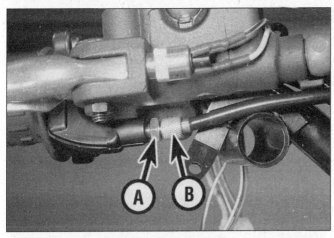

12.22a Loosen the locknut (A) and thread the adjuster (B) fully in

12.22b Undo the screws (arrows) and remove the plate . . .

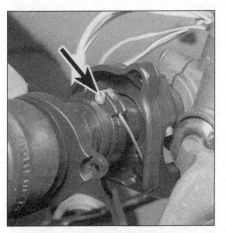

12.22c . . . then detach the cable end (arrow) from its socket

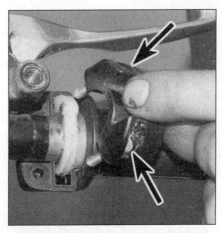

12.22d Undo the screws (arrows) and split the housing . . .

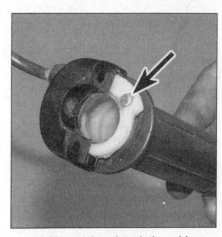

12.22e . . . then detach the cable end (arrow)

(see illustration). Either pull back the twist-grip rubber, then remove the screws securing the cover plate and remove the plate, or undo the twistgrip housing screws and separate the two halves of the housing (see illustrations).

Detach the cable end from its socket, then remove the cable from the housing, noting how it fits.

23 On models with a sliding twistgrip, loosen the screw securing the end of the cable in the

slider, then draw the cable out (see illustrations). Note the distance from the end of the cable where the screw located as an aid for correctly setting the new cable.

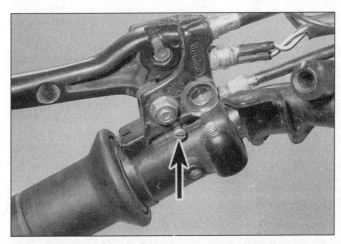

12.23a Loosen the cable clamp screw (arrow) . . .

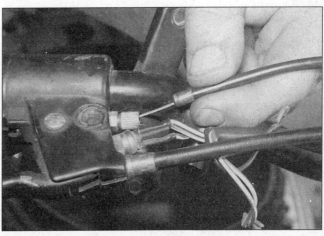

12.23b . . . and pull out the cable

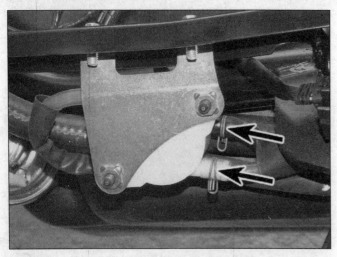

13.3 Location of fuel pump – note the clips (arrows) securing the hoses

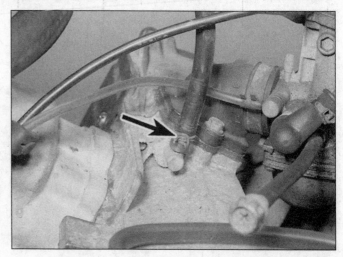

13.5 Check the vacuum hose (arrow) from the crankcase

13 Fuel pump – check and replacement

⚠ **Warning: Refer to the precautions given in Section 1 before proceeding.**

Vacuum fuel pump

Check

1 When the engine is running, the alternating vacuum and pressure in the crankcase opens and closes a diaphragm in the pump. Generally, the pump supplies fuel directly to the carburetor, but on some scooters the pump supplies fuel to a header tank which ensures an immediate supply of fuel to the carburetor when the scooter has been standing unused.

2 The most likely cause of pump failure will be a split in the pump diaphragm.

3 Generally, the fuel pump is mounted on the frame alongside the fuel tank **(see illustration)**. Remove the body panels as required on your scooter to access the pump (see Chapter 9).

4 To check whether the pump is operating, release the clip securing the fuel supply hose to the carburetor, or header tank as applicable, and detach the hose. Place the open end in a container suitable for storing fuel. Turn the engine over on the starter motor and check whether fuel flows from the hose into the container. If fuel flows, the pump is working correctly.

5 If no fuel flows from the pump, first check that this is not due to a blocked filter or fuel hose, or due to a split in the vacuum hose from the crankcase, before replacing the pump **(see illustration)**. Check all the hoses for splits, cracks and kinks, and check that they are securely connected on each end by a good clip. Check that any air vent for the

fuel tank is not blocked. If the filter and hoses are good, replace the pump.

Replacement

6 Release the clips securing the fuel and vacuum hoses and detach them from the pump, noting which fits where. Be prepared to catch any residual fuel in a suitable container. The fuel hoses should be clamped to prevent fuel leaks using any of the methods shown in *Tools and Workshop Tips* in the *Reference* section.

7 Undo the pump fixings and remove the pump, noting which way up it fits.

8 Install the new pump, making sure the hoses are correctly attached and secured with the clips. If the old clips are corroded or deformed, install new ones.

Electric fuel pump (Honda NPS 50 Ruckus)

9 If the engine loses power gradually and stops running, the fuel pump may be at fault.

10 Locate the fuel pump cover, below and behind the right rear corner of the footrest area. Release the latches and open the cover.

11 Turn the key to On, but don't start the engine. You should hear the pump run for about five seconds, then shut off.

12 If there's no sound, unplug the two-wire electrical connector from the pump. Connect a voltmeter between the red/black wire and ground (nearby bare metal). With the key turned to On, the voltmeter should indicate battery voltage. If it doesn't, there may be a break or bad connection in the wiring or the main relay may be at fault. If the wire is good, also check the yellow/white wire from the fuel pump to the engine control module. If the wire is good, have the relay checked by a dealer service department or other qualified shop.

13 Connect a 12-volt battery (the scooter's battery will work if it's fully charged) to the

fuel pump terminals using a pair of jumper wires. The pump should run. If not, it's probably defective.

14 As another check on the pump, connect an ohmmeter between its electrical terminals. The ohmmeter should indicate 2.6 to 3.2 ohms. If it's outside this range, the pump is probably defective.

15 If the pump runs, check its discharge volume. To get to the fuel hose, you'll need to remove the inner cover at the front of the seating area, the seat rail and the floor cover. Once this is done, disconnect the fuel hose from the carburetor and place the end in a graduated container. Run the pump for 30 seconds; it should produce 50 cc (just under 2 fluid ounces) of fuel during that time.

14 Exhaust system – removal and installation

⚠ **Warning: If the engine has been running, the exhaust system will be very hot. Allow the system to cool before carrying out any work.**

Note: *Some scooters are installed with a one-piece exhaust system. Follow the procedure for removing the complete system.*

Downpipe removal

1 Remove the body panels as required on your scooter to access the exhaust system and cylinder head (see Chapter 9).

2 On two-stroke machines equipped with a secondary air system (see Chapter 1, Section 3), loosen the clip securing the air hose to the extension on the exhaust downpipe and disconnect the hose.

14.3a Undo the two nuts (arrows) . . .

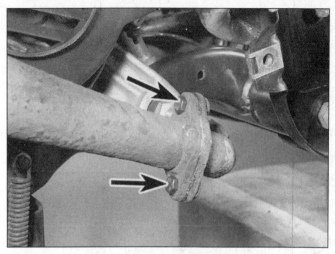

14.3b . . . and the two bolts (arrows)

HAYNES HiNT *Exhaust system fasteners tend to become corroded and seized. It is advisable to spray them with penetrating oil before attempting to loosen them.*

3 Undo the nuts securing the downpipe to the exhaust port in the cylinder or cylinder head, and the fasteners securing the downpipe to the muffler and remove the downpipe **(see illustrations)**. **Note:** *On systems where the downpipe fits inside the muffler and is secured by a clamp, it is necessary to remove the muffler first (see Step 5).*
4 Remove the gasket from the exhaust port and from the downpipe-to-muffler joint and discard them, as new ones must be used **(see illustrations)**.

Muffler removal
5 Undo the fastener securing the muffler to the downpipe **(see illustration 14.3b)** and the bolts securing the muffler, or muffler

bracket, to the engine or frame, and remove the muffler **(see illustration)**. Where installed, remove the gasket from the muffler-to-downpipe joint and discard it, as a new one must be used.

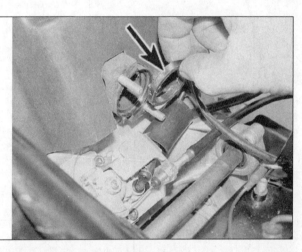

14.4a Remove the gasket from the exhaust port . . .

Complete system removal
6 Follow Steps 1 to 3 to access the exhaust system and disconnect the exhaust pipe from the cylinder or cylinder head. Where

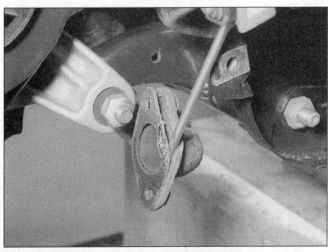

14.4b . . . and the pipe-to-muffler joint

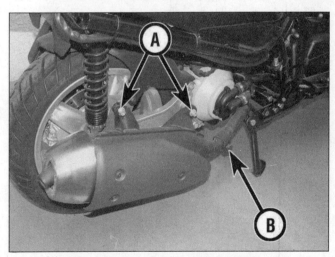

14.5 The muffler is secured to the frame (A) and to the downpipe (B)

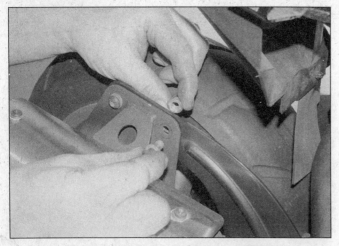

14.7a Undo the bolts securing the muffler . . .

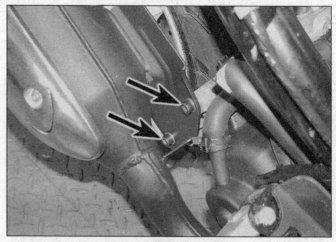

14.7b . . . or muffler bracket . . .

14.7c . . . and lift off the complete system

14.9 Resonator tube on restricted 50cc exhaust system

installed, disconnect the secondary air system.

7 Loosen the bolts securing the muffler, or muffler bracket, then support the exhaust system and remove the bolts. Lift the system off the scooter (see illustrations).

8 Remove the gasket from the exhaust port and discard it, as a new one must be used (see illustration 14.4a).

9 The exhaust system of restricted 50 cc two-stroke machines is installed with a resonator tube (see illustration). If your scooter has been de-restricted and the resonator tube has been removed, check around the welded patch on the exhaust for gas leaks. De-restricting requires a number of modifications to the engine and should only be undertaken by a scooter dealer.

Installation

10 Installation is the reverse of removal, noting the following:

  Clean the exhaust port studs and lubricate them with a suitable copper-based grease before reassembly.

  Clean the jointing surfaces of the exhaust port and the pipe.

  Use new gaskets.

  Smear the port gasket with grease to hold it in place while installing the exhaust system.

  Leave all fasteners finger tight until the system has been installed and correctly aligned, then tighten the exhaust port nuts first.

  Run the engine and check that there are no exhaust gas leaks.

Chapter 5
Ignition systems

Contents

Degrees of difficulty

Easy, suitable for novice with little experience	**Fairly easy,** suitable for beginner with some experience	**Fairly difficult,** suitable for competent DIY mechanic	**Difficult,** suitable for experienced DIY mechanic	**Very difficult,** suitable for expert DIY or professional

Specifications

Refer to the *Data* section at the end of this manual for servicing specifications.

1 General information

All scooters covered by this manual are equipped with a fully-transistorized electronic ignition system. The components which make up the system are the alternator source coil, ignition trigger, pick-up coil, ignition control unit (ICU), coil and spark plug **(see illustration)**.

The ignition trigger, which is on the outside surface of the alternator rotor, operates the pick-up coil as the crankshaft rotates, sending a signal to the ICU which in turn supplies the coil with the power necessary to produce a spark at the plug. The alternator source coil produces the power for the ignition system when the engine is running, and on most machines the battery provides the power for initial starting.

In the typical ignition circuit shown in **illustration 1.1**, the solid black wires show the connection between the ignition system components described above. The role of the ignition switch is to complete the power feed to the starter motor circuit when in the ON position (see Chapter 10) and to divert residual alternator source coil output to ground when turned to the OFF position. The hatched black wires illustrate the ignition switch function.

On some scooters, the coil is integral with the ignition control unit (see Section 3).

The ICU incorporates an ignition advance system controlled by signals from the pick-up coil. This varies the timing of the ignition spark depending on engine speed. Although the ignition timing can be checked on most scooters (see Section 7), there is no provision for adjusting the timing.

Depending upon the model specification, most ignition systems incorporate a safety circuit which prevents the engine from being started unless one of the brake levers is pulled in and/or the side stand is up (refer to your scooter handbook for details). For security, many scooters are installed with an ignition immobilizer (see Section 4).

Due to their lack of mechanical parts, the components of the ignition system are totally maintenance-free. If ignition system troubles occur, and the faulty component can be isolated by a series of checks, the only cure is to replace it. Keep in mind that most electrical parts, once purchased, cannot be returned. To avoid unnecessary expense, make sure the faulty component has been positively identified before buying a new one.

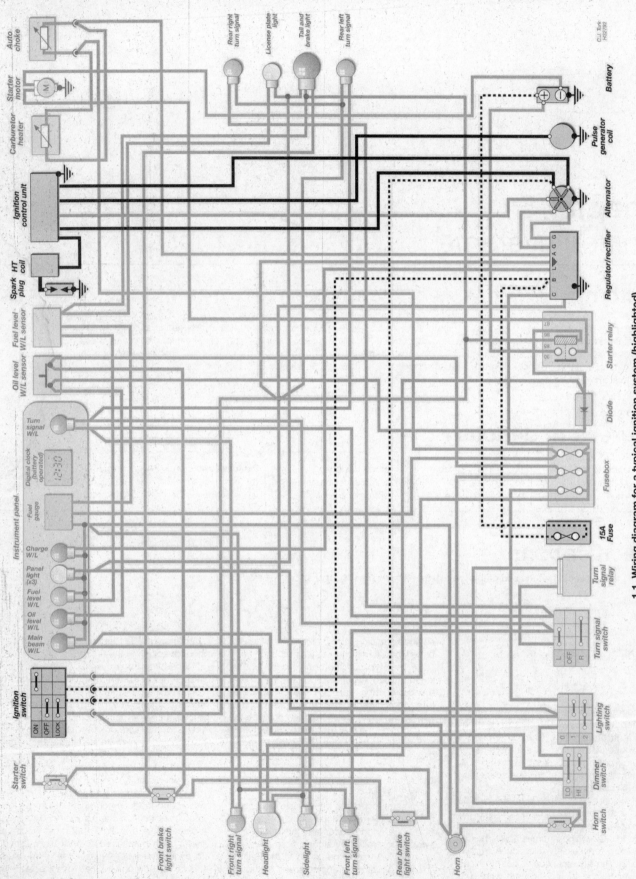

1.1 Wiring diagram for a typical ignition system (highlighted)

Refer to Section 1 on the previous page for an explanation of system operation

2.2 Ground the spark plug and operate the starter

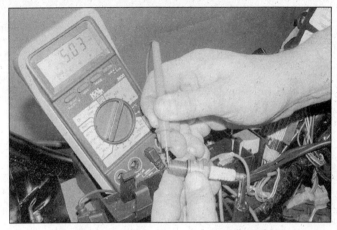

2.4 Measuring the resistance of the spark plug

2 Ignition system – check

⚠️ **Warning: The energy levels in electronic systems can be very high. Under no cicumstances should the ignition be switched on while the plug or plug cap is being held – shocks from the HT circuit can be most unpleasant. Secondly, it is vital that the engine is not turned over with the plug cap removed, and that the plug is grounded when the system is checked for sparking. The ignition system components can be seriously damaged if the HT circuit becomes isolated.**

1 As no means of adjustment is available, any failure of the system can be traced to failure of a system component or a simple wiring fault. Of the two possibilities, the latter is by far the most likely. In the event of failure, check the system in a logical fashion, as described below.

2 Disconnect the spark plug wire from the spark plug. Connect the lead to a new plug of the correct specification and lay the plug on the engine with the thread grounded **(see illustration)**. If necessary, hold the spark plug with an insulated tool.

⚠️ **Warning: Do not remove the spark plug from the engine to perform this check – atomized fuel being pumped out of the open spark plug hole could ignite, causing severe injury!**

3 Having observed the above precautions, turn the ignition switch ON and turn the engine over on the starter motor. If the system is in good condition a regular, fat blue spark should be evident between the plug electrodes. If the spark appears thin or yellowish, or is non-existent, further investigation will be necessary. Before proceeding further, turn the ignition OFF.

Caution: Some ignition systems are

designed for the combined resistance of the spark plug and spark plug cap. To avoid the risk of damaging the ICU, a spark testing tool should not be used.

4 If required, spark plug resistance can be checked with a multimeter. Remove the plug and clean the electrodes (see Chapter 1). Set the multimeter to the K-ohms scale and connect the meter probes to the terminal at the top of the plug and the central electrode **(see illustration)**. Compare the result with the reading from a new plug of the correct specification. If there is a great deal of variance between the readings, discard the old plug.

5 Ignition faults can be divided into two categories, namely those where the ignition system has failed completely, and those which are due to a partial failure. The likely faults are listed below, starting with the most probable source of failure. Work through the list systematically, referring to the subsequent sections for full details of the necessary checks and tests. **Note:** *Before checking the following items, ensure that the battery is fully-charged and that all fuses are in good condition.*

    Loose, corroded or damaged wiring connections, broken or shorted wiring between any of the component parts of the ignition system **(see illustration 1.1).**

    Faulty spark plug with dirty, worn or corroded plug electrodes, or incorrect gap between electrodes (see Chapter 1).
    Faulty coil or spark plug cap.
    Faulty ignition (main) switch (see Chapter 10).
    Faulty immobilizer (where installed).
    Faulty source coil.
    Faulty pick-up coil.
    Faulty ICU.

6 If the above checks don't reveal the cause of the problem, have the ignition system tested by a scooter dealer.

3 Coil and spark plug cap – check, removal and installation

Check

1 Trace the spark plug wire back from the spark plug cap to the coil and remove any body panels as required for access to the coil (see Chapter 9). Disconnect the negative battery cable (see Chapter 10).

2 Pull the spark plug cap off the plug and inspect the cap, spark plug wire and coil for cracks and other damage **(see illustration)**.

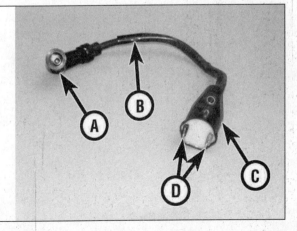

3.2 Spark plug cap (A), spark plug wire (B), coil (C) and primary circuit wiring terminals (D)

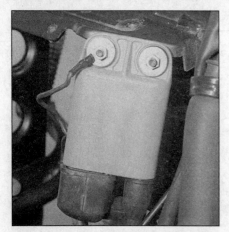

3.3 Combined ignition control unit (ICU) and coil

3 On some scooters, the ICU and coil are integrated in one unit **(see illustration)**. If no test specifications are available in the *Data* section, the only way to determine conclusively that the unit is defective is to substitute it with a known good one. If the fault is rectified, the original unit is faulty.

4 The condition of the coil primary and secondary windings can be checked with a multimeter. Note the position of the primary circuit wiring connectors, then disconnect them **(see illustration)**. **Note:** *If there is only one primary circuit wire, then the coil is grounded through its mounting – use the mounting as a substitute for the ground wire terminal in this check.* Set the multimeter to the appropriate ohms scale and connect the meter probes to the primary circuit wiring terminals **(see illustration)**. This will give a resistance reading for the coil primary windings which should be consistent with the specifications in the *Data* section. If the reading is outside the specified range, it is likely the coil is defective.

5 Set the multimeter to the K-ohms scale and connect the meter probes to the ground primary circuit wiring terminal and the spark plug terminal inside the plug cap **(see illustration)**. This will give a resistance reading for the coil secondary windings. If the reading is not within the specified range, unscrew the plug cap from the spark plug wire and connect the probes to the ground primary circuit wiring terminal and the core of the lead. If the reading is now as specified, the plug cap is suspect. If the reading is still outside the specified range, it is likely that the coil is defective.

6 Should any of the above checks not produce the expected result, have your findings confirmed by a scooter dealer. If the coil is confirmed to be faulty, it must be replaced; the coil is a sealed unit and cannot be repaired.

7 To check the condition of the spark plug cap, set the multimeter to the appropriate ohms scale and connect the meter probes to the spark plug wire and plug terminals inside the cap **(see illustration)**. If the reading is outside the specified range, the cap is defective and a new one must be installed. If the reading is as specified, the cap connection may have been faulty. Remake the connection between the cap and the spark plug wire and check the resistance reading for the coil secondary windings again (see Step 5).

Removal

8 Remove any body panels as required for access (see Chapter 9). Disconnect the neg-

3.4a Disconnect the primary circuit connectors from the coil

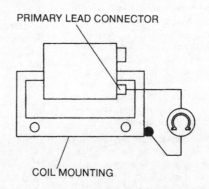

PRIMARY LEAD CONNECTOR

COIL MOUNTING

3.4b Coil primary winding check

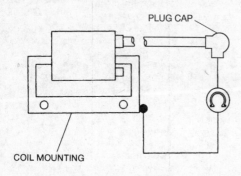

PLUG CAP

COIL MOUNTING

3.5 Coil secondary winding check

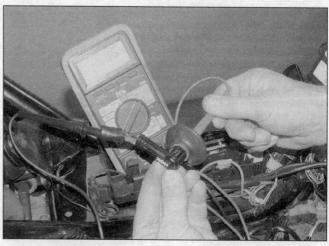

3.7 Measuring the resistance of the spark plug cap

4.6a Transponder antenna (arrow) is clipped to the ignition switch

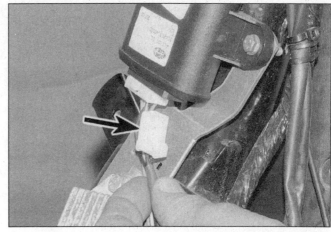

4.6b Disconnect the antenna wiring connector from the immobilizer

ative battery cable (see Chapter 10).

9 Note the position of the primary circuit wiring connectors, then disconnect them **(see illustration 3.4a)**. Disconnect the spark plug wire from the spark plug.

10 Unscrew the fasteners securing the coil to the frame and remove it.

Installation

11 Installation is the reverse of removal. If the coil is grounded through its mounting, ensure the mounting is clean and free from corrosion. Make sure the wiring connectors and spark plug wire are securely connected.

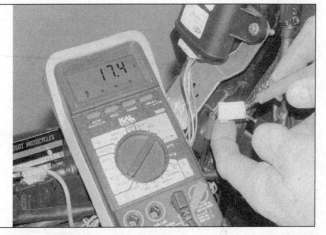

4.6c Measuring the resistance in the transponder antenna

4 Immobilizer system – general information and check

General information

Caution: The use of the correct resistor type, spark plug and suppresser cap is essential to prevent interference with the immobilizer system and possible loss of key programming.

1 The system comprises a security-coded ignition key with integral transponder, the immobilizer and transponder antenna. When the key is inserted into the ignition switch, the security code is transmitted from the key to the immobilizer via the antenna, which is located around the switch. The code deactivates the immobilizer and the warning LED on the instrument panel stops flashing. When the key is removed, the immobilizer is activated and the warning LED starts flashing. **Note:** *To minimize battery discharging, the warning LED goes out after a period of time although the immobilizer system remains active. Disconnecting the battery does not deactivate the immobilizer system.*

2 One master key and several ignition service keys are supplied with each machine from new. The keys and the immobilizer are encoded by the factory. The master key should be kept in a safe place and not used on a day-to-day basis.

3 If an ignition key is lost, obtain a new one from a scooter dealer and have the system recoded. The dealer will require the master key for this purpose. Once the system is recoded, the lost key will not deactivate the immobilizer.

4 The ignition keys can lose their code. If the machine will not start with the ignition switched ON, and the LED continues to flash, use a spare service key or the master key and have the system, including the key that has lost its code, recoded by a scooter dealer.

Check

5 Insert the ignition key into the switch and turn the switch ON. Once the LED stops flashing, the immobilizer has been deactivated; if the machine will not start, the problem lies elsewhere. If the LED continues to flash, and using another key does not deactivate the immobilizer (see Step 4), the immobilizer is suspect.

6 Remove the body panel to access the transponder antenna (see Chapter 9) and disconnect the negative battery cable. Trace the transponder antenna wiring from the ignition switch to the immobilizer and disconnect the wiring **(see illustrations)**. Check the resistance in the antenna with a multimeter set to the appropriate ohms scale. Connect the meter probes to the terminals in the connector and compare the result with the specifications in the *Data* section **(see illustration)**. If the reading is not within the specification, install a new antenna and try starting the machine again.

7 If the machine still will not start, the immobilizer should be checked by a scooter dealer. **Note:** *It is not possible to substitute an immobilizer from another machine, or a second-hand immobilizer, as this will not recognize the security code from your ignition key.*

8 When a new (uncoded) immobilizer is installed, check that it is working before encoding it. Turn the ignition ON and start the engine; the engine should run but will not rev above 2000 rpm. If the engine runs, the immobilizer can be encoded using the master key. **Note:** *Encoding the immobilizer is irreversible – only encode a new immobilizer once you are sure the system is working correctly.*

9 If the engine does not start, the problem lies elsewhere.

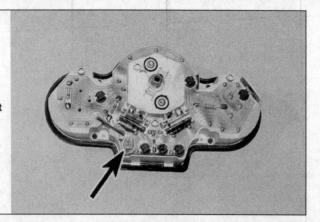

4.10 LED terminals (arrow) on the instrument cluster circuit

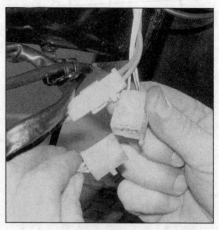

5.2 Disconnect the alternator/pick-up coil wiring connector

10 To check the LED, remove the instrument cluster and test for continuity between the LED terminals **(see illustration)**. There should be continuity in one direction only. If there is no continuity, or continuity in both directions, replace the LED.

Malfunction codes

11 The LED should flash once when the ignition is switched ON. If the LED continues to flash and stays on permanently to indicate an ignition fault, try using the master key to turn the ignition ON. If this works, the service key has lost its program. If the fault persists, refer to your scooter handbook for details of malfunction codes.

5 Source coil and pick-up coil – check and replacement

Check

1 To check the condition of the source coil and the pick-up coil, it is first necessary to identify the wiring for the individual components. Remove the body panels and alternator or engine cover as required according to model (see Chapter 9) and disconnect the negative battery cable.

2 Trace the source coil and pick-up coil wiring from the back of the alternator housing and disconnect it at the connector **(see illustration). Note:** *On some scooters, the wiring will connect directly into the ICU, on others there will be a multi-pin connector where it joins the main wiring loom.* If available, use your scooter's wiring diagram to identify the appropriate wires. Alternatively, check the color-coding of the wires at the source coil (on the alternator stator) and the pick-up coil adjacent to the alternator rotor.

3 Using a multimeter set to the appropriate ohms scale, measure the source coil resistance by connecting the meter probes between the coil terminals on the alternator side of the connector. Now reset the multimeter and measure the pick-up coil resistance by connecting the meter probes between the pick-up terminals in the connector.

4 Compare the readings obtained with those given in the *Data* section. If the readings obtained differ greatly from those given, particularly if the meter indicates a short circuit (no measurable resistance) or an open circuit (infinite, or very high resistance), the alternator stator and pick-up coil assembly must be replaced. However, first check that the fault is not due to a damaged or broken wire from the coil to the connector; pinched or broken wires can usually be repaired.

5 Some scooters are installed with a motorcycle-type alternator with three yellow wires from the stator. Using a multimeter set to the ohms scale, measure resistance of each coil by connecting the meter probes between the yellow wire terminals in the connector. Compare the result with the specifications in the *Data* section. Also check for continuity between each terminal and ground – there should be no continuity.

6 On some scooters, there is a short wiring loom between the multi-pin connector and the ICU. To check the condition of this loom, disconnect the ICU wiring connector and test for continuity between the terminals in the ICU connector and the alternator/pick-up coil multi-pin connector.

Replacement

7 The source coil and pick-up coil are integral with the alternator stator. Refer to the relevant Section of Chapter 2 for the removal and installation procedure.

6 Ignition control unit (ICU) – check, removal and installation

Check

1 If the tests shown in the preceding Sections have failed to isolate the cause of an ignition fault, it is possible that the ICU itself is faulty. In order to determine conclusively that the unit is defective, it should be substituted with a known good one. If the fault is rectified, the original unit is faulty. **Note:** *The ICU unit will be damaged if a non-resistor type spark plug or spark plug cap are installed. When installing a new ICU unit, always ensure the spark plug and cap are of the correct specification before starting the engine.*

Removal

2 Remove the body panels as required according to model (see Chapter 9) and disconnect the negative battery cable. Disconnect the wiring connector(s) from the ICU. Unscrew the nuts and bolts securing the unit to the frame, or unclip it from its fastener, and remove the unit **(see illustrations)**.

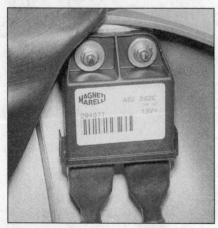

6.2a Undo the ICU fixings . . .

6.2b . . . or unclip it from its holder (arrow)

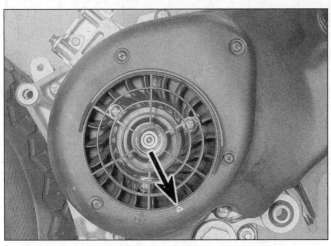

7.3a Static timing mark on the alternator cover

7.3b Timing mark on the alternator rotor (arrow)

Installation

3 Installation is the reverse of removal. Make sure the wiring connector is correctly and securely connected. **Note:** *Some scooters are installted with a combined ICU and ignition immobilizer. When a new unit is installed, it must be encoded by a scooter dealer using your ignition master key.*

| 7 | Ignition timing – general information and check | |

General information

1 Since no provision exists for adjusting the ignition timing and since no component is subject to mechanical wear, there is no need for regular checks; only if investigating a fault - such as a loss of power or a misfire - should the ignition timing be checked.

2 The ignition timing is defined by the relationship between two timing marks – one on the alternator rotor and a static mark on the engine. The alignment of the two marks is checked with the engine running (dynamically) using a stroboscopic lamp. The inexpensive neon lamps should be adequate in theory, but in practice may produce a pulse of such low intensity that the timing mark on the rotor remains indistinct. If possible, one of the more precise xenon tube lamps should be used, powered by an external source of the appropriate voltage. **Note:** *Do not use the machine's own battery, as an incorrect reading may result from stray impulses within the machine's electrical system.*

3 Every engine has two marks – a static mark, either on the alternator cover or on the inside of an inspection hole, and a mark on the alternator rotor or cooling fan **(see illustrations)**. Refer to your scooter handbook for the exact location of the timing marks and the engine speed at which the marks should align.

Check

4 Warm the engine up to normal operating temperature then turn it OFF.

5 Connect the timing lamp to the spark plug wire as described in the manufacturer's instructions.

6 Start the engine and aim the light at the static timing mark. With the machine running at the specified speed, the timing mark on the rotor should align with the idle timing mark.

 The timing marks can be highlighted with white paint to make them more visible under the stroboscope light.

7 Slowly increase the engine speed while observing the timing mark. The timing mark should move counterclockwise, increasing in relation to the engine speed until it reaches the full advance mark (where present).

8 If the ignition timing is incorrect, or suspected of being incorrect, one of the ignition system components is at fault, and the system must be tested as described in the preceding Sections of this Chapter.

Notes

Chapter 6
Transmission: Drive components and gearbox

Contents

Degrees of difficulty

Easy, suitable for novice with little experience	**Fairly easy,** suitable for beginner with some experience	**Fairly difficult,** suitable for competent DIY mechanic	**Difficult,** suitable for experienced DIY mechanic	**Very difficult,** suitable for expert DIY or professional

Specifications

Refer to the *Data* section at the end of this manual for servicing specifications.

1 General information

The transmission on all scooters covered by this manual is fully-automatic in operation.

Power is transmitted from the engine to the rear wheel by belt, via a variable-size drive pulley (the variator), an automatic clutch on the driven pulley, and a reduction gearbox. The variator and the automatic clutch both work on the principal of centrifugal force. **Note:** *On some scooters, the internal compo-nents of the transmission may differ slightly to those described or shown. When disas-sembling, always note the installed position, order and direction of each component as it is removed.*

The transmission can be worked on with the engine in the frame.

2 Drivebelt cover – removal and installation

Removal

1 Remove any body panels as required for access to the transmission casing (see Chapter 9). If required, remove the air filter housing (see Chapter 4).

2 Undo the screw securing the rear brake cable or hydraulic hose bracket to the underside of the transmission casing and remove the bracket **(see illustration)**.

3 Where installed, detach the air cooling duct from the front of the cover **(see illustration)**. On four-stroke engines, where the oil filler plug passes through the cover, remove the plug **(see illustration)**.

4 Some scooters have a plastic trim installed over the main belt cover. If necessary, remove the kickstart lever (see Section 3), then undo the screws securing the trim and remove it. Reinstall the kickstart lever – this is to prevent the kickstart shaft being accidentally knocked through the cover and dislodging

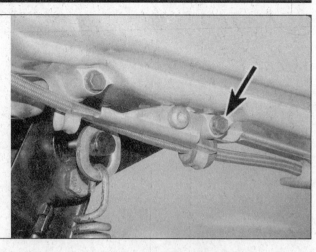

2.2 Undo the screw and remove the brake cable/hose bracket

the mechanism return spring.

5 On some scooters, the gearbox input shaft passes through the drivebelt cover and is supported by a bearing in the cover. To undo the nut on the outer end of the shaft, first unclip the plastic cap on the clutch bearing housing **(see illustration)**. The clutch drum must be locked against the belt cover

to prevent the shaft turning while the nut is undone. Either use a service tool to hold the clutch drum, or insert two large screwdrivers through the holes in the belt cover to engage the holes in the clutch drum. Have an assistant hold the screwdrivers while the nut is undone **(see illustration)**. Remove the nut and washer.

2.3a Detach the air cooling duct (arrow)

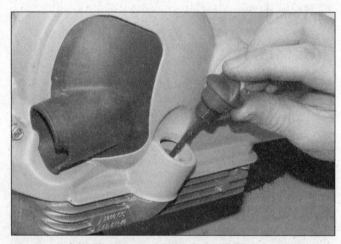

2.3b If necessary, remove the oil filler plug

2.5a Remove the clutch bearing cap

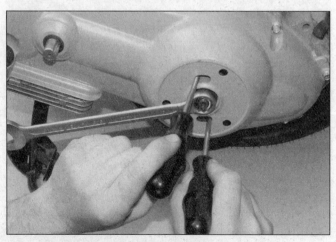

2.5b Lock the clutch drum with two screwdrivers and undo the nut

2.7 Lift off the drivebelt cover

2.8 Note the spacer on the shaft

6 Working in a criss-cross pattern, loosen the drivebelt cover retaining bolts and remove the bolts, noting the position of any clips. **Note:** *On scooters installed with a kickstart lever, it is not necessary to remove the lever before removing the cover.*

HAYNES HINT *Make a cardboard template of the cover and punch a hole for each bolt location. This will ensure all bolts are installed correctly on reassembly – this is important, as some bolts may be of different lengths.*

7 Lift off the cover and note the position of any locating dowels **(see illustration)**. Remove the dowels for safekeeping if they are loose. **Note:** *Sealant should not be used on the cover, but if it will not lift away easily, tap it gently around the edge with a soft-faced hammer.* Some scooters have a cover manufactured from composite material installed with a gasket. If the gasket is damaged, discard it and install a new one on reassembly.

8 On models where the gearbox input shaft passes through the belt cover, note the spacer on the shaft **(see illustration)**.

9 Where installed, note the position of the kickstart quadrant and the engaging pinion **(see illustration 3.2)**. If the starter motor engages with the variator, note how the outer end of the starter motor pinion assembly locates in the cover.

10 If installed, undo the retaining bolt for the air cooling duct and remove the duct. Inspect the duct filter element (see Chapter 1).

11 Clean any dust or dirt from the inside of the casing with a suitable solvent, taking care to avoid contact with the belt and the drive faces of the pulleys. Any evidence of oil inside the casing suggests a worn seal either on the crankshaft or the gearbox input shaft, which must be rectified. Evidence of grease inside the casing suggests worn seals either in the variator or the clutch center, which should also be rectified.

Installation

12 Installation is the reverse of removal, noting the following:

> If removed, install the dowels in the cover.
>
> If required, apply a smear of grease to the end of the starter motor pinion and to the threads of the cover bolts.
>
> On models where the gearbox input shaft passes through the belt cover, ensure the spacer is in place on the shaft.

> Where installed, ensure the kickstart quadrant and engaging pinion are correctly located in the cover.
>
> Tighten the cover bolts evenly in a criss-cross pattern.
>
> Where installed, crank the kickstart lever to ensure the mechanism engages correctly with the kickstart driven gear and that the lever returns to its proper rest position afterwards.

3 Kickstart mechanism – removal, inspection and installation

Removal

1 Remove the drivebelt cover (see Section 2). Where installed, remove the mechanism cover from the inside of the drivebelt cover **(see illustration)**.

2 Pull the engaging pinion out of its recess in the cover, noting how the spring locates **(see illustration)**. Remove the washer from behind the pinion.

3.1 Where installed, remove the kickstart mechanism cover

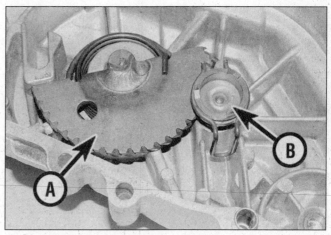

3.2 The kickstart quadrant (A) and engaging pinion (B) are located in the cover

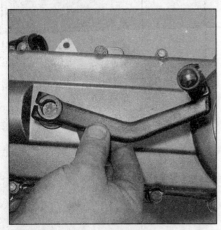

3.3 Undo the pinch-bolt and remove the kickstart lever

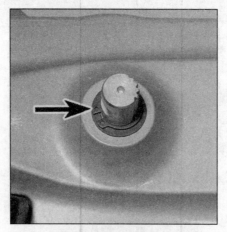

3.4 Remove the snap-ring (arrow) securing the shaft

3.5 Release the tension in the spring and unhook it from the quadrant

3 Note the rest position of the kickstart lever, then undo the lever pinch-bolt and pull the lever off the shaft **(see illustration)**.

4 Remove the snap-ring and washer (if installed) from the kickstart shaft on the outside of the cover **(see illustration)**.

5 Ease the kickstart shaft out of the cover and release the tension on the kickstart return spring. Unhook the spring from the kickstart quadrant and remove the shaft **(see illustration)**.

6 Note how the return spring fits inside the cover and remove the spring **(see illustration)**. If it is a loose fit, lift out the kickstart bushing **(see illustration)**.

7 Clean all the components with a suitable solvent.

Inspection

8 Check the dogs on the end of the engaging pinion and the corresponding dogs on the kickstart driven gear **(see illustration)**. Inspect the teeth on the engaging pinion and the teeth on the kickstart quadrant **(see illustration)**. Check the shafts of the engaging pinion and the kickstart quadrant, and the quadrant bushing, for signs of wear, and inspect the splines on the end of the quadrant shaft for damage. Replace any components that are worn or damaged.

9 Ensure the spring on the engaging pinion is a firm fit and inspect the kickstart return spring for cracks and wear at each end. When installed, the return spring should return the kickstart lever to the rest position and hold it there; if not, it has sagged and should be replaced.

Installation

10 If removed, press the kickstart bushing into the cover, then install the return spring

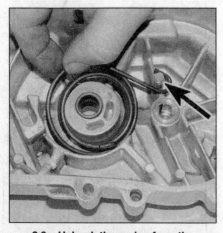

3.6a Unhook the spring from the post (arrow) . . .

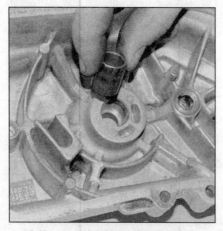

3.6b . . . and remove the kickstart bushing if necessary

3.8a Check the dogs on the engaging pinion and the dogs on the driven gear

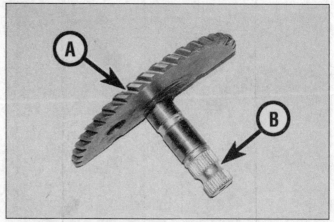

3.8b Inspect the teeth (A) and the splines (B) on the kickstart quadrant

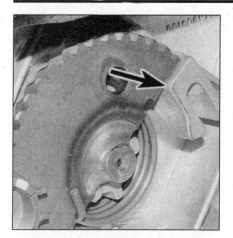

3.11 Quadrant should butt against the stop (arrow) on the inside of the case

3.13 Operate the kickstart lever to draw the pinion into the case

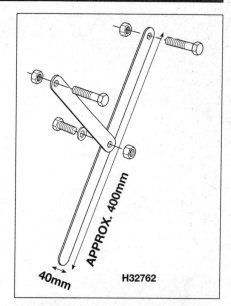

APPROX. 400mm

40mm

H32762

TOOL TiP *A holding tool can be made using two strips of steel bolted together in the middle, and with a nut and bolt through each end which locate into the holes in the pulley.*

with its long end innermost. Hook the long end around the post on the inside of the cover **(see illustration 3.6a)**.

11 Lubricate the kickstart shaft with a smear of molybdenum disulphide grease and insert it through the bushing, then hook the outer end of the return spring onto the quadrant. Rotate the shaft counterclockwise against the spring tension until the quadrant can be butted against the stop on the inside of the case **(see illustration)**. Ensure the shaft is pressed all the way into the case, then install the washer (if equipped) and snap-ring.

12 Install the kickstart lever in the rest position and tighten the pinch-bolt securely. Operate the lever to check that it turns smoothly and returns to its rest position under spring pressure.

13 Lubricate the shaft of the engaging pinion with a smear of grease and install the washer, then install the pinion into the case. Align the spring with the detent in the case, then operate the kickstart lever to engage the pinion with the kickstart quadrant and draw the pinion into the case **(see illustration)**. Check the operation of the mechanism.

14 Install the mechanism cover, if equipped **(see illustration 3.1)**.

15 Reinstall the drivebelt cover (see Section 2).

4 Variator – removal, inspection and installation

Removal

1 Remove the drivebelt cover (see Section 2).

2 To remove the variator center nut, the crankshaft must be locked to stop it turning. On engines with a toothed variator pulley, a service tool which bolts onto the engine case and locates between the teeth on the pulley is available to do this. Alternatively a similar tool can be made **(see illustrations)**. On engines with cooling fan blades on the variator pulley, locate a suitable holding tool in the holes provided in the pulley **(see illustration)**. A holding tool can be made from two strips of steel (see *Tool Tip*). **Note:** *The variator center nut is tight – to avoid damage, ensure the variator pulley is held firmly before attempting to undo the nut.*

4.2a Variator pulley teeth engage in this notch (arrow)

4.2b Lock the crankshaft with the tool (A) and undo the nut (B)

4.2c Using the holding tool to undo the variator center nut

4.3a Note the location of the kickstart driven gear

4.3b Remove the outer half of the pulley

4.3c Mark the direction of rotation on the drivebelt

4.4a Withdraw the center sleeve . . .

3 Undo the variator center nut. **Note:** *Some manufacturers recommend installing a new nut on reassembly – check with a scooter dealer.* On some scooters, the kickstart driven gear is held in place by the nut – note how the gear fits on the outer face of the pulley **(see illustration)**. Remove the outer half

of the variator pulley **(see illustration)**. Move the drivebelt aside – unless you are removing the clutch assembly, leave the belt on the clutch pulley. Mark the belt with a directional arrow if it is removed so that it can be reinstalled in the proper direction **(see illustration)**.

4 Either hold the variator assembly and withdraw the center sleeve, then pull the variator assembly off the crankshaft **(see illustrations)**, or pull the complete variator assembly off the shaft **(see illustration)**. **Note:** *If the variator is just being displaced, grip the assembly so that the ramp plate at the back*

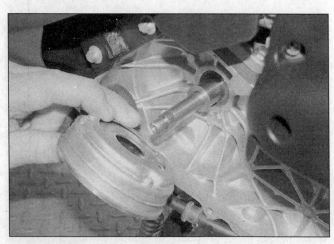

4.4b . . . then pull off the variator assembly

4.4c Hold the ramp plate (arrow) to keep the rollers in place

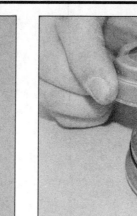
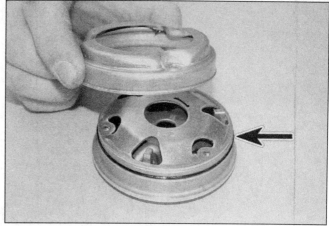

4.6a Undo the screws . . .

4.6b . . . and lift off the cover. Discard the O-ring (arrow)

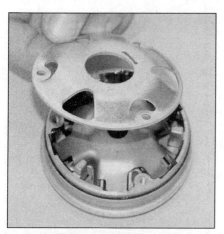

4.6c Where installed, lift out the restrictor plate

4.7a Lift out the ramp plate . . .

4.7b . . . and remove the ramp guides

is held into the variator body as you remove it, otherwise the rollers inside will fall out of their ramps and the variator will have to be disassembled to reposition them.
5 Remove the washer (if installed) from the crankshaft.
6 Where installed, remove the screws or bolts and lift off the variator cover, then remove the

O-ring and discard it, as a new one must be installed on reassembly **(see illustrations)**. Some restricted 50 cc machines have a restrictor plate installed in the variator – lift out the restrictor plate **(see illustration)**.
7 Lift out the ramp plate, noting how it fits, and remove the ramp guides **(see illustrations)**.

8 Lift out the rollers, noting which way they fit **(see illustration)**.
9 Clean all the components using a suitable solvent **(see illustration)**. **Note:** *Some manufacturers lubricate the rollers with high melting-point grease – refer to your scooter handbook for details.*

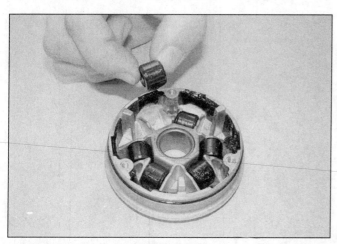

4.8 Lift out the rollers

4.9 Clean the components of the variator thoroughly

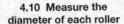
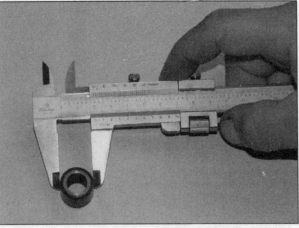

4.10 Measure the diameter of each roller

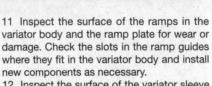

Inspection

10 Measure the diameter of each roller; they should all be the same size **(see illustration)**. Inspect the surface of each roller for flat spots. If any rollers are worn below the size specified in the *Data* section, or have worn flat, replace all the rollers as a set. **Note:** *Variator rollers are not interchangeable between different models. Always specify the year and model of your scooter when buying new rollers.*

4.19a Clean the inner faces of the variator pulley . . .

11 Inspect the surface of the ramps in the variator body and the ramp plate for wear or damage. Check the slots in the ramp guides where they fit in the variator body and install new components as necessary.
12 Inspect the surface of the variator sleeve for wear and install a new one if necessary.
13 Check the condition of the splines in the center of the outer half of the variator pulley and inspect the inner face of the pulley for signs of overheating or blueing, caused by the pulley running out of alignment **(see illustration)**. Replace the pulley half if it is damaged.

Installation

14 If required, lubricate the rollers and the ramps with high melting-point grease, then install the rollers into the variator body **(see illustration 4.8)**. **Note:** *Too much grease in the variator will make it run out of balance and cause vibration.*
15 Check that the ramp guides are correctly installed on the ramp plate and install the plate **(see illustration 4.7b)**.
16 On restricted 50 cc machines, install the restrictor plate.
17 If equipped, install a new O-ring in the groove around the variator body, then install the cover, taking care not to dislodge the O-ring, and tighten the cover screws or bolts securely.

4.13 Check the splines (arrow) for wear and the surface of the pulley for blueing

18 Install the washer (if equipped) on the crankshaft. Grip the variator so that the ramp plate is held into the body and install the assembly and the center sleeve (see Step 4). **Note:** *If the ramp plate moves and the rollers are dislodged, disassemble the variator and reposition the rollers correctly.*
19 Clean both inner faces of the variator pulley with a suitable solvent, then compress the clutch pulley center spring. Press the drivebelt into the clutch pulley to facilitate installing it over the variator pulley **(see illustrations)**.
20 Install the outer half of the variator pulley, ensuring the splines align with the crankshaft. If required, install the kickstart driven gear (see Step 3). Install the center nut finger tight. **Note:** *A new center nut should be installed if recommended by the manufacturer.* Make sure the outer pulley half butts against the center sleeve and is not skewed by the belt.
21 Install the locking tool used on removal (see Step 2) and tighten the center nut to the specified torque setting.
22 Measure the distance between the crankcase face and the edge of the outer pulley half, then rotate the crankshaft and repeat the measuring procedure several times to ensure the outer pulley half is not skewed **(see illustration)**.

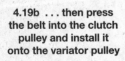

4.19b . . . then press the belt into the clutch pulley and install it onto the variator pulley

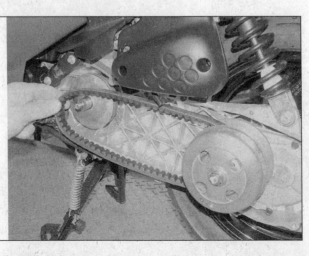

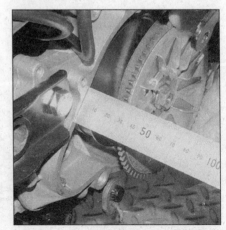

4.22 Check by measuring that the pulley is not skewed

4.23 Ease the belt into place between the two pulleys

23 Ease the drivebelt out of the clutch pulley to reduce the slack in the belt **(see illustration)**, then install the cover (see Section 2).

5 Drivebelt – inspection and replacement

Inspection

1 Most manufacturers specify service intervals for drivebelt inspection and service limits for the width of the belt, but it is good practice to check the condition of the belt whenever the cover is removed (see Section 2).

2 Check along the entire length of the belt for cracks, splits, fraying and damaged teeth and replace the belt if any such damage is found. Measure the belt width and compare the result with the specification in the *Data* section at the end of this manual **(see illustrations)**.

3 The belt will wear during the normal course of use and dust will accumulate inside the cover. However, a large amount of dust or debris inside the cover is an indication of abnormal wear and the cause, such as high spots on the pulleys or the pulleys running out of alignment, should be investigated.

Note: *Drivebelts are not interchangeable*

between different models. Always specify the year and model of your scooter when buying a new belt. If in doubt, check the part number marked on the belt.

4 Oil or grease inside the casing will contaminate the belt and prevent it gripping the pulleys (see Section 2).

Replacement

5 The drivebelt must be replaced at the specified service interval, or earlier dependant on belt condition (see Step 2). Remove the outer half of the variator pulley (see Section 4) and lift the belt off the crankshaft and the clutch pulley without disturbing the variator assembly.

6 Install the new belt, making sure any directional arrows point in the direction of normal rotation, then install the variator outer pulley half (see Section 4).

6 Clutch and clutch pulley – removal, inspection and installation

Removal

1 Remove the drivebelt (see Section 5).

2 To remove the clutch center nut, it is necessary to hold the clutch to prevent it turning. On some scooters, a holding tool that locates in the holes in the clutch drum can be used (see Section 4 *Tool Tip*); alternatively you can use a strap wrench **(see illustrations)**. **Note 1:** *On machines where the gearbox input shaft passes through the drivebelt cover, the clutch center nut will already have been removed. Note any spacer on the gearbox input shaft and remove it.* **Note 2:** *Some*

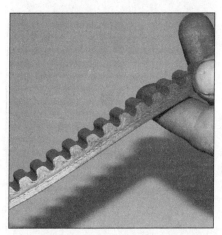

5.2a Check the belt for damage

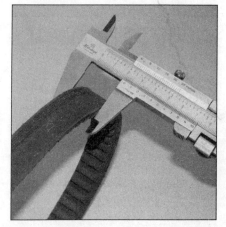

5.2b Measure the belt width

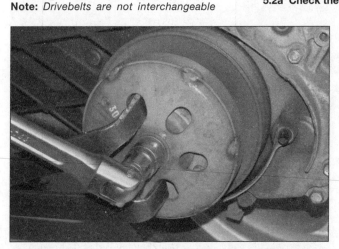

6.2a Prevent the clutch from turning with a home-made tool . . .

6.2b . . . or a strap wrench

6.3 Remove the clutch drum . . .

6.4 . . . then pull the clutch and pulley off the shaft

6.5a To undo the clutch assembly nut (arrow) . . .

6.5b . . . the center spring (arrow) must be compressed

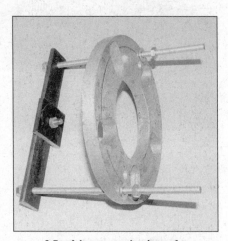

6.5c A home-made clamp for disassembling the clutch

manufacturers recommend installing a new nut on reassembly – check with a scooter dealer.
3 Remove the clutch drum **(see illus-tration)**.
4 Draw the clutch and pulley assembly off the gearbox input shaft **(see illus-tration)**.

5 To disassemble the clutch and pulley assembly, the center spring must be compressed while the assembly nut is undone **(see illustrations)**. Most manufacturers produce a service tool to do this. Alternatively, use the set-up shown, ensuring no pressure is applied to the rim of the pulley and that

there is adequate room to undo the nut **(see illustrations)**.
6 Install a strap wrench around the clutch shoes to hold the assembly while the nut is undone, then release the spring pressure gradually by undoing the clamp **(see illus-tration)**.

6.5d Ensure the clamp does not rest on the rim (arrow) of the pulley

6.6 Hold the clutch with a strap wrench and undo the nut

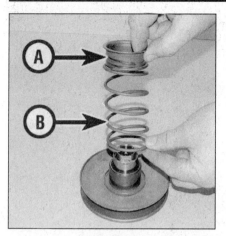

6.7a Lift off the spring seat (A) and spring (B) . . .

6.7b . . . then remove the center sleeve

6.8 Remove the O-rings carefully

7 Remove the clutch shoes and back plate, then remove the spring seat, the spring and the center sleeve **(see illustrations)**.

8 Note the two O-rings installed to the pulley outer half and remove them carefully **(see illustration)**. **Note:** *If the O-rings are damaged, or if grease from the clutch center has worked its way past the O-rings, they should be replaced.*

9 Withdraw the guide pins and separate the pulley halves **(see illustrations)**.

10 Clean all the components with a suitable solvent.

Inspection

11 Check the inner surface of the clutch drum for damage and scoring and inspect the splines in the center; replace it if necessary. Measure the internal diameter of the drum at several points to determine if it is worn or out-of-round **(see illustration)**. If it is worn or out-of-round, replace it.

12 Check the amount of friction material remaining on the clutch shoes **(see illustration)**. If the friction material has worn to the service limit specified in the *Data* section,

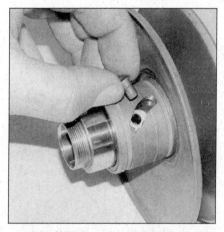

6.9a Withdraw the guide pins . . .

6.9b . . . and separate the pulley halves

down to the shoe, or the shoes are worn unevenly, install a new shoe assembly.

13 Inspect the shoe springs for wear, cracks and stretching. Ensure that the shoes are not seized on their pivot pins and that the retaining snap-rings, where installed, are secure on

the ends of the pins **(see illustration 6.12)**. If any parts are worn or damaged, install a new shoe assembly.

14 Check the condition of the center spring. If it is bent or appears weak, replace it. Measure the free length of the spring and com-

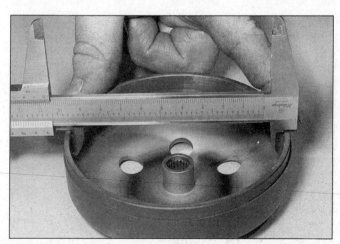

6.11 Measure the internal diameter of the drum as described

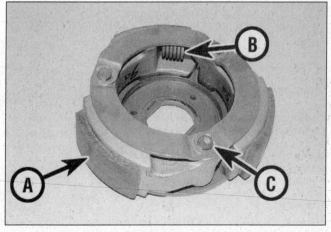

6.12 Check the clutch friction material (A), shoe springs (B) and retaining clips (C)

6.17 Inspect the pulley internal seals (arrows)

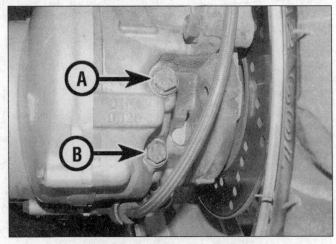

7.2 Gearbox filler plug (A) and drain plug (B)

pare the result with the figure in the *Data* section. Install a new spring if it has worn to less than the service limit.

15 Inspect the inner faces of the clutch pulley for signs of overheating or blueing, caused by the pulley running out of alignment.

16 Inspect the guide pins and the pin slots for wear.

17 Check the seals inside the pulley outer half **(see illustration)**. If the seals are worn or damaged, grease will pass onto the face of the pulley. On most scooters, two bearings are installed in the hub of the pulley inner half; inspect the rollers of the inner bearing for flat spots and ensure the outer sealed ball-bearing turns smoothly (see *Tools and Workshop Tips* in the *Reference* section). If any of the clutch pulley internal components are worn or damaged, they must be replaced. Check with a scooter dealer as to the availability of new parts – details of bearing and seal replacement are given in *Tools and Workshop Tips*. If individual components are not available, or if a number of components are worn, install a new clutch pulley assembly.

Installation

18 Assemble the two halves of the clutch pulley and install the guide pins and the O-rings. Lubricate the pin slots with molybdenum disulphide grease, then install the center sleeve, the center spring and the spring seat.

19 Position the shoe assembly on the spring seat and compress the spring using the same method as for disassembly (see Step 5). Ensure the flats on the shoe back plate are aligned with the pulley hub and install the assembly nut finger tight. Hold the assembly with a strap wrench around the clutch shoes and tighten the nut to the torque setting specified in the *Data* section, then release the clamp **(see illustration 6.6)**.

20 Lubricate the needle bearing in the hub of the pulley inner half with molybdenum disulphide grease and install the clutch and pulley assembly on the input shaft. Install the

clutch drum, ensuring the splines align with the shaft.

21 Install the remaining components in the reverse order of removal, noting the following:

> *Where equipped, install the spacer on the gearbox shaft (see Step 2).*
> *If required, use a new clutch center nut. Tighten the center nut to the specified torque setting.*
> *Clean both inner faces of the clutch pulley with a suitable solvent before installing the drivebelt (see Section 5).*

7 Gearbox – removal, inspection and installation

Removal

1 Remove the clutch and clutch pulley (see Section 6). On scooters equipped with a drum rear brake, remove the rear wheel; on scooters equipped with a disc rear brake, remove the rear wheel, hub and brake disc (see Chapter 8).

2 If a drain plug is installed on the scooter, drain the gearbox oil **(see illustration)**. **Note:** *Remove the filler plug to assist oil drainage.*

3 Unscrew the bolts securing the gearbox cover and remove them **(see illustration)**. **Note:** *Depending on the design of your scooter, the gearbox cover is installed either on the left-hand side of the transmission casing, behind the clutch, or on the right-hand side behind the rear wheel. The cover bolts are usually positioned on the same side as the cover, although on some scooters with a right-hand cover, the bolts pass through the casing from the left.*

 HAYNES HiNT *Make a cardboard template of the gearbox cover and punch a hole for each bolt location. This will ensure all bolts are installed correctly on reassembly – this is important, as some bolts may be of different lengths.*

4 Carefully ease the cover away from the casing and remove it **(see illustration)**. If the cover is stuck, tap around the joint face between the cover and the casing with a soft-faced mallet to free it. Do not try to lever the cover off, as this may damage the sealing surfaces. **Note:** *On gearboxes not*

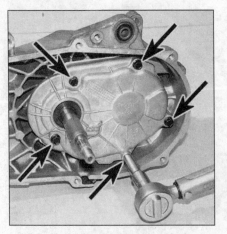

7.3 Undo the gearbox cover bolts

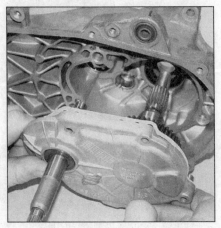

7.4 Lift away the gearbox cover

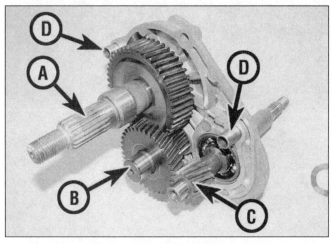

7.6a Output shaft (A), intermediate shaft (B), input shaft (C) and cover dowels (D)

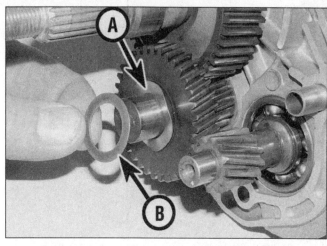

7.6b Note the position of any wave washers (A) or thrustwashers (B) on the shafts

7.6c Lift out the gearbox shafts . . .

7.6d . . . noting how they fit together

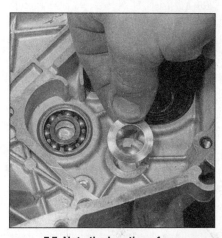

7.7 Note the location of any inner washers

installed with a drain plug, position a tray beneath the casing to catch the oil when the cover is removed.

5 If any of the gearbox shafts come out with the cover, take care not to damage any seals as the shafts are pulled through. Note the position of any dowels on the cover and remove them for safekeeping if they are loose. Discard the gasket, as a new one must be installed on reassembly.

6 All the scooters covered by this manual have three gearbox shafts – the input shaft which carries the clutch, the output shaft which carries the rear wheel, and an intermediate shaft (see illustration). Check the shafts for any thrustwashers or wave washers and remove them, noting where they fit, then lift out the shafts (see illustrations). Note: The input shaft is often a press-fit in its bearing and should not be removed unless the shaft, the bearing or the oil seal is to be replaced.

7 Check the casing and cover for any remaining washers and remove them, noting where they fit (see illustration).

8 Do not remove the gear pinions from the shafts unnecessarily – they should only be removed if components are being replaced.

Inspection

9 Clean all traces of old gasket material from the case and cover mating surfaces, taking care not to scratch or gouge the soft aluminium. Wash all the components in a suitable solvent and dry them with compressed air.

10 Check the pinion teeth for cracking, chipping, pitting and other obvious wear or damage, then check for signs of scoring or blueing on the pinions and shafts caused by overheating due to inadequate lubrication (see illustration).

11 Ensure that all the pinions are a tight fit on their shafts.

12 Inspect the splines and threads on the input and output shafts.

7.10 Check the pinion teeth (A), splines (B) and threads (C) for wear and damage

7.13 Pinion is retained on the shaft by the snap-ring (arrow)

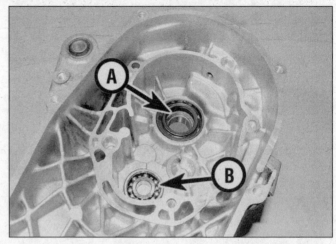

7.16a Check the condition of the oil seals (A) and bearings (B)

13 Replace any damaged or worn components. In some cases, the pinions are a press-fit on the shafts, or are retained by snap-rings allowing components to be replaced individually **(see illustration)**. Some pinions are an integral part of the shaft and on some scooters, shafts are only supplied as matched items. Check with a scooter dealer as to the availability of components.

14 To remove the input shaft, first install the clutch center nut to protect the threads, then drive the shaft out using a soft-faced mallet on the clutch end.

15 Check the intermediate shaft thrustwashers and replace them if they are damaged or worn. Install new ones if in any doubt.

16 Check the condition of the shaft oil seals **(see illustration)**. Some gearboxes are installed with drain holes – if a seal fails, oil will drain out to the underside of the casing **(see illustration)**. Any loss of gearbox oil must be remedied immediately to avoid expensive damage or seizure. If the input shaft oil seal fails, oil will run out of the drain hole (if installed), or into the drivebelt case behind the clutch. If either of the shafts has been removed, it is good practice to install a new seal (see *Tools and Workshop Tips* in the *Reference* section).

17 Inspect the bearings (see *Tools and Workshop Tips* in the *Reference* section). **Note:** *Bearings that are installed into blind holes*

7.16b If the output shaft seal fails, oil will drain at (A); if the input shaft seal fails, oil will drain at (B)

require an internal bearing puller to extract them without damaging the case; consult a scooter dealer or a specialist engineer if they need removing.

Installation

18 Installation is the reverse of removal, noting the following:

Ensure any washers are installed to the shafts before assembly.

Lubricate both ends of the intermediate shaft with molybdenum disulphide grease before installation.

Install any dowels into the cover.

Use a new cover gasket.

Smear the inside of the oil seals with grease before installing the shafts.

Tighten the cover bolts evenly and in a criss-cross pattern to the torque setting specified in the Data section.

If a gearbox drain plug is installed, ensure it is tightened to the specified torque setting.

Fill the gearbox with the specified amount and type of oil (see Chapter 1).

Chapter 7
Frame and suspension

Contents

Degrees of difficulty

Easy, suitable for novice with little experience	**Fairly easy,** suitable for beginner with some experience	**Fairly difficult,** suitable for competent DIY mechanic	**Difficult,** suitable for experienced DIY mechanic	**Very difficult,** suitable for expert DIY or professional

Specifications

Refer to the *Data* section at the end of this manual for servicing specifications.

1 General information

All scooters covered by this manual are equipped with a tubular and pressed steel one-piece frame.

The engine and transmission unit is linked to the frame by a pivoting assembly at the front and by the rear shock absorber(s), making the unit an integral part of the rear suspension.

Front suspension is by a leading or trailing link arrangement with a single shock absorber, or by conventional or upside-down telescopic forks.

Ancillary items such as stands and handlebars are covered in this Chapter.

2 Frame – inspection and repair

1 The frame should not require attention unless accident damage has occurred. In most cases, frame replacement is the only satisfactory remedy for such damage. A few frame specialists have the jigs and other equipment necessary for straightening the frame to the required standard of accuracy, but even then there is no simple way of assessing to what extent the frame may have been over-stressed.

2 After reaching a high mileage, the frame should be examined closely for signs of cracking or splitting at the welded joints. Loose engine mount and suspension bolts can cause ovaling or fracturing of the mounting points. Minor damage can often be repaired by specialist welding, depending on the extent and nature of the damage.

3 Remember that a frame which is out of alignment will cause handling problems. If misalignment is suspected as the result of an accident, it will be necessary to strip the scooter completely so the frame can be thoroughly checked.

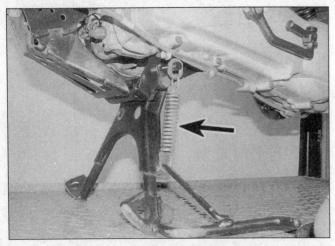

3.2a Note the location of the spring (arrow) . . .

3.2b . . . and remove it carefully

3 Stands – removal and installation

Center stand

1 Support the scooter securely in an upright position using an auxiliary stand. **Note:** *Do not rest the weight of the machine on the bodywork; remove the belly panels to expose the frame (see Chapter 9). Alternatively, have an assistant support the machine.*
2 Unhook the stand spring, noting how it fits, and remove the spring plate, if installed **(see illustrations)**.
3 Unscrew the pivot bolt nut and remove the washer, then withdraw the pivot bolt and remove the stand **(see illustration)**.
4 On scooters with a stand bracket bolted to the underside of the engine, unscrew the nuts and withdraw the bolts securing the bracket, then remove the stand and bracket as an assembly **(see illustration)**.
5 Thoroughly clean the stand and remove all road dirt and old grease. Inspect the pivot bolt and the pivot holes in the bracket for wear and replace them if necessary. Inspect the spring; if it is sagged or cracked, a new spring must be installed. Inspect the rubber stop on the stand and replace it if it is worn or deteriorated.
6 Installation is the reverse of removal, noting the following:

   Apply grease to the pivot bolt and all pivot points.
   Tighten the nuts securely.
   Ensure that the spring holds the stand up securely when it is not in use – an accident is almost certain to occur if the stand extends while the scooter is in motion. If necessary, install a new spring.

Side stand

7 Support the scooter securely in an upright position using an auxiliary stand (see Step 1).
8 Unhook the stand spring, noting how it fits **(see illustration)**.
9 Unscrew the stand pivot bolt and remove the bolt, washer and stand **(see illus-**

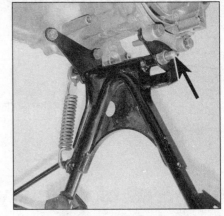

3.3 Unscrew the nut (arrow) and withdraw the pivot bolt

tration 3.8). Note how the contact plate on the stand fits against the safety switch plunger when the stand is lowered.
10 Installation is the reverse of removal, noting the following:

3.4 Remove the stand assembly

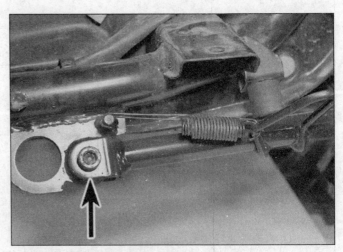

3.8 Unhook the spring and remove the pivot bolt (arrow)

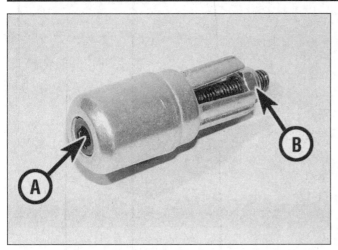

4.3 Loosen the bar end weight center screw (A) to release the nut (B)

4.5 Disconnect the brake light switch wiring connectors

Apply grease to the pivot bolt.
Ensure that the stand contact plate actuates the stand switch when the stand is lowered.
Check the spring tension – it must hold the stand up when it is not in use. If necessary, install a new spring.
Check the operation of the sidestand switch (see Chapter 10, Section 8).

4 Handlebars – removal and installation

Removal

1 Remove the handlebar covers and any body panels as necessary to access the steering stem (see Chapter 9).
2 If required, the handlebars can be displaced from the steering stem for access to the bearings without having to detach any cables, hoses or main wiring looms, or remove the switches, brake levers or master cylinders. If this is the case, ignore the Steps which do not apply.
3 Where installed, loosen the center screws for the bar end weights and withdraw the weights from the handlebars. Take care not to undo the screws too far and lose the nuts on the end of the screws **(see illustration)**.
4 Undo the throttle twistgrip housing screws and slide the twistgrip off the end of the handlebar (see Chapter 4).
5 Disconnect the wiring from each brake light switch **(see illustration)**.
6 Undo the handlebar switch housing screws and displace the housing.
7 Check that no other electrical components are mounted on the handlebars and detach them if necessary.
8 Unscrew the brake master cylinder assembly clamp bolts and position the assembly clear of the handlebar, making sure no strain is placed on the hydraulic hose (see Chapter 8). Keep the master cylinder reservoir upright to

prevent air entering the system. **Note:** *Some scooters are installed with hydraulically-operated front and rear brakes, on others only the front brake is hydraulically-operated.*
9 Remove the left-hand grip; peel the grip off the end of the bar, or if necessary cut it off.
10 On scooters with the handlebars secured by a stem bolt, undo the nut on the stem bolt and remove the nut, washer and shaped spacer, noting how they fit **(see illustration)**. Support the handlebars and withdraw the bolt, then lift the bars off the steering stem.
11 On scooters with the handlebars secured by a clamp and pinch-bolt, undo the nut and bolt, then lift off the bars **(see illustration)**.
12 If the handlebar components have been left attached, position the bars so that no strain is placed on any of the cables, hoses or wiring, and protect the body panels to prevent scratching.

Installation

13 Installation is the reverse of removal, noting the following:
Tighten the handlebar stem bolt to the torque setting specified in the Data *section.*

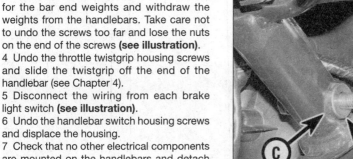

4.10 Remove the nut (A), washer (B) and spacer (C)

Use a suitable adhesive to secure the left-hand grip on the handlebar.
Don't forget to reconnect the brake light switch wiring connectors.
Check the operation of the brakes before riding the scooter.

5 Steering head bearings – adjustment

1 Support the machine on the centerstand with the front wheel raised off the ground. **Note:** *Do not rest the weight of the machine on the bodywork; remove the belly panels to expose the frame (see Chapter 9).*
2 Remove the handlebar covers and any body panels as necessary to access the steering stem (see Chapter 9).
3 If required, displace the handlebars (see Section 4).
4 Some scooters are installed with one locknut above the bearing adjuster nut, others have two locknuts. The locknut and the adjuster nut are usually held in place with a

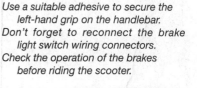

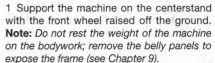

4.11 Undo the nut (A) and withdraw the pinch-bolt (B)

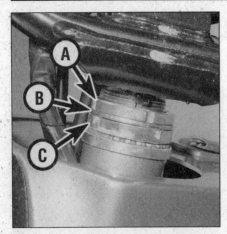

5.4 Locknut (A), washer (B), and adjuster nut (C)

5.6 Remove the locknut (arrow) and discard the lockwasher

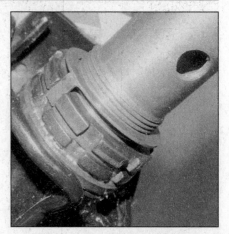

5.7 Location of the tab washer

lock washer **(see illustration)**. Check carefully and refer to your scooter handbook for details.

5 If the lock washer has tabs which locate in notches in the locknut, first pry the tabs out of the notches. **Note:** *A tabbed lock washer should not be re-used; remove the locknut and install a new washer after adjusting the bearings.*

6 If one locknut is installed, loosen it using a suitable wrench, C-spanner or drift **(see illustration)**.

7 If two locknuts are installed, unscrew the top nut then lift the tab washer off the remaining two nuts, noting how it fits **(see illustration)**. Unscrew the second locknut. A rubber washer is installed between the second locknut and the adjuster nut. Discard it if it is crushed or damaged and install a new one on reassembly.

8 Using either a wrench, C-spanner or drift, loosen the adjuster nut slightly to take pressure off the bearing, then tighten the nut until all freeplay is removed. Check that the steering still turns freely from side-to-side. The

object is to set the adjuster nut so that the bearings are under a very light loading, just enough to remove any freeplay.

Caution: Take great care not to apply excessive pressure because this will cause premature failure of the bearings.

9 With the bearings correctly adjusted, the adjuster nut must be held to prevent it from moving while the locknut is tightened. Where necessary, first install a new lockwasher ensuring the tabs locate correctly in the adjuster nut.

10 Where one locknut is installed, tighten the locknut securely, then bend the remaining lockwasher tabs up to secure the locknut. **Note:** *Some manufacturers specify a torque setting for the locknut (see the Data section at the end of this manual); however, to apply this, a service tool or a suitable fabricated tool* **(see illustration 5.11a)** *is required and the handlebars must be displaced (see Section 4).*

11 Where two locknuts are installed, install the rubber washer, then the second locknut, tightening it finger-tight. Hold the adjuster nut

to prevent it turning, then tighten the second locknut only enough to align its notches with the notches in the adjuster nut and install the tab washer **(see illustration 5.7)**. Install the top locknut, then hold the adjuster nut to prevent it turning and tighten the top locknut securely. If the special tool is available, tighten the locknut to the specified torque setting **(see illustrations)**.

12 Check the bearing adjustment and re-adjust if necessary, then install the remaining components in the reverse order of removal.

6 Steering stem – removal and installation

Removal

1 Remove the front wheel and, if applicable, the brake caliper (see Chapter 8). On scooters where the wheel can be removed leaving

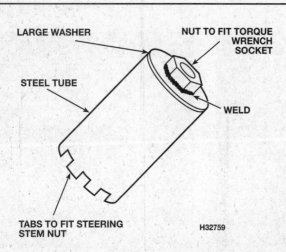

LARGE WASHER

NUT TO FIT TORQUE WRENCH SOCKET

STEEL TUBE

WELD

TABS TO FIT STEERING STEM NUT

H32759

5.11a Tool to adjust the steering head bearings

5.11b Hold the adjuster nut and tighten the locknut with the special tool

the hub in place, remove the hub.

2 If the front fender or fender liner are mounted on the front suspension, remove them (see Chapter 9).

3 Remove the handlebars (see Section 4). **Note:** *The ball-bearings in the lower steering head race may not be retained by a cage – place a clean rag on the floor beneath the steering head to catch the ball-bearings if they are loose when the steering stem is removed.*

4 Unscrew and remove the bearing adjuster locknut(s) and washer (see Section 5).

5 Support the steering stem, then unscrew the bearing adjuster nut and carefully lower the stem out of the steering head **(see illustration)**. Note how the adjuster nut fits.

6 The ball-bearings in the lower race will either fall out of the race or stick to the lower inner race on the steering stem. The top inner race and top bearing will remain in the top of the steering head.

7 If not already done, lift out the top inner race and the top bearing **(see illustration)**. **Note:** *On some scooters, the top inner bearing race is integral with the adjuster nut. The balls of the top bearing may be loose or they may be housed in a cage.*

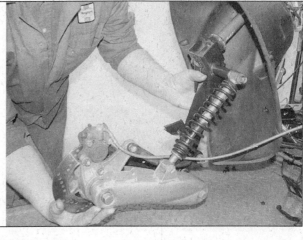

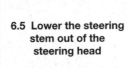

6.5 **Lower the steering stem out of the steering head**

8 Remove all traces of old grease from the ball-bearings and races and inspect them for wear or damage (see Section 7). **Note:** *Do not attempt to remove the outer races from the steering head or the lower bearing inner race from the steering stem unless they are to be replaced.*

Installation

9 Apply a liberal quantity of grease to the bearing inner and outer races and install the top bearing **(see illustration 6.7)**.

10 Assemble the lower race ball-bearings on the lower inner race on the steering stem; if they are a loose assembly, they will be retained by the grease **(see illustration)**.

11 Carefully lift the steering stem up through the steering head, ensuring the lower race ball-bearings remain in place. Either thread the combined top inner bearing race/adjuster nut onto the stem or install the inner race and thread the adjuster nut onto the stem **(see illustrations)**. Ensure the adjuster nut is installed in the correct position.

12 Install the remaining components in the reverse order of removal.

7 Steering head bearings – inspection and replacement

Inspection

1 Remove the steering stem (see Section 6).
2 Remove all traces of old grease from the

6.7 **Top bearing in the top of the steering head**

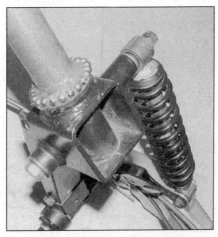

6.10 **Hold the lower race ball-bearings in place with grease**

6.11a **Lift the steering stem into place ...**

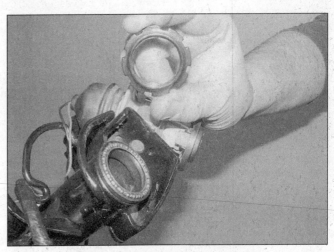

6.11b **... and install the adjuster nut**

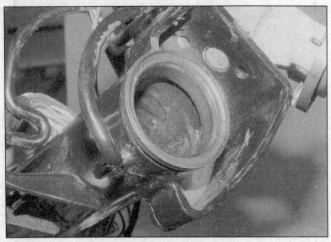

7.3a Inspect the races in the top . . .

7.3b . . . and bottom of the steering head

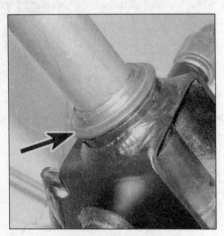

7.3c Lower inner race on the steering stem

bearings and races and check them for wear or damage.

3 The races should be polished and free from indentations **(see illustrations)**. The outer races are in the steering head, the top inner race is either integral with the bearing adjuster nut or it rests on top of the top bearing, and the lower inner race is on the steering stem. Inspect the ball-bearings for signs of wear,

pitting or corrosion, and examine the bearing retainer cage for signs of cracks or splits, where installed. If there are any signs of wear or damage on any of the above components, both upper and lower bearing assemblies must be replaced as a set. Only remove the races from the steering head and the stem if they need to be replaced – do not re-use them once they have been removed.

Replacement

4 The outer races are an interference fit in the frame and can be tapped from position with a suitable drift **(see illustration)**. Tap firmly and evenly around each race to ensure that it is driven out squarely. It may prove advantageous to curve the end of the drift slightly to improve access.

5 Alternatively, the races can be pulled out using a slide-hammer with internal expanding extractor.

6 The new outer races can be pressed into the frame using a drawbolt arrangement **(see illustration)**, or by using a large diameter tubular drift which bears only on the outer edge of the race. Ensure that the drawbolt washer or drift (as applicable) bears only on the outer edge of the race and does not contact the working surface.

Installation of new bearing outer races is made much easier if the races are left overnight in the freezer. This causes them to contract slightly, making them a looser fit.

7 To remove the lower inner race from the steering stem, first drive a chisel between the base of the race and the bottom yoke. Work the chisel around the race to ensure it lifts squarely. Once there is clearance beneath the race, use two levers placed on opposite sides of the race to work it free, using blocks of wood to improve leverage and protect the yoke. If the race is firmly in place, it will be necessary to use a bearing puller.

8 Install the new lower inner race onto the

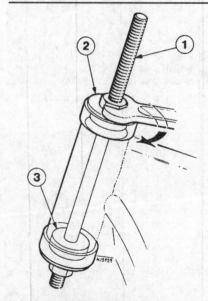

7.6 Using a drawbolt to fit the outer races in the steering head

1 Long bolt or threaded bar
2 Thick washer
3 Guide for lower race

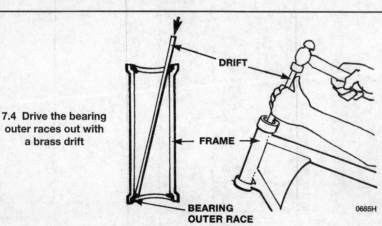

7.4 Drive the bearing outer races out with a brass drift

DRIFT

FRAME

BEARING OUTER RACE

0685H

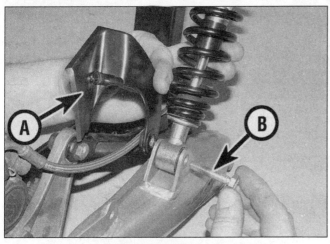

8.2 Remove the bracket (A) and withdraw the lower shock bolt (B)

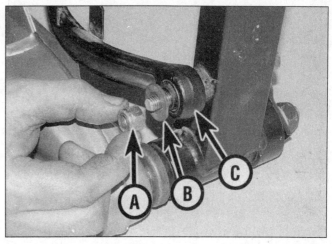

8.4 Remove the nut (A), washer (B) and torque arm (C)

8.6a Undo the pivot bolt nut . . .

8.6b . . . and remove any washers . . .

8.6c . . . or brackets . . .

steering stem. A length of tubing with an internal diameter slightly larger than the steering stem will be needed to tap the new bearing into position. Ensure that the drift bears only on the inner edge of the race and does not contact its working surface.

9 Install the steering stem (see Section 6).

8 Front suspension – disassembly, inspection and reassembly

Note: *Some suspension assemblies use self-locking nuts which should be discarded after use. Always use new self-locking nuts when reassembling the suspension.*

Leading link or monolever

Disassembly

1 Remove the front wheel, hub, caliper bracket and axle (see Chapter 8), and the fender (see Chapter 9).

2 Undo the nut and bolt securing the lower end of the shock absorber to the suspension arm. Support the arm and withdraw the bolt **(see illustration)**.

3 Undo the nut securing the upper end of the shock absorber, then pull off the shock. If required, remove the upper mounting bolt, noting the position of any spacers.

4 Counterhold the bolt and undo the nut securing the brake caliper bracket torque arm to the suspension leg, then remove the nut, washer and torque arm **(see illustration)**. Remove the bolt from the suspension leg if it is loose.

5 On some scooters, the suspension arm pivots on rubber bushings in the bottom of the suspension leg; on others, the arm turns on a pair of bearings. Before separating the arm from the suspension leg, check the condition of the bushings or bearings by moving the arm laterally against the suspension leg. If any play is felt between the arm and the leg, the bushings or bearings must be replaced. Also move the arm up-and-down. If any roughness is felt or the arm does not move smoothly and freely, the bushings, bearings or pivot bolt must be replaced. If there is no play or roughness in the suspension arm movement, there is no need to disassemble the suspension further. **Note:** *Suspension rubber bushings are generally a very tight fit*

which requires a press for removal and installation. Consult a scooter dealer or machine shop if the bushings need replacing.

6 To remove the suspension arm, counterhold the pivot bolt and undo the nut on the opposite end. Remove the nut, noting the position of any washers, spacers or brackets, then withdraw the pivot bolt and arm from the suspension leg **(see illustrations)**. The bolt

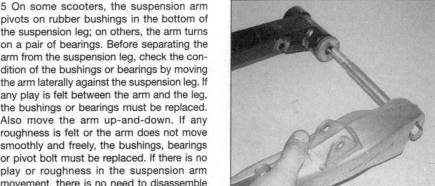

8.6d . . . then withdraw the pivot bolt and arm from the suspension leg

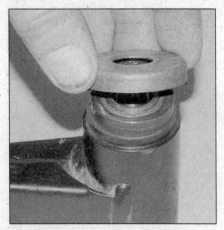

8.7a Remove the dust cap . . .

8.7b . . . and any seals . . .

8.7c . . . or spacers

8.7d Remove the bearing sleeve,
where installed

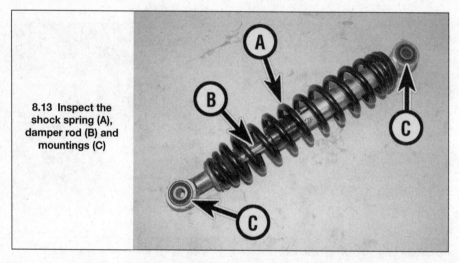

8.13 Inspect the
shock spring (A),
damper rod (B) and
mountings (C)

should be a press-fit in the arm and should not be removed unnecessarily.

7 Remove any dust caps, spacers and seals from either side of the suspension leg, then remove any sleeve from inside the bearings **(see illustrations)**.

Inspection

8 Clean all components thoroughly, removing all traces of dirt, corrosion and grease. Inspect all components closely, looking for obvious signs of wear such as heavy scoring, or for damage such as cracks or distortion.

9 Check the condition of the bearings in the suspension leg (see *Tools and Workshop Tips* in the *Reference* section). **Note:** *If ball-bearings are installed, they can be removed for cleaning and inspection, but needle roller bearings should only be removed if they are going to be replaced.* Check carefully for any retaining snap-rings before attempting to remove the bearings and note the position of the bearings and any sleeves or spacers.

10 Inspect the pivot bolt for wear and remove any corrosion with steel wool. Check the bolt for straightness with a straight-edge. If the bolt is worn, press it out of the suspension arm carefully to avoid damaging the

locating hole and install a new bolt. If the bolt is bent, cut off the damaged section and press the remainder out of the arm.

11 Inspect the condition of the bearing seals and replace them if they show signs of wear or deterioration.

12 Inspect the shock absorber for obvious physical damage and the shock spring for looseness, cracks or signs of fatigue.

13 Inspect the damper rod for signs of bending, pitting and oil leaks, and check the mountings at the top and bottom of the shock for wear or damage **(see illustration)**. If any parts are worn or damaged, a new shock must be installed.

Reassembly

14 If the bearings have been removed, ensure the bearing housings are thoroughly clean, then install the bearings (see *Tools and Workshop Tips* in the *Reference* section). **Note:** *Where a bearing is retained by a snap-ring, drive it in only as far as is necessary to install the snap-ring. Ensure any bearing spacers are in place and lubricate needle roller bearings with molybdenum disulphide grease.*

15 Install any seals, spacers and dust caps

as necessary, then smear the pivot bolt with grease and install it through the bearings, ensuring the seals remain in position. Check that the suspension arm is installed on the correct side of the leg, then install the washers and spacers as necessary and the pivot bolt nut.

16 If the pivot bolt nut retains the fender assembly, tighten the nut sufficiently to allow final positioning of the fender bracket when the fender is installed. Otherwise, tighten the nut to the torque setting specified in the *Data* section at the end of this manual.

17 If removed, install the bolt for the brake caliper bracket torque arm in the suspension leg, then install the arm, washer and nut **(see illustration 8.4)**. Tighten the nut sufficiently to allow final alignment of the torque arm when all the components have been installed.

18 Install the lower end of the shock absorber in the bracket on the monolever arm, then install the bolt. Tighten the bolt finger-tight.

19 Ensure any spacers on the upper shock mounting bolt are correctly positioned, then install the shock onto the bolt and install the nut. Counterhold the bolt and tighten the nut to the specified torque setting.

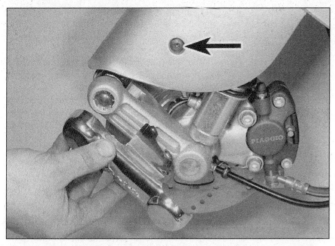

8.24 Undo the screw (arrow) to remove the cover and pull off the trim

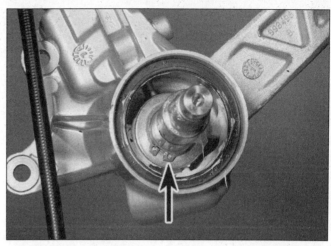

8.25 Remove the circlip (arrow) and slide the bracket off

8.26a Undo the two bolts (arrows) . . .

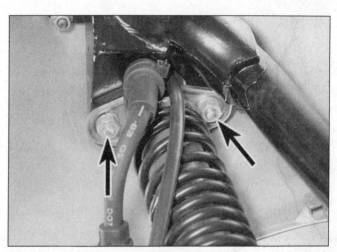

8.26b . . . and the two nuts (arrows) . . .

20 Install the fender (see Chapter 9). If not already done, tighten the pivot bolt nut to the specified torque setting.

21 Install the axle and caliper bracket (see Chapter 8). Counterhold the bolt and tighten the nut securing the caliper bracket torque arm to the suspension leg to the specified torque setting.

22 Tighten the lower shock mounting bolt to the specified torque setting.

23 Install the hub and front wheel (see Chapter 8).

Trailing link monoshock

Disassembly

24 Remove the front wheel and, on disc brake models, the hub assembly (see Chapter 8). Where applicable, remove the suspension cover and the trailing link trim (see illustration).

25 On disc brake models, check for any play in the bearings between the trailing link arm and the brake caliper mounting bracket. Remove the snap-ring and slide the bracket off the arm to inspect the bearings (see illustration).

26 On some scooters, the bottom of the shock absorber is secured by two bolts, and a bracket on the top of the shock is held by two nuts (see illustrations). Alternatively, the shock is secured top and bottom by a single bolt. Loosen the fasteners as appropriate,

noting the position of any washers or spacers, then lift the shock off (see illustration).

27 Before separating the trailing link arm from the suspension leg, check the condition of the bearings by moving the arm laterally against the leg. If any play is felt between

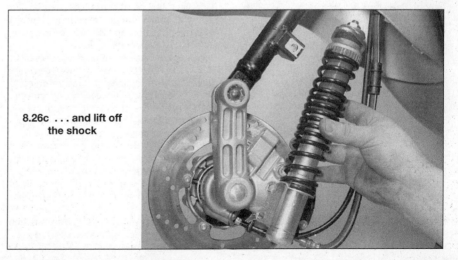

8.26c . . . and lift off the shock

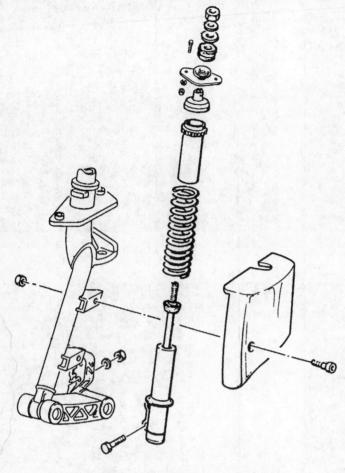

8.37 Front shock absorber components

the arm and the leg, the bearings and spacer pin must be replaced. Also move the arm up-and-down. If any roughness is felt or the arm does not move smoothly and freely, the bearings and spacer pin must be replaced. If there is no play or roughness in the suspension arm movement, there is no need to disassemble the suspension further.

28 To remove the suspension arm, first remove the wheel hub assembly (see Chapter 8).

29 On some scooters, the suspension arm turns on a pivot bolt; counterhold the bolt and undo the nut on the opposite end. Remove the nut, noting the position of any washers or spacers, then withdraw the pivot bolt and arm from the suspension leg.

30 Alternatively, the arm turns on a pin which is secured at each end by a push-in cap. The caps can be removed either by hitting them centrally with a suitable punch or drift, which should be wide enough to cover the raised inner section of the cap, or by prying up the outer tangs of the cap with a screwdriver. Discard the caps, as new ones must be used.

31 Drive or press out the pivot pin from the middle of the arm and separate the arm from

the leg. Note the position of any O-rings and seals.

Inspection

32 Clean all components thoroughly, removing all traces of dirt, corrosion and grease. Inspect all components closely, looking for obvious signs of wear such as heavy scoring, or for damage such as cracks or distortion.

33 Check the condition of the suspension arm and brake caliper mounting bracket bearings (see *Tools and Workshop Tips* in the *Reference* section). **Note:** *If ball-bearings are installed, they can be removed for cleaning and inspection, but needle roller bearings should only be removed if they are going to be replaced. Check carefully for any retaining snap-rings before attempting to remove the bearings and note the position of the bearings and any sleeves or spacers.*

34 Inspect the shock absorber for obvious physical damage and the shock spring for looseness, cracks or signs of fatigue.

35 Inspect the damper rod for signs of bending, pitting and oil leaks **(see illustration 8.13)**.

36 Inspect the mountings at the top and bottom of the shock for wear or damage.

37 On some machines, the shock absorber can be disassembled and individual components replaced **(see illustration)** – check the availability of parts with a scooter dealer. Compress the spring to remove the pressure on the spring seat at the top, then unscrew the top nut. Lift off the components of the upper mounting, noting the order in which they are installed, then carefully release the pressure on the spring. Remove the spring, noting which way up it fits. Install the new components and reassemble the shock in the reverse order of disassembly.

Reassembly

38 If the bearings have been removed, ensure the bearing housings are thoroughly clean, then install the bearings (see *Tools and Workshop Tips* in the *Reference* section). **Note:** *Where a bearing is retained by a snap-ring, drive it in only as far as is necessary to install the snap-ring. Ensure any bearing spacers are in place and lubricate needle roller bearings with molybdenum disulphide grease.*

39 Lubricate the pivot pin with molybdenum disulphide grease. Align the suspension arm with the leg, ensuring it is installed in the correct direction, then press the pin into place.

40 Install new dust seals and O-rings as necessary.

41 Install the new push-in caps and drive them into place using a piece of tubing that bears only on the area between the raised inner section and the raised outer tangs.

42 Install the shock absorber and tighten the nuts and bolts to the specified torque settings.

43 On disc brake models, slide the brake caliper mounting bracket onto the suspension arm and secure it with the snap-ring, making sure it sits properly in its groove (see Step 25). Install the hub assembly (see Step 24).

44 Install the front wheel (see Chapter 8) and the covers, where applicable.

Conventional telescopic fork

Note 1: *Two types of conventional telescopic forks are installed to the scooters covered by this manual. On the first type, the tubes are an integral part of the fork yoke (Steps 45 to 62), on the second, motorcycle-type fork, the tubes are clamped in the yoke and can be removed individually for disassembly (Steps 63 to 92).*

Note 2: *Always disassemble the fork legs separately to avoid interchanging parts. Check the availability of parts and the type and quantity of fork oil required with a scooter dealer before disassembling the forks. Note that on some scooters, the forks are lubricated with grease.*

Disassembly

45 Remove the steering stem (see Section 6).

46 Place a suitable oil drain tray below the fork, then unscrew the bolt in the bottom of the fork slider. Discard the sealing washer, as a new one must be used on reassembly. Pull the slider off the fork tube, then pull the dust

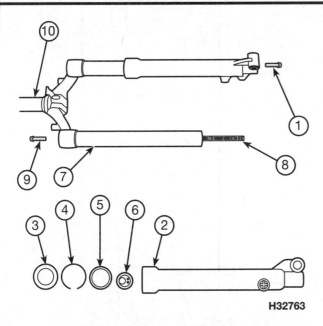

8.46 Typical telescopic fork components

1	Bottom bolt	5	Oil seal	8	Spring
2	Fork slider	6	Compression limiting	9	Top bolt
3	Dust seal		cone	10	Steering stem
4	Snap-ring	7	Fork tube		

seal off the slider and, if applicable, drain the oil from the slider **(see illustration)**.

47 Remove the snap-ring from inside the top of the slider, then carefully pry out the oil seal, taking care not to gouge the rim of the slider when doing this. Discard the seal, as a new one must be installed on reassembly.

48 Remove the compression limiting cone from inside the bottom of the slider, noting how it fits.

49 To remove the spring, unscrew the bolt in the top of the fork tube and draw the spring out of the tube. Hold the spring to prevent it from turning with the bolt. Some forks are installed with a sealed damper unit. Unscrew the top bolt, then unscrew the damper rod from the top bolt and remove damper unit and spring together. **Note:** *Various combinations of spring and damper unit are used – some forks have only one unit installed in one of the legs, others have a damper unit in both legs. Some forks have a damper unit installed in one leg and a spring in the other.*

Inspection

50 Clean all parts in a suitable solvent and dry them with compressed air, if available.

51 Inspect the fork tubes for score marks, pitting or flaking of the chrome finish and excessive or abnormal wear. Check the straightness of the tubes with a straight-edge. If either of the tubes is damaged, worn or bent, install a new fork yoke assembly.

52 Inspect the springs for cracks, sagging and other damage. No service data is available for the springs, but ensure they are both the same length. If one spring is defective,

replace both springs as a pair.

53 If installed, check the operation of the damper unit. Compress the damper rod into the cartridge, then pull it out. Movement of the rod should be slow and gradual – if there is no damping action, or the movement is jerky, install a new unit. **Note:** *If two units are installed, they should be replaced as a pair.*

54 The dust seals should be a sliding fit on the fork legs. Discard the dust seals if they are worn or deteriorated and install new ones (it is good practice to replace the dust seals when the forks are disassembled).

Reassembly

55 Install the compression limiting cone.

56 Lubricate the new oil seal with fork oil or grease, then press it squarely into the slider using a suitable piece of tubing or a socket until the snap-ring groove is visible above the seal.

 HAYNES HINT *Place a suitably-sized washer on top of the oil seal to protect it when pressing it into place.*

57 Once the seal is installed, install the snap-ring, making sure it is correctly located in its groove. **Note:** *If the fork is lubricated with grease, apply the grease to the inside of the slider below the level of the seal.*

58 As required, check that both plugs are in the ends of the spring, then insert the spring into the slider; alternatively, install the damper unit and spring into the slider. Install a new sealing washer to the bottom bolt, then install the bolt into the bottom of the

slider and thread it into the plug in the base of the spring or into the damper unit. Press down on the spring to prevent it from turning and tighten the bolt securely.

59 If applicable, carefully pour the correct quantity of the specified fork oil into the slider (see **Note 2**).

60 Install the dust seal and apply some fork oil to the lips of the seal, then insert the top of the spring into the bottom of the fork tube. Ensure the fork tube fits squarely through the oil seal and into the slider, and install the slider onto the tube until the spring contacts the top of the tube. Hold the slider in position, then install the bolt in the top of the fork tube and thread it into the plug in the top of the spring. Alternatively, extend the damper rod fully, then install the slider onto the tube and thread the damper rod into the top bolt and tighten it securely.

61 Tighten the top bolt securely.

62 Install the steering stem (see Section 6).

Motorcycle-type fork

Note 1: *Two types of conventional telescopic forks are installed to the scooters covered by this manual. On the first type, the tubes are an integral part of the fork yoke (Steps 45 to 62), on the second, motorcycle-type fork, the tubes are clamped in the yoke and can be removed individually for disassembly (Steps 63 to 92).*

Note 2: *Always disassemble the fork legs separately to avoid interchanging parts. Check the availability of parts and the type and quantity of fork oil required with a scooter dealer before disassembling the forks. Note that on some scooters the forks are lubricated with grease.*

Removal

63 Remove the front wheel and, if applicable, the brake caliper (see Chapter 8).

64 If the front fender is mounted on the front suspension, remove it (see Chapter 9).

65 Remove each fork leg individually.

66 If the fork leg is going to be disassembled or the fork oil is going to be changed, loosen the fork top bolt while the leg is still clamped in the fork yoke **(see illustration)**. To do this, first undo the fork leg clamp bolts

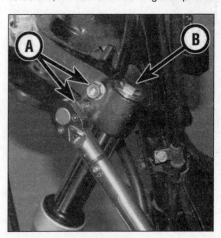

8.66 Fork leg clamp bolts (A) and fork top bolt (B)

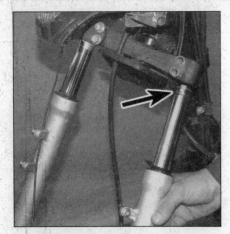

8.67 Pull the leg down – note the groove (arrow)

and push the leg a short distance up through the yoke, then temporarily tighten the clamp bolts. Now loosen the top bolt. **Note:** *Some fork legs have a location groove for one of the clamp bolts – remove the bolt before attempting to move the leg.*

67 Undo the fork clamp bolts and remove the fork leg by twisting it and pulling it downwards **(see illustration).**

 HAYNES HiNT *If the fork legs are seized in the yokes, spray the area with penetrating oil and allow time for it to soak in before trying again.*

Installation

68 Remove all traces of corrosion from the fork tubes and the yokes. Install each fork leg individually. Slide the leg up through the yoke until the top edge of the fork tube is level with the top edge of the yoke. Where applicable, ensure the location groove for the clamp bolt is correctly aligned. **Note:** *If the fork top bolt has not been fully tightened, follow the procedure in Step 66 to tighten it before positioning the leg in the yoke.* Tighten the clamp bolts in the yoke to the torque setting specified in the *Data* section at the end

8.74 Withdraw the fork spring

8.70 Typical motorcycle-type fork components

1   Top bolt
2   Spring
3   Fork tube
4   Sealing ring
5   Damper
6   Rebound spring
7   Spring seat
8   Dust seal
9   Snap-ring
10 Oil seal
11 Fork slider
12 Damper bolt

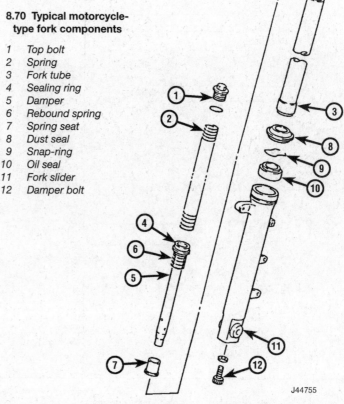

J44755

of this manual.

69 Install the remaining components in the reverse order of removal. Check the operation of the front forks and brake before taking the scooter out on the road.

Disassembly

70 Remove the fork leg (see Steps 63 to 67). Always disassemble the fork legs separately to avoid interchanging parts. Store all components in separate, clearly-marked containers **(see illustration).**

71 The damper bolt should be loosened at this stage. Invert the fork leg and compress

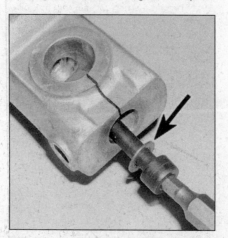

8.76 Remove the damper bolt and sealing washer (arrow)

the fork tube in the slider so that the spring exerts maximum pressure on the damper head, then loosen the bolt in the base of the fork slider **(see illustration 8.76).**

72 If the fork top bolt was not loosened with the fork on the scooter, carefully clamp the fork tube in a vise equipped with soft jaws, taking care not to overtighten or score the tube's surface, and loosen the top bolt.

73 Unscrew the top bolt from the top of the fork tube. If a damper rod is attached to the top bolt, loosen the locknut and unscrew the rod. Note any O-ring installed on the top bolt; if it is damaged, install a new one on reassembly.

⚠ *Warning: The fork spring is pressing on the fork top bolt with considerable pressure. Unscrew the bolt very carefully, keeping a downward pressure on it and release it slowly, as it is likely to spring clear. It is advisable to wear some form of eye and face protection when carrying out this operation.*

74 Slide the fork tube down into the slider and withdraw the spring **(see illustration).** Note which way up the spring is installed.

75 Invert the fork leg over a suitable container and pump the fork vigorously to expel as much fork oil as possible.

76 Remove the previously-loosened damper bolt and its sealing washer from the bottom of the slider **(see illustration).** Discard the sealing washer, as a new one must be

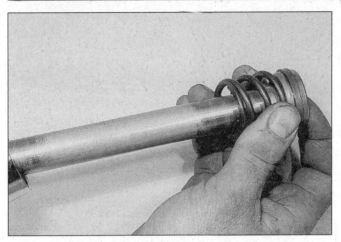

8.78 Withdraw the damper and rebound spring

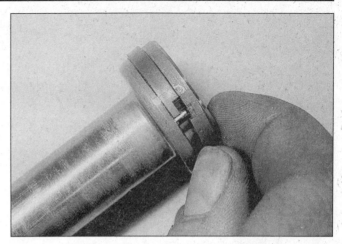

8.82 Check the condition of the sealing ring

used on reassembly. If the damper bolt was not loosened before disassembling the fork, temporarily install the spring and press down on it to prevent the damper from turning.

77 Pull the fork tube out of the slider.

78 Withdraw the damper and, if installed, the rebound spring and spring seat from inside the fork tube **(see illustration)**.

79 Carefully pry out the dust seal from the top of the slider, then remove the retaining clip and pry the oil seal out of the slider. Discard the seals, as new ones must be used on reassembly.

Inspection

80 Follow the procedure in Steps 50 to 54 to clean and check the fork components. If either of the fork tubes appears bent, have them both checked by a scooter dealer or machine shop. If necessary, install new fork tubes - do not have them straightened.

81 Where installed, check the condition of the rebound spring as well as the main spring.

82 On some forks, no damper rod is installed – a sealing ring is installed around the damper which restricts the flow of oil through the fork tube. Inspect the surface of the ring and replace it if it is scored, pitted or

worn **(see illustration)**. **Note:** *Do not remove the ring from the piston unless it requires replacement.*

Reassembly

83 Where installed, slide the rebound spring onto the damper, then insert the damper into the bottom of the fork tube and install the spring seat on the bottom of the damper **(see illustration)**.

84 Lubricate the fork tube with the specified fork oil and insert the assembly into the slider. Install a new sealing washer to the damper bolt and apply a few drops of a suitable, non-permanent thread-locking compound, then install the bolt into the bottom of the slider. Tighten the bolt to the specified torque setting. If the damper rotates inside the tube, hold it with spring pressure as on disassembly (see Step 76).

85 Push the fork tube fully into the slider, then lubricate the inside of the new oil seal with fork oil and slide it over the tube with its markings facing upwards **(see illustration)**. Press the seal into place in the slider. If necessary, use a suitable piece of tubing to tap the seal carefully into place; the tubing must be slightly larger in diameter than the fork tube and slightly smaller in diameter than

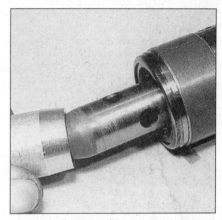

8.83 Install the spring seat on the bottom of the damper

the seal recess in the slider. Take care not to scratch the fork tube during this operation; if the fork tube is pushed fully into the slider any accidental scratching is confined to the area above the seal.

86 Install the retaining clip, making sure it is correctly located in its groove **(see illustration)**.

8.85 Install the oil seal with markings facing up

8.86 Install the oil seal retaining clip . . .

8.87 . . . then the dust seal

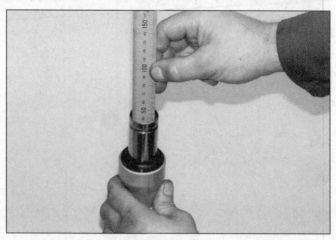

8.88 Measure the oil level with the leg fully compressed

87 Lubricate the inside of the new dust seal, then slide it down the fork tube and press it into position **(see illustration)**.

88 Slowly pour in the correct quantity of the specified grade of fork oil and carefully pump the fork to distribute the oil evenly; the oil level should also be measured and adjustment made by adding or subtracting oil – refer to your scooter handbook for details. Fully compress the fork tube into the slider, then measure the fork oil level from the top of the tube **(see illustration)**.

89 Pull the fork tube out of the slider to its full extension; if applicable, pull the damper rod out also. Install the spring.

90 If necessary, install a new O-ring to the fork top bolt. If applicable, thread the bolt onto the damper rod and tighten the locknut.

91 Keep the fork leg fully extended and press down on the spring while threading the top bolt into the top of the fork tube. Turn the bolt carefully to ensure it is not cross-threaded. **Note:** *The top bolt can be tightened to the specified torque setting when the fork has been installed and is securely held in the bottom yoke.*

⚠️ *Warning: It will be necessary to compress the spring by pressing it down with the top bolt in order to engage the threads of the top bolt with the fork tube. This is a potentially dangerous operation and should be performed with care, using an assistant if necessary. Wipe off any excess oil before starting to prevent the possibility of slipping.*

92 Install the fork leg (see Steps 68 and 69).

Upside-down fork
Seal replacement

93 Remove the front wheel and, if applicable, the brake caliper (see Chapter 8).

94 Where installed, unscrew the bolt from the base of the fork slider which retains the axle/brake caliper bracket and draw the bracket off the slider **(see illustration)**. Where installed, lever the dust seal off the bottom of the fork tube and remove it **(see illustration)**.

95 Where installed, remove the snap-ring, then pry the oil seal out of the bottom of the fork tube, taking care not to gouge the tube or the surface of the slider.

96 Clean the bottom of the slider and the inside of the axle/brake caliper bracket and remove any traces of corrosion.

97 Smear the new oil seal with fork oil or grease, then install it over the slider and press it into position on the bottom of the tube. If applicable, install the snap-ring.

98 If applicable, smear the inside of the new dust seal with fork oil or grease and install the seal.

99 Install the axle/brake caliper bracket and tighten the retaining bolt securely.

100 Install the remaining components in the reverse order of removal.

Disassembly

Note: *Some designs of upside-down forks are difficult to disassemble. If the fork is worn or the fork action is suspect, consult a scooter dealer – it may be more practical to replace the whole assembly. On some scooters, the forks are maintenance-free and no parts are available. Check the availability of parts and the type and quantity of fork oil required with a scooter dealer before disassembling the forks. Note that on some scooters the forks are lubricated with grease.*

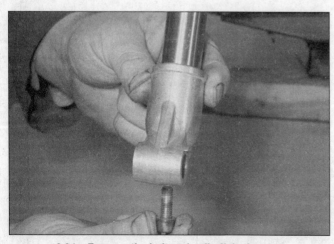

8.94a Remove the bolt and pull off the bracket

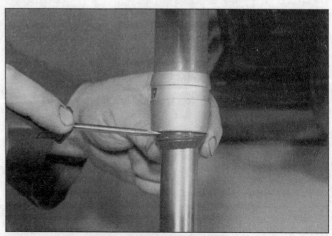

8.94b Lever off the dust seal

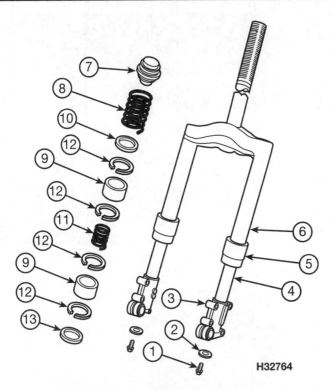

8.101 Typical upside-down fork components

1	Bottom bolt	6	Fork tube	10	Plain washer
2	Washer	7	Buffer	11	Rebound spring
3	Axle bracket	8	Compression spring	12	Snap-ring
4	Fork slider	9	Bush	13	Oil seal
5	Dust seal				

101 Remove the steering stem (see Section 6). Always disassemble the fork legs separately to avoid interchanging parts. Store all components in separate, clearly marked containers (see illustration).
102 Remove the dust and oil seals (see Steps 94 and 95).
103 Remove the lower snap-ring from inside the bottom of the fork tube (see illustration). Pull the slider out of the fork tube, together with the lower bushing and rebound spring. Note the order of the fork components for reassembly. If applicable, drain the fork oil out of the slider.
104 Remove the upper bushing snap-ring, then draw out the upper bushing and remove the upper snap-ring. Discard the snap-rings, as new ones must be installed on reassembly.
105 Withdraw the washer (where installed), compression spring and buffer from the tube.

Inspection

106 Clean all parts in a suitable solvent and dry them with compressed air, if available.
107 Inspect the fork sliders for score marks, pitting or flaking of the chrome finish and excessive or abnormal wear. Check the straightness of the sliders with a straight-edge. If either of the sliders is damaged, worn or bent, install a new fork yoke assembly.

108 Inspect the springs for cracks, sagging and other damage. No service data is available for the springs, but ensure both springs in each pair are the same length. If one spring is defective, replace both springs as a pair.
109 Examine the working surfaces of each bush; if they are worn or scuffed, replace the bushings as a set.

Reassembly

110 Install the various components into the fork tube in the reverse order of removal. If required, pour the correct quantity of the specified fork oil into the slider; alternatively, lubricate the inside of the fork tube and the outside of the slider with grease.
111 Install the buffer, compression spring and washer (where applicable) into the fork tube. Install the new upper bushing and snap-rings using a suitable piece of tubing to ensure they are squarely positioned inside the fork tube. Install the upper snap-ring for the lower bushing inside the fork tube. Install the lower bushing and spring on the slider, then install the slider into the tube, pushing it up into place. Press the lower bushing into place against its upper snap-ring, then secure it with the lower snap-ring.
112 Install the remaining components in the reverse order of removal.

8.103 Removing the circlip

9 Rear shock absorber – removal, inspection and installation

Note: Most scooters covered by this manual have a single rear shock absorber. On scooters with twin rear shocks, the lower end of the right-hand shock is supported by a sub-frame which bolts to the engine case and the rear wheel axle (see Chapter 8).

Removal

1 Support the scooter on its center stand and position a support under the rear wheel so that the engine does not drop when the shock absorber is removed. Make sure that the weight of the scooter is off the rear suspension so that the shock is not compressed.
2 The shock absorber is secured to the frame at the top and the transmission casing at the bottom. To access the upper mounting, remove the body panels as necessary (see Chapter 9). If necessary, remove the air filter housing (see Chapter 4).
3 Undo and remove the nut, or the nut and bolt, securing the top of the shock absorber to the frame (see illustration).

9.3 Upper rear suspension mounting

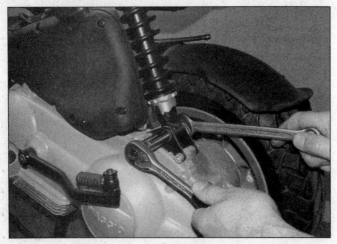

9.4a Undo the lower rear suspension mounting . . .

9.4b . . . then lift out the shock

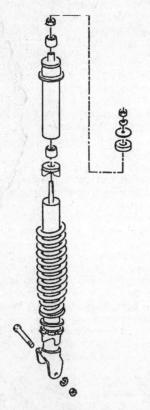

9.7 Rear shock absorber components

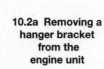

10.2a Removing a hanger bracket from the engine unit

4 Undo the nut and bolt securing the bottom of the shock absorber to the transmission casing; support the shock and remove the bolt, then maneuver the shock away from the scooter (see illustrations).

Inspection

5 Inspect the shock absorber for obvious physical damage and the shock spring for looseness, cracks or signs of fatigue.
6 Inspect the damper rod for signs of bending, pitting and oil leaks and check the mountings at the top and bottom of the shock for wear or damage (see illustration 8.13).
7 On some scooters, the shock absorber can be disassembled and individual components replaced (see illustration) – check the availability of parts with a scooter dealer. Compress the spring to remove the pressure on the spring seat at the top, then unscrew the top nut. Lift off the components of the upper mounting, noting the order in which they are installed, then carefully release the pressure on the spring. Remove the spring, noting which way up it fits. Install the new components and reassemble the shock in the reverse order of disassembly.

Installation

8 Installation is the reverse of removal. Tighten the shock absorber mounting bolts to the specified torque settings.

10 Front engine mounting – removal, inspection and installation

Removal

Note: On some scooters, the front engine mounting is bolted to the front, lower edge of the crankcase, on others a hanger bracket bolts to the top of the crankcase. In all cases, the mounting employs rubber-in-torsion silentbloc bushings and damping rubbers to restrict movement.
1 Remove the engine/transmission unit (see Chapter 2A or 2B).
2 Counterhold the engine bracket bolt(s) and undo the nut(s), then withdraw the bolt(s) and remove the engine mounting (see illustrations).

Inspection

3 Thoroughly clean all components, removing all traces of dirt, corrosion and grease.
4 Inspect the silentbloc bushings closely, looking for obvious signs of deterioration such as compression and cracks, or distortion due to accident damage (see illustration). The bushings are generally a very tight fit which requires a press for removal and installing. Consult a scooter dealer or machine shop if the bushings need replacing.
5 Where the mounting bracket bolts to the front edge of the crankcase, it should be necessary to compress the damping rubber in order to remove and install the engine bracket-to-frame bolt. If the bracket is not

10.2b Withdraw the pivot bolt . . .

10.2c . . . and remove the bracket from the frame

10.4 Inspect the bushes carefully . . .

10.5 . . . and check the condition of the damper rubbers

a tight fit, replace the damping rubber **(see illustration)**.

6 On the hanger bracket type mounting, check for wear on the damping rubbers. If the rubbers have worn, allowing metal-to-metal contact, replace them.

7 Check the bolts for wear and check the holes in the engine bracket for wear. If the bolts are not a precise fit in the bracket, the components must be replaced.

Installation

8 Installation is the reverse of removal. Smear some grease on the engine bracket bolts. Tighten all mounting bolts to the torque setting specified in the *Data* section at the end of this manual.

Notes

Chapter 8
Brakes, wheels and tires

Contents

Degrees of difficulty

Easy, suitable for novice with little experience		Fairly easy, suitable for beginner with some experience		Fairly difficult, suitable for competent DIY mechanic		Difficult, suitable for experienced DIY mechanic		Very difficult, suitable for expert DIY or professional	

Specifications

Refer to the *Data* section at the end of this manual for servicing specifications.

1 General information

The scooters covered by this manual are installed with either hydraulic disc brakes, cable-operated drum brakes, or a combination of disc front and drum rear brakes.

Generally, the hydraulic master cylinder is integral with the brake lever, although occasionally the master cylinder is remotely-mounted and operated by a cable from the brake lever.

In view of the broad variety of wheel types and tire sizes covered, owners are advised to refer to their scooter handbook or consult a tire specialist for the correct size and type of tire.

Caution: Disc brake components rarely require disassembly. Do not disassemble components unless absolutely necessary. If a hydraulic brake hose is loosened, the entire system must be disassembled, drained, cleaned, then properly filled and bled upon reassembly. Do not use solvents on internal brake components. Solvents will cause the seals to swell and distort. Use only clean brake fluid, a dedicated brake cleaner or denatured alcohol for cleaning. Use care when working with brake fluid as it can injure your eyes; it will also damage painted surfaces and plastic parts.

2 Front brake pads – removal, inspection and installation

Warning: The dust created by the brake system is harmful to your health. Never blow it out with compressed air and don't inhale any of it. An approved filtering mask should be worn when working on the brakes.

2.1 Remove the pad cover

2.3a Withdraw the spring wire pins

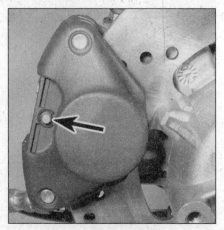

2.3b Remove the E-clip . . .

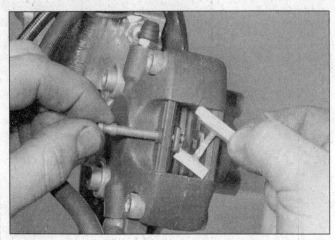

2.3c . . . and withdraw the pin – note the position of the pad spring

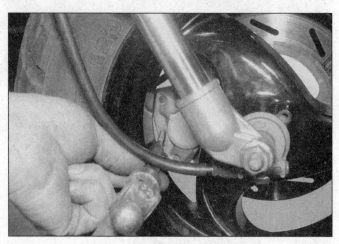

2.3d Drive out the pin and spring clip

1 Where installed, remove the pad cover from the caliper **(see illustration)**.

2 If necessary, unscrew the brake caliper mounting bolts and slide the caliper off the disc (see Section 3). **Note:** *Do not operate the brake lever while the caliper is off the disc.*

3 The pads are retained in the caliper by pad pins. Some calipers have spring wire pins; withdraw the pins, noting how they fit **(see illustration)**. Some calipers have pressed-in steel pins – if the pin is secured with an E-clip, remove the clip and withdraw the pin, noting the position of the pad spring **(see illustrations)**. If the pin is secured with a spring clip, drive out the pin **(see illustration)**. Some calipers have screw-in pins – unscrew the pin plug, then unscrew the pin and withdraw it **(see illustrations)**.

4 If not already done, note the position of any pad springs and remove them, then lift

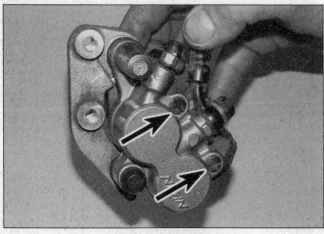

2.3e Unscrew the pin plugs (arrows) . . .

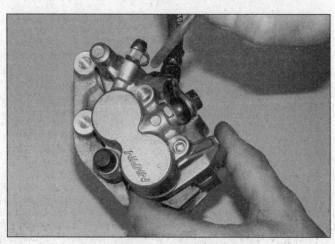

2.3f . . . then unscrew the pad pins

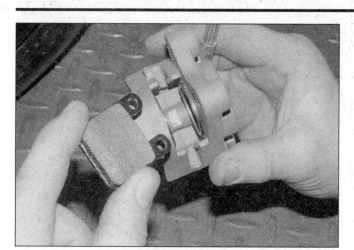

2.4a Lift out the pads

2.4b Note the position of springs (arrows) inside the caliper

out the pads **(see illustration)**. Note the position of any pad springs inside the caliper **(see illustration)**.

5 Inspect the surface of each pad for contamination and check that the friction material has not worn to or beyond the minimum thickness specified in the *Data* section at the end of this manual **(see illustration)**. If either pad is worn down to (or beyond) the service limit, is fouled with oil or grease, or heavily scored or damaged, both pads must be replaced. **Note:** *It is not possible to degrease the friction material; if the pads are contaminated in any way, they must be replaced.*

6 If the pads are in good condition, clean them carefully using a fine wire brush which is completely free of oil and grease to remove all traces of road dirt and corrosion. Spray the caliper with a dedicated brake cleaner to remove any dust and remove any traces of corrosion which might cause sticking of the caliper/pad operation.

7 Remove all traces of corrosion from the pad pins. Inspect the pins for damage and, where applicable, loss of spring tension, and replace them if necessary. If the pins are secured by clips, ensure the clips are a tight fit on the pin, otherwise install new clips on reassembly.

8 Remove all traces of corrosion from the pad springs; if the springs are badly worn or damaged, install new springs.

9 Check the condition of the brake disc (see Section 4).

10 If new pads are being installed, slowly push each piston as far back into the caliper as possible using hand pressure or a piece of wood for leverage. This will displace brake fluid back into the hydraulic reservoir, so it may be necessary to remove the reservoir cap, plate and diaphragm and siphon out some fluid (depending on how much fluid was in there in the first place and how far the pistons have to be pushed in). If a piston is difficult to push back, attach a length of clear hose to the bleed valve and place the open end in a suitable container, then open the valve and try again. Take great care not to

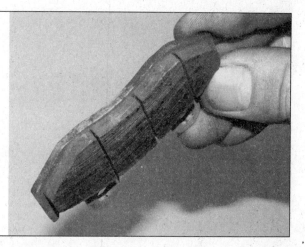

2.5 Measure the amount of friction material on each pad

draw any air into the system and don't forget to tighten the valve once the piston has been sufficiently displaced. If in doubt, bleed the brakes afterwards (see Section 8).

Caution: Never lever the caliper against the brake disc to push a piston back into the caliper, as damage to the disc will result.

11 Smear the pad pins and the backs of the pads with copper-based grease, making sure that none gets on the front or sides of the pads.

12 Installation is the reverse of removal, noting the following:

> If applicable, ensure any pad springs are in place inside the caliper.
> Install the pads into the caliper so that the friction material faces the disc.
> Install the pad pins and, where applicable, the pad spring.
> Check that the pins are correctly locked or clipped in place.
> Install the caliper and operate the brake lever several times to bring the pads into contact with the disc.
> Check the brake fluid level and top-up if necessary (see Daily (pre-ride) checks).

13 Check the operation of the brake before riding the scooter.

3 Front brake caliper – removal, overhaul and installation

Warning: If a caliper indicates the need for replacement (usually due to leaking fluid or sticky operation), all old brake fluid should be flushed from the system at the same time. Also, the dust created by the brake system is harmful to your health. Never blow it out with compressed air and don't inhale any of it. An approved filtering mask should be worn when working on the brakes. Do not, under any circumstances, use petroleum-based solvents to clean brake parts. Use a dedicated brake cleaner or denatured alcohol only, as described. To prevent damage from spilled brake fluid, always cover paintwork when working on the braking system.

3.1a Undo the caliper mounting bolts . . .

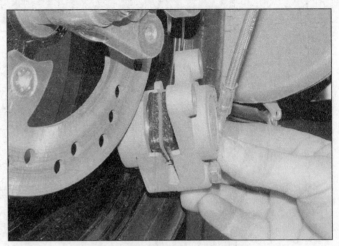

3.1b . . . and slide the caliper off

Note: *On some scooters, the front wheel must be removed before the caliper can be removed (see Section 14).*

Removal

1 Unscrew the brake caliper mounting bolts and slide the caliper off the disc **(see illustrations)**. **Note:** *Do not operate the brake lever while the caliper is off the disc.*

2 If the caliper is just being removed, the brake pads can be left in place. Support the caliper with a cable tie to ensure no strain is placed on the hydraulic hose.

3 If the caliper is being cleaned and inspected, remove the brake pads (see Section 2). **Note:** *It is not necessary to disconnect the brake hose to clean and inspect the caliper.*

4 To remove the caliper from the machine, first note the alignment of the banjo fitting on the caliper, then unscrew the banjo bolt and separate the hose from the caliper **(see illustration)**. Discard the sealing washers, as new ones must be used on installation. Wrap a plastic bag tightly around the end of the hose to prevent dirt entering the system and secure the hose in an upright position

to minimize fluid loss. **Note:** *If you are planning to overhaul the caliper and do not have a source of compressed air to blow out the piston, just loosen the banjo bolt at this stage and retighten it lightly. The hydraulic system can then be used to force the piston out of the caliper. Disconnect the hose once the piston has been sufficiently displaced.*

Overhaul

5 Clean the exterior of the caliper with denatured alcohol or brake system cleaner. Inspect the caliper for signs of damage, especially around the mounting lugs and the bleed screw, and replace it if necessary. If hydraulic fluid is leaking from around the edge of the piston, the internal piston seal has failed **(see illustration)**. If new seals are available, the caliper can be overhauled as follows, otherwise a new caliper will have to be installed. **Note:** *The scooters covered by this manual are installed with single piston, opposed piston or double piston calipers. If there is more than one piston in the caliper, mark each piston head and the caliper body with a suitable marker to ensure that the pistons can be matched to their original bores on reassembly.*

6 Displace the piston from its bore using either compressed air or by carefully operating the front brake lever to pump it out. If the piston is being displaced hydraulically, it may be necessary to top-up the hydraulic reservoir during the procedure. Also, have some clean rag ready to catch any spilled hydraulic fluid when the piston reaches the end of the bore. Where two pistons are installed, ensure that they both move freely and evenly. **Note:** *If the compressed air method is used, direct the air into the fluid inlet on the caliper. Use only low pressure to ease the piston out – if the air pressure is too high and the piston is forced out, the caliper and/or piston may be damaged.*

⚠ *Warning: Never place your fingers in front of a piston in an attempt to catch or protect it when applying compressed air, as serious injury could result.*

7 If a piston sticks in its bore, try to displace it with compressed air (see Step 6). Where two pistons are installed, remove the free piston first, then pack its bore with clean rag and try to displace the stuck piston. If the stuck piston cannot be displaced, a new caliper will have to be installed.

3.4 Unscrew the bolt (arrow) to detach the hose

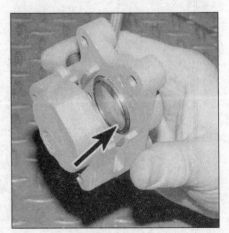

3.5 Fluid leaks indicate a failed seal

3.9 Remove the seals with a soft wooden or plastic tool – a pencil works well

Caution: Do not try to remove a piston by prying it out, or by using pliers or any other grips.

8 On opposed piston calipers, it may not be possible to force the pistons all the way out of their bores. Unscrew the caliper joining bolts and separate the caliper halves, noting the position of any O-rings. Discard the O-rings, as new ones must be installed on reassembly.

9 Remove the dust seal and the piston seal from the piston bore using a soft wooden or plastic tool to avoid scratching the bore **(see illustration)**. Discard the seals, as new ones must be installed.

10 Clean the piston and bore with clean brake fluid or brake system cleaner. If compressed air is available, blow it through the fluid galleries in the caliper to ensure they are clear and use it to dry the parts thoroughly (make sure it is filtered and unlubricated).

Caution: Do not, under any circumstances, use a petroleum-based solvent to clean brake parts.

11 Inspect the bore and piston for signs of corrosion, nicks and burrs and loss of plating. If surface defects are present, the caliper assembly must be replaced. If the caliper

is in bad shape, the master cylinder should also be checked.

12 Lubricate the new piston seal with clean brake fluid and install it in the groove in the caliper bore.

13 Lubricate the new dust seal with clean brake fluid and install it in the groove in the caliper bore.

14 Lubricate the piston with clean brake fluid and install it, closed-end first, into the caliper bore. Using your thumbs, push the piston all the way in, making sure it enters the bore squarely.

15 On opposed piston calipers, smear the new caliper body O-rings with clean brake fluid and install them in one half of the caliper. Assemble the caliper halves and tighten the joining bolts – if required, the bolts can be tightened fully once the caliper has been installed on the scooter.

Installation

16 If the brake pads have been removed, install the pads (see Section 2). If the caliper has just been displaced, install the caliper on the brake disc **(see illustration 3.1b)**.

17 Install the caliper mounting bolts, and tighten them to the torque setting specified in the *Data* section. If required, tighten the

caliper joining bolts (see Step 15).

18 If the caliper was removed from the machine, or a new caliper is being installed, connect the brake hose to the caliper, using new sealing washers on each side of the banjo fitting. Align the banjo fitting as noted on removal. Tighten the banjo bolt to the specified torque setting and top-up the hydraulic reservoir (see *Daily (pre-ride) checks*). Bleed the hydraulic system (see Section 8).

19 Check for fluid leaks and check the operation of the brake before riding the scooter.

4 Front brake disc – inspection, removal and installation

Inspection

1 Visually inspect the surface of the disc for score marks and other damage. Light scratches are normal after use and won't affect brake operation, but deep grooves and heavy score marks will reduce braking efficiency and accelerate pad wear. If a disc is badly grooved it must be machined or replaced.

2 The disc must not be machined or allowed to wear down to a thickness less than the service limit, either as listed in the *Data* section at the end of this manual, or as stamped on the disc **(see illustration)**. Check the thickness of the disc with a micrometer and replace it if necessary **(see illustration)**.

3 To check disc warpage, position the machine upright so that the wheel is raised off the ground. Attach a dial gauge to the suspension with the tip of the gauge touching the surface of the disc about 10 mm from the outer edge. Rotate the wheel and watch the gauge needle; a small amount of movement is acceptable. If excessive movement is indicated, first check the wheel bearings for play (see Section 14). If the bearings are good, the disc is warped and should be replaced.

4.2a Look for the thickness stamped on the disc

4.2b Measuring the thickness of a disc with a micrometer

4.5 Unscrew the bolts (arrows) to remove the disc

4.7 Brake disc directional arrow

Removal

4 Remove the front wheel (see Section 14). On some scooters it may also be necessary to remove the hub assembly.

Caution: Do not lay the wheel down and allow it to rest on the disc – the disc could become warped.

5 If you are not replacing the disc, mark the relationship of the disc to the wheel so that it can be installed in the same position. Unscrew the disc retaining bolts, loosening them a little at a time to avoid distorting the disc, then remove the disc **(see illustration)**.

Installation

6 Before installing the disc, make sure there is no dirt or corrosion where the disc seats on the hub. If the disc does not sit flat when it is bolted down, it will appear to be warped when checked or when the front brake is used.

7 Install the disc, making sure that the directional arrow, if applicable, points in the direction of normal wheel rotation **(see illustration)**. Align the previously applied register marks, if you are reinstalling the original disc.

Install the bolts and tighten them evenly and a little at a time to the torque setting specified in the *Data* section. Clean the disc using acetone or brake system cleaner. If a new brake disc has been installed, remove any protective coating from its working surfaces.

8 If applicable, install the hub assembly, and the front wheel (see Section 14).

9 Operate the brake lever several times to bring the pads into contact with the disc. Check the operation of the brake before riding the scooter.

---

5 Front brake master cylinder – removal, overhaul and installation

Handlebar-mounted

Removal

1 Remove the handlebar covers for access (see Chapter 9).

2 If the master cylinder is just being displaced, ensure the fluid reservoir cover is secure. Unscrew the master cylinder clamp

bolts and remove the back of the clamp **(see illustration)**. Position the assembly clear of the handlebar, making sure no strain is placed on the brake hose and the brake light switch wiring. Keep the fluid reservoir upright to prevent air entering the hydraulic system.

3 If the master cylinder is being removed, disconnect the brake light switch wiring connector and, if required, unscrew the brake light switch.

4 Unscrew the brake hose banjo bolt and detach the banjo fitting, noting its alignment with the master cylinder **(see illustration)**.

5 Once disconnected, secure the hose in an upright position to minimize fluid loss. Wrap a clean plastic bag tightly around the end to prevent dirt entering the system. Discard the sealing washers, as new ones must be installed on reassembly.

6 Undo the master cylinder clamp bolts and remove the back of the clamp **(see illustration 5.2)**. Lift the master cylinder and reservoir away from the handlebar.

7 Undo the reservoir cover retaining screws and lift off the cover, the diaphragm plate and the diaphragm **(see illustration)**. Drain the brake fluid from the reservoir into a suit-

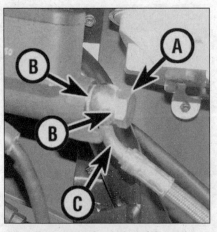

5.2 Unscrew the clamp bolts (arrows)

5.4 Brake hose banjo bolt (A), sealing washers (B) and banjo fitting (C)

5.7 Master cylinder cover, diaphragm plate and diaphragm

5.10 Remove the dust boot to access the pushrod snap-ring

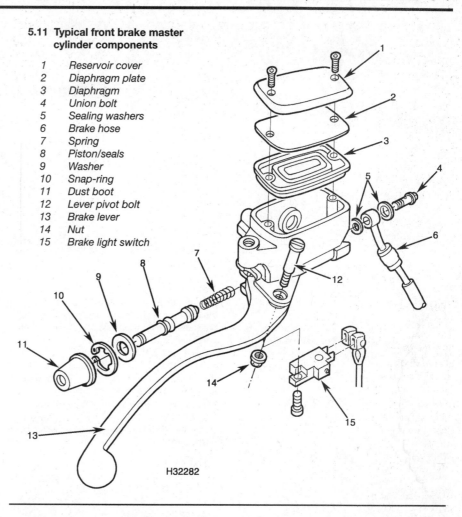

5.11 Typical front brake master cylinder components

1   Reservoir cover
2   Diaphragm plate
3   Diaphragm
4   Union bolt
5   Sealing washers
6   Brake hose
7   Spring
8   Piston/seals
9   Washer
10 Snap-ring
11 Dust boot
12 Lever pivot bolt
13 Brake lever
14 Nut
15 Brake light switch

H32282

able container. Wipe any remaining fluid out of the reservoir with a clean rag.

8 If required, remove the brake lever (see Section 11).

Overhaul

Note: *If the master cylinder is leaking fluid, or if the lever does not produce a firm feel when the brake is applied, bleeding the brakes does not help (see Section 8), and the hydraulic hoses are all in good condition, then the master cylinder must be overhauled or a new one must be installed. Check the availability of parts with a scooter dealer.*

9 Before disassembling the master cylinder, read through the entire procedure and make sure that you have obtained all the new parts required (including some new DOT 4 brake fluid, some clean rags and internal snap-ring pliers).

Caution: Disassembly, overhaul and reassembly of the brake master cylinder must be done in a spotlessly-clean work area to avoid contamination and possible failure of the brake hydraulic system components. To prevent damage to the paint from spilled brake fluid, always cover the fuel tank and fairing when working on the master cylinder.

10 Follow Steps 3 to 8, then carefully remove the dust boot from the master cylinder to reveal the pushrod retaining snap-ring **(see illustration)**.

11 Depress the piston and use snap-ring pliers to remove the snap-ring, then slide out the piston assembly and the spring, noting how they fit **(see illustration)**. If they are difficult to remove, apply low pressure compressed air to the fluid outlet. Lay the parts out in the proper order to prevent confusion during reassembly.

12 Clean all parts with clean brake fluid or brake system cleaner. If compressed air is available, blow it through the fluid galleries to ensure they are clear and use it to dry the parts thoroughly (make sure the air is filtered and unlubricated).

Caution: Do not, under any circumstances, use a petroleum-based solvent to clean brake parts.

13 Check the bore inside the master cylinder for corrosion, scratches, nicks and score marks. If damage or wear is evident, the master cylinder must be replaced. If the master cylinder is in poor condition, then the caliper should be checked as well.

14 The dust boot, snap-ring, piston assembly and spring are included in the master cylinder rebuild kit. Use all of the new parts, regardless of the apparent condition of the old ones. Install them according to the layout of the old piston assembly.

15 Lubricate the piston assembly with clean brake fluid and install the components in the master cylinder in the reverse order of disassembly. Depress the piston and install the new snap-ring, making sure it is properly located in the groove.

16 Install the dust boot, making sure the lip is seated properly in the groove.

17 Inspect the hydraulic reservoir cap, diaphragm plate and diaphragm and replace any parts if they are damaged or deteriorated.

Installation

18 Installation is the reverse of removal, noting the following:

Connect the brake hose to the master cylinder, using new sealing washers on each side of the banjo union.
Align the banjo union as noted on removal.
Ensure the brake light wiring is connected securely.
Fill the fluid reservoir with new brake fluid (see Daily (pre-ride) checks).
Bleed the air from the system (see Section 8).
Ensure the reservoir diaphragm is correctly seated and that the cover screws are tightened securely.

19 Check the operation of the brake before riding the scooter.

Remotely-mounted

Removal

20 On some scooters, the master cylinder is mounted on the steering stem with a separate hydraulic reservoir. The master cylinder is activated by a cable from the brake lever. Remove the handlebar covers and the front body panels as necessary for access (see Chapter 9).

21 Remove the E-clip on the cable pivot pin, then draw out the pin and detach the cable

5.21 Remove the E-clip and draw out the pin

5.22 Unscrew the brake hose union (arrow)

from the master cylinder lever arm **(see illustration)**.

22 Unscrew the brake hose from the master cylinder **(see illustration)**. Secure the hose in an upright position to minimize fluid loss. Wrap a clean plastic bag tightly around the end to prevent dirt entering the system.

5.24 Release the clip (arrow) and detach the reservoir hose

23 Unscrew the reservoir cap and remove the diaphragm plate and diaphragm. Drain the brake fluid from the reservoir into a suitable container.

24 Release the clip securing the reservoir hose to the fitting on the master cylinder, then detach the hose from the fitting **(see illustration)**. Wipe any remaining fluid out of the reservoir with a clean rag.

25 Unscrew the master cylinder mounting bolts and remove the master cylinder **(see illustration)**.

Overhaul

26 If the necessary parts for overhauling the master cylinder are available, follow the procedure in Steps 9 to 17, otherwise install a new master cylinder.

Installation

27 Installation is the reverse of removal, noting the following:

> Ensure the reservoir hose is secured with the clip – if the old clip has weakened, install a new one.
> The E-clip should be a tight fit on the pivot pin – install a new one if necessary.

> Fill the fluid reservoir with new brake fluid (see Daily (pre-ride) checks).
> Bleed the air from the system (see Section 8).
> Ensure the reservoir diaphragm is correctly seated and that the cover is tightened securely.

28 Check the operation of the brake before riding the scooter.

6 Rear disc brake – inspection, removal and installation

1 The procedures for removal, inspection and installation of the rear disc brake pads, caliper, disc and master cylinder are the same as for the front brake. **Note:** *The rear wheel must be displaced before the caliper can be removed (see Section 15).*

2 Note the routing of the rear brake hose before displacing the caliper, then undo any screws securing the hose bracket to the drivebelt cover and remove the bracket **(see illustration)**.

5.25 Master cylinder mounting bolts (arrows)

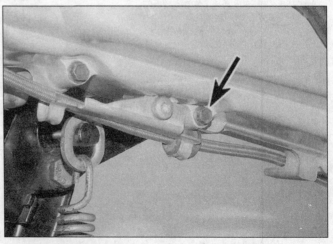

6.2 Undo the screw and remove the bracket

3 The caliper is secured to the transmission casing by two bolts **(see illustration)**.
4 If the caliper is just being displaced, secure it to the machine with a cable tie to avoid straining the hose. **Note:** *Do not operate the brake lever while the caliper is off the disc.*
5 After working on any component in the brake system, always check the operation of the brake before riding the scooter.

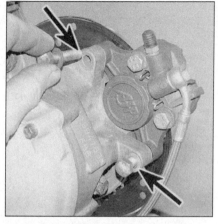

6.3 The brake caliper is secured by two bolts

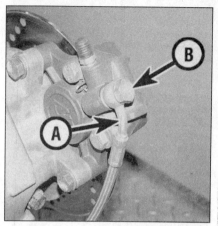

7.5 Note the alignment of the fitting (A) before undoing the bolt (B)

7 Brake hoses and unions – inspection and replacement

Inspection

1 Brake hose condition should be checked regularly and the hose(s) replaced at the specified interval (see Chapter 1).
2 Remove the body panels as necessary (see Chapter 9).
3 Twist and flex the hose while looking for cracks, bulges and seeping fluid. Check extra carefully where the hose connects to the banjo fittings or hose unions, as these are common areas for hose failure.
4 Inspect the banjo fittings and hose unions; if they are rusted, cracked or damaged, install new hoses.

Replacement

5 Most brake hoses have banjo fittings on each end. Cover the surrounding area with plenty of rags and unscrew the banjo bolt, noting the alignment of the fitting with the master cylinder or brake caliper **(see illustration)**. Free the hose from any clips or guides and remove it, noting its routing. Discard the sealing washers. On some hoses, one end is secured by a fitting nut; hold the hose to prevent it twisting while the nut is being undone **(see illustration 5.22)**. **Note:** *Do not operate the brake lever while a brake hose is disconnected.*
6 Position the new hose, making sure it is not twisted or otherwise strained. Ensure that it is correctly routed through any clips or guides and is clear of all moving components.
7 Check that the fittings align correctly, then

install the banjo bolts, using new sealing washers on both sides of the fittings **(see illustration 5.4)**. Tighten the banjo bolts securely. If the hose is secured by a union nut at one end, install that end first to avoid twisting the hose while the nut is being tightened. Take care not to overtighten the fitting nut.
8 Flush the old brake fluid from the system, refill with new brake fluid and bleed the air from the system (see Section 8).
9 Check the operation of the brakes before riding the scooter.

8 Brake system – bleeding and fluid change

Caution: Support the scooter in an upright position and ensure that the hydraulic reservoir is level while carrying out these procedures.

Bleeding

1 Bleeding the brakes is simply the process of removing air from the brake fluid reservoir, master cylinder, the hose and the brake cali-

per. Bleeding is necessary whenever a brake system connection is loosened, or when a component is replaced. Leaks in the system may also allow air to enter, but leaking brake fluid will reveal their presence and warn you of the need for repair.
2 To bleed the brake, you will need some new DOT 4 brake fluid, a small container partially-filled with new brake fluid, a length of clear vinyl or plastic hose, some rags and a wrench to install the brake caliper bleed valve.
3 Remove the handlebar covers or body panels for access to the fluid reservoir (see Chapter 9) and cover any painted components to prevent damage in the event that brake fluid is spilled.
4 Remove the reservoir cover, diaphragm plate and diaphragm, and slowly pump the brake lever a few times until no air bubbles can be seen floating up from the holes in the bottom of the reservoir. This bleeds air from the master cylinder end of the system. Temporarily reinstall the reservoir cover.
5 Pull the dust cap off the caliper bleed valve **(see illustration)**. Attach one end of the clear hose to the bleed valve and submerge the other end in the brake fluid in the container **(see illustration)**. **Note:** *To avoid damag-*

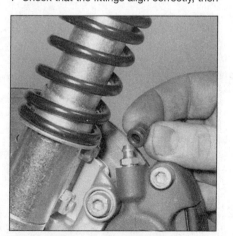

8.5a Pull off the dust cap

8.5b Set-up for bleeding the brakes

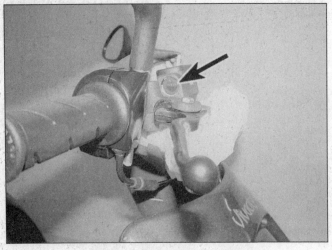

8.6 Check the fluid level regularly

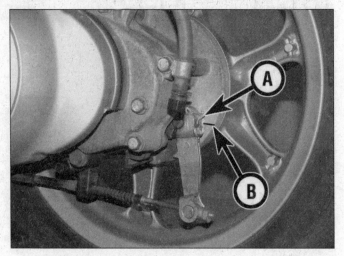

9.1 Brake wear indicator (A) and alignment mark (B)

ing the bleed valve during the procedure, loosen it and then tighten it temporarily with a box-end wrench before attaching the hose. With the hose attached, the valve can then be opened and closed with an open-ended wrench.

6 Check the fluid level in the reservoir. Do not allow the fluid level to drop below the half-way mark during the procedure **(see illustration)**.

7 Carefully pump the brake lever three or four times and hold it in while opening the caliper bleed valve. When the valve is opened, brake fluid will flow out of the caliper into the clear hose and the lever will move toward the handlebar.

8 Tighten the bleed valve, then release the brake lever gradually. Repeat the process until no air bubbles are visible in the brake fluid leaving the caliper and the lever is firm when applied. On completion, disconnect the hose, ensure the bleed valve is tightened securely and install the dust cap.

9 Top-up the reservoir, install the diaphragm, diaphragm plate and cover, and wipe up any spilled brake fluid. Check the entire system for fluid leaks.

 If it's not possible to produce a firm feel to the lever, the fluid may be aerated. Let the brake fluid in the system stabilize for a few hours, then repeat the procedure when the tiny bubbles in the system have settled out. To speed this process up, tie the front brake lever to the handlebar so that the system is pressurized.

Fluid change

Note: Some manufacturers recommend back-filling the hydraulic system with a syringe to avoid troublesome air locks (see Steps 16 to 22).

10 Changing the brake fluid is a similar process to bleeding the brakes and requires

the same materials plus a suitable tool for siphoning the fluid out of the hydraulic reservoir. Also ensure that the container is large enough to take all the old fluid when it is flushed out of the system.

11 Follow the procedure in Step 5, then remove the reservoir cap, diaphragm plate and diaphragm and siphon the old fluid out of the reservoir. Fill the reservoir with new brake fluid, then follow the procedure in Step 7.

12 Retighten the bleed valve, then release the brake lever gradually. Keep the reservoir topped-up with new fluid at all times or air may enter the system and greatly increase the length of the task. Repeat the process until new fluid can be seen emerging from the bleed valve.

 Old brake fluid is invariably much darker in color than new fluid, making it easy to see when all old fluid has been expelled from the system.

13 Disconnect the hose, ensure the bleed valve is tightened securely and install the dust cap.

14 Top-up the reservoir, install the diaphragm, diaphragm plate and cover, and wipe up any spilled brake fluid. Check the entire system for fluid leaks.

15 Check the operation of the brakes before riding the scooter.

16 If, after changing the brake fluid, it proves impossible to obtain a firm feel at the brake lever, it may be necessary to back-fill the system. To back-fill the hydraulic system, remove the reservoir cover, diaphragm plate and diaphragm and siphon the old fluid out of the reservoir. Temporarily reinstall the reservoir cover but do not tighten the screws.

17 Remove the brake caliper and slowly push the pistons as far back into the caliper as possible using hand pressure or a piece of wood for leverage, then siphon any residual fluid from the reservoir. Leave the cover off the reservoir. Reinstall the brake caliper.

18 Fill a suitable syringe with approximately 40 ml of new brake fluid and connect a short length of hose to the syringe. Bleed any air from the syringe and hose, then connect the hose to the caliper bleed valve. **Note:** *To avoid damaging the bleed valve during the procedure, loosen it and then tighten it temporarily with a box-end wrench before attaching the hose. With the hose attached, the valve can then be opened and closed with an open-ended wrench.*

19 Open the bleed valve and carefully inject fluid into the system until the level in the reservoir is up to the half-way mark. Tighten the bleed valve, disconnect the hose and reinstall the dust cap.

20 Operate the brake lever carefully several times to bring the pads into contact with the disc, then check the fluid level in the reservoir and top-up if necessary (see *Daily (pre-ride) checks*).

21 Install the diaphragm, diaphragm plate and cover, and wipe up any spilled brake fluid. Check the system for fluid leaks.

22 Check the operation of the brakes before riding the scooter.

---

9 Drum brakes – inspection, shoe removal and installation

 Warning: The dust created by the brake system is harmful to your health. Never blow it out with compressed air and don't inhale any of it. An approved filtering mask should be worn when working on the brakes.

Inspection

1 Some scooters are equipped with a brake wear indicator; if the wear indicator aligns with the index mark when the brake is

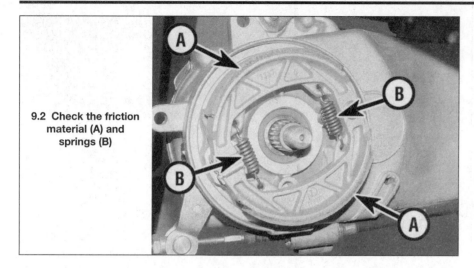

9.2 Check the friction material (A) and springs (B)

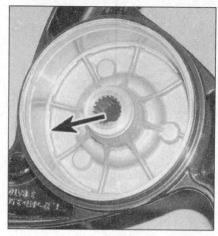

9.6 Check the surface of the brake drum (arrow)

applied, the shoes should be replaced **(see illustration)**.

2 Alternatively, remove the wheel (see Section 14 or 15). On some front suspension types, the brake backing plate will remain on the suspension arm, on others it will be necessary to remove the backing plate from the wheel. Check the amount of friction material on the brake shoes and compare the result with the specification in the *Data* section at the end of this manual **(see illustration)**. If the friction material has worn down to the minimum thickness, install new brake shoes.

3 Inspect the friction material for contamination. If it is fouled with oil or grease, or heavily scored or damaged, both shoes must be replaced as a set. Note that it is not possible to degrease the friction material; if the shoes are contaminated in any way, they must be replaced.

4 If the shoes are in good condition, clean them carefully using a fine wire brush which is completely free of oil and grease to remove all traces of dust and corrosion.

5 Check the condition of the brake shoe springs; they should hold the shoes tightly in place against the operating cam and pivot post **(see illustration 9.2)**. Remove the shoes (see Steps 11 to 12) and replace the springs if they appear weak or are obviously deformed or damaged.

6 Clean the surface of the brake drum using brake system cleaner. Examine the surface for scoring and excessive wear **(see illustration)**. While light scratches are to be expected, any heavy scoring will impair braking and there is no satisfactory way of removing them; in this event the wheel should be replaced, although you could consult a machinist who might be able to machine the surface.

7 Measure the internal diameter of the brake drum with a vernier caliper; take several measurements to ensure the drum has not worn out-of-round. If the drum is out-of-round, install a new wheel.

8 To check and lubricate the brake cam, first remove the brake shoes (see Steps 11 to 12). Note the position of the brake arm and spring, then loosen the brake arm pinch-bolt

and pull the cam out of the backing plate or casing **(see illustration)**. Clean all traces of old grease off the cam and shaft. If the bearing surfaces of the cam or shaft are worn, the cam should be replaced.

9 Lubricate the shaft with a smear of copper grease; position the brake arm and spring and install the cam in the backing plate or casing, then tighten the pinch-bolt securely. Lubricate the cam and the pivot post with a smear of copper grease and install the brake shoes.

Shoe removal and installation

10 Remove the wheel (see Section 14 or 15).

11 If the shoes are not going to be replaced they must be installed in their original positions; mark them to aid reassembly. Note how the springs are installed.

12 Grasp the outer edge of each shoe and fold them inwards towards each other to release the spring tension and remove the shoes **(see illustration)**. Remove the springs from the shoes.

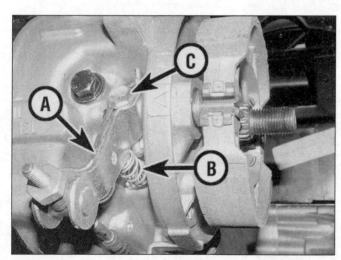

9.8 Brake arm (A), spring (B) and pinch-bolt (C)

9.12 Fold the shoes as shown to release the spring tension

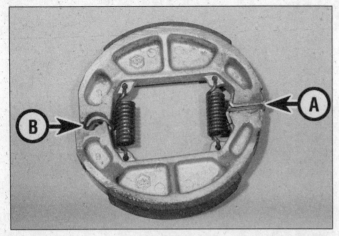

9.13 Assemble the shoes and springs as shown – flat ends (A) and rounded ends (B)

10.2 Release the cable from the brake arm

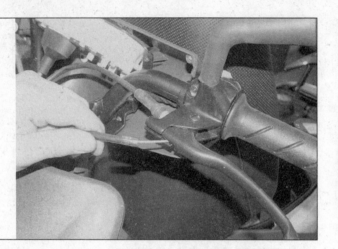

10.4a Pull the cable out of the handlebar bracket . . .

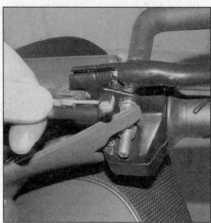

10.4b . . . and release the inner cable end from the lever

11.1 Brake lever pivot bolt locknut

13 To install the shoes, first lubricate the cam and the pivot post with a smear of copper grease and hook the springs into the shoes **(see illustration)**. Position the shoes in a V on the cam and pivot post, then fold them down into position. Operate the brake arm to check that the cam and shoes work correctly.

14 Install the wheel and test the operation of the brake before riding the scooter.

10 Brake cable – replacement

1 Remove the body panels as necessary (see Chapter 9).
2 Fully unscrew the adjuster on the lower end of the cable, then release the cable from the stop on the back plate. Disconnect the cable from the brake arm **(see illustration)**.
3 Free the cable from any clips or guides.
4 Pull the outer cable out of the handlebar lever bracket and free the inner cable end from its socket in the underside of the lever **(see illustrations)**.
5 Withdraw the cable from the scooter, noting its routing.
6 Installation is the reverse of removal. Make sure the cable is correctly routed and clipped into place. Lubricate the cable nipple at the handlebar end with grease before installing it into the lever and adjust the cable freeplay (see Chapter 1).

HAYNES HiNT *When installing a new cable, tape the lower end of the new cable to the upper end of the old cable before removing it from the machine. Slowly pull the lower end of the old cable out, guiding the new cable down into position. Using this method will ensure the cable is routed correctly.*

7 Check the operation of the brake before riding the scooter.

11 Brake levers – removal and installation

Removal

1 Unscrew the lever pivot bolt locknut, then withdraw the pivot bolt and remove the lever **(see illustration)**. Where applicable, loosen the brake cable and detach it from the underside of the lever as you remove it.

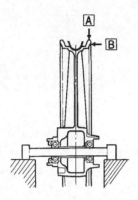

12.2 Check the wheel for radial (out-of-round) runout (A) and axial (side-to-side) runout (B)

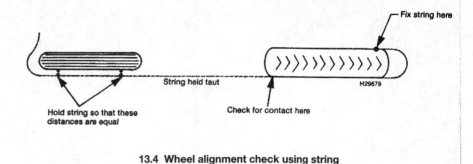

13.4 Wheel alignment check using string

Installation

2 Installation is the reverse of removal. Apply grease to the pivot bolt shank and the contact areas between the lever and its bracket, and to the brake cable nipple (where applicable).

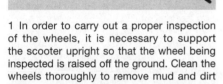

12 Wheels – inspection and repair

1 In order to carry out a proper inspection of the wheels, it is necessary to support the scooter upright so that the wheel being inspected is raised off the ground. Clean the wheels thoroughly to remove mud and dirt that may interfere with the inspection procedure or mask defects. Make a general check of the wheels (see Chapter 1) and tires (see *Daily (pre-ride) checks*).
2 If available, attach a dial gauge to the suspension (front) or the transmission casing (rear) with the tip of the gauge touching the side of the rim. Spin the wheel slowly and check the axial (side-to-side) runout of the rim **(see illustration)**.
3 In order to accurately check radial (out-of-round) runout with the dial gauge, the wheel should be removed from the machine, and the tire removed from the wheel. With the axle clamped in a vise or jig and the dial gauge positioned on the top of the rim, the wheel can be rotated to check the runout.
4 An easier, though slightly less accurate, method is to attach a stiff wire pointer to the front suspension or transmission casing with the end of the pointer a fraction of an inch from the edge of the wheel rim where the wheel and tire join. If the wheel is true, the distance from the pointer to the rim will be constant as the wheel is rotated. **Note:** *If wheel runout is excessive, check the wheel bearings very carefully before replacing the wheel (see Section 16).*
5 The wheels should also be visually inspected for cracks, flat spots on the rim and other damage. Look very closely for dents in the area where the tire bead contacts the rim. Dents in this area may prevent complete sealing of the tire against the rim, which leads to deflation of the tire over a period of time. If damage is evident, or if runout is excessive, the wheel will have to be replaced. Never attempt to repair a damaged cast alloy wheel.

13 Wheels – alignment check

1 Misalignment of the wheels can cause strange and potentially serious handling problems and will most likely be due to bent frame or suspension components as the result of an accident. If the frame or suspension are at fault, repair by a frame specialist or using new parts are the only options.
2 To check wheel alignment you will need an assistant, a length of string or a perfectly straight piece of wood and a ruler. A plumb bob or level for checking that the wheels are vertical will also be required. Support the scooter in an upright position on its center stand.
3 If a string is used, have your assistant hold one end of it about halfway between the floor and the center of the rear wheel, with the string touching the back edge of the rear tire sidewall.
4 Run the other end of the string forward and pull it tight so that it is roughly parallel to the floor. Slowly bring the string into contact with the front sidewall of the rear tire, then turn the front wheel until it is parallel with the string. Measure the distance (offset) from the front tire sidewall to the string **(see illustration)**. **Note:** *Where the same size tire is installed front and rear, there should be no offset.*
5 Repeat the procedure on the other side of the machine. The distance from the front tire sidewall to the string should be equal on both sides.
6 As previously mentioned, a perfectly straight length of wood or metal bar may be substituted for the string **(see illustration)**.
7 If the distance between the string and tire is greater on one side, or if the rear wheel

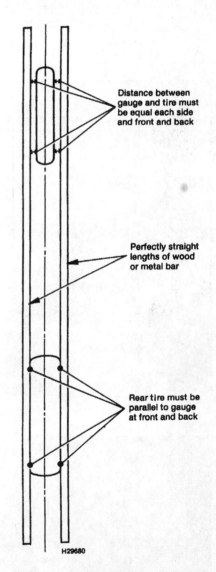

13.6 Wheel alignment check using a straight-edge

appears to be out of alignment, have your machine checked by a scooter dealer.
8 If the front-to-back alignment is correct, the wheels still may be out of alignment vertically.

14.2a Pry off the center cover

14.2b Remove the cotter pin

9 Using a plumb bob or level, check the rear wheel to make sure it is vertical. To do this, hold the string of the plumb bob against the tire upper sidewall and allow the weight to settle just off the floor. If the string touches both the upper and lower tire sidewalls and is perfectly straight, the wheel is vertical. If it is not, adjust the center stand by using spacers under its feet until it is.

10 Once the rear wheel is vertical, check the front wheel in the same manner. If both wheels are not perfectly vertical, the frame and/or major suspension components are bent.

14 Front wheel and hub assembly – removal and installation

Leading and trailing link suspension

Drum brake wheel

1 Support the machine in an upright position with the front wheel off the ground. If required, disconnect the front brake cable from the brake arm and backing plate (see Section 10).

2 On some scooters, the wheel is secured on a fixed axle; pry off the hub center cover using a small flat-bladed screwdriver **(see illustration)**. Where installed, remove the cotter pin from the end of the axle, then remove the cage nut **(see illustration)**. Discard the cotter pin, as a new one must be used. Undo the hub center nut, then remove the washer and lift the wheel off the axle **(see illustrations)**.

3 On some scooters, the wheel is secured on a knock-out axle; counterhold the axle and undo the axle nut, then support the wheel and withdraw the axle. Note how the brake backing plate fits against the suspension arm and how the speedometer drive gearbox fits in the hub.

4 Check the condition of the wheel bearings (see Section 16).

5 If applicable, clean the axle and remove any corrosion using steel wool. Check the axle for straightness by rolling it on a flat surface such as a piece of plate glass. If the axle is bent, replace it.

6 Installation is the reverse of removal – ensure all the components align, then tighten the hub or axle nut to the torque specified in the *Data* section at the end of this manual. Where applicable, install a new cotter pin to secure the cage nut. Adjust the front brake cable (see Chapter 1).

14.2c Undo the center nut . . .

14.2d . . . and remove the washer

14.2e Lift off the wheel

14.14 Front wheel is retained by bolts (arrows)

14.22a Remove the cotter pin (arrow) . . .

Drum brake hub assembly

Note: *On scooters with a separate hub assembly, the assembly incorporates the brake backing plate.*

7 Remove the wheel (see Steps 1 through 5).
8 Remove the suspension shock absorber (see Chapter 7).
9 If necessary, disconnect the speedometer cable from the hub.
10 The hub assembly is secured by a snap-ring; remove the snap-ring and washer, then draw the assembly off the axle.
11 Check the condition of the bearings in the hub (see Section 16). Examine the hub seals for wear and damage – if grease is passing the seals, they should be replaced (see *Tools and Workshop Tips* in the *Reference* section). Clean the axle and remove any corrosion using steel wool.
12 Installation is the reverse of removal, noting the following:

> Lubricate the axle, bearings and speedometer drive with grease.
> Ensure the snap-ring is properly seated in its groove.

Disc brake wheel

Caution: Don't lay the wheel down and allow it to rest on the disc – the disc could become warped. Set the wheel on wood blocks so the disc doesn't support the weight of the wheel.

13 Support the machine in an upright position with the front wheel off the ground.
14 On some scooters, the wheel is secured to the hub assembly; undo the bolts securing the wheel to the hub and lift the wheel off **(see illustration)**. Installation is the reverse of removal – tighten the wheel bolts to the torque specified in the *Data* section.
15 On some scooters, the wheel is secured on a knock-out axle; counterhold the axle and undo the axle nut, then support the wheel and withdraw the axle. Lower the wheel and lift off the speedometer drive gearbox, noting how it fits. Disengage the brake disc from the caliper and remove the wheel. **Note:** *Do not*

14.22b . . . and the cage nut

operate the brake lever while the caliper is off the disc.
16 Note the position of any axle spacers and remove them from the wheel for safe-keeping.
17 Check the condition of the wheel bearings (see Section 16).
18 Clean the axle and remove any corrosion using steel wool. Check the axle for straightness (see Step 5).
19 Installation is the reverse of removal – ensure the speedometer drive gearbox is correctly installed and the axle spacers are in place. Tighten the axle nut to the torque specified in the *Data* section.
20 Check the operation of the front brake before riding the scooter.

Disc brake hub assembly

21 Remove the wheel (see Steps 13 through 18).
22 Where installed, remove the cotter pin from the end of the axle then remove the cage nut **(see illustrations)**. Discard the cotter pin, as a new one must be used. Have an assistant apply the front brake, then loosen the hub center nut. Undo the brake caliper

14.23 Remove the center nut and washer

mounting bolts and remove the caliper (see Section 3). **Note:** *Do not operate the brake lever while the caliper is off the disc.*
23 Unscrew the hub center nut and remove the nut and washer **(see illustration)**.
24 Draw the hub assembly off the axle **(see illustration)**.

14.24 Pull the hub assembly off the axle

14.25a Note how the speedometer drive tabs (arrow) . . .

14.25b . . . locate in the speedometer gearbox (arrows)

25 If applicable, note how the speedometer drive tabs on the back of the hub fit in the speedometer gearbox in the brake caliper bracket **(see illustrations).**

26 Check the condition of the hub bearings and seals, and the axle (see Step 11).

27 If applicable, disconnect the speedometer cable from the speedometer gearbox in the brake caliper bracket. **Note:** *On some scooters, the speedometer is electronically activated and the electrical wire and drive housing are a one-piece unit. Do not attempt to disconnect them.* Undo the bolt securing the brake torque arm to the caliper bracket, then slide the bracket off the axle **(see illustration).**

28 Installation is the reverse of removal, noting the following:

    Lubricate the axle, bearings and speedometer drive with grease.

    Ensure the speedometer drive tabs are correctly located.

    Tighten the hub nut and brake caliper bolts to the torque specified in the Data *section.*

    Where applicable, install a new cotter pin to secure the cage nut.

Telescopic fork

Wheel removal

Caution: Don't lay the wheel down and allow it to rest on the disc – the disc could become warped. Set the wheel on wood blocks so the disc doesn't support the weight of the wheel.

29 Support the machine in an upright position with the front wheel off the ground.

30 On drum brake models, disconnect the brake cable (see Section 10).

31 Unscrew the brake caliper mounting bolts and displace the caliper (see Section 3). **Note:** *Do not operate the brake lever while the caliper is off the disc.*

32 If required, disconnect the speedometer cable from the speedometer gearbox **(see illustration). Note:** *On some scooters, the speedometer is electronically-activated and the electrical wire and drive housing are a one-piece unit. Do not attempt to disconnect them.*

33 Counterhold the axle and undo the axle nut, then support the wheel and withdraw the axle from the wheel and front suspension

(see illustrations). Lower the wheel out of the forks and lift off the speedometer gearbox **(see illustration).**

34 Note the position of any axle spacers and remove them from the wheel for safekeeping.

35 Clean the axle and remove any corrosion using steel wool. Check the axle for straightness by rolling it on a flat surface such as a piece of plate glass. If the axle is bent, replace it.

36 Check the condition of the wheel bearings (see Section 16).

Wheel installation

37 Maneuver the wheel into position, making sure the directional arrow on the tire is pointing in the normal direction of rotation. On models with a cable-activated speedometer, apply some grease to the inside of the speedometer gearbox. Install the speedometer gearbox, ensuring it locates correctly on the wheel hub **(see illustrations).**

38 Lubricate the axle with a smear of grease. Lift the wheel into place between the forks and install any axle spacers. Check that the speedometer gearbox is installed

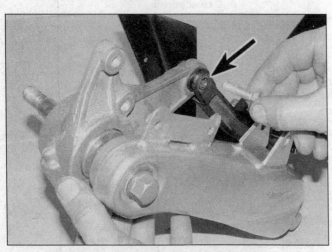

14.27 Undo the torque arm bolt (arrow)

14.32 Disconnect the speedometer cable

14.33a Undo the axle nut . . .

14.33b . . . then support the wheel and withdraw the axle

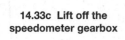

14.33c Lift off the speedometer gearbox

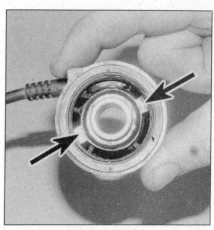

14.37a Tabs in the speedometer gearbox (arrows) . . .

correctly against the inside of the fork (see illustration). On drum brake models, ensure the brake backing plate is installed correctly against the inside of the fork.
39 Slide the axle in carefully, ensuring all the components remain in alignment.
40 Install the axle nut and tighten it to the

torque setting specified in the *Data* section.
41 As necessary, install the brake caliper, making sure the pads sit squarely on each side of the disc (see Section 3). Connect the speedometer cable. On drum brake models, connect the brake cable (see Section 10) and adjust it (see Chapter 1).

42 Move the scooter off its stand, apply the front brake and pump the front forks a few times to settle all components in position.
43 Check the operation of the front brake before riding the scooter.

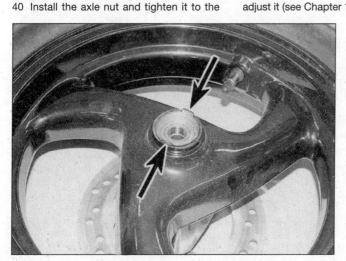

14.37b . . . locate against tabs on the wheel hub (arrows)

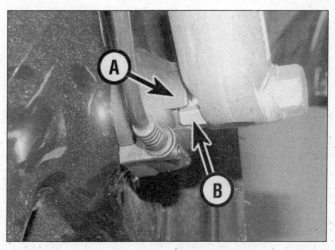

14.38 Note how the speedometer gearbox (A) locates against the fork slider (B)

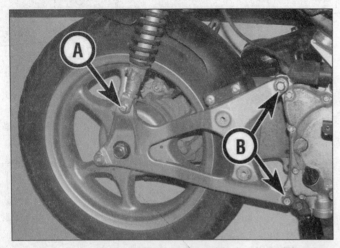

15.3 Bolt (A) secures the shock to the subframe; bolts (B) secure the subframe to the engine

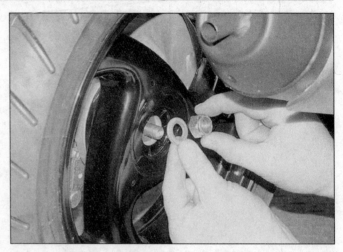

15.5 Remove the hub center nut and washer

15.6 Lift off the rear subframe

15 Rear wheel and hub assembly – removal and installation

Note: *It may not be possible to remove the rear wheel with the exhaust system in place. If necessary, remove the complete system – do not remove the exhaust system mounting bolts and attempt to lever the wheel behind the muffler with the exhaust manifold still connected; damage to the manifold studs and cylinder will result.*

Drum brake models

Wheel

1 Position the scooter on its center stand and support it so that the rear wheel is off the ground.

2 If necessary, remove the exhaust system (see Chapter 4).

3 On scooters with twin rear shock absorbers, undo the bolt securing the lower end of the right-hand shock to the subframe and remove the shock, then undo the bolts securing the subframe to the engine casing **(see illustration)**.

4 Pry the center cover off with a small flat-bladed screwdriver. Where installed, remove the cotter pin from the end of the axle, then remove the cage nut **(see illustrations 14.22a and 14.22b)**. Discard the cotter pin, as a new one must be used.

5 Have an assistant apply the rear brake,

then unscrew the hub center nut and remove the nut and washer **(see illustration)**.

6 If applicable, lift off the rear subframe and slide any spacers off the axle **(see illustration)**. Check the condition of the bearing and seals in the subframe (see *Tools and Workshop Tips* in the *Reference* section). If there is any doubt about the condition of the bearing, replace it.

7 Slide the wheel off the axle and maneuver it out of the back of the scooter **(see illustrations)**.

8 Inspect the splines on the axle and on the inside of the hub for wear and damage **(see illustration)**. If the splines are worn, both components should be replaced. To replace the axle, the gearbox must first be disassembled (see Chapter 6).

9 Installation is the reverse of removal – slide the wheel onto the axle carefully to avoid disturbing the alignment of the brake shoes. Tighten the hub center nut to the torque setting specified in the *Data* section at the end of this manual. Where applicable, install a new cotter pin to secure the cage nut.

10 Check the operation of the rear brake before riding the scooter.

15.7a Slide the wheel off the axle . . .

15.7b . . . and withdraw it from the scooter

15.8 Inspect the splines for wear and damage

15.13 Undo the bolts (arrows) and lift off the wheel

Disc brake models

Wheel

11 Position the scooter on its center stand and support it so that the rear wheel is off the ground.

12 If necessary, remove the exhaust system (see Chapter 4).

13 Have an assistant apply the rear brake, then undo the bolts securing the wheel to the hub assembly and remove the wheel (see illustration). Note: On scooters with twin rear shocks, follow the procedure in Steps 3 and 6 to remove the subframe.

14 Installation is the reverse of removal – tighten the wheel bolts to the torque setting specified in the Data section.

Hub assembly

15 If required, remove the wheel.

16 Lever the center cover off with a small flat-bladed screwdriver. Where installed, remove the cotter pin from the end of the axle then remove the cage nut (see illustrations 14.22a and 14.22b). Discard the cotter pin, as a new one must be used.

17 Have an assistant apply the rear brake,

then loosen the hub center nut.

18 Undo the brake caliper mounting bolts and displace the caliper (see Section 3). Note: Do not operate the brake lever while the caliper is off the disc.

19 Undo the hub center nut and remove the

nut, then draw the hub assembly off the axle (see illustration).

20 Inspect the splines on the axle and on the inside of the hub for wear and damage (see illustrations). If the splines are worn, both components should be replaced. To

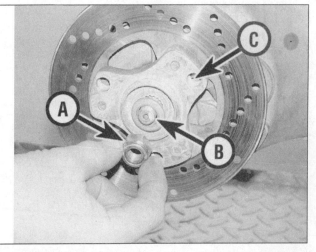

15.19 Remove the nut (A), washer (B) and hub assembly (C)

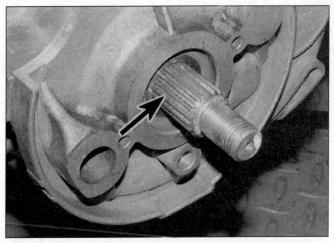

15.20a Inspect the splines on the axle . . .

15.20b . . . and inside the hub (arrow)

16.2a Remove any spacers . . .

16.2b . . . and dust caps

replace the axle, the gearbox must first be disassembled (see Chapter 6).

21 Installation is the reverse of removal – tighten the hub center nut to the torque setting specified in the *Data* section. Where applicable, install a new cotter pin to secure the cage nut.

22 Check the operation of the rear brake before riding the scooter.

16 Wheel bearings – check and replacement

Note: *The front wheel bearings are located inside the wheel hub and, where applicable, inside the separate hub assembly. There are no rear wheel bearings as such, the rear axle/ gearbox output shaft bearings are located inside the gearbox (see Chapter 6). On scooters with twin rear shock absorbers, also check the condition of the bearing in the rear subframe (see Section 15).*

Check

1 Remove the wheel and, if applicable, the hub assembly (see Section 14).

Caution: Don't lay the wheel down and allow it to rest on the brake disc – it could become warped. Set the wheel on wood blocks so the wheel rim supports the weight of the wheel.

2 Remove any spacers and dust caps from the wheel hub **(see illustrations)**.

3 Inspect the bearings (see *Tools and Workshop Tips* in the *Reference* section). If necessary, pry out the bearing seals with a flat-bladed screwdriver to gain access to the bearings and install new seals on reassembly. Wash needle roller bearings with a suitable solvent so that they can be inspected properly. **Note:** *Caged ball-bearings can be removed for checking and re-used if they are good, but needle roller bearings must be replaced once they have been removed.*

4 If there is any doubt about the condition of a bearing, replace it. **Note:** *Always replace the wheel bearings in sets, never individually.*

Replacement

5 If not already done, pry out the bearing seal. Check for any retaining snap-rings and remove them **(see illustration)**.

6 To remove the bearings from the hub assembly, stand the assembly on a suitable spacer to allow the bearings to be driven out. Note the position of the bearings before removing them.

Caution: Don't support the hub on the brake disc when driving out the bearings.

7 To remove a caged ball-bearing, use a metal rod (preferably a brass drift punch) inserted through the center of the bearing on one side of the wheel hub or hub assembly, to tap evenly around the outer race of the bearing on the other side **(see illustrations)**. The bearing spacer will come out with the bearing. Use a drawbolt to remove a needle roller bearing (see *Tools and Workshop Tips* in the *Reference* section).

8 Turn the hub over and remove the remaining bearing using the same procedure.

9 Thoroughly clean the bearing housings

16.5 Remove the snap-ring (arrow)

16.7a Driving a bearing out of the hub

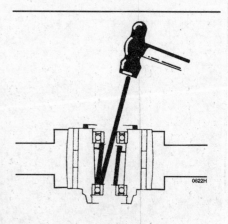

16.7b Position the rod as shown when driving out a bearing

with a suitable solvent and inspect them for scoring and wear. If a housing is damaged, indicating that the bearing has seized and spun in use, it may be possible to secure the new bearing in place with a suitable bearing locking solution.

10 Install a new bearing into its seat in one side of the hub, with the marked or sealed side facing outwards (see *Tools and Workshop Tips* in the *Reference* section), then turn the hub over, install the bearing spacer and install the other new bearing. **Note:** *Needle roller bearings should be installed using a drawbolt.*

11 If applicable, secure the bearing with the snap-ring and ensure the snap-ring is properly located in its groove.

12 Install new bearing seals.

13 Install the hub assembly and/or the wheel as applicable (see Section 14).

17 Tires – general information and installation

General information

1 Tire sizes and tire pressures are given in the *Data* section at the end of this manual.

2 Refer to *Daily (pre-ride) checks* at the beginning of this manual for tire maintenance.

Installing new tires

3 When selecting new tires, refer to the tire information given in the owners handbook. Ensure that front and rear tire types are compatible, the correct size and correct speed rating. If necessary, seek advice from a tire installation specialist.

4 It is recommended that tires are installed by a tire specialist rather than attempted in the home workshop. This is particularly relevant in the case of tubeless tires because the force required to break the seal between the wheel rim and tire bead is substantial, and is usually beyond the capabilities of an individual working with normal tire levers. Additionally, the specialist will be able to balance the wheels after tire installation.

5 Note that although punctured tubeless tires can in some cases be repaired, some manufacturers do not recommend the use of repaired tires.

Notes

Chapter 9
Bodywork

Contents

Degrees of difficulty

Easy, suitable for novice with little experience	**Fairly easy,** suitable for beginner with some experience	**Fairly difficult,** suitable for competent DIY mechanic	**Difficult,** suitable for experienced DIY mechanic	**Very difficult,** suitable for expert DIY or professional

1 General information

Almost all the functional components of the scooters covered by this manual are enclosed by body panels, making removal of relevant panels a necessary part of most servicing and maintenance procedures. Panel removal is straightforward, and as well as facilitating access to mechanical components, it avoids the risk of accidental damage to the panels.

Most panels are retained by screws and interlocking tabs, although in some cases trim clips are used (see Section 5). Always check the details in your scooter handbook and follow the advice given at the beginning of Section 8 before removing the panels.

2 Rear view mirrors – removal and installation

Removal

Note: *If the mirror stem is covered by a rub-* *ber boot, pull back the lower end of the boot to expose the attachment point.*

1 Where the mirror threads into a housing, loosen the locknut, then unscrew the mirror **(see illustrations)**.

2 Where the mirror passes through a bore and is secured by a nut, unscrew the nut from the underside and remove the mirror **(see illustration)**.

Installation

3 Installation is the reverse of removal. Position the mirror as required, then hold it in place and tighten the nut.

4 Some mirrors have adjuster screws on the

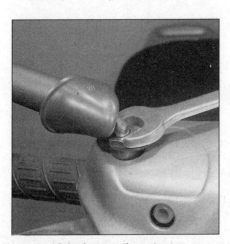

2.1a Loosen the nut . . .

2.1b . . . then unscrew the mirror

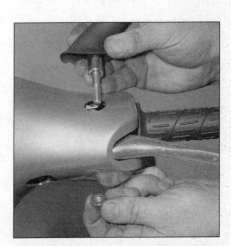

2.2 Undo the nut from the bottom of the stem and remove the mirror

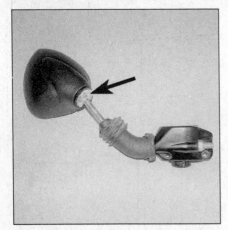

2.4 Rear view mirror adjuster screws

3.1 Remove the cotter pin (A) to release the pivot pin. Note the detent plate (B) and ball (C)

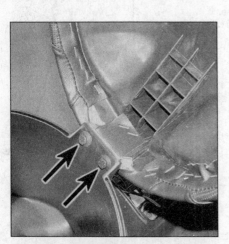

4.2 Undo the hinge bolts to remove the seat

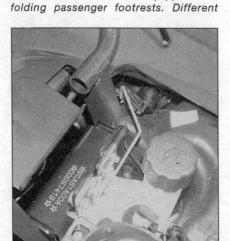

4.3a The latch mechanism is actuated either by a rod . . .

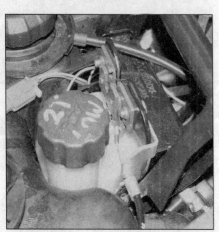

4.3b . . . or by a cable

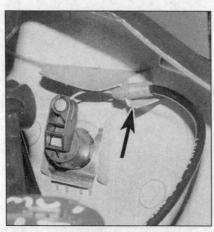

4.3c Unclip the cable from the stop on the panel . . .

4.3d . . . then from the back of the lock

back of the mirror head. To adjust the angle of the mirror, pull back the upper end of the boot on the stem to expose the adjuster screws **(see illustration)**. Loosen the screws and set the mirror to the required position, then tighten the screws and reinstall the boot.

---

3   Passenger footrests – removal and installation

Note: Some scooters are equipped with folding passenger footrests. Different methods of securing the footrests are employed – study the design before attempting to remove the footrest.

Removal

1 If applicable, remove the cotter pin and washer or spring clip from the bottom of the footrest pivot pin, then withdraw the pivot pin and remove the footrest **(see illustration)**. Some footrests are held in position with a detent plate, ball and spring; note how they are installed and take care that they do not spring out when removing the footrest.
2 On some scooters, the footrest is secured by a pivot bolt. Counterhold the bolt and undo the nut on the underside of the footrest **(see illustration)**. **Note:** *It may be necessary to remove a cover or lift a floor mat to access the bolt.* Withdraw the bolt and slide the footrest out of the bracket.

Installation

3 Installation is the reverse of removal. Apply a smear of grease to the pivot pin or bolt and ensure any washers or spacers are installed on the bolt before it is installed. If

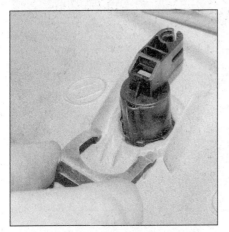

4.4 Pull off the clip to remove the lock

4.8 Remove the collars from the fuel and oil tank filler necks

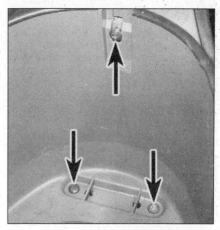

4.9a The storage compartment is retained by screws . . .

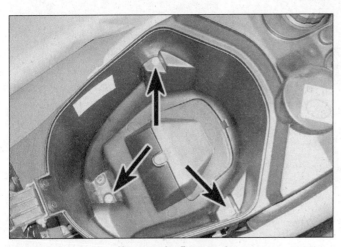

4.9b . . . or by flange nuts

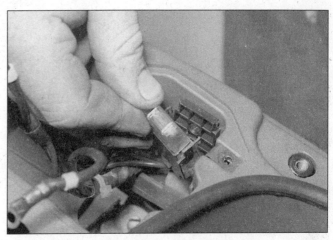

4.10 Detach any electrical components from the compartment

applicable, tighten the nut enough to allow the footrest to pivot without binding in the bracket. Alternatively, install the spring clip, ensuring it is a firm fit, or install a new cotter pin.

| 4 | Seat and storage compartment – removal and installation | |

Seat

1 Release the seat catch and swing the seat upright.
2 The seat is retained by the hinge at the front of the seat base (see illustration). Support the seat and undo the hinge bolts, then lift the seat away.
3 The seat latch mechanism is actuated either by a rod or cable from the seat lock (see illustrations). To remove the seat lock, first remove the storage compartment (see Steps 7 to 10). Unclip the rod from the lock or unclip the cable from the back of the side panel and the lock (see illustrations), then remove the side panel (see Section 8).

4 The lock is retained in a recess in the panel by a spring clip. Pull off the spring clip, note how the lock locates in the panel recess, then remove the lock (see illustration).
5 Check the operation of the latch mechanism and lubricate it with a smear of grease.
6 Installation is the reverse of removal.

⚠️ Warning: Ensure the actuating rod or cable is properly connected to the lock before closing the seat, otherwise you will have no way of releasing the latch.

Storage compartment

7 Unlock the seat and swing it upright. Generally, an engine access panel is installed in the bottom of the compartment, although this offers limited access to the engine; for better access, remove the storage compartment as follows. Note: On most scooters, the storage compartment can be removed with the seat attached.
8 Where installed, remove any sealing collars from around the fuel and oil tank filler necks – it will be necessary to unscrew the tank caps to remove the collars (see illustra-

tion). Reinstall the tank caps.
9 Undo the screws or flange nuts securing the storage compartment to the frame edge (see illustrations). Note that on some scooters, the screws also secure some body panels.
10 Check that no electrical components such as relays or fuseboxes are clipped to the compartment, then lift it out (see illustration).
11 Installation is the reverse of removal.

| 5 | Panel fasteners – removal and installation | |

1 Before removing any body panel, study it closely, noting the position of the fasteners and associated fittings.
2 Once the evident fasteners have been removed, try to remove the panel but DO NOT FORCE IT – if it will not release, check that all fasteners have been removed. On some panels, fasteners are located inside glove compartments or fuel filler flaps, or

5.2a Check for fasteners inside compartments . . .

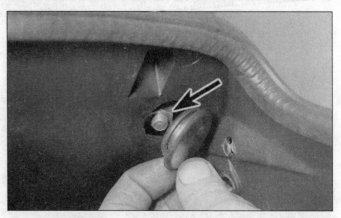

5.2b . . . or behind blanking plugs

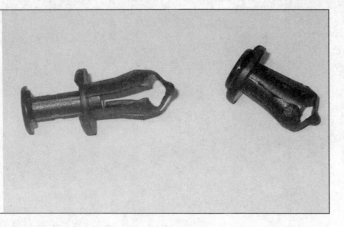

5.6 Pry up the center pin to unlock the clip (left); push the center post down to lock it in place (right)

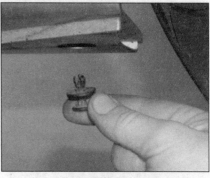

5.7 After the center pin has been pulled out, the clip can be removed

behind blanking plugs **(see illustrations)**. **Note:** *Adjacent panels are often joined together by tabs and slots (see Step 16).*
3 Note all the fasteners and associated fittings removed with the panel to be sure of returning everything to its correct place on installation.

 *Make a cardboard template of the panel and punch a hole for each fastener location. This will ensure all fasteners are installed correctly on reassembly – this is important, as some fasteners may be of different sizes or lengths.*

5.11 U-clip (arrow) should be a firm fit

4 Before installing a panel, check that all fasteners and fittings are in good condition and replace any that are damaged.
5 Tighten the fasteners securely, but be careful not to overtighten any of them or the panel may break (not always immediately) due to uneven stress. Take particular care when tightening self-tapping screws into plastic lugs on the backs of panels – if the lugs break, the panel will have to be replaced.

Trim clips

6 Two types of trim clips are used. If the center pin is flush with the head of the trim clip, push the center into the body, then draw the clip out of the panel **(see illustration)**. Before installing the this type of trim clip, first push the center back out so that it protrudes from the top of the clip **(see illustration)**. Install the clip into its hole, then push the center in so that it is flush with the top of the clip.
7 Alternatively, if the center pin has a raised head, pull the pin out, then draw the clip out of the panel **(see illustration)**. To install the clip, install the clip into its hole, then push the center in until it clicks into place.

Quick-release screws

8 To undo a quick-release screw, turn it counterclockwise until resistance is felt – the screw will normally turn between 90° and 180°. As the

panel is removed, note the alignment between the screw and its retaining mechanism.
9 To install a quick-release screw, first ensure it is correctly aligned, then turn it clockwise until resistance is felt – the screw should now be locked.

Self-tapping screws

10 When the panel is removed, note the location of the screws. If they engage in plastic lugs on the back of an adjacent panel, check the condition of each lug and ensure it is not split or the thread stripped. If necessary, repair a damaged lug with a proprietary repair kit (see Section 6).
11 If the screws engage in U-clips, check that the clips are a firm fit on the mounting lug and that they are not sprained **(see illustration)**. If necessary, install new U-clips.

Shouldered screws

12 Shouldered screws are designed to retain a panel in conjunction with a spacer or rubber bushing **(see illustration)**. Ensure the correct components are in place on the screw before installing it, otherwise the panel will not be held firmly. Do not pack a shouldered screw with washers – this will place undue pressure on the panel and cause cracking.

Wellnuts

13 Wellnuts have a metal thread retained inside a rubber bushing; the bushing is a firm

5.12 Shouldered screw and rubber bushing

5.13 Wellnut threads are retained inside a rubber bushing

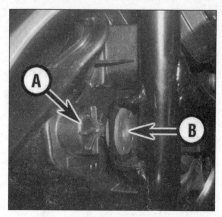

5.14 Peg (A) is secured in rubber grommet (B)

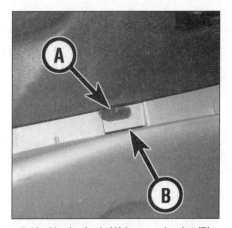

5.16 Hooked tab (A) locates in slot (B)

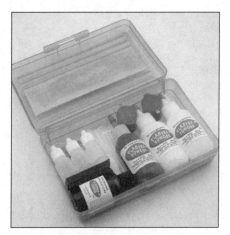

6.2 A typical repair kit

press-fit in a body panel or windshield **(see illustration)**. Avoid overtightening the screw, otherwise the bushing will twist in the panel and damage the locating hole.

Peg and grommet

14 Ease the panel back and exert firm, even pressure to pull the peg out of the rubber grommet **(see illustration)**. If the peg is a tight fit, use a lubricating spray to release it. Do not rock the panel, as the peg may snap.

15 If the grommet has split or hardened with age, replace it.

 Note that a small amount of lubricant (liquid soap or similar) applied to rubber mounting grommets will assist the lugs to engage without the need for undue pressure.

Tab and slot

16 The edges of adjacent panels are often joined by tabs and slots – once all the screws have been removed, slide these panels apart rather than pull them **(see illustration)**.

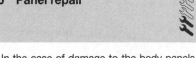
6 Panel repair

1 In the case of damage to the body panels, it is usually necessary to remove the broken panel and use a new (or second-hand) one. There are however some shops that specialize in plastic welding, so it may be worthwhile seeking the advice of one of these specialists before scrapping an expensive component.

2 Proprietary repair kits can be obtained for repair of small components **(see illustration)**.

---

7 Fuel and oil tanks – removal and installation

 Warning: Refer to the precautions given in Chapter 4, Section, 1 before proceeding.

Fuel tank

1 Generally, the fuel tank is located under-

neath the seat, although on some scooters the tank is underneath the floor panel. The location of the fuel filler is a good guide to the location of the tank.

2 Remove the body panels as necessary on your scooter to access the tank (see Section 8).

3 Disconnect the negative battery cable and disconnect the fuel gauge sender wiring connector (see Chapter 10).

4 If the tank is located underneath the seat, fuel flow to the carburetor will be controlled by a tap on the underside of the tank. Disconnect the fuel and vacuum hoses from the tap (see Chapter 4). Drain any residual fuel in the fuel hose into a suitable container.

5 If the tank is located underneath the floor panel, fuel flow to the carburetor will be controlled by a pump mounted on the frame alongside the fuel tank. Disconnect the fuel hose between the tank and the pump at the pump, and drain any residual fuel in the hose into a suitable container. The fuel hose should be clamped to prevent fuel leakage using any of the methods shown in *Tools and Workshop Tips* in the *Reference* section.

6 Undo the fasteners securing the tank to the frame, noting the location of any washers, then lift out the tank. Note the routing of any tank vent hoses.

 Warning: If the fuel tank is removed from the scooter, it should not be placed in an area where sparks or open flames could ignite the fumes coming out of the tank. Be especially careful inside garages where a gas-type appliance is located, because it could cause an explosion.

7 Installation is the reverse of removal, noting the following:

Ensure no wiring is trapped between the tank and the frame.

Tighten the fasteners securely.

Ensure the fuel and vacuum hoses are tightened securely.

Ensure any vent hoses are correctly routed.

8.6a Handlebar covers are usually screwed together . . .

8.6b . . . and secured to the handlebars

Oil tank

8 Generally, the oil tank is located underneath the seat, either alongside or below the fuel tank. If necessary, remove the fuel tank (see Steps 1 through 6).

9 Disconnect the oil level warning light sensor wiring connector.

10 Release the clip securing the oil hose from the tank to the oil filter and detach the hose from the filter. Clamp the hose to prevent oil loss (see Step 5). Wrap a clean plastic bag around the oil filter to prevent dirt entering the system and secure the filter in an upright position to minimize oil loss.

11 Undo the tank fasteners, noting the location of any washers, then lift out the tank.

12 Installation is the reverse of removal, noting the following:

Ensure no wiring is trapped between the tank and the frame.

Tighten the fasteners securely.

Ensure the oil hose is pushed fully onto the fitting on the filter and secure it with the clip.

Bleed any air trapped in the filter (see Chapter 1).

8 Body panels – removal and installation

1 In most cases, adjacent body panels are linked together with some form of fastener, and it is usually necessary to remove panels in a specific order – refer to your scooter handbook for details. Removing service panels, rear carriers and the under seat storage compartment often allows access to concealed panel fasteners.

2 In some cases, the aid of an assistant will be required when removing panels, to avoid the risk of straining tabs or damaging paintwork. Where assistance was required to remove a panel, make sure your assistant is on hand to install it.

3 Check that all mounting brackets are straight and repair or replace them if necessary before attempting to install a panel.

4 The following information is intended as a general guide to panel removal.

Handlebar covers

5 Remove the handlebar covers to gain access to the instrument cluster, brake master cylinder(s) and, where applicable, the headlight unit.

6 The covers are usually screwed and clipped together – remove the fasteners and ease them apart carefully (see illustrations).

7 If the instrument cluster is located in the top cover, ease the cover up and disconnect the speedometer cable and wiring connectors before removing the cover.

8 Note any cut-out in the covers for the throttle cable.

9 On some scooters, the handlebar switches are located in the covers – take care not to strain the switch wiring when removing the covers.

10 On some scooters, the handlebars must be removed in order to remove the lower cover (see Chapter 7).

Front panel

11 Generally, the front panel is secured by fasteners through the kick panel and, where installed, the glove compartment. Also check

8.11a Front panel fixings in the kick panel . . .

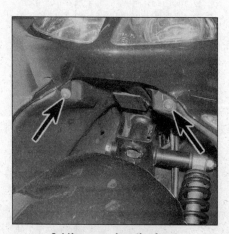

8.11b . . . and on the front underside (arrows)

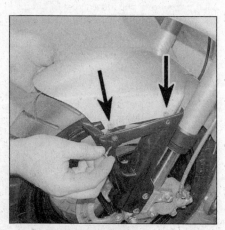

8.14 Front fender secured by screws (arrows) to separate bracket

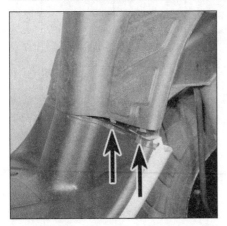

8.17 Check for tabs (arrows) between the floor and kick panels

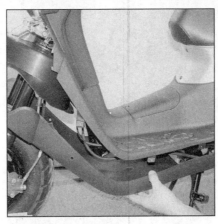

8.20a Remove the belly panel carefully . . .

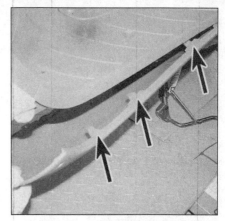

8.20b . . . to avoid breaking the tabs (arrows)

for fasteners underneath the front of the panel above the front wheel **(see illustrations)**.
12 If the headlight unit is located in the front panel, ease the panel forward and disconnect the light wiring connectors before removing the panel.
13 On some liquid-cooled scooters, the radiator is located behind the front panel. The grille in the front panel should be kept free from obstructions.

Front fender
14 On some scooters, the fender is mounted on the front suspension, on others it is secured to the front body panels **(see illustration)**.
15 It may be necessary to remove the front wheel before removing the fender.
16 Note the location of any guides for the speedometer cable and front brake hose/cable on the fender. Ensure the cables are correctly routed on installation.

Kick panel
17 Generally, the kick panel is secured to the main frame tube and is clipped to the

floor panel along its lower edge **(see illustration)**.
18 Remove the kick panel to gain access to the main headlight/ignition wiring loom and the throttle cable. On some two-stroke scooters with a cable-operated oil pump, the cable splitter is located behind the kick panel.

Belly panel
19 The belly panel may be either a one or two-piece assembly; check along the center of the panel underneath the scooter for joining screws.
20 On some scooters, the top edge of the belly panel is secured to the floor panel with tabs and slots; check carefully before removing the panel to avoid breaking the tabs **(see illustrations)**.

Side panels
21 Remove the side panels to gain access to the engine, fuel tank and carburetor, and upper rear suspension mounting(s).
22 On some scooters, the side panels

can be removed as an assembly once the seat and storage compartment have been removed; on others, a separate rear cowling is installed **(see illustrations)**.
23 Note the location of the tail light unit. On some scooters, the tail light is located

8.22a Side panels may be removed as an assembly . . .

8.22b . . . or individually, depending on design

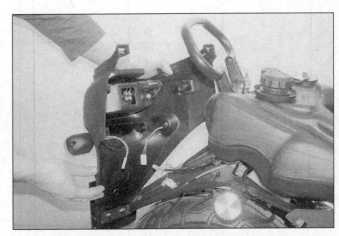

8.22c Some scooters have a separate rear cowling

8.26a Check for floor panel fasteners behind plugs or covers . . .

8.26b . . . underneath floor mats . . .

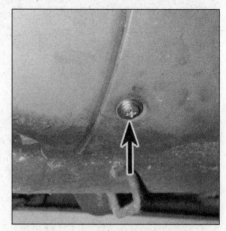

8.26c . . . and on the underside of the panel

in a body panel assembly; disconnect the light wiring connectors before removing the assembly. On some scooters, it is necessary to remove the light lens to access panel screws.

24 If applicable, note the position of the seat lock and disconnect the latch mechanism before removing the appropriate panel (see Section 4).

Floor panel

25 The floor panel is secured to the main frame tube and support brackets. On most scooters, it is necessary to remove some of the adjacent panels before the floor panel will lift off. Check for tab and slot fasteners to the kick panel, belly panel and the side panels.

26 Panel fixings are often located underneath rubber mats, metal trim panels or behind blanking plugs; also check on the underside of the floor panel **(see illustrations)**.

27 It may be necessary to remove the passenger footrests before the floor panel will lift off (see Section 3).

28 On installation, ensure no cables, hoses or wiring are trapped between the panel and the frame.

Rear fender

29 On most scooters, the fender is secured to the rear of the frame underneath the side panels or rear cowling **(see illustration)**.

30 Check the location of the rear turn signals and, where installed, the license plate light, and disconnect the wiring if applicable before removing the fender.

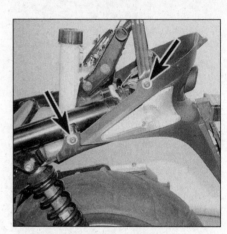

8.29 Fender fasteners (arrows). Note the turn signals and license plate light are part of the assembly

Chapter 10
Electrical systems

Contents

Degrees of difficulty

Easy, suitable for novice with little experience	Fairly easy, suitable for beginner with some experience	Fairly difficult, suitable for competent DIY mechanic	Difficult, suitable for experienced DIY mechanic	Very difficult, suitable for expert DIY or professional

Specifications

Refer to the *Data* section at the end of this manual for servicing specifications.

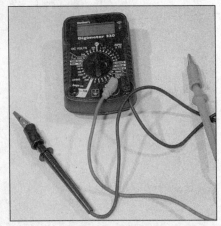

2.5 A multimeter is capable of reading ohms, amps and volts

2.6a A test light . . .

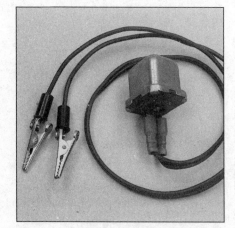

2.6b . . . or buzzer can be used for simple voltage checks

1 General information

All the scooters covered by this manual have 12 volt electrical systems charged by a three-phase alternator with a separate regulator/rectifier. The regulator maintains the charging system output within a speci-fied range to prevent overcharging, and the rectifier converts the AC (alternating current) output of the alternator to DC (direct current) to power the lights and other components, and to charge the battery.

The four electrical systems covered in this Chapter – lighting, signalling, starting and charging – are each illustrated by a general wiring diagram which shows how the system components are linked together. Follow the diagrams when tracing faults and compare them with the wiring diagram in your scooter handbook, noting any additional features specific to your scooter.

The location of electrical components such as relays, resistors and diodes varies enormously; refer to the wiring diagram in your handbook and trace the wiring to the component, removing any body panels as necessary to gain access (see Chapter 9). **Note:** *Keep in mind that electrical parts, once purchased, cannot be returned. To avoid unnecessary expense, make very sure the faulty compo-nent has been positively identified before buying a new part.*

2 Electrical systems – fault finding

⚠️ *Warning: To prevent the risk of short circuits, the ignition (main) switch must always be OFF and the negative battery cable should be disconnected before any of the scooter's other electrical components are disturbed. Don't forget to reconnect the terminal securely once work is finished or if battery power is needed for circuit testing.*

Tracing faults

1 A typical electrical circuit consists of an electrical component, the switches, relays, etc, related to that component, and the wir-ing and connectors that link the component to both the battery and the frame. To aid in locating any electrical problem, refer to the relevant system wiring diagram in this manual and to the diagram in your scooter hand-book.

2 Study the wiring diagram thoroughly to get a complete picture of what makes up each individual circuit. Trouble spots, for instance, can often be narrowed down by noting if other components related to that circuit are operat-ing properly or not. If several components or circuits fail at one time, chances are the fault lies in the system fuse or ground connection.

3 Electrical problems often stem from simple causes, such as loose or corroded connections or a blown fuse. Prior to any electrical fault finding, always check the condition of the fuse, wires and connections in the problem circuit. Intermittent failures can be especially frustrat-ing, since you can't always duplicate the failure when it's convenient to test. In such situations, a good practice is to clean all connections in the affected circuit, whether or not they appear to be good. All of the connections and wires should also be wiggled to check for looseness which can cause intermittent failure.

4 If testing instruments are going to be used, use the wiring diagram to plan where you will make the necessary connections in order to accurately pinpoint the trouble spot.

Using test equipment

5 The basic tools needed for electrical fault finding include a battery and bulb test circuit, a continuity tester, a test light, and a jumper wire. A multimeter capable of reading volts, ohms and amps is also very useful as an alternative to the above, and is necessary for performing more extensive tests and checks (see illustration).

6 Voltage checks should be performed if a circuit is not functioning properly. Connect one lead of a test light or voltmeter to either the negative battery terminal or a known good ground (see illustrations). Connect the other lead to a connector in the circuit being tested, preferably nearest to the battery or fuse. If the bulb lights, voltage is reaching that point, which means the part of the circuit between that connector and the battery is problem-free. Continue checking the remainder of the circuit in the same manner. When you reach a point where no voltage is present, the prob-lem lies between there and the last good test point. Most of the time the problem is due to a loose connection. Keep in mind that some circuits only receive voltage when the ignition is ON.

7 One method of finding short circuits is to remove the fuse and connect a test light or voltmeter to the fuse terminals. There should be no load in the circuit (it should be switched off). Move the wiring harness from side-to-side while watching the test light. If the bulb lights, there is a short to ground somewhere in that area, probably where insulation has rubbed off a wire. The same test can be per-formed on other components in the circuit, including the switch.

8 A ground check should be done to see if a component is grounded properly. Discon-nect the battery and connect one lead of a self-powered test light (continuity tester) to a known good ground (see illustrations). Connect the other lead to the wire or ground connection being tested. If the bulb lights, the ground is good. If the bulb does not light, the ground is not good.

9 A continuity check is performed to see if a circuit, section of circuit or individual compo-nent is capable of passing electricity through it. Disconnect the battery and connect one lead of a self-powered test light (continuity

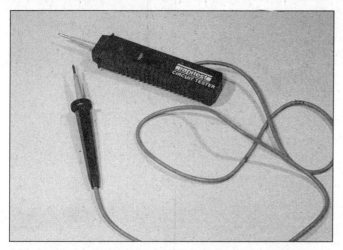

2.8a Continuity can be checked with a battery powered tester . . .

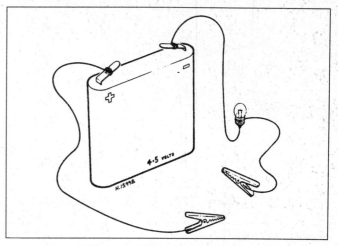

2.8b . . . or a battery and bulb circuit

tester) to one end of the circuit being tested and the other lead to the other end of the circuit. If the bulb lights, there is continuity, which means the circuit is passing electricity through it properly. Switches can be checked in the same way.

 Remember that all electrical circuits are designed to conduct electricity from the battery, through the wires, switches, relays, etc, to the electrical component (light bulb, motor, etc). From there it is directed to the frame (ground) where it is passed back to the battery. Electrical problems are basically an interruption in the flow of electricity from the battery or back to it.

3 Battery – removal, installation and checks

⚠️ *Warning: Be extremely careful when handling or working around the battery. Do not allow electrolyte to come in contact with your skin, or painted or plastic surfaces of the scooter. Rinse off any spills immediately with plenty of water. Check with the local authorities about disposing of an old battery. Many communities will have collection centers which will see that batteries are disposed of safely.*

Removal and installation

1 Refer to your scooter handbook and remove the battery access panel.
2 Undo the negative terminal screw first and disconnect the cable from the battery, then unscrew the positive terminal screw and disconnect the cable **(see illustration)**.
3 Undo the battery strap or displace the

strap and lift the battery from its holder.
4 Before installation, clean the battery terminals, terminal screws, nuts and cable ends with a wire brush, knife or steel wool to ensure a good electrical connection.
5 Install the battery, then reconnect the cables, connecting the positive cable first, and secure the battery strap.

 Battery corrosion can be kept to a minimum by applying a layer of petroleum jelly to the terminals after the cables have been connected.

6 Install the battery access panel.

Inspection and maintenance
Conventional battery

7 The battery installed on most scooters covered by this manual is of the conventional lead-acid type, requiring regular checks of the electrolyte level (see Chapter 1) in addition to those detailed below.
8 Check the battery terminals and leads for tightness and corrosion. If corrosion is evident, undo the terminal screws and disconnect the cables from the battery, disconnect-

ing the negative battery cable first. Wash the terminals and cable ends in a solution of baking soda and hot water and dry them thoroughly. If necessary, further clean the terminals and cable ends with a wire brush, knife or steel wool. Reconnect the cables, connecting the negative cable last, and apply a thin coat of petroleum jelly to the connections to slow further corrosion.
9 The battery case should be kept clean to prevent current leakage, which can discharge the battery over a period of time (especially when it sits unused). Wash the outside of the case with a solution of baking soda and water. Rinse the battery thoroughly, then dry it.
10 Look for cracks in the case and replace the battery if any are found. If acid has been spilled on the battery holder or surrounding bodywork, neutralize it with a baking soda and water solution, dry it thoroughly, then touch up any damaged paint.
11 If the machine is not used for long periods of time, disconnect the cables from the battery terminals, negative cable first. Refer to Section 4 and charge the battery once every month to six weeks.

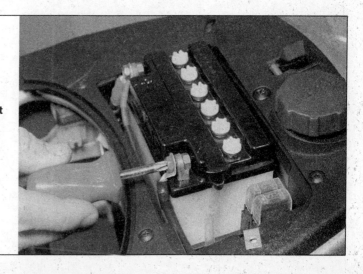

3.2 Disconnect the negative battery cable first, then the positive cable

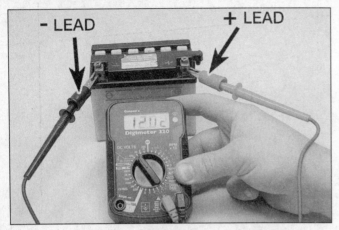

3.12 Measuring battery open-circuit voltage

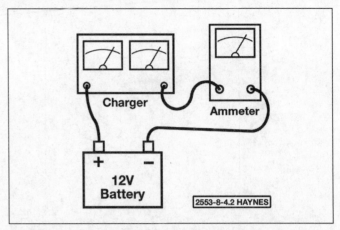

4.3 If the charger doesn't have an ammeter built in, connect one in series as shown; DO NOT connect the ammeter between the battery terminals or it will be ruined

12 The condition of the battery can be assessed by measuring the voltage present at the battery terminals with a multimeter. Connect the meter positive probe to the battery positive terminal, and the negative probe to the battery negative terminal (see illustration). Compare the reading with the specifications given in the *Data* section at the end of this manual. If the voltage falls below 12 volts, the battery must be removed, disconnecting the negative cable first, and recharged as described in Section 4. **Note:** *Before taking the measurement, wait at least 30 minutes after any charging has taken place (including running the engine).*

13 If battery condition is suspect, connect the multimeter to the battery terminals as before (see Step 12), turn the ignition ON and press the starter button. If the meter reading drops below 8 volts, a new battery is required.

Maintenance-free (MF) battery

14 If your scooter is equipped with an MF battery, inspect the terminals and case as for a conventional battery (see Steps 8 to 10). If the machine is not used for long periods of time, disconnect the cables from the battery terminals and charge the battery periodically (see Step 11).

15 Battery condition can be assessed as for a conventional battery (see Steps 12 and 13).

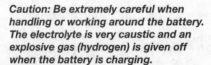

4 Battery – charging

Caution: Be extremely careful when handling or working around the battery. The electrolyte is very caustic and an explosive gas (hydrogen) is given off when the battery is charging.

1 Ensure the charger is suitable for charging a 12V battery.

2 Remove the battery (see Section 3). Connect the charger to the battery **BEFORE** switching the charger on. Make sure that the positive lead on the charger is connected to the positive terminal on the battery, and the negative lead is connected to the negative terminal.

3 Refer to your scooter handbook for the recommend battery charging rate – manufacturers generally recommend a rate of no more than 0.5 amps. Exceeding this figure can cause the battery to overheat, buckling the plates and rendering it useless. Few owners will have access to an expensive current controlled charger, so if a normal domestic charger is used, check that after a possible initial peak, the charge rate falls to a safe level (see illustration). If the battery becomes hot during charging, **STOP**. Further charging will cause damage.

4 When charging a maintenance-free battery, make sure that you use a regulated battery charger.

5 If the recharged battery discharges rapidly if left disconnected, it is likely that an internal short caused by physical damage or sulphation has occurred. A new battery will be required. A sound battery will tend to lose its charge at about 1% per day.

6 Install the battery (see Section 3).

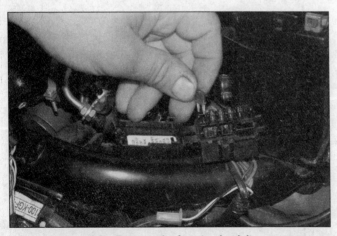

5.2a Remove the fuse to check it

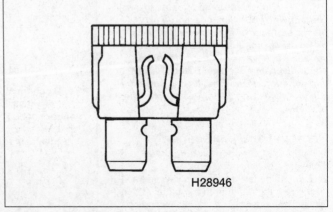

H28946

5.2b A blown fuse can be identified by a break in the element

5 Fuses – check and replacement

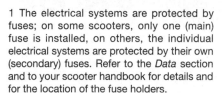

1 The electrical systems are protected by fuses; on some scooters, only one (main) fuse is installed, on others, the individual electrical systems are protected by their own (secondary) fuses. Refer to the *Data* section and to your scooter handbook for details and for the location of the fuse holders.

2 A blown fuse is easily identified by a break in the element – pull the fuse out of its holder to check it visually **(see illustrations)**. The fuse is clearly marked with its rating and must only be replaced with a fuse of the correct rating. It is advisable to carry spare fuses on the scooter at all times.

 Warning: Never put in a fuse of a higher rating or bridge the terminals with any other substitute, however temporary it may be. Serious damage may be done to the circuit, or a fire may start.

3 If the fuse blows, be sure to check the wiring circuit very carefully for evidence of a short-circuit. Look for bare wires and chafed, melted or burned insulation. If the fuse is replaced before the cause is located, the new fuse will blow immediately.

4 Occasionally the fuse will blow or cause an open-circuit for no obvious reason. Corrosion of the fuse ends and fuse holder terminals may occur and cause poor fuse contact. If this happens, remove the corrosion with a wire brush or steel wool, then spray the fuse ends and fuse holder terminals with electrical contact cleaner.

6 Lighting system – check

1 The lighting system consists of the headlight, sidelight, tail light, brake light, instru-

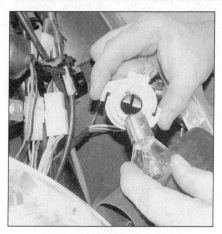

6.3a Checking the headlight bulb terminals . . .

ment panel lights, handlebar switches and fuse **(see illustration on next page)**.

2 On most of the scooters covered by this manual, the engine must be running for any of the lights to work. If none of the lights work, always check the fuse (where installed) and alternator lighting coil before proceeding (see Section 9). If applicable, check the condition of the lighting resistor (see Step 11).

Lights

Note: *To remove the bulbs, refer to your scooter handbook for details.*

3 If a light fails to work, first check the bulb and the terminals in the bulbholder or the bulb wiring connector **(see illustrations)**.
Note: *If the headlight bulb is of the quartz-halogen type, do not touch the bulb glass as skin acids will shorten the bulb's service life. If the bulb is accidentally touched, it should be wiped carefully when cold with a rag soaked in alcohol and dried before installation.*

 Warning: Allow the bulb time to cool before removing it if the headlight has just been on.

6.3b . . . and the tail light terminals (arrows)

4 Next check for voltage on the supply side of the bulbholder or wiring connector with a test light or multimeter with the light switch ON. Don't forget that the engine may have to be running to do this check (see Step 2). When checking the headlight, select either high or low beam at the handlebar switch. When checking the brake light, pull the brake lever in.

5 If no voltage is indicated, check the wiring between the bulbholder and the light switch, then check the switch (see Steps 12 to 16).

6 If voltage is indicated, check for continuity between the ground wire terminal and a ground point on the scooter frame. If there is no continuity, check the ground circuit for a broken or poor connection.

Instrument panel lights

Note: *On some scooters, the panel is illuminated with LEDs. If an LED fails, it may be necessary to replace the complete panel circuit – check the availability of parts with a scooter dealer.*

7 If one light fails to work, check the bulb and the bulb terminals **(see illustration)**. If none of the lights work, refer to the wiring diagram in your scooter handbook, then check for voltage on the supply side of the instrument cluster wiring connector, if necessary with the engine running and light switch ON **(see illustration)**.

8 If no voltage is indicated, check the wiring between the connector, the light switch and the ignition switch, then check the switches themselves.

9 If voltage is indicated, disconnect the connector and check for continuity between the power supply wire terminal on the instrument cluster and the corresponding terminals in the bulbholders; no continuity indicates a break in the circuit.

10 If continuity is present, check for continuity between the ground wire terminal in the wiring connector and a ground point on the scooter frame. If there is no continuity, check the ground circuit for a broken or poor connection.

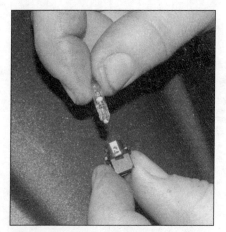

6.7a Pull the instrument panel bulb out of its holder

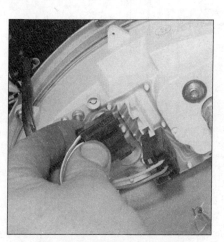

6.7b Instrument cluster wiring connectors

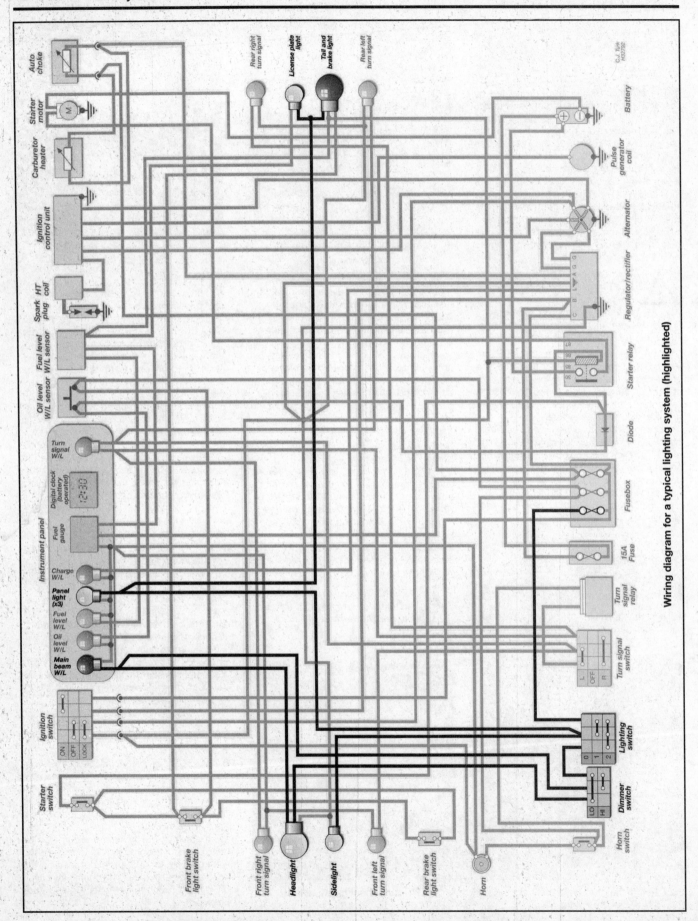

Wiring diagram for a typical lighting system (highlighted)

6.11 A typical lighting system resistor

Lighting system resistor

11 On some scooters, the lighting system is protected by a resistor **(see illustration)**. To test the resistor, substitute it with a known good one or have the resistance checked by a scooter dealer.

Handlebar switches

12 Generally speaking, the switches are reliable and trouble-free. Most problems, when they do occur, are caused by dirty or corroded contacts, but wear and breakage of internal parts is a possibility that should not be overlooked when tracing a fault. If breakage does occur, the entire switch and related wiring harness will have to be replaced, as individual parts are not available.

13 The switches can be checked for continuity using a multimeter or test light and battery. Always disconnect the negative battery cable, which will prevent the possibility of a short circuit, before making the checks.

14 Remove the body panels as necessary to trace the wiring from the switch in question back to its connector (see Chapter 9). Disconnect the relevant wiring connector **(see illustrations)**. Refer to the wiring diagram in your scooter handbook and check for continuity between the terminals of the switch wiring with the switch in the various positions (switch OFF – no continuity; switch ON – continuity).

15 If the checks indicate a problem exists,

remove the switch housing and spray the switch contacts with electrical contact cleaner. If they are accessible, the contacts can be scraped clean carefully with a knife or polished with crocus cloth. If switch components are damaged or broken, it will be obvious when the switch is disassembled.

16 Clean the inside of the switch body thoroughly and smear the contacts with suitable grease before reassembly.

Brake light switches

17 Remove the handlebar cover (see Chapter 9), then disconnect the switch wiring connectors **(see illustration)**. Using a continuity tester, connect a probe to each terminal on the switch. With the brake lever at rest, there should be no continuity. Pull the brake lever in – there should now be continuity **(see illustration)**. If not, install a new switch.

18 If the switch is good, refer to the wiring diagram in your scooter handbook to check the brake light circuit using a multimeter or test light (see Section 2).

6.14a Trace the wiring to the connectors . . .

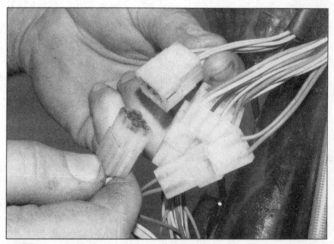

6.14b . . . and disconnect them to test the handlebar switches

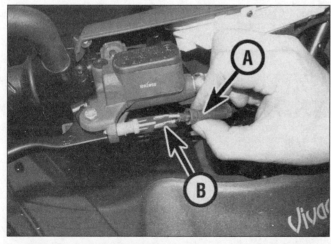

6.17a Pull back the boot (A) and disconnect the wires (B)

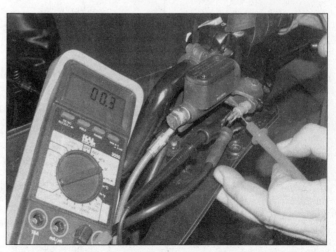

6.17b Testing the continuity of the brake light switch

7.4 A typical turn signal relay

8.4 Starter motor relay

7 Turn signal system – check

1 The turn signal system consists of the turn signal lights, instrument panel light, handlebar switch, relay and fuse (see illustration on next page).

2 On most of the scooters covered by this manual, the engine must be running for the turn signal lights to work. If none of the lights work, always check the fuse (where installed) and alternator lighting coil before proceeding (see Section 9).

Turn signal lights

3 Most turn signal problems are the result of a failed bulb or corroded socket. This is especially true when the turn signals function properly in one direction, but not in the other. Follow the procedures described in Section 6 to check the bulbs and the sockets, the operation of the turn signal switch and the turn signal warning light in the instrument cluster.

Turn signal relay

4 If the bulbs and sockets are good, test the power supply to the turn signal relay (see illustration). Disconnect the relay wiring connector and check for voltage at the input wire terminal in the connector with the engine running, using a multimeter or test light connected to a good ground. Turn the engine OFF. If there is no voltage, use the wiring diagram in your scooter handbook to check the supply circuit.

5 If there is voltage, reconnect the wiring connector to the relay and use a test light to check for voltage on the output side of the relay wiring connector with the engine running. The light should flash; if it does not, install a new relay.

8 Starter system – check

1 The starter system consists of the starter switch, starter motor, battery, relay and fuse (see illustration on page 10•10). On some scooters, one or both of the brake light switches and, where installed, the side stand switch, are part of a safety circuit which prevents the engine starting unless the brake is held on and the side stand is up.

2 On most two-stroke engined scooters, a diode links the starter circuit with the oil level warning light; this serves to check that the warning light bulb is sound. A similar system may also be installed to check that the fuel level warning light bulb is sound.

3 If the starter circuit is faulty, first check the fuse (see Section 5). Also check that the battery is fully-charged (see Section 3).

Starter relay

4 To locate the starter relay, either trace the lead from the positive terminal of the battery to the relay, or trace the lead back from the starter motor to the relay (see illustration).

5 Disconnect the starter motor lead from the relay. With the ignition switch ON, press the starter switch. The relay should be heard to click. Switch the ignition OFF.

6 If the relay wasn't heard to click in the test above, remove it from the scooter for further testing. Ensure that the ignition is OFF and disconnect the negative battery cable beforehand. Take note of the wire connections to the starter relay, then disconnect the heavy gauge battery and starter motor cables from the relay terminals, followed by the wire connector. Move the relay to the bench for testing. Connect a multimeter set to the ohms (resistance) range across the battery and starter motor terminals of the relay (these are the terminals for the heavy gauge cables). Using a fully charged battery (the scooter's

battery will do) and short jumper wires, connect the other terminals of the relay to the battery (see illustration). If the relay is working correctly, continuity should be indicated on the meter when battery power is applied. Note that the wire terminal numbers shown in the illustration may be stamped on the relay, particularly on European models.

7 If the relay is good, refer to the wiring diagram in your scooter handbook and check the other components in the starter circuit as described below. If all components are good, check the wiring between the various components.

Oil level warning light and diode

8 The oil level warning light in the instrument cluster should come on temporarily when the starter button is pressed as a check of the warning bulb. If the light fails to come on, first check the bulb (see Section 6), then

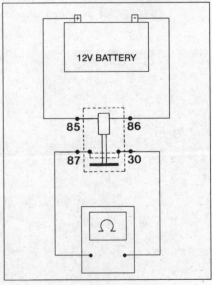

8.6 Starter relay test

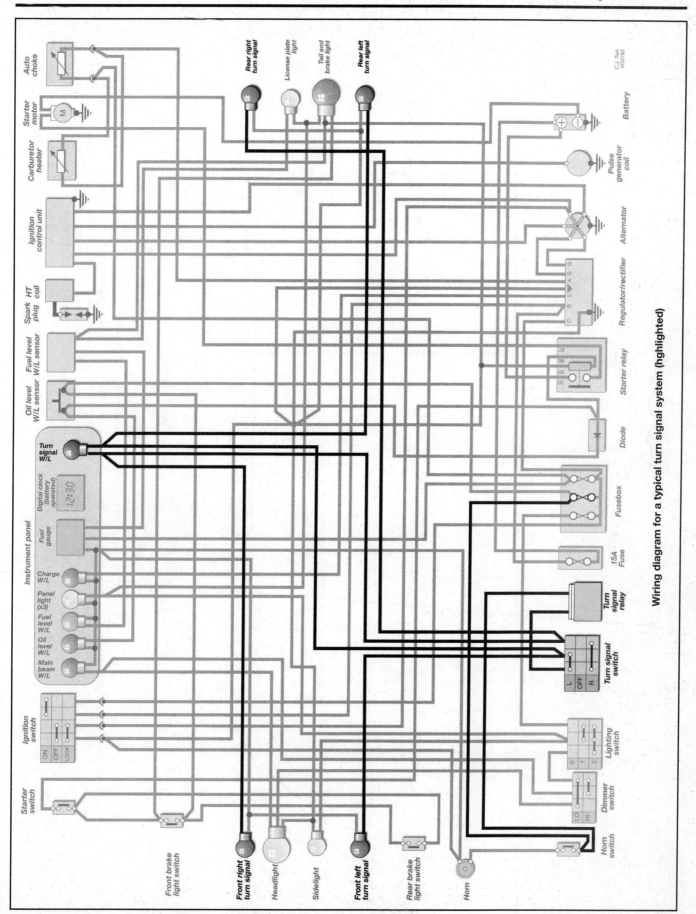

Wiring diagram for a typical turn signal system (hghlighted)

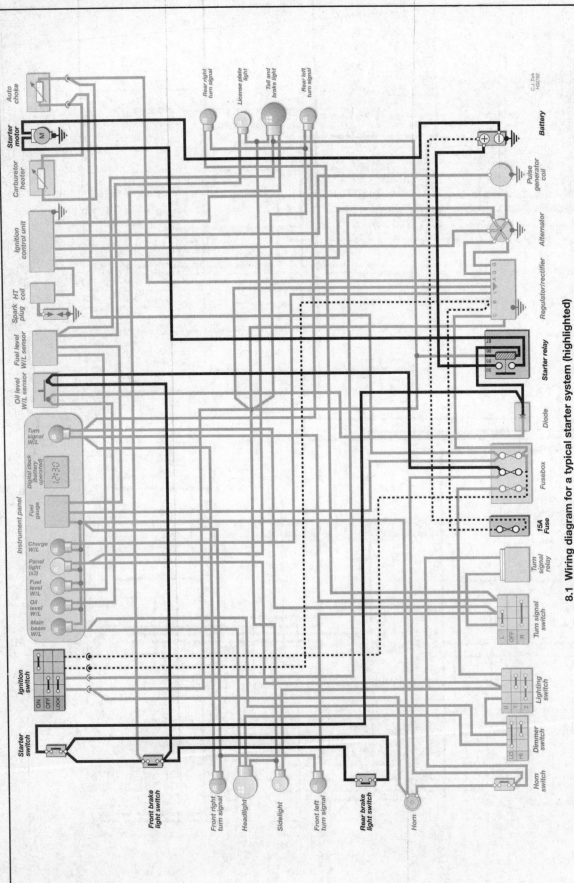

8.1 Wiring diagram for a typical starter system (highlighted)

The hatched black wires show the feed from the battery, through the main fuse and ignition switch to the fusebox containing the circuit fuses. The solid black wires illustrate the starter circuit: Power is fed from the starter circuit fuse, via the oil level sensor to the brake lever switches. Closing either brake lever switch allows current to flow to the starter switch on the handlebar. When the starter switch is closed, current flows to the coil of the starter relay and then to ground, completing the circuit and activating the relay contacts to bridge the heavy gauge cables between the battery and starter motor.

An additional feature on many two-stroke engined scooters is the link with the oil level warning light. When the starter switch is closed (button pressed), power is also fed to the warning light with the oil level warning light. In normal operation (engine running), if the oil level sensor contacts close due to the oil level dropping to a low level, light via a diode. This serves as a check of the warning light bulb. When the starter switch is closed (button pressed), power is also fed to the warning current is routed from the starter circuit fuse side of the circuit to the oil level warning light.

8.12 Location of the side stand switch

8.15 Disconnect the wire from the starter motor terminal

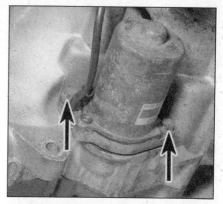

8.16 Remove the two bolts, noting the ground cable where installed

check the wiring between the instrument cluster and the diode.

9 The diode will only allow current to pass in one direction. This is usually represented by an arrowhead on the diode housing and may also be shown on the wiring diagram.

10 Unplug the diode from the wiring harness, taking note of the wire locations. Use a multimeter set to the ohms or diode test function, connect its probes across the two terminals of the diode. Continuity (zero resistance) should be indicated when connecting the probes one way, then no continuity (infinite resistance) should be shown when reversing the probes.

11 If the tests indicate the same condition in both directions, the diode is faulty.

Side stand switch

12 The side stand switch is mounted on the stand bracket (see illustration). To test the switch, trace the wiring back to the connector and disconnect it.

13 Connect a multimeter or continuity tester to the terminals on the switch side of the connector. With the sidestand up, there should be continuity (zero resistance) between the terminals; with the stand down, there should be no continuity (infinite resistance).

14 If the switch does not work as expected, check that the fault is not caused by a sticking switch plunger; spray the switch with

WD-40, or equivalent. If the switch still does not work, it is defective and must be replaced.

Starter motor

15 To remove the starter motor, first disconnect the negative battery cable. If accessible, disconnect the wire from the starter motor terminal (see illustration). Alternatively, trace the wire from the starter motor terminal and disconnect it at the connector.

16 Unscrew the two bolts securing the starter motor to the crankcase; note any ground wire secured by the bolts (see illustration).

17 Withdraw the starter motor. If not already done, disconnect the wire from the motor terminal. Remove the O-ring from the end of the motor body and discard it, as a new one must be installed on reassembly (see illustration).

18 Installation is the reverse of removal. Where installed, apply a smear of engine oil to the new body O-ring and secure the ground wire with one of the mounting bolts.

19 The parts of the starter motor that are most likely to wear are the brushes, the commutator and the bearings. If the motor is suspect, it can be inspected as follows.

Note: A number of different starter motors are installed across the range of scooters covered by this manual. Before disassembling the motor, check the availability of new

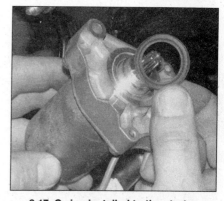

8.17 O-ring installed to the starter motor body

parts with a scooter dealer. If parts are not available, it may be worthwhile consulting an auto-electrician before buying a new motor, as sometimes, depending on the nature of the fault, they can be repaired. When disassembling the motor, carefully note the correct installed position of each component before removing it, as the procedure given below is general and does not cover the specific components of each type of motor.

20 Remove the starter motor (see Steps 15 to 17), then undo the screws or bolts securing the housing to the end cover and draw the housing off, leaving the armature in place in the cover (see illustrations). Note the

8.20a Undo the screws . . .

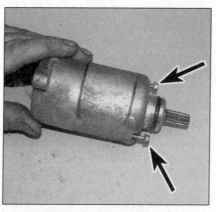

8.20b . . . or the bolts . . .

8.20c . . . and remove the housing

8.21 Withdraw the armature, noting
how it fits

8.22a Remove the brushes . . .

8.22b . . . and remove the brush springs

8.23 Brushes mounted on separate
brush plate

8.24 Inspect the commutator
bars (arrow)

position of any housing seals and remove them carefully. **Note:** *If there is oil inside the starter motor, the internal cover seal has failed – check the availability of a new seal or cover assembly with a scooter dealer.*
21 Withdraw the armature from the cover, noting any shims or washers on either or both ends of the armature shaft, and noting

how the brushes fit on the commutator **(see illustration).**
22 Slide the brushes out from their holders; note the position of the brush springs and remove them for safekeeping if they are loose **(see illustrations).**
23 Check that the brushes are firmly attached to their terminals. If the brushes are

excessively worn, cracked or chipped, they should be replaced, otherwise a new starter motor must be installed. Note that some starter motors are installed with separate brush plates **(see illustration).**
24 Inspect the commutator bars on the armature for scoring, scratches and discoloration **(see illustration).** The commutator can be cleaned and polished with crocus cloth, but do not use sandpaper or emery paper. After cleaning, wipe away any residue with a cloth soaked in electrical system cleaner or alcohol.
25 Using an multimeter or test light and battery, check for continuity between the commutator bars **(see illustration).** Continuity (zero resistance) should exist between each bar and all of the others.
26 Also, check for continuity between the commutator bars and the armature shaft **(see illustration).** There should be no continuity (infinite resistance) between the commutator and the shaft. If the checks indicate otherwise, the armature is defective.
27 Check the front end of the armature shaft for worn or chipped teeth. Check the condition of the bearing, which may be either on the armature or in the motor cover **(see illustration).**

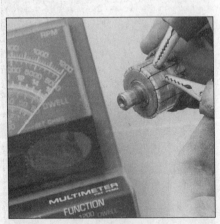

8.25 Continuity should exist between the
commutator bars

8.26 There should be no continuity
between the commutator bars and the
armature shaft

8.27 Bearing (arrow) located in starter
motor cover

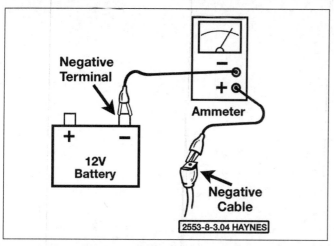

9.5 Checking for a battery drain with an ammeter

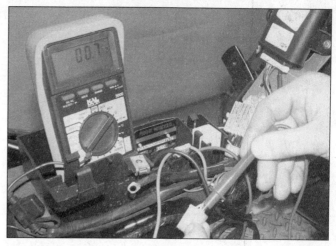

9.15 Checking the resistance in the alternator coils

28 Reassemble the starter motor in the reverse order of disassembly, noting the following:

Press the brushes into their holders against the pressure of their springs, then install the armature into the end cover carefully to avoid damaging the seal.

Ensure each brush is pressed against the commutator by its spring and is free to move easily in its holder.

Lubricate the bushing in the end of the housing with a smear of grease.

9 Charging system – check

1 If the performance of the charging system is suspect, the system as a whole should be checked first, followed by testing of the individual components and circuits **(see illustration on next page)**. Note: *Before beginning the checks, make sure the battery is fully charged and that all circuit connections are clean and tight.*

2 Checking the output of the charging system and the performance of the various components within the charging system requires the use of a multimeter – if a multimeter is not available, have the system tested by a scooter dealer or auto-electrician.

3 When making the checks, follow the procedures carefully to prevent incorrect connections or short circuits, as irreparable damage to electrical system components may result if short circuits occur.

Leakage test

4 Disconnect the negative battery cable.

5 Set the multimeter to the amps function and connect its negative probe to the negative battery terminal, and positive probe to the disconnected negative cable **(see illustration)**. Always set the meter to a high amps

range initially, then bring it down to the mA (milliAmps) range; if there is a high current flow in the circuit, it may blow the meter's fuse.

Caution: Always connect an ammeter in series, never in parallel with the battery, otherwise it will be damaged. Do not turn the ignition ON or operate the starter motor when the meter is connected – a sudden surge in current will blow the meter's fuse.

6 While manufacturers figures may vary, if the current leakage indicated exceeds 1 mA, there is probably a short circuit in the wiring. Disconnect the meter and reconnect the negative cable to the battery, tightening it securely,

7 If current leakage is indicated, refer to the wiring diagram in your scooter handbook and systematically disconnect individual electrical components and repeat the test until the source is identified.

Alternator

Regulated output test

8 Start the engine and warm it up to normal operating temperature, then stop the engine and turn the ignition OFF.

9 Support the scooter on its center stand with the rear wheel clear of the ground.

10 To check the regulated voltage output, set the multimeter to the 0 to 50 volts DC scale (voltmeter). Connect the meter positive probe to the positive battery terminal, and the negative probe to the negative battery terminal.

11 Start the engine and slowly increase the engine speed to a fast idle; the regulated voltage should be as specified in the *Data* section at the end of this manual. Now turn the headlight ON and note the reading – there should be no significant change in the output voltage. **Note:** *As a general rule, if a regulated voltage is not specified, the meter reading should be between 13 to 16 volts.*

12 If the voltage is not within these limits, there is a fault either in the regulator/rectifier

or the alternator itself. If available, substitute the regulator/rectifier with a known good unit and test again; if the voltage is still outside the specified limits, check the alternator coil resistance (see Steps 14 to 17).

13 Some manufacturers only specify an unregulated alternator output. This check requires a wiring diagram and test details specific to your scooter, and is best undertaken by a scooter dealer or auto-electrician.

 Clues to a faulty regulator are constantly blowing bulbs, with brightness varying considerably with engine speed, and battery overheating.

Coils resistance test

14 Disconnect the negative battery cable. Trace the wiring from the alternator cover and disconnect it at the connector.

15 Refer to the wiring diagram in your scooter handbook and identify the wire terminals for the charging coil and lighting coil in the alternator side of the connector. **Note:** *For alternators with three charging coil wires of the same color code, see Step 16.* Set the multimeter to the ohms x 1 scale and connect the meter probes to the charging coil wire terminal and to ground, and then to the lighting coil terminal and ground. This will give resistance readings for the coils which should be consistent with the specifications in the *Data* section **(see illustration)**.

16 Alternatively, set the multimeter to the ohms x 1 scale and check the resistance between one pair of wire terminals at a time and note the three readings obtained. Also check for continuity between each terminal and ground. The readings should be consistent with the specifications in the *Data* section and there should be no continuity (infinite resistance) between any of the terminals and ground.

17 If the readings obtained differ greatly from those given in the *Data* section, particularly if the meter indicates a short circuit (no measurable resistance) or an open circuit (infinite,

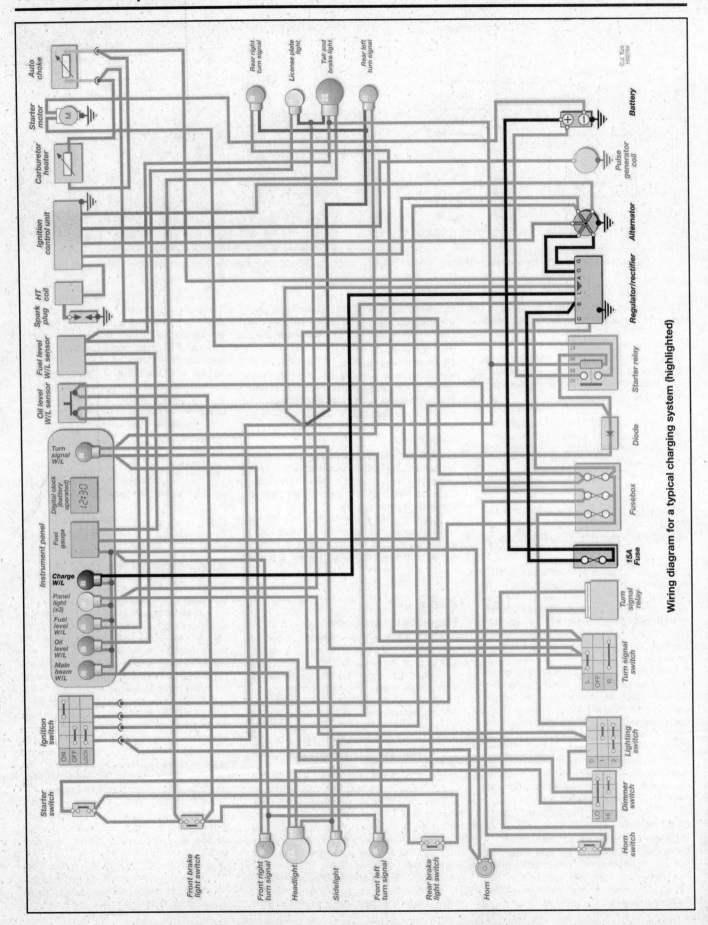

Wiring diagram for a typical charging system (highlighted)

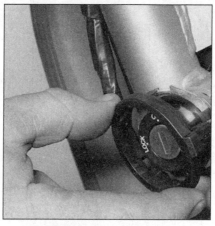

10.1 Disconnect the ignition switch wiring connector

10.4 Where installed, unclip the immobilizer ring

10.5 Ignition switch is secured by a shear bolt (arrow)

or very high resistance), the alternator stator assembly must be replaced. However, first check that the fault is not due to a damaged or broken wire from the alternator to the connector; pinched or broken wires can usually be repaired.

18 Refer to the procedure in Chapter 2A or 2B, as applicable, for details of alternator removal and installation.

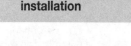

10 Ignition (main) switch – check, removal and installation

⚠ **Warning: To prevent the risk of short circuits, disconnect the negative battery cable before making any ignition (main) switch checks.**

Check

1 Remove any body panels as required for access (see Chapter 9). Ensure the negative battery cable is disconnected, then pull back the boot on the wiring connector and disconnect the connector **(see illustration)**.

2 Refer to the wiring diagram in your scooter handbook, then using a multimeter or continuity tester, check the continuity of the connector terminal pairs. Continuity should exist between the connected terminals when the switch is in the indicated position.

3 If the switch fails any of the tests, replace it.

Removal

4 Disconnect the negative battery cable and the switch wiring connector (see Step 1). If applicable, unclip the immobilizer transponder antenna from the front of the switch **(see illustration)**.

5 The switch is secured to the frame by a shear bolt **(see illustration)**. To remove the bolt, drill off the bolt head, then remove the switch. The threaded section of the bolt can then be unscrewed with pliers.

Installation

6 Installation is the reverse of removal. Operate the key to ensure the steering lock mechanism is correctly aligned with the frame and steering stem before tightening the shear bolt, then tighten the bolt until the head snaps off.

7 Reconnect the negative battery cable once all electrical connections have been made to the switch.

11 Horn – check and replacement

Check

1 Remove any body panels as required for access to the horn (see Chapter 9).

2 Disconnect the wiring connectors from the horn and ensure that the contacts are clean and free from corrosion **(see illustration)**.

3 To test the horn, use jumper wires to connect one of the horn terminals to the positive battery terminal and the other horn terminal to the negative battery terminal. If the horn

sounds, check the handlebar switch (see Section 6) and the wiring between the switch and the horn.

4 If the horn doesn't sound, replace it.

Replacement

5 Disconnect the wiring connectors from the horn, then unscrew the bolt securing the horn and remove it.

6 Install the horn and tighten the mounting bolt securely. Connect the wiring connectors and test the horn.

12 Fuel gauge and level sender – check and replacement

⚠ **Warning: Gasoline is extremely flammable, so take extra precautions when you work on any part of the fuel system. Don't smoke or allow open flames or bare light bulbs near the work area, and don't work in a garage where a gas-type appliance is present. If you spill any fuel on your skin, rinse it off immediately**

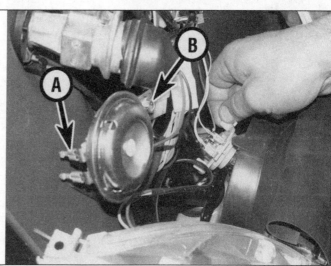

11.2 Horn wiring connectors (A) and mounting bolt (B)

12.1 Fuel level sender wiring connector

12.3 Fuel level sender unit

with soap and water. **When you perform any kind of work on the fuel system, wear safety glasses and have a fire extinguisher suitable for a class B type fire (flammable liquids) on hand.**

Fuel gauge
Check
1 Disconnect the wiring connector from the top of the fuel level sender **(see illustration)**.
2 Connect a jumper wire between the terminals on the wiring loom side of the connector. With the ignition switched ON, the fuel gauge should read FULL. If it doesn't, check the wiring between the connector and the gauge. If the wiring is good, then the gauge is confirmed faulty. **Note:** *On most scooters, the fuel gauge is integral with the instru-*

ment cluster, for which no individual parts are available. If the fuel gauge is faulty, the entire cluster must be replaced.

Fuel level sender
Check
3 Disconnect the wiring connector from the fuel level sender (see Step 1), then unscrew the sender from the tank and remove the sender unit **(see illustration)**. **Note:** *On some scooters the sender is retained by a locking ring.*

 Warning: Block the opening in the tank to prevent the escape of gasoline fumes and accidental fuel spillage.

4 Check the operation of the sender; the arm should move freely without binding.

Also check that the float is held securely on the arm and that it is not damaged. This will usually be apparent by the presence of fuel inside the float. If any of the component parts are faulty or damaged, install a new sender.
5 If the sender is good, check the wiring between the sender and the gauge.
6 If a fault persists with the fuel gauge and both the gauge and sender appear good, have the sender resistance checked by a scooter dealer.

Replacement
7 Check the condition of the sender O-ring and install a new one if it is deformed or deteriorated. Insert the sender carefully into the tank, then lock it in position.

Data section
Contents

Wheelbase

Contents (continued)

Daelim A-Four, 2006 and later

Engine	49.5 cc single-cylinder 2-stroke
Cooling system	Air cooled
Fuel system	CV carburetor
Ignition system	CDI
Transmission	Variable speed automatic, belt driven
Suspension	Telescopic front, swingarm with single shock rear
Brakes	Disc front, drum rear
Tires	
Front	120/70-12 58L
Rear	130/70-12 62L
Wheelbase	1260 mm (49.6 inches)
Weight (dry)	92 kg (202.4 lbs)
Fuel tank capacity	6 liters (1.58 gallons)

Engine

Spark plug type	NGK BR8HSA
Electrode gap	0.6 to 0.7 mm (0.024 to 0.028 inch)
Idle speed (rpm)	1700 +/- 100 rpm
Engine oil type	2-stroke oil (DMC Ultra 2 or equivalent)
Engine oil capacity	1.2 liters (1.1 qt)
Bore x stroke	39.0 x 41.1 mm (1.181 x 1.618 inch)
Piston diameter (service limit, all grade marks)	38.9 mm (1.531 inches)
Piston to bore clearance (service limit)	0.10 mm (0.004 inch)
Piston ring installed end gap (top and second)	
Standard	0.10 to 0.25 mm (0.004 to 0.009 inch)
Limit	0.40 mm (0.016 inch)

Fuel system

Throttle twistgrip freeplay	2 to 6 mm (3/32 to 1/4 inch)
Main jet	65
Slow jet	38
Needle type/position	Not specified
Air screw setting	1-1/4 turns out

Ignition system

Ignition coil peak primary voltage	120 volts minimum
Ignition pulse generator peak voltage	1.5 volts minimum
Ignition pulse generator resistance	100 ohms +/- 20 percent
Ignition coil primary resistance	0.1 to 0.5 ohms
Ignition coil secondary resistance (cap installed)	6.5 to 9.5 k-ohms

Transmission

Belt width (service limit)	16.5 mm (0.649 inch)
Weight roller outer diameter	
Standard	15.920 to 16.080 mm (0.627 to 0.633 inch)
Limit	15.4 mm (0.606 inch)
Clutch lining thickness (service limit)	2.0 mm (0.079 inch)
Clutch spring free length (service limit)	92.8 mm (3.653 inches)

Brakes

Brake fluid	DOT 4
Disc thickness (limit)	3.0 mm (0.118 inch)
Pad wear limit	To wear line
Brake lever freeplay (front and rear)	10 to 20 mm (3/8 to 3/4 inch)
Rear brake shoe wear limit	When wear indicator marks align or 2.0 mm (0.078 inch)
Rear brake drum diameter (limit)	111 mm (4.370 inches)

Tire pressures

Front	25 psi
Rear	29 psi

Daelim A-Four, 2006 and later (continued)

Electrical system

Battery
Capacity	12V-3Ah
Voltage (fully charged)	13.0 to 13.2 volts

Alternator
Output (regulated)	14.0 to 15.0 volts
Charging coil resistance	0.8 ohms +/- 20 per cent
Fuse	7 amps

Torque wrench settings

Note: One foot-pound (ft-lb) of torque is equivalent to 12 inch-pounds (in-lbs) of torque. Torque values below approximately 15 foot-pounds are expressed in inch-pounds, because most foot-pound torque wrenches are not accurate at these smaller values.

Transmission oil check bolt	13 Nm (112 inch-lbs)
Cylinder head nuts	10 Nm (87 inch-lbs)
Clutch drive bolts face nut	54 Nm (40 ft-lbs)
Driven pulley locknut	39 Nm (29 ft-lbs)
Clutch outer nut	39 Nm (29 ft-lbs)
Alternator rotor nut	39 Nm (29 ft-lbs)
Starter clutch Allen bolts	29 Nm (22 ft-lbs) (2)
Crankcase bolts	10 Nm (87 inch-lbs)
Engine hanger bracket to engine	49 Nm (36 ft-lbs)
Engine hanger bracket to frame	72 Nm (53 ft-lbs)
Front axle nut	59 Nm (43 ft-lbs)
Rear axle nut	Not specified
Handlebar to steering stem bolt	49 Nm (36 ft-lbs)

Steering stem bearing adjustment nut
First step	10 Nm (87 inch-lbs)
Second step	Loosen 1/8 turn
Steering stem locknut	68 Nm (51 ft-lbs)
Steering stem to fork bolt	34 to 44 Nm (25 to 32 ft-lbs)
Front fork damper rod bolts	20 Nm (14 ft-lbs)
Front fork to triple clamp bolts	39 Nm (29 ft-lbs)
Rear shock bolts (upper and lower)	34 to 44 Nm (25 to 32 ft-lbs)
Swingarm mounting bolts	49 Nm (36 ft-lbs)

Front brake bolts
Caliper bracket bolts	26 Nm (20 ft-lbs)
Caliper pin bolt	Not specified
Caliper brake hose union bolt	34 Nm (25 ft-lbs)

Daelim Cordi, 2006 and later

Engine	49.5 cc single-cylinder 2-stroke
Cooling system	Air cooled
Fuel system	Slide piston carburetor
Ignition system	CDI
Transmission	Variable speed automatic, belt driven
Suspension	Telescopic front, swingarm with single shock rear
Brakes	Disc front, drum rear
Tires (front and rear)	90/90-10-50J
Wheelbase	1227 mm (48.3 inches)
Weight (dry)	76.5 kg (168.3 lbs)
Fuel tank capacity	4.8 liters (1.18 gallons)

Engine

Spark plug type	
Standard	NGK BP6HS or BPR6HS
Low speed riding	NGK B46HSA or BR46HSA
High speed riding	NGK BP7HS or BPR7HS
Electrode gap	0.6 to 0.7 mm (0.024 to 0.028 inch)
Idle speed (rpm)	1800 to 2000 rpm
Engine oil type	2-stroke oil (Motix or equivalent)
Engine oil capacity	1.2 liters (1.1 qt)
Bore x stroke	40 x 39.4 mm (1.575 x 1.552 inch)
Piston diameter	
ID mark A	39.955 to 39.960 mm (1.5730 to 1.5732 inch)
No ID mark	39.960 to 39.965 mm (1.5734 to 1.5736 inch)
ID mark B	39.965 to 39.970 mm (1.5734 to 1.5736 inch)
Service limit, all grade marks	39.90 mm (1.570 inches)
Piston to bore clearance	
Standard	0.40 to 0.55 mm (0.016 to 0.021 inch)
Limit	0.13 mm (0.005 inch)
(Piston ring installed end gap (top and second)	0.15 to 0.30 mm (0.006 to 0.012 inch)

Fuel system

Throttle twistgrip freeplay	2 to 6 mm (3/32 to 1/4 inch)
Main jet	77
Slow jet	38
Needle type/position	Not specified
Air screw setting	1-1/2 turns out
Float level	8 mm (5/16 inch)

Ignition system

Ignition coil peak primary voltage	300 volts minimum
Ignition pulse generator peak voltage	2.8 volts minimum
Ignition pulse generator resistance	400 to 800 ohms
Exciter coil resistance	50 to 200 ohms
Ignition coil primary resistance	0.1 to 0.5 ohms
Ignition coil secondary resistance (cap installed)	6.3 to 10.3 k-ohms

Transmission

Belt width (service limit)	15.5 mm (0.610 inch)
Weight roller outer diameter	
Standard	15.920 to 16.080 mm (0.627 to 0.633 inch)
Limit	15.4 mm (0.606 inch)
Clutch lining thickness (service limit)	2.0 mm (0.079 inch)
Clutch spring free length	98.1 mm (3.862 inches)

Daelim Cordi, 2006 and later (continued)

Brakes

Brake fluid	DOT 4
Disc thickness (limit)	2.5 mm (0.098 inch)
Pad wear limit	To wear line
Brake lever freeplay (front and rear)	10 to 20 mm (3/8 to 3/4 inch)
Rear brake shoe wear limit	When wear indicator marks align or 2.0 mm (0.078 inch)
Rear brake drum diameter (limit)	95.5 mm (3.759 inches)

Tire pressures

Front	25 psi
Rear	29 psi

Electrical system

Battery	
Capacity	12V-3Ah
Voltage (fully charged)	13.0 to 13.2 volts
Alternator	
Output (regulated)	13.0 to 15.0 volts
Charging coil resistance	0.4 to 1.0 ohms
Fuse	7 amps

Torque wrench settings

Note: One foot-pound (ft-lb) of torque is equivalent to 12 inch-pounds (in-lbs) of torque. Torque values below approximately 15 foot-pounds are expressed in inch-pounds, because most foot-pound torque wrenches are not accurate at these smaller values.

Transmission oil check bolt	13 Nm (112 inch-lbs)
Cylinder head nuts	10 Nm (87 inch-lbs)
Drive pulley nut	54 Nm (40 ft-lbs)
Clutch driven face nut	54 Nm (40 ft-lbs)
Clutch outer nut	39 Nm (29 ft-lbs)
Alternator rotor nut	39 Nm (29 ft-lbs)
Crankcase bolts	10 Nm (87 inch-lbs)
Engine hanger bracket nut	
To engine	49 Nm (36 ft-lbs)
To frame	72 Nm (53 ft-lbs)
Front axle nut	59 Nm (43 ft-lbs)
Rear axle nut	108 Nm (80 ft-lbs)
Handlebar to steering stem post nut	49 Nm (36 ft-lbs)
Handlebar to steering stem bolt	49 Nm (36 ft-lbs)
Steering stem bearing adjustment nut	
First step	10 Nm (87 inch-lbs)
Second step	Loosen 1/8 turn
Steering stem locknut	68 Nm (51 ft-lbs)
Steering stem to fork bolt	34 to 44 Nm (25 to 32 ft-lbs)
Front fork damper rod bolts	20 Nm (15 ft-lbs)
Front fork to triple clamp bolts	40 Nm (28 ft-lbs)
Rear shock bolts (upper and lower)	40 Nm (28 ft-lbs)
Swingarm mounting bolts	49 Nm (36 ft-lbs)
Front brake bolts	
Caliper bracket bolts	27 Nm (20 ft-lbs)
Caliper pad pins	18 Nm (156 inch-lbs)
Caliper slide pins	23 Nm (17 ft-lbs)
Brake hose union bolts	35 Nm (25 ft-lbs)
Rear brake arm bolt	6 Nm (52 inch-lbs)

Daelim Delfino, 2006 and later

Engine	99.7 cc single-cylinder 2-stroke
Cooling system	Air cooled
Fuel system	Slide piston carburetor
Ignition system	CDI
Transmission	Variable speed automatic, belt driven
Suspension	Telescopic front, swingarm with single shock rear
Brakes	Disc front, drum rear
Tires (front and rear)	100/90-10 56J
Wheelbase	1290 mm (50.787 inches)
Weight (dry)	220 kg (8.661 inch)
Fuel tank capacity	7.2 liters (1.77 gallons)

Engine

Spark plug type	NGK BR8HS
Electrode gap	0.6 to 0.7 mm (0.024 to 0.028 inch)
Idle speed (rpm)	1800 +/- rpm
Engine oil type	2-stroke oil (DMC Ultra or equivalent)
Engine oil capacity	1.2 liters (1.1 qt)
Bore x stroke	50.6 x 49.6 mm (1.992 x 1.953 inches)
Piston diameter (3mm [1/8-inch] up from bottom of skirt)	
ID mark B	50.565 to 50.569 mm (1.9909 to 1.9911 inches)
ID mark A	50.570 to 50.574 mm (1.991 to 1.991 inches)
No ID mark	50.575 to 50.579 mm (1.9911 to 1.9912 inches)
Piston to bore clearance (limit)	0.10 mm (0.004 inch)
Piston ring installed end gap	
Top	
Standard	0.15 to 0.35 mm (0.006 to 0.014 inch)
Limit	0.60 mm (0.023 inch)
Second	
Standard	0.15 to 0.35 mm (0.006 to 0.014 inch)
Limit	0.40 mm (0.016 inch)

Fuel system

Throttle twistgrip freeplay	2 to 6 mm (3/32 to 1/4 inch)
Main jet	88
Slow jet	38
Needle type/position	Not specified
Air screw setting	1-1/8 turns out
Float level	8 mm (5/16 inch)

Ignition system

Ignition pulse generator resistance	50 to 200 ohms
Ignition coil primary resistance	0.1 to 0.3 ohms
Ignition coil secondary resistance (cap installed)	7.5 to 8.6 k-ohms
Ignition coil secondary resistance (without cap)	2.7 to 3.5 k-ohms

Transmission

Belt width (service limit)	16.5 mm (0.649 inch)
Weight roller outer diameter	
Standard	15.920 to 16.080 mm (0.627 to 0.633 inch)
Limit	15.4 mm (0.606 inch)
Clutch lining thickness (service limit)	2.0 mm (0.079 inch)
Clutch spring free length (limit)	137.5 mm (5.413 inches)

Daelim Delfino, 2006 and later (continued)

Brakes

Brake fluid .... DOT 4
Disc thickness (limit)... 3.0 mm (0.118 inch)
Pad wear limit.. To wear line
Rear brake lever freeplay.. 10 to 20 mm (3/8 to 3/4 inch)
Rear brake shoe wear limit.. When wear indicator marks align or 2.0 mm (0.078 inch)
Rear brake drum diameter (limit)............................... 111 mm (4.370 inches)

Tire pressures

Front .... 22 psi
Rear
    Rider only .... 25 psi
    Rider and passenger.. 32 psi

Electrical system

Battery
    Capacity 12V-3Ah
    Voltage (fully charged)....................................... 13.0 to 13.2 volts
Alternator
    Output (regulated).. 13.0 to 15.0 volts
    Charging coil resistance..................................... 0.3 to 1.2 ohms
Fuse .... 7 amps

Torque wrench settings

Note: One foot-pound (ft-lb) of torque is equivalent to 12 inch-pounds (in-lbs) of torque. Torque values below approximately 15 foot-pounds are expressed in inch-pounds, because most foot-pound torque wrenches are not accurate at these smaller values.

Transmission oil check bolt....................................... 18 Nm (156 inch-lbs)
Cylinder head bolts .... 10 Nm (87 inch-lbs)
Drive pulley nut... 44 Nm (32 ft-lbs)
Clutch driven face nut .... 54 Nm (40 ft-lbs)
Clutch outer nut.. 39 Nm (28 ft-lbs)
Alternator rotor nut... 39 Nm (28 ft-lbs)
Crankcase bolts .... Not specified
Engine hanger bracket nut.. 70 Nm (51 ft-lbs)
Front axle nut .... 58 Nm (42 ft-lbs)
Rear axle nut .... 117 Nm (86 ft-lbs)
Steering stem locknut .... 68 Nm (50 Nm)
Handlebar to steering stem bolt................................ 44 Nm (32 ft-lbs)
Steering stem bearing adjustment nut
    First step .... 10 Nm (87 inch-lbs)
    Second step.. Loosen 1/8 turn
Rear shock bolts
    Upper .... 39 Nm (29 ft-lbs)
    Lower .... 25 Nm (18 ft-lbs)
Swingarm mounting bolts .... 48 Nm (35 ft-lbs)
Front brake bolts
    Caliper bracket bolts... 28 Nm (21 ft-lbs)
    Caliper pad pins... 18 Nm (156 inch-lbs)
    Caliper slide pins... 23 Nm (17 ft-lbs)
    Brake hose union bolts .... 34 Nm (25 ft-lbs)
Rear brake arm bolt.. 6 Nm (52 inch-lbs)

Daelim E-5, S-5, 2006 and later

Engine	49.5 cc single-cylinder 2-stroke
Cooling system	Air cooled
Fuel system	Piston valve carburetor
Ignition system	CDI
Transmission	Variable speed automatic, belt driven
Suspension	Telescopic front, swingarm with single shock rear
Brakes	Disc front, drum rear
Tires	130/90-10 61J
Wheelbase	1260 mm (49.6 inches)
Weight (dry)	
E-5	86 kg (189.2 lbs)
S-5	94 kg (207 lbs)
Fuel tank capacity	6 liters (1.58 gallons)

Engine

Spark plug type	
E-5	NGK B7HS
S-5	NGK B8HSA
Electrode gap	0.6 to 0.7 mm (0.024 to 0.028 inch)
Idle speed (rpm)	1800 +/- 100 rpm
Engine oil type	2-stroke oil (DMC Ultra 2 or equivalent
Engine oil capacity	1.2 liters (1.1 qt)
Bore x stroke	39.0 x 41.1 mm (1.181 x 1.618 inch)
Piston diameter (service limit, all grade marks)	38.9 mm (1.531 inches)
Piston to bore clearance (service limit)	0.10 mm (0.004 inch)
Piston ring installed end gap (top and second)	
Standard	0.10 to 0.25 mm (0.004 to 0.009 inch)
Limit	0.40 mm (0.016 inch)

Fuel system

Throttle twistgrip freeplay	2 to 6 mm (3/32 to 1/4 inch)
Main jet	75
Slow jet	38
Needle type/position	Not specified
Air screw setting	1-1/4 turns out
Float level	8 mm (5/16 inch)

Ignition system

Ignition coil peak primary voltage	120 volts minimum
Ignition pulse generator peak voltage	1.5 volts minimum
Ignition pulse generator resistance	100 ohms +/- 20 per cent
Ignition coil primary resistance	0.1 to 0.5 ohms
Ignition coil secondary resistance (cap installed)	6.5 to 9.5 k-ohms

Transmission

Belt width (service limit)	16.5 mm (0.649 inch)
Weight roller outer diameter	
Standard	15.920 to 16.080 mm (0.627 to 0.633 inch)
Limit	15.4 mm (0.606 inch)
Clutch lining thickness (service limit)	2.0 mm (0.079 inch)
Clutch spring free length (service limit)	98.1 mm (3.862 inches)

Brakes

Brake fluid	DOT 4
Disc thickness (limit)	3.0 mm (0.118 inch)
Pad wear limit	To wear line
Brake lever freeplay (front and rear)	10 to 20 mm (3/8 to 3/4 inch)
Rear brake shoe wear limit	When wear indicator marks align or 2.0 mm (0.078 inch)
Rear brake drum diameter (limit)	111 mm (4.370 inches)

Daelim E-5, S-5, 2006 and later (continued)

Tire pressures

Front .... 25 psi
Rear .... 29 psi

Electrical system

Battery
    Capacity 12V-3Ah
    Voltage (fully charged)... 13.0 to 13.2 volts
Alternator
    Output (regulated)... 14.0 to 15.0 volts
    Charging coil resistance.. 0.8 ohms +/- 20 percent
Fuse .... 7 amps

Torque wrench settings

Note: One foot-pound (ft-lb) of torque is equivalent to 12 inch-pounds (in-lbs) of torque. Torque values below approximately 15 foot-pounds are expressed in inch-pounds, because most foot-pound torque wrenches are not accurate at these smaller values.

Transmission oil check bolt...	13 Nm (112 inch-lbs)
Cylinder head nuts	10 Nm (87 inch-lbs)
Clutch driven face nut	54 Nm (40 ft-lbs)
Drive face nut	39 Nm (29 ft-lbs)
Clutch outer nut..	39 Nm (29 ft-lbs)
Alternator rotor nut	39 Nm (29 ft-lbs)
Starter clutch Allen bolts	28 Nm (21 ft-lbs) (2)
Crankcase bolts	10 Nm (87 inch-lbs)
Engine hanger bracket nut	
To engine	49 Nm (36 ft-lbs)
To frame	72 Nm (53 ft-lbs)
Front axle nut	59 Nm (43 ft-lbs)
Rear axle nut	Not specified
Handlebar to steering stem bolt.....................................	49 Nm (36 ft-lbs)
Steering stem bearing adjustment nut	
First step	10 Nm (87 inch-lbs)
Second step..	Loosen 1/8 turn
Steering stem locknut	68 Nm (51 ft-lbs)
Steering stem to fork bolt...	34 to 44 Nm (25 to 32 ft-lbs)
Front fork damper rod bolts	20 Nm (14 ft-lbs)
Front fork to triple clamp bolts.......................................	Not specified
Rear shock bolts (upper and lower)	39 Nm (29 ft-lbs)
Swingarm mounting bolts	48 Nm (35 ft-lbs)
Front brake bolts	
Caliper bracket bolts...	26 Nm (20 ft-lbs)
Caliper pin bolt..	Not specified
Caliper pad pins..	18 Nm (156 inch-lbs)
Caliper brake hose union bolt	34 Nm (25 ft-lbs)
Rear brake arm bolt..	Not specified

Daelim History, 2006 and later

Engine	124.9 cc single-cylinder 4-stroke
Cooling system	Air-oil cooled
Fuel system	CV carburetor
Ignition system	CDI
Transmission	Variable speed automatic, belt driven
Suspension	Telescopic front, swingarm with single shock rear
Brakes	Disc front and rear, drum parking brake
Tires	
Front	120/70-12 53K
Rear	130/70-12 62K
Wheelbase	1350 mm (53.15 inches)
Weight (dry)	125 kg (275 lbs)
Fuel tank capacity	
Total capacity	8.0 liters (1.97 gallons)
Reserve	1.7 liters (0.42 gallon)

Engine

Spark plug type	NGK CR8EH-9
Electrode gap	0.8 to 0.9 mm (0.032 to 0.036 inch)
Idle speed (rpm)	1800 +/- 100 rpm
Engine oil type	API Service SE, SF or SH
Engine oil capacity (oil and filter change)	0.8 liters (0.85 qt)
Valve clearance (intake and exhaust, engine cool)	0.12 +/- 0.12 mm (0.005 +/- 0.005 inch)
Bore x stroke	56 x 50.7 mm (2.204 x 1.996 inches)
Piston diameter	55.925 to 55.945 mm (2.202 to 2.203 inches)
Piston to bore clearance	
Standard	0.055 to 0.090 mm (0.022 to 0.035 inch)
Limit	0.2 mm (0.008 inch)
Piston ring installed end gap	
Top and second	0.10 to 0.25 mm (0.004 to 0.010 inch)
Oil ring	0.20 to 0.70 mm (0.008 inch to 0.027 inch)
Piston ring side clearance	
Top	0.040 to 0.67 mm (0.016 to 0.026 inch)

Fuel system

Throttle twistgrip freeplay	2 to 6 mm (3/32 to 1/4 inch)
Main jet	95
Slow jet	Not specified
Needle type/position	Not specified
Pilot screw setting	1-1/2 turns out
Float level	13 mm (1/2 inch)

Ignition system

Ignition pulse generator peak voltage	21.5 volts minimum
Ignition pulse generator resistance	90 to 150 ohms
Exciter coil resistance	50 to 200 ohms
Ignition coil primary resistance	0.1 to 0.2 ohms
Ignition coil secondary resistance (cap installed)	7.3 to 11.0 k-ohms
Ignition coil secondary resistance (without spark plug cap)	3.6 to 4.6 k-ohms

Transmission

Belt width (service limit)	20.5 mm (0.8 inch)
Weight roller outer diameter	
Standard	19.95 to 20.02 mm (0.785 to 0.788 inch)
Limit	19.5 mm (0.768 inch)
Clutch lining thickness (service limit)	2.0 mm (0.079 inch)
Clutch spring free length	90.0 mm (3.354 inches)

Daelim History, 2006 and later (continued)

Brakes

Brake fluid	DOT 4
Disc thickness (limit)	Not specified
Pad wear limit	To wear line

Tire pressures

Front	29 psi
Rear	
Rider only	29 psi
Rider and passenger	36 psi

Electrical system

Battery	
Capacity	12V-10Ah
Voltage (fully charged)	13.0 to 13.2 volts
Alternator	
Output (regulated)	14.0 to 15.0 volts
Charging coil resistance	0.1 to 1.0 ohms
Fuse	15 amps

Torque wrench settings

Note: One foot-pound (ft-lb) of torque is equivalent to 12 inch-pounds (in-lbs) of torque. Torque values below approximately 15 foot-pounds are expressed in inch-pounds, because most foot-pound torque wrenches are not accurate at these smaller values.

Engine oil drain plug	20 to 30 Nm (14 to 22 ft-lbs)
Transmission oil check bolt	9 Nm (78 inch-lbs)
Valve cover bolts	10 Nm (87 inch-lbs)
Camshaft holder nuts	20 Nm (14 ft-lbs) (1)
Cylinder head bolts	10 Nm (87 inch-lbs)
Drive pulley nut	74 Nm (54 ft-lbs)
Clutch driven face nut	Not specified
Clutch outer bolt	54 Nm (40 ft-lbs)
Alternator rotor nut	54 Nm (40 ft-lbs)
Starter clutch locknut	93 Nm (69 ft-lbs)
Crankcase bolts	Not specified
Engine hanger bracket nut	44 Nm (32 ft-lbs)
Front axle nut	49 to 68 Nm (36 to 51 ft-lbs)
Rear axle nut	Not specified
Handlebar to steering stem post nut	59 Nm (43 ft-lbs)
Steering stem bearing adjustment nut	
First step	2 Nm (17 inch-lbs)
Second step	Loosen 1/8 turn
Steering stem locknut	68 Nm (51 ft-lbs)
Steering stem to fork bolt	Not specified
Front fork damper rod bolts	20 Nm (14 ft-lbs) (2)
Front fork to triple clamp bolts	75 Nm (55 ft-lbs)
Rear shock bolts (upper and lower)	39 Nm (29 ft-lbs)
Swingarm mounting bolts	Not specified
Front brake bolts	
Caliper bracket bolts	26 Nm (20 ft-lbs)
Caliper bracket pin bolt	18 Nm (156 inch-lbs) (2)
Caliper slide pins	23 Nm (17 ft-lbs)
Brake hose union bolts	29 Nm (22 ft-lbs)
Rear brake arm flange bolt	98 Nm (72 ft-lbs)

1. *Apply engine oil to the threads.*
2. *Apply non-permanent thread locking agent to the threads.*

Daelim S2-250, 2006 and later

Engine	249 cc single-cylinder 4-stroke
Cooling system	Liquid cooled
Fuel system	CV carburetor
Ignition system	CDI
Transmission	Variable speed automatic, belt driven
Suspension	Telescopic front, swingarm with twin shock rear
Brakes	Disc front and rear
Tires	
Front	120/70-12
Rear	140/60-12
Wheelbase	1481 mm (58.3 inches)
Weight (dry)	164 kg (360.8 lbs)
Fuel tank capacity	
Total capacity	11.0 liters (2.9 gallons)
Reserve	2.8 liters (0.74 gallon)

Engine

Spark plug type	NGK DPR7EA-9
Electrode gap	0.9 mm (0.036 inch)
Idle speed (rpm)	1700 +/- 100 rpm
Engine oil type	API Service SJ, 15W-40 or 10W-30
Engine oil capacity (oil and filter change)	0.95 liters (1.0 qt)
Coolant type	Ethylene glycol-based antifreeze and water, 60/40 mixture
Coolant capacity	1.0 liters (1.1 qt)
Valve clearance (intake and exhaust, engine cool)	0.1 mm (0.004 inch)
Bore x stroke	72.7 x 60 mm (2.850 x 2.362 inches)
Piston diameter	72.67 to 72.69 mm (2.861 to 2.862 inches)
Piston to bore clearance	
Standard	0.01 to 0.04 mm (0.0004 to 0.0016 inch)
Limit	0.10 mm (0.004 inch)
Piston ring installed end gap	
Top	0.10 to 0.25 mm (0.004 to 0.010 inch)
Second	0.15 to 0.30 mm (0.006 to 0.012 inch)
Oil ring	0.25 to 0.70 mm (0.010 to 0.027 inch)
Piston ring side clearance	
Top	
Standard	0.2 mm (0.008 inch)
Limit	0.9 mm (0.035 inch)

Fuel system

Throttle twistgrip freeplay	2 to 6 mm (3/32 to 1/4 inch)
Main jet	102
Slow jet	Not specified
Needle type/position	Not specified
Pilot screw setting	2-1/2 turns out
Float level	18.5 mm (3/4 inch)

Ignition system

Ignition pulse generator peak voltage	Not specified
Ignition pulse generator resistance	90 to 150 ohms
Exciter coil resistance	23 to 35 ohms
Ignition coil primary resistance	1.5 to 3.5 ohms
Ignition coil secondary resistance (cap installed)	12 to 16 k-ohms
Ignition coil secondary resistance (without spark plug cap)	Not specified

Transmission

Belt width (service limit)	22.0 mm (0.866 inch)
Weight roller outer diameter	
Standard	22.92 to 23.08 mm (0.902 to 0.908 inch)
Limit	22.0 mm (0.866 inch)
Clutch lining thickness (service limit)	2.0 mm (0.079 inch)
Clutch spring free length	90.0 mm (3.354 inches)

Daelim S2-250, 2006 and later (continued)

Brakes
Brake fluid	DOT 4
Disc thickness (limit)	3.0 mm (0.118 inch)
Pad wear limit	To wear line

Tire pressures
Front	29 psi
Rear	
Rider only	29 psi
Rider and passenger	36 psi

Electrical system
Battery	
Capacity	12V-10Ah
Voltage (fully charged)	13.0 to 13.2 volts
Alternator	
Output (regulated)	14.0 to 15.0 volts
Charging coil resistance	0.6 to 1.6 ohms
Fuse	Not specified

Torque wrench settings
Note: *One foot-pound (ft-lb) of torque is equivalent to 12 inch-pounds (in-lbs) of torque. Torque values below approximately 15 foot-pounds are expressed in inch-pounds, because most foot-pound torque wrenches are not accurate at these smaller values.*

Engine oil filler screen cap	14 Nm (128 inch-lbs)
Engine oil drain plug	14 Nm (128 inch-lbs)
Transmission oil check bolt	Not specified
Valve cover bolts	Not specified
Camshaft holder nuts	24 Nm (18 ft-lbs) (1)
Cylinder head bolts	30 Nm (22 ft-lbs)
Cam chain tensioner bolt	12 Nm (106 inch-lbs)
Cam chain tensioner slipper bolt	10 Nm (87 inch-lbs)
Drive pulley nut	55 Nm (40 ft-lbs)
Water pump impeller	10 to 13 Nm (87 to 119 inch-lbs)
Clutch drive pulley nut	88 to 98 Nm (64 to 71 ft-lbs)
Clutch driven pulley nut	55 Nm (40 ft-lbs)
Alternator rotor nut	58 Nm (43 ft-lbs)
Starter clutch bolts	10 to 14 Nm (87 to 120 inch-lbs)
Crankcase bolts	Not specified
Engine hanger bracket nut	
To engine	48 Nm (35 ft-lbs)
To frame	38 Nm (28 ft-lbs)
Front axle nut	59 Nm (43 ft-lbs)
Rear axle nut	Not specified
Steering stem nut	68 Nm (51 ft-lbs)
Steering stem bearing adjustment nut	
First step	2.45 Nm (22 inch-lbs)
Second step	Loosen 1/8 turn
Handlebar to steering stem bolt	38 to 48 Nm (28 to 35 ft-lbs)
Steering stem locknut	68 Nm (51 ft-lbs)
Steering stem to fork bolt	60 Nm (43 ft-lbs)
Front fork damper rod bolts	20 Nm (14 ft-lbs) (2)
Front fork to triple clamp bolts	Not specified
Rear shock bolts	
Upper	38 Nm (28 ft-lbs)
Lower	19 to 29 Nm (14 to 21 ft-lbs)
Swingarm mounting bolts	Not specified
Front brake bolts	
Caliper bolts	30 Nm (22 ft-lbs)
Brake hose union bolts	34 Nm (25 ft-lbs)
Rear caliper bolt	19 to 29 Nm (14 to 21 ft-lbs)

1. *Apply engine oil to the threads.*
2. *Apply non-permanent thread locking agent to the threads.*

Honda CHF50 Metropolitan, 2002 and later

Engine	49.4 cc single-cylinder OHC 4-stroke
Cooling system	Liquid cooled
Fuel system	Flat valve CV carburetor
Ignition system	DC-CDI
Transmission	Variable speed automatic, belt driven
Suspension	Telescopic fork front, swingarm with single shock rear
Brakes	Drum front and rear
Tires	90/90-10 50J front and rear
Wheelbase	1190 mm (46.9 inches)
Curb weight	
2002 through 2005	79 kg (174 lbs)
2006 and later	80 kg (176 lbs)
Fuel tank capacity	Not specified

Engine

Spark plug type	
Standard	NGK CR8EH-9, ND U24FER-9
Cold climates	NGK CR7EH-9 ND U22FER-9
Extended high speed riding	NGK CR9EH-9, ND U27FER-9
Electrode gap	0.8 to 0.9 mm (0.031 to 0.035 inch)
Idle speed (rpm)	2000 +/-100 rpm
Engine oil type	SG or higher 4-stroke engine oil, JASO standard MA, (without moly additives), SAE 10W-30
Engine oil capacity (drain and fill)	600 cc (20 fl oz)
Engine coolant type	50/50 ethylene glycol antifreeze and soft water
Engine coolant capacity	
Radiator and engine	300 cc (10 fl oz)
Reserve tank	180 cc (6 fl oz)
Bore x stroke	37.8 x 44.0 mm (1.49 x 1.73 inches)
Piston diameter (service limit)	37.72 mm (1.485 inches)
Piston to bore clearance (service limit)	0.08 mm (0.003 inch)
Piston ring installed end gap	
Top	
Standard	0.05 to 0.015 mm (0.002 to 0.006 inch)
Limit	0.40 mm (0.016 inch)
Second	
Standard	0.05 to 0.017 mm (0.002 to 0.007 inch)
Limit	0.40 mm (0.016 inch)
Oil ring side rail	
Standard	0.10 to 0.60 mm (0.004 to 0.024 inch)
Limit	0.80 mm (0.031 inch)
Piston ring side clearance	
Top	
Standard	0.020 to 0.050 mm (0.0008 to 0.0020 inch)
Limit	0.08 mm (0.003 inch)
Second	
Standard	0.015 to 0.050 mm (0.0006 to 0.0020 inch)
Limit	0.08 mm (0.003 inch)

Fuel system

Throttle twistgrip freeplay	2 to 6 mm (1/8 to 1/4 inch)
Main jet	72
Slow jet	35 x 35
Needle type/position	Not specified
Pilot screw setting	
2002 through 2005	
All except P-type	2-3/4 turns out
P-type	2-1/8 turns out
2006 and later	2-1/4 turns out
Float level	13 mm (0.5 inch)

Honda CHF50 Metropolitan, 2002 and later (continued)

Ignition system

Ignition coil peak voltage	80 volts minimum
Ignition pulse generator peak voltage	0.7 volts minimum

Transmission and final drive

Belt width (service limit)	17.15 mm (0.68 inch)
Weight roller outer diameter	
Standard	15.92 to 16.08 mm (0.627 to 0.623 inch)
Limit	15.4 mm (0.61 inch)
Clutch lining thickness (service limit)	2.0 mm (0.08 inch)
Clutch spring free length (service limit)	75.3 mm (2.96 inch)

Brakes

Drum internal diameter (service limit, front and rear)	95.5 mm (3.76 inch)
Brake lining thickness (service limit)	1.0 mm (0.04 inch)
Brake freeplay (front and rear)	10 to 20 mm (3/8 to 3/4 inch)

Tire pressures

Front and rear	18 psi

Electrical system

Battery	
Capacity	12V-6Ah
Voltage (fully charged)	13.0 to 13.2 volts
Alternator	
Output (regulated)	15.5 volts at 5000 rpm
Charging coil resistance	0.05 to 0.5 ohms
Fuse	
Main	15 amps
Secondary	10 amps

Torque wrench settings

Note: One foot-pound (ft-lb) of torque is equivalent to 12 inch-pounds (in-lbs) of torque. Torque values below approximately 15 foot-pounds are expressed in inch-pounds, because most foot-pound torque wrenches are not accurate at these smaller values.

Valve cover bolts	Not specified
Cylinder head bolts	12 Nm (108 inch-lbs)
Cam chain tensioner lifter screw (2002 through 2005)	3.9 Nm (35 inch-lbs)
Cam sprocket bolts	8.8 Nm (78 inch-lbs)
Drive pulley face nut	32 Nm (24 ft-lbs)*
Driven pulley nut	39 Nm (29 ft-lbs)
Gearbox oil check bolt	13 Nm (108 inch-lbs)
Engine oil drain bolt	25 Nm (18 ft-lbs)
Engine oil strainer cap	20 Nm (14 ft-lbs)
Alternator rotor nut	44 Nm (33 ft-lbs)
Alternator cooling fan bolts	12 Nm (108 inch-lbs)
Crankcase bolts	12 Nm (108 inch-lbs)
Front axle nut	44 Nm (33 ft-lbs)
Rear axle nut	118 Nm (87 ft-lbs)
Handlebar post nut	42 Nm (31 ft-lbs)
Steering stem top cone race	
First step	11 Nm (96 inch-lbs)
Second step	Loosen 45-degrees
Third step	Hand tighten
Steering stem bearing locknut	69 Nm (51 ft-lbs)
Front brake arm nut	5.8 Nm (52 inch-lbs)
Rear brake arm bolt	4.9 Nm (46 inch-lbs)
Front fork pinch bolts	Not specified
Rear shock absorber bolts	26 Nm (20 ft-lbs)

*Coat the threads and flange surface with engine oil.

Honda NB50 Aero, 1985 through 1987

Engine	49.3 cc single-cylinder 2-stroke
Cooling system	Air cooled
Fuel system	Piston valve carburetor
Ignition system	CDI
Transmission	Variable speed automatic, belt driven
Suspension	Trailing link front, swingarm with single shock rear
Brakes	Drum front and rear
Tires	2.75-10 front and rear
Wheelbase	1130 mm (44.5 inches)
Weight (dry)	
1985	57 kg (125.8 lbs)
1986 and later	58 kg (127.9 lbs)
Fuel tank capacity	3.7 liters (1 gal)

Engine

Spark plug type	
Standard	
1985	NGK BPR6HS, ND W20FPR
1986 and later	NGK BPR6HSA, ND W20FPR-L
Cold climates	
1985	NGK BPR4HS, ND W14FPR-L
1986 and later	NGK BPR4HSA, ND W14FPR-L
Extended high speed riding	
1985	NGK BPR8HS, ND W24FPR
1986 and later	NGK BPR8HSA, ND W24FPR-L
Electrode gap	0.6 to 0.7 mm (0.024 to 0.028 inch)
Idle speed (rpm)	1800 +/-100 rpm
Engine oil type	Honda 2-stroke injector oil or equivalent
Oil tank capacity	800 cc (27 fl oz)
Bore x stroke	41.0 x 37.4 mm (1.61 x 1.47 inches)
Piston diameter (service limit)	40.9 mm (1.610 inches)
Piston to bore clearance (service limit)	0.10 mm (0.004 inch)
Piston ring installed end gap (top and second)	
Standard	0.10 to 0.25 mm (0.004 to 0.010 inch)
Limit	0.50 mm (0.020 inch)

Fuel system

Throttle twistgrip freeplay	2 to 6 mm (1/8 to 1/4 inch)
Main jet	Not specified
Slow jet	Not specified
Needle type/position	Not specified
Air screw setting	
1985	1-1/4 turns out
1986 and later	1-3/4 turns out
Float level	12.2 mm (0.48 inch)

Ignition system

Ignition coil primary resistance	0.2 to 0.3 ohm
Ignition coil secondary resistance	
Without spark plug cap installed	3.4 to 4.2 k-ohms
With spark plug cap installed	8.0 to 11.5 k-ohms
Ignition pulse generator resistance	50 to 200 ohms

Transmission

Belt width (service limit)	14.0 mm (0.55 inch)
Weight roller outer diameter	
Standard	15.92 to 16.08 mm (0.627 to 0.633 inch)
Limit	15.4 mm (0.606 inch)
Clutch lining thickness (service limit)	2.0 mm (0.08 inch)
Clutch spring free length (service limit)	88.8 mm (3.50 inch)

Honda NB50 Aero, 1985 through 1987 (continued)

Brakes
Drum internal diameter (service limit)
    Front .... 80.5 mm (3.17 inches)
    Rear .... 95.5 mm (3.76 inches)
Brake lining thickness (service limit)................................ 2.0 mm (0.08 inch)
Brake freeplay (front and rear)....................................... 10 to 20 mm (3/8 to 3/4 inch)

Tire pressures
Front .... 21 psi
Rear .... 28 psi

Electrical system
Battery
    Capacity 12V-3Ah
    Voltage (fully charged)... 13.1 volts
Alternator
    Output (regulated) .... 14 to 15 volts
    Stator coil resistance
        White to ground.. 0.2 to 0.9 ohms
        Yellow to ground... 0.1 to 0.8 ohms
    Exciter coil resistance .... 600 to 1000 ohms
    Fuse .... 7 amps

Torque wrench settings
Note: One foot-pound (ft-lb) of torque is equivalent to 12 inch-pounds (in-lbs) of torque. Torque values below approximately 15 foot-pounds are expressed in inch-pounds, because most foot-pound torque wrenches are not accurate at these smaller values.

Cylinder head bolts .... 9 to 12 Nm (84 to 108 inch-lbs)*
Drive and driven pulley nuts.. 35 to 40 Nm (25 to 29 ft-lbs)
Alternator rotor nut... 35 to 40 Nm (25 to 29 ft-lbs)
Engine mounting bolt .... 32 to 38 Nm (23 to 27 ft-lbs)
Crankcase bolts .... Not specified
Front axle nut .... 40 to 50 Nm (29 to 36 ft-lbs)
Rear axle nut .... 100 to 120 Nm (72 to 87 ft-lbs)
Steering stem bearing top cone race.............................. Snug, then back off 1/8 turn
Steering stem bearing locknut .... 5 to 13 Nm (48 to 120 inch-lbs)
Steering stem nut .... 80 to 120 Nm (58 to 87 ft-lbs)
Fork pivot arm .... 24 to 30 Nm (17 to 22 ft-lbs)
Front shock absorber upper mounting bolt .... 20 to 30 Nm (14 to 22 ft-lbs)
Front shock absorber lower mounting bolt .... 0.8 to 1.2 Nm (7 to 11 inch-lbs)
Front shock absorber lower mounting nut .... 15 to 20 Nm (11 to 14 ft-lbs)
Rear shock absorber upper bolt .... 30 to 40 Nm (22 to 29 ft-lbs)
Rear shock absorber lower bolt .... 20 to 30 Nm (14 to 22 ft-lbs)
Front and rear brake arms... 4 to 7 Nm (36 to 60 inch-lbs)

Tighten with the engine cold.

Honda NPS 50 Ruckus, 2003 and later

Engine	49.4 cc single-cylinder OHC 4-stroke
Cooling system	Liquid cooled
Fuel system	Flat valve CV carburetor
Ignition system	DC-CDI
Transmission	Variable speed automatic, belt driven
Suspension	Telescopic front, swingarm with single shock rear
Brakes	Drum front and rear
Tires	
2003 through 2005	
Front	120/90-10 54J
Rear	120/90-10 57J
2006 and later	
Front	130/90-10 59J
Rear	130/90-10 61J
Wheelbase	1265 mm (49.8 inches)
Weight (dry)	82 kg (181 lbs)
Fuel tank capacity	Not specified

Engine

Spark plug type	
2003 through 2005	
Standard	NGK CR8EH-9, ND U24FER-9
Cold climates	NGK CR7EH-9, ND U22FER-9
Extended high speed riding	NGK CR9EH-9, ND U27FER-9
2006 and later	
Standard	NGK CR8EH-9
Cold climates	NGK CR7EH-9
Extended high speed riding	NGK CR9EF-9
Electrode gap	0.8 to 0.9 mm (0.031 to 0.035 inch)
Idle speed (rpm)	2000 +/-100 rpm
Engine oil type	SG or higher 4-stroke engine oil, SAE 10W-30, JASO standard MA
Engine oil capacity (drain and fill)	600 cc (20 fl oz)
Engine coolant type	50/50 ethylene glycol antifreeze and soft water
Engine coolant capacity	
Radiator end engine	0.48 liter (16 fl oz)
Reserve tank	0.28 liter (5 fl oz)
Bore x stroke	37.8 x 44.0 mm (1.49 x 1.73 inches)
Piston diameter (service limit)	37.72 mm (1.485 inches)
Piston to bore clearance (service limit)	0.08 mm (0.003 inch)
Piston ring installed end gap	
Top	
Standard	0.05 to 0.015 mm (0.002 to 0.006 inch)
Limit	0.40 mm (0.016 inch)
Second	
Standard	0.05 to 0.017 mm (0.002 to 0.007 inch)
Limit	0.40 mm (0.016 inch)
Oil ring side rail	
Standard	0.10 to 0.60 mm (0.004 to 0.024 inch)
Limit	0.80 mm (0.031 inch)
Piston ring side clearance	
Top	
Standard	0.020 to 0.050 mm (0.0008 to 0.0020 inch)
Limit	0.08 mm (0.003 inch)
Second	
Standard	0.015 to 0.050 mm (0.0006 to 0.0020 inch)
Limit	0.08 mm (0.003 inch)

Fuel system

Throttle twistgrip freeplay	2 to 6 mm (1/8 to 1/4 inch)
Main jet	75
Slow jet	35 x 35
Needle type/position	Not specified
Pilot screw setting	2-1/4 turns out
Float level	13 mm (0.5 inch)

Honda NPS 50 Ruckus, 2003 and later (continued)

Ignition system
Ignition coil peak voltage	80 volts minimum
Ignition pulse generator peak voltage	0.7 volts minimum

Transmission and final drive
Belt width (service limit)	17.15 mm (0.68 inch)
Weight roller outer diameter	
Standard	15.92 to 16.08 mm (0.627 to 0.623 inch)
Limit	15.4 mm (0.61 inch)
Clutch lining thickness (service limit)	2.0 mm (0.08 inch)
Clutch spring free length (service limit)	86.0 mm (3.39 inches)

Brakes
Drum internal diameter (service limit, front and rear)	95.5 mm (3.76 inches)
Brake lining thickness (service limit)	1.0 mm (0.04 inch)
Brake freeplay (front and rear)	10 to 20 mm (3/8 to 3/4 inch)

Tire pressures
Front and rear	25 psi

Electrical system
Battery	
Capacity	12V-6Ah
Voltage (fully charged)	13.0 to 13.2 volts
Alternator	
Output (regulated)	15.5 volts at 5000 rpm
Charging coil resistance	0.05 to 0.5 ohms
Fuse	
Main	20 amps
Secondary	10 amps
Final drive oil	
Type	SAE 90 gear oil
Capacity	0.1 liter (3-1/3 fl oz)
Coolant temperature sensor resistance	
At 50-degrees C/122-degrees F	690 to 860 ohms
At 130-degrees C/266-degrees F	2.6 to 3.2 ohms

Torque wrench settings
Note: One foot-pound (ft-lb) of torque is equivalent to 12 inch-pounds (in-lbs) of torque. Torque values below approximately 15 foot-pounds are expressed in inch-pounds, because most foot-pound torque wrenches are not accurate at these smaller values.

Valve cover bolts	Not specified
Cylinder head bolts	12 Nm (108 inch-lbs)
Cam chain tensioner lifter screw (2003 through 2005)	4.2 Nm (37 inch-lbs)
Cam sprocket bolt	8.8 Nm (78 inch-lbs)
Drive pulley face nut	32 Nm (24 ft-lbs)
Driven pulley nut	39 Nm (29 ft-lbs)
Gearbox drain plug	13 Nm (108 inch-lbs)
Engine oil drain bolt	25 Nm (18 ft-lbs)
Alternator rotor nut	44 Nm (33 ft-lbs)
Alternator cooling fan bolts	7.8 Nm (70 inch-lbs)
Crankcase bolts	12 Nm (108 inch-lbs)
Front axle nut	44 Nm (33 ft-lbs)
Rear axle nut	118 Nm (87 ft-lbs)*
Handlebar post nut	42 Nm (31 ft-lbs)
Steering stem top cone race	
First step	11 Nm (96 inch-lbs)
Second step	Loosen 45-degrees
Third step	Hand tighten
Steering stem locknut	69 Nm (51 ft-lbs)
Front brake arm nut	5.4 Nm (48 inch-lbs)
Rear brake arm bolt	4.9 Nm (43 inch-lbs)
Front fork pinch bolts	Not specified
Rear shock absorber upper bolt	38 Nm (28 ft-lbs)
Rear shock absorber lower bolt	26 Nm (20 ft-lbs)

1. Coat the threads with engine oil.
2. Replace the bolt with a new one whenever it's removed.

Honda NQ50 Spree, 1984 through 1987

Engine	49 cc single-cylinder 2-stroke
Cooling system	Air cooled
Fuel system	Piston valve carburetor
Ignition system	CDI
Transmission	Variable speed automatic, belt driven
Suspension	Telescopic fork front, swingarm with single shock rear
Brakes	Drum front and rear
Tires	2.50-10 front and rear
Wheelbase	1065 mm (41.9 inches)
Weight (dry)	
1984 and 1985	39 kg (86 lbs)
1986	41.8 kg (92 lbs)
1987	42.5 kg (94 lbs)
Fuel tank capacity	2.5 liters (0.66 gal)

Engine

Spark plug type	
Standard	
1984 and 1985	NGK BPR6HS, ND W20FPR
1986 and later	NGK BPR6HSA, ND W20FPR-L
Cold climates	
1984 and 1985	NGK BPR4HS, ND W14FPR-L
1986 and later	NGK BPR4HSA, ND W14FPR-L
Extended high speed riding	
1984 and 1985	NGK BPR8HS, ND W24FPR
1986 and later	NGK BPR8HSA, ND W24FPR-L
Electrode gap	0.6 to 0.7 mm (0.024 to 0.028 inch)
Idle speed (rpm)	1800 +/-100 rpm
Engine oil type	Honda 2-stroke injector oil or equivalent
Oil tank capacity	800 cc (27 fl oz)
Bore x stroke	41.0 x 37.4 mm (1.61 x 1.47 inches)
Piston diameter (service limit)	40.9 mm (1.610 inches)
Piston to bore clearance (service limit)	0.10 mm (0.004 inch)
Piston ring installed end gap (top and second)	
Standard	0.10 to 0.25 mm (0.004 to 0.010 inch)
Limit	0.50 mm (0.020 inch)

Fuel system

Throttle twistgrip freeplay	2 to 6 mm (1/8 to 1/4 inch)
Main jet	Not specified
Slow jet	Not specified
Needle type/position	Not specified
Air screw setting	
1984 and 1985	1-7/8 turns out
1986	1-1/2 turns out
1987	1-3/8 turns out
Float level	12.2 mm (0.48 inch)

Ignition system

Ignition coil primary resistance	0.1 to 0.3 ohm
Ignition coil secondary resistance (without spark plug cap)	7.4 to 11.0 k-ohms
Ignition pulse generator resistance	50 to 200 ohms

Transmission

Belt width (service limit)	10.5 mm (0.41 inch)
Weight roller outer diameter	Not applicable
Standard	15.92 to 16.08 mm (0.627 to 0.633 inch)
Limit	15.4 mm (0.606 inch)
Clutch lining thickness (service limit)	1.5 mm (0.06 inch)
Clutch spring free length (service limit)	68.0 mm (2.7 inches)

Honda NQ50 Spree, 1984 through 1987 (continued)

Brakes

Drum internal diameter (service limit)
  Front .... Not specified
  Rear .... 80.5 mm (3.17 inches)
Brake lining thickness (service limit)
  Front .... Not specified
  Rear .... 1.5 mm (0.06 inch)
Brake freeplay (front and rear) .... 10 to 20 mm (3/8 to 3/4 inch)

Tire pressures

Front .... 18 psi
Rear .... 24 psi

Electrical system

Battery
  Capacity 12V-3Ah
  Voltage (fully charged) .... 13.1 volts
Alternator
  Output (regulated) .... 14 to 15 volts
  Charging coil resistance
    1984 and 1985 .... 0.5 to 3.0 ohms
    1986 and later .... 0.2 to 0.9 ohms
  Lighting coil resistance (yellow to ground)
    1984 and 1985 .... 0.3 to 2.0 ohms
    1986 and later .... 0.1 to 0.8 ohms
  Exciter coil resistance .... 750 to 1200 ohms
  Fuse .... 7 amps

Torque wrench settings

Note: One foot-pound (ft-lb) of torque is equivalent to 12 inch-pounds (in-lbs) of torque. Torque values below approximately 15 foot-pounds are expressed in inch-pounds, because most foot-pound torque wrenches are not accurate at these smaller values.

Cylinder head bolts .... 8 to 12 Nm (72 to 108 inch-lbs)*
Drive and driven pulley nuts .... 35 to 40 Nm (25 to 29 ft-lbs)
Alternator rotor nut .... 35 to 40 Nm (25 to 29 ft-lbs)
Engine hanger bolt .... 35 to 45 Nm (25 to 33 ft-lbs)
Crankcase bolts .... Not specified
Front axle nut .... 40 to 50 Nm (29 to 36 ft-lbs)
Rear axle nut .... 65 to 80 Nm (47 to 58 ft-lbs)
Handlebar pinch bolt .... 40 to 50 Nm (29 to 36 ft-lbs)
Steering stem bearing nut
  First step .... 5 to 13 Nm (48 to 108 inch-lbs)
  Second step .... Loosen 1/8 turn
Steering stem locknut
  1984 through 1986 .... 80 to 120 Nm (58 to 87 ft-lbs)
  1987 .... 60 to 80 Nm (43 to 58)
Rear shock absorber upper bolt
  1984 through 1986 .... 30 to 45 Nm (22 to 33 ft-lbs)
  1987 .... 24 to 30 Nm (17 to 22 ft-lbs)
Rear shock absorber lower bolt .... 20 to 30 Nm (14 to 22 ft-lbs)
Front and rear brake arms .... 4 to 7 Nm (36 to 60 inch-lbs)

Tighten with the engine cold.

Honda SA50 Elite, 1988 through 2001

Engine	49.4 cc single-cylinder 2-stroke
Cooling system	Air cooled
Fuel system	Piston valve carburetor
Ignition system	CDI
Transmission	Variable speed automatic, belt driven
Suspension	Trailing link front, swingarm with single shock rear
Brakes	Drum front and rear
Tires	
1988 through 1993	3.00-10 4PR front and rear
1994 through 2001	3.00-10 42J front and rear
Wheelbase	
1988 through 1993	1160 mm (45.7 inches)
1994 through 2001	1170 mm (46.1 inches)
Weight (dry)	
1988 through 1993	62.4 kg (138 lbs)
1994 through 2001	
SA50	65.0 kg (143 lbs)
SA50P	65.2 kg (144 lbs)
Fuel tank capacity	4.6 liters (1.22 gal)

Engine

Spark plug type	
Standard	
1988 through 1993	NGK BPR6HSA, ND W20FPR-L
1994 through 2001	NGK BR6HSA, ND W20FR-L
Cold climates	
1988 through 1993	NGK BPR4HSA, ND W14FPR-L
1994 through 2001	NGK BR4HSA, ND W14FR-L
Extended high speed riding	
1988 through 1993	NGK BPR8HSA, ND W24FPR-L
1994 through 2001	NGK BR48SA, ND W24FR-L
Electrode gap	0.6 to 0.7 mm (0.024 to 0.028 inch)
Idle speed (rpm)	1800 +/-100 rpm
Engine oil type	Honda 2-stroke injector oil or equivalent
Oil tank capacity	800 cc (27 fl oz)
Bore x stroke	
1988 through 1993	41.0 x 37.4 mm (1.61 x 1.47 inches)
1994 through 2001	39.0 x 41.4 mm (1.54 x 1.63 inches)
Piston diameter (service limit)	
1998 through 1993	40.9 mm (1.610 inches)
1994 through 2001	38.9 mm (1.531 inches)
Piston to bore clearance (service limit)	Not specified
Piston ring installed end gap (top and second)	
Standard	0.10 to 0.25 mm (0.004 to 0.010 inch)
Limit	
1988 through 1993	0.50 mm (0.020 inch)
1994 through 2001	0.40 mm (0.016 inch)

Fuel system

Throttle twistgrip freeplay	2 to 6 mm (1/8 to 1/4 inch)
Main jet	
1988 through 1993	88
1994 through 2001	
SA50	78
SA50P	68
Slow jet	35
Needle type/position	Not specified/second groove
Air screw setting	
1988 through 1993	1-3/8 turns out
1994 through 2001	
SA50	1-7/8 turns out
SA50P	1-3/4 turns out
Float level	12.2 mm (0.48 inch)

Honda SA50 Elite, 1988 through 2001 (continued)

Ignition system
Ignition coil primary resistance
    1988 and 1989 .... 0.1 to 0.2 ohms
    1990 through 1993 .... 0.1 to 0.3 ohms
    1994 through 2001 .... 0.1 to 0.4 ohms
Ignition coil secondary resistance
    Without spark plug cap installed
        1988 and 1989 .... 3.7 to 4.5 k-ohms
        1990 and 1993 .... 2.7 to 4.5 k-ohms
        1994 through 2001 .... 2.2 to 4.4 k-ohms
    With spark plug cap installed
        1988 and 1989 .... 7.4 to 11.0 k-ohms
        1990 and 1993 .... 6.4 to 11.0 k-ohms
        1994 through 2001 .... 5.0 to 11.0 k-ohms
Ignition pulse generator resistance .... 50 to 200 ohms

Transmission
Belt width (service limit) .... 15.0 mm (0.59 inch)
Weight roller outer diameter
    Standard .... 15.92 to 16.08 mm (0.627 to 0.633 inch)
    Limit .... 15.4 mm (0.606 inch)
Clutch lining thickness (service limit) .... 2.0 mm (0.08 inch)
Clutch spring free length (service limit) .... 92.8 mm (3.65 inch)

Brakes
Drum internal diameter (service limit)
    Front .... 80.5 mm (3.17 inches)
    Rear .... 95.5 mm (3.76 inches)
Brake lining thickness (service limit) .... 2.0 mm (0.08 inch)
Brake freeplay (front and rear) .... 10 to 20 mm (3/8 to 3/4 inch)

Tire pressures
Front .... 21 psi
Rear .... 28 psi

Electrical system
Battery
    Capacity 12V-3Ah
    Voltage (fully charged) .... 12.3 volts minimum
Alternator
    Output (regulated) .... 13.5 to 15 volts
    Lighting coil resistance .... 0.1 to 0.8 ohms
    Charging coil resistance .... 0.2 to 0.9 ohms
    Fuse .... 10 amps

Torque wrench settings
Note: One foot-pound (ft-lb) of torque is equivalent to 12 inch-pounds (in-lbs) of torque. Torque values below approximately 15 foot-pounds are expressed in inch-pounds, because most foot-pound torque wrenches are not accurate at these smaller values.

Cylinder head bolts .... 10 Nm (84 inch-lbs)*
Drive pulley nut
    1988 through 1993 .... 38 Nm (27 ft-lbs)
    1994 through 2001 .... 60 Nm (43 ft-lbs)*
Driven pulley nut
    1988 through 1993 .... 38 Nm (27 ft-lbs)
    1994 through 2001 .... 40 Nm (29 ft-lbs)
Clutch locknut
    1988 through 1993 .... 38 Nm (27 ft-lbs)
    1994 and later .... 55 Nm (40 ft-lbs)
Alternator rotor nut .... 38 Nm (27 ft-lbs)
Engine mounting bolt .... 50 Nm (36 ft-lbs)
Engine bracket bolt .... 50 Nm (36 ft-lbs)
Crankcase bolts .... 10 Nm (84 inch-lbs)

Apply engine oil to the threads and seating surfaces.

Front axle nut	45 Nm (33 ft-lbs)
Rear axle nut	
1988 through 1993	110 Nm (80 ft-lbs)
1994 through 2001	120 Nm (87 ft-lbs)
Steering stem bearing top cone race	Snug, then loosen 1/8 turn
Steering stem bearing locknut	9 Nm (78 inch-lbs)
Steering stem locknut	100 Nm (72 ft-lbs)
Fork pivot arm	27 Nm (20 ft-lbs)
Front shock absorber upper mounting bolt	27 Nm (20 ft-lbs)
Front shock absorber lower mounting bolt	1 Nm (9 inch-lbs)
Front shock absorber lower mounting nut	18 Nm (159 inch-lbs)
Rear shock absorber upper bolt	40 Nm (29 ft-lbs)
Rear shock absorber lower bolt	25 Nm (18 ft-lbs)
Front brake arm	6 Nm (52 inch-lbs)
Rear brake arm	5 Nm (43 inch-lbs)

Honda SB50 Elite, 1988 through 2001

Engine	49 cc single-cylinder 2-stroke
Cooling system	Air cooled
Fuel system	Piston valve carburetor
Ignition system	CDI
Transmission	Variable speed automatic, belt driven
Suspension	Telescopic front, swingarm with single shock rear
Brakes	Drum front and rear
Tires	250-10 4PR front and rear
Wheelbase	1090 mm (42.9 inches)
Weight (dry)	49 kg (108 lbs)
Fuel tank capacity	Not specified

Engine

Spark plug type	
Standard	NGK BPR6HSA, ND W20FPR-L
Cold climates	NGK BPR4HSA, ND W14FPR-L
Extended high speed riding	NGK BPR8HSA, ND W24FPR-L
Electrode gap	0.6 to 0.7 mm (0.024 to 0.028 inch)
Idle speed (rpm)	1800 +/-100 rpm
Engine oil type	Honda 2-stroke injector oil or equivalent
Oil tank capacity	Not specified
Bore x stroke	41.0 x 37.4 mm (1.61 x 1.47 inches)
Piston diameter (service limit)	40.9 mm (1.610 inches)
Piston to bore clearance (service limit)	0.10 mm (0.004 inch)
Piston ring installed end gap (top and second)	
Standard	0.10 to 0.25 mm (0.004 to 0.010 inch)
Limit	0.40 mm (0.016 inch)

Fuel system

Throttle twistgrip freeplay	2 to 6 mm (1/8 to 1/4 inch)
Main jet	68
Slow jet	Not specified
Needle type/position	Not specified/second groove
Air screw setting	
SB50	1-7/8 turns out
SB50P	1-3/4 turns out
Float level	12.2 mm (0.48 inch)

Honda SB50 Elite, 1988 through 2001 (continued)

Ignition system
Ignition coil primary resistance... 0.2 to 0.2 ohm
Ignition coil secondary resistance (with plug cap installed) .... 8.2 to 9.3 k-ohms
Ignition pulse generator resistance .... 50 to 200 ohms

Transmission
Belt width (service limit)... 10.4 mm (0.41 inch)
Clutch lining thickness (service limit)................................... 1.5 mm (0.06 inch)
Clutch spring free length (service limit) .... 56.0 mm (2.20 inches)

Brakes
Drum internal diameter (service limit, front and rear) .... 80.5 mm (3.17 inches)
Brake lining thickness (service limit).................................... 1.5 mm (0.06 inch)
Brake freeplay (front and rear) .... 10 to 20 mm (3/8 to 3/4 inch)

Tire pressures
Front .... 22 psi
Rear .... 33 psi

Electrical system
Battery
  Capacity 12V-3Ah
  Voltage (fully charged).. Not specified
Alternator
  Output (regulated) .... 13.5 to 15.5 volts
  Lighting coil resistance .... 0.2 to 0.8 ohms
  Charging coil resistance.. 0.3 to 0.9 ohms
  Exciter coil resistance .... 500 to 900 ohms
  Fuse .... 7 amps

Torque wrench settings
Note: *One foot-pound (ft-lb) of torque is equivalent to 12 inch-pounds (in-lbs) of torque. Torque values below approximately 15 foot-pounds are expressed in inch-pounds, because most foot-pound torque wrenches are not accurate at these smaller values.*

Cylinder head bolts .... 10 Nm (84 inch-lbs)*
Drive and driven pulley nuts .... 38 Nm (27 ft-lbs)
Clutch locknut (28 mm) .... 38 Nm (27 ft-lbs)
Alternator rotor nut .... 38 Nm (27 ft-lbs)
Engine mounting bolt .... 40 Nm (29 ft-lbs)
Engine bracket bolt .... 55 Nm (40 ft-lbs)
Crankcase bolts .... 10 Nm (84 inch-lbs)
Front axle nut .... 45 Nm (33 ft-lbs)
Rear axle nut .... 73 Nm (53 ft-lbs)
Steering stem bearing nut .... Hand tight (no vertical play)
Steering stem locknut .... 70 Nm (51 ft-lbs)
Handlebar pinch bolt .... 45 Nm (33 ft-lbs)
Rear shock absorber upper nut .... 38 Nm (27 ft-lbs)
Rear shock absorber lower bolt .... 27 Nm (20 ft-lbs)
Front and rear brake arms... 6 Nm (52 inch-lbs)

Tighten while the engine is cold.

Honda SE50 Elite, 1987

Engine	49.4 cc single-cylinder 2-stroke
Cooling system	Air cooled
Fuel system	Piston valve carburetor
Ignition system	CDI
Transmission	Variable speed automatic, belt driven
Suspension	Trailing link front, swingarm with single shock rear
Brakes	Drum front and rear
Tires	2.75-10 front and rear
Wheelbase	1180 mm (46.5 inches)
Weight (dry)	57.5 kg (125.8 lbs)
Fuel tank capacity	Not specified

Engine

Spark plug type	
Standard	NGK BR6HSA, ND W20FPR-L
Cold climates	NGK BPR4HSA, ND W14FPR-L
Extended high speed riding	NGK BPR8HSA, ND W24FPR
Electrode gap	0.6 to 0.7 mm (0.024 to 0.028 inch)
Idle speed (rpm)	1800 +/-100 rpm
Engine oil type	Honda 2-stroke injector oil or equivalent
Oil tank capacity	900 cc (30 fl oz)
Bore x stroke	41.0 x 37.4 mm (1.61 x 1.47 inches)
Piston diameter (service limit)	40.9 mm (1.610 inches)
Piston to bore clearance (service limit)	0.10 mm (0.004 inch)
Piston ring installed end gap (top and second)	
Standard	0.10 to 0.25 mm (0.004 to 0.010 inch)
Limit	0.40 mm (0.020 inch)

Fuel system

Throttle twistgrip freeplay	2 to 6 mm (1/8 to 1/4 inch)
Main jet	
SE50	85
SE50P	82
Slow jet	35
Needle type/position	Not specified
Air screw setting	
SE50	1-3/4 turns out
SE50P	1-1/2 turns out
Float level	12.2 mm (0.48 inch)

Ignition system

Ignition coil primary resistance	0.1 to 0.2 ohm
Ignition coil secondary resistance	
Without spark plug cap installed	3.6 to 4.6 k-ohms
With spark plug cap installed	8.6 to 9.6 k-ohms
Ignition pulse generator resistance	50 to 200 ohms

Transmission

Belt width (service limit)	14.5 mm (0.57 inch)
Weight roller outer diameter	
Standard	15.92 to 16.08 mm (0.627 to 0.633 inch)
Limit	15.4 mm (0.606 inch)
Clutch lining thickness (service limit)	2.0 mm (0.08 inch)
Clutch spring free length (service limit)	88.8 mm (3.50 inches)

Brakes

Drum internal diameter (service limit)	
Front	80.5 mm (3.17 inches)
Rear	95.5 mm (3.76 inches)
Brake lining thickness (service limit)	2.0 mm (0.08 inch)
Brake freeplay (front and rear)	10 to 20 mm (3/8 to 3/4 inch)

Honda SE50 Elite, 1987 (continued)

Tire pressures

Front .... 18 psi
Rear .... 28 psi

Electrical system

Battery
    Capacity 12V-3Ah
    Voltage (fully charged)................................. 13.0 to 13.2 volts
Alternator
    Output (regulated).. 13.5 to 15.5 volts
    Charging coil resistance.............................. 0.2 to 0.9 ohms
    Lighting coil resistance .... 0.1 to 0.8 ohms
    Fuse .... 10 amps

Torque wrench settings

Note: One foot-pound (ft-lb) of torque is equivalent to 12 inch-pounds (in-lbs) of torque. Torque values below approximately 15 foot-pounds are expressed in inch-pounds, because most foot-pound torque wrenches are not accurate at these smaller values.

Cylinder head bolts	8 to 12 Nm (72 to 108 inch-lbs)
Drive pulley nut..	50 to 60 Nm (36 to 43ft-lbs)
Driven pulley nut..	35 to 40 Nm (25 to 29 ft-lbs)
Driven pulley 28 mm nut..	35 to 40 Nm (25 to 29 ft-lbs)
Drive face seal bolts	3 to 6 Nm (24 to 48 inch-lbs)
Alternator rotor nut	35 to 40 Nm (25 to 29 ft-lbs)
Engine mounting bolt	32 to 38 Nm (23 to 27 ft-lbs)
Engine mounting bracket bolt	35 to 45 Nm (25 to 33 ft-lbs)
Crankcase bolts	Not specified
Front axle nut	40 to 50 Nm (29 to 36 ft-lbs)
Rear axle nut	100 to 120 Nm (72 to 87 ft-lbs)
Steering stem bearing top cone race...................................	Hand tight, no vertical play
Steering stem locknut	60 to 80 Nm (43 to 58 ft-lbs)
Fork pivot arm	24 to 30 Nm (17 to 22 ft-lbs)
Front shock absorber upper mounting bolt	24 to 30 Nm (17 to 22 ft-lbs)
Front shock absorber lower mounting bolt	0.8 to 1.2 Nm (7 to 11 inch-lbs)
Front shock absorber lower mounting nut	15 to 20 Nm (11 to 14 ft-lbs)
Rear shock absorber upper bolt	30 to 45 Nm (22 to 29 ft-lbs)
Rear shock absorber lower bolt	20 to 30 Nm (14 to 22 ft-lbs)
Front and rear brake arms...	4 to 7 Nm (36 to 60 inch-lbs)

Honda NH80 Aero, 1985

Engine	80 cc single-cylinder 2-stroke
Cooling system	Air cooled
Fuel system	Piston valve carburetor
Ignition system	CDI
Transmission	Variable speed automatic, belt driven
Suspension	Trailing link front, swingarm with single shock rear
Brakes	Drum front and rear
Tires	3.50-10 front and rear
Wheelbase	1185 mm (36.6 inches)
Weight (dry)	77 kg (170.0 lbs)
Fuel tank capacity	4.8 liters (1.2 gal)

Engine

Spark plug type	
Standard	NGK BPR6HSA, ND W20FPR-L
Cold climates	NGK BPR4HSA, ND W14FPR-L
Extended high speed riding	NGK BPR8HSA, ND W24FPR-L
Electrode gap	0.6 to 0.7 mm (0.024 to 0.028 inch)
Idle speed (rpm)	1800 +/-100 rpm
Engine oil type	Honda 2-stroke injector oil or equivalent
Oil tank capacity	1.2 liters (1.3 qt)
Bore x stroke	48.0 x 44.0 mm (1.89 x 1.73 inches)
Piston diameter (service limit)	47.9 mm (1.886 inches)
Piston to bore clearance (service limit)	0.10 mm (0.004 inch)
Piston ring installed end gap (top and second)	
Standard	0.15 to 0.35 mm (0.006 to 0.015 inch)
Limit	0.60 mm (0.024 inch)

Fuel system

Throttle twistgrip freeplay	2 to 6 mm (1/8 to 1/4 inch)
Main jet	88
Slow jet	Not specified
Needle type/position	Not specified
Air screw setting	1-3/8 turns out
Float level	8.5 mm (0.33 inch)

Ignition system

Ignition coil primary resistance	0.2 to 0.3 ohm
Ignition coil secondary resistance	
Without spark plug cap installed	3.4 to 4.2 k-ohms
With spark plug cap installed	8.0 to 8.5 k-ohms
Ignition pulse generator resistance	
Black/red to ground	100 to 400 ohms
Blue/yellow to ground	10 to 100 ohms

Transmission

Belt width (service limit)	13.5 mm (0.531 inch)
Weight roller outer diameter	
Standard	17.92 to 18.08 mm (0.706 to 0.712 inch)
Limit	17.4 mm (0.69 inch)
Clutch lining thickness (service limit)	2.0 mm (0.08 inch)
Clutch spring free length (service limit)	77.6 mm (3.06 inches)

Brakes

Drum internal diameter (service limit)	
Front	80.5 mm (3.17 inches)
Rear	95.5 mm (3.76 inches)
Brake lining thickness (service limit)	2.0 mm (0.08 inch)
Brake freeplay (front and rear)	10 to 20 mm (3/8 to 3/4 inch)

Honda NH80 Aero, 1985 (continued)

Tire pressures
Front .... 21 psi
Rear
    Up to 90 kg (200 lbs) load.. 24 psi
    90 kg (200 lbs) to maximum rated load .... 32 psi

Electrical system
Battery
    Capacity 12V-4Ah
    Voltage (fully charged)... 13.0 to 13.2 volts
Alternator
    Output (regulated) .... 14 to 15 volts
    Stator coil resistance
        White to ground... 0.2 to 0.9 ohms
        Yellow to ground.. 0.1 to 0.5 ohms
    Fuse .... 10 amps

Torque wrench settings
Note: *One foot-pound (ft-lb) of torque is equivalent to 12 inch-pounds (in-lbs) of torque. Torque values below approximately 15 foot-pounds are expressed in inch-pounds, because most foot-pound torque wrenches are not accurate at these smaller values.*

Cylinder head bolts	8 to 12 Nm (72 to 108 inch-lbs)*
Drive and driven pulley nuts	35 to 40 Nm (25 to 29 ft-lbs)
Alternator rotor nut	35 to 40 Nm (25 to 29 ft-lbs)
Crankcase bolts	8 to 12 Nm (72 to 108 inch-lbs)
Engine mounting bolt	27 to 33 Nm (20 to 24 ft-lbs)
Front axle nut	50 to 70 Nm (36 to 51 ft-lbs)
Rear axle nut	80 to 100 Nm (58 to 72 ft-lbs)
Steering stem bearing top cone race	Snug, then loosen 1/8 turn
Steering stem bearing nut	5 to 13 Nm (48 to 120 inch-lbs)
Steering stem locknut	120 to 150 Nm (87 to 108 ft-lbs)
Fork pivot arm bolt	24 to 30 Nm (17 to 22 ft-lbs)
Front shock absorber upper mounting bolt	20 to 24 Nm (14 to 17 ft-lbs)
Front shock absorber lower mounting bolt	0.8 to 1.2 Nm (7 to 11 inch-lbs)
Front shock absorber lower mounting nut	15 to 20 Nm (11 to 14 ft-lbs)
Rear shock absorber upper bolt	30 to 45 Nm (22 to 32 ft-lbs)
Rear shock absorber lower bolt	20 to 30 Nm (14 to 22 ft-lbs)
Front brake arm bolt	8 to 12 Nm (72 to 108 inch-lbs)
Front brake torque link bolt	24 to 30 Nm (17 to 22 ft-lbs)
Rear brake arm bolt	4 to 7 Nm (36 to 60 inch-lbs)

Tighten with the engine cold.

Honda CH80 Elite, 1985 through 2007

Engine	49.5 cc single-cylinder OHC 4-stroke
Cooling system	Air cooled
Fuel system	Change valve type carburetor
Ignition system	CDI
Transmission	Variable speed automatic, belt driven
Suspension	Pivot arm front, swingarm with single shock rear
Brakes	Drum front and rear
Tires	3.50-10 front and rear
Wheelbase	1170 mm (46.1 inches)
Weight (dry)	78 kg (172 lbs)
Fuel tank capacity	5.0 liters (1.3 gal)

Engine

Spark plug type	
Standard	NGK CR7HS, ND U22FSR-U
Cold climates	NGK CR6HS, ND U20FSR-U
Extended high speed riding	NGK CR8HS, ND U24FSR-U
Electrode gap	0.6 to 0.7 mm (0.024 to 0.028 inch)
Idle speed (rpm)	1700 +/-100 rpm
Engine oil type	SG or higher 4-stroke engine oil, SAE 10W-30, JASO standard MA
Engine oil capacity (drain and fill)	600 cc (20 fl oz)
Bore x stroke	49.5 x 41.1 mm (1.95 x 1.63 inches)
Piston diameter (service limit)	49.4 mm (1.945 inches)
Piston to bore clearance (service limit)	0.15 mm (0.006 inch)
Piston ring installed end gap	
Top	
Standard	0.1 to 0.3 mm (0.004 to 0.012 inch)
Limit	0.50 mm (0.020 inch)
Oil ring side rail	0.2 to 0.7 mm (0.008 to 0.028 inch)

Fuel system

Throttle twistgrip freeplay	2 to 6 mm (1/8 to 1/4 inch)
Main jet	88
Slow jet	40
Needle type/position	Not specified
Air screw setting	
1985	1-7/8 turns out
1986 and later	1-1/2 turns out
Float level	10.7 mm (0.42 inch)

Ignition system

Ignition coil primary resistance	0.1 to 0.3 ohm
Ignition coil secondary resistance	
Without spark plug cap installed	3.7 to 4.5 k-ohms
With spark plug cap installed	7.4 to 11.0 k-ohms
Ignition pulse generator resistance	50 to 200 ohms

Transmission

Belt width (service limit)	15.0 mm (0.59 inch)
Weight roller outer diameter	
Standard	17.92 to 18.08 mm (0.706 to 0.712 inch)
Limit	17.4 mm (0.69 inch)
Clutch lining thickness (service limit)	2.0 mm (0.08 inch)
Clutch spring free length (service limit)	86.3 mm (3.40 inches)

Brakes

Drum internal diameter (service limit)	
Front	111.0 mm (4.37 inches)
Rear	95.5 mm (3.76 inches)
Brake lining thickness (service limit)	2.0 mm (0.08 inch)
Brake freeplay (front and rear)	10 to 20 mm (3/8 to 3/4 inch)

Honda CH80 Elite, 1985 through 2007 (continued)

Tire pressures

Front	22 psi
Rear	
Up to 90 kg (200 lbs) load	25 psi
90 kg (200 lbs) to maximum rated load	33 psi

Electrical system

Battery	
Capacity	
1985	12V-5Ah
1986 and later	12V-4Ah
Voltage (fully charged)	13.0 to 13.2 volts
Alternator	
Output (regulated)	14 to 15 volts
Charging coil resistance	0.3 to 1.5 ohms
Lighting coil resistance	0.1 to 1.0 ohms
Exciter coil resistance	800 to 1200 ohms
Fuse	
1985	7 amps
1986 and later	10 amps

Torque wrench settings

Note: One foot-pound (ft-lb) of torque is equivalent to 12 inch-pounds (in-lbs) of torque. Torque values below approximately 15 foot-pounds are expressed in inch-pounds, because most foot-pound torque wrenches are not accurate at these smaller values.

Valve cover bolts	10 to 14 Nm (84 to 120 inch-lbs)
Rocker assembly/camshaft holder nuts	10 to 14 Nm (84 to 120 inch-lbs)
Cylinder head-to-cylinder bolt	8 to 12 Nm (72 to 108 inch-lbs)
Cam chain tensioner sealing bolt	38 to 45 Nm (27 to 33 ft-lbs)
Cam chain tensioner bolt	13 to 17 Nm (108 to 144 inch-lbs)
Cam chain guide roller bolt	9 to 14 Nm (72 to 120 inch-lbs)
Clutch drive face (28 mm locknut)	35 to 40 Nm (25 to 29 ft-lbs)
Drive and driven pulley nuts	35 to 40 Nm (25 to 29 ft-lbs)
Moveable face seal bolts	3 to 6 Nm (27 to 51 inch-lbs)
Gearbox drain plug	10 to 14 Nm (84 to 120 inch-lbs)
Final gear case bolt	9 to 12 Nm (84 to 108 inch-lbs)
Alternator rotor nut	35 to 40 Nm (25 to 29 ft-lbs)
Crankcase bolts	9 to 12 Nm (84 to 108 inch-lbs)
Front axle nut	50 to 70 Nm (36 to 51 ft-lbs)
Rear axle nut	
1985 and 1986	80 to 100 Nm (58 to 72 ft-lbs)
1987 and later	100 to 120 Nm (72 to 87 ft-lbs)
Steering stem bearing top cone race	Snug, then loosen 1/8 turn
Steering stem bearing nut	5 to 13 Nm (48 to 108 inch-lbs)
Steering stem locknut	80 to 120 Nm (58 to 87 ft-lbs)
Fork pivot arm	27 to 33 Nm (20 to 24 ft-lbs)
Front shock absorber upper	
1985 and 1986	30 to 36 Nm (22 to 26 ft-lbs)
1987 and later	27 to 33 Nm (20 to 24 ft-lbs)
Rear shock absorber upper bolt	30 to 45 Nm (22 to 33 ft-lbs)
Rear shock absorber lower bolt	25 to 35 Nm (18 to 25 ft-lbs)

Honda CH150 Elite, 1985 through 1987

Engine	153 cc single-cylinder OHC 4-stroke
Cooling system	Liquid cooled
Fuel system	Round slide CV carburetor
Ignition system	CDI
Transmission	Variable speed automatic, belt driven
Suspension	Pivot arm front, swingarm with twin shocks rear
Brakes	Drum front and rear
Tires	3.50-10 front and rear
Wheelbase	
1985 and 1986	1200 mm (47.2 inches)
1987	1255 mm (49.4 inches)
Weight (dry)	105 kg (232 lbs)
Fuel tank capacity	Not specified

Engine

Spark plug type	
Standard	NGK DPR7EA-9, ND X22EPR-U9
Cold weather	NGK DPR6EA-9, X20EPR-U9
Electrode gap	0.8 to 0.9 mm (0.031 to 0.035 inch)
Idle speed (rpm)	1500 +/-100 rpm
Engine oil type	SE or SF 4-stroke engine oil, SAE 10W-40
Engine oil capacity (drain and fill)	0.8 liter (0.8 qt)
Valve clearance (cold, intake and exhaust)	0.1 mm (0.004 inch)
Bore x stroke	58.0 x 57.8 mm (2.283 x 2.275 inches)
Piston diameter (service limit)	57.9 mm (2.280 inches)
Piston to bore clearance (service limit)	0.10 mm (0.004 inch)
Piston ring installed end gap	
Top and second	
Standard	0.15 to 0.30 mm (0.006 to 0.012 inch)
Limit	0.50 mm (0.020 inch)
Oil ring side rail	0.2 to 0.9 mm (0.008 to 0.035 inch)

Fuel system

Throttle twistgrip freeplay	2 to 6 mm (1/8 to 1/4 inch)
Main jet	
Standard	
1985 and 1986	100
1987	102
High altitude	
1985 and 1986	95
1987	98
Slow jet	35
Needle type/position	Not specified
Pilot screw setting	Not specified
Float level	18.5 mm (0.73 inch)

Ignition system

Ignition coil primary resistance	0.1 to 0.2 ohm
Ignition coil secondary resistance	
Without spark plug cap installed	3.6 to 4.6 k-ohms
With spark plug cap installed	7.4 to 11.0 k-ohms
Ignition pulse generator resistance	
1985 and 1986	Not specified
1987	50 to 170 ohms

Transmission

Belt width (service limit)	17.5 mm (0.689 inch)
Weight roller outer diameter	
Standard	19.95 to 20.10 mm (0.785 to 0.791 inch)
Limit	19.5 mm (0.77 inch)
Clutch lining thickness (service limit)	2.0 mm (0.08 inch)
Clutch spring free length (service limit)	83.2 mm (3.28 inch)

Honda CH150 Elite, 1985 through 1987 (continued)

Brakes

Drum internal diameter (service limit, front and rear)	111.0 mm (4.37 inches)
Brake lining thickness (service limit)...	2.0 mm (0.08 inch)
Brake freeplay	
Front	10 to 20 mm (3/8 to 3/4 inch)
Rear	20 to 30 mm (3/4 to 1-1/8 inch)

Tire pressures

Front	21 psi
Rear	
Up to 90 kg (200 lbs) load...	29 psi
90 kg (200 lbs) to maximum rated load	36 psi

Electrical system

Battery	
Capacity	12V-9Ah
Voltage (fully charged)...	12.5 volts
Alternator	
Output (regulated)...	14 to 15 volts
Charging coil resistance	
1985 and 1986...	Not specified
1987	0.1 to 1.0 ohms
Exciter coil resistance	50 to 350 ohms
Fuses	
Main	20 amps
Fan motor (1987)...	5 amps
All others	10 amps

Torque wrench settings

Note: One foot-pound (ft-lb) of torque is equivalent to 12 inch-pounds (in-lbs) of torque. Torque values below approximately 15 foot-pounds are expressed in inch-pounds, because most foot-pound torque wrenches are not accurate at these smaller values.

Oil screen filter cap...	19 to 25 Nm (15 to 18 ft-lbs)
Transmission oil drain bolt..	10 to 14 Nm (84 to 120 inch-lbs)
Transmission oil level check bolt...	10 to 15 Nm (84 to 132 inch-lbs)
Oil pump mounting bolt...	8 to 12 Nm (72 to 108 inch-lbs)
Valve cover bolts	8 to 12 Nm (72 to 108 inch-lbs)
Cylinder head cap nuts	20 to 24 Nm (14 to 17 ft-lbs)
Cylinder head-to-cylinder bolt...	8 to 12 Nm (72 to 108 inch-lbs)
Cam chain tensioner sealing bolt	
1985 and 1986..	4 to 6 Nm (34 to 51 inch-lbs)
1987	8 to 12 Nm (72 to 108 inch-lbs)
Cam chain tensioner bolts	
1985 and 1986..	6 to 10 Nm (51 to 86 inch-lbs)
1987	12 to 16 Nm (108 to 144 inch-lbs)
Cam chain guide pivot bolt	12 to 16 Nm (108 to 144 inch-lbs)
External oil line upper banjo bolts.......................................	8 to 12 Nm (72 to 108 inch-lbs)
External oil line lower banjo bolt	18 to 22 Nm (13 to 16 ft-lbs)
Clutch drive face (28 mm locknut).......................................	50 to 60 Nm (36 to 43 ft-lbs)
Drive pulley nut..	50 to 60 Nm (36 to 43 ft-lbs)
Driven pulley nut..	35 to 40 Nm (25 to 29 ft-lbs)
Face seal cover bolts	3 to 5 Nm (25 to 43 inch-lbs)
Alternator rotor nut...	50 to 60 Nm (36 to 43 ft-lbs)
Crankcase bolts	8 to 12 Nm (72 to 108 inch-lbs)
Engine mounting bolts/nuts	
1985 and 1986	
Engine hanger stopper bolt	24 to 30 Nm (17 to 22 ft-lbs)
Engine hanger bracket bolt	35 to 45 Nm (25 to 32 ft-lbs)
Engine hanger bolt...	35 to 45 Nm (25 to 32 ft-lbs)
Engine mounting bolt..	35 to 45 Nm (25 to 32 ft-lbs)

Engine mounting bolts/nuts (continued)
　1987
　　　Engine hanger stopper nut .... 18 to 22 Nm (13 to 16 ft-lbs)
　　　Engine hanger bracket nut .... 40 to 50 Nm (29 to 36 ft-lbs)
　　　Engine hanger bolt.. 40 to 50 Nm (29 to 36 ft-lbs)
　　　Engine hanger mounting bolt .... 35 to 45 Nm (25 to 32 ft-lbs)
Front axle nut .... 50 to 70 Nm (36 to 51 ft-lbs)
Rear axle nut
　1985 and 1986 .... 80 to 100 Nm (58 to 72 ft-lbs)
　1987 .... 100 to 120 Nm (72 to 87 ft-lbs)
Steering stem bearing top cone race.................................... 2 to 3 Nm (17 to 26 inch-lbs)
Steering stem bearing locknut
　1985 and 1986 .... 10 to 20 Nm (84 to 168 inch-lbs)
　1987 .... 5 to 13 Nm (48 to 108 inch-lbs)
Steering stem nut
　1985 and 1986 .... 130 to 150 Nm (74 to 108 ft-lbs)
　1987 .... 120 to 150 Nm (87 to 108 ft-lbs)
Fork pivot arm
　1985 and 1986 .... 20 to 24 Nm (14 to 17 ft-lbs)
　1987 .... 24 to 30 Nm (17 to 22 ft-lbs)
Front shock absorber upper bolt
　1985 and 1986 .... 30 to 36 Nm (22 to 26 ft-lbs)
　1987 .... 24 to 30 Nm (17 to 22 ft-lbs)
Front shock absorber lower mounting bolt .... 0.8 to 1.2 Nm (7 to 11 inch-lbs)
Front shock absorber lower mounting nut .... 15 to 20 Nm (11 to 14 ft-lbs)
Rear shock bolts (upper and lower) .... 24 to 30 Nm (17 to 22 ft-lbs)
Brake torque link bolts .... 27 to 33 Nm (20 to 24 ft-lbs)
Brake arm bolt.. 8 to 12 Nm (72 to 108 inch-lbs)

Honda CH250 Elite, 1985 through 1988

Engine .... 244.3 cc single-cylinder OHC 4-stroke
Cooling system.. Liquid cooled
Fuel system .... CV carburetor
Ignition system .... CDI
Transmission .... Variable speed automatic, belt driven
Suspension .... Pivot arm front, swingarm with twin shocks rear
Brakes .... Drum front and rear
Tires .... 4.00-10 4 PR front and rear
Wheelbase .... 1260 mm (49.6 inches)
Weight (dry)
　1985 .... 122 kg (269 lbs)
　1986 .... 126 kg (278 lbs)
　1987 and later .... 127 kg (280 lbs)
Fuel tank capacity .... 8 liters (2.1 gal)

Engine

Spark plug type
　Standard .... NGK DPR6EA-9, ND X20EPR-U9
　Cold weather .... NGK DPR5EA-9, X16EPR-U9
　Extended high speed riding .... NGK DPR7EA-9, ND X22EPR-U9
Electrode gap .... 0.8 to 0.9 mm (0.031 to 0.035 inch)
Idle speed (rpm).. 1500 +/-100 rpm
Engine oil type... SE or SF 4-stroke engine oil, SAE 10W-30
Engine oil capacity (drain and fill).. 800 cc (27 fl oz)
Valve clearance (cold, intake and exhaust) .... 0.08 to 0.12 mm (0.003 to 0.005 inch)
Bore x stroke .... 72.0 x 60.0 mm (2.83 x 2.36 inches)
Piston diameter (service limit) .... 71.9 mm (2.831 inches)
Piston to bore clearance (service limit)................................ 0.10 mm (0.004 inch)
Piston ring installed end gap
　Top and second
　　Standard .... 0.15 to 0.35 mm (0.006 to 0.014 inch)
　　Limit .... 0.50 mm (0.020 inch)
　　Oil ring side rail .... 0.2 to 0.7 mm (0.008 to 0.028 inch)

Honda CH250 Elite, 1985 through 1988 (continued)

Fuel system

Throttle twistgrip freeplay	2 to 6 mm (1/8 to 1/4 inch)
Main jet	
1985	115
1986 and later	112
Slow jet	38
Needle type/position	Not specified
Pilot screw setting	
1985 and 1986	
Standard	2 turns out
High altitude	1-3/4 turns out
1987 and later	
Standard	2-1/2 turns out
High altitude	2-1/4 turns out
Float level	18.5 +/- 1.0 mm (0.73+/-0.04 inch)

Ignition system

Ignition coil primary resistance	0.1 to 0.2 ohm
Ignition coil secondary resistance without	
spark plug cap installed	3.6 to 4.6 k-ohms
Ignition pulse generator resistance	50 to 180 ohms

Transmission

Belt width (service limit)	21.0 mm (0.83 inch)
Weight roller outer diameter	
Standard	23.8 mm (0.94 inch)
Limit	23.2 mm (0.91 inch)
Clutch lining thickness (service limit)	2.0 mm (0.08 inch)
Clutch spring free length (service limit)	94.0 mm (3.70 inch)

Brakes

Drum internal diameter (service limit, front and rear)	111.0 mm (4.37 inches)
Brake lining thickness (service limit)	2.0 mm (0.08 inch)
Brake freeplay	
Front	10 to 20 mm (3/8 to 3/4 inch)
Rear	20 to 30 mm (3/4 to 1-1/8 inch)

Tire pressures

Front	25 psi
Rear	
Rider only	29 psi
Rider and passenger	36 psi

Electrical system

Battery	
Capacity	
1985 and 1986	12V-12Ah
1987 and later	12V-10Ah
Voltage (fully charged)	13.0 to 13.2 volts
Alternator	
Output (regulated)	14 to 15 volts
Exciter coil resistance	50 to 250 ohms
Fuses	
Main	20 amps
Fan motor	5 amps
Key light	5 amps
Horn	5 amps
Turn, stop, gauge	10 amps
Head and taillights	10 amps

Torque wrench settings

Note: One foot-pound (ft-lb) of torque is equivalent to 12 inch-pounds (in-lbs) of torque. Torque values below approximately 15 foot-pounds are expressed in inch-pounds, because most foot-pound torque wrenches are not accurate at these smaller values.

Oil screen filter cap	18 to 22 Nm (13 to 16 ft-lbs)
Transmission oil drain bolt	10 to 14 Nm (84 to 120 inch-lbs)
Engine oil drain plug	20 to 25 Nm (14 to 18 ft-lbs)
Valve cover bolts	
1985 and 1986	10 to 14 Nm (84 to 120 inch-lbs)
1987 and later	8 to 12 Nm (72 to 108 inch-lbs)
Cylinder head cap nuts	22 to 26 Nm (16 to 19 ft-lbs)
Camshaft holder bolts	8 to 12 Nm (72 to 108 inch-lbs)
Cam chain tensioner sealing bolt	8 to 12 Nm (72 to 108 inch-lbs)
Cam chain tensioner bolts	Not specified
External oil pipe lower banjo fitting	18 to 22 Nm (13 to 16 ft-lbs)
External oil pipe center banjo bolt (silver)	8 to 12 Nm (72 to 108 inch-lbs)
External oil pipe upper banjo bolt (black)	8 to 12 Nm (72 to 108 inch-lbs)
Clutch driven face nut (30 mm locknut)	70 to 90 Nm (51 to 65 ft-lbs)
Drive pulley nut	80 to 100 Nm (58 to 72 ft-lbs)
Driven pulley nut	50 to 60 Nm (36 to 43 ft-lbs)
Face seal cover bolts	2.5 to 4.0 Nm (22 to 34 inch-lbs)
Alternator rotor nut	
1985 and 1986	90 to 100 Nm (65 to 72 ft-lbs)
1987 and 1988	105 to 115 Nm (76 to 83 ft-lbs)
Starter clutch Allen bolts	28 to 32 Nm (21 to 24 ft-lbs)
Crankcase bolts	8 to 12 Nm (72 to 108 inch-lbs)
Engine mounting bolts/nuts	
Engine hanger bolt	100 to 120 Nm (72 to 87 ft-lbs)
Engine hanger joint bolt	
1985 through 1987	40 to 55 Nm (29 to 40 ft-lbs)
1988	55 to 70 Nm (40 to 50 ft-lbs)
Engine hanger rubber stopper bolt	24 to 30 Nm (17 to 22 ft-lbs)
Engine mounting bolt	40 to 55 Nm (29 to 40 ft-lbs)
Front axle nut	50 to 70 Nm (36 to 51 ft-lbs)
Front wheel hub nut	28 to 32 Nm (20 to 23 ft-lbs)
Rear axle nut	80 to 100 Nm (58 to 72 ft-lbs)
Rear wheel hub nut	28 to 32 Nm (20 to 23 ft-lbs)
Steering stem bearing top cone race	
1985	Snug, then back out 1/8 turn
1986 and later	2 to 3 Nm (17 to 26 inch-lbs)
Steering stem bearing locknut	
1985	5 to 13 Nm (48 to 108 inch-lbs)
1986 and later	10 to 20 Nm (84 to 168 inch-lbs)
Steering stem nut	
1985	120 to 150 Nm (87 to 108 ft-lbs)
1986 and later	130 to 150 Nm (74 to 108 ft-lbs)
Front shock absorber	
Upper bolt	35 to 45 Nm (25 to 33 ft-lbs)
Clevis locknut	15 to 25 Nm (11 to 18 ft-lbs)
Lower mounting screw	0.8 to 1.2 Nm (7 to 11 inch-lbs)
Lower nut	15 to 20 Nm (11 to 14 ft-lbs)
Rear shock bolts (upper and lower)	24 to 30 Nm (17 to 22 ft-lbs)
Front brake torque link bolts	
To panel	24 to 30 Nm (17 to 22 ft-lbs)
To fork	35 to 45 Nm (25 to 33 ft-lbs)
Brake arm bolts (front and rear)	8 to 12 Nm (72 to 108 inch-lbs)

Honda CH250 Elite, 1989 and 1990

Engine	244.3 cc single-cylinder OHC 4-stroke
Cooling system	Liquid cooled
Fuel system	CV carburetor
Ignition system	CDI
Transmission	Variable speed automatic, belt driven
Suspension	Pivot arm front, swingarm with twin shocks rear
Brakes	Drum front and rear
Tires	
Front	110/90-10 61J
Rear	120/90-10 65J
Wheelbase	1300 mm (51.2 inches)
Weight (dry)	130 kg (287 lbs)
Fuel tank capacity	9.2 liters (2.43 gal)

Engine

Spark plug type	
Standard	NGK DPR6EA-9, ND X20EPR-U9
Cold weather	NGK DPR5EA-9, X16EPR-U9
Extended high speed riding	NGK DPR7EA-9, ND X22EPR-U9
Electrode gap	0.8 to 0.9 mm (0.031 to 0.035 inch)
Idle speed (rpm)	1500 +/-100 rpm
Engine oil type	SF or SG 4-stroke engine oil, SAE 10W-40
Engine oil capacity (drain and fill)	1.1 liters (1.16 qts)
Valve clearance (cold, intake and exhaust)	0.10 to 0.14 mm (0.004 to 0.006 inch)
Bore x stroke	72.0 x 60.0 mm (2.83 x 2.36 inches)
Piston diameter (service limit)	71.9 mm (2.831 inches)
Piston to bore clearance (service limit)	0.10 mm (0.004 inch)
Piston ring installed end gap (top and second)	
Standard	0.15 to 0.35 mm (0.006 to 0.014 inch)
Limit	0.50 mm (0.020 inch)

Fuel system

Throttle twistgrip freeplay	Not specified
Main jet	
Standard	112
High altitude	110
Slow jet	40
Needle type/position	Not specified
Pilot screw setting	
Standard	2-1/8 turns out
High altitude	1/2 turn in from standard
Float level	18.5 mm (0.73 inch)

Ignition system

Ignition coil primary resistance	0.2 to 0.3 ohm
Ignition coil secondary resistance	
Without spark plug cap installed	2.5 to 3.5 k-ohms
With spark plug cap installed	6.0 to 10.0 k-ohms
Ignition pulse generator resistance	190 to 250 ohms

Transmission

Belt width (service limit)	21.0 mm (0.83 inch)
Weight roller outer diameter	
Standard	23.8 mm (0.94 inch)
Limit	23.2 mm (0.91 inch)
Clutch lining thickness (service limit)	0.5 mm (0.02 inch)
Clutch spring free length (service limit)	94.0 mm (3.70 inches)

Brakes

Drum internal diameter (service limit, front and rear)	131.0 mm (5.16 inches)
Brake lining thickness (service limit)	2.0 mm (0.08 inch)

Brakes
Brake freeplay
    Front .... 10 to 20 mm (3/8 to 3/4 inch)
    Rear .... Not specified

Tire pressures
Front .... 25 psi
Rear
    Rider only.. 29 psi
    Rider and passenger.. 33 psi

Electrical system
Battery
    Capacity 12V-10Ah
    Voltage (fully charged)... 13.0 to 13.2 volts
Alternator
    Output (regulated) .... 14 to 15 volts
    Charging coil resistance.. 0.1 to 0.5 ohms
Fuses
    Main .... 30 amps
    Horn/turn signals .... 10 amps
    Front position, tail, gauge and license plate light .... 5 amps
    Front and rear brake lights, starter............................ 10 amps
    Ignition .... 5 amps
    Headlight .... 10 amps
    Fan motor.. 5 amps
    Accessory .... 5 amps

Torque wrench settings
Note: One foot-pound (ft-lb) of torque is equivalent to 12 inch-pounds (in-lbs) of torque. Torque values below approximately 15 foot-pounds are expressed in inch-pounds, because most foot-pound torque wrenches are not accurate at these smaller values.

Oil screen filter cap... 20 Nm (15 ft-lbs)
Transmission oil drain and check bolts .... 13 Nm (132 inch-lbs)
Valve cover bolts .... 12 Nm (108 inch-lbs)
Cylinder head cap nuts .... 24 Nm (18 ft-lbs)
Cylinder head bolts .... Not specified
Camshaft holder bolts .... 9 Nm (84 inch-lbs)
Cam chain tensioner sealing bolt..................................... 22 Nm (16 ft-lbs)
Cam chain tensioner bolts... 12 Nm (108 inch-lbs)
Clutch driven face nut (30 mm locknut) .... 80 Nm (58 ft-lbs)
Drive pulley nut... 110 Nm (80 ft-lbs)
Driven pulley nut... 75 Nm (54 ft-lbs)
Face seal cover bolts .... 3.3 Nm (29 inch-lbs)
Alternator rotor nut .... 110 Nm (80 ft-lbs)
Starter clutch Allen bolts .... 30 Nm (22 ft-lbs)*
Crankcase bolts .... 12 Nm (108 inch-lbs)
Crankcase cover bolts... 12 Nm (108 inch-lbs)
Engine mounting bolts/nuts
    Engine hanger pivot nut to frame............................... 80 Nm (50 ft-lbs)
    Tension rod U-nut .... 20 Nm (15 ft-lbs)
    Engine hanger adjusting bolt .... 30 Nm (22 ft-lbs)
    Engine hanger locknut .... 45 Nm (33 ft-lbs)
Front axle nut .... 70 Nm (51 ft-lbs)
Rear axle nut .... 110 Nm (80 ft-lbs)
Steering stem bearing top cone race .... Snug, then back out 1/8 turn
Steering stem bearing locknut .... 15 Nm (130 inch-lbs)
Steering stem nut .... 140 Nm (101 ft-lbs)
Front shock absorber
    Upper mounting bolt.. 40 Nm (29 ft-lbs)
    Lower mounting bolt.. 1.0 Nm (8 inch-lbs)
    Lower mounting nut.. 18 Nm (13 ft-lbs)
Rear shock absorber
    Upper nut... 26 Nm (19 ft-lbs)
    Lower nut (right side) .... 45 Nm (33 ft-lbs)
    Lower nut (left side).. 40 Nm (29 ft-lbs)

Apply non-permanent thread locking agent to the threads.

Honda CN250 Helix, 1986 through 2001

Engine	244 cc single-cylinder OHC 4-stroke
Cooling system	Liquid cooled
Fuel system	CV carburetor
Ignition system	CDI
Transmission	Variable speed automatic, belt driven
Suspension	Pivot arm front, swingarm with twin shocks rear
Brakes	Disc front, drum rear
Tires	
Front	110/100-12 67J
Rear	120/90-10 65J
Wheelbase	1620 mm (63.8 inches)
Weight (dry)	
1986 and 1987	155 kg (342 lbs)
1988 through 1991	Not specified
1992 through 2001	158.5 kg (349 lbs)
Fuel tank capacity	Not specified

Engine

Spark plug type	
Standard	NGK DPR6EA-9, ND X20EPR-U9
Cold weather	NGK DPR5EA-9, X16EPR-U9
Extended high speed riding	NGK DPR7EA-9, ND X22EPR-U9
Electrode gap	0.8 to 0.9 mm (0.031 to 0.035 inch)
Idle speed (rpm)	1500 +/- 100 rpm
Engine oil type	SF or SG 4-stroke engine oil, SAE 10W-40
Engine oil capacity (drain and fill)	800 cc (27 fl oz)
Coolant capacity	
Radiator and engine	1.42 liter (1.5 qts)
Reserve tank	0.4 liter (13 fl oz)
Valve clearance (cold, intake and exhaust)	0.08 to 0.12 mm (0.003 to 0.005 inch)
Bore x stroke	72.0 x 60.0 mm (2.83 x 2.36 inches)
Piston diameter (service limit)	71.9 mm (2.831 inches)
Piston to bore clearance (service limit)	0.10 mm (0.004 inch)
Piston ring installed end gap	
Top and second	
Standard	0.15 to 0.35 mm (0.006 to 0.014 inch)
Limit	0.50 mm (0.020 inch)
Oil ring side rail	0.2 to 0.7 mm (0.008 to 0.028 inch)

Fuel system

Throttle twistgrip freeplay	2 to 6 mm (1/8 to 1/4 inch)
Main jet	110
Slow jet	38
Needle type/position	Not specified
Pilot screw setting	
1986 and 1987	2-1/2 turns out
1988 through 1990	Not specified
1991 through 2001	2-1/4 turns out
Float level	18.5 +/- 1.0 mm (0.73 +/- 0.04 inch)

Ignition system

Ignition coil primary resistance	0.1 to 0.2 ohm
Ignition coil secondary resistance	
Without spark plug cap installed	3.6 to 4.6 k-ohms
With spark plug cap installed	7.3 to 11.0 k-ohms
Ignition pulse generator resistance	50 to 170 ohms

Transmission

Belt width (service limit)	21.0 mm (0.83 inch)
Weight roller outer diameter	
Standard	23.8 mm (0.94 inch)
Limit	23.2 mm (0.91 inch)

Transmission (continued)

Clutch lining thickness (service limit)	
1985	1.5 mm (0.06 inch)
1986 through 2001	0.5 mm (0.02 inch)
Clutch spring free length (service limit)	94.0 mm (3.70 inches)

Brakes

Disc thickness (limit, front)	4.0 mm (0.16 inch)
Pad wear limit, front	To wear line
Drum internal diameter (service limit, rear)	131.0 mm (5.16 inches)
Brake lining thickness (service limit)	2.0 mm (0.08 inch)
Brake freeplay (rear only)	20 to 30 mm (3/4 to 1-1/8 inch)

Tiire pressures

Front	24 psi
Rear	
Up to 90 kg (200 lbs) load	28 psi
Up to maximum load	32 psi

Electrical system

Battery	
Capacity	12V-10Ah
Voltage (fully charged)	13.0 to 13.2 volts
Alternator	
Output (regulated)	14 to 15 volts
Charging coil resistance	0.1 to 1.0 ohms
Fuses	
Main	20 amps
Fuel pump, charging system, starter	5 amps
Fan	5 amps
Turn signals, horn, brake light, gauge illumination	10 amps
Headlight, taillight, front position light	10 amps
Clock, accessories	5 amps

Torque wrench settings

Note: One foot-pound (ft-lb) of torque is equivalent to 12 inch-pounds (in-lbs) of torque. Torque values below approximately 15 foot-pounds are expressed in inch-pounds, because most foot-pound torque wrenches are not accurate at these smaller values.

Oil screen filter cap	18 to 22 Nm (13 to 16 ft-lbs)
Transmission oil check bolt	10 to 15 Nm (84 to 180 inch-lbs)
Valve cover bolts	8 to 12 Nm (72 to 108 inch-lbs)
Cylinder head cap nuts	22 to 26 Nm (16 to 19 ft-lbs)
Valve cover pan screw	3.5 to 5.0 Nm (30 to 43 inch-lbs)*
Cam chain tensioner sealing bolt	8 to 12 Nm (72 to 108 inch-lbs)
Cam chain tensioner bolts	8 to 12 Nm (72 to 108 inch-lbs)
Clutch driven face nut (30 mm locknut)	70 to 90 Nm (51 to 65 ft-lbs)
Drive pulley nut	
1986, 1997 and 1992	80 to 100 Nm (58 to 72 ft-lbs)
1988 through 1991	Not specified
1993 and later	90 to 100 Nm (65 to 72 ft-lbs)
Driven pulley nut	50 to 60 Nm (36 to 43 ft-lbs)
Face seal cover bolts	2.5 to 4.0 Nm (22 to 34 inch-lbs)
Alternator rotor nut	105 to 115 Nm (76 to 83 ft-lbs)
Starter clutch Allen bolts	28 to 32 Nm (20 to 23 ft-lbs)
Crankcase bolts	8 to 12 Nm (72 to 108 inch-lbs)
Engine mounting bolts/nuts	
Engine hanger rubber stopper bolt	18 to 22 Nm (13 to 16 ft-lbs)
Engine hanger tension arm nut	24 to 30 Nm (17 to 22 ft-lbs)
Engine hanger nut	55 to 70 Nm (40 to 51 ft-lbs)
Engine pivot collar	25 to 35 Nm (18 to 25 ft-lbs)
Pivot collar locknut	35 to 50 Nm (22 to 36 ft-lbs)
Engine hanger through bolt and nut	70 to 90 Nm (51 to 65 ft-lbs)
Engine mount through-bolt	40 to 55 Nm (29 to 40 ft-lbs)

*Apply non-permanent thread locking agent to the threads.

Honda CN250 Helix, 1986 trough 2001 (continued)

Torque wrench settings

Note: One foot-pound (ft-lb) of torque is equivalent to 12 inch-pounds (in-lbs) of torque. Torque values below approximately 15 foot-pounds are expressed in inch-pounds, because most foot-pound torque wrenches are not accurate at these smaller values.

Front axle nut	60 to 80 Nm (43 to 58 ft-lbs)
Front wheel hub nut	28 to 32 Nm (20 to 23 ft-lbs)
Rear axle nut	
1986 and 1987	100 to 120 Nm (72 to 87 ft-lbs)
1988 through 1991	Not specified
1992 and later	110 to 130 Nm (80 to 94 ft-lbs)
Rear wheel hub nut	28 to 32 Nm (20 to 23 ft-lbs)
Steering stem bearing adjusting nut	
First step	30 to 40 Nm (22 to 29 ft-lbs)
Second step	Loosen
Third step	2.5 to 3.5 Nm (22 to 30 inch-lbs)
Steering stem nut	80 to 120 Nm (58 to 87 ft-lbs)
Front shock absorber	
Upper bolt	35 to 45 Nm (25 to 33 ft-lbs)
Lower mounting screw	0.8 to 1.2 Nm (7 to 11 inch-lbs)
Lower nut	15 to 20 Nm (11 to 14 ft-lbs)
Rear shock bolts	
Upper bolt	24 to 30 Nm (17 to 22 ft-lbs)
Lower left nut	35 to 45 Nm (25 to 33 ft-lbs)
Lower left stud	40 to 50 Nm (29 to 36 ft-lbs)
Lower right bolt	24 to 30 Nm (17 to 22 ft-lbs)
Front brake bolts	
1986 and 1987, 1992 and 1993	
Caliper pin bolt	25 to 30 Nm (18 to 22 ft-lbs)
Caliper mounting bolt	20 to 25 Nm (14 to 18 ft-lbs)
Pad pin retainer bolt	8 to 13 Nm (72 to 108 inch-lbs)
1988 through 1991	Not specified
1994 and later	
Caliper pin bolt	25 to 30 Nm (18 to 22 ft-lbs)
Caliper bracket pin bolt	10 to 15 Nm (84 to 132 inch-lbs)
Pad pins	15 to 20 Nm (11 to 14 ft-lbs)
Master cylinder mounting bolts	10 to 14 Nm (84 to 120 inch-lbs)
Brake hose bolt	25 to 35 Nm (18 to 25 ft-lbs)
Torque link	
To caliper bracket	30 to 40 Nm (22 to 29 ft-lbs)
To fork	35 to 45 Nm (25 to 33 ft-lbs)
Brake arm bolt (rear)	8 to 12 Nm (72 to 108 inch-lbs)
Brake stopper bolt (rear)	10 to 14 Nm (84 to 120 inch-lbs)

Honda CN250 Helix, 2004 and later

Engine	244 cc single-cylinder OHC 4-stroke
Cooling system	Liquid cooled
Fuel system	CV carburetor
Ignition system	CDI
Transmission	Variable speed automatic, belt driven
Suspension	Pivot arm front, swingarm with twin shocks rear
Brakes	Disc front, drum rear
Tires	
Front	110/100-12 67J
Rear	120/90-10 66J
Wheelbase	1620 mm (63.8 inches)
Weight (dry)	158.5 kg (349 lbs)
Fuel tank capacity	12 liters (3.17 gal)

Engine

Spark plug type	
Standard	NGK DPR6EA-9, ND X20EPR-U9
Cold weather	NGK DPR5EA-9, X16EPR-U9
Extended high speed riding	NGK DPR7EA-9, ND X22EPR-U9
Electrode gap	0.8 to 0.9 mm (0.031 to 0.035 inch)
Idle speed (rpm)	1500 +/-100 rpm
Engine oil type	SG or better 4-stroke engine oil meeting JASO MA standard, SAE 10W-40
Engine oil capacity (drain and fill)	800 cc (27 fl oz)
Coolant capacity	
Radiator and engine	1.42 liter (1.5 qts)
Reserve tank	0.4 liter (13 fl oz)
Valve clearance (cold, intake and exhaust)	0.08 to 0.12 mm (0.003 to 0.005 inch)
Bore x stroke	72.0 x 60.0 mm (2.83 x 2.36 inches)
Piston diameter (service limit)	71.9 mm (2.831 inches)
Piston to bore clearance (service limit)	0.10 mm (0.004 inch)
Piston ring installed end gap	
Top and second	
Standard	0.15 to 0.30 mm (0.006 to 0.012 inch)
Limit	0.50 mm (0.020 inch)
Oil ring side rail	
Standard	0.2 to 0.7 mm (0.008 to 0.028 inch)
Limit	0.9 mm (0.040 inch)

Fuel system

Throttle twistgrip freeplay	2 to 6 mm (1/8 to 1/4 inch)
Main jet	110
Slow jet	38
Needle type/position	Not specified
Pilot screw setting	
First step	2-1/4 turns out
Second step	Turn in until engine speed drops 100 rpm
Third step	One turn out from second step
Float level	18.5 mm (0.73 inch)

Ignition system

Ignition coil primary peak voltage	100 volts minimum
Exciter coil peak voltage	100 volts minimum
Ignition pulse generator peak voltage	0.7 volts minimum

Transmission

Belt width (service limit)	21.0 mm (0.83 inch)
Weight roller outer diameter	
Standard	23.8 mm (0.94 inch)
Limit	23.2 mm (0.91 inch)

Honda CN250 Helix, 2004 and later (continued)

Transmission (continued)

Clutch lining thickness (service limit)	1.5 mm (0.06 inch)
Clutch spring free length (service limit)	94.0 mm (3.70 inches)

Brakes

Brake fluid, front	DOT 4
Disc thickness (limit, front)	4.0 mm (0.16 inch)
Pad wear limit, front	To wear line
Drum internal diameter (service limit, rear)	131.0 mm (5.16 inches)
Brake lining thickness (service limit)	2.0 mm (0.08 inch)
Brake freeplay (rear only)	20 to 30 mm (3/4 to 1-1/8 inch)

Tire pressures

Front	25 psi
Rear	
Up to 90 kg (200 lbs) load	29 psi
Up to maximum load	33 psi

Electrical system

Battery	
Capacity	12V-10Ah
Voltage (fully charged)	13.0 to 13.2 volts
Alternator	
Output (regulated)	14 to 15 volts
Charging coil resistance	0.1 to 1.0 ohms
Fuses	
Main	20 amps
Fuel pump, charging system, starter	5 amps
Fan	5 amps
Turn signals, horn, brake light, gauge illumination	10 amps
Headlight, taillight, front position light	10 amps
Clock, accessories	5 amps

Torque wrench settings

Note: One foot-pound (ft-lb) of torque is equivalent to 12 inch-pounds (in-lbs) of torque. Torque values below approximately 15 foot-pounds are expressed in inch-pounds, because most foot-pound torque wrenches are not accurate at these smaller values.

Oil screen filter cap	20 Nm (14 ft-lbs)
Transmission oil check bolt	13 Nm (108 inch-lbs)
Transmission oil drain bolt	10 Nm (84 inch-lbs)
Valve cover bolts	10 Nm (84 inch-lbs)
Cylinder head cap nuts	24 Nm (17 ft-lbs)
Valve cover pan screw	3.9 Nm (35 inch-lbs) (1)
Cam chain tensioner sealing bolt	10 Nm (84 inch-lbs)
Cam chain tensioner bolts	10 Nm (84 inch-lbs)
Clutch driven face nut (30 mm locknut)	78 Nm (58 ft-lbs)
Drive pulley nut	93 Nm (69 ft-lbs) (2)
Driven pulley nut	74 Nm (54 ft-lbs)
Face seal cover bolts	2.9 Nm (26 inch-lbs)
Alternator rotor nut	108 Nm (80 ft-lbs)
Starter clutch Allen bolts	29 Nm (22 ft-lbs)
Crankcase bolts	10 Nm (84 inch-lbs)
Engine mounting bolts/nuts	
Tension rod pivot nut	26 Nm (20 ft-lbs)
Tension rod stopper nut	20 Nm (14 ft-lbs)
Engine hanger joint nut	62 Nm (46 ft-lbs)
Engine hanger mounting nut	78 Nm (58 ft-lbs)
Engine hanger adjusting bolt	29 Nm (22 ft-lbs)
Engine hanger adjusting bolt locknut	42 Nm (31 ft-lbs)
Lower front through-bolt and nut	47 Nm (35 ft-lbs)
Front axle nut	59 Nm (43 ft-lbs)
Rear axle nut	118 Nm (87 ft-lbs)
Front suspension pivot arm nut	39 Nm (29 ft-lbs)

Front suspension pivot arm cover bolt	4.9 Nm (43 inch-lbs)
Upper fork bridge to fork tubes	54 Nm (40 ft-lbs)
Steering stem bearing adjusting nut	
First step	27 Nm (20 ft-lbs)
Second step	Loosen
Third step	3.9 Nm (35 inch-lbs)
Steering stem nut	103 Nm (76 ft-lbs)
Front shock absorber	
Upper bolt	39 Nm (29 ft-lbs)
Lower mounting screw	1.0 Nm (9 inch-lbs)
Lower nut	18 Nm (13 ft-lbs)
Rear shock bolts	
Upper bolt	Not specified
Lower left stud	44 Nm (33 ft-lbs)
Lower left nut	39 Nm (29 ft-lbs)
Lower right bolt	Not specified
Front brake bolts	
Caliper pin bolt	23 Nm (17 ft-lbs)
Caliper bracket pin bolt	13 Nm (108 inch-lbs)
Torque link to fork bolt	39 Nm (29 ft-lbs)
Torque link to caliper bracket bolt	26 Nm (20 ft-lbs)
Pad pin	18 Nm (13 ft-lbs)
Pad pin plug	2.9 Nm (26 inch-lbs)
Master cylinder mounting bolts	12 Nm (108 inch-lbs)
Brake hose bolt	34 Nm (25 ft-lbs)
Brake arm bolt (rear)	10 Nm (84 inch-lbs)

1. *Apply non-permanent thread locking agent to the threads.*
2. *Apply engine oil to the threads and seating surface of the nut.*

Honda NS250 Reflex, 2001 and later

Engine	249 cc single-cylinder OHC 4-stroke
Cooling system	Liquid cooled
Fuel system	CV carburetor
Ignition system	CDI
Transmission	Variable speed automatic, belt driven
Suspension	Telescopic front, swingarm with twin shocks rear
Brakes	Disc front and rear
Tires	
Front	110/90-13 M/C 56L
Rear	130/70-12 62L
Wheelbase	1545 mm (60.8 inches)
Weight (dry)	
NSS250	170.0 kg (374.8 lbs)
NSS250A/AS	172.0 kg (379.2 lbs)
NSS250S	169.0 kg (372.6 lbs)
Fuel tank capacity	12.0 liters (3.17 gal)

Engine

Spark plug type	
Standard	NGK DPR7EA-9, ND X22EPR-U9
Cold weather	NGK DPR6EA-9, X20EPR-U9
Extended high speed riding	NGK DPR8EA-9, ND X24EPR-U9
Electrode gap	0.8 to 0.9 mm (0.031 to 0.035 inch)
Idle speed (rpm)	1500 +/-100 rpm
Engine oil type	API SG or better 4-stroke engine oil meeting JASO MA standard, SAE 10W-30
Engine oil capacity (drain and fill)	1.1 liter (1.2 qt)
Coolant capacity	
Radiator and engine	1.2 liter (1.3 qt)
Reserve tank	0.2 liter (6 fl oz)
Valve clearance (cold, intake and exhaust)	One graduation mark from resistance point
Bore x stroke	72.7 x 60.0 mm (2.86 x 2.36 inches)

Honda NS250 Reflex, 2001 and later (continued)

Piston diameter (service limit) .... 72.65 mm (2.860 inches)
Piston to bore clearance (service limit) .... 0.10 mm (0.004 inch)
Piston ring installed end gap
  Top
    Standard .... 0.15 to 0.30 mm (0.006 to 0.012 inch)
    Service limit .... 0.5 mm (0.020 inch)
  Second
    Standard .... 0.30 to 0.45 mm (0.012 to 0.018 inch)
    Service limit .... 0.65 mm (0.065 inch)
  Oil ring side rail
    Standard .... 0.2 to 0.7 mm (0.008 to 0.028 inch)
    Service limit .... 0.90 mm (0.035 inch)
Piston ring side clearance
  Top and second
    Standard .... 0.15 to 0.50 mm (0.006 to 0.0020 inch)
    Limit .... 0.09 mm (0.004 inch)

Fuel system

Throttle twistgrip freeplay .... 2 to 6 mm (1/8 to 1/4 inch)
Main jet 102
Slow jet 40
Needle type/position .... Not specified
Pilot screw setting
  First step .... 2-1/8 turns out
  Second step .... Set idle to specifications
  Third step .... Turn pilot screw for highest idle speed
  Fourth step .... Reset idle to specifications
Float level .... 18.5 mm (0.73 inch)

Ignition system

Ignition coil primary peak voltage .... 100 volts minimum
Exciter coil peak voltage .... 100 volts minimum
Ignition pulse generator peak voltage .... 0.7 volts minimum

Transmission

Belt width (service limit) .... 22.3 mm (0.88 inch)
Weight roller outer diameter
  Standard .... 22.92 to 23.08 mm (0.902 to 0.909 inch)
  Limit .... 22.5 mm (0.89 inch)
Clutch lining thickness (service limit) .... 0.5 mm (0.02 inch)
Clutch spring free length (service limit) .... 108.6 mm (4.28 inches)

Brakes

Brake fluid .... DOT 4
Disc thickness (limit)
  Front .... 3.5 mm (0.14 inch)
  Rear .... 4.0 mm (0.16 inch)
Pad wear limit
  Front .... Replace when wear limit groove is worn away
  Rear .... Replace when wear indicators align

Tire pressures

Front .... 25 psi
Rear
  Rider only .... 29 psi
  Rider and passenger .... 36 psi

Electrical system

Battery
  Capacity 12V-11Ah
  Voltage (fully charged) .... 13.0 to 13.2 volts
Alternator
  Output (regulated) .... 15.5 volts
  Charging coil resistance .... 0.1 to 0.5 ohms

Fuses

Main	30 amps
Clock, back-up light, luggage light	10 amps
Ignition, starter, fuel pump	10 amps
Fan	10 amps
Headlight	15 amps
Turn/brake/tail/meter lights, horn	15 amps
Anti-lock brakes main	10 amps
Anti-lock brakes fail-safe relay	20 amps
Anti-lock brakes motor	30 amps

Torque wrench settings

Note: One foot-pound (ft-lb) of torque is equivalent to 12 inch-pounds (in-lbs) of torque. Torque values below approximately 15 foot-pounds are expressed in inch-pounds, because most foot-pound torque wrenches are not accurate at these smaller values.

Oil screen filter cap	20 Nm (14 ft-lbs)
Transmission oil check bolt	13 Nm (108 inch-lbs)
Transmission oil drain bolt	13 Nm (108 inch-lbs)
Valve cover bolts	Not specified
Cylinder head nuts	24 Nm (17 ft-lbs)
Cam chain tensioner sealing bolt	22 Nm (16 ft-lbs)
Cam chain tensioner bolts	Not specified
Cam chain guide pivot bolt	10 Nm (84 inch-lbs)
Clutch driven face nut (30 mm locknut)	78 Nm (58 ft-lbs)
Drive pulley nut	93 Nm (69 ft-lbs)
Driven pulley nut	78 Nm (58 ft-lbs)
Alternator rotor nut	116 Nm (85 ft-lbs) (1)
Starter clutch Allen bolts	29 Nm (22 ft-lbs) (2)
Crankcase bolts	Not specified
Engine mounting bolts/nuts	
Tension rod nut	20 Nm (14 ft-lbs)
Engine hanger locknut	42 Nm (31 ft-lbs)
Engine hanger pivot nut	78 Nm (58 ft-lbs)
Engine hanger adjusting bolt	15 Nm (132 inch-lbs)
Sub-bracket pivot nut	69 Nm (51 ft-lbs)
Sub-bracket stopper nut	26 Nm (20 ft-lbs)
Engine mounting nut	59 Nm (43 ft-lbs)
Handlebar clamp bolts	
NSS250S, NSS250AS	27 Nm (20 ft-lbs)
NSS250, NSS250A	Not specified
Front axle nut	69 Nm (51 ft-lbs)
Rear axle nut	118 Nm (87 ft-lbs)
Front fork pinch bolts	49 Nm (36 ft-lbs)
Front fender Allen bolts	12 Nm (108 inch-lbs)
Steering stem bearing adjusting nut	
First step	2.5 Nm (22 inch-lbs)
Second step	Loosen
Third step	2.5 Nm (22 inch-lbs)
Steering stem bearing locknut	74 Nm (54 ft-lbs)
Rear shock bolts (upper and lower)	39 Nm (29 ft-lbs)
Swingarm mounting bolts	49 Nm (36 ft-lbs)
Front brake bolts	
Caliper mounting bolts	31 Nm (23 ft-lbs) (3)
Caliper body assembly bolts	32 Nm (24 ft-lbs (3)
Front caliper pin bolts	23 Nm (17 ft-lbs) (2)
Front caliper bracket pin bolts	13 Nm (108 inch-lbs)
Pad pin	18 Nm (13 ft-lbs)
Pad pin plug	2.5 Nm (22 inch-lbs)
Master cylinder mounting bolts	12 Nm (108 inch-lbs)
Brake hose banjo fitting	34 Nm (25 ft-lbs)
Rear caliper mounting bolts	31 Nm (23 ft-lbs)

1. Apply engine oil to the threads and seating surface of the nut.
2. Apply non-permanent thread locking agent to the threads.
3. Self-locking bolts. Replace with new ones whenever they're removed.

Honda PS250 Big Ruckus, 2005 and 2006

Engine	249 cc single-cylinder 4-stroke
Cooling system	Liquid cooled
Fuel system	CV carburetor
Ignition system	CDI
Transmission	Variable speed automatic, belt driven
Suspension	Telescopic front, swingarm with single shock rear
Brakes	Disc front, drum rear
Tires	
Front	110/90-12 64L
Rear	1130/70-12 56L
Wheelbase	1455 mm (57.3 inches)
Weight (dry)	164 kg (362 lbs)
Fuel tank capacity	Not specified

Engine

Spark plug type	
Standard	NGK DPR7EA-9, ND X22EPR-U9
Cold weather	NGK DPR6EA-9, ND X20EPR-U9
Extended high speed riding	NGK DPR8EA-9, ND X24EPR-U9
Electrode gap	0.8 to 0.9 mm (0.031 to 0.035 inch)
Idle speed (rpm)	1500 +/- 100 rpm
Engine oil type	API SG or better engine oil meeting JASO MA standard, SAE 10W-40
Engine oil capacity (drain and fill)	1.1 liter (1.2 qt)
Coolant capacity	
Radiator and engine	1.2 liter (1.3 qt)
Reserve tank	0.2 liter (6 fl oz)
Valve clearance (cold, intake and exhaust)	One graduation mark from resistance point
Bore x stroke	72.7 x 60.0 mm (2.86 x 2.36 inches)
Piston diameter (service limit)	72.65 mm (2.860 inches)
Piston to bore clearance (service limit)	0.10 mm (0.004 inch)
Piston ring installed end gap	
Top	
Standard	0.15 to 0.30 mm (0.006 to 0.012 inch)
Limit	0.50 mm (0.020 inch)
Second	
Standard	0.30 to 0.45 mm (0.012 to 0.018 inch)
Limit	0.65 mm (0.026 inch)
Oil ring side rail	
Standard	0.20 to 0.70 mm (0.008 to 0.028 inch)
Limit	0.90 mm (0.035 inch)
Piston ring side clearance	
Top and second	
Standard	0.015 to 0.050 mm (0.0006 to 0.0020 inch)
Limit	0.09 mm (0.004 inch)

Fuel system

Throttle twistgrip freeplay	3 to 6 mm (1/8 to 1/4 inch)
Main jet	98
Slow jet	40
Needle type/position	Not specified
Pilot screw setting	
First step	1-3/4 turns out
Second step	Set idle speed to specifications
Third step	Turn pilot screw for highest idle speed
Fourth step	Rev engine two or three times, then reset idle speed
Fifth step	Turn pilot screw in until idle speed drops 100 rpm
Sixth step	Turn pilot screw 1/2 turn out
Float level	18.5 mm (0.73 inch)

Ignition system

Ignition coil peak primary voltage	100 volts minimum
Ignition pulse generator peak voltage	0.7 volts minimum

Transmission

Belt width (service limit)	22.3 mm (0.88 inch)
Weight roller outer diameter	
Standard	22.92 to 23.08 mm (0.902 to 0.909 inch)
Limit	22.5 mm (0.89 inch)
Clutch lining thickness (service limit)	0.5 mm (0.020 inch)
Clutch spring free length (service limit)	125.8 mm (4.95 inches)

Brakes

Brake fluid	DOT 4
Disc thickness (limit)	3.5 mm (0.14 inch)
Pad wear limit	To bottom of wear groove
Rear brake lever freeplay	20 to 30 mm (3/4 to 1-1/4 inch)
Rear brake shoe wear limit	When wear indicator marks align
Rear brake drum diameter (limit)	161 mm (6.3 inches)

Tire pressures

Front	25 psi
Rear	
Up to 90 kg (200 lbs) load	29 psi
Up to maximum weight capacity	33 psi

Electrical system

Battery	
Capacity	12V-11Ah
Voltage (fully charged)	13.0 to 13.2 volts
Alternator	
Output (regulated)	Not specified
Charging coil resistance	0.1 to 0.5 ohms
Fuses	
Main fuse	30 amps
All others	10 amps

Torque wrench settings

Note: One foot-pound (ft-lb) of torque is equivalent to 12 inch-pounds (in-lbs) of torque. Torque values below approximately 15 foot-pounds are expressed in inch-pounds, because most foot-pound torque wrenches are not accurate at these smaller values.

Oil screen filter cap	20 Nm (15 ft-lbs) (1)
Transmission oil check, filler and drain bolts	13 Nm (108 inch-lbs)
Valve cover bolts	Not specified
Cylinder head nuts	24 Nm (18 ft-lbs)
Cam chain tensioner sealing bolt	22 Nm (16 ft-lbs)
Cam chain tensioner bolt	10 Nm (84 inch-lbs)
Clutch driven face nut (30 mm locknut)	79 Nm (58 ft-lbs)
Drive pulley nut	94 Nm (69 ft-lbs)
Driven pulley nut	74 Nm (55 ft-lbs)
Alternator rotor nut	116 Nm (86 ft-lbs) (1)
Starter clutch Allen bolts	29 Nm (22 ft-lbs) (2)
Crankcase bolts	Not specified
Engine mounting bolts/nuts	
Tension rod nut	20 Nm (15 ft-lbs)
Engine hanger locknut	42 Nm (31 ft-lbs)
Engine hanger pivot nut	78 Nm (58 ft-lbs)
Sub-bracket pivot nut	62 Nm (46 ft-lbs)
Engine mounting nut	59 Nm (44 ft-lbs)
Front axle nut	68 Nm (50 ft-lbs)
Rear axle nut	118 Nm (87 ft-lbs)

1. *Apply engine oil to the threads and seating surface of the cap.*
2. *Apply non-permanent thread locking agent to the threads.*
3. *Self-locking bolts. Replace with new ones whenever they're removed.*

Honda PS250 Big Ruckus, 2005 and 2006 (continued)

Torque wrench settings (continued)

Note: One foot-pound (ft-lb) of torque is equivalent to 12 inch-pounds (in-lbs) of torque. Torque values below approximately 15 foot-pounds are expressed in inch-pounds, because most foot-pound torque wrenches are not accurate at these smaller values.

Handlebar clamp bolts	26 Nm (19 ft-lbs)
Steering stem bearing adjustment nut	
First step	2.5 Nm (22 inch-lbs)
Second step	Loosen
Third step	2.5 Nm (22 inch-lbs)
Steering stem locknut	74 Nm (55 ft-lbs)
Rear shock bolts	
Upper	49 Nm (36 ft-lbs)
Lower	39 Nm (29 ft-lbs)
Swingarm mounting bolts	49 Nm (36 ft-lbs)
Front brake bolts	
Caliper mounting bolts	30 Nm (22 ft-lbs) (3)
Caliper pin bolt	22 Nm (16 ft-lbs)
Caliper bracket pin bolt	12 Nm (108 inch-lbs)
Rear brake arm bolt	29 Nm (22 ft-lbs)
Rear thrust cylinder mounting bolt	27 Nm (20 ft-lbs) (3)

1. Apply engine oil to the threads and seating surface of the cap.
2. Apply non-permanent thread locking agent to the threads.
3. Self-locking bolts. Replace with new ones whenever they're removed.

Kymco Agility 50, 2006 and later

Engine	49.5 cc single-cylinder 4-stroke
Cooling system	Air cooled
Fuel system	CV carburetor
Ignition system	CDI
Transmission	Variable speed automatic, belt driven
Suspension	Telescopic front, swingarm with single shock rear
Brakes	Disc or drum front, drum rear
Tires	
Front	120/70-12
Rear	130/70-12
Wheelbase	1325 mm (52.16 inches)
Weight (dry)	92.5 kg (203.5 lbs)
Fuel tank capacity	5.0 liters (1.32 gallons)

Engine

Spark plug type	
Standard	NGK C7HSA
Hot plug	NGK C6HSA
Cold plug	NGK C8HSA
Electrode gap	0.6 to 0.7 mm (0.028 to 0.031 inch)
Idle speed (rpm)	1900 +/- 100 rpm
Engine oil type	Not specified
Engine oil capacity (drain and fill)	0.7 liter (0.75 qt)
Valve clearance (intake and exhaust, engine cool)	0.4 mm (0.016 inch)
Bore x stroke	39.0 x 41.4 mm (1.534 x 1.618 inches)
Piston diameter	
Standard	39.985 to 39.995 mm (1.574 to 1.575 inches)
Service limit	39.9 mm (1.570 inches)
Piston to bore clearance	
Standard	0.010 to 0.040 mm (0.004 to 0.016 inch)
Limit	0.1 mm (0.005 inch)
Piston ring installed end gap	
Top	
Standard	0.08 to 0.20 mm (0.003 to 0.008 inch)
Limit	0.45 mm (0.018 inch)
Second	
Standard	0.05 to 0.20 mm (0.002 to 0.008 inch)
Limit	0.05 to 0.20 mm (0.002 to 0.008 inch)
Oil ring side rail	0.20 to 0.70 mm (0.008 to 0.035 inch)

Fuel system

Throttle twistgrip freeplay	2 to 6 mm (3/32 to 1/4 inch)
Main jet	82
Slow jet	35
Needle type/position	Not specified
Air screw setting	2-1/2 turns out
Float level	17 mm (0.669 inch)

Ignition system

Ignition pulse generator resistance	40 to 300 ohms
Exciter coil resistance	Not specified
Ignition coil primary resistance	0.1 to 1.0 ohms
Ignition coil secondary resistance (spark plug cap installed)	7 to 12 k-ohms
Ignition coil secondary resistance (spark plug cap removed)	3 to 5 k-ohms

Transmission

Belt width (service limit)	16.5 mm (0.650 inch)
Weight roller outer diameter	
Standard	15.920 to 16.080 mm (0.627 to 0.633 inch)
Limit	15.4 mm (0.606 inch)
Clutch lining thickness (service limit)	1.5 mm (0.059 inch)
Clutch spring free length	154.6 mm (6.141 inches)

Kymco Agility 50, 2006 and later (continued)

Brakes

Brake fluid	Not applicable
Brake drum diameter (limit) (front and rear)	111 mm (4.370 inches)
Drum brake lining thickness (limit)	2.0 mm (0.079 inch)
Rear brake lever freeplay	10 to 20 mm (3/8 to 3/4 inch)
Rear brake shoe wear limit	When wear indicator marks align

Tire pressures

Front
Rider only	22 psi
Rider and passenger	25 psi

Rear
Rider only	28 psi
Rider and passenger	32 psi

Electrical system

Battery
Capacity	12V-4Ah
Voltage (fully charged)	13.0 to 13.2 volts

Alternator
Output (regulated)	1.0 to 15.0 volts
Charging coil resistance	0.2 to 1.2 ohms
Fuse	Not specified

Torque wrench settings

Note: One foot-pound (ft-lb) of torque is equivalent to 12 inch-pounds (in-lbs) of torque. Torque values below approximately 15 foot-pounds are expressed in inch-pounds, because most foot-pound torque wrenches are not accurate at these smaller values.

Oil screen filter cap	10 to 12 Nm (87 to 104 inch-lbs)
Transmission oil drain bolt	8 to 12 Nm (69 to 104 inch-lbs)
Cylinder head nuts	18 to 22 Nm (13 to 16 ft-lbs) (1)
Cam chain tensioner slipper bolt	8 to 12 Nm (69 to 104 inch-lbs)
Drive pulley nut	34 to 39 Nm (25 to 29 ft-lbs)
Centrifugal clutch outer nut	49 to 59 Nm (36 to 43 ft-lbs)
Driven pulley nut	34 to 44 Nm (25 to 32 ft-lbs)
Alternator rotor nut	34 to 44 Nm (25 to 32 ft-lbs)
Crankcase bolts	8 to 12 Nm (69 to 104 inch-lbs)
Engine mounting bolt	44 to 54 Nm (32 to 40 ft-lbs)
Engine hanger bracket bolt	44 to 54 Nm (32 to 40 ft-lbs)
Front axle nut	49 to 68 Nm (36 to 51 ft-lbs)
Rear axle nut	108 to 127 Nm (80 to 94 ft-lbs)
Handlebar bolt	44 to 54 Nm (32 to 40 ft-lbs)
Steering stem bearing adjustment nut	5 to 13 Nm (43 to 112 inch-lbs)
Steering stem locknut	59 to 78 Nm (43 to 58 ft-lbs)
Steering stem to fork bolt	34 to 44 Nm (25 to 32 ft-lbs)
Front fork damper rod bolts	Not specified
Front fork to triple clamp bolts	Not specified
Rear shock bolts	
Upper	34 to 44 Nm (25 to 32 ft-lbs)
Lower	24 to 29 Nm (17 to 22 ft-lbs)
Front brake bolts	
Caliper bracket bolts (front disc brake)	24 to 34 Nm (18 to 25 ft-lbs)
Caliper pad pins	15 to 20 Nm (11 to 15 ft-lbs)
Caliper slide pins	Not specified
Brake hose union bolts	24 to 34 Nm (18 to 25 ft-lbs)
Front brake arm bolt	8 to 12 Nm (69 to 104 inch-lbs)

1. *Apply engine oil to the threads.*

Kymco People S-50, 2006 and later

Engine	49.5 cc single-cylinder 4-stroke
Cooling system	Air cooled
Fuel system	CV carburetor
Ignition system	CDI
Transmission	Variable speed automatic, belt driven
Suspension	Telescopic front, swingarm with single shock rear
Brakes	Disc front, drum rear
Tires	
Front	100/80-16 50P
Rear	120/80-16 50P
Wheelbase	1360 mm (53.54 inches)
Weight (dry)	102 kg (224.4 lbs)
Fuel tank capacity	6.8 liters (1.67 gallons)

Engine

Spark plug type	NGK CR7HSA
Electrode gap	0.6 to 0.7 mm (0.028 to 0.031 inch)
Idle speed (rpm)	1900 +/- 100 rpm
Engine oil type	API service SG, 15W-40
Engine oil capacity (drain and fill)	0.7 liter (0.75 qt)
Valve clearance (intake and exhaust, engine cool)	0.04 mm (0.0016 inch)
Bore x stroke	39.0 x 41.4 mm (1.534 x 1.618 inches)
Piston diameter	
Standard	39.985 to 39.995 mm (1.574 to 1.575 inches)
Service limit	39.9 mm (1.570 inches)
Piston to bore clearance	
Standard	0.010 to 0.040 mm (0.004 to 0.016 inch)
Limit	0.1 mm (0.005 inch)
Piston ring installed end gap	
Top and second	
Standard	0.10 to 0.30 mm (0.004 to 0.012 inch)
Limit	0.5 mm (0.020 inch)
Oil ring side rail	0.20 to 0.70 mm (0.008 to 0.035 inch)

Fuel system

Throttle twistgrip freeplay	2 to 6 mm (3/32 to 1/4 inch)
Main jet	80
Slow jet	35
Needle type/position	Not specified
Pilot screw setting	1-3/4 +/- 1/2 turns out
Float level	17 mm (0.669 inch)

Ignition system

Ignition pulse generator resistance	70 to 130 ohms
Exciter coil resistance	Not specified
Ignition coil primary resistance	0.1 to 1.0 ohms
Ignition coil secondary resistance (spark plug cap installed)	7 to 12 k-ohms
Ignition coil secondary resistance (spark plug cap removed)	2 to 4 k-ohms

Transmission

Belt width (service limit)	17 mm (0.669 inch)
Weight roller outer diameter	
Standard	15.920 to 16.080 mm (0.627 to 0.633 inch)
Limit	15.4 mm (0.606 inch)
Clutch lining thickness (service limit)	1.5 mm (0.059 inch)
Clutch spring free length	154.6 mm (6.141 inches)

Kymco People S-50, 2006 and later (continued)

Brakes

Brake fluid	DOT 4
Disc thickness (limit)	3.0 mm (0.118 inch)
Brake drum diameter (limit)	111 mm (4.370 inches)
Drum brake lining thickness (limit)	2.0 mm (0.079 inch)
Brake lever freeplay	10 to 20 mm (3/8 to 3/4 inch)
Rear brake shoe wear limit	When wear indicator marks align

Tire pressures

Front	25 psi
Rear	
Rider only	29 psi
Rider and passenger	36 psi

Electrical system

Battery	
Capacity	12V-6Ah
Voltage (fully charged)	13.0 to 13.2 volts
Alternator	
Output (regulated)	13.5 to 15.5 volts
Charging coil resistance	0.2 to 1.2 ohms
Fuse	15 amps

Torque wrench settings

Note: One foot-pound (ft-lb) of torque is equivalent to 12 inch-pounds (in-lbs) of torque. Torque values below approximately 15 foot-pounds are expressed in inch-pounds, because most foot-pound torque wrenches are not accurate at these smaller values.

Oil screen filter cap	10 to 20 Nm (87 to 174 inch-lbs)
Transmission oil check bolt	12 Nm (104 inch-lbs)
Engine oil drain bolt	10 Nm (87 inch-lbs)
Cylinder head nuts	20 Nm (14 ft-lbs) (1)
Cam chain tensioner slipper bolt	10 Nm (87 inch-lbs)
Drive pulley nut	54 Nm (40 ft-lbs)
Centrifugal clutch outer nut	54 Nm (40 ft-lbs)
Driven pulley nut	54 Nm (40 ft-lbs)
Starter clutch locknut	93 Nm (69 ft-lbs)
Alternator rotor nut	54 Nm (40 ft-lbs)
Crankcase bolts	9 Nm (78 inch-lbs)
Engine mounting bolts	49 Nm (36 ft-lbs)
Front axle nut	48 to 68 Nm (36 to 51 ft-lbs)
Rear axle nut	108 to 127 Nm (80 to 94 ft-lbs)
Handlebar bolt	39 to 49 Nm (29 to 36 ft-lbs)
Steering stem bearing adjustment nut	5 to 13 Nm (43 to 112 inch-lbs)
Steering stem locknut	68 to 78 Nm (51 to 58 ft-lbs)
Steering stem to fork bolt	44 Nm (32 ft-lbs)
Front fork damper rod bolts	Not specified
Front fork to triple clamp bolts	Not specified
Rear shock bolts	
Upper	39 Nm (29 ft-lbs)
Lower	27 Nm (19 ft-lbs)
Front brake bolts	
Caliper bracket bolts (front disc brake)	28 to 34 Nm (21 to 20 ft-lbs)
Caliper pad pins	15 to 20 Nm (11 to 15 ft-lbs)
Caliper slide pins	Not specified
Brake hose union bolts	29 to 39 Nm (22 to 25 ft-lbs)
Rear brake arm bolt	10 Nm (87 inch-lbs)

1. *Apply engine oil to the threads.*

Kymco Agility 125, 2006 and later

Engine	124.6 cc single-cylinder 4-stroke
Cooling system	Air cooled
Fuel system	CV carburetor
Ignition system	CDI
Transmission	Variable speed automatic, belt driven
Suspension	Telescopic front, swingarm with single shock rear
Brakes	Disc or drum front, drum rear
Tires	
Front	120/70-12 56J
Rear	130/70-12 56J
Wheelbase	1300 mm (51.2 inches)
Weight (dry)	109.5 kg (240.9 lbs)
Fuel tank capacity	5.0 liters (1.23 gallons)

Engine

Spark plug type	Champion P-RZ9 HC
Electrode gap	0.6 to 0.7 mm (0.028 to 0.031 inch)
Idle speed (rpm)	1900 +/- 100 rpm
Engine oil type	API service SG, 15W-40
Engine oil capacity (drain and fill)	0.8 liter (0.81 qt)
Valve clearance (intake and exhaust, engine cool)	0.04 mm (0.0016 inch)
Bore x stroke	52.4 x 57.8 mm (2.062 to 2.275 inches)
Piston diameter	
Standard	52.370 to 52.390 mm (2.061 to 2.062 inches)
Service limit	52.30 mm (2.059 inches)
Piston to bore clearance	
Standard	0.010 to 0.040 mm (0.004 to 0.016 inch)
Limit	0.1 mm (0.005 inch)
Piston ring installed end gap	
Top and second	
Standard	0.10 to 0.25 mm (0.004 to 0.010 inch)
Limit	0.5 mm (0.020 inch)
Oil ring side rail	0.20 to 0.70 mm (0.008 to 0.035 inch)
Piston ring side clearance (top and second)	
Standard	0.015 to 0.055 mm (0.0006 to 0.002 inch)
Limit	0.09 mm (0.003 inch)

Fuel system

Throttle twistgrip freeplay	2 to 6 mm (3/32 to 1/4 inch)
Main jet	105
Slow jet	35
Needle type/position	Not specified
Pilot screw setting	3 +/- 1/2 turns out
Float level	17.5+ mm (0.689 inch)

Ignition system

Ignition pulse generator resistance	40 to 300 ohms
Exciter coil resistance	Not specified
Ignition coil primary resistance	0.1 to 1.0 ohms
Ignition coil secondary resistance (spark plug cap installed)	7 to 12 k-ohms
Ignition coil secondary resistance (spark plug cap removed)	2 to 4 k-ohms

Transmission

Belt width (service limit)	16.5 mm (0.646 inch)
Weight roller outer diameter	
Standard	15.920 to 16.080 mm (0.627 to 0.633 inch)
Limit	15.4 mm (0.606 inch)
Clutch lining thickness (service limit)	1.5 mm (0.059 inch)
Clutch spring free length	154.6 mm (6.141 inches)

Kymco Agility 125, 2006 and later (continued)

Brakes

Brake fluid	DOT 4
Disc thickness (limit)	3.0 mm (0.118 inch)
Front brake pad thickness	2.0 mm (0.079 inch)
Brake drum diameter (limit)	111 mm (4.370 inches)
Drum brake lining thickness (limit)	2.0 mm (0.079 inch)
Brake lever freeplay	10 to 20 mm (3/8 to 3/4 inch)
Rear brake shoe wear limit	When wear indicator marks align

Tire pressures

Front	
Rider only	21 psi
Rider and passenger	25 psi
Rear	
Rider only	28 psi
Rider and passenger	32 psi

Electrical system

Battery	
Capacity	12V-7Ah
Voltage (fully charged)	13.0 to 13.2 volts
Alternator	
Output (regulated)	14 to 15 volts
Charging coil resistance	0.2 to 1.2 ohms
Fuse	15 amps

Torque wrench settings

Note: One foot-pound (ft-lb) of torque is equivalent to 12 inch-pounds (in-lbs) of torque. Torque values below approximately 15 foot-pounds are expressed in inch-pounds, because most foot-pound torque wrenches are not accurate at these smaller values.

Oil screen filter cap	10 to 20 Nm (87 to 174 inch-lbs)
Transmission oil check and drain bolts	8 to 12 Nm (69 to 104 inch-lbs)
Engine oil drain bolt	10 Nm (87 inch-lbs)
Cylinder head nuts	20 Nm (14 ft-lbs) (1)
Cam chain tensioner slipper bolt	8 to 12 Nm (69 to 104 inch-lbs)
Drive pulley face nut	54 to 64 Nm (40 to 47 ft-lbs)
Centrifugal clutch outer nut (driven pulley)	34 to 44 Nm (25 to 32 ft-lbs)
Drive plate nut	49 to 50 Nm (36 to 43 ft-lbs)
Starter clutch locknut	93 Nm (69 ft-lbs)
Starter clutch cover bolts	12 Nm (104 inch-lbs)
Alternator rotor nut	34 to 44 Nm (25 to 32 ft-lbs)
Crankcase bolts	8 to 12 Nm (69 to 104 inch-lbs)
Engine mounting bolt	68 Nm (51 ft-lbs)
Front axle nut	49 to 68 Nm (36 to 51 ft-lbs)
Rear axle nut	108 to 127 Nm (80 to 94 ft-lbs)
Handlebar bolt	44 to 54 Nm (32 to 40 ft-lbs)
Steering stem bearing adjustment nut	5 to 13 Nm (43 to 112 inch-lbs)
Steering stem locknut	68 to 78 Nm (51 to 58 ft-lbs)
Steering stem to fork bolt	44 Nm (32 ft-lbs)
Front fork damper rod bolts	29 Nm (22 ft-lbs) (1)
Front fork to triple clamp bolts	Not specified
Rear shock bolts	
Upper	39 Nm (29 ft-lbs)
Lower	27 Nm (19 ft-lbs)
Front disc brake bolts	
Caliper bracket bolts (front disc brake)	28 to 34 Nm (21 to 20 ft-lbs)
Caliper pad pins	15 to 20 Nm (11 to 15 ft-lbs)
Caliper slide pins	Not specified
Brake hose union bolts	24 to 34 Nm (18 to 25 ft-lbs)
Brake arm bolt (front and rear drum brakes)	8 to 12 Nm (69 to 104 inch-lbs)

1. Apply engine oil to the threads

Kymco People S-125, 2006 and later

Engine	125 cc single-cylinder 4-stroke
Cooling system	Air cooled
Fuel system	CV carburetor
Ignition system	CDI
Transmission	Variable speed automatic, belt driven
Suspension	Telescopic front, swingarm with twin shock rear
Brakes	Disc front, drum rear
Tires	
Front	100/80-16 50P
Rear	120/80-16 50P
Wheelbase	1350 mm (53.15 inches)
Weight (dry)	122 kg (268.4 lbs)
Fuel tank capacity	6.8 liters (1.67 gallons)

Engine

Spark plug type	
Standard	NGK C7HSA
Hot plug	NGK C6HSA
Cold plug	NGK C8HSA
Electrode gap	0.6 to 0.7 mm (0.028 to 0.031 inch)
Idle speed (rpm)	1700 +/- 100 rpm
Engine oil type	API service SG, 15W-40
Engine oil capacity (drain and fill)	0.8 liter (0.81 qt)
Valve clearance (intake and exhaust, engine cool)	0.12 mm (0.005 inch)
Bore x stroke	52.4 x 57.8 mm (2.062 to 2.275 inches)
Piston diameter	
Standard	52.370 to 52.390 mm (2.061 to 2.062 inches)
Service limit	52.30 mm (2.059 inches)
Piston to bore clearance	
Standard	0.010 to 0.040 mm (0.004 to 0.016 inch)
Limit	0.1 mm (0.005 inch)
Piston ring installed end gap	
Top and second	
Standard	0.10 to 0.25 mm (0.004 to 0.010 inch)
Limit	0.5 mm (0.020 inch)
Oil ring side rail	0.20 to 0.70 mm (0.008 to 0.035 inch)
Piston ring side clearance (top and second)	
Standard	0.015 to 0.055 mm (0.0006 to 0.002 inch)
Limit	0.09 mm (0.003 inch)

Fuel system

Throttle twistgrip freeplay	2 to 6 mm (3/32 to 1/4 inch)
Main jet	114
Slow jet	35
Needle type/position	Not specified
Pilot screw setting	2-3/8 +/- 3/4 turns out
Float level	17 mm (0.669 inch)

Ignition system

Ignition pulse generator resistance	70 to 130 ohms
Exciter coil resistance	Not specified
Ignition coil primary resistance	0.1 to 1.0 ohms
Ignition coil secondary resistance (spark plug cap installed)	7 to 12 k-ohms
Ignition coil secondary resistance (spark plug cap removed)	2 to 4 k-ohms

Transmission

Belt width (service limit)	19.0 mm (0.748 inch)
Weight roller outer diameter	
Standard	15.920 to 16.080 mm (0.627 to 0.633 inch)
Limit	15.4 mm (0.606 inch)
Clutch lining thickness (service limit)	1.5 mm (0.059 inch)
Clutch spring free length	154.6 mm (6.141 inches)

Kymco People S-125, 2006 and later (continued)

Brakes

Brake fluid	DOT 4
Disc thickness (limit)	3.0 mm (0.118 inch)
Front brake pad thickness	2.75 mm (0.108 inch)
Brake drum diameter (limit)	131 mm (5.157 inches)
Drum brake lining thickness (limit)	2.0 mm (0.079 inch)
Brake lever freeplay	10 to 20 mm (3/8 to 3/4 inch)
Rear brake shoe wear limit	When wear indicator marks align

Tire pressures

Front	25 psi
Rear	
Rider only	29 psi
Rider and passenger	36 psi

Electrical system

Battery	
Capacity	12V-6Ah
Voltage (fully charged)	13.0 to 13.2 volts
Alternator	
Output (regulated)	13.5 to 15.5 volts
Charging coil resistance	0.2 to 1.2 ohms
Fuse	15 amps

Torque wrench settings

Note: One foot-pound (ft-lb) of torque is equivalent to 12 inch-pounds (in-lbs) of torque. Torque values below approximately 15 foot-pounds are expressed in inch-pounds, because most foot-pound torque wrenches are not accurate at these smaller values.

Oil screen filter cap	15 Nm (130 inch-lbs)
Transmission oil check bolt	10 to 15 Nm (87 to 130 inch-lbs)
Engine oil drain bolt	10 Nm (87 inch-lbs)
Cylinder head nuts	20 Nm (14 ft-lbs) (1)
Cam chain tensioner slipper bolt	10 Nm (87 inch-lbs)
Drive pulley nut	54 Nm (40 ft-lbs)
Centrifugal clutch outer nut	54 Nm (40 ft-lbs)
Driven pulley nut	54 Nm (40 ft-lbs)
Starter clutch locknut	93 Nm (69 ft-lbs)
Alternator rotor nut	54 Nm (40 ft-lbs)
Crankcase bolts	9 Nm (78 inch-lbs)
Engine mounting bolts	49 Nm (36 ft-lbs)
Front axle nut	59 Nm (43 ft-lbs)
Rear axle nut	118 Nm (87 ft-lbs)
Handlebar bolt	39 to 49 Nm (29 to 36 ft-lbs)
Steering stem bearing adjustment nut	5 to 13 Nm (43 to 112 inch-lbs)
Steering stem locknut	68 to 78 Nm (51 to 58 ft-lbs)
Steering stem to fork bolt	44 Nm (32 ft-lbs)
Front fork damper rod bolts	20 to 25 Nm (15 to 18 ft-lbs)
Front fork to triple clamp bolts	Not specified
Rear shock bolts	
Upper	39 Nm (29 ft-lbs)
Lower	27 Nm (19 ft-lbs)
Front brake bolts	
Caliper bracket bolts (front disc brake)	28 to 34 Nm (21 to 25 ft-lbs)
Caliper pad pins	15 to 20 Nm (11 to 15 ft-lbs)
Caliper slide pins	Not specified
Brake hose union bolts	29 to 39 Nm (22 to 25 ft-lbs)
Rear brake arm bolt	10 Nm (87 inch-lbs)

1. *Apply engine oil to the threads.*

Kymco People S-200, 2006 and later

Engine	163 cc single-cylinder 4-stroke
Cooling system	Air cooled
Fuel system	CV carburetor
Ignition system	CDI
Transmission	Variable speed automatic, belt driven
Suspension	Telescopic front, swingarm with twin shock rear
Brakes	Disc front, drum rear
Tires	
Front	100/80-16 50P
Rear	120/80-16 50P
Wheelbase	1350 mm (53.15 inches)
Weight (dry)	116 kg (255.2 lbs)
Fuel tank capacity	6.8 liters (1.67 gallons)

Engine

Spark plug type	
Standard	NGK C7HSA
Hot plug	NGK C6HSA
Cold plug	NGK C8HSA
Electrode gap	0.6 to 0.7 mm (0.028 to 0.031 inch)
Idle speed (rpm)	1700 +/- 100 rpm
Engine oil type	API service SG, 15W-40
Engine oil capacity (drain and fill)	0.8 liter (0.81 qt)
Valve clearance (intake and exhaust, engine cool)	0.12 mm (0.005 inch)
Bore x stroke	60 x 57.8 mm (2.362 x 2.244 inches)
Piston diameter	
Standard	59.993 to 59.995 mm (2.361 to 2.362 inches)
Service limit	59.5 mm (2.358 inches)
Piston to bore clearance	
Standard	0.010 to 0.040 mm (0.004 to 0.016 inch)
Limit	0.1 mm (0.005 inch)
Piston ring installed end gap	
Top and second	
Standard	0.15 to 0.55 mm (0.006 to 0.021 inch)
Limit	0.5 mm (0.020 inch)
Oil ring side rail	0.20 to 0.70 mm (0.008 to 0.035 inch)
Piston ring side clearance (top and second)	
Standard	0.015 to 0.055 mm (0.0006 to 0.002 inch)
Limit	0.09 mm (0.003 inch)

Fuel system

Throttle twistgrip freeplay	2 to 6 mm (3/32 to 1/4 inch)
Main jet	118
Slow jet	35
Needle type/position	Not specified
Pilot screw setting	2-3/8 +/- 3/4 turns out
Float level	17 mm (0.669 inch)

Ignition system

Ignition pulse generator resistance	70 to 130 ohms
Exciter coil resistance	Not specified
Ignition coil primary resistance	0.1 to 1.0 ohms
Ignition coil secondary resistance (spark plug cap installed)	7 to 12 k-ohms
Ignition coil secondary resistance (spark plug cap removed)	2 to 4 k-ohms

Transmission

Belt width (service limit)	19.0 mm (0.748 inch)
Weight roller outer diameter	
Standard	15.920 to 16.080 mm (0.627 to 0.633 inch)
Limit	15.4 mm (0.606 inch)
Clutch lining thickness (service limit)	1.5 mm (0.059 inch)
Clutch spring free length	154.6 mm (6.141 inches)

Kymco People S-200, 2006 and later (continued)

Brakes

Brake fluid	DOT 4
Disc thickness (limit)	3.0 mm (0.118 inch)
Front brake pad thickness	2.75 mm (0.108 inch)
Brake drum diameter (limit)	131 mm (5.157 inches)
Drum brake lining thickness (limit)	2.0 mm (0.079 inch)
Brake lever freeplay	10 to 20 mm (3/8 to 3/4 inch)
Rear brake shoe wear limit	When wear indicator marks align

Tire pressures

Front	25 psi
Rear	
Rider only	29 psi
Rider and passenger	36 psi

Electrical system

Battery	
Capacity	12V-6Ah
Voltage (fully charged)	13.0 to 13.2 volts
Alternator	
Output (regulated)	13.5 to 15.5 volts
Charging coil resistance	0.2 to 1.2 ohms
Fuse	15 amps

Torque wrench settings

Note: One foot-pound (ft-lb) of torque is equivalent to 12 inch-pounds (in-lbs) of torque. Torque values below approximately 15 foot-pounds are expressed in inch-pounds, because most foot-pound torque wrenches are not accurate at these smaller values.

Oil screen filter cap	15 Nm (130 inch-lbs)
Transmission oil check bolt	10 to 15 Nm (87 to 130 inch-lbs)
Engine oil drain bolt	10 Nm (87 inch-lbs)
Cylinder head nuts	20 Nm (14 ft-lbs) (1)
Cam chain tensioner slipper bolt	10 Nm (87 inch-lbs)
Drive pulley nut	54 Nm (40 ft-lbs)
Centrifugal clutch outer nut	54 Nm (40 ft-lbs)
Driven pulley nut	54 Nm (40 ft-lbs)
Starter clutch locknut	93 Nm (69 ft-lbs)
Alternator rotor nut	54 Nm (40 ft-lbs)
Crankcase bolts	9 Nm (78 inch-lbs)
Engine mounting bolts	49 Nm (36 ft-lbs)
Front axle nut	59 Nm (43 ft-lbs)
Rear axle nut	118 Nm (87 ft-lbs)
Handlebar bolt	39 to 49 Nm (29 to 36 ft-lbs)
Steering stem bearing adjustment nut	5 to 13 Nm (43 to 112 inch-lbs)
Steering stem locknut	68 to 78 Nm (51 to 58 ft-lbs)
Steering stem to fork bolt	44 Nm (32 ft-lbs)
Front fork damper rod bolts	20 to 25 Nm (15 to 18 ft-lbs)
Front fork to triple clamp bolts	Not specified
Rear shock bolts	
Upper	39 Nm (29 ft-lbs)
Lower	27 Nm (19 ft-lbs)
Front brake bolts	
Caliper bracket bolts (front disc brake)	28 to 34 Nm (21 to 20 ft-lbs)
Caliper pad pins	15 to 20 Nm (11 to 15 ft-lbs)
Caliper slide pins	Not specified
Brake hose union bolts	29 to 39 Nm (22 to 25 ft-lbs)
Rear brake arm bolt	10 Nm (87 inch-lbs)

1. Apply engine oil to the threads.

Piaggio Typhoon 50, 2005 and later

Engine	49.4 cc single cylinder 2-stroke
Cooling system	Air cooled
Fuel system	Dell'orto carburetor
Ignition system	CDI
Transmission	Variable speed automatic, belt driven
Suspension	Telescopic front, swingarm with single shock rear
Brakes	Disc front and rear
Tires (front and rear)	120/90-10
Wheelbase	1260 mm (49.6 inches)
Weight (curb)	83 kg (182.6 lbs)
Fuel tank capacity	5.5 liters (1.35 gallons)

Engine

Spark plug type	Champion RGN 2C
Electrode gap	0.6 to 0.7mm (0.024 to 0.028 inch)
Idle speed (rpm)	1800 to 2000 rpm
Engine oil type	Synthetic 2-stroke oil meeting API TC++ specification
Oil capacity	1.2 liters (1.27 quarts)
Bore x stroke	40 x 39.3 mm (1.574 x 1.447 inches)
Piston diameter	
M piston	39.943 to 39.950 mm (1.5725 to 1.5728 inches)
N piston	39.950 to 39.957 mm (1.5728 to 1.5731 inches)
O piston	39.957 to 39.964 mm (1.5731 to 1.5733 inches)
P piston	39.964 to 39.971 mm (1.5733 to 1.5736 inches)
Piston to bore clearance (all)	0.055 to 0.069 mm (0.002 to 0.003 inch)
Piston ring installed end gap	0.10 to 0.25 mm (0.004 to 0.0120 inch)

Fuel system

Throttle twistgrip freeplay	Not specified
Main jet	Not specified
Slow jet	Not specified
Needle position	1 notch from top
Pilot screw setting (Keihin)	1-1/2 turns out
Float level	Not specified

Ignition system

Ignition pulse generator resistance	90 to 140 ohms
Exciter coil resistance	Not specified
Ignition coil primary resistance	Not specified
Ignition coil secondary resistance (spark plug cap installed)	Not specified
Ignition coil secondary resistance (spark plug cap removed)	Not specified

Transmission

Belt width (service limit)	17.5 mm (0.688 inch)
Clutch lining thickness (service limit)	1.0 mm (0.039 inch)
Clutch spring free length (service limit)	113 mm (4.448 inches)

Brakes

Brake fluid	DOT 4
Disc thickness (limit)	3.5 mm (0.137 inch)
Front brake pad thickness	1.5 mm (0.059 inch)
Brake drum diameter (limit)	Not applicable
Drum brake lining thickness (limit)	Not applicable
Brake lever freeplay	10 to 20 mm (3/8 to 3/4 inch)
Rear brake shoe wear limit	Not applicable

Tire pressures

Tire pressures	Not specified

Piaggio Typhoon 50, 2005 and later (continued)

Electrical system

Battery	
Capacity	12V-4Ah
Minimum voltage	12.6 volts
Alternator	
Output (unregulated)	25 to 30 volts AC at 3000 rpm
Charging voltage (between battery terminals)	13 volts DC
Charging coil resistance	800 to 1100 ohms
Fuse	7.5 amps

Torque wrench settings

Note: One foot-pound (ft-lb) of torque is equivalent to 12 inch-pounds (in-lbs) of torque. Torque values below approximately 15 foot-pounds are expressed in inch-pounds, because most foot-pound torque wrenches are not accurate at these smaller values.

Transmission oil drain bolt	Not specified
Cylinder head nuts	10 to 11 Nm (89 to 97 inch-lbs)
Driven pulley shaft nut	40 to 44 Nm (29 to 32 ft-lbs)
Drive pulley nut	
First step	18 to 20 Nm (13 to 15 ft-lbs)
Second step	Tighten an additional 90-degrees
Starter clutch mounting bolts	Not specified
Starter motor mounting bolts	Not specified
Alternator rotor nut	40 to 44 Nm (29 to 32 ft-lbs)
Crankcase bolts	11 to 13 Nm (97 to 115 inch-lbs)
Swingarm to engine	33 to 41 Nm (24 to 30 ft-lbs)
Swingarm to frame	64 to 72 Nm (47 to 53 ft-lbs)
Front axle nut	45 to 50 Nm (33 to 37 ft-lbs)
Rear axle nut	104 to 126 Nm (77 to 93 ft-lbs)
Handlebar bolt	45 to 50 Nm (32 to 37 ft-lbs)
Steering stem bearing adjustment nut	8 to 10 Nm (71 to 84 inch-lbs)
Steering stem locknut	35 to 40 Nm (26 to 29 ft-lbs)
Front fork damper rod bolts	20 to 25 Nm (15 to 18 ft-lbs)
Front fork to triple clamp bolts	Not specified
Rear shock to engine	33 to 41 Nm (24 to 30 ft-lbs)
Rear shock to frame	20 to 25 Nm (15 to 18 ft-lbs)
Front drum brake lining thickness (limit)	Not applicable
Front and rear disc brake bolts	
Caliper bracket bolts	20 to 25 Nm (15 to 18 ft-lbs)
Caliper assembly bolts	20 to 25 Nm (15 to 18 ft-lbs)
Brake hose to caliper	20 to 25 Nm (15 to 18 ft-lbs)
Brake hose to master cylinder	13 to 18 Nm (115 to 159 inch-lbs)
Brake arm bolt (front and rear drum brakes)	Not applicable

1. *Apply engine oil to the threads.*

Piaggio FLY150, 2005 and later

Engine	150 cc single-cylinder 4-stroke
Cooling system	Air cooled
Fuel system	CV carburetor
Ignition system	CDI
Transmission	Variable speed automatic, belt driven
Suspension	Telescopic front, swingarm with single shock rear
Brakes	Disc front, drum rear
Tires	120/70-12 (front and rear)
Wheelbase	1330 mm (52.36 inches)
Weight (dry)	112 kg (246.4 lbs)
Fuel tank capacity	7.2 liters (1.9 gal)

Engine

Spark plug type	Champion RG6YC
Electrode gap	0.7 to 0.8 mm (0.028 to 0.031 inch)
Idle speed (rpm)	1600 to 1800 rpm
Engine oil type	Synthetic API SG, 5W-40
Oil capacity (with filter change)	1.1 liters (1.16 qt)*
Bore x stroke	62.6 x 48.6 mm (2.464 x 1.913 inches)
Piston to bore clearance (service limit)	0.040 to 0.054 mm (0.0016 to 0.0021 inch)
Piston ring installed end gap	
Compression (standard)	0.15 to 0.30 mm (0.006 to 0.012 inch)
Oil (standard)	0.2 to 0.4 mm (0.008 to 0.016 inch)

Fuel system

Throttle twistgrip freeplay	Not specified
Minimum jet	35
Starter jet	33
Needle type/position	5CI3/not specified
Pilot screw setting	1-3/4 turns out
Float height	Bottom edge parallel to gasket face

Ignition system

Ignition coil primary resistance	0.4 to 0.5 ohms
Ignition coil secondary resistance	3 k-ohms +/- 10%
Pick-up coil resistance	Not specified

Transmission

Belt width (service limit)	21.5 mm (0.846 inch)
Clutch lining thickness (standard)	1.0 mm (0.039 inch)
Clutch spring free length (standard)	106 mm (4.17 inch)

Brakes

Front brake pad thickness (service limit)	1.5 mm (1/16 inch)
Front brake disc runout (service limit)	0.1 mm (0.004 inch)

Tire pressures

Front	26 psi
Rear	
Rider only	29 psi
Rider and passenger	33 psi

Electrical system

Battery	
Capacity	12V 9 Ah
Open-circuit voltage (maintenance-free battery, minimum)	12.6 volts
Specific gravity (fillable battery)	1.270 @ 20-degrees C/68-degrees F
Alternator	
Regulated voltage (no load)	14.0 to 15.2 volts
Charging coil resistance	0.7 to 0.9 ohms
Fuses	
Main fusible link	15 amps
Fuses	7 and 5 amps

*Total capacity. Start by adding the same amount that was drained, then let the engine idle for a few minutes, shut it off, wait 5 minutes and recheck the level. Do not fill beyond the MAX mark.

Torque wrench settings

Note: One foot-pound (ft-lb) of torque is equivalent to 12 inch-pounds (in-lbs) of torque. Torque values below approximately 15 foot-pounds are expressed in inch-pounds, because most foot-pound torque wrenches are not accurate at these smaller values.

Cylinder head cover	11 to 13 Nm (96 to 112 inch-lbs)
Cylinder head nuts	28 to 30 Nm (21 to 22 ft-lbs)
Cylinder head external screws	11 to 13 Nm (96 to 112 inch-lbs)
Camshaft sprocket screws	12 to 14 Nm (108 to 120 inch-lbs)
Timing chain tensioner sliding block screws	10 to 14 Nm (89 to 120 inch-lbs)
Drive pulley screw	75 to 83 Nm (55 to 61 ft-lbs)
Centrifugal clutch housing nut	45 to 50 Nm (33 to 44 ft-lbs)

Piaggio FLY150, 2005 and later (continued)

Torque wrench settings (continued)

Note: One foot-pound (ft-lb) of torque is equivalent to 12 inch-pounds (in-lbs) of torque. Torque values below approximately 15 foot-pounds are expressed in inch-pounds, because most foot-pound torque wrenches are not accurate at these smaller values.

Driven pulley nut	54 to 60 Nm (40 to 44 ft-lbs)
Alternator rotor nut	52 to 58 Nm (38 to 42 ft-lbs)
Front axle nut	45 to 50 Nm (33 to 44 ft-lbs)
Rear axle nut	104 to 126 Nm (77 to 92 ft-lbs)
Handlebar clamp bolts	50 to 55 Nm (33 to 40 ft-lbs)
Steering stem bearing lower nut	8 to 10 Nm (72 to 86 inch-lbs)
Steering stem bearing upper nut	35 to 40 Nm (25 to 29 ft-lbs)
Front fork lower attaching screws	15 to 20 Nm (11 to 14 ft-lbs)
Rear shock absorber to chassis	20 to 25 Nm (14 to 18 ft-lbs)
Rear shock absorber bracket to chassis	20 to 25 Nm (14 to 18 ft-lbs)
Front brake caliper setscrews	24 to 27 Nm (18 to 20 ft-lbs)
Brake disc mounting screws	8 to 10 Nm (72 to 89 inch-lbs)

Piaggio BV200, 2002 and later

Engine	198 cc single-cylinder 4-stroke
Cooling system	Liquid cooled
Fuel system	Walbro or Keihin CV carburetor
Ignition system	CDI
Transmission	Variable speed automatic, belt driven
Suspension	Telescopic front, swingarm with dual shock rear
Brakes	Disc front and rear
Tires	
Front	110/70-16 M/C 52P
Rear	140/70-16 M/C 65P
Wheelbase	1475 mm (58.07 inches)
Weight (dry)	149 kg (328.5 lbs)
Fuel tank capacity	7.2 liters (1.9 gal)

Engine

Spark plug type	Champion RG6YC
Electrode gap	0.7 to 0.8 mm (0.028 to 0.031 inch)
Idle speed (rpm)	1650 +/- 50 rpm
Engine oil type	Synthetic API SG, 5W-40
Oil capacity (with filter change)	1.1 liters (1.16 qt)*
Bore x stroke	72.0 x 48.6 mm (2.83 x 1.913 inches)
Piston to bore clearance (service limit)	0.040 to 0.054 mm (0.0016 to 0.0021 inch)
Piston ring installed end gap (service limit)	1.0 mm (0.039 inch)
Piston ring side clearance (service limit)	0.07 mm (0.0027 inch)

*Total capacity. Start by adding the same amount that was drained, then let the engine idle for a few minutes, shut it off, wait 5 minutes and recheck the level. Do not fill beyond the MAX mark.

Fuel system

Throttle twistgrip freeplay	Not specified
Walbro carburetor	
Max jet	95
Slow running jet	33
Main air jet	120
Idle air jet	55
Minimum jet	35
Starter jet	33
Needle type	495
Pilot screw setting	1-1/2 to 2-1/2 turns out
Float height	Bottom edge parallel to gasket face

Keihin carburetor
Max jet 92
Slow running jet 38
Main air jet 70
Idle air jet 115
Starter jet 42
Needle type.. NDAA
Pilot screw setting... 2 to 2-1/2 turns out
Float height .... Bottom edge parallel to gasket face

Ignition system
Ignition coil primary resistance.. 0.4 to 0.5 ohms
Ignition coil secondary resistance .... 3 k-ohms +/- 10%
Pick-up coil resistance .... Not specified

Transmission
Belt width (service limit)... Not specified
Clutch lining thickness (standard) .... 1.0 mm (0.039 inch)
Clutch spring free length (standard)................................... 106 mm (4.17 inches)

Brakes
Front brake pad thickness (service limit)........................... 1.5 mm (1/16 inch)
Front brake disc runout (service limit) .... 0.1 mm (0.004 inch)

Tire pressures
Front .... 26 psi
Rear
Rider only.. 29 psi
Rider and passenger..................................... 32 psi

Electrical system
Battery
Capacity .... 12V 12 Ah
Open-circuit voltage (maintenance-free battery, minimum)........ 12.6 volts
Specific gravity (fillable battery) .... 1.270 @ 20-degrees C/68-degrees F
Alternator
Regulated voltage (no load) .... 14.0 to 15.2 volts
Charging coil resistance............................... 0.7 to 0.9 ohms
Fuses .... 15, 10, 7.5 (3) and 5 (2) amps

Torque wrench settings
Note: One foot-pound (ft-lb) of torque is equivalent to 12 inch-pounds (in-lbs) of torque. Torque values below approximately 15 foot-pounds are expressed in inch-pounds, because most foot-pound torque wrenches are not accurate at these smaller values.

Cylinder head cover .... 12 to 14 Nm (106 to 123 inch-lbs)
Cylinder head nuts
First step .... 7 +/- 1 Nm (63 +/- 8.4 inch-lbs)
Second step.. One additional half-turn
Cylinder head external screws .... 11 to 13 Nm (96 to 112 inch-lbs)
Camshaft retaining plate screws .... 4 to 6 Nm (2.9 to 4.4 ft-lbs)
Timing chain tensioner sliding block screws................... 10 to 14 Nm (89 to 124 inch-lbs)
Drive pulley nut.. 75 to 83 Nm (55 to 61 ft-lbs)
Centrifugal clutch housing nut .... 55 to 60 Nm (41 to 44 ft-lbs)
Driven pulley nut.. 54 to 60 Nm (40 to 44 ft-lbs)
Alternator rotor nut .... 52 to 58 Nm (38 to 42 ft-lbs)
Front axle nut .... 75 to 90 Nm (55 to 66 ft-lbs)
Rear axle nut .... 104 to 126 Nm (77 to 92 ft-lbs)
Handlebar clamp bolts .... 45 to 50 Nm (33 to 36 ft-lbs)
Steering stem bearing lower nut .... 8 to 10 Nm (71 to 89 inch-lbs)
Steering stem bearing upper nut.................................. 30 to 40 Nm (22 to 29 ft-lbs)
Front shock absorber plate to caliper screws................. 20 to 27 Nm (15 to 20 ft-lbs)
Rear shock absorber upper end................................... 20 to 25 Nm (14 to 18 ft-lbs)
Rear shock absorber support plate to crankcase............ 20 to 25 Nm (14 to 18 ft-lbs)
Rear shock absorber lower end .... 33 to 41 Nm (24 to 30 ft-lbs)
Front brake caliper to shock absorber plate .... 20 to 25 Nm (14 to 18 ft-lbs)
Brake disc mounting screws .... 6 Nm (53 inch-lbs)

Piaggio BV250, 2005 and later

Engine	244 cc single-cylinder 4-stroke
Cooling system	Liquid cooled
Fuel system	Walbro or Keihin carburetor
Ignition system	CDI
Transmission	Variable speed automatic, belt driven
Suspension	Telescopic front, swingarm with dual shock rear
Brakes	Disc front and rear
Tires	
Front	110/70-16 MC 52P
Rear	140/70-16 MC 65P
Wheelbase	1455 mm
Weight (curb)	149 kg (327.8 lbs)
Fuel tank capacity	10 liters (2.64 gallons), including 2.5 liters (0.66 gallon) reserve

Engine

Spark plug type	Champion RG 4 HC
Electrode gap	0.7 to 0.8 mm (0.028 to 0.031 inch)
Idle speed (rpm)	1650 +/- 50
Engine oil type	Synthetic API SJ, 5W-40
Oil capacity (with filter change)	1.2 liters (1.27 quarts)
Valve clearance	
Intake	0.10 mm (0.004 inch)
Exhaust	0.15 mm (0.006 inch)
Bore x stroke	72. x 60 mm (2.835 to 2.362 inches)
Piston diameter	
A piston	71.953 to 71.960 mm (2.832 to 2.833 inches)
B piston	71.960 to 71.967 mm (2.8330 to 2.8333 inches)
C piston	71.967 to 71.974 mm (2.8333 to 2.8334 inches)
D piston	71.974 to 71.981 mm (2.8334 to 2.8338 inches)
Piston to bore clearance	0.030 to 0.040 mm (0.012 to 0.016 inch)
Piston ring installed end gap	
Top and second	0.15 to 0.30 mm (0.0006 to 0.0012 inch)
Oil ring side rail	0.20 to 0.40 mm (0.008 to 0.016 inch)
Piston ring side clearance (all rings, service limit)	0.07 mm (0.003 inch)

Fuel system

Throttle twistgrip freeplay	Not specified
Main jet (Keihin)	100
Slow jet (Keihin)	38
Main jet (Walbro)	118
Slow jet (Walbro)	34
Needle type/position	Not specified
Pilot screw setting (Keihin)	2-1/2 +/- 1/4 turns out
Pilot screw setting (Walbro)	3-1/2 +/- 1/2 turns out
Float level	17.5+ mm (0.689 inch)

Ignition system

Ignition pulse generator resistance	105 to 124 ohms
Exciter coil resistance	Not specified
Ignition coil primary resistance	0.4 to 0.5 ohms
Ignition coil secondary resistance (spark plug cap installed)	Not specified
Ignition coil secondary resistance (spark plug cap removed)	2000 ohms +/- 300 ohms

Transmission

Belt width (service limit)	19.5 mm (0.767 inch)
Weight roller outer diameter	
Standard	20.5 to 20.7 mm (0.807 to 0.814 inch)
Limit	20 mm (0.787 inch)
Clutch lining thickness (service limit)	1.0 mm (0.039 inch)
Clutch spring free length (service limit)	118 mm (4.645 inches)

Brakes

Brake fluid	DOT 4
Disc thickness (limit)	3.5 mm (0.137 inch)

Front brake pad thickness	1.5 mm (0.059 inch)
Brake drum diameter (limit)	Not applicable
Drum brake lining thickness (limit)	Not applicable
Brake lever freeplay	10 to 20 mm (3/8 to 3/4 inch)
Rear brake shoe wear limit	Not applicable

Tire pressures

Front	30 psi
Rear	
Rider only	33 psi
Rider and passenger	36 psi

Electrical system

Battery	
Capacity	12V-12Ah
Voltage (fully charged)	13.0 to 13.2 volts
Alternator	
Output (regulated)	14.0 to 15.2 volts
Charging coil resistance	0.7 to 0.9 ohms
Fuses	2-15 amps, 1-10 amps, 2-7.5 amps, 3-4 amps

Torque wrench settings

Note: One foot-pound (ft-lb) of torque is equivalent to 12 inch-pounds (in-lbs) of torque. Torque values below approximately 15 foot-pounds are expressed in inch-pounds, because most foot-pound torque wrenches are not accurate at these smaller values.

Engine oil drain plug	24 to 30 Nm (18 to 22 ft-lbs)
Transmission oil drain bolt	15 to 17 Nm (133 to 150 inch-lbs)
Cylinder head nuts (1)	
First step	7 +/- 1 Nm (62 +/- 9 inch-lbs)
Second step	10 +/- 1 Nm (89 +/- 9 inch-lbs)
Third step	An additional 3/4-turn
Cam chain tensioner pivot bolt	10 to 14 Nm (89 to 124 inch-lbs)
Pulley shaft nut	54 to 60 Nm (39 to 44 ft-lbs)
Drive pulley nut	75 to 83 Nm (55 to 61 ft-lbs)
Starter clutch mounting bolts	13 to 15 Nm (115 to 132 inch-lbs)
Starter motor mounting bolts	11 to 13 Nm (97 to 115 inch-lbs)
Alternator rotor nut	94 to 102 Nm (69 to 75 ft-lbs)
Crankcase bolts	11 to 13 Nm (97 to 115 inch-lbs)
Frame arm to engine arm link nut	33 to 41 Nm (24 to 30 ft-lbs)
Spacer - clamping threaded bushing	13 to 17 Nm (115 to 150 inch-lbs)
Threaded bushing counternut	90 to 110 Nm (66 to 81 ft-lbs)
Silentbloc support plate bolt	64 to 72 Nm (47 to 53 ft-lbs)
Front axle nut	45 to 50 Nm (33 to 37 ft-lbs)
Rear axle nut	104 to 126 Nm (77 to 93 ft-lbs)
Handlebar bolt	45 to 50 Nm (33 to 37 ft-lbs)
Rear wheel bolts	34 to 38 Nm (25 to 28 ft-lbs)
Steering stem bearing adjustment nut	
First step	10 to 13 Nm (89 to 115 inch-lbs)
Second step	Loosen 90-degrees
Steering stem locknut	30 to 36 Nm (22 to 26 ft-lbs)
Front fork damper rod bolts	20 to 25 Nm (15 to 18 ft-lbs)
Front fork to triple clamp bolts	Not specified
Rear shock bolts (upper and lower)	33 to 41 Nm (24 to 30 ft-lbs)
Shock absorber lower left support bolt	20 to 25 Nm (15 to 18 ft-lbs)
Swingarm pivot bolt to engine	64 to 72 Nm (47 to 53 ft-lbs)
Swingarm pivot bolt to frame	64 to 72 Nm (47 to 53 ft-lbs)
Front drum brake lining thickness (limit)	Not applicable
Front and rear disc brake bolts	
Caliper bracket bolts	20 to 25 Nm (15 to 18 ft-lbs)
Caliper pad pins	20 to 25 Nm (15 to 18 ft-lbs)
Caliper slide pins	20 to 25 Nm (15 to 18 ft-lbs)
Brake hose union bolts	16 to 20 Nm (12 to 15 ft-lbs)
Rear brake hose to metal tube	9 to 11 Nm (80 to 97 inch-lbs)
Brake arm bolt (front and rear drum brakes)	Not applicable

1. Apply engine oil to the threads.

Vespa LX50, 2005

Engine	50 cc single-cylinder 4-stroke
Cooling system	Air cooled
Fuel system	CV carburetor
Ignition system	CDI
Transmission	Variable speed automatic, belt driven
Suspension	Pivot arm front, swingarm with single shock rear
Brakes	Disc front, drum rear
Tires	
Front	110/70-11
Rear	120/70-11
Wheelbase	1290 mm (50.79 inches)
Weight (dry)	Not specified
Fuel tank capacity	8.5 liters (2.24 gal)

Engine

Spark plug type	NGK CR8EB
Electrode gap	0.7 to 0.8 mm (0.028 to 0.031 inch)
Idle speed (rpm)	1900 to 2000 rpm
Engine oil type	Synthetic API SG, 5W-40
Oil capacity (with filter change)	850 cc (29 fl oz)*
Bore x stroke	39.0 x 41.8 mm (1.535 x 1.645 inches)
Piston ring installed end gap (service limit)	1.0 mm (0.039 inch)
Piston ring side clearance (service limit)	0.07 mm (0.0027 inch)

Total capacity. Start by adding the same amount that was drained, then let the engine idle for a few minutes, shut it off, wait 5 minutes and recheck the level. Do not fill beyond the MAX mark.

Fuel system

Throttle twistgrip freeplay	Not specified
Idle air jet	1.4
Needle type	NGBA
Pilot screw setting	1-3/4 turns out
Float height	Bottom edge parallel to gasket face

Transmission

Belt width (service limit)	17.5 mm (0.689 inch)
Clutch lining thickness (standard)	1.0 mm (0.039 inch)
Clutch spring free length (standard)	118 mm (4.645 inches)

Brakes

Front brake pad thickness (service limit)	1.5 mm (1/16 inch)
Front brake disc runout (service limit)	0.1 mm (0.004 inch)

Tire pressures

Front	23 psi
Rear	29 psi

Electrical system

Battery	
Capacity	12V 9 Ah
Open-circuit voltage (maintenance-free battery, minimum)	12.6 volts
Specific gravity (fillable battery)	1.270 @ 20-degrees C/68-degrees F
Alternator	
Regulated voltage (no load)	14.0 to 14.5 volts
Charging coil resistance	1 ohms
Fuse	10 amps

Torque wrench settings

Note: One foot-pound (ft-lb) of torque is equivalent to 12 inch-pounds (in-lbs) of torque. Torque values below approximately 15 foot-pounds are expressed in inch-pounds, because most foot-pound torque wrenches are not accurate at these smaller values.

Cylinder head cover	12 to 14 Nm (106 to 123 inch-lbs)
Cylinder head stud bolts	
First step	6 to 7 Nm (53 to 62 inch-lbs)
Second step	An additional 1/4 turn
Third step	Another additional 1/4 turn

Cylinder head and cylinder screws	8 to 10 Nm (71 to 89 inch-lbs)
Camshaft pulley screw	12 to 14 Nm (106 to 124 inch-lbs)
Rocker arm shaft to camshaft bearing screw	3 to 4 Nm (27 to 35 inch-lbs)
Drive pulley nut	
First step	20 Nm (15 ft-lbs)
Second step	An additional 1/4-turn
Centrifugal clutch housing nut	55 to 60 Nm (41 to 44 ft-lbs)
Driven pulley nut	40 to 44 Nm (29 to 32 ft-lbs)
Alternator rotor nut	52 to 58 Nm (38 to 42 ft-lbs)
Front axle nut	75 to 90 Nm (55 to 66 ft-lbs)
Rear axle nut	104 to 126 Nm (77 to 92 ft-lbs)
Handlebar clamp bolt	50 Nm (36 ft-lbs)
Steering stem bearing lower nut	8 to 10 Nm (71 to 89 inch-lbs)
Steering stem bearing upper nut	30 to 40 Nm (22 to 29 ft-lbs)
Front shock absorber plate to caliper screws	20 to 27 Nm (15 to 20 ft-lbs)
Rear shock absorber upper nut	20 to 25 Nm (14 to 18 ft-lbs)
Rear shock absorber to engine	33 to 41 Nm (24 to 30 ft-lbs)
Front brake caliper mounting bolts	20 to 25 Nm (14 to 18 ft-lbs)
Brake disc mounting screws	5.0 to 6.5 Nm (44 to 57 inch-lbs)

Vespa ET-4 150, 2001 and later

Engine	150 cc single-cylinder 4-stroke
Cooling system	Air cooled
Fuel system	Walbro carburetor
Ignition system	CDI
Transmission	Variable speed automatic, belt driven
Suspension	Telescopic front, swingarm with dual shock rear
Brakes	Disc front, drum rear
Tires	Not specified
Wheelbase	1455 mm
Weight (curb)	149 kg (327.8 lbs)
Fuel tank capacity	10 liters (2.64 gallons), including 2.5 liters (0.66 gallon) reserve

Engine

Spark plug type	Champion RG6 YC
Electrode gap	0.8 mm to 0.9 mm 0.031 to 0.035 inch)
Idle speed (rpm)	1650 +/- 50
Engine oil type	Synthetic API SJ, 5W-40
Oil capacity (with filter change)	1.0 liters (1.057 quart)
Valve clearance	
Intake	0.10 mm (0.004 inch)
Exhaust	0.15 mm (0.006 inch)
Bore x stroke	62.6 x 48.6 mm (2.5 x 1.9 inches)
Piston diameter	62.533 to 62.540 mm (2.462 to 2.4622 inches)
Piston to bore clearance	0.040 to 0.054 mm (0.0015 to 0.0021 inch)
Piston ring installed end gap	
Top	
Standard	0.15 to 0.30 mm (0.0006 to 0.0012 inch)
Limit	0.4 mm (0.015 inch)
Second and oil ring	
Standard	0.20 to 0.40 mm (0.008 to 0.016 inch)
Limit	0.5 mm (0.020 inch)
Piston ring side clearance	
Top	
Standard	0.025 to 0.070 mm (0.0009 to 0.0027 inch)
Limit	0.08 mm (0.003 inch)
Second and oil rings	
Standard	0.015 to 0.060 mm (0.0005 to 0.0023 inch)
Limit	0.07 mm (0.0027 inch)

Vespa ET-4 150, 2001 and later (continued)

Fuel system

Throttle twistgrip freeplay	Not specified
Main jet	82
Slow jet	34
Needle position	3 notches from top
Pilot screw setting	3 +/- 1/2 turns out
Float level	Not specified

Ignition system

Ignition pulse generator resistance	105 to 124 ohms
Exciter coil resistance	Not specified
Ignition coil minimum peak voltage	100 ohms
Ignition coil primary resistance	0.4 to 0.5 ohms
Spark plug cap resistance	5000 ohms
Ignition coil secondary resistance (spark plug cap removed)	3000 ohms +/- 300 ohms

Transmission

Belt width (service limit)	21.5 mm (0.84 inch)
Weight roller outer diameter	
Standard	18.9 mm (0.74 inch)
Limit	18.5 mm (0.72 inch)
Clutch lining thickness (service limit)	Not specified
Clutch spring free length (service limit)	Not specified

Brakes

Brake fluid	DOT 4
Disc thickness (limit)	Not specified
Front brake pad thickness	1.5 mm (0.059 inch)
Brake drum diameter (limit)	Not specified
Drum brake lining thickness (limit)	When wear marks align
Brake lever freeplay	10 mm (3/8 inch)
Rear brake shoe wear limit	Not applicable

Tire pressures

Tire pressures	Not specified

Electrical system

Battery	
Capacity	12V-10Ah
Voltage (fully charged)	13.0 to 13.2 volts
Alternator	
Output (regulated)	14.0 to 15.2 volts
Charging coil resistance	0.7 to 0.9 ohms
Fuses	15 amps, 7.5 amps

Torque wrench settings

Note: One foot-pound (ft-lb) of torque is equivalent to 12 inch-pounds (in-lbs) of torque. Torque values below approximately 15 foot-pounds are expressed in inch-pounds, because most foot-pound torque wrenches are not accurate at these smaller values.

Engine oil drain plug	24 to 30 Nm (18 to 22 ft-lbs)
Engine oil drain plug	15 to 17 Nm (133 to 150 inch-lbs)
Transmission oil drain bolt	15 to 17 Nm (133 to 150 inch-lbs)
Valve cover bolts	11 to 13 Nm (97 to 115 inch-lbs)
Carburetor inlet duct to engine	11 to 13 Nm (97 to 115 inch-lbs)
Cylinder head nuts (1)	
First step	12 +/- 1 Nm (106 +/- 9 inch-lbs)
Second step	16 +/- 1 Nm (141 +/- 9 inch-lbs)
Third step	An additional 1/4-turn
Cylinder head bolts	11 to 13 Nm (97 to 115 inch-lbs)
Camshaft sprocket counterweight bolt	11 to 15 Nm (97 to 133 inch-lbs)
Cam chain tensioner mounting bolts	11 to 13 Nm (97 to 115 inch-lbs)
Clutch locknut	45 to 50 Nm (33 to 37 ft-lbs)
Driven pulley shaft nut	54 to 60 Nm (39 to 44 ft-lbs) (2)
Drive pulley nut	75 to 83 Nm (55 to 61 ft-lbs) (2, 3)

Starter clutch mounting bolts	Not specified
Starter motor mounting bolts	11 to 13 Nm (97 to 115 inch-lbs)
Alternator rotor nut	52 to 58 Nm (38 to 43 ft-lbs)
Crankcase bolts	11 to 13 Nm (97 to 115 inch-lbs)
Engine mounting bolt	33 to 41 Nm (24 to 30 ft-lbs)
Front axle nut	75 to 90 Nm (55 to 66 ft-lobs)
Rear axle nut	104 to 126 Nm (77 to 93 ft-lbs)
Handlebar bolt	50 to 60 Nm (37 to 44 ft-lbs)
Front wheel bolts	20 to 25 Nm (15 to 18 ft-lbs)
Steering stem bearing adjustment nut	8 to 10 Nm (71 to 88 inch-lbs)
Steering stem locknut	30 to 40 Nm (22 to 29 ft-lbs)
Front fork damper rod bolts	Not specified
Front fork to triple clamp bolts	Not specified
Rear shock bolts (upper and lower)	33 to 41 Nm (24 to 30 ft-lbs)
Front drum brake lining thickness (limit)	Not applicable
Front and rear disc brake bolts	
Caliper bracket bolts	20 to 27 Nm (15 to 20 ft-lbs)
Caliper to bracket bolts	20 to 25 Nm (15 to 18 ft-lbs)
Brake hose to caliper	20 to 25 Nm (15 to 18 ft-lbs)
Rear brake cam	11 to 13 Nm (97 to 115 inch-lbs)

1. *Apply engine oil to the threads.*
2. *Apply Loctite Super Rapid 242E thread locking compound or equivalent to the threads.*
3. *Replace the nut with a new one whenever it's removed.*

Vespa LX150, 2005 and later

Engine	150 cc single-cylinder 4-stroke
Cooling system	Air cooled
Fuel system	CV carburetor
Ignition system	CDI
Transmission	Variable speed automatic, belt driven
Suspension	Telescopic front, swingarm with single shock rear
Brakes	Disc front, drum rear
Tires	
Front	110/70-11
Rear	120/70-10
Wheelbase	1280 mm (50.39 inches)
Weight (curb)	110 +/- 5 kg (220 +/- 11 lbs)
Fuel tank capacity	8.5 liters (2.24 gal)

Engine

Spark plug type	Champion RG6YC, NGK CR7EB
Electrode gap	0.7 to 0.8 mm (0.028 to 0.031 inch)
Idle speed (rpm)	1650 to 1800 rpm
Engine oil type	Synthetic API SG, 5W-40
Oil capacity (with filter change)	1.0 liters (1.06 qt)*
Bore x stroke	62.6 x 48.6 mm (2.464 x 1.913 inches)
Piston to bore clearance (service limit)	0.040 to 0.054 mm (0.0016 to 0.0021 inch)
Piston ring installed end gap	
Compression (standard)	0.15 to 0.30 mm (0.006 to 0.012 inch)
Oil (standard)	0.2 to 0.4 mm (0.008 to 0.016 inch)

Total capacity. Start by adding the same amount that was drained, then let the engine idle for a few minutes, shut it off, wait 5 minutes and recheck the level. Do not fill beyond the MAX mark.

Fuel system

Throttle twistgrip freeplay	Not specified
Minimum jet	35
Starter jet	42
Needle type/position	NELA
Pilot screw setting	1-3/4 turns out
Float height	Bottom edge parallel to gasket face

Vespa LX150, 2005 and later (continued)

Ignition system
Spark plug cap resistance.. 5000 ohms
Ignition coil primary resistance.. 0.4 to 0.5 ohms
Ignition coil secondary resistance... 3000 +/- 300 ohms
Pick-up coil resistance .... 105 to 124 ohms

Transmission
Belt width (service limit).. Not specified
Clutch lining thickness (standard) .... 1.0 mm (0.039 inch)
Clutch spring free length (standard)... 106 mm (4.17 inches)

Brakes
Front brake pad thickness (service limit)....................................... 1.5 mm (1/16 inch)
Front brake disc runout (service limit) .... 0.1 mm (0.004 inch)

Tire pressures
Front .... 26 psi
Rear
    Rider only.. 29 psi
    Rider and passenger.. 33 psi

Electrical system
Battery
    Capacity .... 12V 9 Ah
    Open-circuit voltage (maintenance-free battery, minimum)......... 12.6 volts
    Specific gravity (fillable battery) .... 1.270 @ 20-degrees C/68-degrees F
Alternator
    Regulated voltage (no load) .... 14.0 to 15.2 volts
    Charging coil resistance.. 0.7 to 0.9 ohms
Fuses .... 15 and 7.5 amps

Torque wrench settings
Note: One foot-pound (ft-lb) of torque is equivalent to 12 inch-pounds (in-lbs) of torque. Torque values below approximately 15 foot-pounds are expressed in inch-pounds, because most foot-pound torque wrenches are not accurate at these smaller values.

Cylinder head cover .... 11 to 13 Nm (97 to 115 inch-lbs)
Cylinder head nuts .... 28 to 30 Nm (21 to 22 ft-lbs)
Cylinder head external screws .... 11 to 13 Nm (97 to 115 inch-lbs)
Camshaft sprocket screws .... 12 to 14 Nm (106 to 124 inch-lbs)
Timing chain tensioner sliding block screws.................................. 10 to 14 Nm (89 to 124 inch-lbs)
Drive pulley screw .... 75 to 83 Nm (55 to 61 ft-lbs)
Centrifugal clutch housing nut .... 45 to 50 Nm (33 to 36 ft-lbs)
Driven pulley nut .... 54 to 60 Nm (40 to 44 ft-lbs)
Alternator rotor nut .... 52 to 58 Nm (38 to 42 ft-lbs)
Front axle nut .... 75 to 90 Nm (55 to 66 ft-lbs)
Rear axle nut .... 104 to 126 Nm (77 to 92 ft-lbs)
Handlebar clamp bolts .... 50 to 55 Nm (36 to 40 ft-lbs)
Steering stem bearing lower nut .... 12 to 14 Nm (106 to 124 inch-lbs)
Steering stem bearing upper nut... 35 to 40 Nm (25 to 29 ft-lbs)
Front shock absorber upper nut.. 20 to 30 Nm (14 to 22 ft-lbs)
Front shock absorber upper bracket bolt .... 20 to 25 Nm (14 to 18 ft-lbs)
Front shock absorber lower bolts .... 20 to 27 Nm (14 to 20 ft-lbs)
Rear shock absorber lower end .... 33 to 41 Nm (24 to 30 ft-lbs)
Rear shock absorber bracket to chassis....................................... 20 to 25 Nm (14 to 18 ft-lbs)
Front brake caliper setscrews .... 24 to 27 Nm (18 to 20 ft-lbs)
Brake disc mounting screws .... 5.0 to 6.5 Nm (44 to 57 inch-lbs)

Vespa GT200, 2004 and later

Engine	198 cc single-cylinder 4-stroke
Cooling system	Liquid cooled
Fuel system	Walbro or Keihin CV carburetor
Ignition system	CDI
Transmission	Variable speed automatic, belt driven
Suspension	Telescopic front, swingarm with dual shock rear
Brakes	Disc front and rear
Tires	
Front	120/70-12
Rear	130/70-12
Wheelbase	1395 mm (54.92 inches)
Weight (dry)	140 kg (308 lbs)
Fuel tank capacity	9.5 liters (2.5 gal)

Engine

Spark plug type	Champion RG6YC
Electrode gap	0.7 to 0.8 mm (0.028 to 0.031 inch)
Idle speed (rpm)	1650 +/- 50 rpm
Engine oil type	Synthetic API SG, 5W-40
Oil capacity (with filter change)	1.0 liters (1.06 qt)*
Bore x stroke	72.0 x 48.6 mm (2.83 x 1.913 inches)
Piston ring installed end gap	
Compression (standard)	0.15 to 0.30 mm (0.005 to 0.011 inch)
Oil ring (standard)	0.2 to 0.4 mm (0.007 to 0.015 inch)

Total capacity. Start by adding the same amount that was drained, then let the engine idle for a few minutes, shut it off, wait 5 minutes and recheck the level. Do not fill beyond the MAX mark.

Fuel system

Throttle twistgrip freeplay	Not specified
Walbro carburetor	
Max jet	95
Slow running jet	33
Main air jet	120
Idle air jet	55
Starter jet	45
Needle type	495
Pilot screw setting	1-1/2 to 2-1/2 turns out
Float height	Bottom edge parallel to gasket face
Keihin carburetor	
Max jet	92
Slow running jet	38
Main air jet	70
Idle air jet	115
Starter jet	42
Needle type	NDAA
Pilot screw setting	2 to 2-1/2 turns out
Float height	Bottom edge parallel to gasket face

Ignition system

Ignition coil primary resistance	0.4 to 0.5 ohms
Ignition coil secondary resistance	3 k-ohms +/- 10%
Pick-up coil resistance	Not specified

Transmission

Belt width (service limit)	19.5 mm (0.76 inch)
Clutch lining thickness (standard)	1.0 mm (0.039 inch)
Clutch spring free length (standard)	118 mm (4.65 inches)

Brakes

Front brake pad thickness (service limit)	1.5 mm (1/16 inch)
Front brake disc runout (service limit)	0.1 mm (0.004 inch)

Vespa GT200, 2004 and later (continued)

Tire pressures

Front	26 psi
Rear	
Rider only	29 psi
Rider and passenger	32 psi

Electrical system

Battery	
Capacity	12V 12 Ah
Open-circuit voltage (maintenance-free battery, minimum)	12.6 volts
Specific gravity (fillable battery)	1.270 @ 20-degrees C/68-degrees F
Alternator	
Regulated voltage (no load)	14.0 to 15.2 volts
Charging coil resistance	0.7 to 0.9 ohms
Fuses	15, 10, 7.5 (3) and 5 (2) amps

Torque wrench settings

Note: One foot-pound (ft-lb) of torque is equivalent to 12 inch-pounds (in-lbs) of torque. Torque values below approximately 15 foot-pounds are expressed in inch-pounds, because most foot-pound torque wrenches are not accurate at these smaller values.

Cylinder head cover	6 to 7 Nm (53 to 62 inch-lbs)
Cylinder head nuts	
First step	7 +/- 1 Nm (63 +/- 8.4 inch-lbs)
Second step	One additional half-turn
Cylinder head external screws	11 to 13 Nm (97 to 115 inch-lbs)
Camshaft retaining plate screws	4 to 6 Nm (27 to 39 inch-lbs)
Timing chain tensioner sliding block screws	10 to 14 Nm (89 to 120 inch-lbs)
Drive pulley nut	75 to 83 Nm (55 to 61 ft-lbs)
Centrifugal clutch housing nut	55 to 60 Nm (41 to 44 ft-lbs)
Driven pulley nut	54 to 60 Nm (40 to 44 ft-lbs)
Alternator rotor nut	52 to 58 Nm (38 to 42 ft-lbs)
Front axle nut	75 to 90 Nm (55 to 66 ft-lbs)
Rear axle nut	104 to 126 Nm (77 to 92 ft-lbs)
Handlebar clamp bolts	45 to 50 Nm (33 to 36 ft-lbs)
Steering stem bearing lower nut	8 to 10 Nm (71 to 89 inch-lbs)
Steering stem bearing upper nut	30 to 40 Nm (22 to 29 ft-lbs)
Front shock absorber plate to caliper screws	20 to 27 Nm (14 to 20 ft-lbs)
Rear shock absorber upper end	20 to 25 Nm (14 to 18 ft-lbs)
Rear shock absorber support plate to crankcase	20 to 25 Nm (14 to 18 ft-lbs)
Rear shock absorber lower end	33 to 41 Nm (24 to 30 ft-lbs)
Front brake caliper to shock absorber plate	20 to 25 Nm (14 to 18 ft-lbs)
Brake disc mounting screws	6 Nm (53 inch-lbs)

Yamaha CA50 Riva, 1985 and 1986

Engine	49 cc single-cylinder 2-stroke
Cooling system	Air cooled
Fuel system	Piston valve carburetor
Ignition system	CDI
Transmission	Variable speed automatic, belt driven
Suspension	Trailing link front, swingarm with single shock rear
Brakes	Drum front and rear
Tires	2.75-10 front and rear
Wheelbase	1125 mm (44.3 inches)
Weight (with oil and full fuel tank)	62 kg (137 lbs)
Fuel tank capacity	3.8 liters (1 gal)

Engine

Spark plug type	NGK BP6HS
Electrode gap	0.6 to 0.7 mm (0.024 to 0.028 inch)
Idle speed (rpm)	1700 rpm
Engine oil type	Yamaha Autolube oil or equivalent
Oil tank capacity	1.0 liters (1.06 qt)
Bore x stroke	40.0 x 39.2 mm (1.57 x 1.54 inches)
Piston diameter (service limit)	39.94 mm (1.572 inches)
Piston to bore clearance (service limit)	0.05 mm (0.002 inch)
Piston ring installed end gap (top and second)	0.15 to 0.35 mm (0.006 to 0.014 inch)

Fuel system

Throttle twistgrip freeplay	3 to 7 mm (1/8 to 17/64 inch)
Main jet	74
Pilot jet	40
Needle type/position	Not specified
Air screw setting	1-5/8 +/- 1/4 turns out
Float height	15 +/- 0.05 mm (0.59 +/- 0.02 inch)

Ignition system

Ignition coil primary resistance	1.6 ohm +/- 10%
Ignition coil secondary resistance (without spark plug cap installed)	6.6 k-ohms +/- 10%
Pick-up coil resistance	30 ohms +/- 10%

Transmission

Belt width (service limit)	14.0 mm (0.55 inch)
Clutch lining thickness	4.0 mm (0.16 inch)
Clutch spring free length (service limit)	27.5 mm (1.083 inches)

Brakes

Drum internal diameter (service limit)	
Front	80.5 mm (3.17 inches)
Rear	95.5 mm (3.76 inches)
Brake lining thickness (service limit)	2.0 mm (0.08 inch)
Brake freeplay (front and rear)	10 to 20 mm (3/8 to 3/4 inch)

Tire pressures

Front	18 psi
Rear	32 psi

Electrical system

Battery	
Capacity	6V-8Ah
Specific gravity	1.280 @ 20-degrees C/68-degrees F

Yamaha CA50 Riva, 1985 and 1986 (continued)

Electrical system

Alternator
Output	1.3 amps @ 3000 rpm
Source coil resistance	385 +/- 10%
Charge coil resistance	0.32 ohms +/- 10%
Lighting coil resistance	0.2 ohms +/- 10%
Fuses (main and reserve)	10 amps

Torque wrench settings

Note: One foot-pound (ft-lb) of torque is equivalent to 12 inch-pounds (in-lbs) of torque. Torque values below approximately 15 foot-pounds are expressed in inch-pounds, because most foot-pound torque wrenches are not accurate at these smaller values.

Cylinder head nuts	10 Nm (87 inch-lbs)
Drive pulley nut	30 Nm (22 ft-lbs)
Driven pulley nut	50 Nm (36 ft-lbs)
Centrifugal clutch housing nut	40 Nm (29 ft-lbs)
Alternator rotor nut	43 Nm (31 ft-lbs)
Engine mounting bracket to engine and frame	42 Nm (30 ft-lbs)
Crankcase bolts	8 Nm (70 inch-lbs)
Front axle nut	35 Nm (25 ft-lbs)
Rear axle nut	95 Nm (68 ft-lbs)
Steering stem bearing upper nut	
First step	30 Nm (22 ft-lbs)
Second step	Loosen 1/4 to 1/3 turn
Steering stem bearing locknut	30 Nm (22 ft-lbs)
Handlebar bolt and nut	30 Nm (22 ft-lbs)
Fork pivot arm	22 Nm (16 ft-lbs)
Front shock mounting bolts (upper and lower)	26 Nm (19 ft-lbs)
Rear shock absorber to frame nut	32 Nm (23 ft-lbs)
Rear shock absorber to crankcase bolt	18 Nm (156 inch-lbs)
Rear brake arm	6 Nm (52 inch-lbs)
Rear brake panel bolts	18 Nm (156 inch-lbs)

Yamaha CE50 and CG50 Jog, 1986 through 1988

Engine	49 cc single-cylinder 2-stroke
Cooling system	Air cooled
Fuel system	Piston valve carburetor
Ignition system	CDI
Transmission	Variable speed automatic, belt driven
Suspension	Telescopic front, swingarm with single shock rear
Brakes	Drum front and rear
Tires	2.75-10 front and rear
Wheelbase	1085 mm (42.7 inches)
Weight (with oil and full fuel tank)	55.5 kg (122 lbs)
Fuel tank capacity	2.9 liters (0.77 gal)

Engine

Spark plug type	
1986 and 1987	NGK BP6HS-10
1988	NGK BP7HS
Electrode gap	
1986 and 1987	0.9 to 1.0 mm (0.036 to 0.039 inch)
1988	0.6 to 0.7 mm (0.024 to 0.028 inch)
Idle speed (rpm)	1500 to 2100 rpm
Engine oil type	Yamaha Autolube oil or equivalent
Oil tank capacity	800 cc (27 fl oz)
Bore x stroke	40.0 x 39.2 mm (1.57 x 1.54 inches)
Piston diameter (standard)	40.0 mm (1.575 inches)
Piston to bore clearance (service limit)	0.05 mm (0.002 inch)
Piston ring installed end gap (top and second)	0.15 to 0.35 mm (0.006 to 0.014 inch)
Piston ring side clearance (top and second)	0.03 to 0.05 mm (0.0012 to 0.0020 inch)

Fuel system

Throttle twistgrip freeplay	3 to 7 mm (1/8 to 17/64 inch)
Main jet	82
Pilot jet	42
Needle type/position	Not specified
Air screw setting	Not specified
Float height	16 +/- 1.0 mm (0.63 +/- 0.04 inch)

Ignition system

Ignition coil primary resistance	
1986 and 1987	1.44 to 1.76 ohms
1988	0.56 to 0.84 ohms
Ignition coil secondary resistance (without spark plug cap installed)	
1986 and 1987	5.28 to 7.92 ohms
1988	5.68 to 8.52 k-ohms
Pick-up coil resistance	
1986	24 to 36 ohms
1987	27 to 33 ohms
1988	400 to 600 ohms

Transmission

Belt width (service limit)	13.5 mm (0.53 inch)
Clutch lining thickness (service limit)	2.5 mm (0.10 inch)
Clutch spring free length (service limit)	94.0 mm (3.70 inches)

Brakes

Drum internal diameter (service limit)	
Front	80.5 mm (3.17 inches)
Rear	95.5 mm (3.76 inches)
Brake lining thickness (service limit)	2.0 mm (0.08 inch)
Brake freeplay (front and rear)	10 to 20 mm (3/8 to 3/4 inch)

Yamaha CE50 and CG50 Jog, 1986 through 1988 (continued)

Tire pressures

Front	18 psi
Rear	32 psi

Electrical system

Battery
Capacity	12V-4Ah
Specific gravity	1.280 @ 20-degrees C/68-degrees F

Alternator
Output	13.0 to 17.5 volts @ 4000 rpm

Source coil resistance
1986	264 to 396 ohms
1987	216 to 264 ohms
1988	640 to 960 ohms

Charge coil resistance
1986	0.56 to 0.84 ohms
1987	0.63 to 0.77 ohms
1988	0.48 to 0.72 ohms

Lighting coil resistance
1986 and 1987	0.27 to 0.33 ohms
1988	0.4 to 0.6 ohms
Fuse	7 amps

Torque wrench settings

Note: One foot-pound (ft-lb) of torque is equivalent to 12 inch-pounds (in-lbs) of torque. Torque values below approximately 15 foot-pounds are expressed in inch-pounds, because most foot-pound torque wrenches are not accurate at these smaller values.

Cylinder head nuts	10 Nm (87 inch-lbs)
Drive pulley nut	30 Nm (22 ft-lbs)
Driven pulley nut	50 Nm (36 ft-lbs)
Centrifugal clutch housing nut	40 Nm (29 ft-lbs)
Alternator rotor nut	43 Nm (31 ft-lbs)
Engine mounting bracket to engine and frame	42 Nm (30 ft-lbs)
Crankcase bolts	8 Nm (70 inch-lbs)
Front axle nut	35 Nm (25 ft-lbs)
Rear axle nut	93 Nm (67 ft-lbs)
Steering stem bearing upper race	Not specified
Steering stem ring nut	30 Nm (22 ft-lbs)*

Handlebar
1986	29 Nm (21 ft-lbs)
1987	60 Nm (43 ft-lbs)
Rear shock absorber to frame nut	32 Nm (23 ft-lbs)
Rear shock absorber to crankcase bolt	17 Nm (148 inch-lbs)
Rear brake arm	6 Nm (52 inch-lbs)
Rear brake panel bolts	18 Nm (156 inch-lbs)

Handlebars must move easily from lock to lock with no looseness or binding after adjustment.

Yamaha CW50 Zuma/Zuma II, 1997 through 2000

Engine	49 cc single-cylinder 2-stroke
Cooling system	Air cooled
Fuel system	Piston valve carburetor
Ignition system	CDI
Transmission	Variable speed automatic, belt driven
Suspension	Telescopic front, swingarm with single shock rear
Brakes	
1997 and 1998	Drum front and rear
1999 and 2000	Disc front, drum rear
Tires	
Front	120/90-10
Rear	130/90-10
Wheelbase	1170 mm (46.0 inches)
Weight (with oil and full fuel tank)	78.0 kg (172 lbs)
Fuel tank capacity	4.6 liters (1.21 gal)

Engine

Spark plug type	NGK BR8HS
Electrode gap	0.5 to 0.7 mm (0.020 to 0.028 inch)
Idle speed (rpm)	1800 +/- 200
Engine oil type	Yamaha Autolube oil or equivalent
Oil tank capacity	1.3 liters (44 fl oz)
Bore x stroke	40.0 x 39.2 mm (1.57 x 1.54 inches)
Piston diameter (service limit)	39.952 mm (1.574 inches)
Piston to bore clearance (service limit)	0.1 mm (0.004 inch)
Piston ring installed end gap (top and second)	
Standard	0.15 to 0.30 mm (0.006 to 0.012 inch)
Service limit	0.70 mm (0.028 inch)

Fuel system

Throttle twistgrip freeplay	1.5 to 3.0 mm (1/16 to 1/8 inch)
Main jet	93
Pilot jet	36
Needle type/position	Not specified
Air screw setting	1-5/8 +/- 1/4 turn out
Float height	16 +/- 1.0 mm (0.63 +/- 0.04 inch)

Ignition system

Ignition coil primary resistance	0.56 to 0.84 ohms
Ignition coil secondary resistance (without spark plug cap installed)	5.28 to 7.92 ohms
Spark plug cap resistance	5 k-ohms
Pick-up coil resistance	400 to 600 ohms

Transmission

Belt width (service limit)	
1997 and 1998	13.5 mm (0.53 inch)
1999 and 2000	14.85 mm (0.58 inch)
Clutch lining thickness (service limit)	2.5 mm (0.10 inch)
Clutch spring free length (service limit)	26.2 mm (1.03 inches)

Brakes

Front disc thickness (1999 and 2000, service limit)	3.0 mm (0.12 inch)
Pad thickness (1999 and 2000, service limit)	0.55 mm (0.02 inch)
Drum internal diameter (service limit, front and rear)	110.5 mm (4.35 inches)
Brake lining thickness (service limit)	2.0 mm (0.08 inch)
Brake freeplay (front and rear)	10 to 20 mm (3/8 to 3/4 inch)

Tire pressures

Front	15 psi
Rear	
Up to 90 kg (200 lbs) load	18 psi
Above 90 kg (200 lbs) load	21 psi

Yamaha CW50 Zuma/Zuma II, 1997 through 2000 (continued)

Electrical system
Battery
Capacity	12V-4Ah
Specific gravity	1.280 @ 20-degrees C/68-degrees F

Alternator
Output (regulated)	13 to 14 volts
Source coil resistance	640 to 960 ohms

Lighting coil resistance
Yellow to red/black	0.32 to 0.48 ohms
White to black	0.48 to 0.72 ohms
Fuse	7 amps

Torque wrench settings
Note: One foot-pound (ft-lb) of torque is equivalent to 12 inch-pounds (in-lbs) of torque. Torque values below approximately 15 foot-pounds are expressed in inch-pounds, because most foot-pound torque wrenches are not accurate at these smaller values.

Cylinder head nuts	10 Nm (87 inch-lbs)
Drive pulley nut	30 Nm (22 ft-lbs)
Driven pulley nut	50 Nm (36 ft-lbs)
Centrifugal clutch housing nut	40 Nm (29 ft-lbs)
Alternator rotor nut	37.5 Nm (27 ft-lbs)
Engine mounting bolt	42 Nm (30 ft-lbs)
Crankcase bolt	13 Nm (113 inch-lbs)
Front axle nut	35 Nm (25 ft-lbs)

Rear axle nut
1997 and 1998	103.5 Nm (75 ft-lbs)
1999 and 2000	105 Nm (76 ft-lbs)
Steering stem ring nut	Tighten to remove bearing play
Steering stem locknut	22.5 Nm (16 ft-lbs)
Handlebar	60 Nm (43 ft-lbs)
Front fork Allen bolts (1999 and 2000)	23 Nm (17 ft-lbs)
Front fork pinch bolts (1999 and 2000)	30 Nm (22 ft-lbs)
Rear shock absorber upper bolt	32 Nm (23 ft-lbs)
Rear shock absorber lower bolt	17 Nm (148 inch-lbs)

Front disc brake
Caliper mounting bolts	23 Nm (17 ft-lbs)
Caliper assembly bolts	22 Nm (16 ft-lbs)
Brake disc mounting bolts	23 Nm (17 ft-lbs)
Brake hose banjo bolts	23 Nm (17 ft-lbs)
Rear brake arm	9.7 Nm (84 inch-lbs)

Yamaha CW50 Zuma, 1989 and 1990

Engine	49 cc single-cylinder 2-stroke
Cooling system	Air cooled
Fuel system	Piston valve carburetor
Ignition system	CDI
Transmission	Variable speed automatic, belt driven
Suspension	Telescopic front, swingarm with single shock rear
Brakes	Drum front and rear
Tires	
Front	120/90-10 54J
Rear	130/90-10 59J
Wheelbase	1170 mm (68.3 inches)
Weight (with oil and full fuel tank)	70 kg (154 lbs)
Fuel tank capacity	3.3 liters (0.87 gal)

Engine

Spark plug type	NGK BPR7HS or ND W22FPR-U
Electrode gap	0.6 to 0.7 mm (0.024 to 0.028 inch)
Idle speed (rpm)	1800
Engine oil type	Yamaha Autolube oil or equivalent
Oil tank capacity	1.1 liter (1.1 qt)
Bore x stroke	40.0 x 39.2 mm (1.57 x 1.54 inches)
Piston diameter (service limit)	39.952 mm (1.573 inches)
Piston to bore clearance (standard)	0.034 to 0.047 mm (0.0013 to 0.0018 inch)
Piston ring installed end gap (top and second, standard)	0.15 to 0.35 mm (0.006 to 0.014 inch)
Piston ring side clearance (top and second)	0.03 to 0.05 mm (0.0012 to 0.0020 inch)

Fuel system

Throttle twistgrip freeplay	2 to 4 mm (5/63 to 5/32 inch)
Main jet	90
Pilot jet	50
Needle type/position	Not specified
Air screw setting	1-1/2 turns out
Float height	16 +/- 1.0 mm (0.63 +/- 0.04 inch)

Ignition system

Ignition coil primary resistance	0.56 to 0.84 ohms
Ignition coil secondary resistance (without spark plug cap installed)	5.68 to 8.52 k-ohms
Pick-up coil resistance	640 to 960 ohms

Transmission

Belt width (service limit)	13.5 mm (0.53 inch)
Weight roller outer diameter (service limit)	14.5 mm (0.571 inch)
Clutch lining thickness (service limit)	2.5 mm (0.10 inch)
Clutch spring free length (service limit)	106.7 mm (0.4.59 inch)

Brakes

Drum internal diameter (service limit, front and rear)	110.5 mm (4.35 inches)
Brake lining thickness (service limit)	2.0 mm (0.08 inch)
Brake freeplay (front and rear)	10 to 20 mm (3/8 to 3/4 inch)

Tire pressures

Front	14 psi
Rear	18 psi

Yamaha CW50 Zuma, 1989 and 1990 (continued)

Electrical system

Battery
Capacity	12V-4Ah
Specific gravity	1.280 @ 20-degrees C/68-degrees F

Alternator
Charging voltage	13 to 14 volts @ 4000 rpm
Source coil resistance	400 to 600 ohms
Charge coil resistance	0.52 to 0.78 ohms
Lighting coil resistance	0.36 to 0.54 ohms
Fuse	7 amps

Torque wrench settings

Note: One foot-pound (ft-lb) of torque is equivalent to 12 inch-pounds (in-lbs) of torque. Torque values below approximately 15 foot-pounds are expressed in inch-pounds, because most foot-pound torque wrenches are not accurate at these smaller values.

Cylinder head nuts	10 Nm (87 inch-lbs)
Drive pulley nut	33 Nm (24 ft-lbs)
Driven pulley nut	50 Nm (36 ft-lbs)
Centrifugal clutch housing nut	40 Nm (29 ft-lbs)
Alternator rotor nut	38 Nm (27 ft-lbs)
Engine mounting bracket to frame and engine	42 Nm (30 ft-lbs)
Crankcase bolt	12 Nm (104 inch-lbs)
Front axle nut	35 Nm (25 ft-lbs)
Rear axle nut	95 Nm (68 ft-lbs)
Steering stem ring nut	30 Nm (22 ft-lbs)*
Handlebar	60 Nm (43 ft-lbs)
Rear shock absorber upper nut	32 Nm (23 ft-lbs)
Rear shock absorber lower bolt	18 Nm (156 inch-lbs)
Front and rear brake arms	10 Nm (87 inch-lbs)

*Handlebars must move easily from lock to lock with no looseness or binding after adjustment.

Yamaha CY50 Riva/Riva Jog, 1992 and later

Engine	49 cc single-cylinder 2-stroke
Cooling system	Air cooled
Fuel system	Piston valve carburetor
Ignition system	CDI
Transmission	Variable speed automatic, belt driven
Suspension	Telescopic front, swingarm with single shock rear
Brakes	Drum front and rear
Tires	80/90-10 34J front and rear
Wheelbase	1115 mm (43.9 inches)
Weight (with oil and full fuel tank)	65 kg (143 lbs)
Fuel tank capacity	3.5 liters (0.92 gal)

Engine

Spark plug type	NGK BPR7HS or ND W22FPR-U
Electrode gap	0.6 to 0.7 mm (0.024 to 0.028 inch)
Idle speed (rpm)	1800
Engine oil type	Yamaha Autolube oil or equivalent
Oil tank capacity	800 cc (27 fl oz)
Bore x stroke	40.0 x 39.2 mm (1.57 x 1.54 inches)
Piston diameter (service limit)	39.953 mm (1.573 inches)
Piston to bore clearance (service limit)	0.1 mm (0.004 inch)
Piston ring installed end gap (top and second)	
Standard	0.15 to 0.35 mm (0.006 to 0.014 inch)
Service limit	0.70 mm (0.028 inch)
Piston ring side clearance (top and second)	0.03 to 0.05 mm (0.0012 to 0.0020 inch)

Fuel system

Throttle twistgrip freeplay	1.5 to 3.0 mm (1/16 to 1/8 inch)
Main jet	76
Pilot jet	42
Needle type/position	Not specified
Air screw setting	1-5/8 turns out
Float height	16 +/- 1.0 mm (0.63 +/- 0.04 inch)

Ignition system

Ignition coil primary resistance	0.56 to 0.84 ohms
Ignition coil secondary resistance (without spark plug cap installed)	5.68 to 8.52 k-ohms
Pick-up coil resistance	400 to 600 ohms

Transmission

Belt width (service limit)	15.2 mm (0.60 inch)
Clutch lining thickness (service limit)	2.0 mm (0.08 inch)
Clutch spring free length (service limit)	95.4 mm (3.76 inches)

Brakes

Drum internal diameter (service limit)

Front	80.5 mm (3.17 inches)
Rear	95.5 mm (3.76 inches)
Brake lining thickness (service limit)	2.0 mm (0.08 inch)
Brake freeplay (front and rear)	10 to 20 mm (3/8 to 3/4 inch)

Tire pressures

Front	18 psi
Rear	32 psi

Electrical system

Battery

Capacity	12V-3Ah
Specific gravity	1.320 @ 20-degrees C/68-degrees F

Alternator

No-load regulated voltage	13.5 to 14.5 volts @ 4000 rpm
Source coil resistance	640 to 960 ohms
Charge coil resistance	0.48 to 0.72 ohms

Lighting coil resistance

Yellow/red to black	0.4 to 0.6 ohms
White to black	0.48 to 0.72 ohms
Fuse	7 amps

Torque wrench settings

Note: One foot-pound (ft-lb) of torque is equivalent to 12 inch-pounds (in-lbs) of torque. Torque values below approximately 15 foot-pounds are expressed in inch-pounds, because most foot-pound torque wrenches are not accurate at these smaller values.

Cylinder head nuts	14 Nm (120 inch-lbs)
Drive pulley nut	33 Nm (24 ft-lbs)
Driven pulley nut	50 Nm (36 ft-lbs)
Centrifugal clutch housing nut	40 Nm (29 ft-lbs)
Alternator rotor nut	38 Nm (27 ft-lbs)
Engine mounting bracket to frame	46 Nm (33 ft-lbs)
Engine mounting bracket to engine	84 Nm (61 ft-lbs)
Crankcase bolt	9 Nm (75 inch-lbs)
Front axle nut	47 Nm (34 ft-lbs)
Rear axle nut	104 Nm (76 ft-lbs)
Steering stem bearing upper race	4 Nm (35 inch-lbs)*
Steering stem ring nut	30 Nm (22 ft-lbs)*
Handlebar	60 Nm (43 ft-lbs)
Rear shock absorber upper nut	32 Nm (23 ft-lbs)
Rear shock absorber lower bolt	18 Nm (156 inch-lbs)
Front brake arm	4 Nm (35 inch-lbs)
Rear brake arm	8 Nm (70 inch-lbs)

*Handlebars must move easily from lock to lock with no looseness or binding after adjustment.

Yamaha XC50 Vino, 2006 and later

Engine	49 cc single-cylinder 4-stroke
Cooling system	Liquid cooled
Fuel system	Keihin CV
Ignition system	CDI
Transmission	Variable speed automatic, belt driven
Suspension	Telescopic front, single shock swingarm rear
Brakes	Drum front and rear
Tires (front and rear)	90/90-10 50J
Wheelbase	1160 mm (45.7 inches)
Weight (with oil and full fuel tank)	81 kg (179 lbs)
Fuel tank capacity	4.5 liters (1.18 gallons)

Engine

Spark plug type	NGK CR7E
Electrode gap	0.7 to 0.8 mm (0.028 to 0.031 inch)
Idle speed (rpm)	2000 to 2400 rpm
Engine oil type	SAE 10W-40
Engine oil capacity (drain and fill)	0.73 to 0.83 liters (0.8 to 0.9 qt)
Bore x stroke	38.0 x 43.5 mm (2.318 x 2.653 inches)
Piston diameter (service limit)	37.975 to 37.990 mm (1.574 to 1.496 inches)
Piston to bore clearance (service limit)	0.150 mm (0.006 inch)
Piston ring installed end gap	
Top	
Standard	0.05 to 0.15 mm (0.002 to 0.006 inch)
Service limit	0.40 mm (0.016 inch)
Second	
Standard	0.05 to 0.17 mm (0.002 to 0.0066 inch)
Service limit	0.52 mm (0.020 inch)
Piston ring side clearance	
Top	
Standard	0.02 to 0.08 mm (0.0008 to 0.0032 inch)
Service limit	0.12 mm (0.005 inch)

Fuel system

Throttle twistgrip freeplay	1.5 to 3.5 mm (0.059 to 0.138 inch)
Main jet	82
Main air jet	80
Needle type	N425-36628
Choke jet	38
Float level	6.6 to 7.6 mm (0.259 to 0.299 inch)

Ignition system

Ignition coil primary resistance	0.168 to 0.252 ohms
Ignition coil secondary resistance (without spark plug cap installed)	2.4 to 3.6 k-ohms

Transmission

Belt width (service limit)	15.8 mm (0.622 inch)
Clutch lining thickness (limit)	2.0 mm (0.078 inch)
Clutch spring free length	
Shoe spring	30.1 +/- 0.04 mm (1.185 +/- 0.042 inches)
Compression spring	76.4 mm (3.004 inches)

Brakes

Drum internal diameter (service limit)	110.5 mm (4.350 inches)
Brake lining thickness (service limit)	2.0 mm (0.08 inch)
Brake lever freeplay	10 to 20 mm (3/8 to 3/4 inch)

Tire pressure

Front and rear	22 psi

Electrical system
Battery
  Capacity 12V 4Ah
  Specific gravity................... 1.330
Alternator
  No-load regulated voltage .... 14.1 to 14.9 volts
  Stator coil resistance .... 0.288 to 0.432 ohms
  Fuse .... 7.5 amps

Torque wrench settings
Note: One foot-pound (ft-lb) of torque is equivalent to 12 inch-pounds (in-lbs) of torque. Torque values below approximately 15 foot-pounds are expressed in inch-pounds, because most foot-pound torque wrenches are not accurate at these smaller values.

Cylinder head nuts	10 Nm (87 inch-lbs)
Drive pulley but	55 Nm (40 ft-lbs)
Driven pulley nut	30 Nm (22 ft-lbs)
Centrifugal clutch housing nut	40 Nm (29 ft-lbs)
Alternator rotor nut	43 Nm (31 ft-lbs)
Engine mounting bracket to frame	46 Nm (33 ft-lbs)
Engine mounting bolt/nut	58 Nm (42 ft-lbs)
Crankcase bolt	10 Nm (87 inch-lbs)
Front axle nut	48 Nm (35 ft-lbs)
Rear axle nut	104 Nm (75 ft-lbs)
Steering stem bearing adjusting nut	7 Nm (61 inch-lbs)
Steering stem ring nut	30 Nm (22 ft-lbs)
Handlebar pinch bolt	60 Nm (43 ft-lbs)
Rear shock absorber upper nut	30 Nm (22 ft-lbs)
Rear shock absorber lower bolt	16 Nm (144 inch-lbs)
Front brake arm	8 Nm (70 inch-lbs)
Rear brake arm	7 Nm (61 inch-lbs)

Yamaha YJ50 Vino, 2001 through 2004

Engine	49 cc single-cylinder 2-stroke
Cooling system	Air cooled
Fuel system	Piston valve carburetor
Ignition system	CDI
Transmission	Variable speed automatic, belt driven
Suspension	Link front, swingarm with single shock rear
Brakes	Drum front and rear
Tires	80/90-10 34J front and rear
Wheelbase	1159 mm (45.3 inches)
Weight (with oil and full fuel tank)	74 kg (163 lbs)
Fuel tank capacity	6 liters (1.57 gal)

Engine

Spark plug type	NGK BPR7HS or ND W22FPR-U
Electrode gap	0.6 to 0.7 mm (0.024 to 0.028 inch)
Idle speed (rpm)	1800
Engine oil type	Yamaha Autolube oil or equivalent
Oil tank capacity	1.4 liters (1.5 qt)
Bore x stroke	40.0 x 39.2 mm (1.57 x 1.54 inches)
Piston diameter (service limit)	39.953 mm (1.573 inches)
Piston to bore clearance (service limit)	0.1 mm (0.004 inch)
Piston ring installed end gap (top and second)	
Standard	0.15 to 0.35 mm (0.006 to 0.014 inch)
Service limit	0.70 mm (0.028 inch)
Piston ring side clearance (top and second)	
Standard	0.03 to 0.05 mm (0.0012 to 0.0020 inch)
Service limit	0.10 mm (0.004 inch)

Yamaha YJ50 Vino, 2001 through 2004 (continued)

Fuel system

Throttle twistgrip freeplay	1.5 to 3.5 mm (1/16 to 17/64 inch)
Main jet	64
Pilot jet	46
Needle type/position	Not specified
Air screw setting	1-5/8 turns out
Float height	16 +/- 1.0 mm (0.63 +/- 0.04 inch)

Ignition system

Ignition coil primary resistance	0.18 to 0.28 ohms
Ignition coil secondary resistance (without spark plug cap installed)	6.32 to 9.48 k-ohms
Pick-up coil resistance	248 to 372 ohms

Transmission

Belt width (service limit)	15.0 mm (0.59 inch)
Clutch lining thickness (service limit)	1.0 mm (0.04 inch)
Clutch spring free length (service limit)	29.9 mm (1.18 inches)

Brakes

Drum internal diameter (service limit, front and rear)	110.5 mm (4.35 inches)
Brake lining thickness (service limit)	2.0 mm (0.08 inch)
Brake freeplay (front and rear)	10 to 20 mm (3/8 to 3/4 inch)

Tire pressures

Front	22 psi
Rear	25 psi

Electrical system

Battery	
Capacity	12V-2.5Ah
Specific gravity	1.350 @ 20-degrees C/68-degrees F
Alternator	
No-load regulated voltage	14 to 15 volts
Stator coil resistance	0.29 to 0.43 ohms
Fuse	7.5 amps

Torque wrench settings

Note: One foot-pound (ft-lb) of torque is equivalent to 12 inch-pounds (in-lbs) of torque. Torque values below approximately 15 foot-pounds are expressed in inch-pounds, because most foot-pound torque wrenches are not accurate at these smaller values.

Cylinder head nuts	14 Nm (120 inch-lbs)
Drive pulley nut	30 Nm (22 ft-lbs)
Driven pulley nut	50 Nm (36 ft-lbs)
Centrifugal clutch housing nut	40 Nm (29 ft-lbs)
Alternator rotor nut	38 Nm (27 ft-lbs)
Engine mounting bracket to frame	46 Nm (33 ft-lbs)
Engine mounting bolt/nut	84 Nm (61 ft-lbs)
Crankcase bolt	9 Nm (75 inch-lbs)
Front axle nut	48 Nm (35 ft-lbs)
Rear axle nut	105 Nm (75 ft-lbs)
Steering stem bearing adjusting nut	7 Nm (61 inch-lbs)
Steering stem ring nut	33 Nm (24 ft-lbs)
Handlebar clamp bolts	10 Nm (87 inch-lbs)
Rear shock absorber upper nut	30 Nm (22 ft-lbs)
Rear shock absorber lower bolt	15 Nm (132 inch-lbs)
Front brake arm	4 Nm (35 inch-lbs)
Rear brake arm	7 Nm (61 inch-lbs)

Yamaha YW50 Zuma, 2002 through 2004

Engine	49 cc single-cylinder 2-stroke
Cooling system	Air cooled
Fuel system	Piston valve carburetor
Ignition system	CDI
Transmission	Variable speed automatic, belt driven
Suspension	Telescopic fork front, swingarm with single shock rear
Brakes	Disc front, drum rear
Tires	
Front	120/90-10 56J
Rear	130/90-10 59J
Wheelbase	1275 mm (50.2 inches)
Weight (with oil and full fuel tank)	94 kg (207 lbs)
Fuel tank capacity	5.7 liters (1.5 gal)

Engine

Spark plug type	NGK BPR7HS
Electrode gap	0.6 to 0.7 mm (0.024 to 0.028 inch)
Idle speed (rpm)	1750 to 1850 rpm
Engine oil type	Yamaha Autolube oil or equivalent
Oil tank capacity	1.4 liters (1.5 qt)
Bore x stroke	40.0 x 39.2 mm (1.57 x 1.54 inches)
Piston diameter (service limit)	39.958 mm (1.573 inches)
Piston to bore clearance (service limit)	0.1 mm (0.004 inch)
Piston ring installed end gap (top and second)	
Standard	0.15 to 0.35 mm (0.006 to 0.014 inch)
Service limit	0.60 mm (0.024 inch)
Piston ring side clearance (top and second)	
Standard	0.03 to 0.05 mm (0.0012 to 0.0020 inch)
Service limit	0.10 mm (0.004 inch)

Fuel system

Throttle twistgrip freeplay	3 to 5 mm (1/8 to 3/16 inch)
Main jet	80
Pilot jet	44
Needle type/position	3N24-3/5
Air screw setting	1-5/8 turns out
Float height	16 +/- 1.0 mm (0.63 +/- 0.04 inch)

Ignition system

Ignition coil primary resistance	0.32 to 0.48 ohms
Ignition coil secondary resistance (without spark plug cap installed)	5.68 to 8.52 k-ohms
Spark plug cap resistance	5 k-ohms
Pick-up coil resistance	248 to 372 ohms

Transmission

Belt width (service limit)	14.6 mm (0.57 inch)
Clutch lining thickness (service limit)	2.5 mm (0.1 inch)
Clutch spring free length (service limit)	91 mm (3.58 inches)

Brakes

Drum internal diameter (service limit, front and rear)	110.5 mm (4.35 inches)
Brake lining thickness (service limit)	2.0 mm (0.08 inch)
Brake freeplay (front and rear)	10 to 20 mm (3/8 to 3/4 inch)

Tire pressures

Front	22 psi
Rear	25 psi

Yamaha YW50 Zuma, 2002 through 2004 (continued)

Electrical system

Battery

Capacity	12V-2.5Ah
Specific gravity	1.350 @ 20-degrees C/68-degrees F

Alternator

Charging voltage	13 to 14 volts @ 4000 rpm
Charging coil resistance	0.48 to 0.72 ohms
Lighting coil resistance	0.4 to 0.6 ohms
Fuse	7 amps

Torque wrench settings

Note: One foot-pound (ft-lb) of torque is equivalent to 12 inch-pounds (in-lbs) of torque. Torque values below approximately 15 foot-pounds are expressed in inch-pounds, because most foot-pound torque wrenches are not accurate at these smaller values.

Cylinder head nuts	14 Nm (120 inch-lbs)
Drive pulley nut	45 Nm (33 ft-lbs)
Driven pulley nut	50 Nm (36 ft-lbs)
Centrifugal clutch housing nut	40 Nm (29 ft-lbs)
Alternator rotor nut	38 Nm (27 ft-lbs)
Engine mounting bracket to frame	84 Nm (61 ft-lbs)
Engine bracket to engine	45 Nm (31 ft-lbs)
Crankcase bolt	12 Nm (101 inch-lbs)
Front axle nut	70 Nm (51 ft-lbs)
Rear axle nut	120 Nm (87 ft-lbs)
Steering stem bearing adjusting nut	
First step	22 Nm (16 ft-lbs)
Second step	Loosen 1/4 turn
Third step	Install rubber washer
Fourth step	Align tabs of first and second nuts
Fifth step	Install tab washer over both nuts
Sixth step	Tighten third nut to 66 Nm (48 ft-lbs)
Handlebar pinch bolt and nut	43 Nm (37 ft-lbs)
Fork caps	38 Nm (27 ft-lbs)
Fork pinch bolts	40 Nm (29 ft-lbs)
Fork bottom Allen bolts	23 Nm (17 ft-lbs)*
Rear shock absorber nuts/bolts	Not specified
Rear shock absorber lower bolt	15 Nm (132 inch-lbs)
Front brake caliper mounting bolts	23 Nm (17 ft-lbs)
Front brake pad pin bolt	23 Nm (17 ft-lbs)
Rear brake arm	10 Nm (87 inch-lbs)

Apply non-permanent thread locking agent to the threads.

Yamaha CV80 Zuma, 1984 through 1987

Engine	79 cc single-cylinder 2-stroke
Cooling system	Air cooled
Fuel system	CV carburetor
Ignition system	CDI
Transmission	Variable speed automatic, belt driven
Suspension	Pivot front, swingarm with single shock rear
Brakes	Drum front and rear
Tires	3.50/10 4PR front and rear
Wheelbase	1200 mm (47.2 inches)
Weight (with oil and full fuel tank)	87 kg (191 lbs)
Fuel tank capacity	4.7 liters (1.3 gal)

Engine

Spark plug type	
1984	NGK BP7HS
1985 through 1987	NGK BP8HS
Electrode gap	
1984	0.6 to 0.7 mm (0.024 to 0.028 inch)
1985 through 1987	0.5 to 0.6 mm (0.020 to 0.024 inch)
Idle speed (rpm)	1500 to 1700 rpm
Engine oil type	Yamaha Autolube oil or equivalent
Oil tank capacity	1.1 liters (37 fl oz)
Bore x stroke	49.0 x 42.0 mm (1.93 x 1.65 inches)
Piston diameter (service limit)	49.0 mm (1.93 inches)
Bore diameter (service limit)	49.020 mm (1.9308 inches)
Piston to bore clearance (service limit)	
1984	0.1 mm (0.004 inch)
1985 and later	0.04 mm (0.0016 inch)
Piston ring installed end gap	
1984 (top and second)	0.15 to 0.30 mm (0.006 to 0.010 inch)
1985 and later	
Top	0.2 to 0.4 mm (0.008 to 0.016 inch)
Second	0.15 to 0.30 mm (0.006 to 0.012 inch)
Piston ring side clearance	
1984 (top and second)	0.03 to 0.05 mm (0.0012 to 0.0020 inch)
1985 and later	
Top	0.02 to 0.06 mm (0.0008 to 0.0024 inch)
Second	0.03 to 0.05 mm (0.0012 to 0.0020 inch)

Fuel system

Throttle twistgrip freeplay	3 to 7 mm (1/8 to 17/64 inch)
Main jet	
1984	75
1985 and later	95
Pilot jet	
1984	20
1985 and later	27.5
Needle type/position	
1984	3T12-1
1985 and later	3F23-1
Air screw setting	Not specified
Float height	14.5 +/- 1.0 mm (0.57 +/- 0.04 inch)

Ignition system

Ignition coil primary resistance	1.6 ohms +/- 10%
Ignition coil secondary resistance (without spark plug cap installed)	6.6 k-ohms +/- 10%
Pick-up coil resistance	34 ohms +/- 10%

Yamaha CV80 Zuma, 1984 through 1987 (continued)

Transmission

Belt width (service limit)	15.5 mm (0.61 inch)
Clutch lining thickness (service limit)	
1984	2.5 mm (0.1 inch)
1985 and later	2.0 mm (0.08 inch)
Clutch spring free length (service limit)	25.9 mm (1.02 inch)

Brakes

Drum internal diameter (service limit, front and rear)	110.5 mm (4.35 inches)
Brake lining thickness (service limit)	2.0 mm (0.08 inch)
Brake freeplay (front and rear)	10 to 20 mm (3/8 to 3/4 inch)

Tire pressures

Front	14 psi
Rear	
Rider only	22 psi
Rider and passenger	
1984	36 psi
1985 and later	32 psi

Electrical system

Battery	
Capacity	6V-11Ah
Specific gravity	1.280 @ 20-degrees C/68-degrees F
Alternator	
Regulated voltage (no load)	7.5 volts
Charging coil resistance	
1984	378 ohms +/- 10%
1985 and later	0.6 ohms +/- 20%
Fuses (main and reserve)	10 amps

Torque wrench settings

Note: One foot-pound (ft-lb) of torque is equivalent to 12 inch-pounds (in-lbs) of torque. Torque values below approximately 15 foot-pounds are expressed in inch-pounds, because most foot-pound torque wrenches are not accurate at these smaller values.

Cylinder head nuts	15 Nm (132 inch-lbs)
Drive pulley nut	30 Nm (22 ft-lbs)
Driven pulley nut	50 Nm (36 ft-lbs)
Centrifugal clutch housing nut (1985 and later)	60 Nm (43 ft-lbs)
Alternator rotor nut	43 Nm (31 ft-lbs)
Engine mounting bracket to frame	42 Nm (30 ft-lbs)
Engine mounting bracket to engine	
1984	42 Nm (30 ft-lbs)
1985 and later	74 Nm (54 ft-lbs)
Crankcase bolts	8 Nm (70 inch-lbs)
Front axle nut	35 Nm (25 ft-lbs)
Rear axle nut	95 Nm (70 ft-lbs)
Handlebar to steering shaft	34 Nm (24 ft-lbs)
Steering stem bearing adjusting nut	
First step	30 Nm (22 ft-lbs)
Second step	Loosen 1/4 to 1/3 turn
Third step	Tighten locknut to 30 Nm (22 ft-lbs)
Front shock absorber upper bolts	26 Nm (19 ft-lbs)
Front shock absorber lower bolts	50 Nm (36 ft-lbs)
Rear shock absorber to frame bolt	40 Nm (29 ft-lbs)
Rear shock absorber to engine bolt	
1984	50 Nm (36 ft-lbs)
1985 and later	49 Nm (35 ft-lbs)
Rear brake arm	
1984	10 Nm (87 inch-lbs)
1985 and later	8 Nm (70 inch-lbs)

Yamaha XC125 Riva, 1985 through 2001

Engine	124 cc single-cylinder 4-stroke
Cooling system	Air cooled
Fuel system	CV carburetor
Ignition system	CDI
Transmission	Variable speed automatic, belt driven
Suspension	Pivot front, swingarm with twin shocks rear
Brakes	Drum front and rear
Tires	
Front	3.50-10 4PR
Rear	3.50-10 REINF
Wheelbase	1250 mm (49.2 inches)
Weight (with oil and full fuel tank)	102 kg (225 lbs)
Fuel tank capacity	7.0 liters (1.8 gal)

Engine

Spark plug type	NGK C6HSA or ND U20FS-U
Electrode gap	0.6 to 0.7 mm (0.024 to 0.028 inch)
Idle speed (rpm)	1400 +/- 50 rpm
Engine oil type	
Above 5-degrees C (40-degrees F)	API SE, 20W-40
Below 15-degrees C (60-degrees F)	API SE, 10W-30
Oil capacity	1.0 liters (1.1 qt)
Bore x stroke	49.0 x 66.0 mm (1.93 x 2.60 inches)
Piston diameter (service limit)	48.945 mm (1.927 inches)
Bore diameter (service limit)	49.01 mm (1.9294 inches)
Piston to bore clearance (service limit)	0.04 mm (0.0016 inch)
Piston ring installed end gap	
Top and second	0.15 to 0.30 mm (0.006 to 0.010 inch)
Oil	0.3 to 0.9 mm (0.012 to 0.035 inch)
Piston ring side clearance	
Top	0.03 to 0.07 mm (0.0012 to 0.0028 inch)
Second	0.02 to 0.06 mm (0.0008 to 0.0024 inch)
Oil ring	None

Fuel system

Throttle twistgrip freeplay	1.5 to 3.5 mm (1/16 to 17/64 inch)
Main jet	108
Pilot jet	34
Pilot air jet	140
Needle type/position	Not specified
Pilot screw setting	Not specified
Float height	27 +/- 1.0 mm (1.063 +/- 0.04 inch)

Ignition system

Ignition coil primary resistance	2.7 ohms +/- 10%
Ignition coil secondary resistance	13.2 k-ohms +/- 20%
Pick-up coil resistance	112.5 ohms +/- 20%

Transmission

Belt width (service limit)	17.5 mm (0.689 inch)
Clutch lining thickness (service limit)	2.0 mm (0.08 inch)
Clutch spring free length (service limit)	71.0 mm (2.80 inches)

Brakes

Drum internal diameter (service limit, front and rear)	131 mm (5.16 inches)
Brake lining thickness (service limit)	2.0 mm (0.08 inch)
Brake freeplay	
Front	10 to 20 mm (3/8 to 3/4 inch)
Rear	5 to 15 mm (3/16 to 9/16 inch)

Yamaha XC125 Riva, 1985 through 2001 (continued)

Tire pressures

Front .... 21 psi

Rear

    Up to 90 kg (200 lbs) load.............................. 28 psi

    90 kg (200 lbs) to maximum load................................. 43 psi

Electrical system

Battery

    Capacity 12V-7Ah

    Specific gravity.. 1.280 @ 20-degrees C/68-degrees F

Alternator

    Regulated voltage (no load) .... 14.5 volts

    Charging coil resistance................................ 0.8 ohms +/- 20%

    Fuses (main and reserve) .... 20 amps

Torque wrench settings

Note: One foot-pound (ft-lb) of torque is equivalent to 12 inch-pounds (in-lbs) of torque. Torque values below approximately 15 foot-pounds are expressed in inch-pounds, because most foot-pound torque wrenches are not accurate at these smaller values.

Cylinder head main bolts.. 22 Nm (16 ft-lbs)

Cylinder head small bolt... 10 Nm (87 inch-lbs)

Camshaft sprocket bolt.. 28 Nm (20 ft-lbs)

Camshaft bearing retainer bolt... 7 Nm (61 inch-lbs)

Drive pulley nut... 55 Nm (40 ft-lbs)

Driven pulley nut... 90 Nm (36 ft-lbs)

Centrifugal clutch housing nut .... 60 Nm (43 ft-lbs)

Alternator rotor nut.. 70 Nm (50 ft-lbs)

Engine mounting bolt... 74 Nm (53 ft-lbs)

Crankcase bolts .... 10 Nm (87 inch-lbs)

Front axle nut .... 70 Nm (50 ft-lbs)

Rear axle nut .... 105 Nm (75 ft-lbs)

Handlebar mounting bolt.. 34 Nm (24 ft-lbs)

Steering stem bearing adjusting nut

    First step .... 30 Nm (22 ft-lbs)

    Second step.. Loosen 1/4 to 1/3 turn

    Third step .... Tighten locknut to 30 Nm (22 ft-lbs)

Front shock absorber upper and lower bolts .... 19 Nm (13 ft-lbs)

Front pivot arm nuts and bolts .... 40 Nm (29 ft-lbs)

Rear shock absorber mounting arm bolts......................... 23 Nm (17 ft-lbs)

Rear shock absorber mounting bolts................................ 19 Nm (13 ft-lbs)

Rear brake arm.. 10 Nm (87 inch-lbs)

Rear brake panel mounting bolts .... 19 Nm (13 ft-lbs)

Yamaha YJ125 Vino, 2004

Engine	125 cc single-cylinder 4-stroke
Cooling system	Air cooled
Fuel system	CV carburetor
Ignition system	CDI
Transmission	Variable speed automatic, belt driven
Suspension	Telescopic front, swingarm with single shock rear
Brakes	Disc front, drum rear
Tires	3.50-10 51J (front and rear)
Wheelbase	1230 mm (48.4 inches)
Weight (with oil and full fuel tank)	109 kg (240 lbs)
Fuel tank capacity	4.5 liters (1.18 gal)

Engine

Spark plug type	NGK CR7E
Electrode gap	0.7 to 0.8 mm (0.028 to 0.032 inch)
Idle speed (rpm)	1600 to 1700 rpm
Engine oil type	API SE, 20W-40
Oil capacity (with filter change)	1.2 liters (1.31 qt)
Bore x stroke	51.5 x 60.0 mm (2.027 x 2.362 inches)
Piston diameter (service limit)	51.470 mm (inch)
Bore diameter (service limit)	49.01 mm (1.9294 inches)
Piston to bore clearance (service limit)	0.15 mm (0.006 inch)
Piston ring installed end gap	
Top	
Standard	0.10 to 0.20 mm (0.004 to 0.008 inch)
Service limit	0.45 mm (0.018 inch)
Second	
Standard	0.20 to 0.30 mm (0.008 to 0.012 inch)
Service limit	0.65 mm (0.025 inch)
Oil	0.2 to 0.7 mm (0.008 to 0.028 inch)
Piston ring side clearance	
Top	0.02 to 0.08 mm (0.0008 to 0.0031 inch)
Second	0.02 to 0.06 mm (0.0008 to 0.0024 inch)

Fuel system

Throttle twistgrip freeplay	3 to 5 mm (1/8 to 3/16 inch)
Main jet	97.5
Needle type/position	4Dx16-1
Pilot screw setting	Not specified
Float height	27 +/- 1.0 mm (1.063 +/- 0.04 inches)
Fuel level	6.5 to 7.5 mm (0.256 to 0.295 inch)

Ignition system

Ignition coil primary resistance	0.184 to 0.276 ohms
Ignition coil secondary resistance	6.32 to 9.48 k-ohms
Spark plug cap resistance	8 to 12 k-ohms
Pick-up coil resistance	304 to 456 ohms

Transmission

Belt width (service limit)	19.5 mm (0.768 inch)
Weight roller outer diameter (standard)	19.9 to 20.1 mm (0.783 to 0.791 inch)
Clutch lining thickness (service limit)	2.0 mm (0.08 inch)
Clutch spring free length (standard)	113.6 mm (4.472 inches)

Yamaha YJ125 Vino, 2004 (continued)

Brakes
Front brake pad thickness (service limit).. 0.8 mm (0.031 inch)
Front brake thickness (service limit) .... 3.5 mm (0.138 inch)
Rear drum brake
    Drum internal diameter (service limit).. 111 mm (4.37 inches)
    Brake lining thickness (service limit) .... 2.0 mm (0.08 inch)
Brake freeplay
    Front   .... 3 to 5 mm (1/8 to 3/16 inch)
    Rear   .... 5 to 15 mm (3/16 to 9/16 inch)

Tire pressures
Front   .... 22 psi
Rear
    Up to 90 kg (200 lbs) load... 29 psi
    90 kg (200 lbs) to maximum load... 32 psi

Electrical system
Battery
    Capacity 12V-6Ah
    Specific gravity.. 1.330 @ 20-degrees C/68-degrees F
Alternator
    Regulated voltage (no load) .... 14 to 15 volts
    Lighting coil resistance .... 0.28 to 0.42 ohms
Fuses (main and reserve).. 10 amps

Torque wrench settings
Note: One foot-pound (ft-lb) of torque is equivalent to 12 inch-pounds (in-lbs) of torque. Torque values below approximately 15 foot-pounds are expressed in inch-pounds, because most foot-pound torque wrenches are not accurate at these smaller values.

Cylinder head nuts .... 22 Nm (16 ft-lbs)
Cylinder head bolts .... 12 Nm (104 inch-lbs)
Camshaft sprocket bolt... 30 Nm (22 ft-lbs)
External oil line banjo bolt .... 10 Nm (87 inch-lbs)
External oil line retaining bolt .... 8 Nm (70 inch-lbs)
Timing chain tensioner sealing bolt .... 8 Nm (70 inch-lbs)
Timing chain tensioner mounting bolts .... 10 Nm (86 inch-lbs)
Drive pulley nut... 55 Nm (40 ft-lbs)
Driven pulley nut... 90 Nm (36 ft-lbs)
Centrifugal clutch housing nut .... 60 Nm (43 ft-lbs)
Alternator rotor nut... 70 Nm (50 ft-lbs)
Engine mounting through-bolt .... 42 Nm (30 ft-lbs)
Engine mounting bracket bolts .... 32 Nm (23 ft-lbs)
Crankcase bolts .... 12 Nm (104 inch-lbs)
Front axle nut .... 70 Nm (50 ft-lbs)
Rear axle nut .... 105 Nm (75 ft-lbs)
Handlebar clamp bolts .... 30 Nm (22 ft-lbs)
Steering stem bearing adjusting nut
    First step   .... 28 Nm (20 ft-lbs)
    Second step.. Loosen completely
    Third step .... Tighten locknut to 9 Nm (78 inch ft-lbs)
    Fourth step.. Align tabs of first and second nuts
    Fifth step .... Install tab washer over both nuts
    Sixth step .... Tighten third nut to 75 Nm (54 ft-lbs)
Front fork pinch bolts .... 23 Nm (17 ft-lbs)
Front fork top plugs .... 45 Nm (33 ft-lbs)
Front fork bottom Allen bolts... 30 Nm (22 ft-lbs)*
Front pivot arm nuts and bolts .... 40 Nm (29 ft-lbs)
Rear shock absorber mounting arm bolts.. 23 Nm (17 ft-lbs)
Rear shock absorber mounting bolts... 19 Nm (13 ft-lbs)
Front brake caliper mounting bolts .... 35 Nm (25 ft-lbs)
Front brake hose banjo bolt .... 23 Nm (17 ft-lbs)
Rear brake arm... 10 Nm (87 inch-lbs)
Rear brake panel mounting bolts .... 19 Nm (13 ft-lbs)

Apply non-permanent thread locking agent to the threads.

Yamaha XC200 Riva, 1987 through 1991

Engine	200 cc single-cylinder 4-stroke
Cooling system	Air cooled
Fuel system	CV carburetor
Ignition system	CDI
Transmission	Variable speed automatic, belt driven
Suspension	Link front, swingarm with single shock rear
Brakes	Drum front and rear
Tires	400-10 (front and rear)
Wheelbase	1290 mm (50.8 inches)
Weight (with oil and full fuel tank)	128 kg (282 lbs)
Fuel tank capacity	6.5 liters (1.72 gal)

Engine

Spark plug type	NGK DPR7EA-9 or ND X22EPR-U9
Electrode gap	0.8 to 0.9 mm (0.032 to 0.035 inch)
Idle speed (rpm)	1250 to 1350 rpm
Engine oil type	
Above 5-degrees C (40-degrees F)	API SE, 20W-40
Below 15-degrees C (60-degrees F)	API SE, 20W-40
Oil capacity (with filter change)	1.0 liters (1.1 qt)
Bore x stroke	68.0 x 55.0 mm (2.677 x 2.125 inches)
Piston diameter (service limit)	69.75 mm (2.675 inches)
Bore diameter (service limit)	Not specified
Piston to bore clearance (service limit)	0.04 mm (0.0016 inch)
Piston ring installed end gap	
Top and second (standard)	0.30 to 0.45 mm (0.012 to 0.018 inch)
Oil (standard)	0.2 to 0.7 mm (0.008 to 0.028 inch)
Piston ring side clearance	
Top	0.03 to 0.07 mm (0.0012 to 0.0028 inch)
Second	0.02 to 0.06 mm (0.0008 to 0.0024 inch)

Fuel system

Throttle twistgrip freeplay	3 to 7 mm (1/8 to 17/64 inch)
Main jet	128
Needle jet	95
Pilot jet	36
Needle type/position	5CI3/not specified
Pilot screw setting	Two turns out
Float height	27 +/- 1.0 mm (1.063 +/- 0.04 inches)

Ignition system

Ignition coil primary resistance	2.7 ohms +/- 10%
Ignition coil secondary resistance	13.2 k-ohms +/- 10%
Pick-up coil resistance	114.5 ohms +/- 15%

Transmission

Belt width (service limit)	20.0 mm (0.787 inch)
Clutch lining thickness (standard)	4.0 mm (0.157 inch)
Clutch spring free length (standard)	96.7 mm (3.81 inches)

Brakes

Drum internal diameter (service limit)	
Front	131 mm (5.16 inches)
Rear	151 mm (5.94 inches)
Brake lining thickness (service limit)	2.0 mm (0.08 inch)
Brake freeplay	
Front	10 to 20 mm (3/8 to 3/4 inch)
Rear	5 to 15 mm (3/16 to 9/16 inch)

Yamaha XC200 Riva, 1987 through 1991 (continued)

Tire pressures

Front	21 psi
Rear	
Up to 90 kg (200 lbs) load	28 psi
90 kg (200 lbs) to maximum load	35 psi

Electrical system

Battery	
Capacity	12V-10Ah
Specific gravity	1.280 @ 20-degrees C/68-degrees F
Alternator	
Regulated voltage (no load)	14 to 15 volts
Charging coil resistance	0.44 ohms +/- 15%
Fuses (main and reserve)	10 amps

Torque wrench settings

Note: *One foot-pound (ft-lb) of torque is equivalent to 12 inch-pounds (in-lbs) of torque. Torque values below approximately 15 foot-pounds are expressed in inch-pounds, because most foot-pound torque wrenches are not accurate at these smaller values.*

Cylinder head cover	20 Nm (14 ft-lbs)
Cylinder head nuts	22 Nm (16 ft-lbs)
Cylinder base bolts	10 Nm (87 inch-lbs)
Camshaft sprocket bolt	30 Nm (22 ft-lbs)
Drive pulley nut	50 Nm (36 ft-lbs)
Driven pulley nut	90 Nm (36 ft-lbs)
Centrifugal clutch housing nut	50 Nm (36 ft-lbs)
Alternator rotor nut	35 Nm (25 ft-lbs)
Engine pivot shaft	80 Nm (56 ft-lbs)
Connecting rod nuts	18 Nm (13 ft-lbs)
Crankcase bolts	12 Nm (104 inch-lbs)
Front axle nut	70 Nm (50 ft-lbs)
Rear axle nut	100 Nm (72 ft-lbs)
Steering stem bearing adjusting nut	
First step	30 Nm (22 ft-lbs)
Second step	Loosen completely
Third step	Tighten to 3 Nm (26 inch-lbs)
Fourth step	Tighten locknut (upper nut) to 30 Nm (22 ft-lbs)
Front shock absorber upper bolts	35 Nm (25 ft-lbs)
Front shock absorber lower bolts	20 Nm (14 ft-lbs)
Front pivot arm nuts	45 Nm (32 ft-lbs)
Rear shock absorber bolts (upper and lower)	50 Nm (36 ft-lbs)
Front brake tension bar nut	45 Nm (32 ft-lbs)
Front and rear brake arms	10 Nm (87 inch-lbs)
Rear brake panel mounting bolts	18 Nm (13 ft-lbs)

*Apply non-permanent thread locking agent to the threads.

Wiring diagrams on the following pages

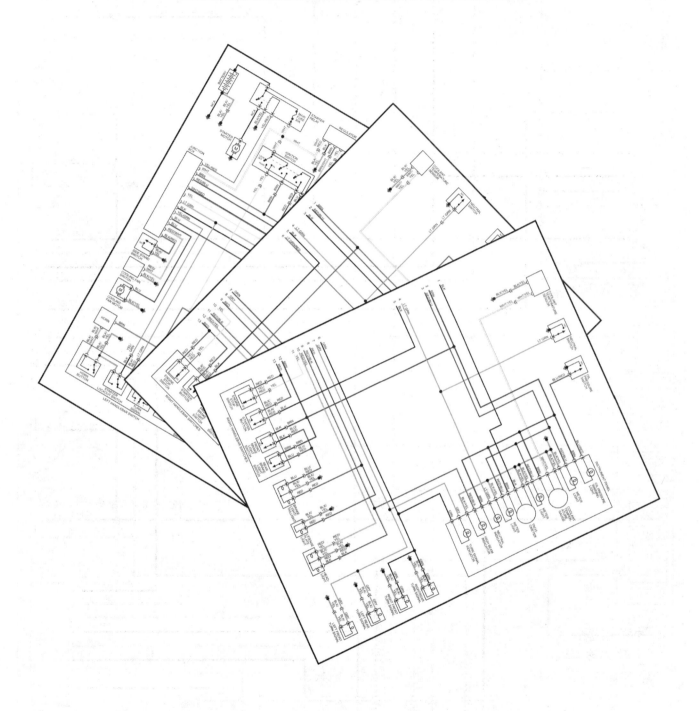

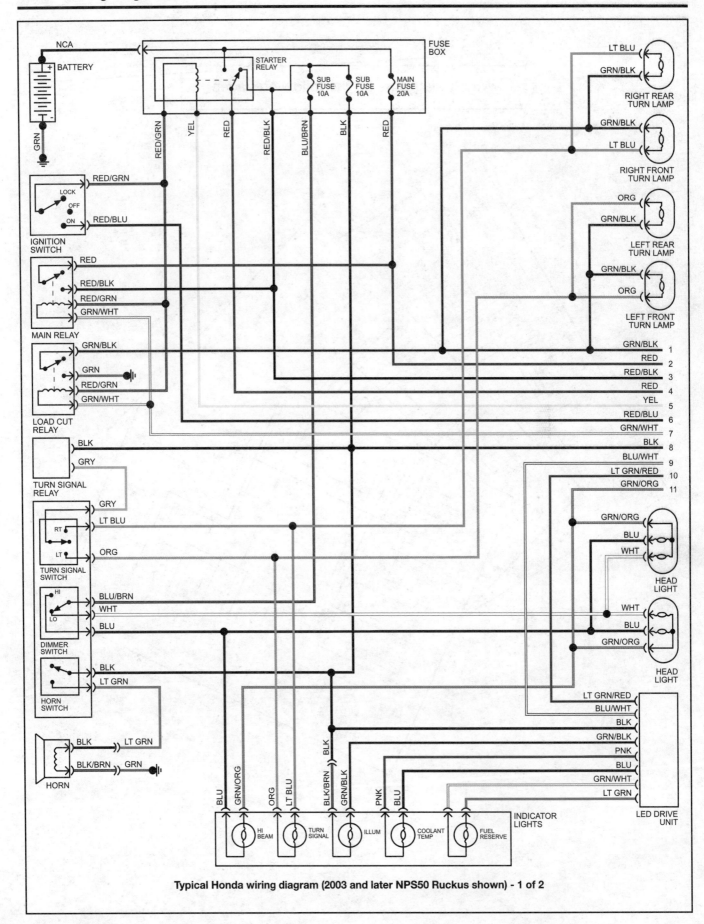

Typical Honda wiring diagram (2003 and later NPS50 Ruckus shown) - 1 of 2

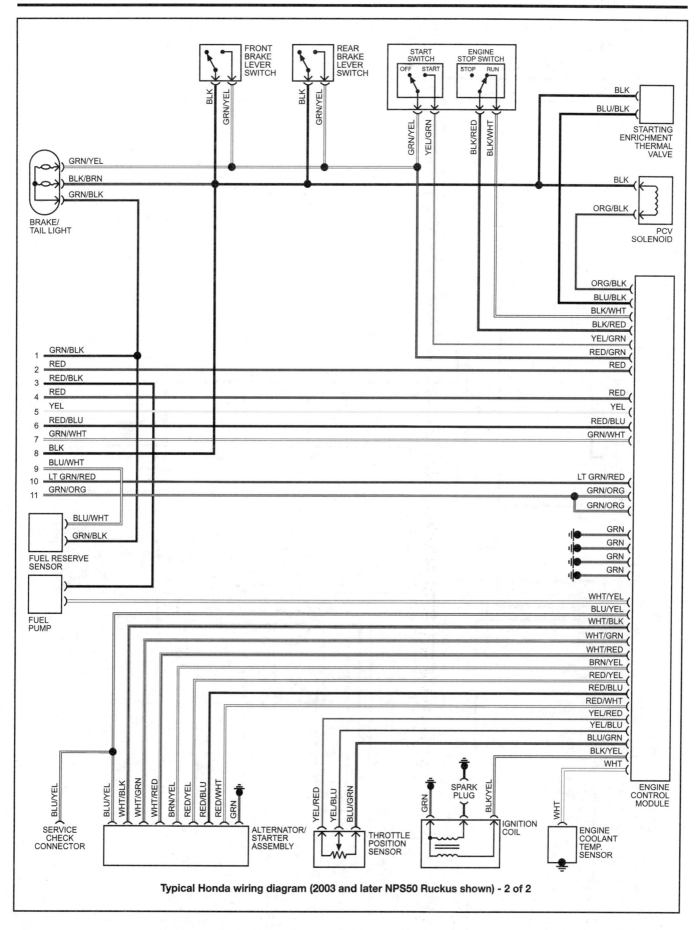

Typical Honda wiring diagram (2003 and later NPS50 Ruckus shown) - 2 of 2

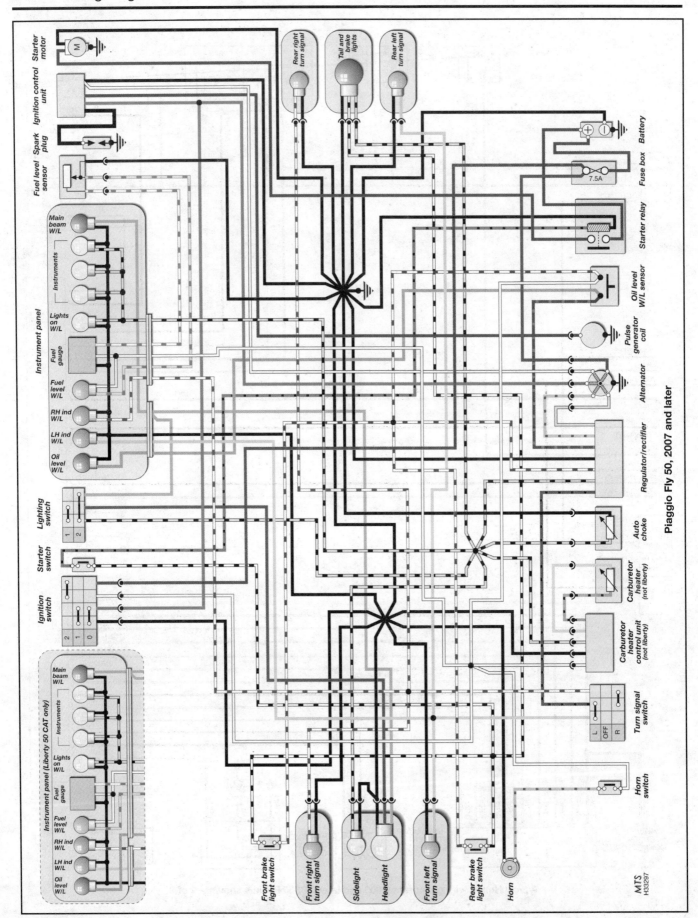

Piaggio Fly 50, 2007 and later

MTS
H33297

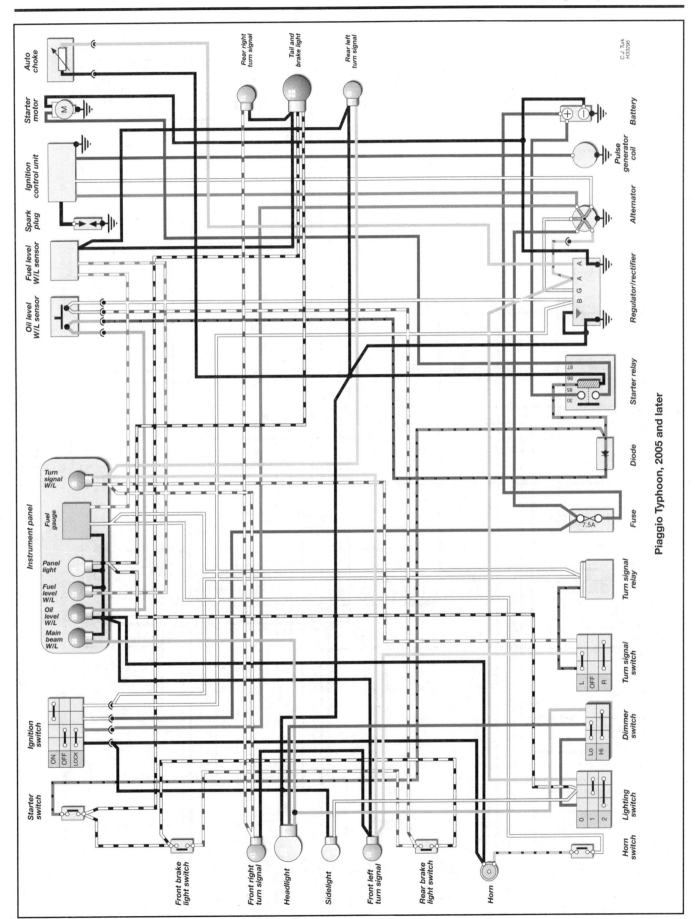

Piaggio Typhoon, 2005 and later

C.J. Turk
H33295

Auto choke

Starter motor

Ignition control unit

Spark plug

Fuel level W/L sensor

Oil level W/L sensor

Rear right turn signal

Tail and brake light

Rear left turn signal

Battery

Pulse generator coil

Alternator

Regulator/rectifier

Starter relay

Diode

Fuse

7.5A

Turn signal relay

Turn signal switch

Dimmer switch

Lighting switch

Horn switch

Instrument panel

Turn signal W/L

Fuel gauge

Panel light

Fuel level W/L

Oil level W/L

Main beam W/L

Ignition switch

ON
OFF
LOCK

Starter switch

Front brake light switch

Front right turn signal

Headlight

Sidelight

Front left turn signal

Rear brake light switch

Horn

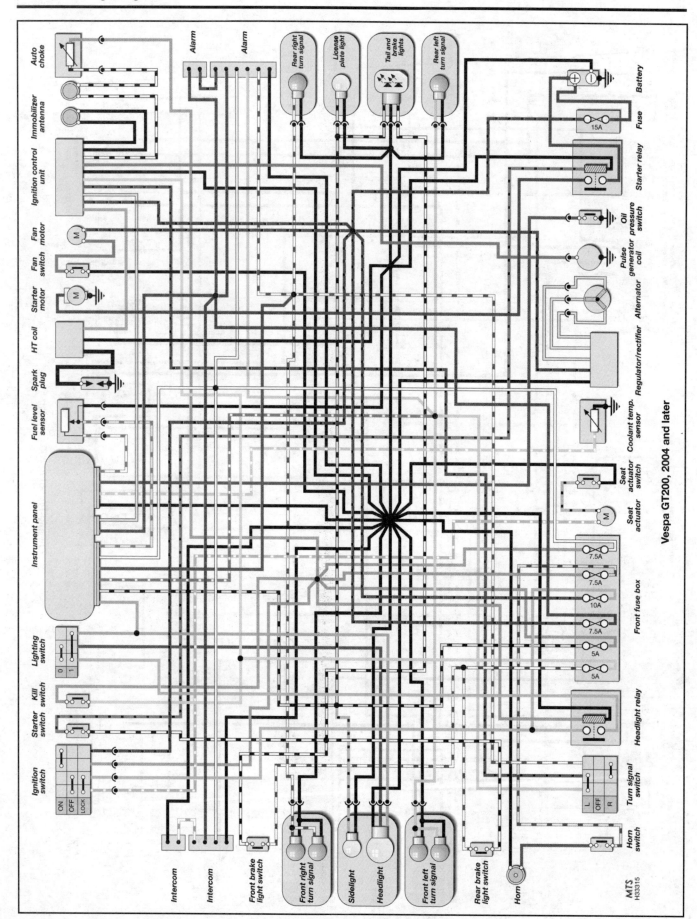

Vespa GT200, 2004 and later

MTS
H33315

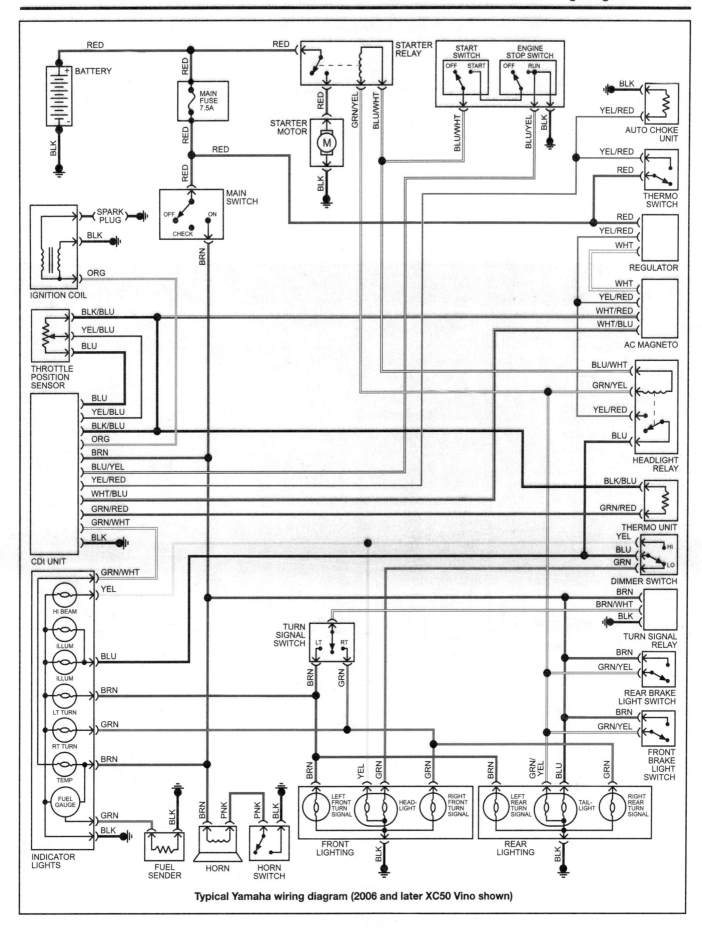

Typical Yamaha wiring diagram (2006 and later XC50 Vino shown)

Notes

Reference

Service record

Date	Mileage/hours	Work performed

Tools and Workshop Tips

Buying tools

A good set of tools is a fundamental requirement for servicing and repairing a scooter. Although there will be an initial expense in building up enough tools for servicing, this will soon be offset by the savings made by doing the job yourself. As experience and confidence grow, additional tools can be added to enable the repair and overhaul of the scooter. Many of the special tools are expensive and not often used so it may be preferable to rent them, or for a group of friends or scooter club to join in the purchase.

As a rule, it is better to buy more expensive, good quality tools. Cheaper tools are likely to wear out faster and need to be replaced more often, nullifying the original savings.

 Warning: To avoid the risk of a poor quality tool breaking in use, causing injury or damage to the component being worked on, always aim to purchase tools which meet the relevant national safety standards.

The following lists of tools do not represent the manufacturer's service tools, but serve as a guide to help the owner decide which tools are needed for this level of work. In addition, items such as an electric drill, hacksaw, files, soldering iron and a workbench equipped with a vise, may be needed. Although not classed as tools, a selection of bolts, screws, nuts, washers and pieces of tubing always come in useful.

For more information about tools, refer to the Haynes *Motorcycle Workshop Practice Techbook* (Bk. No. 3470).

Manufacturer's service tools

Inevitably certain tasks require the use of a service tool. Where possible, an alternative tool or method of approach is recommended, but sometimes there is no option if personal injury or damage to the component is to be avoided. Where required, service tools are referred to in the relevant procedure.

Service tools can usually only be purchased from a scooter dealer and are identified by a part number. Some of the commonly-used tools, such as rotor pullers, are available in aftermarket form from mail-order tool and accessory suppliers.

Maintenance and minor repair tools

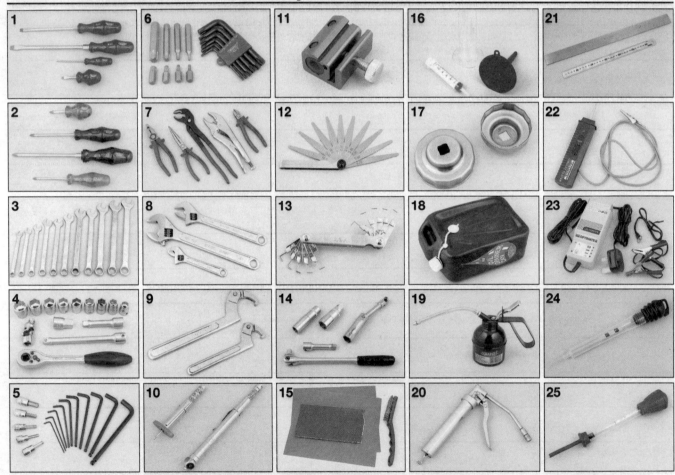

1 *Set of flat-bladed screwdrivers*
2 *Set of Phillips head screwdrivers*
3 *Combination open-end and box wrenches*
4 *Socket set (3/8 inch or 1/2 inch drive)*
5 *Set of Allen keys or bits*
6 *Set of Torx keys or bits*
7 *Pliers, cutters and self-locking grips (vise grips)*
8 *Adjustable wrenches*
9 *C-spanners*
10 *Tread depth gauge and tire pressure gauge*
11 *Cable oiler clamp*
12 *Feeler gauges*
13 *Spark plug gap measuring tool*
14 *Spark plug wrench or deep plug sockets*
15 *Wire brush and emery paper*
16 *Calibrated syringe, measuring cup and funnel*
17 *Oil filter adapters*
18 *Oil drainer can or tray*
19 *Pump type oil can*
20 *Grease gun*
21 *Straight-edge and steel rule*
22 *Continuity tester*
23 *Battery charger*
24 *Hydrometer (for battery specific gravity check)*
25 *Antifreeze tester (for liquid-cooled engines)*

Repair and overhaul tools

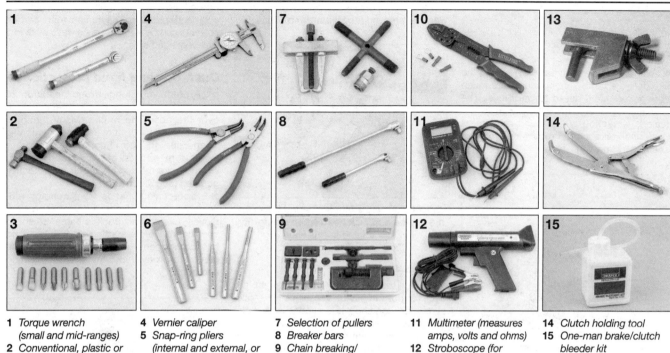

1 Torque wrench
(small and mid-ranges)
2 Conventional, plastic or
soft-faced hammers
3 Impact driver set

4 Vernier caliper
5 Snap-ring pliers
(internal and external, or
combination)
6 Set of cold chisels
and punches

7 Selection of pullers
8 Breaker bars
9 Chain breaking/
riveting tool set
10 Wire stripper and
crimper tool

11 Multimeter (measures
amps, volts and ohms)
12 Stroboscope (for
dynamic timing checks)
13 Hose clamp
(wingnut type shown)

14 Clutch holding tool
15 One-man brake/clutch
bleeder kit

Special tools

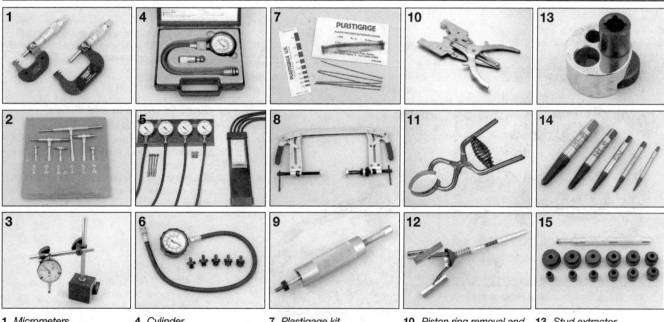

1 Micrometers
(external type)
2 Telescoping gauges
3 Dial gauge

4 Cylinder
compression gauge
5 Vacuum gauges (left) or
manometer (right)
6 Oil pressure gauge

7 Plastigage kit
8 Valve spring compressor
(4-stroke engines)
9 Piston pin drawbolt tool

10 Piston ring removal and
installation tool
11 Piston ring clamp
12 Cylinder bore hone
(stone type shown)

13 Stud extractor
14 Screw extractor set
15 Bearing driver set

1 Workshop equipment and facilities

The workbench

● Work is made much easier by raising the bike up on a ramp - components are much more accessible if raised to waist level. The hydraulic or pneumatic types seen in the dealer's workshop are a sound investment if you undertake a lot of repairs or overhauls **(see illustration 1.1)**.

1.1 Hydraulic ramp

● If raised off ground level, the bike must be supported on the ramp to avoid it falling. Most ramps incorporate a front wheel locating clamp which can be adjusted to suit different diameter wheels. When tightening the clamp, take care not to mark the wheel rim or damage the tire - use wood blocks on each side to prevent this.
● Secure the bike to the ramp using tie-downs **(see illustration 1.2)**. If the bike has only a sidestand, and hence leans at a dangerous angle when raised, support the bike on an auxiliary stand.

1.2 Tie-downs are used around the passenger footrests to secure the bike

● Auxiliary (paddock) stands are widely available from mail order companies or scooter dealers and attach either to the wheel axle or swingarm pivot. If the scooter has a centerstand, you can support it under the crankcase to prevent it toppling while either wheel is removed **(see illustration 1.3)**.

1.3 Always use a block of wood between the engine and jack head when supporting the engine in this way

Fumes and fire

● Refer to the *Safety first!* page at the beginning of the manual for full details. Make sure your workshop is equipped with a fire extinguisher suitable for fuel-related fires (Class B fire - flammable liquids) - it is not sufficient to have a water-filled extinguisher.
● Always ensure adequate ventilation is available. Unless an exhaust gas extraction system is available for use, ensure that the engine is run outside of the workshop.
● If working on the fuel system, make sure the workshop is ventilated to avoid a build-up of fumes. This applies equally to fume build-up when charging a battery. Do not smoke or allow anyone else to smoke in the workshop.

Fluids

● If you need to drain fuel from the tank, store it in an approved container marked as suitable for the storage of gasoline **(see illustration 1.4)**. Do not store fuel in glass jars or bottles.
● Use proprietary engine degreasers or solvents which have a high flash-point, such

1.4 Use an approved can only for storing gasoline

as kerosene, for cleaning off oil, grease and dirt - never use gasoline for cleaning. Wear rubber gloves when handling solvent and engine degreaser. The fumes from certain solvents can be dangerous - always work in a well-ventilated area.

Dust, eye and hand protection

● Protect your lungs from inhalation of dust particles by wearing a filtering mask over the nose and mouth. Many frictional materials still contain asbestos which is dangerous to your health. Protect your eyes from spouts of liquid and sprung components by wearing a pair of protective goggles **(see illustration 1.5)**.
● Protect your hands from contact with solvents, fuel and oils by wearing rubber gloves. Alternatively apply a barrier cream to your hands before starting work. If handling hot components or fluids, wear suitable gloves to protect your hands from scalding and burns.

1.5 A fire extinguisher, goggles, mask and protective gloves should be at hand in the workshop

What to do with old fluids

● Old cleaning solvent, fuel, coolant and oils should not be poured down domestic drains or onto the ground. Package the fluid up in old oil containers, label it accordingly, and take it to a garage or disposal facility. Contact your local disposal company for location of such sites.

Note: It is illegal to dump oil down the drain. Check with your local auto parts store, disposal facility or environmental agency to see if they accept the oil for recycling.

2 Fasteners - screws, bolts and nuts

Fastener types and applications

Bolts and screws

● Fastener head types are either of hexagonal, Torx or splined design, with internal and external versions of each type **(see illustrations 2.1 and 2.2)**; splined head fasteners are not in common use on scooters. The conventional slotted or Phillips head design is used for certain screws. Bolt or screw length is always measured from the underside of the head to the end of the item **(see illustration 2.11)**.

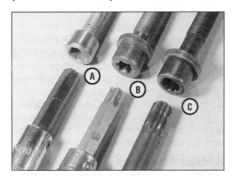

2.1 Internal hexagon/Allen (A), Torx (B) and splined (C) fasteners, with corresponding bits

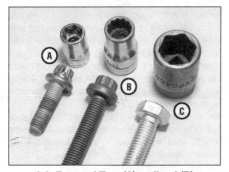

2.2 External Torx (A), splined (B) and hexagon (C) fasteners, with corresponding sockets

● Certain fasteners on the scooter have a tensile marking on their heads, the higher the marking the stronger the fastener. High tensile fasteners generally carry a 10 or higher marking. Never replace a high tensile fastener with one of a lower tensile strength.

Washers (see illustration 2.3)

● Plain washers are used between a fastener head and a component to prevent damage to the component or to spread the load when torque is applied. Plain washers can also be used as spacers or shims in certain assemblies. Copper or aluminum plain washers are often used as sealing washers on drain plugs.

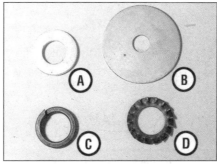

2.3 Plain washer (A), penny washer (B), spring washer (C) and serrated washer (D)

● The split-ring spring washer works by applying axial tension between the fastener head and component. If flattened, it is fatigued and must be replaced. If a plain (flat) washer is used on the fastener, position the spring washer between the fastener and the plain washer.

● Serrated star type washers dig into the fastener and component faces, preventing loosening. They are often used on electrical ground connections to the frame.

● Cone type washers (sometimes called Belleville) are conical and when tightened apply axial tension between the fastener head and component. They must be installed with the dished side against the component and often carry an OUTSIDE marking on their outer face. If flattened, they are fatigued and must be replaced.

● Tab washers are used to lock plain nuts or bolts on a shaft. A portion of the tab washer is bent up hard against one flat of the nut or bolt to prevent it loosening. Due to the tab washer being deformed in use, a new tab washer should be used every time it is removed.

● Wave washers are used to take up endfloat on a shaft. They provide light springing and prevent excessive side-to-side play of a component. Can be found on rocker arm shafts.

Nuts and cotter pins

● Conventional plain nuts are usually six-sided **(see illustration 2.4)**. They are sized by thread diameter and pitch. High tensile nuts carry a number on one end to denote their tensile strength.

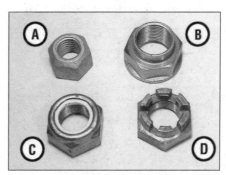

2.4 Plain nut (A), shouldered locknut (B), nylon insert nut (C) and castellated nut (D)

● Self-locking nuts either have a nylon insert, or two spring metal tabs, or a shoulder which is staked into a groove in the shaft - their advantage over conventional plain nuts is a resistance to loosening due to vibration. The nylon insert type can be used a number of times, but must be replaced when the friction of the nylon insert is reduced, i.e. when the nut spins freely on the shaft. The spring tab type can be reused unless the tabs are damaged. The shouldered type must be replaced every time it is removed.

● Cotter pins are used to lock a castellated nut to a shaft or to prevent loosening of a plain nut. Common applications are wheel axles and brake torque arms. Because the cotter pin arms are deformed to lock around the nut, a new cotter pin must always be used on installation - always use the correct size cotter pin which will fit snugly in the shaft hole. Make sure the cotter pin arms are correctly located around the nut **(see illustrations 2.5 and 2.6)**.

2.5 Bend cotter pin arms as shown (arrows) to secure a castellated nut

2.6 Bend cotter pin arms as shown to secure a plain nut

Caution: If the castellated nut slots do not align with the shaft hole after tightening to the torque setting, tighten the nut until the next slot aligns with the hole - never loosen the nut to align its slot.

● R-pins (shaped like the letter R), or slip pins as they are sometimes called, are sprung and can be reused if they are otherwise in good condition. Always install R-pins with their closed end facing forwards **(see illustration 2.7)**.

2.7 Correct fitting of R-pin. Arrow indicates forward direction

Snap-rings (see illustration 2.8)

● Snap-rings (sometimes called circlips) are used to retain components on a shaft or in a housing and have corresponding external or internal ears to permit removal. Parallel-sided (machined) snap-rings can be installed either way round in their groove, whereas stamped snap-rings (which have a chamfered edge on one face) must be installed with the chamfer facing away from the direction of thrust load **(see illustration 2.9)**.

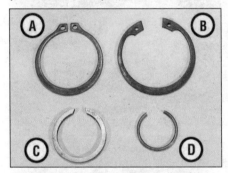

2.8 External stamped snap-ring (A), internal stamped snap-ring (B), machined snap-ring (C) and wire snap-ring (D)

● Always use snap-ring pliers to remove and install snap-rings; expand or compress them just enough to remove them. After installation, rotate the snap-ring in its groove to ensure it is securely seated. If installing a snap-ring on a splined shaft, always align its opening with a shaft channel to ensure the snap-ring ends are well supported and unlikely to catch **(see illustration 2.10)**.

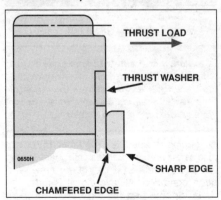

2.9 Correct fitting of a stamped snap-ring

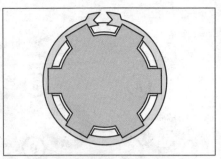

2.10 Align snap-ring opening with shaft channel

● Snap-rings can wear due to the thrust of components and become loose in their grooves, with the subsequent danger of becoming dislodged in operation. For this reason, replacement is advised every time a snap-ring is disturbed.

● Wire snap-rings are commonly used as piston pin retaining clips. If a removal tang is provided, long-nosed pliers can be used to dislodge them, otherwise careful use of a small flat-bladed screwdriver is necessary. Wire snap-rings should be replaced every time they are disturbed.

Thread diameter and pitch

● Diameter of a male thread (screw, bolt or stud) is the outside diameter of the threaded portion **(see illustration 2.11)**. Most motorcycle manufacturers use the ISO (International Standards Organization) metric system expressed in millimeters. For example, M6 refers to a 6 mm diameter thread. Sizing is the same for nuts, except that the thread diameter is measured across the valleys of the nut.

● Pitch is the distance between the peaks of the thread **(see illustration 2.11)**. It is expressed in millimeters, thus a common bolt size may be expressed as 6.0 x 1.0 mm (6 mm thread diameter and 1 mm pitch). Generally pitch increases in proportion to thread diameter, although there are always exceptions.

● Thread diameter and pitch are related for conventional fastener applications and the accompanying table can be used as a guide. Additionally, the AF (Across Flats), wrench or socket size dimension of the bolt or nut **(see illustration 2.11)** is linked to thread and pitch specification. Thread pitch can be measured with a thread gauge **(see illustration 2.12)**.

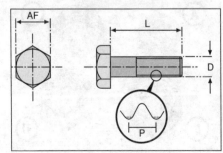

2.11 Fastener length (L), thread diameter (D), thread pitch (P) and head size (AF)

2.12 Using a thread gauge to measure pitch

AF size	Thread diameter x pitch (mm)
8 mm	M5 x 0.8
8 mm	M6 x 1.0
10 mm	M6 x 1.0
12 mm	M8 x 1.25
14 mm	M10 x 1.25
17 mm	M12 x 1.25

● The threads of most fasteners are of the right-hand type, and they are turned clockwise to tighten, and counterclockwise to loosen. The reverse situation applies to left-hand thread fasteners, which are turned counter-clockwise to tighten and clockwise to loosen. Left-hand threads are used where rotation of a component might loosen a conventional right-hand thread fastener.

Seized fasteners

● Corrosion of external fasteners due to water or reaction between two dissimilar metals can occur over a period of time. It will build up sooner in wet conditions or in areas where salt is used on the roads during the winter. If a fastener is severely corroded it is likely that normal methods of removal will fail, and result in its head being ruined. When you attempt removal, the fastener thread should be heard to crack free and unscrew easily - if it doesn't, stop there before damaging something.

● A sharp tap on the head of the fastener will often succeed in breaking free corrosion which has occurred in the threads **(see illustration 2.13)**.

● An aerosol penetrating fluid (such as WD-40) applied the night beforehand may work its way down into the thread and ease removal. Depending on the location, you may be able to make up a modeling-clay well around the

2.13 A sharp tap on the head of a fastener will often break free a corroded thread

fastener head and fill it with penetrating fluid.
● If you are working on an engine internal component, corrosion will most likely not be a problem due to the well lubricated environment. However, components can be very tight and an impact driver is a useful tool in freeing them (see illustration 2.14).

**2.14 Using an impact driver
to free a fastener**

● Where corrosion has occurred between dissimilar metals (like steel and aluminum alloy), the application of heat to the fastener head will create a disproportionate expansion rate between the two metals and break the seizure caused by the corrosion. Whether heat can be applied depends on the location of the fastener - any surrounding components likely to be damaged must first be removed (see illustration 2.15). Heat can be applied using a paint stripper heat gun or clothes iron, or by immersing the component in boiling water - wear protective gloves to prevent scalding or burns to the hands.

2.15 Using heat to free a seized fastener

● As a last resort, it is possible to use a hammer and cold chisel to work the fastener head unscrewed (see illustration 2.16). This will damage the fastener, but more importantly, extreme care must be taken not to damage the surrounding component.

Caution: Remember that the component being secured is generally of more value than the bolt, nut or screw - when the fastener is freed, do not unscrew it with force, instead work the fastener back and forth when resistance is felt to prevent thread damage.

**2.16 Using a hammer and chisel
to free a seized fastener**

Broken fasteners and damaged heads

● If the shank of a broken bolt or screw is accessible, you can grip it with self-locking grips. The knurled wheel type stud extractor tool or self-gripping stud puller tool is particularly useful for removing the long studs which screw into the cylinder mouth surface of the crankcase, or bolts and screws from which the head has broken off (see illustration 2.17). Studs can also be removed by locking two nuts together on the threaded end of the stud and using a wrench on the lower nut (see illustration 2.18).

**2.17 Using a stud extractor tool to remove
a broken crankcase stud**

**2.18 Two nuts can be locked together to
unscrew a stud from a component**

● A bolt or screw which has broken off below or level with the casing must be extracted using a screw extractor set. Centerpunch the fastener to centralize the drill bit, then drill a hole in the fastener (see illustration 2.19). Select a drill bit which is approximately half to three-quarters the diameter of the fastener

**2.19 When using a screw extractor,
first drill a hole in the fastener . . .**

and drill to a depth which will accommodate the extractor. Use the largest size extractor possible, but avoid leaving too small a wall thickness, otherwise the extractor will merely force the fastener walls outwards, wedging it in the casing thread.
● If a spiral type extractor is used, thread it counterclockwise into the fastener. As it is screwed in, it will grip the fastener and unscrew it from the casing (see illustration 2.20).

**2.20 . . . then thread the extractor
counterclockwise into the fastener**

● If a taper type extractor is used, tap it into the fastener so that it is firmly wedged in place. Unscrew the extractor (counterclockwise) to draw the fastener out.

⚠ *Warning: Stud extractors are very hard and may break off in the fastener if care is not taken - ask a machine shop about spark erosion (electronic tap removal) if this happens.*

● Alternatively, the broken bolt/screw can be drilled out and the hole retapped for an oversize bolt/screw or a diamond-section thread insert. It is essential that the drilling is carried out squarely and to the correct depth, otherwise the casing may be ruined - if in doubt, entrust the work to a machine shop.
● Bolts and nuts with rounded corners cause the correct size wrench or socket to slip when force is applied. Of the types of wrench/socket available always use a six-point type rather than an eight or twelve-point type - better grip

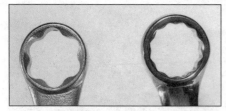

2.21 Comparison of surface drive box wrench (left) with 12-point type (right)

is obtained. Surface drive wrenches grip the middle of the hex flats, rather than the corners, and are thus good in cases of damaged heads **(see illustration 2.21)**.

● Slotted-head or Phillips-head screws are often damaged by the use of the wrong size screwdriver. Allen-head and Torx-head screws are much less likely to sustain damage. If enough of the screw head is exposed you can use a hacksaw to cut a slot in its head and then use a conventional flat-bladed screwdriver to remove it. Alternatively use a hammer and cold chisel to tap the head of the fastener around to loosen it. Always replace damaged fasteners with new ones, preferably Torx or Allen-head type.

A dab of valve grinding compound between the screw head and screwdriver tip will often give a good grip.

Thread repair

● Threads (particularly those in aluminum alloy components) can be damaged by overtightening, being assembled with dirt in the threads, or from a component working loose and vibrating. Eventually the thread will fail completely, and it will be impossible to tighten the fastener.

● If a thread is damaged or clogged with old locking compound it can be renovated with a thread repair tool (thread chaser) **(see illustrations 2.22 and 2.23)**; special thread

2.22 A thread repair tool being used to correct an internal thread

2.23 A thread repair tool being used to correct an external thread

chasers are available for spark plug hole threads. The tool will not cut a new thread, but clean and true the original thread. Make sure that you use the correct diameter and pitch tool. Similarly, external threads can be cleaned up with a die or a thread restorer file **(see illustration 2.24)**.

2.24 Using a thread restorer file

● It is possible to drill out the old thread and retap the component to the next thread size. This will work where there is enough surrounding material and a new bolt or screw can be obtained. Sometimes, however, this is not possible - such as where the bolt/screw passes through another component which must also be suitably modified, also in cases where a spark plug or oil drain plug cannot be obtained in a larger diameter thread size.

● The diamond-section thread insert (often known by its popular trade name of Heli-Coil) is a simple and effective method of replacing the thread and retaining the original size. A kit can be purchased which contains the tap, insert and installing tool **(see illustration 2.25)**. Drill out the damaged thread with the size drill specified **(see illustration 2.26)**. Carefully retap the thread **(see illustration 2.27)**. Install the

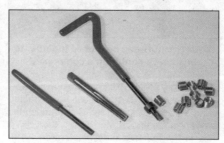

2.25 Obtain a thread insert kit to suit the thread diameter and pitch required

2.26 To install a thread insert, first drill out the original thread . . .

2.27 . . . tap a new thread . . .

2.28 . . . fit the insert on the installing tool . . .

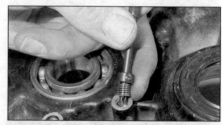

2.29 . . . and thread it into the component . . .

2.30 . . . break off the tang when complete

insert on the installing tool and thread it slowly into place using a light downward pressure **(see illustrations 2.28 and 2.29)**. When positioned between a 1/4 and 1/2 turn below the surface withdraw the installing tool and use the break-off tool to press down on the tang, breaking it off **(see illustration 2.30)**.

● There are epoxy thread repair kits on the market which can rebuild stripped internal threads, although this repair should not be used on high load-bearing components.

Thread locking and sealing compounds

● Locking compounds are used in locations where the fastener is prone to loosening due to vibration or on important safety-related items which might cause loss of control of the scooter if they fail. It is also used where important fasteners cannot be secured by other means such as lockwashers or cotter pins.

● Before applying locking compound, make sure that the threads (internal and external) are clean and dry with all old compound removed. Select a compound to suit the component being secured - a non-permanent general locking and sealing type is suitable for most applications, but a high strength type is needed for permanent fixing of studs in castings. Apply a drop or two of the compound to the first few threads of the fastener, then thread it into place and tighten to the specified torque. Do not apply excessive thread locking compound otherwise the thread may be damaged on subsequent removal.

● Certain fasteners are impregnated with a dry film type coating of locking compound on their threads. Always replace this type of fastener if disturbed.

● Anti-seize compounds, such as copper-based greases, can be applied to protect threads from seizure due to extreme heat and corrosion. A common instance is spark plug threads and exhaust system fasteners.

3 Measuring tools and gauges

Feeler gauges

● Feeler gauges (or blades) are used for measuring small gaps and clearances (see illustration 3.1). They can also be used to measure endfloat (sideplay) of a component on a shaft where access is not possible with a dial gauge.

● Feeler gauge sets should be treated with care and not bent or damaged. They are etched with their size on one face. Keep them clean and very lightly oiled to prevent corrosion build-up.

3.1 Feeler gauges are used for measuring small gaps and clearances - thickness is marked on one face of gauge

● When measuring a clearance, select a gauge which is a light sliding fit between the two components. You may need to use two gauges together to measure the clearance accurately.

Micrometers

● A micrometer is a precision tool capable of measuring to 0.01 or 0.001 of a millimeter. It should always be stored in its case and not in the general toolbox. It must be kept clean and never dropped, otherwise its frame or measuring anvils could be distorted, resulting in inaccurate readings.

● External micrometers are used for measuring outside diameters of components and have many more applications than internal micrometers. Micrometers are available in different size ranges, typically 0 to 25 mm, 25 to 50 mm, and upwards in 25 mm steps; some large micrometers have interchangeable anvils to allow a range of measurements to be taken. Generally the largest precision measurement you are likely to take on a scooter is the piston diameter.

● Internal micrometers (or bore micrometers) are used for measuring inside diameters, such as valve guides and cylinder bores. Telescoping gauges and small hole gauges are used in conjunction with an external micrometer, whereas the more expensive internal micrometers have their own measuring device.

External micrometer

Note: The conventional analog type instrument is described. Although much easier to read, digital micrometers are considerably more expensive.

● Always check the calibration of the micrometer before use. With the anvils

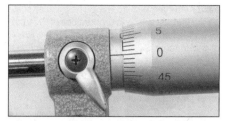

3.2 Check micrometer calibration before use

closed (0 to 25 mm type) or set over a test gauge (for the larger types) the scale should read zero (see illustration 3.2); make sure that the anvils (and test piece) are clean first. Any discrepancy can be adjusted by referring to the instructions supplied with the tool. Remember that the micrometer is a precision measuring tool - don't force the anvils closed, use the ratchet (4) on the end of the micrometer to close it. In this way, a measured force is always applied.

● To use, first make sure that the item being measured is clean. Place the anvil of the micrometer (1) against the item and use the thimble (2) to bring the spindle (3) lightly into contact with the other side of the item (see illustration 3.3). Don't tighten the thimble down because this will damage the micrometer - instead use the ratchet (4) on the end of the micrometer. The ratchet mechanism applies a measured force preventing damage to the instrument.

● The micrometer is read by referring to the linear scale on the sleeve and the annular scale on the thimble. Read off the sleeve first to obtain the base measurement, then add the fine measurement from the thimble to obtain the overall reading. The linear scale on the sleeve represents the measuring range of the

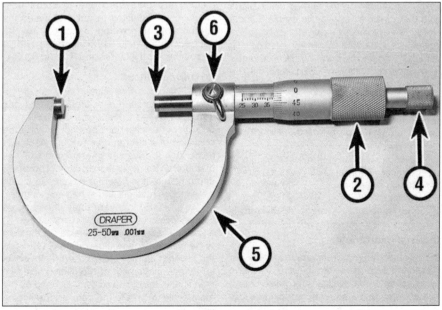

3.3 Micrometer component parts

1 Anvil	3 Spindle	5 Frame
2 Thimble	4 Ratchet	6 Locking lever

micrometer (eg 0 to 25 mm). The annular scale on the thimble will be in graduations of 0.01 mm (or as marked on the frame) - one full revolution of the thimble will move 0.5 mm on the linear scale. Take the reading where the datum line on the sleeve intersects the thimble's scale. Always position the eye directly above the scale, otherwise an inaccurate reading will result.

In the example shown, the item measures 2.95 mm **(see illustration 3.4):**

Linear scale	2.00 mm
Linear scale	0.50 mm
Annular scale	0.45 mm
Total figure	**2.95 mm**

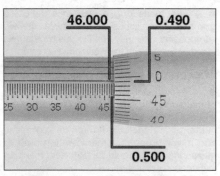

3.5 Micrometer reading of 46.99 mm on linear and annular scales . . .

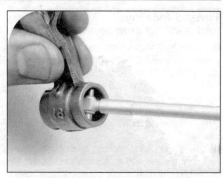

3.7 Expand the telescoping gauge in the bore, lock its position . . .

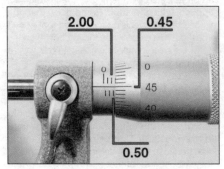

3.4 Micrometer reading of 2.95 mm

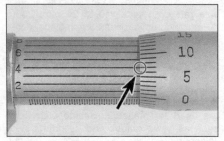

3.6 . . . and 0.004 mm on vernier scale

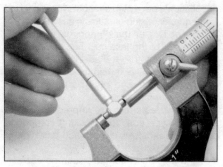

3.8 . . . then measure the gauge with a micrometer

Most micrometers have a locking lever (6) on the frame to hold the setting in place, allowing the item to be removed from the micrometer.
● Some micrometers have a vernier scale on their sleeve, providing an even finer measurement to be taken, in 0.001 increments of a millimeter. Take the sleeve and thimble measurement as described above, then check which graduation on the vernier scale aligns with that of the annular scale on the thimble **Note:** *The eye must be perpendicular to the scale when taking the vernier reading - if necessary rotate the body of the micrometer to ensure this.* Multiply the vernier scale figure by 0.001 and add it to the base and fine measurement figures.

In the example shown, the item measures 46.994 mm **(see illustrations 3.5 and 3.6):**

Linear scale (base)	46.000 mm
Linear scale (base)	00.500 mm
Annular scale (fine)	00.490 mm
Vernier scale	00.004 mm
Total figure	**46.994 mm**

Internal micrometer

● Internal micrometers are available for measuring bore diameters, but are expensive and unlikely to be available for home use. It is suggested that a set of telescoping gauges and small hole gauges, both of which must be used with an external micrometer, will suffice for taking internal measurements on a scooter.
● Telescoping gauges can be used to

measure internal diameters of components. Select a gauge with the correct size range, make sure its ends are clean and insert it into the bore. Expand the gauge, then lock its position and withdraw it from the bore **(see illustration 3.7).** Measure across the gauge ends with a micrometer **(see illustration 3.8).**
● Very small diameter bores (such as valve guides) are measured with a small hole gauge. Once adjusted to a slip-fit inside the component, its position is locked and the gauge withdrawn for measurement with a micrometer **(see illustrations 3.9 and 3.10).**

Vernier caliper

Note: *The conventional linear and dial gauge type instruments are described. Digital types are easier to read, but are far more expensive.*
● The vernier caliper does not provide the precision of a micrometer, but is versatile in being able to measure internal and external diameters. Some types also incorporate a depth gauge. It is ideal for measuring clutch plate friction material and spring free lengths.
● To use the conventional linear scale vernier, loosen off the vernier clamp screws (1) and set its jaws over (2), or inside (3), the item to be measured **(see illustration 3.11).** Slide the jaw into contact, using the thumb-wheel (4) for fine movement of the sliding scale (5) then tighten the clamp screws (1). Read off the main scale (6) where the zero on the sliding scale (5) intersects it, taking the whole number to the left of the zero; this provides the base measurement. View along the sliding scale and select the division which lines up exactly

3.9 Expand the small hole gauge in the bore, lock its position . . .

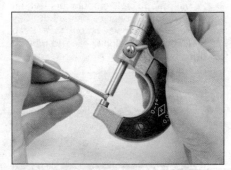

3.10 . . . then measure the gauge with a micrometer

with any of the divisions on the main scale, noting that the divisions usually represents 0.02 of a millimeter. Add this fine measurement to the base measurement to obtain the total reading.

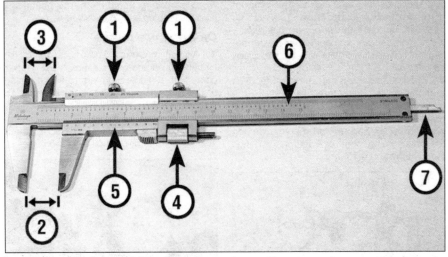

3.11 Vernier component parts (linear gauge)

1 Clamp screws   3 Internal jaws   5 Sliding scale   7 Depth gauge
2 External jaws   4 Thumbwheel   6 Main scale

In the example shown, the item measures 55.92 mm **(see illustration 3.12)**:

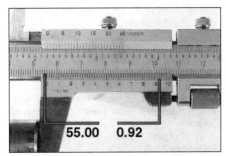

3.12 Vernier gauge reading of 55.92 mm

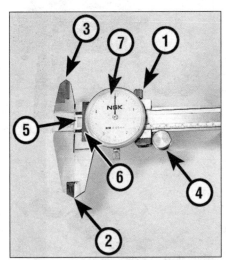

3.13 Vernier component parts (dial gauge)

1 Clamp screw   5 Main scale
2 External jaws   6 Sliding scale
3 Internal jaws   7 Dial gauge
4 Thumbwheel

Base measurement	55.00 mm
Fine measurement	00.92 mm
Total figure	**55.92 mm**

● Some vernier calipers are equipped with a dial gauge for fine measurement. Before use, check that the jaws are clean, then close them fully and check that the dial gauge reads zero. If necessary adjust the gauge ring accordingly. Slacken the vernier clamp screw (1) and set its jaws over (2), or inside (3), the item to be measured **(see illustration 3.13)**. Slide the jaws into contact, using the thumbwheel (4) for fine movement. Read off the main scale (5) where the edge of the sliding scale (6) intersects it, taking the whole number to the left of the zero; this provides the base measurement. Read off the needle position on the dial gauge (7) scale to provide the fine measurement; each division represents 0.05 of a millimeter. Add this fine measurement to the base measurement to obtain the total reading.

In the example shown, the item measures 55.95 mm **(see illustration 3.14)**:

Base measurement	55.00 mm
Fine measurement	00.95 mm
Total figure	**55.95 mm**

3.14 Vernier gauge reading of 55.95 mm

Plastigage

● Plastigage is a plastic material which can be compressed between two surfaces to measure the oil clearance between them. The width of the compressed Plastigage is measured against a calibrated scale to determine the clearance.

● Common uses of Plastigage are for measuring the clearance between crankshaft journal and main bearing inserts, between crankshaft journal and big-end bearing inserts, and between camshaft and bearing surfaces. The following example describes big-end oil clearance measurement.

● Handle the Plastigage material carefully to prevent distortion. Using a sharp knife, cut a length which corresponds with the width of the bearing being measured and place it carefully across the journal so that it is parallel with the shaft **(see illustration 3.15)**. Carefully install both bearing shells and the connecting rod. Without rotating the rod on the journal tighten its bolts or nuts (as applicable) to the specified torque. The connecting rod and bearings are then disassembled and the crushed Plastigage examined.

3.15 Plastigage placed across shaft journal

● Using the scale provided in the Plastigage kit, measure the width of the material to determine the oil clearance **(see illustration 3.16)**. Always remove all traces of Plastigage after use using your fingernails.

> **Caution: Arriving at the correct clearance demands that the assembly is torqued correctly, according to the settings and sequence (where applicable) provided by the scooter manufacturer.**

3.16 Measuring the width of the crushed Plastigage

Dial gauge or DTI (Dial Test Indicator)

● A dial gauge can be used to accurately measure small amounts of movement. Typical uses are measuring shaft runout or shaft endfloat (sideplay) and setting piston position for ignition timing on two-strokes. A dial gauge set usually comes with a range of different probes and adapters and mounting equipment.

● The gauge needle must point to zero when at rest. Rotate the ring around its periphery to zero the gauge.

● Check that the gauge is capable of reading the extent of movement in the work. Most gauges have a small dial set in the face which records whole millimeters of movement as well as the fine scale around the face periphery which is calibrated in 0.01 mm divisions. Read off the small dial first to obtain the base measurement, then add the measurement from the fine scale to obtain the total reading.

In the example shown the gauge reads 1.48 mm **(see illustration 3.17)**:

Base measurement	1.00 mm
Fine measurement	0.48 mm
Total figure	**1.48 mm**

3.17 Dial gauge reading of 1.48 mm

● If measuring shaft runout, the shaft must be supported in vee-blocks and the gauge mounted on a stand perpendicular to the shaft. Rest the tip of the gauge against the center of the shaft and rotate the shaft slowly while watching the gauge reading **(see illustration 3.18)**. Take several measurements along the length of the shaft and record the

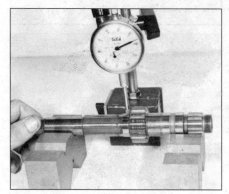

3.18 Using a dial gauge to measure shaft runout

maximum gauge reading as the amount of runout in the shaft. **Note:** *The reading obtained will be total runout at that point - some manufacturers specify that the runout figure is halved to compare with their specified runout limit.*

● Endfloat (sideplay) measurement requires that the gauge is mounted securely to the surrounding component with its probe touching the end of the shaft. Using hand pressure, push and pull on the shaft noting the maximum endfloat recorded on the gauge **(see illustration 3.19)**.

3.19 Using a dial gauge to measure shaft endfloat

● A dial gauge with suitable adapters can be used to determine piston position BTDC on two-stroke engines for the purposes of ignition timing. The gauge, adapter and suitable length probe are installed in the place of the spark plug and the gauge zeroed at TDC. If the piston position is specified as 1.14 mm BTDC, rotate the engine back to 2.00 mm BTDC, then slowly forwards to 1.14 mm BTDC.

Cylinder compression gauges

● A compression gauge is used for measuring cylinder compression. Either the rubber-cone type or the threaded adapter type can be used. The latter is preferred to ensure a perfect seal against the cylinder head. A 0 to 300 psi (0 to 20 Bar) type gauge (for gasoline engines) will be suitable for scooters.

● The spark plug is removed and the gauge either held hard against the cylinder head (cone type) or the gauge adapter screwed into the cylinder head (threaded type) **(see illustration 3.20)**. Cylinder compression is measured with the engine turning over, but not running - carry out the compression test as described in

3.20 Using a rubber-cone type cylinder compression gauge

Troubleshooting Equipment. The gauge will hold the reading until manually released.

Oil pressure gauge

● An oil pressure gauge is used for measuring engine oil pressure. Most gauges come with a set of adapters to fit the thread of the take-off point **(see illustration 3.21)**. If the take-off point specified by the scooter manufacturer is an external oil pipe union, make sure that the specified replacement union is used to prevent oil starvation.

3.21 Oil pressure gauge and take-off point adapter (arrow)

● Oil pressure is measured with the engine running (at a specific rpm) and often the manufacturer will specify pressure limits for a cold and hot engine.

Straight-edge and surface plate

● If checking the gasket face of a component for warpage, place a steel rule or precision straight-edge across the gasket face and measure any gap between the straight-edge and component with feeler gauges **(see illustration 3.22)**. Check diagonally across the component and between mounting holes **(see illustration 3.23)**.

3.22 Use a straight-edge and feeler gauges to check for warpage

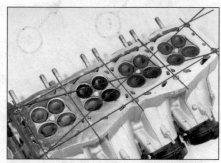

3.23 Check for warpage in these directions

- Checking individual components for warpage, such as clutch plain (metal) plates, requires a perfectly flat plate or piece of plate glass and feeler gauges.

4 Torque and leverage

What is torque?

- Torque describes the twisting force around a shaft. The amount of torque applied is determined by the distance from the center of the shaft to the end of the lever and the amount of force being applied to the end of the lever; distance multiplied by force equals torque.
- The manufacturer applies a measured torque to a bolt or nut to ensure that it will not loosen in use and to hold two components securely together without movement in the joint. The actual torque setting depends on the thread size, bolt or nut material and the composition of the components being held.
- Too little torque may cause the fastener to loosen due to vibration, whereas too much torque will distort the joint faces of the component or cause the fastener to shear off. Always stick to the specified torque setting.

Using a torque wrench

- Check the calibration of the torque wrench and make sure it has a suitable range for the job. Torque wrenches are available in Nm (Newton-meters), kgf m (kilograms-force meter), lbf ft (pounds-feet), lbf in (inch-pounds). Do not confuse lbf ft with lbf in.
- Adjust the tool to the desired torque on the scale **(see illustration 4.1)**. If your torque wrench is not calibrated in the units specified, carefully convert the figure (see *Conversion Factors*). A manufacturer sometimes gives a torque setting as a range (8 to 10 Nm) rather than a single figure - in this case set the tool midway between the two settings. The same torque may be expressed as 9 Nm ± 1 Nm. Some torque wrenches have a method of locking the setting so that it isn't inadvertently altered during use.

4.1 Set the torque wrench index mark to the setting required, in this case 12 Nm

- Install the bolts/nuts in their correct location and secure them lightly. Their threads must be clean and free of any old locking compound. Unless specified the threads and flange should be dry - oiled threads are necessary in certain circumstances and the manufacturer will take this into account in the specified torque figure. Similarly, the manufacturer may also specify the application of thread-locking compound.
- Tighten the fasteners in the specified sequence until the torque wrench clicks, indicating that the torque setting has been reached. Apply the torque again to double-check the setting. Where different thread diameter fasteners secure the component, as a rule tighten the larger diameter ones first.
- When the torque wrench has been finished with, release the lock (where applicable) and fully back off its setting to zero - do not leave the torque wrench tensioned. Also, do not use a torque wrench for loosening a fastener.

Angle-tightening

- Manufacturers often specify a figure in degrees for final tightening of a fastener. This usually follows tightening to a specific torque setting.
- A degree disc can be set and attached to the socket **(see illustration 4.2)** or a protractor can be used to mark the angle of movement on the bolt/nut head and the surrounding casting **(see illustration 4.3)**.

4.2 Angle tightening can be accomplished with a torque-angle gauge . . .

4.3 . . . or by marking the angle on the surrounding component

Loosening sequences

- Where more than one bolt/nut secures a component, loosen each fastener evenly a little at a time. In this way, not all the stress of the joint is held by one fastener and the components are not likely to distort.
- If a tightening sequence is provided, work in the REVERSE of this, but if not, work from the outside in, in a criss-cross sequence **(see illustration 4.4)**.

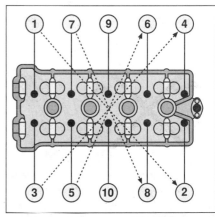

4.4 When loosening, work from the outside inwards

Tightening sequences

- If a component is held by more than one fastener it is important that the retaining bolts/nuts are tightened evenly to prevent uneven stress build-up and distortion of sealing faces. This is especially important on high-compression joints such as the cylinder head.
- A sequence is usually provided by the manufacturer, either in a diagram or actually marked in the casting. If not, always start in the center and work outwards in a criss-cross pattern **(see illustration 4.5)**. Start off by securing all bolts/nuts finger-tight, then set the torque wrench and tighten each fastener by a small amount in sequence until the final torque is reached. By following this practice,

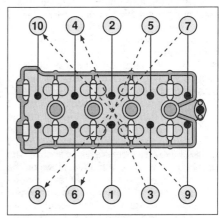

4.5 When tightening, work from the inside outwards

the joint will be held evenly and will not be distorted. Important joints, such as the cylinder head and big-end fasteners often have two- or three-stage torque settings.

Applying leverage

● Use tools at the correct angle. Position a socket or wrench on the bolt/nut so that you pull it towards you when loosening. If this can't be done, push the wrench without curling your fingers around it (see illustration 4.6) - the wrench may slip or the fastener loosen suddenly, resulting in your fingers being crushed against a component.

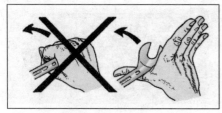

4.6 If you can't pull on the wrench to loosen a fastener, push with your hand open

● Additional leverage is gained by extending the length of the lever. The best way to do this is to use a breaker bar instead of the regular length tool, or to slip a length of tubing over the end of the wrench or socket.
● If additional leverage will not work, the fastener head is either damaged or firmly corroded in place (see Fasteners).

5 Bearings

Bearing removal and installation

Drivers and sockets

● Before removing a bearing, always inspect the casing to see which way it must be driven out - some casings will have retaining plates or a cast step. Also check for any identifying markings on the bearing and, if installed to a certain depth, measure this at this stage. Some roller bearings are sealed on one side - take note of the original installed position.
● Bearings can be driven out of a casing using a bearing driver tool (with the correct size head) or a socket of the correct diameter. Select the driver head or socket so that it contacts the outer race of the bearing, not the balls/rollers or inner race. Always support the casing around the bearing housing with wood blocks, otherwise there is a risk of fracture. The bearing is driven out with a few blows on the driver or socket from a heavy mallet. Unless access is severely restricted (as with wheel bearings), a pin-punch is not recommended unless it is moved around the bearing to keep it square in its housing.

● The same equipment can be used to install bearings. Make sure the bearing housing is supported on wood blocks and line up the bearing in its housing. Install the bearing as noted on removal - generally they are installed with their marked side facing outwards. Tap the bearing squarely into its housing using a driver or socket which bears only on the bearing's outer race - contact with the bearing balls/rollers or inner race will destroy it (see illustrations 5.1 and 5.2).
● Check that the bearing inner race and balls/rollers rotate freely.

5.1 Using a bearing driver against the bearing's outer race

5.2 Using a large socket against the bearing's outer race

Pullers and slide-hammers

● Where a bearing is pressed on a shaft a puller will be required to extract it (see illustration 5.3). Make sure that the puller clamp or legs fit securely behind the bearing and are unlikely to slip out. If pulling a bearing

5.3 This bearing puller clamps behind the bearing and pressure is applied to the shaft end to draw the bearing off

off a gear shaft for example, you may have to locate the puller behind a gear pinion if there is no access to the race and draw the gear pinion off the shaft as well (see illustration 5.4).

> *Caution: Ensure that the puller's center bolt locates securely against the end of the shaft and will not slip when pressure is applied. Also ensure that puller does not damage the shaft end.*

5.4 Where no access is available to the rear of the bearing, it is sometimes possible to draw off the adjacent component

● Operate the puller so that its center bolt exerts pressure on the shaft end and draws the bearing off the shaft.
● When installing the bearing on the shaft, tap only on the bearing's inner race - contact with the balls/rollers or outer race will destroy the bearing. Use a socket or length of tubing as a drift which fits over the shaft end (see illustration 5.5).

5.5 When installing a bearing on a shaft, use a piece of tubing which bears only on the bearing's inner race

● Where a bearing locates in a blind hole in a casing, it cannot be driven or pulled out as described above. A slide-hammer with knife-edged bearing puller attachment will be required. The puller attachment passes through the bearing and when tightened expands to fit firmly behind the bearing (see illustration 5.6). By operating the slide-hammer part of the tool the bearing is jarred out of its housing (see illustration 5.7).
● It is possible, if the bearing is of reasonable weight, for it to drop out of its housing if the casing is heated as described opposite. If

5.6 Expand the bearing puller so that it locks behind the bearing . . .

5.7 . . . attach the slide hammer to the bearing puller

this method is attempted, first prepare a work surface which will enable the casing to be tapped face down to help dislodge the bearing - a wood surface is ideal since it will not damage the casing's gasket surface. Wearing protective gloves, tap the heated casing several times against the work surface to dislodge the bearing under its own weight **(see illustration 5.8)**.

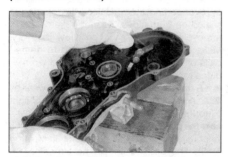

5.8 Tapping a casing face down on wood blocks can often dislodge a bearing

● Bearings can be installed in blind holes using the driver or socket method described above.

Drawbolts

● Where a bearing or bushing is set in the eye of a component, such as a suspension linkage arm or connecting rod small-end, removal by drift may damage the component. Furthermore, a rubber bushing in a shock absorber eye cannot successfully be driven out of position. If access is available to a hydraulic press, the task is straightforward. If not, a drawbolt can be fabricated to extract the bearing or bushing.

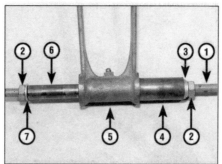

5.9 Drawbolt component parts assembled on a suspension arm

1 Bolt or length of threaded bar
2 Nuts
3 Washer (external diameter greater than tubing internal diameter)
4 Tubing (internal diameter sufficient to accommodate bearing)
5 Suspension arm with bearing
6 Tubing (external diameter slightly smaller than bearing)
7 Washer (external diameter slightly smaller than bearing)

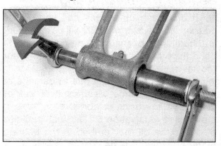

5.10 Drawing the bearing out of the suspension arm

● To extract the bearing/bushing you will need a long bolt with nut (or piece of threaded bar with two nuts), a piece of tubing which has an internal diameter larger than the bearing/bushing, another piece of tubing which has an external diameter slightly smaller than the bearing/bushing, and a selection of washers **(see illustrations 5.9 and 5.10)**. Note that the pieces of tubing must be of the same length, or longer, than the bearing/bushing.
● The same kit (without the pieces of tubing) can be used to draw the new bearing/bushing back into place **(see illustration 5.11)**.

Temperature change

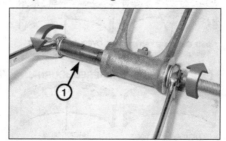

5.11 Installing a new bearing (1) in the suspension arm

● If the bearing's outer race is a tight fit in the casing, the aluminum casing can be heated to release its grip on the bearing. Aluminum will expand at a greater rate than the steel bearing outer race. There are several ways to do this, but avoid any localized extreme heat (such as a blow torch) - aluminum alloy has a low melting point.
● Approved methods of heating a casing are using a domestic oven (heated to 100°C/200°F) or immersing the casing in boiling water **(see illustration 5.12)**. Low temperature range localized heat sources such as a paint stripper heat gun or clothes iron can also be used **(see illustration 5.13)**. Alternatively, soak a rag in boiling water, wring it out and wrap it around the bearing housing.
● If heating the whole casing note that

> ⚠️ **Warning: All of these methods require care in use to prevent scalding and burns to the hands. Wear protective gloves when handling hot components.**

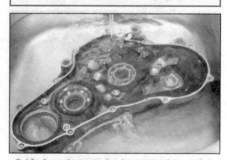

5.12 A casing can be immersed in a sink of boiling water to aid bearing removal

5.13 Using a localized heat source to aid bearing removal

plastic components, such as the neutral switch, may suffer - remove them beforehand.
● After heating, remove the bearing as described above. You may find that the expansion is sufficient for the bearing to fall out of the casing under its own weight or with a light tap on the driver or socket.
● If necessary, the casing can be heated to aid bearing installation, and this is sometimes the recommended procedure if the scooter manufacturer has designed the housing and bearing fit with this intention.

● Installation of bearings can be eased by placing them in a freezer the night before installation. The steel bearing will contract slightly, allowing easy insertion in its housing. This is often useful when installing steering head outer races in the frame.

Bearing types and markings

● Plain shell bearings, ball bearings, needle roller bearings and tapered roller bearings will all be found on scooters (see illustrations 5.14 and 5.15). The ball and roller types are usually caged between an inner and outer race, but uncaged variations may be found.

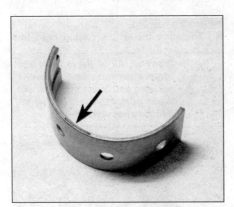

5.14 Shell bearings are either plain or grooved. They are usually identified by color code (arrow)

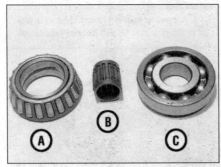

5.15 Tapered roller bearing (A), needle roller bearing (B) and ball journal bearing (C)

● Shell bearings (often called inserts) are usually found at the crankshaft main and connecting rod big-end where they are good at coping with high loads. They are made of a phosphor-bronze material and are impregnated with self-lubricating properties.

● Ball bearings and needle roller bearings consist of a steel inner and outer race with the balls or rollers between the races. They require constant lubrication by oil or grease and are good at coping with axial loads. Taper roller bearings consist of rollers set in a tapered cage set on the inner race; the outer race is separate. They are good at coping with axial loads and prevent movement along the shaft - a typical application is in the steering head.

5.16 Typical bearing marking

● Bearing manufacturers produce bearings to ISO size standards and stamp one face of the bearing to indicate its internal and external diameter, load capacity and type (see illustration 5.16).

● Metal bushings are usually of phosphor-bronze material. Rubber bushings are used in suspension mounting eyes. Fiber bushings have also been used in suspension pivots.

Bearing troubleshooting

● If a bearing outer race has spun in its housing, the housing material will be damaged. You can use a bearing locking compound to bond the outer race in place if damage is not too severe.

● Shell bearings will fail due to damage of their working surface, as a result of lack of lubrication, corrosion or abrasive particles in the oil (see illustration 5.17). Small particles of dirt in the oil may embed in the bearing material whereas larger particles will score the bearing and shaft journal. If a number of short journeys are made, insufficient heat will be generated to drive off condensation which has built up on the bearings.

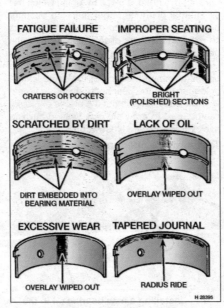

5.17 Typical bearing failures

5.18 Example of ball journal bearing with damaged balls and cages

5.19 Hold outer race and listen to inner race when spun

● Ball and roller bearings will fail due to lack of lubrication or damage to the balls or rollers. Tapered-roller bearings can be damaged by overloading them. Unless the bearing is sealed on both sides, wash it in kerosene to remove all old grease, then allow it to dry. Make a visual inspection looking to dented balls or rollers, damaged cages and worn or pitted races (see illustration 5.18).

● A ball bearing can be checked for wear by listening to it when spun. Apply a film of light oil to the bearing and hold it close to the ear - hold the outer race with one hand and spin the inner race with the other hand (see illustration 5.19). The bearing should be almost silent when spun; if it grates or rattles it is worn.

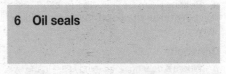

6 Oil seals

Oil seal removal and installation

● Oil seals should be replaced every time a component is dismantled. This is because the seal lips will become set to the sealing surface and will not necessarily reseal.

● Oil seals can be pried out of position using a large flat-bladed screwdriver (see illustration 6.1). In the case of crankcase seals, check first that the seal is not lipped on the inside, preventing its removal with the crankcases joined.

6.1 Pry out oil seals with a large flat-bladed screwdriver

● New seals are usually installed with their marked face (containing the seal reference code) outwards and the spring side towards the fluid being retained. In certain cases, such as a two-stroke engine crankshaft seal, a double lipped seal may be used due to there being fluid or gas on each side of the joint.

● Use a bearing driver or socket which bears only on the outer hard edge of the seal to install it in the casing - tapping on the inner edge will damage the sealing lip.

Oil seal types and markings

● Oil seals are usually of the single-lipped type. Double-lipped seals are found where a liquid or gas is on both sides of the joint.

● Oil seals can harden and lose their sealing ability if the scooter has been in storage for a long period - replacement is the only solution.

● Oil seal manufacturers also conform to the ISO markings for seal size - these are molded into the outer face of the seal **(see illustration 6.2)**.

6.2 These oil seal markings indicate inside diameter, outside diameter and seal thickness

7 Gaskets and sealants

Types of gasket and sealant

● Gaskets are used to seal the mating surfaces between components and keep lubricants, fluids, vacuum or pressure contained within the assembly. Aluminum gaskets are sometimes found at the cylinder joints, but most gaskets are paper-based. If the mating surfaces of the components being joined are undamaged, the gasket can be installed dry, although a dab of sealant or grease will be useful to hold it in place during assembly.

● RTV (Room Temperature Vulcanizing) silicone rubber sealants cure when exposed to moisture in the atmosphere. These sealants are good at filling pits or irregular gasket faces, but will tend to be forced out of the joint under very high torque. They can be used to replace a paper gasket, but first make sure that the width of the paper gasket is not essential to the shimming of internal components. RTV sealants should not be used on components containing gasoline.

● Non-hardening, semi-hardening and hard setting liquid gasket compounds can be used with a gasket or between a metal-to-metal joint. Select the sealant to suit the application: universal non-hardening sealant can be used on virtually all joints; semi-hardening on joint faces which are rough or damaged; hard setting sealant on joints which require a permanent bond and are subjected to high temperature and pressure. **Note:** *Check first if the paper gasket has a bead of sealant impregnated in its surface before applying additional sealant.*

● When choosing a sealant, make sure it is suitable for the application, particularly if being applied in a high-temperature area or in the vicinity of fuel. Certain manufacturers produce sealants in either clear, silver or black colors to match the finish of the engine. This has a particular application on scooters where much of the engine is exposed.

● Do not over-apply sealant. That which is squeezed out on the outside of the joint can be wiped off, whereas an excess of sealant on the inside can break off and clog oilways.

Breaking a sealed joint

● Age, heat, pressure and the use of hard setting sealant can cause two components to stick together so tightly that they are difficult to separate using finger pressure alone. Do not resort to using levers unless there is a pry point provided for this purpose **(see illustration 7.1)**, or else the gasket surfaces will be damaged.

● Use a soft-faced hammer **(see illustration 7.2)** or a wood block and conventional hammer to strike the component near the mating surface. Avoid hammering against cast

extremities since they may break off. If this method fails, try using a wood wedge between the two components.

Caution: If the joint will not separate, double-check that you have removed all the fasteners.

7.1 If a pry point is provided, apply gentle pressure with a flat-bladed screwdriver

7.2 Tap around the joint with a soft-faced mallet if necessary - don't strike cooling fins

Most components have one or two hollow locating dowels between the two gasket faces. If a dowel cannot be removed, do not resort to gripping it with pliers - it will almost certainly be distorted. Install a close-fitting socket or Phillips screwdriver into the dowel and then grip the outer edge of the dowel to free it.

Removal of old gasket and sealant

● Paper gaskets will most likely come away complete, leaving only a few traces stuck on the sealing faces of the components. It is imperative that all traces are removed to ensure correct sealing of the new gasket.

● Very carefully scrape all traces of gasket away, making sure that the sealing surfaces are not gouged or scored by the scraper (**see illustrations 7.3, 7.4 and 7.5**). Stubborn deposits can be removed by spraying with an aerosol gasket remover. Final preparation

of the gasket surface can be made with very fine abrasive paper or a plastic kitchen scourer (**see illustrations 7.6 and 7.7**).

● Old sealant can be scraped or peeled off components, depending on the type originally used. Note that gasket removal compounds are available to avoid scraping the components clean; make sure the gasket remover suits the type of sealant used.

7.3 Paper gaskets can be scraped off with a gasket scraper tool . . .

7.4 . . . a knife blade . . .

7.5 . . . or a household scraper

7.6 Fine abrasive paper is wrapped around a flat file to clean up the gasket face

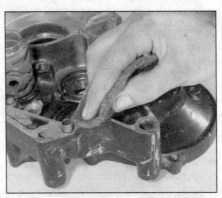

7.7 A kitchen scourer can be used on stubborn deposits

8 Hoses

Clamping to prevent flow

● Small-bore flexible hoses can be clamped to prevent fluid flow while a component is worked on. Whichever method is used, ensure that the hose material is not permanently distorted or damaged by the clamp.

a) A brake hose clamp available from auto parts stores (**see illustration 8.1**).

b) A wingnut type hose clamp (**see illustration 8.2**).

c) Two sockets placed on each side of the hose and held with straight-jawed self-locking pliers (**see illustration 8.3**).

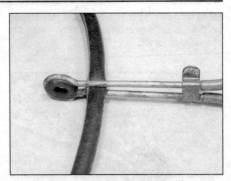

8.1 Hoses can be clamped with an automotive brake hose clamp . . .

8.2 . . . a wingnut type hose clamp . . .

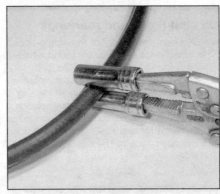

8.3 . . . two sockets and a pair of self-locking grips . . .

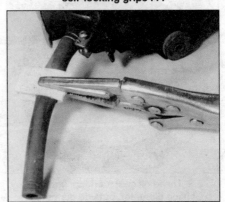

8.4 . . . or thick card and self-locking grips

8.5 Cutting a coolant hose free with a sharp knife

d) *Thick card stock on each side of the hose held between straight-jawed self-locking pliers (see illustration 8.4).*

Freeing and fitting hoses

● Always make sure the hose clamp is moved well clear of the hose end. Grip the hose with your hand and rotate it while pulling it off the union. If the hose has hardened due to age and will not move, slit it with a sharp knife and peel its ends off the union **(see illustration 8.5)**.

● Resist the temptation to use grease or soap on the unions to aid installation; although it helps the hose slip over the union it will equally aid the escape of fluid from the joint. It is preferable to soften the hose ends in hot water and wet the inside surface of the hose with water or a fluid which will evaporate.

Conversion Factors

Length (distance)

Inches (in)	X	25.4	= Millimeters (mm)	X	0.0394	= Inches (in)
Feet (ft)	X	0.305	= Meters (m)	X	3.281	= Feet (ft)
Miles	X	1.609	= Kilometers (km)	X	0.621	= Miles

Volume (capacity)

Cubic inches (cu in; in³)	X	16.387	= Cubic centimeters (cc; cm³)	X	0.061	= Cubic inches (cu in; in³)
Imperial pints (Imp pt)	X	0.568	= Liters (l)	X	1.76	= Imperial pints (Imp pt)
Imperial quarts (Imp qt)	X	1.137	= Liters (l)	X	0.88	= Imperial quarts (Imp qt)
Imperial quarts (Imp qt)	X	1.201	= US quarts (US qt)	X	0.833	= Imperial quarts (Imp qt)
US quarts (US qt)	X	0.946	= Liters (l)	X	1.057	= US quarts (US qt)
Imperial gallons (Imp gal)	X	4.546	= Liters (l)	X	0.22	= Imperial gallons (Imp gal)
Imperial gallons (Imp gal)	X	1.201	= US gallons (US gal)	X	0.833	= Imperial gallons (Imp gal)
US gallons (US gal)	X	3.785	= Liters (l)	X	0.264	= US gallons (US gal)

Mass (weight)

Ounces (oz)	X	28.35	= Grams (g)	X	0.035	= Ounces (oz)
Pounds (lb)	X	0.454	= Kilograms (kg)	X	2.205	= Pounds (lb)

Force

Ounces-force (ozf; oz)	X	0.278	= Newtons (N)	X	3.6	= Ounces-force (ozf; oz)
Pounds-force (lbf; lb)	X	4.448	= Newtons (N)	X	0.225	= Pounds-force (lbf; lb)
Newtons (N)	X	0.1	= Kilograms-force (kgf; kg)	X	9.81	= Newtons (N)

Pressure

Pounds-force per square inch (psi; lbf/in²; lb/in²)	X	0.070	= Kilograms-force per square centimeter (kgf/cm²; kg/cm²)	X	14.223	= Pounds-force per square inch (psi; lbf/in²; lb/in²)
Pounds-force per square inch (psi; lbf/in²; lb/in²)	X	0.068	= Atmospheres (atm)	X	14.696	= Pounds-force per square inch (psi; lbf/in²; lb/in²)
Pounds-force per square inch (psi; lbf/in²; lb/in²)	X	0.069	= Bars	X	14.5	= Pounds-force per square inch (psi; lbf/in²; lb/in²)
Pounds-force per square inch (psi; lbf/in²; lb/in²)	X	6.895	= Kilopascals (kPa)	X	0.145	= Pounds-force per square inch (psi; lbf/in²; lb/in²)
Kilopascals (kPa)	X	0.01	= Kilograms-force per square centimeter (kgf/cm²; kg/cm²)	X	98.1	= Kilopascals (kPa)

Torque (moment of force)

Pounds-force inches (lbf in; lb in)	X	1.152	= Kilograms-force centimeter (kgf cm; kg cm)	X	0.868	= Pounds-force inches (lbf in; lb in)
Pounds-force inches (lbf in; lb in)	X	0.113	= Newton meters (Nm)	X	8.85	= Pounds-force inches (lbf in; lb in)
Pounds-force inches (lbf in; lb in)	X	0.083	= Pounds-force feet (lbf ft; lb ft)	X	12	= Pounds-force inches (lbf in; lb in)
Pounds-force feet (lbf ft; lb ft)	X	0.138	= Kilograms-force meters (kgf m; kg m)	X	7.233	= Pounds-force feet (lbf ft; lb ft)
Pounds-force feet (lbf ft; lb ft)	X	1.356	= Newton meters (Nm)	X	0.738	= Pounds-force feet (lbf ft; lb ft)
Newton meters (Nm)	X	0.102	= Kilograms-force meters (kgf m; kg m)	X	9.804	= Newton meters (Nm)

Vacuum

Inches mercury (in. Hg)	X	3.377	= Kilopascals (kPa)	X	0.2961	= Inches mercury
Inches mercury (in. Hg)	X	25.4	= Millimeters mercury (mm Hg)	X	0.0394	= Inches mercury

Power

Horsepower (hp)	X	745.7	= Watts (W)	X	0.0013	= Horsepower (hp)

Velocity (speed)

Miles per hour (miles/hr; mph)	X	1.609	= Kilometers per hour (km/hr; kph)	X	0.621	= Miles per hour (miles/hr; mph)

Fuel consumption*

Miles per gallon, Imperial (mpg)	X	0.354	= Kilometers per liter (km/l)	X	2.825	= Miles per gallon, Imperial (mpg)
Miles per gallon, US (mpg)	X	0.425	= Kilometers per liter (km/l)	X	2.352	= Miles per gallon, US (mpg)

Temperature

Degrees Fahrenheit = (°C x 1.8) + 32   Degrees Celsius (Degrees Centigrade; °C) = (°F - 32) x 0.56

*It is common practice to convert from miles per gallon (mpg) to liters/100 kilometers (l/100km), where mpg (Imperial) x l/100 km = 282 and mpg (US) x l/100 km = 235

A number of chemicals and lubricants are available for use in scooter maintenance and repair. They include a wide variety of products ranging from cleaning solvents and degreasers to lubricants and protective sprays for rubber, plastic and vinyl.

• **Contact point/spark plug cleaner** is a solvent used to clean oily film and dirt from points, grime from electrical connectors and oil deposits from spark plugs. It is oil free and leaves no residue. It can also be used to remove gum and varnish from carburetor jets and other orifices.

• **Carburetor cleaner** is similar to contact point/spark plug cleaner but it usually has a stronger solvent and may leave a slight oily residue. It is not recommended for cleaning electrical components or connections.

• **Brake system cleaner** is used to remove brake dust, grease and brake fluid from the brake system, where clean surfaces are absolutely necessary. It leaves no residue and often eliminates brake squeal caused by contaminants.

• **Silicone-based lubricants** are used to protect rubber parts such as hoses and grommets, and are used as lubricants for hinges and locks.

• **Multi-purpose grease** is an all purpose lubricant used wherever grease is more practical than a liquid lubricant such as oil. Some multi-purpose grease is colored white and specially formulated to be more resistant to water than ordinary grease.

• **Gear oil** (sometimes called gear lube) is a specially designed oil used in transmissions and final drive units, as well as other areas where high friction, high temperature lubrication is required. It is available in a number of viscosities (weights) for various applications.

• **Motor oil** is the lubricant formulated for use in engines. It normally contains a wide variety of additives to prevent corrosion and reduce foaming and wear. Motor oil comes in various weights (viscosity ratings) from 0 to 50. The recommended weight of the oil depends on the season, temperature and the demands on the engine. Light oil is used in cold climates and under light load conditions. Heavy oil is used in hot climates and where high loads are encountered. Multi-viscosity oils are designed to have characteristics of both light and heavy oils and are available in a number of weights from 0W-20 to 20W-50.

• **Gasoline additives** perform several functions, depending on their chemical makeup. They usually contain solvents that help dissolve gum and varnish that build up on carburetor and inlet parts. They also serve to break down carbon deposits that form on the inside surfaces of the combustion chambers. Some additives contain upper cylinder lubricants for valves and piston rings.

• **Brake and clutch fluid** is a specially formulated hydraulic fluid that can withstand the heat and pressure encountered in break/clutch systems. Care must be taken that this fluid does not come in contact with painted surfaces or plastics. An opened container should always be resealed to prevent contamination by water or dirt.

• **Degreasers** are heavy duty solvents used to remove grease and grime that may accumulate on the engine and frame components. They can be sprayed or brushed on and, depending on the type, are rinsed with either water or solvent.

• **Solvents** are used alone or in combination with degreasers to clean parts and assemblies during repair and overhaul. The home mechanic should use only solvents that are non-flammable and that do not produce irritating fumes.

• **Gasket sealing compounds** may be used in conjunction with gaskets, to improve their sealing capabilities, or alone, to seal metal-to-metal joints. Many gasket sealers can withstand extreme heat, some are impervious to gasoline and lubricants, while others are capable of filling and sealing large cavities. Depending on the intended use, gasket sealers either dry hard or stay relatively soft and pliable. They are usually applied by hand, with a brush or are sprayed on the gasket sealing surfaces.

• **Thread locking compound** is an adhesive locking compound that prevents threaded fasteners from loosening because of vibration. It is available in a variety of types for different applications.

• **Moisture dispersants** are usually sprays that can be used to dry out electrical components such as the fuse block and wiring connectors. Some types an also be used as treatment for rubber and as a lubricant for hinges, cables and locks.

• **Waxes and polishes** are used to help protect painted and plated surfaces from the weather. Different types of pain may require the use of different types of wax polish. Some polishes utilize a chemical or abrasive cleaner to help remove the top layer of oxidized (dull) paint on older vehicles. In recent years, many non-wax polishes (that contain a wide variety of chemicals such as polymers and silicones) have been introduced. These non-wax polishes are usually easier to apply and last longer than conventional waxes and polishes.

Preparing for storage

Before you start

If repairs or an overhaul is needed, see that this is carried out now rather than left until you want to ride the bike again.

Give the bike a good wash and scrub all dirt from its underside. Make sure the bike dries completely before preparing for storage.

Engine

● Remove the spark plug(s) and lubricate the cylinder bores with approximately one teaspoon of motor oil using a spout-type oil can (see illustration 1). Reinstall the spark plug(s). Crank the engine over a couple of times to coat the piston rings and bores with oil. If the bike has a kickstart, use this to turn the engine over. If not, flick the kill switch to the OFF position and crank the engine over on the starter (see illustration 2). If the nature of the ignition system prevents the starter operating with the kill switch in the OFF position, remove the spark plugs and fit them back in their caps; ensure that the plugs are grounded against the cylinder head when the starter is operated (see illustration 3).

> ⚠️ **Warning: It is important that the plugs are grounded away from the spark plug holes otherwise there is a risk of atomized fuel from the cylinders igniting.**

> **HAYNES HiNT** *On a single cylinder four-stroke engine, you can seal the combustion chamber completely by positioning the piston at TDC on the compression stroke.*

● Drain the carburetor(s), otherwise there is a risk of jets becoming blocked by gum deposits from the fuel (see illustration 4).

● If the bike is going into long-term storage, consider adding a fuel stabilizer to the fuel in the tank. If the tank is drained completely, corrosion of its internal surfaces may occur if left unprotected for a long period. The tank can be treated with a rust preventative especially for this purpose. Alternatively, remove the tank and pour half a liter of motor oil into it, install the filler cap and shake the tank to coat its internals with oil before draining off the excess. The same effect can also be achieved by spraying WD40 or a similar water-dispersant around the inside of the tank via its flexible nozzle.

● Make sure the cooling system contains the correct mix of antifreeze. Antifreeze also contains important corrosion inhibitors.

● The air intakes and exhaust can be sealed off by covering or plugging the openings. Ensure that you do not seal in any condensation; run the engine until it is hot, then switch off and allow to cool. Tape a

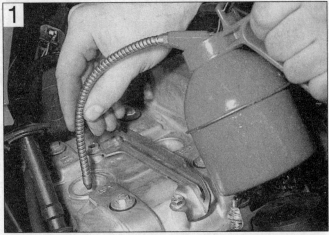

Squirt a drop of motor oil into each cylinder

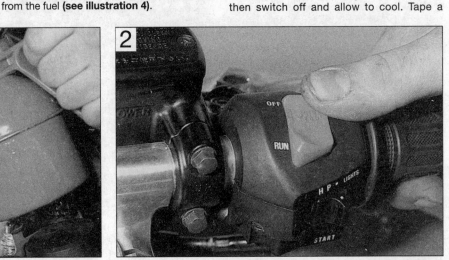

Flick the kill switch to OFF . . .

. . . and ensure that the metal bodies of the plugs (arrows) are grounded against the cylinder head

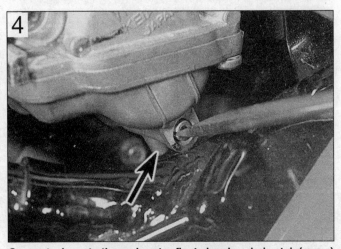

Connect a hose to the carburetor float chamber drain stub (arrow) and unscrew the drain screw

Exhausts can be sealed off with a plastic bag

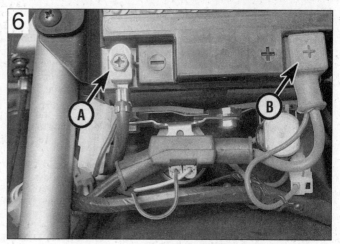

Disconnect the negative lead (A) first, followed by the positive lead (B)

piece of thick plastic over the silencer end(s) **(see illustration 5)**. Note that some advocate pouring a tablespoon of motor oil into the silencer(s) before sealing them off.

Battery

● Remove it from the bike - in extreme cases of cold the battery may freeze and crack its case **(see illustration 6)**.
● Check the electrolyte level and top up if necessary (conventional refillable batteries). Clean the terminals.
● Store the battery off the motorcycle and away from any sources of fire. Position a wooden block under the battery if it is to sit on the ground.
● Give the battery a trickle charge for a few hours every month **(see illustration 7)**.

Tires

● Place the bike on its centerstand or an auxiliary stand which will support the motorcycle in an upright position. Position wood blocks under the tires to keep them off the ground and to provide insulation from damp. If the bike is being put into long-term

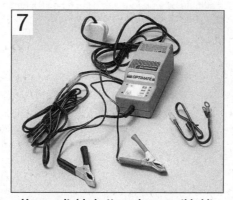

Use a suitable battery charger - this kit also assesses battery condition

storage, ideally both tires should be off the ground; not only will this protect the tires, but will also ensure that no load is placed on the steering head or wheel bearings.
● Deflate each tire by 5 to 10 psi, no more or the beads may unseat from the rim, making subsequent inflation difficult on tubeless tires.

Pivots and controls

● Lubricate all lever, pedal, stand and footrest pivot points. If grease nipples are fitted to the rear suspension components, apply lubricant to the pivots.
● Lubricate all control cables.

Cycle components

● Apply a wax protectant to all painted and plastic components. Wipe off any excess, but don't polish to a shine. Where fitted, clean the screen with soap and water.
● Coat metal parts with Vaseline (petroleum jelly). When applying this to the fork tubes, do not compress the forks, otherwise the seals will rot from contact with the Vaseline.
● Apply a vinyl cleaner to the seat.

Storage conditions

● Aim to store the bike in a shed or garage which does not leak and is free from damp.
● Drape an old blanket or bedspread over the bike to protect it from dust and direct contact with sunlight (which will fade paint). Beware of tight-fitting plastic covers which may allow condensation to form and settle on the bike.

Getting back on the road

Engine and transmission

● Change the oil and replace the oil filter. If this was done prior to storage, check that the oil hasn't emulsified - a thick whitish substance which occurs through condensation.
● Remove the spark plug(s). Using a spout-type oil can, squirt a few drops of oil into the cylinder(s). This will provide initial lubrication as the piston rings and bores comes back into contact. Service the spark plugs, or buy new

ones, and install them in the engine.
● If the air intakes or silencer end(s) were blocked off, remove the plug or cover used.
● If the fuel tank was coated with a rust preventative, oil or a stabilizer added to the fuel, drain and flush the tank and dispose of the fuel sensibly. If no action was taken with the fuel tank prior to storage, it is advised that the old fuel is disposed of since it will go bad over a period of time. Refill the fuel tank with fresh fuel.

Frame and running gear

● Oil all pivot points and cables.
● Check the tire pressures. They will definitely need inflating if pressures were reduced for storage.
● Lubricate the final drive chain (where applicable).
● Remove any protective coating applied to the fork tubes (stanchions) since this may well destroy the fork seals. If the fork tubes weren't

protected and have picked up rust spots, remove them with very fine abrasive paper and refinish with metal polish.

● Check that both brakes operate correctly. Apply each brake hard and check that it's not possible to move the scooter forwards, then check that the brake frees off again once released. Brake caliper pistons can stick due to corrosion around the piston head, or on the sliding caliper types, due to corrosion of the slider pins. If the brake doesn't free after repeated operation, take the caliper off for examination. Similarly, drum brakes can stick due to a seized operating cam, cable or rod linkage.

● If the scooter has been in long-term storage, replace the brake fluid and clutch fluid (where applicable).

● Depending on where the bike has been stored, the wiring, cables and hoses may have been nibbled by rodents. Make a visual check and investigate disturbed wiring loom tape.

Battery

● If the battery has been previously removed and given top up charges, it can simply be reconnected. Remember to connect the positive cable first and the negative cable last.

● On conventional refillable batteries, if the battery has not received any attention, remove it from the scooter and check its electrolyte level. Top up if necessary, then charge the battery. If the battery fails to hold a charge and a visual check shows heavy white sulfation of the plates, the battery is probably defective and must be replaced. This is particularly likely if the battery is old. Confirm battery condition with a specific gravity check.

● On sealed (MF) batteries, if the battery has not received any attention, remove it from the scooter and charge it according to the information on the battery case - if the battery fails to hold a charge it must be replaced.

Starting procedure

● If a kickstart is installed, turn the engine over a couple of times with the ignition OFF to distribute oil around the engine. If no kickstart is installed, flick the engine kill switch OFF and the ignition ON and crank the engine over a couple of times to work oil around the upper cylinder components. If the nature of the ignition system is such that the starter won't work with the kill switch OFF, remove the spark plugs, fit them back into their caps and ground their bodies on the cylinder head. Reinstall the spark plugs afterwards.

● Switch the kill switch to RUN, operate the choke and start the engine. If the engine won't start, don't continue cranking the engine - not only will this flatten the battery, but the starter motor will overheat. Switch the ignition off and try again later. If the engine refuses to start, go through the troubleshooting procedures in this manual. **Note:** *If the bike has been in storage for a long time, old fuel or a carburetor blockage may be the problem. Gum deposits in carburetors can block jets - if a carburetor cleaner doesn't prove successful, the carburetors must be disassembled for cleaning.*

● Once the engine has started, check that the lights, turn signals and horn work properly.

● Treat the bike gently for the first ride and check all fluid levels on completion. Settle the bike back into the maintenance schedule.

This Section provides an easy reference-guide to the more common faults that are likely to afflict your machine. Obviously, the opportunities are almost limitless for faults to occur as a result of obscure failures, and to try and cover all eventualities would require a book. Indeed, a number have been written on the subject.

Successful troubleshooting is not a mysterious 'black art' but the application of a bit of knowledge combined with a systematic and logical approach to the problem. Approach any troubleshooting by first accurately identifying the symptom and then checking through the list of possible causes, starting with the simplest or most obvious and progressing in stages to the most complex.

Take nothing for granted, but above all apply liberal quantities of common sense.

The main symptom of a fault is given in the text as a major heading below which are listed the various systems or areas which may contain the fault. Details of each possible cause for a fault and the remedial action to be taken are given, in brief, in the paragraphs below each heading. Further information should be sought in the relevant Chapter.

1 Engine doesn't start or is difficult to start
- Starter motor doesn't rotate
- Starter motor rotates but engine does not turn over
- Starter works but engine won't turn over (seized)
- No fuel flow
- Engine flooded
- No spark or weak spark
- Compression low
- Stalls after starting
- Rough idle

2 Poor running at low speed
- Spark weak
- Fuel/air mixture incorrect
- Compression low
- Poor acceleration

3 Poor running or no power at high speed
- Firing incorrect
- Fuel/air mixture incorrect
- Compression low
- Knocking or pinging
- Miscellaneous causes

4 Overheating
- Engine overheats
- Firing incorrect
- Fuel/air mixture incorrect
- Compression too high
- Engine load excessive
- Lubrication inadequate
- Miscellaneous causes

5 Transmission problems
- No drive to rear wheel
- Vibration
- Poor performance
- Clutch not disengaging completely

6 Abnormal engine noise
- Knocking or pinging
- Piston slap or rattling
- Valve noise
- Other noise

7 Abnormal frame and suspension noise
- Front end noise
- Shock absorber noise
- Brake noise

8 Excessive exhaust smoke
- White smoke (four-stroke engines)
- White/blue smoke (two-stroke engines)
- Black smoke
- Brown smoke

9 Poor handling or stability
- Handlebar hard to turn
- Handlebar shakes or vibrates excessively
- Handlebar pulls to one side
- Poor shock absorbing qualities

10 Braking problems – disc brakes
- Brakes are ineffective
- Brake lever pulsates
- Brakes drag

11 Braking problems – drum brakes
- Brakes are ineffective
- Brake lever pulsates
- Brakes drag

12 Electrical problems
- Battery dead or weak
- Battery overcharged

1 Engine doesn't start or is difficult to start

Starter motor doesn't rotate

☐ Fuse blown. Check fuse and starter circuit (Chapter 10).
☐ Battery voltage low. Check and recharge battery (Chapter 10).
☐ Starter motor defective. Make sure the wiring to the starter is secure. Make sure the starter relay clicks when the start button is pushed. If the relay clicks, then the fault is in the wiring or motor.
☐ Starter relay faulty. Check it (Chapter 10).
☐ Starter switch on handlebar not contacting. The contacts could be wet, corroded or dirty. Disassemble and clean the switch (Chapter 10).
☐ Wiring open or shorted. Check all wiring connections and harnesses to make sure that they are dry, tight and not corroded. Also check for broken or frayed wires that can cause a short to ground.
☐ Ignition (main) switch defective. Check the switch according to the procedure in Chapter 10. Replace the switch if it is defective.

Starter motor rotates but engine does not turn over

☐ Starter pinion assembly or starter clutch defective. Inspect and repair or replace (Chapter 2A or 2B).
☐ Damaged pinion assembly or starter gears. Inspect and replace the damaged parts (Chapter 2A or 2B).

Starter works but engine won't turn over (seized)

☐ Seized engine caused by one or more internally damaged components. Failure due to wear, abuse or lack of lubrication. On all engines damage can include piston, cylinder, connecting rod, crankshaft, bearings and additionally on four-strokes, valves, camshaft, camchain. Refer to Chapter 2A or 2B for engine disassembly.

No fuel flow

☐ No fuel in tank.
☐ Fuel hose or tank vent hose trapped. Check the hoses.
☐ Fuel filter clogged. Remove the tap and clean the filter, or check the in-line fuel filter.
☐ Fuel tap vacuum hose split or detached. Check the hose.
☐ Fuel tap diaphragm split. Replace the tap (Chapter 4).
☐ Fuel hose clogged. Remove the fuel hose and carefully blow through it.
☐ Float needle valve or carburetor jets clogged. The carburetor should be removed and overhauled if draining the float chamber doesn't solve the problem.

Engine flooded

☐ Float height or fuel level too high. Check as described in Chapter 4.
☐ Float needle valve worn or stuck open. A piece of dirt, rust or other debris can cause the valve to seat improperly, causing excess fuel to be admitted to the float chamber. In this case, the float chamber should be cleaned and the needle valve and seat inspected. If the needle and seat are worn, then the leaking will persist and the parts should be replaced (Chapter 4).

No spark or weak spark

☐ Ignition switch OFF.
☐ Battery voltage low. Check and recharge the battery as necessary (Chapter 10).
☐ Spark plug dirty, defective or worn out. Locate the reason for the fouled plug using the spark plug condition chart at the end of this manual and follow the plug maintenance procedures (Chapter 1).

Condition is especially applicable to two-stroke engines due to the oily nature of their lubrication system.
☐ Spark plug cap or secondary (HT) wiring faulty. Check condition. Replace either or both components if cracks or deterioration are evident (Chapter 5).
☐ Spark plug cap not making good contact. Make sure that the plug cap fits snugly over the plug end.
☐ Ignition control unit (ICU) defective. Check the unit, referring to Chapter 5 for details.
☐ Pick-up coil or source coil defective. Check the unit, referring to Chapter 5 for details.
☐ Ignition HT coil defective. Check the coil, referring to Chapter 5.
☐ Ignition switch shorted. This is usually caused by water, corrosion, damage or excessive wear. The switch can be disassembled and cleaned with electrical contact cleaner. If cleaning does not help, replace the switch (Chapter 10).
☐ Wiring shorted or broken. Make sure that all wiring connections are clean, dry and tight. Look for chafed and broken wires (Chapters 5 and 10).

Compression low

☐ Spark plug loose. Remove the plug and inspect its threads (Chapter 1).
☐ Cylinder head not sufficiently tightened down. If the cylinder head is suspected of being loose, then there's a chance that the gasket or head is damaged if the problem has persisted for any length of time. The head nuts should be tightened to the proper torque in the correct sequence (Chapter 2A or 2B).
☐ Low crankcase compression on two-stroke engines due to worn crankshaft oil seals. Condition will upset the fuel/air mixture. Replace the seals (Chapter 2A).
☐ Improper valve clearance (four-strokes). This means that the valve is not closing completely and compression pressure is leaking past the valve. Check and adjust the valve clearances (Chapter 1).
☐ Cylinder and/or piston worn. Excessive wear will cause compression pressure to leak past the rings. This is usually accompanied by worn rings as well. A top-end overhaul is necessary (Chapter 2A or 2B).
☐ Piston rings worn, weak, broken, or sticking. Broken or sticking piston rings usually indicate a lubrication or carburetion problem that causes excess carbon deposits or seizures to form on the pistons and rings. Top-end overhaul is necessary (Chapter 2A or 2B).
☐ Cylinder head gasket damaged. If a head is allowed to become loose, or if excessive carbon build-up on the piston crown and combustion chamber causes extremely high compression, the head gasket may leak. Retorquing the head is not always sufficient to restore the seal, so gasket replacement is necessary (Chapter 2A or 2B).
☐ Cylinder head warped. This is caused by overheating or improperly tightened head nuts. Machine shop resurfacing or head replacement is necessary (Chapter 2A or 2B).
☐ Valve spring broken or weak (four-stroke engines). Caused by component failure or wear; the springs must be replaced (Chapter 2B).
☐ Valve not seating properly (four-stroke engines). This is caused by a bent valve (from over-revving or improper valve adjustment), burned valve or seat (improper carburetion) or an accumulation of carbon deposits on the seat (from carburetion or lubrication problems). The valves must be cleaned and/or replaced and the seats serviced if possible (Chapter 2B).

Stalls after starting

☐ Faulty automatic choke. Check connections and movement (Chapter 4).
☐ Ignition malfunction (Chapter 5).
☐ Carburetor malfunction (Chapter 4).
☐ Fuel contaminated. The fuel can be contaminated with either dirt or water, or can change chemically if the machine is allowed to sit for several months or more. Drain the tank and carburetor (Chapter 4).
☐ Intake air leak. Check for loose carburetor-to-intake manifold connection, loose carburetor top (Chapter 4).
☐ Engine idle speed incorrect. Turn idle adjusting screw until the engine idles at the specified rpm (Chapter 1).

Rough idle

☐ Ignition malfunction (Chapter 5).
☐ Idle speed incorrect (Chapter 1).
☐ Carburetor malfunction (Chapter 4).
☐ Fuel contaminated. The fuel can be contaminated with either dirt or water, or can change chemically if the machine is allowed to sit for several months or more. Drain the tank and carburetor (Chapter 4).
☐ Intake air leak. Check for loose carburetor-to-intake manifold connection, loose carburetor top (Chapter 4).
☐ Air filter clogged. Clean or replace the air filter element (Chapter 1).

2 Poor running at low speeds

Spark weak

☐ Battery voltage low. Check and recharge battery (Chapter 10).
☐ Spark plug fouled, defective or worn out. Refer to Chapter 1 for spark plug maintenance.
☐ Spark plug cap or HT wiring defective. Refer to Chapter 5 for details on the ignition system.
☐ Spark plug cap not making contact.
☐ Incorrect spark plug. Wrong type, heat range or cap configuration. Check and install correct plug listed in Chapter 1.
☐ Ignition control unit (ICU) defective. See Chapter 5.
☐ Pick-up coil defective. See Chapter 5.
☐ Ignition HT coil defective. See Chapter 5.

Fuel/air mixture incorrect

☐ Pilot screw out of adjustment (Chapter 4).
☐ Pilot jet or air passage clogged. Remove and clean the carburetor (Chapter 4).
☐ Air bleed hole clogged. Remove carburetor and blow out all passages (Chapter 4).
☐ Air filter clogged, poorly sealed or missing (Chapter 1).
☐ Air filter housing poorly sealed. Look for cracks, holes or loose screws and replace or repair defective parts.
☐ Fuel level too high or too low. Check the float height and fuel level (Chapter 4).
☐ Carburetor intake manifold loose. Check for cracks, breaks, tears or loose fixings.

Compression low

☐ Spark plug loose. Remove the plug and inspect its threads (Chapter 1).
☐ Cylinder head not sufficiently tightened down. If the cylinder head is suspected of being loose, then there's a chance that the gasket or head is damaged if the problem has persisted for any length of time. The head nuts should be tightened to the proper torque in the correct sequence (Chapter 2A or 2B).
☐ Improper valve clearance (four-stroke engines). This means that the valve is not closing completely and compression pressure is leaking past the valve. Check and adjust the valve clearances (Chapter 1).
☐ Low crankcase compression on two-stroke engines due to worn crankshaft oil seals. Condition will upset the fuel/air mixture. Replace the seals (Chapter 2A).
☐ Cylinder and/or piston worn. Excessive wear will cause compression pressure to leak past the rings. This is usually accompanied by worn rings as well. A top-end overhaul is necessary (Chapter 2A or 2B).
☐ Piston rings worn, weak, broken, or sticking. Broken or sticking piston rings usually indicate a lubrication or carburetion problem that causes excess carbon deposits or seizures to form on the pistons and rings. Top-end overhaul is necessary (Chapter 2A or 2B).
☐ Cylinder head gasket damaged. If a head is allowed to become loose, or if excessive carbon build-up on the piston crown and combustion chamber causes extremely high compression, the head gasket may leak. Retorquing the head is not always sufficient to restore the seal, so gasket replacement is necessary (Chapter 2A or 2B).
☐ Cylinder head warped. This is caused by overheating or improperly tightened head nuts. Machine shop resurfacing or head replacement is necessary (Chapter 2A or 2B).
☐ Valve spring broken or weak (four-stroke engines). Caused by component failure or wear; the springs must be replaced (Chapter 2B).
☐ Valve not seating properly (four-stroke engines). This is caused by a bent valve (from over-revving or improper valve adjustment), burned valve or seat (improper carburetion) or an accumulation of carbon deposits on the seat (from carburetion or lubrication problems). The valves must be cleaned and/or replaced and the seats serviced if possible (Chapter 2B).

Poor acceleration

☐ Carburetor leaking or dirty. Overhaul the carburetor (Chapter 4).
☐ Faulty automatic choke (Chapter 4).
☐ Timing not advancing. The pick-up coil or the ignition control unit (ICU) may be defective (Chapter 5). If so, they must be replaced, as they can't be repaired.
☐ Engine oil viscosity too high (four-stroke engines). Using a heavier oil than that recommended in Chapter 1 can damage the oil pump or lubrication system and cause drag on the engine.
☐ Brakes dragging. On disc brakes, usually caused by debris which has entered the brake piston seals, or from a warped disc or bent axle, or cable out of adjustment where appropriate. On drum brakes, cable out of adjustment, shoe return spring broken. Repair as necessary (Chapter 8).
☐ Clutch slipping, drive belt worn, or variator (automatic transmission) faulty (Chapter 6).

3 Poor running or no power at high speed

Firing incorrect

☐ Air filter clogged. Clean or replace filter (Chapter 1).
☐ Spark plug fouled, defective or worn out. See Chapter 1 for spark plug maintenance.
☐ Spark plug cap or HT wiring defective. See Chapter 5 for details of the ignition system.
☐ Spark plug cap not in good contact (Chapter 5).
☐ Incorrect spark plug. Wrong type, heat range or cap configuration. Check and install correct plug listed in Chapter 1.
☐ Ignition control unit or HT coil defective (Chapter 5).

Fuel/air mixture incorrect

☐ Main jet clogged. Dirt, water or other contaminants can clog the main jet. Clean the fuel tap filter, the in-line filter, the float chamber and the jets and carburetor orifices (Chapter 4).
☐ Main jet wrong size. The standard jetting is for sea level atmospheric pressure and oxygen content.
☐ Air bleed holes clogged. Remove and overhaul carburetor (Chapter 4).
☐ Air filter clogged, poorly sealed, or missing (Chapter 1).
☐ Air filter housing or duct poorly sealed. Look for cracks, holes or loose clamps or screws, and replace or repair defective parts.
☐ Fuel level too high or too low. Check the float height or fuel level (Chapter 4).
☐ Carburetor intake manifold loose. Check for cracks, breaks, tears or loose fixings.

Compression low

☐ Spark plug loose. Remove the plug and inspect its threads. Reinstall and tighten to the specified torque (Chapter 1).
☐ Cylinder head not sufficiently tightened down. If the cylinder head is suspected of being loose, then there's a chance that the gasket or head is damaged if the problem has persisted for any length of time. The head nuts should be tightened to the proper torque in the correct sequence (Chapter 2A or 2B).
☐ Improper valve clearance (four-stroke engines). This means that the valve is not closing completely and compression pressure is leaking past the valve. Check and adjust the valve clearances (Chapter 1).
☐ Low crankcase compression on two-stroke engines due to worn crankshaft oil seals. Condition will upset the fuel/air mixture. Replace the seals (Chapter 2A).
☐ Cylinder and/or piston worn. Excessive wear will cause compression pressure to leak past the rings. This is usually accompanied by worn rings as well. A top-end overhaul is necessary (Chapter 2A or 2B).
☐ Piston rings worn, weak, broken, or sticking. Broken or sticking piston rings usually indicate a lubrication or carburetion problem that causes excess carbon deposits or seizures to form on the pistons and rings. Top-end overhaul is necessary (Chapter 2A or 2B).
☐ Cylinder head gasket damaged. If a head is allowed to become loose, or if excessive carbon build-up on the piston crown and combustion chamber causes extremely high compression, the head gasket may leak. Retorquing the head is not always sufficient to restore the seal, so gasket replacement is necessary (Chapter 2A or 2B).
☐ Cylinder head warped. This is caused by overheating or improperly tightened head nuts. Cylinder head skimming or head replacement is necessary (Chapter 2A or 2B).
☐ Valve spring broken or weak (four-stroke engines). Caused by component failure or wear; the springs must be replaced (Chapter 2B).
☐ Valve not seating properly (four-stroke engines). This is caused by a bent valve (from over-revving or improper valve adjustment), burned valve or seat (improper carburetion) or an accumulation of carbon deposits on the seat (from carburetion or lubrication problems). The valves must be cleaned and/or replaced and the seats serviced if possible (Chapter 2B).

Knocking or pinging

☐ Carbon build-up in combustion chamber. Use of a fuel additive that will dissolve the adhesive bonding the carbon particles to the crown and chamber is the easiest way to remove the build-up. Otherwise, the cylinder head will have to be removed and decarbonized (Chapter 2A or 2B). On two-stroke engines, the regular service interval for cylinder head decarbonization should be adhered to.
☐ Incorrect or poor quality fuel. Old or improper grades of fuel can cause detonation. This causes the piston to rattle, thus the knocking or pinging sound. Drain old fuel and always use the recommended fuel grade.
☐ Spark plug heat range incorrect. Uncontrolled detonation indicates the plug heat range is too hot. The plug in effect becomes a glow plug, raising cylinder temperatures. Install the proper heat range plug (Chapter 1).
☐ Improper air/fuel mixture. This will cause the cylinders to run hot, which leads to detonation. Clogged jets or an air leak can cause this imbalance. See Chapter 4.

Miscellaneous causes

☐ Throttle valve doesn't open fully. Adjust the throttle twistgrip freeplay (Chapter 1).
☐ Clutch slipping, drive belt worn, or speed governor faulty (Chapter 6).
☐ Timing not advancing (Chapter 5).
☐ Engine oil viscosity too high (four-stroke engines). Using a heavier oil than the one recommended in Chapter 1 can damage the oil pump or lubrication system and cause drag on the engine.
☐ Brakes dragging. On disc brakes, usually caused by debris which has entered the brake piston seals, or from a warped disc or bent axle, or cable out of adjustment where appropriate. On drum brakes, cable out of adjustment, shoe return spring broken. Repair as necessary (Chapter 8).

4 Overheating

Engine overheats – liquid-cooled engines

- ☐ Coolant level low. Check and add coolant (Chapter 1).
- ☐ Leak in cooling system. Check cooling system hoses and radiator for leaks and other damage. Repair or replace parts as necessary (Chapter 3).
- ☐ Thermostat sticking open or closed. Check and replace as described in Chapter 3.
- ☐ Coolant passages clogged. Drain and flush the entire system, then refill with fresh coolant.
- ☐ Water pump defective. Remove the pump and check the components (Chapter 3).
- ☐ Clogged radiator fins. Clean them by blowing compressed air through the fins from the back of the radiator.
- ☐ Cooling fan or fan switch fault (Chapter 3).

Engine overheats – air-cooled engines

- ☐ Air cooling ducts or engine cowling blocked or incorrectly installed.
- ☐ Problem with cooling fan.

Firing incorrect

- ☐ Spark plug fouled, defective or worn out. See Chapter 1 for spark plug maintenance.
- ☐ Incorrect spark plug.
- ☐ Ignition control unit defective (Chapter 5).
- ☐ Faulty ignition HT coil (Chapter 5).

Fuel/air mixture incorrect

- ☐ Main jet clogged. Dirt, water or other contaminants can clog the main jet. Clean the fuel tap filter, the in-line filter, the float chamber and the jets and carburetor orifices (Chapter 4).
- ☐ Main jet wrong size. The standard jetting is for sea level atmospheric pressure and oxygen content.
- ☐ Air bleed holes clogged. Remove and overhaul carburetor (Chapter 4).
- ☐ Air filter clogged, poorly sealed, or missing (Chapter 1).
- ☐ Air filter housing or duct poorly sealed. Look for cracks, holes or loose clamps or screws, and replace or repair defective parts.
- ☐ Fuel level too high or too low. Check the float height or fuel level (Chapter 4).
- ☐ Carburetor intake manifold loose. Check for cracks, breaks, tears or loose fixings.

Compression too high

- ☐ Carbon build-up in combustion chamber. Use of a fuel additive

that will dissolve the adhesive bonding the carbon particles to the piston crown and chamber is the easiest way to remove the build-up. Otherwise, the cylinder head will have to be removed and decarbonized (Chapter 2A or 2B). On two-stroke engines, the regular service interval for cylinder head decarbonization should be adhered to.
- ☐ Improperly machined head surface or installation of incorrect size cylinder base gasket during engine assembly.

Engine load excessive

- ☐ Clutch slipping, drive belt worn, or variator faulty (Chapter 6).
- ☐ Engine oil level too high (four-stroke engines). The addition of too much oil will cause pressurization of the crankcase and inefficient engine operation. Check Specifications and drain to proper level (Chapter 1).
- ☐ Engine oil viscosity too high (four-stroke engines). Using a heavier oil than the one recommended in Chapter 1 can damage the oil pump or lubrication system as well as cause drag on the engine.
- ☐ Brakes dragging. On disc brakes, usually caused by debris which has entered the brake piston seals, or from a warped disc or bent axle, or cable out of adjustment where appropriate. On drum brakes, cable out of adjustment, shoe return spring broken. Repair as necessary (Chapter 8).

Lubrication inadequate

- ☐ Engine oil level too low (four-stroke engines). Friction caused by intermittent lack of lubrication or from oil that is overworked can cause overheating. The oil provides a definite cooling function in the engine. Check the oil level (Chapter 1).
- ☐ Oil pump out of adjustment (two-stroke engines) . Adjust pump cable (Chapter 1).
- ☐ Poor quality oil or incorrect viscosity or type. Oil is rated not only according to viscosity but also according to type. Some oils are not rated high enough for use in this engine. Check the Specifications section and change to the correct oil (Chapter 1). On two-stroke engines, make sure that you use a two-stroke oil which is suitable for oil injection engines.

Miscellaneous causes

- ☐ Modification to exhaust system. Most aftermarket exhaust systems cause the engine to run leaner, which makes them run hotter. When installing an accessory exhaust system, always obtain advice on rejetting the carburetor.

5 Transmission problems

No drive to rear wheel

☐ Drive belt broken (Chapter 6).
☐ Clutch not engaging (Chapter 6).
☐ Clutch or drum excessively worn (Chapter 6).

Transmission noise or vibration

☐ Bearings worn. Also includes the possibility that the shafts are worn. Overhaul the transmission (Chapter 6).
☐ Gears worn or chipped (Chapter 6).
☐ Clutch drum worn unevenly (Chapter 6).
☐ Worn bearings or bent shaft (Chapter 6).
☐ Loose clutch nut or drum nut (Chapter 6).

Poor performance

☐ Variator (automatic transmission) worn or insufficiently greased (Chapter 6).
☐ Weak or broken driven pulley spring (Chapter 6).
☐ Clutch or drum excessively worn (Chapter 6).
☐ Grease on clutch friction material (Chapter 6).
☐ Drive belt excessively worn (Chapter 6).

Clutch not disengaging completely

☐ Weak or broken clutch springs (Chapter 6).
☐ Engine idle speed too high (Chapter 1).

6 Abnormal engine noise

Knocking or pinging

☐ Carbon build-up in combustion chamber. Use of a fuel additive that will dissolve the adhesive bonding the carbon particles to the piston crown and chamber is the easiest way to remove the build-up. Otherwise, the cylinder head will have to be removed and decarbonized (Chapter 2A or 2B). On two-stroke engines, always decarbonize the cylinder head and piston crown at the recommended service interval (Chapter 1).
☐ Incorrect or poor quality fuel. Old or improper fuel can cause detonation. This causes the pistons to rattle, thus the knocking or pinging sound. Drain the old fuel and always use the recommended grade fuel (Chapter 4).
☐ Spark plug heat range incorrect. Uncontrolled detonation indicates that the plug heat range is too hot. The plug in effect becomes a glow plug, raising cylinder temperatures. Install the proper heat range plug (Chapter 1).
☐ Improper air/fuel mixture. This will cause the cylinder to run hot and lead to detonation. Clogged jets or an air leak can cause this imbalance. See Chapter 4.

Piston slap or rattling

☐ Cylinder-to-piston clearance excessive. Caused by improper assembly. Inspect and overhaul top-end parts (Chapter 2A or 2B).
☐ Connecting rod bent. Caused by over-revving, trying to start a badly flooded engine or from ingesting a foreign object into the combustion chamber. Replace the damaged parts (Chapter 2A or 2B).
☐ Piston pin or piston pin bore worn or seized from wear or lack of lubrication. Replace damaged parts (Chapter 2A or 2B).
☐ Piston ring(s) worn, broken or sticking. Overhaul the top-end (Chapter 2A or 2B).

☐ Piston seizure damage. Usually from lack of lubrication or overheating. Replace the piston and where possible, rebore the cylinder, as necessary (Chapter 2A or 2B). On two-stroke engines, check that the oil pump is correctly adjusted.
☐ Connecting rod upper or lower end clearance excessive. Caused by excessive wear or lack of lubrication. Replace worn parts.

Valve noise – four-stroke engines

☐ Incorrect valve clearances. Adjust the clearances by referring to Chapter 1.
☐ Valve spring broken or weak. Check and replace weak valve springs (Chapter 2B).
☐ Camshaft bearings worn or damaged. Lack of lubrication at high rpm is usually the cause of damage. Insufficient oil or failure to change the oil at the recommended intervals are the chief causes. (Chapter 2B).

Other noise

☐ Exhaust pipe leaking at cylinder head connection. Caused by improper fit of pipe or loose exhaust flange. All exhaust fasteners should be tightened evenly and carefully. Failure to do this will lead to a leak.
☐ Crankshaft runout excessive. Caused by a bent crankshaft (from over-revving) or damage from an upper cylinder component failure.
☐ Engine mounting bolts loose. Tighten all engine mount bolts (Chapter 2A or 2B).
☐ Crankshaft bearings worn (Chapter 2A or 2B).
☐ Camshaft drive gear assembly defective (four-stroke engines). Replace according to the procedure in Chapter 2B.

7 Abnormal frame and suspension noise

Front end noise

☐ Steering head bearings loose or damaged. Clicks when braking. Check and adjust or replace as necessary (Chapters 1 and 7).
☐ Bolts loose. Make sure all bolts are tightened to the specified torque (Chapter 7).
☐ Fork tube bent. Good possibility if machine has been in a collision. Replace the tube or the fork assembly (Chapter 7).
☐ Front axle nut loose. Tighten to the specified torque (Chapter 8).
☐ Loose or worn wheel or hub bearings. Check and replace as needed (Chapter 8).

Shock absorber noise

☐ Fluid level incorrect. Indicates a leak caused by defective seal. Shock will be covered with oil. Replace the shock (Chapter 7).
☐ Defective shock absorber with internal damage. This is in the body of the shock and can't be remedied. The shock must be replaced (Chapter 7).
☐ Bent or damaged shock body. Replace the shock (Chapter 7).
☐ Loose or worn suspension linkage components. Check and replace as necessary (Chapter 7).

Brake noise

☐ Squeal caused by dust on brake pads or shoes. Usually found in combination with glazed pads or shoes. Clean using brake cleaning solvent (Chapter 8).
☐ Contamination of brake pads or shoes. Oil or brake fluid causing brake to chatter or squeal. Replace pads or shoes (Chapter 8).
☐ Pads or shoes glazed. Caused by excessive heat from prolonged use or from contamination. Do not use sandpaper, emery cloth, or any other abrasive to roughen the pad surfaces as abrasives will stay in the pad material and damage the disc or drum. A very fine flat file can be used, but pad or shoe replacement is advised (Chapter 8).
☐ Disc or drum warped. Can cause a chattering, clicking or intermittent squeal. Usually accompanied by a pulsating lever and uneven braking. Check the disc runout and the drum ovality (Chapter 8).
☐ Loose or worn wheel (front) or transmission (rear) bearings. Check and replace as needed (Chapters 8 or 6).

8 Excessive exhaust smoke

White smoke – four-stroke engines (oil burning)

☐ Piston oil ring worn. The ring may be broken or damaged, causing oil from the crankcase to be pulled past the piston into the combustion chamber. Replace the rings (Chapter 2B).
☐ Cylinder worn, or scored. Caused by overheating or oil starvation. The cylinder will have to be rebored and an oversize piston installed (Chapter 2B).
☐ Valve stem oil seal damaged or worn. Replace oil seals (Chapter 2B).
☐ Valve guide worn. Inspect the valve guides and if worn, seek the advice of a scooter dealer (Chapter 2B).
☐ Engine oil level too high, which causes the oil to be forced past the rings. Drain oil to the proper level (Daily (pre-ride) checks).
☐ Head gasket broken between oil return and cylinder. Causes oil to be pulled into the combustion chamber. Replace the head gasket and check the head for warpage (Chapter 2B).
☐ Abnormal crankcase pressurization, which forces oil past the rings.

White/blue smoke – two-stroke engines (oil burning)

☐ Oil pump cable adjustment incorrect. Check throttle cable/oil pump cable adjustment (Chapter 1).
☐ Accumulated oil deposits in the exhaust system. If the scooter is used for short journeys only, the oil residue from the exhaust gases will condense in the cool muffler. Take the scooter for a long run to burn off the accumulated oil residue.

Black smoke (over-rich mixture)

☐ Air filter clogged. Clean or replace the element (Chapter 1).
☐ Main jet too large or loose. Compare the jet size to the Specifications (Chapter 4).
☐ Automatic choke faulty (Chapter 4).
☐ Fuel level too high. Check and adjust the float height or fuel level as necessary (Chapter 4).
☐ Float needle valve held off needle seat. Clean the float chamber and fuel line and replace the needle and seat if necessary (Chapter 4).

Brown smoke (lean mixture)

☐ Main jet too small or clogged. Lean condition caused by wrong size main jet or by a restricted orifice. Clean float chamber and jets and compare jet size to specifications (Chapter 4).
☐ Fuel flow insufficient. Float needle valve stuck closed due to chemical reaction with old fuel. Float height or fuel level incorrect. Restricted fuel hose. Clean hose and float chamber and adjust float if necessary.
☐ Carburetor intake manifold clamp loose (Chapter 4).
☐ Air filter poorly sealed or not installed (Chapter 1).
☐ Ignition timing incorrect (Chapter 5).

9 Poor handling or stability

Handlebar hard to turn

- ☐ Steering head bearing adjuster nut too tight. Check adjustment as described in Chapter 1.
- ☐ Bearings damaged. Roughness can be felt as the bars are turned from side-to-side. Replace bearings and races (Chapter 7).
- ☐ Races dented or worn. Denting results from wear in only one position (for example, straight ahead), from a collision or hitting a pothole or from dropping the machine. Replace races and bearings (Chapter 7).
- ☐ Steering stem lubrication inadequate. Causes are grease getting hard from age or being washed out by high pressure car washes. Disassemble steering head and repack bearings (Chapter 7).
- ☐ Steering stem bent. Caused by a collision, hitting a pothole or by dropping the machine. Replace damaged part. Don't try to straighten the steering stem (Chapter 7).
- ☐ Front tire air pressure too low (*Daily (pre-ride) checks*).

Handlebar shakes or vibrates excessively

- ☐ Tires worn (Chapter 8).
- ☐ Suspension pivots worn. Replace worn components (Chapter 7).
- ☐ Wheel rim(s) warped or damaged. Inspect wheels for runout (Chapter 8).
- ☐ Wheel bearings worn. Worn wheel bearings (front) or transmission bearings (rear) can cause poor tracking. Worn front bearings will cause wobble (Chapter 8).
- ☐ Handlebar mountings loose (Chapter 7).
- ☐ Front suspension bolts loose. Tighten them to the specified torque (Chapter 7).

- ☐ Engine mounting bolts loose. Will cause excessive vibration with increased engine rpm (Chapter 2A or 2B).

Handlebar pulls to one side

- ☐ Frame bent. Definitely suspect this if the machine has been in a collision. May or may not be accompanied by cracking near the bend. Replace the frame (Chapter 7).
- ☐ Wheels out of alignment. Caused by improper location of axle spacers or from bent steering stem or frame (Chapter 7 or 8).
- ☐ Steering stem bent. Caused by impact damage or by dropping the machine. Replace the steering stem (Chapter 7).
- ☐ Fork tube bent (telescopic fork models). Disassemble the forks and replace the damaged parts (Chapter 7).

Poor shock absorbing qualities

Too hard:
  a) *Fork grease or oil quantity excessive (Chapter 7).*
  b) *Fork grease or oil viscosity too high. Refer to your scooter handbook or check with a scooter dealer.*
  c) *Suspension bent. Causes a harsh, sticking feeling (Chapter 7).*
  d) *Fork or front shock internal damage (Chapter 7).*
  e) *Rear shock internal damage (Chapter 7).*
  f) *Tire pressure too high (Chapter 1).*
Too soft:
  a) *Fork grease or oil viscosity too light. Refer to your scooter handbook or check with a scooter dealer.*
  b) *Fork or shock spring(s) weak or broken (Chapter 7).*
  c) *Shock internal damage or leakage (Chapter 7).*

10 Braking problems – disc brakes

Brakes are ineffective

- ☐ Air in brake hose. Caused by inattention to master cylinder fluid level or by leakage. Locate problem and bleed brake (Chapter 8).
- ☐ Pads or disc worn (Chapter 8).
- ☐ Brake fluid leak. Locate problem and rectify (Chapter 8).
- ☐ Contaminated pads. Caused by contamination with oil, grease, brake fluid, etc. Replace pads. Clean disc thoroughly with brake cleaner (Chapter 8).
- ☐ Brake fluid deteriorated. Fluid is old or contaminated. Drain system, replenish with new fluid and bleed the system (Chapter 8).
- ☐ Master cylinder internal parts worn or damaged, causing fluid to bypass (Chapter 8).
- ☐ Master cylinder bore scratched by foreign material or broken spring. Repair or replace master cylinder (Chapter 8).
- ☐ Disc warped. Replace disc (Chapter 8).
- ☐ On some scooters, the master cylinder is operated by a short cable from the handlebar lever. Check that the cable is correctly adjusted and moves freely (Chapter 8).

Brake lever pulsates

- ☐ Disc warped. Replace disc (Chapter 8).
- ☐ Axle bent. Replace axle (Chapter 8).
- ☐ Brake caliper bolts loose (Chapter 8).
- ☐ Wheel warped or otherwise damaged (Chapter 8).
- ☐ Wheel or hub bearings damaged or worn (Chapter 8).

Brakes drag

- ☐ Master cylinder piston seized. Caused by wear or damage to piston or cylinder bore (Chapter 8).
- ☐ Lever balky or stuck. Check pivot and lubricate (Chapter 8).
- ☐ Brake caliper piston seized in bore. Caused by wear or ingestion of dirt past deteriorated seal (Chapter 8).
- ☐ Brake pads damaged. Pad material separated from backing plate. Usually caused by faulty manufacturing process or from contact with chemicals. Replace pads (Chapter 8).
- ☐ Pads improperly installed (Chapter 8).

11 Braking problems – drum brakes

Brakes are ineffective

- [ ] Cable incorrectly adjusted. Check cable (Chapter 1).
- [ ] Shoes or drum worn (Chapter 8).
- [ ] Contaminated shoes. Caused by contamination with oil, grease, brake fluid, etc. Replace shoes. Clean drum thoroughly with brake cleaner (Chapter 8).
- [ ] Brake lever arm incorrectly positioned, or cam excessively worn (Chapter 8).

Brake lever pulsates

- [ ] Drum warped. Replace drum (Chapter 8).
- [ ] Axle bent. Replace axle (Chapter 8).
- [ ] Wheel warped or otherwise damaged (Chapter 8).
- [ ] Wheel/hub bearings (front) or transmission bearings (rear) damaged or worn (Chapter 8).

Brakes drag

- [ ] Cable incorrectly adjusted or requires lubrication. Check cable (Chapter 1).
- [ ] Shoe return springs broken (Chapter 8).
- [ ] Lever balky or stuck. Check pivot and lubricate (Chapter 8).
- [ ] Lever arm or cam binds. Caused by inadequate lubrication or damage (Chapter 8).
- [ ] Brake shoe damaged. Friction material separated from shoe. Usually caused by faulty manufacturing process or from contact with chemicals. Replace shoes (Chapter 8).
- [ ] Shoes improperly installed (Chapter 8).

12 Electrical problems

Battery dead or weak

- [ ] Battery faulty. Caused by sulphated plates which are shorted through sedimentation. Also, broken battery terminal making only occasional contact (Chapter 10).
- [ ] Battery cables making poor electrical contact (Chapter 10).
- [ ] Load excessive. Caused by addition of high wattage lights or other electrical accessories.
- [ ] Ignition (main) switch defective. Switch either grounds internally or fails to shut off system. Replace the switch (Chapter 10).
- [ ] Regulator/rectifier defective (Chapter 10).
- [ ] Alternator stator coil open or shorted (Chapter 10).
- [ ] Wiring faulty. Wiring either shorted to ground or connections loose in ignition, charging or lighting circuits (Chapter 10).

Battery overcharged

- [ ] Regulator/rectifier defective. Overcharging is noticed when battery gets excessively warm (Chapter 10).
- [ ] Battery defective. Replace battery (Chapter 10).
- [ ] Battery amperage too low, wrong type or size. Install manufacturer's specified amp-hour battery to handle charging load (Chapter 10).

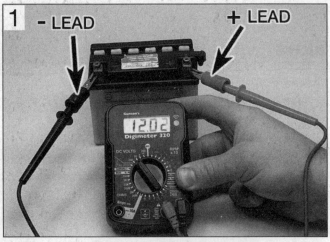

Measuring open-circuit battery voltage

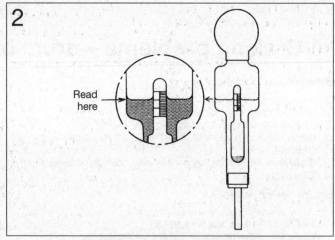

Float-type hydrometer for measuring battery specific gravity

Checking engine compression

● Low compression will result in exhaust smoke, heavy oil consumption, poor starting and poor performance. A compression test will provide useful information about an engine's condition and if performed regularly, can give warning of trouble before any other symptoms become apparent.
● A compression gauge will be required, along with an adapter to suit the spark plug hole thread size. Note that the screw-in type gauge/adapter set up is preferable to the rubber cone type.
● Before carrying out the test, first check the valve clearances as described in Chapter 1.
● Compression testing procedures for the scooters covered in this manual are described in Chapter 2.

Checking battery open-circuit voltage

 Warning: The gases produced by the battery are explosive - never smoke or create any sparks in the vicinity of the battery. Never allow the electrolyte to contact your skin or clothing - if it does, wash it off and seek immediate medical attention.

● Before any electrical fault is investigated, the battery should be checked.
● You'll need a dc voltmeter or multimeter to check battery voltage. Check that the leads are inserted in the correct terminals on the meter, red lead to positive (+), black lead to negative (-). Incorrect connections can damage the meter.
● A sound, fully-charged 12 volt battery should produce between 12.3 and 12.6 volts across its terminals (12.8 volts for a maintenance-free battery). On machines with a 6 volt battery, voltage should be between 6.1 and 6.3 volts.
1 Set a multimeter to the 0 to 20 volts dc range and connect its probes across the battery terminals. Connect the meter's positive (+) probe, usually red, to the battery positive (+) terminal, followed by the meter's negative (-) probe, usually black, to the battery negative terminal (-) **(see illustration 1)**.
2 If battery voltage is low (below 10 volts on a 12 volt battery or below 4 volts on a six volt battery), charge the battery and test the voltage again. If the battery repeatedly goes flat, investigate the scooter's charging system.

Checking battery specific gravity (SG)

 Warning: The gases produced by the battery are explosive - never smoke or create any sparks in the vicinity of the battery. Never allow the electrolyte to contact your skin or clothing - if it does, wash it off and seek immediate medical attention.

● The specific gravity check gives an indication of a battery's state of charge.
● A hydrometer is used for measuring specific gravity. Make sure you purchase one which has a small enough hose to insert in the aperture of a scooter battery.
● Specific gravity is simply a measure of the electrolyte's density compared with that of water. Water has an SG of 1.000, and fully-charged battery electrolyte is about 26% heavier, at 1.260.
● Specific gravity checks are not possible on maintenance-free batteries. Testing the open-circuit voltage is the only means of determining their state of charge.
1 To measure SG, remove the battery from the scooter and remove the first cell cap. Draw some electrolyte into the hydrometer and note the reading **(see illustration 2)**. Return the electrolyte to the cell and install the cap.
2 The reading should be in the region of 1.260 to 1.280. If SG is below 1.200, the battery needs charging. Note that SG will vary with temperature; it should be measured at 20°C (68°F). Add 0.007 to the reading for every 10°C above 20°C, and subtract 0.007 from the reading for every 10°C below 20°C. Add 0.004 to the reading for every 10°F above 68°F, and subtract 0.004 from the reading for every 10°F below 68°F.
3 When the check is complete, rinse the hydrometer thoroughly with clean water.

Checking for continuity

● The term continuity describes the uninterrupted flow of electricity through an electrical circuit. A continuity check will determine whether an **open-circuit** situation exists.
● Continuity can be checked with an ohmmeter, multimeter, continuity tester or battery and bulb test circuit **(see illustrations 3, 4 and 5)**.
● All of these instruments are self-powered by a battery, therefore the checks are made with the ignition OFF.
● As a safety precaution, always disconnect the battery negative (-) lead before making checks, particularly if ignition switch checks are being made.
● If using a meter, select the appropriate

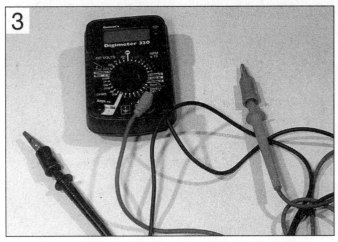

Digital multimeter can be used for all electrical tests

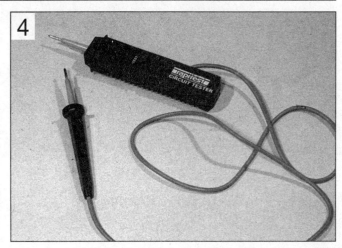

Battery-powered continuity tester

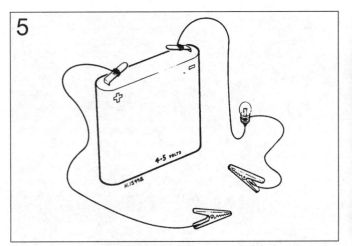

Battery and bulb test circuit

Continuity check of front brake light switch using a meter - note cotter pins used to access connector terminals

ohms scale and check that the meter reads infinity (∞). Touch the meter probes together and check that meter reads zero; where necessary adjust the meter so that it reads zero.

● After using a meter, always switch it OFF to conserve its battery.

Switch checks

1 If a switch is at fault, trace its wiring up to the wiring connectors. Separate the wire connectors and inspect them for security and condition. A build-up of dirt or corrosion here will most likely be the cause of the problem - clean up and apply a water dispersant such as WD40.

2 If using a test meter, set the meter to the ohms x 10 scale and connect its probes across the wires from the switch **(see illustration 6)**. Simple ON/OFF type switches, such as brake light switches, only have two wires whereas combination switches, like the ignition switch, have many internal links. Study the wiring diagram to ensure that you are connecting across the correct pair of wires. Continuity (low or no measurable resistance - 0 ohms) should be indicated with the switch ON and no continuity (high resistance) with it OFF.

3 Note that the polarity of the test probes doesn't matter for continuity checks, although care should be taken to follow specific test procedures if a diode or solid-state component is being checked.

4 A continuity tester or battery and bulb circuit can be used in the same way. Connect its probes as described above **(see illustration 7)**. The light should come on to indicate continuity in the ON switch position, but should extinguish in the OFF position.

Wiring checks

● Many electrical faults are caused by damaged wiring, often due to incorrect routing or chaffing on frame components.

● Loose, wet or corroded wire connectors

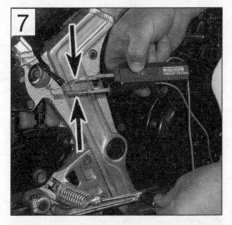

Continuity check of rear brake light switch using a continuity tester

can also be the cause of electrical problems, especially in exposed locations.

Continuity check of front brake light switch sub-harness

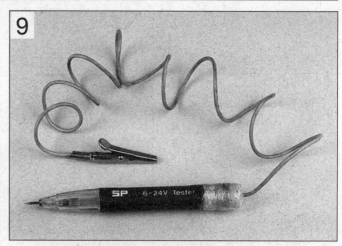

A simple test light can be used for voltage checks

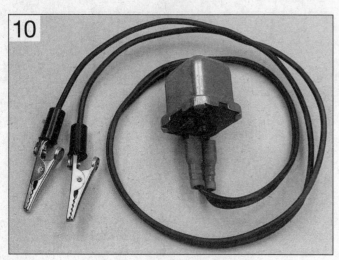

A buzzer is useful for voltage checks

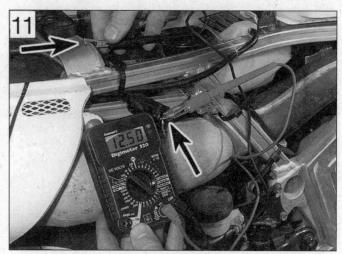

Checking for voltage at the rear brake light power supply wire using a meter . . .

1 A continuity check can be made on a single length of wire by disconnecting it at each end and connecting a meter or continuity tester across both ends of the wire (see illustration 8).

2 Continuity (low or no resistance - 0 ohms) should be indicated if the wire is good. If no continuity (high resistance) is shown, suspect a broken wire.

Checking for voltage

● A voltage check can determine whether current is reaching a component.

● Voltage can be checked with a dc voltmeter, multimeter set on the dc volts scale, test light or buzzer (see illustrations 9 and 10). A meter has the advantage of being able to measure actual voltage.

● When using a meter, check that its leads are inserted in the correct terminals on the meter, red to positive (+), black to negative (-). Incorrect connections can damage the meter.

● A voltmeter (or multimeter set to the dc volts scale) should always be connected in parallel (across the load). Connecting it in series will destroy the meter.

● Voltage checks are made with the ignition ON.

1 First identify the relevant wiring circuit by referring to the wiring diagram at the end of this manual. If other electrical components share the same power supply (they are fed from the same fuse), take note whether they are working correctly - this is useful information in deciding where to start checking the circuit.

2 If using a meter, check first that the meter leads are plugged into the correct terminals on the meter (see above). Set the meter to the dc volts function, at a range suitable for the battery voltage. Connect the meter red probe (+) to the power supply wire and the black probe to a good metal ground on the scooter's frame or directly to the battery negative (-) terminal (see illustration 11). Battery voltage should be shown on the meter with the ignition switched ON.

3 If using a test light or buzzer, connect its positive (+) probe to the power supply terminal and its negative (-) probe to a good ground on the scooter's frame or directly to the battery negative (-) terminal (see illustration 12). With the ignition ON, the test light should illuminate or the buzzer sound.

4 If no voltage is indicated, work back towards the fuse continuing to check for voltage. When you reach a point where there is voltage, you know the problem lies between that point and your last check point.

Checking the ground

● Ground connections are made either

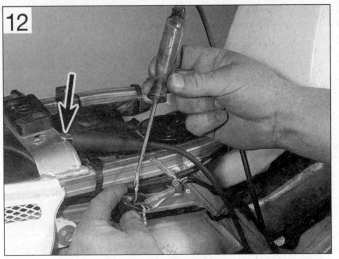

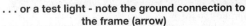

. . . or a test light - note the ground connection to the frame (arrow)

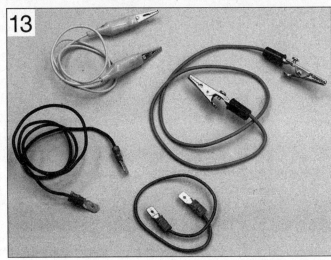

A selection of jumper wires for making ground checks

directly to the engine or frame (such as sensors, neutral switch etc. which only have a positive feed) or by a separate wire into the ground circuit of the wiring harness. Alternatively a short ground wire is sometimes run directly from the component to the scooter's frame.

● Corrosion is often the cause of a poor ground connection.

● If total failure is experienced, check the security of the main ground lead from the negative (-) terminal of the battery and also the main ground point on the wiring harness. If corroded, dismantle the connection and clean all surfaces back to bare metal.

1 To check the ground on a component, use an insulated jumper wire to temporarily bypass its ground connection **(see illustration 13)**. Connect one end of the jumper wire between the ground terminal or metal body of the

component and the other end to the scooter's frame.

2 If the circuit works with the jumper wire installed, the original ground circuit is faulty. Check the wiring for open-circuits or poor connections. Clean up direct ground connections, removing all traces of corrosion and remake the joint. Apply petroleum jelly to the joint to prevent future corrosion.

Tracing a short-circuit

● A short-circuit occurs where current shorts to ground bypassing the circuit components. This usually results in a blown fuse.

● A short-circuit is most likely to occur where the insulation has worn through due to wiring chafing on a component, allowing a direct path to ground on the frame.

1 Remove any body panels necessary to access the circuit wiring.

2 Check that all electrical switches in the circuit are OFF, then remove the circuit fuse and connect a test light, buzzer or voltmeter (set to the dc scale) across the fuse terminals. No voltage should be shown.

3 Move the wiring from side to side while observing the test light or meter. When the test light comes on, buzzer sounds or meter shows voltage, you have found the cause of the short. It will usually shown up as damaged or burned insulation.

4 Note that the same test can be performed on each component in the circuit, even the switch.

Introduction

In less time than it takes to read this introduction, a thief could steal your scooter. Returning only to find your scooter has gone is one of the worst feelings in the world. Even if the scooter is insured against theft, once you've got over the initial shock, you will have the inconvenience of dealing with the police and your insurance company.

The scooter is an easy target for the professional thief and the joyrider alike and the official figures on motorcycle theft make for depressing reading; on average a motorcycle is stolen every 16 minutes!

Motorcycle and scooter thefts fall into two categories, those stolen "to order" and those taken by opportunists. The thief stealing to order will be on the look out for a specific make and model and will go to extraordinary lengths to obtain that motorcycle. The opportunist thief on the other hand will look for easy targets which can be stolen with the minimum of effort and risk.

While it is never going to be possible to make your machine 100% secure, it is estimated that around half of all stolen bikes are taken by opportunist thieves. Remember that the opportunist thief is always on the look out for the easy option: if there are two similar scooters parked side-by-side, they will target the one with the lowest level of security. By taking a few precautions, you can reduce the chances of your scooter being stolen.

Security equipment

There are many specialized scooter security devices available and the following text summarizes their applications and their good and bad points.

Once you have decided on the type of security equipment which best suits your needs, we recommended that you read one of the many equipment tests regularly carried out by the motorcycle press. These tests compare the products from all the major manufacturers and give impartial ratings on their effectiveness, value-for-money and ease of use.

No one item of security equipment can provide complete protection. It is highly recommended that two or more of the items described below are combined to increase the security of your scooter (a lock and chain plus an alarm system is just about ideal). The more security installed on the scooter, the less likely it is to be stolen.

Ensure the lock and chain you buy is of good quality and long enough to shackle your scooter to a solid object

Lock and chain

Pros: *Very flexible to use; can be used to secure the scooter to almost any immovable object. On some locks and chains, the lock can be used on its own as a disc lock (see below).*

Cons: *Can be very heavy and awkward to carry on the scooter, although some types will be supplied with a carry bag which can be strapped to the pillion seat.*

● Heavy-duty chains and locks are an excellent security measure **(see illustration 1)**. Whenever the scooter is parked, use the lock and chain to secure the machine to a solid, immovable object such as a post or railings. This will prevent the machine from being ridden away or being lifted into the back of a van.

● When fitting the chain, always ensure the chain is routed around the scooter frame or swingarm **(see illustrations 2 and 3)**. Never merely pass the chain around one of the wheel rims; a thief may unbolt the wheel and lift the rest of the machine into a van, leaving you with just the wheel! Try to avoid having excess chain free, thus making it difficult to use cutting tools, and keep the chain and lock off the ground to prevent thieves attacking it with a cold chisel. Position the lock so that its lock barrel is facing downwards; this will make it harder for the thief to attack the lock mechanism.

Pass the chain through the scooter's frame, rather than just through a wheel . . .

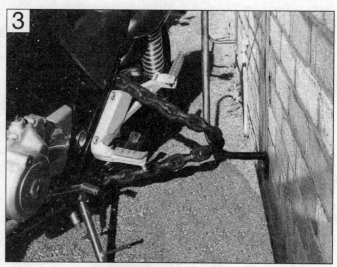

. . . and loop it around a solid object

U-locks

Pros: *Highly effective deterrent which can be used to secure the scooter to a post or railings. Most U-locks come with a carrier which allows the lock to be easily carried on the scooter.*

Cons: *Not as flexible to use as a lock and chain.*

● These are solid locks which are similar in use to a lock and chain. U-locks are lighter than a lock and chain but not so flexible to use. The length and shape of the lock shackle limit the objects to which the scooter can be secured **(see illustration 4)**.

Disc locks

Pros: *Small, light and very easy to carry; most can be stored underneath the seat.*

Cons: *Does not prevent the scooter being lifted into a van. Can be very embarrassing if you*

U-locks can be used to secure the scooter to a solid object – ensure you purchase one which is long enough

forget to remove the lock before attempting to ride off!

● Disc locks are designed to be attached to the front brake disc. The lock passes through one of the holes in the disc and prevents the wheel rotating by jamming against the fork/ brake caliper **(see illustration 5)**. Some are equipped with an alarm siren which sounds if the disc lock is moved; this not only acts as a theft deterrent but also as a handy reminder if you try to move the scooter with the lock still installed.

● Combining the disc lock with a length of cable which can be looped around a post or railings provides an additional measure of security **(see illustration 6)**.

Alarms and immobilizers

Pros: *Once installed it is completely hassle-free to use. In some cases, insurance companies may give you a discount.*

Cons: *Can be expensive to buy and complex to install. No system will prevent the scooter from being lifted into a van and taken away.*

● Electronic alarms and immobilizers are available to suit a variety of budgets. There are three different types of system available: pure alarms, pure immobilizers, and the more expensive systems which are combined alarm/immobilizers **(see illustration 7)**.
● An alarm system is designed to emit an audible warning if the scooter is being tampered with.
● An immobilizer prevents the scooter being started and ridden away by disabling its electrical systems.
● When purchasing an alarm/immobilizer system, check the cost of installing the system unless you are able to do it yourself. If the scooter is not used regularly, another consideration is the current drain of the system. All alarm/immobilizer systems are powered by the scooter's battery; purchasing a system with a very low current drain could prevent the battery losing its charge while the scooter is not being used.

A typical disc lock attached through one of the holes in the disc

A disc lock combined with a security cable provides additional protection

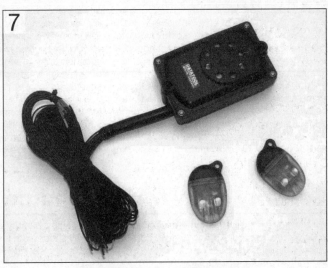

A typical alarm/immobilizer system

8

Indelible markings can be applied to most areas of the scooter – always apply the manufacturer's sticker to warn off thieves

9

Chemically-etched code numbers can be applied to main body panels . . .

10

. . . again, always ensure that the kit manufacturer's sticker is applied in a prominent position

Security marking kits

Pros: *Very cheap and effective deterrent. Many insurance companies will give you a discount on your insurance premium if a recognized security marking kit is used on your scooter.*

Cons: *Does not prevent the scooter being stolen by joyriders.*

● There are many different types of security marking kits available. The idea is to mark as many parts of the scooter as possible with a unique security number **(see illustrations 8, 9 and 10)**. A form will be included with the kit to register your personal details and those of the scooter with the kit manufacturer. This register is made available to the police to help them trace the rightful owner of any scooter or components which they recover should all other forms of identification have been removed. Always apply the warning stickers provided with the kit to deter thieves.

Ground anchors, wheel clamps and security posts

Pros: *An excellent form of security which will deter all but the most determined of thieves.*

Cons: *Awkward to install and can be expensive.*

● While the scooter is at home, it is a good idea to attach it securely to the floor or a solid wall, even if it is kept in a securely locked garage. Various types of ground anchors, security posts and wheel clamps are available for this purpose **(see illustration 11)**. These security devices are either bolted to a solid concrete or brick structure or can be cemented into the ground.

11

Permanent ground anchors provide an excellent level of security when the scooter is at home

Security at home

A high percentage of scooter thefts are from the owner's home. Here are some things to consider whenever your scooter is at home:
✔ Where possible, always keep the scooter in a securely locked garage. Never rely solely on the standard lock on the garage door, these are usually hopelessly inadequate. Install an additional locking mechanism to the door and consider having the garage alarmed. A security light, activated by a movement sensor, is also a good investment.

✔ Always secure the scooter to the ground or a wall, even if it is inside a securely locked garage.
✔ Do not regularly leave the scooter outside your home, try to keep it out of sight wherever possible. If a garage is not available, fit a scooter cover over the scooter to disguise its true identity.
✔ It is not uncommon for thieves to follow a rider home to find out where the scooter is kept. They will then return at a later date. Be aware of this whenever you are returning home

on your scooter. If you suspect you are being followed, do not return home, instead ride to a garage or shop and stop as a precaution.
✔ When selling a scooter, do not provide your home address or the location where the scooter is normally kept. Arrange to meet the buyer at a location away from your home. Thieves have been known to pose as potential buyers to find out where scooters are kept and then return later to steal them.

Security away from the home

As well as installing security equipment to your scooter, here are a few general rules to follow whenever you park your scooter.
✔ Park in a busy, public place.
✔ Use parking lots which incorporate security features, such as CCTV.

✔ At night, park in a well-lit area, preferably directly underneath a street light.
✔ Engage the steering lock.
✔ Secure the scooter to a solid, immovable object such as a post or railings with an additional lock. If this is not possible, secure

the scooter to a friend's scooter. Some public parking places provide security loops for scooters.
✔ Never leave your helmet or luggage attached to the scooter. Take them with you at all times.

A

ABS (Anti-lock braking system) A system, usually electronically controlled, that senses incipient wheel lockup during braking and relieves hydraulic pressure at wheel which is about to skid.

Aftermarket Components suitable for the scooter, but not produced by the scooter manufacturer.

Allen key A hexagonal wrench which fits into a recessed hexagonal hole.

Alternating current (ac) Current produced by an alternator. Requires converting to direct current by a rectifier for charging purposes.

Alternator Converts mechanical energy from the engine into electrical energy to charge the battery and power the electrical system.

Ampere (amp) A unit of measurement for the flow of electrical current. Current = Volts ÷ Ohms.

Ampere-hour (Ah) Measure of battery capacity.

Angle-tightening A torque expressed in degrees. Often follows a conventional tightening torque for cylinder head or main bearing fasteners **(see illustration)**.

Angle-tightening cylinder head bolts

Antifreeze A substance (usually ethylene glycol) mixed with water, and added to the cooling system, to prevent freezing of the coolant in winter. Antifreeze also contains chemicals to inhibit corrosion and the formation of rust and other deposits that would tend to clog the radiator and coolant passages and reduce cooling efficiency.

Anti-dive System attached to the fork lower leg (slider) to prevent fork dive when braking hard.

Anti-seize compound A coating that reduces the risk of seizing on fasteners that are subjected to high temperatures, such as exhaust clamp bolts and nuts.

API American Petroleum Institute. A quality standard for 4-stroke motor oils.

Asbestos A natural fibrous mineral with great heat resistance, commonly used in the composition of brake friction materials. Asbestos is a health hazard and the dust created by brake systems should never be inhaled or ingested.

ATF Automatic Transmission Fluid. Often used in front forks.

ATU Automatic Timing Unit. Mechanical device for advancing the ignition timing on early engines.

ATV All Terrain Vehicle. Often called a Quad.

Axial play Side-to-side movement.

Axle A shaft on which a wheel revolves. Also known as a spindle.

B

Backlash The amount of movement between meshed components when one component is held still. Usually applies to gear teeth.

Ball bearing A bearing consisting of a hardened inner and outer race with hardened steel balls between the two races.

Bearings Used between two working surfaces to prevent wear of the components and a build-up of heat. Four types of bearing are commonly used on scooters: plain shell bearings, ball bearings, tapered roller bearings and needle roller bearings.

Bevel gears Used to turn the drive through 90°. Typical applications are shaft final drive and camshaft drive **(see illustration)**.

BHP Brake Horsepower. A measurement for engine power output. Power output is also expressed in kilowatts (kW).

Bevel gears are used to turn the drive through 90°

Bias-belted tire Similar construction to radial tire, but with outer belt running at an angle to the wheel rim.

Bleeding The process of removing air from a hydraulic system via a bleed nipple or bleed screw.

Bottom-end A description of an engine's crankcase components and all components contained therein.

BTDC Before Top Dead Center in terms of piston position. Ignition timing is often expressed in terms of degrees or millimeters BTDC.

Bushing A cylindrical metal or rubber component used between two moving parts.

Burr Rough edge left on a component after machining or as a result of excessive wear.

C

Cam chain The chain which takes drive from the crankshaft to the camshaft(s).

Canister The main component in an evaporative emission control system (California market only); contains activated charcoal granules to trap vapors from the fuel system rather than allowing them to vent to the atmosphere.

Castellated Resembling the parapets along the top of a castle wall. For example, a castellated wheel axle or spindle nut.

Catalytic converter A device in the exhaust system of some machines which converts certain pollutants in the exhaust gases into less harmful substances.

Charging system Description of the components which charge the battery, like the alternator, rectifier and regulator.

Cush drive rubber segments dampen out transmission shocks

Clearance The amount of space between two parts. For example, between a piston and a cylinder, between a bearing and a journal, etc.

Coil spring A spiral of elastic steel found in various sizes throughout a vehicle, for example as a springing medium in the suspension and in the valve train.

Compression Reduction in volume, and increase in pressure and temperature, of a gas, caused by squeezing it into a smaller space.

Compression damping Controls the speed the suspension compresses when hitting a bump.

Compression ratio The relationship between cylinder volume when the piston is at top dead center and cylinder volume when the piston is at bottom dead center.

Connecting rod bearing The bearing in the end of the connecting rod that's attached to the crankshaft.

Continuity The uninterrupted path in the flow of electricity. Little or no measurable resistance.

Continuity tester Self-powered bleeper or test light which indicates continuity.

Cp Candlepower. Bulb rating commonly found on US scooters.

Crossply tire Tire plies arranged in a criss-cross pattern. Usually four or six plies used, hence 4PR or 6PR in tire size codes.

Cush drive Rubber damper segments installed between the rear wheel and final drive sprocket to absorb transmission shocks **(see illustration)**.

D

Degree disc Calibrated disc for measuring piston position. Expressed in degrees.

Dial gauge Clock-type gauge with adapters for measuring runout and piston position. Expressed in mm or inches.

Diaphragm The rubber membrane in a master cylinder or carburetor which seals the upper chamber.

Diaphragm spring A single sprung plate often used in clutches.

Direct current (dc) Current produced by a dc generator.

Decarbonization The process of removing carbon deposits - typically from the combustion chamber, valves and exhaust port/system.

Detonation Destructive and damaging explosion of fuel/air mixture in combustion chamber instead of controlled burning.

Diode An electrical valve which only allows current to flow in one direction. Commonly used in rectifiers and starter interlock systems.

Disc valve (or rotary valve) An induction system used on some two-stroke engines.

Double-overhead camshaft (DOHC) An engine that uses two overhead camshafts, one for the intake valves and one for the exhaust valves.

Drivebelt A toothed belt used to transmit drive to the rear wheel on some scooters. A drivebelt has also been used to drive the camshafts. Drivebelts are usually made of Kevlar.

Driveshaft Any shaft used to transmit motion. Commonly used when referring to the final driveshaft on shaft drive scooters.

E

ECU (Electronic Control Unit) A computer which controls (for instance) an ignition system, or an anti-lock braking system.

EGO Exhaust Gas Oxygen sensor. Some-times called a Lambda sensor.

Electrolyte The fluid in a lead-acid battery.

EMS (Engine Management System) A computer controlled system which manages the fuel injection and the ignition systems in an integrated fashion.

Endplay The amount of lengthwise movement between two parts. As applied to a crankshaft, the distance that the crankshaft can move side-to-side in the crankcase.

Endless chain A chain having no joining link. Common use for cam chains and final drive chains.

EP (Extreme Pressure) Oil type used in locations where high loads are applied, such as between gear teeth.

Evaporative emission control system Describes a charcoal filled canister which stores fuel vapors from the tank rather than allowing them to vent to the atmosphere. Usually only fitted to California models and referred to as an EVAP system.

Expansion chamber Section of two-stroke engine exhaust system so designed to improve engine efficiency and boost power.

F

Feeler blade or gauge A thin strip or blade of hardened steel, ground to an exact thickness, used to check or measure clearances between parts.

Final drive Description of the drive from the transmission to the rear wheel. Usually by chain or shaft, but sometimes by belt.

Firing order The order in which the engine cylinders fire, or deliver their power strokes, beginning with the number one cylinder.

Flooding Term used to describe a high fuel level in the carburetor float chambers, leading to fuel overflow. Also refers to excess fuel in the combustion chamber due to incorrect starting technique.

Free length The no-load state of a component when measured. Clutch, valve and fork spring lengths are measured at rest, without any preload.

Freeplay The amount of travel before any action takes place. The looseness in a linkage, or an assembly of parts, between the initial application of force and actual movement. For example, the distance the rear brake pedal moves before the rear brake is actuated.

Fuel injection The fuel/air mixture is metered electronically and directed into the engine intake ports (indirect injection) or into the cylinders (direct injection). Sensors supply information on engine speed and conditions.

Fuel/air mixture The charge of fuel and air going into the engine. See *Stoichiometric ratio*.

Fuse An electrical device which protects a circuit against accidental overload. The typical fuse contains a soft piece of metal which is calibrated to melt at a predetermined current flow (expressed as amps) and break the circuit.

G

Gap The distance the spark must travel in jumping from the center electrode to the side electrode in a spark plug. Also refers to the distance between the ignition rotor and the pickup coil in an electronic ignition system.

Gasket Any thin, soft material - usually cork, cardboard, asbestos or soft metal - installed between two metal surfaces to ensure a good seal. For instance, the cylinder head gasket seals the joint between the block and the cylinder head.

Gauge An instrument panel display used to monitor engine conditions. A gauge with a movable pointer on a dial or a fixed scale is an analog gauge. A gauge with a numerical readout is called a digital gauge.

Gear ratios The drive ratio of a pair of gears in a gearbox, calculated on their number of teeth.

Glaze-busting see **Honing**

Grinding Process for renovating the valve face and valve seat contact area in the cylinder head.

Ground return The return path of an electrical circuit, utilizing the scooter's frame.

Gudgeon pin The shaft which connects the connecting rod small-end with the piston. Often called a piston pin or wrist pin.

H

Helical gears Gear teeth are slightly curved and produce less gear noise that straight-cut gears. Often used for primary drives.

Helicoil A thread insert repair system. Commonly used as a repair for stripped spark plug threads **(see illustration)**.

Installing a Helicoil thread insert in a cylinder head

Honing A process used to break down the glaze on a cylinder bore (also called glaze-busting). Can also be carried out to roughen a rebored cylinder to aid ring bedding-in.

HT (High Tension) Description of the electrical circuit from the secondary winding of the ignition coil to the spark plug.

Hydraulic A liquid filled system used to transmit pressure from one component to another. Common uses on scooters are brakes and clutches.

Hydrometer An instrument for measuring the specific gravity of a lead-acid battery.

Hygroscopic Water absorbing. In scooter applications, braking efficiency will be reduced if DOT 3 or 4 hydraulic fluid absorbs water from the air - care must be taken to keep new brake fluid in tightly sealed containers.

I

lbf ft Pounds-force feet. A unit of torque. Sometimes written as ft-lbs.

lbf in Pound-force inch. A unit of torque, applied to components where a very low torque is required. Sometimes written as inch-lbs.

IC Abbreviation for Integrated Circuit.

Ignition advance Means of increasing the timing of the spark at higher engine speeds. Done by mechanical means (ATU) on early engines or electronically by the ignition control unit on later engines.

Ignition timing The moment at which the spark plug fires, expressed in the number of crankshaft degrees before the piston reaches the top of its stroke, or in the number of millimeters before the piston reaches the top of its stroke.

Infinity (∞) Description of an open-circuit electrical state, where no continuity exists.

Inverted forks (upside down forks) The sliders or lower legs are held in the yokes and the fork tubes or stanchions are connected to the wheel axle (spindle). Less unsprung weight and stiffer construction than conventional forks.

J

JASO Japan Automobile Standards Organization. JASO MA is a standard for scooter oil equivalent to API SJ, but designed to prevent problems with wet-type scooter clutches.

Joule The unit of electrical energy.

Journal The bearing surface of a shaft.

K

Kickstart Mechanical means of turning the engine over for starting purposes.

Only usually installed on mopeds, small capacity scooters and off-road motorcycles.

Kill switch Handebar-mounted switch for emergency ignition cut-out. Cuts the ignition circuit on all models, and additionally prevent starter motor operation on others.

km Symbol for kilometer.

kmh Abbreviation for kilometers per hour.

L

Lambda sensor A sensor fitted in the exhaust system to measure the exhaust gas oxygen content (excess air factor). Also called oxygen sensor.

Lapping see **Grinding**.

LCD Abbreviation for Liquid Crystal Display.

LED Abbreviation for Light Emitting Diode.

Liner A steel cylinder liner inserted in an aluminum alloy cylinder block.

Locknut A nut used to lock an adjustment nut, or other threaded component, in place.

Lockstops The lugs on the lower triple clamp (yoke) which abut those on the frame, preventing handlebar-to-fuel tank contact.

Lockwasher A form of washer designed to prevent an attaching nut from working loose.

LT Low Tension Description of the electrical circuit from the power supply to the primary winding of the ignition coil.

M

Main bearings The bearings between the crankshaft and crankcase.

Maintenance-free (MF) battery A sealed battery which cannot be topped up.

Manometer Mercury-filled calibrated tubes used to measure intake tract vacuum. Used to synchronize carburetors on multi-cylinder engines.

Tappet shims are measured with a micrometer

Micrometer A precision measuring instrument that measures component outside diameters **(see illustration)**.

MON (Motor Octane Number) A measure of a fuel's resistance to knock.

Monograde oil An oil with a single viscosity, eg SAE80W.

Monoshock A single suspension unit linking the swingarm or suspension linkage to the frame.

mph Abbreviation for miles per hour.

Multigrade oil Having a wide viscosity range (eg 10W40). The W stands for Winter, thus the viscosity ranges from SAE10 when cold to SAE40 when hot.

Multimeter An electrical test instrument with the capability to measure voltage, current and resistance. Some meters also incorporate a continuity tester and buzzer.

N

Needle roller bearing Inner race of caged needle rollers and hardened outer race. Examples of uncaged needle rollers can be found on some engines. Commonly used in rear suspension applications and in two-stroke engines.

Nm Newton meters. A unit of measure for torque.

NOx Oxides of Nitrogen. A common toxic pollutant emitted by gasoline engines at higher temperatures.

O

Octane The measure of a fuel's resistance to knock.

OE (Original Equipment) Relates to components installed on a scooter as standard or replacement parts supplied by the scooter manufacturer.

Ohm The unit of electrical resistance. Ohms = Volts ÷ Current.

Ohmmeter An instrument for measuring electrical resistance.

Oil cooler System for diverting engine oil outside of the engine to a radiator for cooling purposes.

Oil injection A system of two-stroke engine lubrication where oil is pump-fed to the engine in accordance with throttle position.

Open-circuit An electrical condition where there is a break in the flow of electricity - no continuity (high resistance).

O-ring A type of sealing ring made of a special rubber-like material; in use, the O-ring is compressed into a groove to provide the sealing action.

Oversize (OS) Term used for piston and ring size options fitted to a rebored cylinder.

Overhead cam (sohc) engine An engine with single camshaft located on top of the cylinder head.

Overhead valve (ohv) engine An engine with the valves located in the cylinder head, but with the camshaft located in the engine block or crankcase.

Oxygen sensor A device installed in the exhaust system which senses the oxygen content in the exhaust and converts this information into an electric current. Also called a Lambda sensor.

P

Plastigage A thin strip of plastic thread, available in different sizes, used for measuring clearances. For example, a strip of Plastigage is laid across a bearing journal. The parts are assembled and dismantled; the width of the crushed strip indicates the clearance between journal and bearing.

Polarity Either negative or positive ground, determined by which battery lead is connected to the frame (ground return). Modern scooters are usually negative ground.

Pre-ignition A situation where the fuel/air mixture ignites before the spark plug fires. Often due to a hot spot in the combustion chamber caused by carbon build-up. Engine has a tendency to run-on.

Pre-load (suspension) The amount a spring is compressed when in the unloaded state. Preload can be applied by gas, spacer or mechanical adjuster.

Premix The method of engine lubrication on some gasoline two-stroke engines. Engine oil is mixed with the gasoline in the fuel tank in a specific ratio. The fuel/oil mix is sometimes referred to as "petrol."

Primary drive Description of the drive from the crankshaft to the clutch. Usually by gear or chain.

PS Pferdestärke - a German interpretation of BHP.

PSI Pounds-force per square inch. Imperial measurement of tire pressure and cylinder pressure measurement.

PTFE Polytetrafluoroethylene. A low friction substance.

Pulse secondary air injection system A process of promoting the burning of excess fuel present in the exhaust gases by routing fresh air into the exhaust ports.

Q

Quartz halogen bulb Tungsten filament surrounded by a halogen gas. Typically used for the headlight **(see illustration)**.

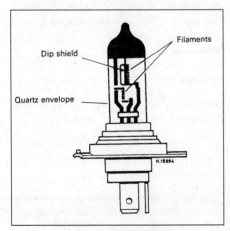

Quartz halogen headlight bulb construction

R

Rack-and-pinion A pinion gear on the end of a shaft that mates with a rack (think of a geared wheel opened up and laid flat). Sometimes used in clutch operating systems.

Radial play Up and down movement around a shaft.

Radial ply tires Tire plies run across the tire (from bead to bead) and around the circumference of the tire. Less resistant to tread distortion than other tire types.

Radiator A liquid-to-air heat transfer device designed to reduce the temperature of the coolant in a liquid cooled engine.

Rake A feature of steering geometry - the angle of the steering head in relation to the vertical **(see illustration)**.

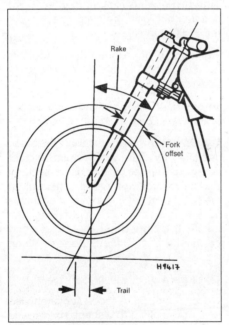

Steering geometry

Rebore Providing a new working surface to the cylinder bore by boring out the old surface. Necessitates the use of oversize piston and rings.

Rebound damping A means of controlling the oscillation of a suspension unit spring after it has been compressed. Resists the spring's natural tendency to bounce back after being compressed.

Rectifier Device for converting the ac output of an alternator into dc for battery charging.

Reed valve An induction system commonly used on two-stroke engines.

Regulator Device for maintaining the charging voltage from the generator or alternator within a specified range.

Relay A electrical device used to switch heavy current on and off by using a low current auxiliary circuit.

Resistance Measured in ohms. An electrical component's ability to pass electrical current.

RON (Research Octane Number) A measure of a fuel's resistance to knock.

rpm revolutions per minute.

Runout The amount of wobble (in-and-out movement) of a wheel or shaft as it's rotated. The amount a shaft rotates "out-of-true." The out-of-round condition of a rotating part.

S

SAE (Society of Automotive Engineers) A standard for the viscosity of a fluid.

Sealant A liquid or paste used to prevent leakage at a joint. Sometimes used in conjunction with a gasket.

Service limit Term for the point where a component is no longer useable and must be replaced.

Shaft drive A method of transmitting drive from the transmission to the rear wheel.

Shell bearings Plain bearings consisting of two shell halves. Most often used as connecting rod and main bearings in a four-stroke engine. Often called bearing inserts.

Shim Thin spacer, commonly used to adjust the clearance or relative positions between two parts. For example, shims inserted into or under tappets or followers to control valve clearances. Clearance is adjusted by changing the thickness of the shim.

Short-circuit An electrical condition where current shorts to ground bypassing the circuit components.

Skimming Process to correct warpage or repair a damaged surface, for example, on brake discs or drums.

Slide-hammer A special puller that screws into or hooks onto a component such as a shaft or bearing; a heavy sliding handle on the shaft bottoms against the end of the shaft to knock the component free.

Small-end bearing The bearing in the upper end of the connecting rod at its joint with the gudgeon pin.

Snap-ring A ring-shaped clip used to prevent endwise movement of cylindrical parts and shafts. An internal snap-ring is installed in a groove in a housing; an external snap-ring fits into a groove on the outside of a cylindrical piece such as a shaft. Also known as a circlip.

Spalling Damage to camshaft lobes or bearing journals shown as pitting of the working surface.

Specific gravity (SG) The state of charge of the electrolyte in a lead-acid battery. A measure of the electrolyte's density compared with water.

Straight-cut gears Common type gear used on gearbox shafts and for oil pump and water pump drives.

Stanchion The inner sliding part of the front forks, held by the yokes. Often called a fork tube.

Stoichiometric ratio The optimum chemical air/fuel ratio for a gasoline engine, said to be 14.7 parts of air to 1 part of fuel.

Sulphuric acid The liquid (electrolyte) used in a lead-acid battery. Poisonous and extremely corrosive.

Surface grinding (lapping) Process to correct a warped gasket face, commonly used on cylinder heads.

T

Tapered-roller bearing Tapered inner race of caged needle rollers and separate tapered outer race. Examples of taper roller bearings can be found on steering heads.

Tappet A cylindrical component which transmits motion from the cam to the valve stem, either directly or via a pushrod and rocker arm. Also called a cam follower.

TCS Traction Control System. An electronically-controlled system which senses wheel spin and reduces engine speed accordingly.

TDC Top Dead Center denotes that the piston is at its highest point in the cylinder.

Thread-locking compound Solution applied to fastener threads to prevent loosening. Select type to suit application.

Thrust washer A washer positioned between two moving components on a shaft. For example, between gear pinions on gearshaft.

Timing chain See **Cam Chain**.

Timing light Stroboscopic lamp for carrying out ignition timing checks with the engine running.

Top-end A description of an engine's cylinder block, head and valve gear components.

Torque Turning or twisting force around a shaft.

Torque setting A prescribed tightness specified by the scooter manufacturer to ensure that the bolt or nut is secured correctly. Undertightening can result in the bolt or nut coming loose or a surface not being sealed. Overtightening can result in stripped threads, distortion or damage to the component being retained.

Torx key A six-point wrench.

Tracer A stripe of a second color applied to a wire insulator to distinguish that wire from another one with the same color insulator. For example, Br/W is often used to denote a brown insulator with a white tracer.

Trail A feature of steering geometry. Distance from the steering head axis to the tire's central contact point.

Triple clamps The cast components which extend from the steering head and support the fork stanchions or tubes. Often called fork yokes.

Turbocharger A centrifugal device, driven by exhaust gases, that pressurizes the intake air. Normally used to increase the power output from a given engine displacement.

TWI Abbreviation for Tire Wear Indicator. Indicates the location of the tread depth indicator bars on tires.

U

Universal joint or U-joint (UJ) A double-pivoted connection for transmitting power from a driving to a driven shaft through an angle. Typically found in shaft drive assemblies.

Unsprung weight Anything not supported by the bike's suspension (the wheel, tires, brakes, final drive and bottom [moving] part of the suspension).

V

Vacuum gauges Clock-type gauges for measuring intake tract vacuum. Used for carburetor synchronization on multi-cylinder engines.

Valve A device through which the flow of liquid, gas or vacuum may be stopped, started or regulated by a moveable part that opens, shuts or partially obstructs one or more ports or passageways. The intake and exhaust valves in the cylinder head are of the poppet type.

Valve clearance The clearance between the valve tip (the end of the valve stem) and the rocker arm or tappet/follower. The valve clearance is measured when the valve is closed. The correct clearance is important - if too small, the valve won't close fully and will burn out, whereas if too large, noisy operation will result.

Valve lift The amount a valve is lifted off its seat by the camshaft lobe.

Valve timing The exact setting for the opening and closing of the valves in relation to piston position.

Vernier caliper A precision measuring instrument that measures inside and outside dimensions. Not quite as accurate as a micrometer, but more convenient.

VIN Vehicle Identification Number. Term for the bike's engine and frame numbers.

Viscosity The thickness of a liquid or its resistance to flow.

Volt A unit for expressing electrical "pressure" in a circuit. Volts = current x ohms.

W

Water pump A mechanically-driven device for moving coolant around the engine.

Watt A unit for expressing electrical power. Watts = volts x current.

Wet liner arrangement

Wear limit see **Service limit**

Wet liner A liquid-cooled engine design where the pistons run in liners which are directly surrounded by coolant (**see illustration**).

Wheelbase Distance from the center of the front wheel to the center of the rear wheel.

Wiring harness or loom Describes the electrical wires running the length of the scooter and enclosed in tape or plastic sheathing. Wiring coming off the main harness is usually referred to as a sub harness.

Woodruff key A key of semi-circular or square section used to locate a gear to a shaft. Often used to locate the alternator rotor on the crankshaft.

Wrist pin Another name for gudgeon or piston pin.

Notes

Note: *References throughout this index are in the form "Chapter Number" • "Page Number"*